1000 Best Courses in Britain and Ireland

1000
Best Courses
in Britain and Ireland

AURUM PRESS

This revised edition first published 2004 by Aurum Press

First published in Great Britain 1999 by Aurum Press Ltd
25 Bedford Avenue, London WC1B 3AT

A catalogue record for this book is available from the British Library.

ISBN 1 85410 980 4

1 3 5 7 9 10 8 6 4 2
2004 2006 2008 2007 2005

Text compiled and written by Linda Manigan, Kevin Brown and Peter Masters
All information correct at time of going to press
Text design by Don Macpherson
Cover design by Julian Cooke
Cover photograph by Angus Murray

Typeset by Action Publishing Technology
Printed and bound in Great Britain by CPD Group, Wales

Contents

Preface

Welcome to the 2004 edition of *Golf World*'s *1000 Best Courses in Britain and Ireland*.

These are exciting times for golf, with so much choice and fantastic value for money to be enjoyed at an ever-increasing wealth of golf courses, whether it be a newly opened gem or a long-standing, well-established course that continues to delight visitors and members alike.

This new edition has been thoroughly updated to include changes to green fees, contact numbers and any new course information that is available. It is a comprehensive and invaluable guide that will enable you to make the right decision about which course to visit in the confidence that *Golf World*'s experts have given you all the information you need. Our ratings evaluate the total golf experience: the course itself, the quality of the welcome, the catering, and overall value for money.

It all adds up to an invitation to sample the best courses around. Don't wait too long before you make that special trip.

Good golfing!

David Clarke
Publishing Editor-in-Chief
Golf World

Introduction

Wherever you may be in the British Isles, here is a book geared to finding you the best and most memorable places to play golf while on your travels. Welcome to the new, revamped third edition of the *Golf World* guide to the best 1000 courses in the British Isles.

Based on an exclusive nationwide survey of our readers, we have aimed to produce the first independent and authoritative guide reflecting the thoughts and experiences of ordinary golfers. Lists of the best places to play are typically selected by professionals, course designers and other figures of authority within the golf industry. Unlike the golfing cognoscenti, the green-fee-paying golfer is out there playing courses day in day out, and therefore he or she is often better placed to identify the strengths and weaknesses of the top courses.

Upon this premise we asked our readers to evaluate 1000 pre-selected courses in eight different categories: value for money, course presentation, course difficulty, quality of food and drink, quality of pro shop, quality of practice facilities, quality of welcome, and finally, they were asked to give an overall rating that accurately reflected the quality of the golf experience.

By ranking the courses in these categories, we aimed to answer the questions that the typical golfer might ask before visiting a new course. Is it worth the money? Is the course too hard for a player of my standard? Where will I be made welcome? We also wanted to know what, in the opinion of the grass-roots golfers, were the best courses in Britain and Ireland.

While the ratings and rankings achieved the purpose of grading each course, we also wanted golfers' personal comments about them. At the foot of each entry in this guide you will find individual comments about the course from people who have played there; in many cases, the comments are as illuminating as the ratings.

Any guide that attempts to grade courses is open to criticism. People like different courses for different reasons, just as people enjoy playing golf for different reasons. We are acutely aware of this fact and have tried to balance the ratings and comments to achieve a fair, rational view. Hopefully, you will agree. If not, it should cause a lively debate in the club bar, and we certainly welcome any views or comments you have about this guide.

How to use this guide

The book is split into three sections. In the first section are the rankings of the Top 100 Courses, the 20 Most Difficult Courses, the Top 10 Heathland, Top 10 Parkland and Top 10 Links Courses in Britain and Ireland. In the second section are the star ratings for all 1000 courses, rated from five star to one star as follows:

★★★★★ – Exceptional. The best.
★★★★   – Excellent. An outstanding day's golf.
★★★   – Very good.
★★   – Good, but not great.
★   – Standard. Nothing special.

The third section is the main part of the book, listing all 1000 courses. Here you will find all the information you need to organise a game. The listing starts county by county with England, followed by Scotland, Wales and Ireland. The division of courses in Scotland and Wales has been chosen for simplicity rather than to adhere to the new county boundaries. A review of *Golf World*'s favourite course in the area appears at the beginning of each county listing (with the exceptions of Tyne & Wear and East Yorkshire).

This is a typical entry:

Royal Cromer Golf Club   ★★★

145 Overstrand Road, Cromer, NR27 0JH
Website: www.royalcromergolfclub.com
E-mail: general.manager@royal-cromer.com
Nearest main town: Cromer

Secretary:	Mrs D. Hopkins	Tel: 01263 512884
		Fax: 01263 512430
Professional:	Mr L. Patterson	Tel: 01263 512267

Playing: Midweek: round n/a; day £37.00. Weekend: round n/a; day £50.00.

Facilities: Bar: 11am–11pm. Food: Lunch and dinner from 11am–7pm. Bar snacks.

Comments: Always a pleasure to play ... Very tough in the wind ... Can get very windy ... Set on a cliff edge, Cromer is an experience not to be missed ... Awaken your senses at Cromer.

– The information listed is accurate at the time of going to press. The bar and catering hours given are expected opening times during the summer. In many cases, bar and catering hours are likely to be shorter during the winter due to the early close of play.

– There are four possible green-fee prices: for weekday round/day and weekend round/day. Where there is no price next to an entry, it means that price is not available at the club.

Advice for visitors

It often feels like you need a special handshake to get into some golf courses. Clubs tend to be protective of their courses, much as a child guards his or her favourite toy. Provided you have a handicap and are clear on golf etiquette, there are just a few simple rules to smooth the way.

The majority of the courses listed in the book require visitors to contact the club in advance and be able to produce a handicap certificate on the day of play. That is normally sufficient. When approaching some of the more exclusive courses, it is recommended that you write a letter of introduction direct to the secretary or organise a letter of introduction from your own club secretary.

With the exception of a very few clubs, there is nothing to stop you playing the best courses in the country, provided you follow these basic instructions. If you do not have a handicap, then the best advice is to follow the normal procedures and hope for the best – you may be asked to prove your ability when you arrive at the club.

Clubs have many competition and society days during the year, so find out the best days for visitors before you go. If you just turn up at the door, you may be disappointed. Also, gentlemen should remember to pack a jacket and tie, as many clubs have a dress code in the bar and dining room.

Good golfing!

TOP 100 COURSES

1. Muirfield	45. Hunstanton
2. Royal County Down	46. Prestwick
3. Westin Turnberry (Ailsa)	47. Royal Cinque Ports
4. St Andrews (Old)	48. The Berkshire (Blue)
5. Royal Birkdale	49. Silloth-on-Solway
6. Loch Lomond	50. Rye
7. Portmarnock (Old)	51. Mount Juliet
8. Royal Portrush (Dunluce)	52. Blairgowrie (Rosemount)
9. Woodhall Spa (Hotchkin)	53. Royal Worlington & Newmarket
10. Ballybunion (Old)	54. Formby
11. Sunningdale (Old)	55. Alwoodley
12. Carnoustie (Links)	56. Ballyliffin (Glashedy)
13. Kingsbarns	57. Cruden Bay
14. Ganton	58. Machrie Hotel
15. Royal Dornoch	59. Woburn (Marquess)
16. Royal St George's	60. Killarney (Killeen)
17. Gleneagles (King's)	61. Hillside (White)
18. Walton Heath (Old)	62. North Berwick
19. Wentworth (West)	63. St Enodoc (Church)
20. Royal Troon (Old)	64. Wisley
21. The European Club	65. Macrihanish
22. Royal Lytham & St Annes	66. Donegal
23. Waterville	67. Worplesdon
24. Royal Liverpool	68. Lindrick
25. Notts (Hollinwell)	69. Saunton (West)
26. Swinley Forest	70. The Island
27. County Louth	71. Killarney (Mahoney's Point)
28. Sunningdale (New)	72. Burnham & Berrow
29. Saunton (East)	73. Woburn (Duchess)
30. Lahinch (Old)	74. Aberdovey
31. West Sussex	75. Woburn (Dukes)
32. Royal Porthcawl	76. Tenby
33. Royal St David's	77. Druids Glen
34. Nairn	78. Gullane (No.1)
35. Royal West Norfolk	79. K Club (North Course)
36. Royal Aberdeen	80. Hankley Common
37. Western Gailes	81. Ferndown (Old)
38. St Andrews (New)	82. Castletown
39. The Berkshire (Red)	83. Nefyn
40. St George's Hill	84. Southerness
41. Wentworth (East)	85. Skibo Castle
42. Little Aston	86. Woking
43. Gleneagles (Queen's)	87. Moortown Parkstone
44. County Sligo	

88. Portstewart (Strand)
89. Luffness
90. Aldeburgh
91. Southport & Ainsdale
92. New Zealand
93. The Roxburghe
94. Royal Ashdown Forest (Old)

95. West Hill
96. Tralee
97. Enniscone
98. West Lancashire
99. Old Head of Kinsale
100. Royal North Devon

20 MOST DIFFICULT COURSES

1. Carnoustie
2. St Mellion (Nicklaus)
3. Royal Portrush (Dunluce)
4. Silloth-on-Solway
5. Royal County Down
6. Muirfield
7. Royal Dornoch
8. Western Gailes
9. Royal St George's
10. Royal Birkdale
11. Sunningdale (New)
12. Royal Troon
13. Royal St David's
14. St Andrews (Jubilee)
15. Carne
16. Burnham & Berrow
17. Moortown
18. Waterville
19. The Alwoodley
20. Royal Worlington & Newmarket

TOP 10 HEATHLAND COURSES

1. Sunningdale (Old)
2. Gleneagles (King's)
3. Woodhall Spa (Hotchkin)
4. Wentworth (West)
5. Ganton
6. Walton Heath (Old)
7. Swinley Forest
8. The Berkshire (Red)
9. Blairgowrie (Rosemount)
10. West Sussex

TOP 10 PARKLAND COURSES

1. Loch Lomond
2. Mount Juliet
3. Royal Worlington & Newmarket
4. Notts (Hollinwell)
5. Alwoodley
6. Little Aston
7. Ferndown (Old)
8. Killarney (Killeen)
9. Moortown
10. The Grove

TOP 10 LINKS COURSES

1. Muirfield
2. Royal County Down
3. Westin Turnberry (Ailsa)
4. Royal Birkdale
5. Ballybunion (Old)
6. Portmarnock (Old)
7. St Andrews (Old)
8. Royal Dornoch
9. Royal Portrush (Dunluce)
10. Carnoustie

STAR RATINGS

★★★★★

Ballybunion (Old)
The Berkshire (Blue)
The Berkshire (Red)
Carnoustie
County Louth
County Sligo
The European Club
Ganton
Gleneagles (King's)
Gleneagles (Queen's)
Hunstanton
Kingsbarns
Lahinch (Old)
Little Aston
Loch Lomond
Muirfield
Nairn
Notts (Hollinwell)
Portmarnock (Old)
Prestwick
Royal Aberdeen
Royal Birkdale
Royal Cinque Ports
Royal County Down
Royal Dornoch

Royal Liverpool
Royal Lytham & St Annes
Royal Porthcawl
Royal Portrush (Dunluce)
Royal St David's
Royal St George's
Royal Troon (Old)
Royal West Norfolk
Rye
St Andrews New
St Andrews Old
St George's Hill
Saunton (East)
Silloth-on-Solway
Sunningdale (New)
Sunningdale (Old)
Swinley Forest
Walton Heath (Old)
Waterville
Wentworth (East)
Wentworth (West)
West Sussex
Western Gailes
Westin Turnberry (Ailsa)
Woodhall Spa (Hotchkin)

★★★★

Aberdovey
Adare Manor
The Addington
Aldeburgh
The Alwoodley
Ashburnham
Ashridge
Aspley Guise & Woburn Sands
Ballybunion (Cashen)
Ballyliffin (Glashedy)
Ballyliffin (Old)

Bamburgh Castle
Barton-on-Sea
Bearwood Lakes
Beau Desert
Belleisle
Belvoir Park
Berwick-on-Tweed (Goswick)
Bingley St Ives
Blackmoor
Blairgowrie (Rosemount)
Boat of Garten

Bolton
Bolton Old Links
Borth & Ynyslas
Brancepeth Castle
Broadstone
Brookmans Park
The Buckinghamshire
Burnham & Berrow
Carden Park
Carlisle
Carlow
Carlyon Bay
Carne
Carnegie (Skibo Castle)
Carton House
Castlerock
Castletown
Cavendish
Chart Hills
Connemara
Conwy
Cork
County Tipperary
Crail (Balcomie)
Crieff
Cruden Bay
Cumberwell Park
Dalmahoy
Dartmouth
Delamere Forest
Dingle Links/Ceann Sibeal
Donegal
Dooks
Doonbeg
The Dorset
Downfield
Druid's Glen
Druids Heath
Duff House Royal
Dunbar
East Berkshire
East Sussex National
Edzell
Enniscrone
Ferndown (Old)
Forest of Arden

Forest Pines
Formby
Foxhills (Chertsey)
Frilford Heath (Red)
Fulford
Fulford Heath
Gainsborough (Karsten)
Glasgow Gailes
Glasson
Glen
Gleneagles (PGA Centenary)
Gog Magog
Goring & Streatley
The Grove
Gullane (No.1)
Gullane (No.3)
Hadley Wood
Hanbury Manor
Hankley Common
Harrogate
Hawkstone Park Hotel
Hayling
Hesketh
Heswall
Hillside
Hindhead
Ilkley
Irvine
The Island
Isle of Purbeck
John O'Gaunt (Main)
K Club (North)
K Club (South)
The Kendleshire
Killarney (Killeen)
Killarney (Mahoney's Point)
Kilmarnock (Barrassie)
Kingussie
La Moye
Ladybank
Lahinch (Castle)
Lanhydrock
Leven Links
Lindrick
Liphook
Littlestone

Llanymynech
The London Club (Heritage)
Longcliffe
Luffenham Heath
Luffness (New)
Lundin
Lytham Green Drive
Machrie Hotel
Machrihanish
Manchester
Mannings Heath (Waterfall)
Manor House
Monifieth (Medal)
Montrose (Medal)
Moor Allerton
Moor Park (High)
Moortown
Moray (Old)
Mount Juliet
Murcar
Nefyn & District
New Zealand
Nizels
North Berwick
North Foreland
North Hants
Northamptonshire County
Old Head of Kinsale
Parkstone
Pennard
Perranporth
Piltdown
The Players
Portmarnock Links
Portpatrick Dunskey
Portsalon
Portstewart (Strand)
Powfoot
Prince's
Pyle & Kenfig
Rathsallagh
Rosapenna
Ross-on-Wye
Rotherham
The Roxburghe
Royal Ashdown Forest (Old)

Royal Dublin
Royal Jersey
Royal Musselburgh
Royal North Devon
Royal Portrush (Valley)
Royal Worlington & Newmarket
St Andrews Bay (Devlin)
St Andrews Dukes
St Andrews Eden
St Andrews Jubilee
St Enodoc
St Mellion (Nicklaus)
St Pierre
Sand Moor
Sandiway
Saunton (West)
Scarcroft
Scotscraig
Seacroft
Seaford
Seaton Carew
Shanklin & Sandown
Sherwood Forest
Slaley Hall
Southerndown
Southerness
Southport & Ainsdale
Stoke Park
Stoneham
Tadmarton Heath
Tain
Tandridge
Tenby
Thorpeness
Thurlestone
Tilgate Forest
Tralee
Tramore
Trevose
Tytherington
Wallasey
Welcombe Hotel
Wellingborough
West Cornwall
West Derby
West Hill

West Lancashire
West Surrey
Wisley
Woburn (Duchess)
Woburn (Dukes)

Woburn (Marquess)
Woking
Worksop
Worplesdon
York

★★★

Aberdour
Abridge
Alderney
Alloa
Alyth
Ardglass
Army
Ashdown Forest (Hotel)
Ashdown Forest (Old)
Athlone
Auchterarder
Badgemore Park
Balbirnie Park
Ballater
Ballybofey & Stranorlar
Ballycastle
Ballykisteen
Balmoral
Bangor
Barnard Castle
Bath
Beaconsfield
Beaufort
Bedford & County
The Belfry (Brabazon)
The Belfry (PGA National)
Belmont Lodge
Belton Woods (Lakes)
Berkhamsted
Bigbury
Birchwood
Bothwell Castle
Bowood
Braemar
Brampton (Talkin Tarn)
Brampton Park
Branston

Bristol & Clifton
Broadway
Brockenhurst Manor
Brocton Hall
Brora
Bruntsfield Links
Buchanan Castle
Bude & North Cornwall
Burhill
Burnham Beeches
Bury St Edmunds
Cairndhu
Callander
Camberley Heath
Came Down
Cardrona
Cardross
Carnoustie Burnside
Castletroy
Cathkin Braes
Cawder
Charlesland
Charleville
Chesfield Downs
Chesterfield
The Childwall
Chiltern Forest
China Fleet
Chorlton-cum-Hardy
Church Stretton
Churston
Clandaboye (Ava)
Clandeboye (Dufferin)
Clevedon
Clitheroe
Collingtree Park
Cooden Beach

Coombe Hill
Copthorne
Corhampton
Courtown
Coventry
Coxmoor
Cradoc
Crow Wood
Crowborough Beacon
Deer Park (Ireland)
Deeside
Denham
Drift
Dromoland
Drumpellier
Duddingston
Dumfries & County
Dummer
Dundalk
Dungannon
Dunstable Downs
Eaglescliffe
East Devon
East Renfrewshire
Eaton (Cheshire)
Eaton (Norfolk)
Eden
Edgbaston
Effingham
Elgin
Ellesborough
Enville (Highgate)
Enville (Lodge)
Erskine
Exeter
Fairhaven
Faithlegg
Farrington (Main)
Faversham
Felixstowe Ferry
Five Lakes (Lakes)
Fleetwood
Forfar
Forres
Fortrose & Rosemarkie
Freshwater Bay

Frilford Heath (Blue)
Frilford Heath (Green)
Frodsham
Fulwell
Galway
Galway Bay
Garforth
Gerrards Cross
Glasgow
Gleddoch
Glenbervie
Golf House
Golspie
Grange Park
Grantown-on-Spey
Great Yarmouth and Caister
Guildford
Gullane (No.2)
Haggs Castle
Halifax
Hallamshire
Harleyford
Hartlepool
Hawick
Headfort
Hellidon Lakes
Henley
Hermitage
Hever Castle
High Post
Hill Valley (Emerald)
Hill Valley (Sapphire)
Hillsborough
Hilton Park (Hilton)
Hockley
Holyhead
Hopeman
Horsley Lodge
Huddersfield
Huntercombe
Ilfracombe
Inverness
Ipswich (Purdis Heath)
Kedleston Park
Kelso
Kenmare

Keswick
Kilkenny
Killorgin
Kilmacolm
Kilspindie
King James VI
King's Lynn
Kings Acre
Kington
Kirkbymoorside
Kirkcaldy
Kirkistown Castle
Knock
Knole Park
Lakeside Lodge
The Lambourne
Lancaster
Langdon Hills
Langley Park
Lee Valley
Letham Grange (Old)
Limerick County
Linden Hall
Littlehampton
London Club (International)
Long Ashton
Longniddry
Lullingstone Park
Luttrellstown Castle
Maesdu
Malone
Mannings Heath (Kingfisher)
Massereene
Mendip Spring
Meon Valley
Mere
Merrist Wood
Mill Hill
Mill Ride
Millbrook
Millport
Moffat
Monifieth (Ashludie)
Moray (New)
Mottram Hall
Mount Temple

Murrayshall House
Musselburgh
Nairn Dunbar
Narin & Portnoo
Nevill
Newburgh-on-Ythan
Newbury & Crookham
Newmachar (Hawkshill)
Newport
Newtonmore
North Shore Hotel
Northcliffe
Northop
Oake Manor
Orchardleigh
Ormskirk
The Oxfordshire
Panmure
Pannal
Parknasilla
Peebles
Penrith
Peterborough Milton
Pitlochry
Pollok
Portal
Portal Premier
Porters Park
Porthmadog
Portlethen
Powerscourt
Prestbury
Prestwick St Cuthberts
Pyrford
Radisson Roe Park
Ratho Park
Reading
Reddish Vale
Redlibbets
Rolls of Monmouth
Romanby
Romford
Roserrow
Rosslare
Royal Blackheath
Royal Burgess

Royal Cromer
Royal Eastbourne (Devonshire)
Royal Epping Forest
Royal Guernsey
Royal Mid-Surrey (Outer)
Royal Norwich
Royal Winchester
Rudding Park
Rushmere
St Annes Old Links
St Margarets
Salisbury & South Wilts
Sandford Springs
Scarborough North Cliff
Scarborough South Cliff
Seahouses
Seascale
Seckford
Selsdon Park Hotel
Shannon
Shaw Hill
Sherborne
Sheringham
Shifnal
Shipley
Shiskine
The Shropshire
Silecroft
Slieve Russell
South Herts
South Winchester
Southfield
Southport Old Links
Standish Court
Staverton Park
Stock Brook Manor
Stockley Park
Stockport
Stocks Hotel
Stoke-by-Nayland (Gainsborough)
Stonehaven
Stranraer
Stratford-upon-Avon
Strathaven
Strathpeffer Spa
The Suffolk

Sundridge Park (East)
Sundridge Park (West)
Sutton Coldfield
Swindon
Taymouth Castle
Telford
Temple
Thetford
Thorndon Park
Thorpe Wood
Three Rivers (Kings)
Tidworth Garrison
Torquay
Troon Portland
Tullamore
Ulverston
Verulam
Wakefield
The Wales National
Walton Heath (New)
The Warwickshire (SE)
Waterlooville
West Berkshire
West Byfleet
West Essex
West Linton
West Lothian
West Waterford
Westin Turnberry (Arran)
Westport
Whitekirk
Whittington Heath
Whittlebury Park
Wick
Wildwood
Windyhill
Wollaton Park
Woodbridge
Woodbrook
Woodbury Park
Woodenbridge
Woodhall Spa (Bracken)
Workington
Worthing (Lower)
The Wychwood
Yeovil (Old)

★★

Abbotsley (Abbotsley)
Abbotsley (Cromwell)
Aberystwyth
Aboyne
Aldenham (Old)
Alnmouth
Appleby
Arbroath
Austin Lodge
Baberton
Ballochmyle
Barrow
Basingstoke
Beadlow Manor
Beamish Park
Bellingham
Belton Park
Beverley & East Riding
Birch Hall
Black Bush
Blairgowrie (Lansdowne)
Bognor Regis
Boldon
Braehead
Braintree
Bramshaw (Manor)
Breadsall Priory (Priory)
Brechin
Broomieknowie
Brunston Castle
Bull Bay
Burghill Valley
The Burstead
Buxton & High Peak
Caerphilly
Calcot Park
Caldy
Camperdown
Cams Hall Estate (Creek)
Canterbury
Castle Eden & Peterlee
Castle Hume
Castle Royle
Cathcart Castle

Celtic Manor (Coldra)
Celtic Manor (Roman Road)
Chapel-en-le-Frith
Chelmsford
Cherry Lodge
Chichester (Cathedral)
Chichester (Tower)
Chigwell
Chipping Sodbury
Chorley
Cleeve Hill
Cleveland
Cochrane Castle
Cocksford
Cold Ashby
Copt Heath
Cotgrave Place
County Cavan
Cowglen
Cruit Island
Cullen
Dainton Park
Dalmilling
Dean Wood
Deer Park (Scotland)
Dinsdale Spa
Doncaster
Downshire
Drayton Park
Drumoig
Dudsbury
Duke's Dene
Dullatur
Dunfermline
Dungarvan
Dunham Forest
Dunmurry
Dunstanburgh Castle
East Herts
Eastbourne Downs
Elton Furze
Epsom
The Essex (County)
Falmouth

Farnham
Farnham Park
Five Lakes (Links)
Flackwell Heath
Forest Park (Old Foss)
Fraserburgh
Frinton (Long)
Furness
Garesfield
Gatton Manor
George Washington Hotel
Girvan
Goodwood
Gorleston
Gourock
Great Hadham
Greenburn
Greenore
Greetham Valley
Haddington
Hallowes
Ham Manor
Haydock Park
Hazelhead
Headingley
Henbury
Herons Reach
Hexham
Heyrose
Hollywood Lakes
Hornsea
Hoylake
Huntly
Invergordon
Isle of Wedmore
Jarvis Gloucester Hotel
John O'Gaunt (Carthagena)
Keighley
Kemnay
Kendal
Kilkeel
Killeen
Kilworth Springs
Kings Norton
Kintore
Kirkby Lonsdale

Kirriemuir
Knockanally
Knowle
Lanark
Largs
Launceston
Leeds
Leek
Leigh
Leighton Buzzard
Letchworth
Liberton
Lisburn
Llandrindod Wells
Lochranza
Longridge
Looe
Lothianburn
Loudoun Gawf
Lurgan
Mahee Island
Maidenhead
Malahide
Mallow
Malton & Norton
Mapperley
Market Harborough
Marlborough
Mentmore
Mid Sussex
Milngavie
Minchinhampton (Avening)
Minchinhampton (Cherington)
Minehead & West Somerset
Moatlands
Mortonhall
Mount Murray
Mount Wolseley
Mullingar
Mullion
Newark
Newmachar (Swailend)
Newton Stewart
North Middlesex
North Wilts
Northenden

Nuremore
Oakdale
Oakridge
Old Thorns
Orsett
Paisley
Panshanger
Patshull Park
Penrhos
Peterculter
Peterhead
Pitreavie (Dunfermline)
Prestonfield
Prestwick St Nicholas
Puckrup Hall
Pype Hayes
Ralston
Ramsdale Park (High)
Ramside Hall
Reigate Heath
Robin Hood
Rochester & Cobham Park
Rowlands Castle
Royal Belfast
Royal Tarlair
Royal Wimbledon
Ruddington Grange
Rufford Park
St Augustines
St Austell
St David's City
St Helens Bay
St Mellons
Sandwell Park
Sandy Lodge
Seaford Head
Sedlescombe
Seedy Mill
Shirley Park
Shrigley Hall
Sickleholme
Sonning
South Beds
South Kyme
South Moor
Southampton

Spalding
Stapleford Abbotts (Abbotts)
Stinchcombe Hill
Stoke-by-Nayland (Constable)
Swinton Park
Tavistock
Teignmouth
Tewkesbury Park
Theydon Bois
Tiverton
Tracy Park
Traigh
Tudor Park Hotel
Ufford Park Hotel
Ullesthorpe Court
Upavon
Upminster
Walmer & Kingsdown
Warrenpoint
The Warwickshire (NW)
Waterford
Waterford Castle
Waterstock
Wearside
Wensum Valley (Valley)
West Herts
West Hove
West Kilbride
West Wilts
Western Park
Westerwood
Weston Turville
Weston-super-Mare
Westwood (Leek)
Weymouth
Wharton Park
Whipsnade Park
Whitefield
Wicklow
Wilmslow
The Wiltshire
Windermere
Windlesham
Winter Hill
Woodham
Woodlands

Woodlands Manor
Woodsome Hall
Woodspring
Worcester

The Wrekin
Wyboston Lakes
Yelverton

★

Allendale
Arscott
Bank House
Barnham Broom Hotel (Valley)
Bawburgh
Beacon Park
Bedlingtonshire
Bidford Grange
Bishop Auckland
Blackburn
Bondhay
Boston
Botley Park
Braid Hills
Brailes
Brett Vale
Bridgnorth
Bridlington
Bridport & West Dorset
Broome Park
Burton-on-Trent
Cambridge National
Cape Cornwall
Carholme
Carradale
Castlewarden
Catterick
Cave Castle
Chalgrave Manor
Channels
Chesterton Country
Chipping Norton
Chirk
Churchill & Blakedown
Clonmel
Clontarf
Cockermouth
Colmworth & North Bedfordshire

Cosby
Cottesmore (Griffin)
Delvin Castle
Disley
Duns
Dunscar
Dyke
Edmondstown
Elderslie
Ennis
Executive of Cranbrook
Filton
Flamborough Head
Forest Hills
Gainsborough (Thonock)
Glamorganshire
Glencruitten
Gort
Grange Fell
Grange-over-Sands
Hagley
Halifax Bradley Hall
Hayston
The Heath (Portlaoise)
Hennerton
Herefordshire
Hintlesham Hall
Kilkea Castle
Kingsthorpe
Kirkhill
Leamington & County
Leominster
Letterkenny
Lochwinnoch
Loughrea
Lydd
Magdalene Fields
Manor of Groves

Mendip
Mid Kent
Mid Yorkshire
Mile End
Mill Green
Monkstown
Monmouthshire
Morecambe
Morlais Castle
Moseley
Mountrath
Muir of Ord
Muskerry
New Forest
Newbiggin-by-the-Sea
Newquay
The Norfolk
North West
North Worcestershire
Northumberland
Northwood
Oakmere Park (Admirals)
Ogbourne Downs
Old Conna
Otley
Oundle
Park Hill
Parklands
Penwortham
Pleasington
Pontypridd
Port Glasgow
Portadown
Pwllheli
Pyecombe

Radyr
Ranfurly Castle
Richmond
Richmond Park
Romiley
Rush
Shirehampton Park
Shirland
Silkstone
Singing Hills
Slinford Park
South Shields
Stand
Stirling
Strandhill
Strathlene
Tankersley Park
Test Valley
Trentham Park
Vale
Vale of Leven
Warren
Weald of Kent
West Bowling
West Monmouthshire
Whitefields Hotel
Whitley Bay
Whitsand Bay
Wimbledon Common
Windmill Village
Windwhistle
Wooler
Worfield
Worsley

ENGLAND

Bedfordshire

John O'Gaunt Golf Club (Main)　　　★★★★

Sutton Park, Sandy, Biggleswade, SG19 2LY
Website: www.johnogauntgolfclub.co.uk
E-mail: admin@johnogauntgolfclub.co.uk
Nearest main town: Biggleswade

Fred Hawtree is primarily known in the British Isles for his work on Hillside, the less illustrious but gorgeous neighbour of Royal Birkdale in Southport. One of the lesser works on his CV is the Main course at John O'Gaunt, a course located not far outside Biggleswade in Bedfordshire. Cut through parkland, it is a course with a wonderfully British feel and design.

British golfers generally have a preference for links, heathland and woodland golf (in roughly that order), so it comes as no surprise that John O'Gaunt is never too busy and can, as a result, usually be found in exceptional condition. It is by far the best course in the county, and holds all the important county and regional competitions.

In truth, it is part woodland and part parkland, but the trees rarely interfere with your line of sight and merely provide the backdrop for the two par-5s and three par-3s. It is long at around 6500 yards. There are a number of par-4s of over 400 yards, the pick being a 472-yard par-4 that the members grudgingly approach as if it were a par-5. Two of the finest holes on the course are the 10th, a par-3 where trouble lurks all around, and the 17th, where the green is located on an old castle mound.

With the fairways cut to curb aggression, and the greens small and well-protected, John O'Gaunt could be labelled unfair. You may even feel that there are not enough par-5s and par-3s to break the monotony of the 13 par-4s. But you're unlikely to come away from John O'Gaunt being anything but impressed with its condition and certain that there is nothing to beat it in the area.

Secretary:	Mr S. Anthony	Tel: 01767 260360
	(General Manager)	Fax: 01767 262834
Professional:	Mr L. Scarbrow	Tel: 01767 260094
		Fax: 01767 260080
Playing:	Midweek: round £50.00; day £50.00. Weekend: round £60.00; day £60.00.	

Facilities: Bar: 11am–11pm. Food: Breakfast, lunch and dinner from 9am–9pm. Bar snacks.

Comments: Can be unwelcoming for non-members … Challenging with delightful, changing views … A very natural course with a river influencing play on four holes … Far better than the Carthagena … Very exciting … Wonderful feel to this club.

Aspley Guise & Woburn Sands Golf Club   ★★★★

West Hill, Aspley Guise, Milton Keynes, MK17 8DX
Nearest main town: Milton Keynes

Secretary:	Mr R. Norris	Tel: 01908 583596
		Fax: 01908 583596
Professional:	Mr C. Clingan	Tel: 01908 582974

Playing: Midweek: round £28.00; day n/a. Weekend: round £38.00 (prior booking only); day n/a.

Facilities: Bar: 11.30am–10.30pm. Food: Lunch and dinner from 11am–11pm. Bar snacks.

Comments: This course just makes you feel good – enough said … Heavenly greens, accuracy at a premium … Play the percentages here as there are plenty of big trees … Undulating heathland with silver birch … Make your score on the front nine … Heathland beauty in area bereft of good golf.

Beadlow Manor Hotel Golf & Country Club   ★★

Beadlow, Shefford, SG17 5PH
Nearest main town: Shefford

Secretary:	None	Tel: 01525 860666
		Fax: 01525 861345
Professional:	Messrs S. & G. Allen & Morris	Tel: 01525 860666
		Fax: 01525 861345

Playing: Midweek: round £12.00; day n/a. Weekend: round £20.00; day n/a.

Facilities: Bar: 11am–11pm. Food: Lunch and dinner from 11am–11pm. Bar snacks.

Comments: Excellent facilities at this parkland course ... Condition varies but nice amateur course ... 36-hole complex with little to choose between the two courses ... US-style layout with plenty of water hazards ... Courses could be better given the standard of facilities ... Fair value.

Bedford & County Golf Club ★★★

Green Lane, Clapham, MK41 6ET
Website: www.bedfordandcountygolfclub.co.uk
E-mail: olga@bedcounty.fsnet.uk.co
Nearest main town: Bedford

Secretary:	Mr R. Walker	Tel: 01234 352617
	(General Manager)	Fax: 01234 357195
Professional:	Mr R. Tattersall	Tel: 01234 359189
		Fax: 01234 340322

Playing: Midweek: round £26.00; day £32.00. Weekend: round members and guests only; day n/a.

Facilities: Bar: 11am–10pm. Food: Lunch from 11am–6pm. Bar snacks.

Comments: Pleasing, straightforward parkland course ... Mature layout which can play long at times ... 15th the highlight of this cheerful course ... Quiet club in quiet golfing region.

Chalgrave Manor Golf Club ★

Dunstable Road, Chalgrave, Toddington, LU5 6JN
E-mail: chalgravegolf@onetel.net.uk
Nearest main town: Dunstable

Secretary:	Mr S. Rumball	Tel: 01525 876556
		Fax: 01525 876556
Professional:	Mr G. Swain	

Playing: Midweek: round £20.00 (visitors); day n/a. Weekend: round £30.00 (visitors); day n/a.

Facilities: Bar: 11am–10pm. Food: Bar snacks.

Comments: Fun starts on the back nine ... Average condition ... Simple with plenty of birdie chances ... Adequate facilities.

Colmworth & North Bedfordshire Golf Club   ★

New Road, Colmworth, MK44 2NV
Website: www.colmworthgolfclub.co.uk
E-mail: colmworthgc@btopenworld.com
Nearest main town: Bedford

Secretary:	Mr A. Willis	Tel: 01234 378181	
		Fax: 01234 376678	
Professional:	Mr G. Bithrey	Tel: 01234 378181	
		Fax: 01234 376678	

Playing: Midweek: round £14.00; day n/a. Weekend: round
£20.00 (visitors after 10am); day n/a.

Facilities: Bar: 8am–10pm. Food: Breakfast, lunch and dinner
from 8am–10pm. Bar snacks.

Comments: A 'second shot' course ... Just about worth it for the
weekday rate ... Very friendly club.

Dunstable Downs Golf Club   ★★★

Whipsnade Road, Dunstable, LU6 2NB
Website: www.dunstable-golf.co.uk   E-mail: ddgc@btconnect.com
Nearest main town: Dunstable

Secretary:	Mr J. Nolan	Tel: 01582 604472
		Fax: 01582 478700
Professional:	Mr M. Weldon	Tel: 01582 662806

Playing: Midweek: round £28.50; day n/a. Weekend: round n/a;
day n/a.

Facilities: Bar: Members only. Food: Members only.

Comments: Dramatic course with elevated tees above sweeping
fairways ... Consistently surprising and interesting down-
land/parkland course ... Few memorable holes with the
exception of the 9th ... Edged out by John O'Gaunt as
best Beds course.

John O'Gaunt Golf Club (Carthagena)   ★★

Sutton Park, Sandy, Biggleswade, SG19 2LY
Website: www.johnogauntgolfclub.co.uk
E-mail: admin@johnogauntgolfclub.co.uk
Nearest main town: Biggleswade

Secretary: Mr S. Anthony   Tel: 01767 260360
(General Manager) Fax: 01767 262834
Professional: Mr L. Scarbrow   Tel: 01767 260094
                                   Fax: 01767 260080

Playing: Midweek: round £50.00; day £50.00. Weekend: round £60.00; day £60.00.

Facilities: Bar: 11am–11pm. Food: Breakfast, lunch and dinner from 9am–9pm. Bar snacks.

Comments: Not as mature or natural as the main course ... Very challenging holes ... Shorter than main course and short on challenge ... If you're in the area, play the main course.

Leighton Buzzard Golf Club   ★★

Plantation Road, Leighton Buzzard, LU7 3JF
Website: www.leightonbuzzardgolf.net
E-mail: secretary@leightonbuzzardgolf.net
Nearest main town: Leighton Buzzard

Secretary: Mr D. Mutton   Tel: 01525 244800
                                  Fax: 01525 244801
Professional: Mr M. Campbell Tel: 01525 244815
                                  Fax: 01525 244801

Playing: Midweek: round £34.00 (18 holes); day £36.00 (36 holes). Weekend: round with member only; day n/a.

Facilities: Bar: 11am–11pm. Food: Lunch from 11.30am–2.30pm. Dinner from 5pm–8.30pm.

Comments: Tree-lined, mature course ... Can be very busy ... Members a little protective ... Overshadowed by nearby Woburn ... Great finish.

Mentmore Golf & Country Club   ★★

Mentmore, Leighton Buzzard, LU7 0UA
Website: www.clubhaus.com   E-mail: mentmore@clubhaus.com
Nearest main town: Leighton Buzzard

Secretary: None   Tel: 01296 662020
                               Fax: 01296 662592
Professional: Mr R. Davies Tel: 01296 662020

Playing: Midweek: round prices on application; day n/a. Weekend: round n/a; day n/a.

Facilities: Bar: 11am–11pm. Food: Lunch on Sundays only from 12pm–4pm. Dinner bookings for Friday and Saturday from 7pm–10pm.

Comments: For all the grace and splendour of the main building, the course has a long way to go ... Not much between the two 18-hole courses, but both short of highest order ... Good day out with all the facilities.

The Millbrook Golf Club   ★★★

Millbrook, Ampthill, MK45 2JB
Website: www.themillbrook.com
Nearest main town: Ampthill

Secretary: Mr D. Cooke   Tel: 01525 840252
                  (Manager)   Fax: 01525 406249
Professional: Mr G. Dixon   Tel: 01525 402269

Playing: Midweek: round £22.00; day n/a. Weekend: round £28.00 (after 12pm); day n/a.

Facilities: Bar: 11am–9pm. Food: Bar snacks.

Comments: You need to be fit to play here ... Quite challenging ... Long course through woodland on rolling hills ... Good value ... Playable most of the year ... Progressive club ... Value golf.

South Beds Golf Club   ★★

Warden Hill Road, Luton, LU2 7AE
Nearest main town: Luton

Secretary: Mr R. Wright   Tel: 01582 591500
                                        Fax: 01582 495381
Professional: Mr E. Cogle   Tel: 01582 591209

Playing: Midweek: round prices on application; day n/a. Weekend: round n/a; day n/a.

Facilities: Bar: 11.30am–11pm. Food: Lunch and dinner from 11.30am–11pm. Bar snacks.

Comments: Plenty of holes (27), but all of average quality ... Normally in good condition ... Very busy ... Worth a try once ... Downland course with some dramatic holes.

Wyboston Lakes Golf Club   ★★

Wyboston Lakes, Wyboston, MK44 3AL
Website: www.wybostonlakes.co.uk
Nearest main town: St Neots

Secretary:	Mrs M. Oldfield	Tel: 01480 880350
Professional:	Mr P. Ashwell	Tel: 01480 223004
		Fax: 01480 407330

Playing: Midweek: round £13.75; day n/a. Weekend: round £18.00; day n/a.

Facilities: Bar: 11.30am–11pm. Food: Lunch and dinner from 11.30am–10pm. Bar snacks.

Comments: Beginners' course ... Terrific facilities and a worthy challenge ... A cheap course, not far behind some of the better ones in Beds ... Practice areas high class.

Berkshire

The Berkshire (Red & Blue) Golf Club ★★★★★

Swinley Road, Ascot, SL5 8AY
Nearest main town: Ascot

Some golfers swear that the perfect golfing day out is to be had not on the links courses of Britain and Ireland but just off the M3 near Bracknell. Thirty-six holes of golf, playing the Red and Blue courses at the Berkshire, one either side of lunch, is, they say, sheer golfing heaven and a wonderful escape from the outside world.

The peace and tranquillity that can be found on these fairways, carved out of pine, chestnut and birch forest, is truly intoxicating. Not even the great heath and heather courses of nearby Surrey have quite the same feel as a late afternoon in the forest at the Berkshire. Which course you play matters little, as there is no general consensus as to which is the best, and no one knows which one the designer, Herbert Fowler (he of Walton Heath and Saunton fame), preferred.

The Red course is certainly more interesting, mixing six par-3s, six par-4s and six par-5s, a very modern blend of holes that many players wish they could have more of. The par-5s are really needed because of the depth and difficulty of the par-3s, many of which require long irons to tiny greens protected on all sides. The 221-yard 16th, where the plateau green can only be held with a shot to the centre, is a good example. Indeed, it is a very tough track, where, even if you do manage to keep out of the trees, you are still likely to get tangled up in heather.

For a more traditional round, the Blue course may appeal more. The hazards are essentially the same as those of the Red, with a stream coming into play on several fairways. It is shorter and perhaps a little easier than the Red, although the bunkering appears to be more precise and more thought is needed when you are standing on the tee.

Some say when you make a composite course of the two, as they do for competitions, you have the perfect golf course. Play this course on a crisp autumn or spring day, and you won't disagree.

Secretary: Col J. Hunt   Tel: 01344 621496/621495
Professional: Mr P. Anderson   Tel: 01344 622351
Fax: 01344 873090

Playing: Midweek: round £75.00; day £95.00. Weekend: round members only; day n/a.

Facilities: Bar: Members only. Food: Members only

Comments: It just gets tougher and tougher – a wonderful design ... Attractive heather ... Both courses are what golf is all about ... Stuffy atmosphere, but who cares when the golf is this good ... Classic heathland course where you can contemplate amongst the trees.

Swinley Forest Golf Club ★★★★★

Coronation Road, Ascot, SL5 9LE
E-mail: swinleyfgc@aol.com
Nearest main town: Ascot

Hidden in the heathland folds of the Berkshire stockbroker belt, Swinley has that 'land that time forgot' feel about it. The atmosphere lends itself to a feeling of exclusivity which sits comfortably on the club's shoulders. They are off the beaten track and rather pleased about it.

If you're fortunate enough to play Swinley, you are in for a rare treat. The work of Harry Colt, this is a fine example of traditional heathland design. The course is not long, but can be quite punishing for those who venture off line. Heather clings to the edges of fairways that have an adventurous ride over the humps and hollows of the woodlands that flank the Ascot horse-racing circuit. This heather, its delicate purple flowers adding a splash of colour to an already inspirational canvas, can be a golfer's nightmare. It wraps itself round your club with a vice-like grip, ensuring that anyone trying to gain a little too much ground gets adequately punished.

There are two moments in a round of golf at Swinley that stick in the memory. At the latter end of a glorious front nine, it is the 9th that sends the temperature soaring, particularly if you are a fan of a good driving hole. The fairway is inviting from an elevated tee, but you would do well to hug the left-hand side to get the shortest route to the pin.

Another vivid memory comes on the approach to the par-4 12th. The green is quite large and inviting and behind it climbs a grandstand of rhododendrons, whose blooms peer over one another to get a better view.

Secretary: Mr I. Pearce   Tel: 01344 874979
                                 Fax: 01344 874733
Professional: Mr S. Hill   Tel: 01344 874811

Playing: Midweek: round n/a; day £80.00. Weekend: round no visitors; day n/a.

Facilities: Bar: 11am–11.30pm. Food: Lunch and dinner served. Bar snacks.

Comments: One of the golfing gems of England ... Premium on shot-making ... Very traditional – be on your best behaviour.

Bearwood Lakes Golf Club   ★★★★

Bearwood Road, Sindlesham, RG41 4SJ
Website: www.bearwoodlakes.co.uk
E-mail: golf@bearwoodlakes.co.uk
Nearest main town: Wokingham

Secretary:	Mr S. Evans	Tel: 0118 979 7900
	(General Manager)	Fax: 0118 979 2911
Professional:	Mr T. Waldron	Tel: 0118 978 3030
		Fax: 0118 979 2911

Playing: Midweek: round members and guests only; day n/a. Weekend: round n/a; day n/a.

Facilities: Bar: Members only. Food: Members only.

Comments: Modern design ... No two holes are the same ... One of the best courses to open in the last few years ... Very helpful pro shop ... Parkland course with a smattering of water ... Best holes on the back nine around the lake.

Calcot Park Golf Club   ★★

Bath Road, Calcot, RG31 7RN
Website: www.calcotpark.fsworld.co.uk   E-mail: info@calcotpark.com
Nearest main town: Reading

Secretary:	Ms K. Brake	Tel: 0118 942 7124
		Fax: 0118 945 3373
Professional:	Mr I. Campbell	Tel: 0118 942 7797
		E-mail: ian.campbell@virgin.net

Playing: Midweek: round £40.00; day n/a. Weekend: round n/a; day n/a.

Facilities: Bar: 11am–11pm. Food: Lunch and dinner from 11am–9pm. Bar snacks.

Comments: Undulating, open fairways ... Get out the driver ... 6th worth looking out for ... Interesting water features ... Company helped me enjoy this tough, changing track ... Fun to play with friends.

Castle Royle Golf Club ★★

Bath Road, Knowl Hill, Reading, RG10 9XA
Nearest main town: Reading

Secretary:	Mr B. Lee	Tel: 01628 829252
Professional:	Mr P. Stanwick	Tel: 01628 825442

Playing: Midweek: round £35.00; day n/a. Weekend: round £45.00; day n/a.

Facilities: Bar: 7.30am–10.30pm. Food: Breakfast, lunch and dinner from 7.30am–8pm. Bar snacks.

Comments: Fairly unremarkable land for a golf course ... Way too pricey ... Neil Coles did a good job with raw materials ... Plenty of water ... Too expensive ... Views of Windsor Castle.

Downshire Golf Club ★★

Easthampstead Park, Wokingham, RG40 3DH
Website: www.bracknell-forest.gov.uk/downshiregc
E-mail: downshiregc@bracknell-forest.gov.uk
Nearest main town: Wokingham

Secretary:	Mr P. Stanwick	Tel: 01344 422708
		Fax: 01344 301020
Professional:	Mr W. Owers	Tel: 01344 302030
		Fax: 01344 301020

Playing: Midweek: round £17.60; day n/a. Weekend: round £21.75; day n/a.

Facilities: Bar: 11am–11pm. Food: Breakfast and lunch from 7am–4pm. Dinner by arrangement.

Comments: Course catering for all standards ... Extremely good pay-and-play ... Mature public parkland course, hard to beat for municipal golf ... 7th and 15th stand out here ... Well done Downshire, best municipal in the land!

East Berkshire Golf Club ★★★★

Ravenswood Avenue, Crowthorne, RG45 6BD
E-mail: thesecretary@eastberksgc.fsnet.co.uk
Nearest main town: Crowthorne

Secretary:	Mr D. Kelly	Tel: 01344 772041
		Fax: 01344 777378
Professional:	Mr J. Brant	Tel: 01344 774112

Playing: Midweek: round £46.00; day n/a. Weekend: round n/a; day no visitors.

Facilities: Bar: 11am–8pm. Food: Lunch from 11am–5pm. Bar snacks.

Comments: Not far behind the Berkshire ... Very easy on the eye ... First-rate course in heavenly countryside ... The smell of heather and pine simply intoxicating ... Not as hilly as other nearby courses ... A picture ... Heather makes life very tough.

Goring & Streatley Golf Club   ★★★★

Rectory Road, Streatley-on-Thames, RG8 9QA
E-mail: goringgc@aol.com
Nearest main town: Reading

Secretary:	Mr I. McColl	Tel: 01491 873229
		Fax: 01491 875224
Professional:	Mr J. Hadland	Tel: 01491 873715

Playing: Midweek: round £28.00; day £35.00. Weekend: round £28.00; day £35.00.

Facilities: Bar: 10.30am–11pm. Food: Lunch and dinner from 11am–8pm. Bar snacks.

Comments: Hilly course ... Sloping lies and high scores ... Wonderful views of the River Thames ... Very friendly club – wish you could say the same about the course ... Views of the Ridgeway on this up-and-down course.

Hennerton Golf Club   ★

Crazies Hill Road, Wargrave, RG10 8LT
Website: www.hennertongolfclub.co.uk
E-mail: info@hennertongolfclub.co.uk
Nearest main town: Wargrave

Secretary:	Ms Z. Hearn	Tel: 0118 940 1000
		Fax: 0118 940 1042
Professional:	Mr W. Farrow	Tel: 0118 940 4778
		Fax: 0118 940 1042

Playing: Midweek: round visitors £17.00 (18 holes), £12.00 (9 holes); day n/a. Weekend: round visitors £20.00 (18 holes), £15.00 (9 holes); day n/a.

Facilities: Bar: 11am–11pm. Food: Lunch and dinner from 10am–8pm. Bar snacks.

Comments: Not many nine-holers in the area but this is the best ... Very natural ... Good value for nine holes ... Good for anyone who can't cope with a full round ... Fun for beginners, swerve it if you know the game.

Maidenhead Golf Club   ★★

Shoppenhangers Road, Maidenhead, SL6 2PZ
Website: www.maidenheadgolf.co.uk
E-mail: manager@maidenheadgolf.co.uk
Nearest main town: Maidenhead

Secretary:	None	Tel: 01628 624693
		Fax: 01628 780758
Professional:	Mr S. Geary	Tel: 01628 624067
		Fax: 01628 780758

Playing: Midweek: round £35.00; day n/a. Weekend: round n/a; day n/a.

Facilities: Bar: 11am–10pm. Food: Lunch from 11am–6pm. Bar snacks.

Comments: Par-3s really stand out ... Very flat and fairly simple ... Good short holes ... Parkland course, but there is better in Berkshire.

Mill Ride Golf Club   ★★★

Mill Ride, Ascot, SL5 8LT
Website: www.mill-ride.com
Nearest main town: Ascot

Secretary:	Mr A. Gillies	Tel: 01344 886777
		Fax: 01344 886820
Professional:	Mr T. Wyld	Tel: 01344 886777
		Fax: 01344 886820

Playing: Midweek: round n/a; day £50.00. Weekend: round n/a; day £75.00.

Facilities: Bar: 7.30am–11pm. Food: Breakfast and lunch from 7.30am–6pm.

Comments: New course with plenty of character ... A little expensive ... Best yet to come ... Very challenging ... Overpriced, like all the courses in this area.

Newbury & Crookham Golf Club   ★★★

Burys Bank Road, Greenham, Newbury, RG19 8BZ
E-mail: june.hearsey@newburygolf.co.uk
Nearest main town: Newbury

Secretary:	Mrs J. Hearsey	Tel: 01635 40035
		Fax: 01635 40045
Professional:	Mr D. Harris	Tel: 01635 31201

Playing: Midweek: round £25.00; day n/a. Weekend: round £25.00; day n/a.

Facilities: Bar: 11am–11pm. Food: Lunch from 11am–2pm. Bar snacks. Dinner by arrangement.

Comments: Decent value for a hugely underrated course ... Interesting parkland ... Think carefully around this strategic track ... Trees seemingly in the way all the time ... Good value ... Condition varies and facilities a little poor ... Best course for miles around.

Reading Golf Club   ★★★

Kidmore End Road, Emmer Green, Reading, RG4 8SG
E-mail: secretary@readinggolfclub.golfagent.co.uk
Nearest main town: Reading

Secretary:	Mr R. Brown	Tel: 0118 947 2909
		Fax: 0118 946 4468
Professional:	Mr S. Fotheringham	Tel: 0118 947 6115

Playing: Midweek: round n/a; day £33.00. Weekend: round n/a; day n/a.

Facilities: Bar: 11am–11pm. Food: Bar snacks.

Comments: Very friendly and simple club ... Par-3 the highlight ... Not much to get excited about.

Sonning Golf Club ★★

Duffield Road, Sonning-on-Thames, Reading, RG4 6GJ
E-mail: atanner@sonning-golf-club.co.uk
Nearest main town: Reading

Secretary: Mr A. Tanner   Tel: 0118 969 3332
                              Fax: 0118 944 8409
Professional: Mr R. McDougall   Tel: 0118 969 2910

Playing: Midweek: round £25.00 (18 holes); day £35.00 (36 holes). Weekend: round members only; day n/a.

Facilities: Bar: 11am–11pm. Food: Lunch from 12pm–2pm. Dinner from 6pm–9pm.

Comments: Flat, but long and hard course ... Fairly flat and dull ... Key is driving the ball well ... Pretty straightforward and open – just how I like it ... By no means in the top echelon in Berkshire, but lovely feel to this club ... Clubhouse recently improved, much overdue.

Temple Golf Club ★★★

Henley Road, Hurley, SL6 5LH
E-mail: templegolfclub@btconnect.com
Nearest main town: Maidenhead

Secretary: Mr K. Adderley   Tel: 01628 824795
                               Fax: 01628 828119
Professional: Mr J. Whiteley   Tel: 01628 824254

Playing: Midweek: round £40.00; day £52.00. Weekend: round £50.00; day £60.00.

Facilities: Bar: 11am–10pm. Food: Bar snacks. Dinner by arrangement.

Comments: Nobble your opening tee shot and the ball just scampers down the hill ... Great variety at this exclusive bolt-hole near Marlow ... The punchbowl green at the 12th throws out the rulebook ... Some monster par-4s with long iron approaches ... A fine parkland course with great value and service ... Lovely autumn course when the colours are so bold ... 11th is the toughest hole here.

West Berkshire Golf Club ★★★

Chaddleworth, Newbury, RG20 7DU
E-mail: thewestberkshire@tesco.net
Nearest main town: Newbury

Secretary:	Mr T. Eyres	Tel: 01488 638574
		Fax: 01488 638781
Professional:	Mr P. Simpson	Tel: 01488 638851

Playing: Midweek: round £20.00; day n/a. Weekend: round £30.00 (pm only); day n/a.

Facilities: Bar: 11am–11pm. Food: 9am–4.30pm. Bar snacks.

Comments: Goes on forever ... Decent value ... Long and not that interesting ... Expected heath and heather but got a flat-tish, nondescript course ... Not blessed with area's fine scenery ... Good value ... Easy walking for a long course ... Par-5 5th is one of longest in England at over 600 yards ... Get a buggy ... Long par-5 is just a joke.

Winter Hill Golf Club ★★

Grange Lane, Cookham, SL6 9RP
Nearest main town: Maidenhead

Secretary:	Mr M. Goodenough	Tel: 01628 527613
		Fax: 01628 527479
Professional:	Mr R. Frost	Tel: 01628 527610
		Fax: 01628 527479

Playing: Midweek: round n/a; day £31.00. Weekend: round n/a; day n/a.

Facilities: Bar: 11.30am–9.30pm. Food: Bar snacks from 11.30am–5pm.

Comments: Views overlooking the River Thames towards Cliveden don't disguise how average this course is ... Straightforward course with many uninteresting holes ... Very open, bad shots not always punished ... Not on my list in Berkshire.

Buckinghamshire

Woburn Golf & Country Club (Dukes)   ★★★★

Little Brickhill, Milton Keynes, MK17 9LJ
Website: www.woburngolf.com   E-mail: enquiries@woburngolf.com
Nearest main town: Milton Keynes

One of the best-known and most popular courses in England, Woburn consistently justifies its position as a favourite among discerning golfers. Few other courses in the country have as much appeal as Woburn, a feeling that was perpetuated by the flattering television pictures of the course when the British Masters was held there on a regular basis. Although it no longer hosts top tournaments, the condition of the course is always good and provides a quality golfing day out, particularly for golf societies that aspire to deliver a quality course for their members at reasonable rates. As a consequence, the course can get busy and it's worth checking out in advance when you can play. The Woburn experience is not something that you can keep to yourself.

The course is certainly demanding, and is not recommended for the inexperienced, who will find it a long slog and a hopeless criss-cross across fairways to find the ball in woods. Woburn is essentially a driver's course, and the player who can hit it long and straight can invariably score well as there are few dangers around the greens. Most of the fairways are bordered by magnificent pines, so there is no real need for any rough at Woburn, except on some of the more exposed holes around the turn. One of the hardest shots you will have to master here is how to play your ball off pine needles, which really need to be nipped off a tight lie. This is particularly the case at the 4th, a wonderful dogleg played through a funnel of pines. It is arguably the strongest hole on a front nine that must rank as the best in British golf. That really is no exaggeration, and if the Dukes had a more inspiring mid-section it would rival Sunningdale as the top inland course in England. Practice facilities here are some of the best in Europe, while the club lunch is legendary. No one who plays Woburn should leave without dining here. The advice is not to have something too big at breakfast, as portions at lunch are more than generous. You'll enjoy the quality of the food as you will the course. And that goes for both the Duchess and Marquess courses as well.

Secretary: Mrs G. Beasley   Tel: 01908 370756
                                        Fax: 01908 378436

Professional: Mr L. Blacklock   Tel: 01908 626600

Playing: Midweek: round prices on application; day n/a. Weekend: round members and guests only; day n/a.

Facilities: Bar: 10.30am–11pm. Food: Lunch from 12pm–2.30pm.

Comments: Just a fine golfing experience – perfect ... Fantastic day's golf ... Cut out of a forest, this course is simply superb ... Outstanding day out spoilt by the cost of play ... Most imaginatively designed course in the south of England ... Quality course demanding quality golf.

Beaconsfield Golf Club ★★★

Farm Lane, Seer Green, Beaconsfield, HP9 2UR
E-mail: secretary@beaconsfieldgolfclub.co.uk
Nearest main town: Beaconsfield

Secretary: Mr K. Wilcox   Tel: 01494 676545
                                 Fax: 01494 681148
Professional: Mr M. Brothers   Tel: 01494 676616

Playing: Midweek: round £36.00; day £50.00. Weekend: round members' guests only; day n/a.

Facilities: Bar: 11am–9.30pm. Food: Breakfast and lunch from 9am–5pm. Dinner by arrangement.

Comments: Played here in abysmal weather but not one blade of grass was out of place ... Good, interesting parkland course requiring a subtle short game to score well ... Much improved over the last two years ... Not particularly welcoming but the course makes up for it ... Cracking clubhouse and the course, well, I didn't want to leave ... Arresting course that never takes the driver out of your hands ... Better than Stoke Poges and more homely for the visitor ... Could not wait to play after glimpsing it from the railway ... Super finish to elegant course.

The Buckinghamshire Golf Club ★★★★

Denham Court Mansion, Denham Court Drive, Denham, UB9 5PG
Website: www.buckinghamshire-golfclub.co.uk
E-mail: enquiries@bucks.dircon.co.uk
Nearest main town: Uxbridge

Secretary:	Mr E. Roca	Tel: 01895 835777
		Fax: 01895 835210
Professional:	Mr J. O'Leary	Tel: 01895 835777
		Fax: 01895 835210

Playing: Midweek: round £80.00; day n/a. Weekend: round £90.00; day n/a.

Facilities: Bar: 11am–11pm. Food: Lunch from 12pm–2pm. Dinner from 7pm–9pm.

Comments: Fantastic greens all year round ... A real pleasure to play ... Greens just perfect ... Super greens – slick but holding ... A good test in unrivalled atmosphere ... Best course in the UK, fantastic practice facilities and excellent clubhouse ... A course that feels as if it's been around for years ... Don't miss it.

Burnham Beeches Golf Club   ★★★

Green Lane, Burnham, Slough, SL1 8EG
Website: www.bbgc.co.uk   E-mail: enquiries@bbgc.co.uk
Nearest main town: Slough

Secretary:	Mr T. Jackson	Tel: 01628 661448
		Fax: 01628 668968
Professional:	Mr R. Bolton	Tel: 01628 661661

Playing: Midweek: round £38.00; day n/a. Weekend: round n/a; day n/a.

Facilities: Bar: 11am–10pm. Food: Lunch and dinner from 10am–8pm.

Comments: Traditional parkland golf ... Value given its proximity to some pricey courses ... Continues to be a proper golf club ... Almost as good as nearby Stoke Poges ... If you go, take time to enjoy the woods ... Surprisingly open, welcoming club – usually quiet.

Chiltern Forest Golf Club   ★★★

Aston Hill, Halton, HP22 5NQ
Website: www.chilternforest.co.uk
E-mail: secretary@chilternforest.co.uk
Nearest main town: Aylesbury

Secretary:	Mr B. Cliff	Tel: 01296 631267
		Fax: 01296 632709
Professional:	Mr A. Lavers	Tel: 01296 631817

Playing: Midweek: round £30.00; day n/a. Weekend: round with member only; day n/a.

Facilities: Bar: 11am–11pm. Food: Lunch and dinner from 12pm–6pm. Bar snacks.

Comments: Very underrated ... Scenic but don't be fooled by the course ... Danger everywhere you look ... Great-looker but not that difficult.

Denham Golf Club   ★★★

Tilehouse Lane, Denham, UB9 5DE
Website: www.denhamgolfclub
E-mail: club.secretary@denhamgolfclub.co.uk
Nearest main town: Denham

Secretary:	Mr M. Miller	Tel: 01895 832022
		Fax: 01895 835340
Professional:	Mr S. Campbell	Tel: 01895 832801
		Fax: 01895 835743

Playing: Midweek: round £55.00 (Mon–Thurs, 18 holes), £75.00 (18+); day n/a. Weekend: round members' guests only; day n/a.

Facilities: Bar: 11am–8pm. Food: Lunch from 11am–4pm. Bar snacks.

Comments: Dropped in by chance and felt thoroughly welcome ... So nice, so close to London ... Its difficulty is somewhat reliant on the weather ... Beguiling parkland/heathland ... Top of the tree in Bucks ... Hilly, but you don't mind here.

Ellesborough Golf Club   ★★★

Butlers Cross, Aylesbury, HP17 0TZ
Nearest main town: Aylesbury

Secretary:	Mr P. York	Tel: 01296 622114
		Fax: 01296 622114
Professional:	Mr M. Squire	Tel: 01296 623126

Playing: Midweek: round £30.00; day £40.00. Weekend: round n/a; day n/a.

Facilities: Bar: 11am–11pm. Food: Breakfast and lunch from 11am–7pm.

Comments: Interesting course with scenery to match ... Not too difficult to master and excellent facilities ... Too hilly to be considered top class ... Dreary downland track.

Farnham Park (Bucks) Golf Club   ★★

Park Road, Stoke Poges, SL2 4PJ
Website: www.farnhampark.co.uk
E-mail: farnhamparkgolfclub@btopenworld.com
Nearest main town: Stoke Poges

Secretary: Mrs M. Brooker   Tel: 01753 647065
                                       Fax: 01753 647065
Professional: Mr P. Warner   Tel: 01753 643332
                                       Fax: 01753 643332

Playing: Midweek: round £13.00 (reductions for seniors); day n/a. Weekend: round £18.00 (reductions for juniors); day n/a.

Facilities: Bar: 11am–11pm. Food: Lunch and dinner from 11am–11pm. Bar snacks.

Comments: Pay-and-play that is consistently good ... A quality pay-and-play ... Mix of bland and interesting holes ... 9th is particularly good driving over the corner of a lake ... Some class holes on the front nine ... Condition not great but well worth it for the price ... Can get a bit boggy.

Flackwell Heath Golf Club   ★★

Treadaway Road, Flackwell Heath, High Wycombe, HP10 9PE
Website: www.flackwellheathgolfclub.co.uk
E-mail: info@flackwellheathgolfclub.co.uk
Nearest main town: High Wycombe

Secretary: Mr S. Chandler   Tel: 01628 520929
                                       Fax: 01628 530040
Professional: Mr P. Watson   Tel: 01628 523017
                                       Fax: 01628 529662

Playing: Midweek: round £25.00; day £38.00. Weekend: round n/a; day n/a.

Facilities: Bar: 11am–8pm. Food: Lunch from 12pm–2pm.
Dinner from 6pm–9pm. Bar snacks.

Comments: Clip on the crampons ... Very hilly with good par-3s ...
Long 7th next to the M40 is a very unattractive hole ...
15th is a cracker ... Short front nine consistently
interesting, although a little easy ... Not the best in Bucks.

Gerrards Cross Golf Club   ★★★

Chalfont Park, Gerrards Cross, SL9 0QA
Website: www.gxgolf.co.uk   E-mail: secretary@gxgolf.demon.co.uk
Nearest main town: Gerrards Cross

Secretary: Mr B. Cable   Tel: 01753 883263
                                        Fax: 01753 883593
Professional: Mr M. Barr   Tel: 01753 885300
                                        Fax: 01753 883593

Playing: Midweek: round £38.00; day n/a. Weekend: round n/a;
day n/a.

Facilities: Bar: 11am–11pm. Food: Breakfast, lunch and dinner
available 8am–10pm. Bar snacks.

Comments: Sensational unknown course that never fails to surprise
... Nice doglegs and straightaway holes ... Par-3s are
the highlight of this well-prepared and exclusive course
... This and Beaconsfield are superb to play and just
sublime on warm summer evenings ... Can't pick
between this and Beaconsfield.

Harleyford Golf Club   ★★★

Harleyford Estate, Henley Road, Marlow, SL7 2SP
Website: www.harleyfordgolf.co.uk   E-mail: info@harleyfordgolf.co.uk
Nearest main town: Marlow

Secretary: Mr G. Ivory   Tel: 01628 816167
                                        Fax: 01628 816160
Professional: Mr L. Jackson   Tel: 01628 816162
                                        Fax: 01628 816160

Playing: Midweek: round £45.00; day n/a. Weekend: round
£65.00; day n/a.

Facilities: Bar: 11am–11pm. Food: Lunch and dinner from
10am–9pm. Bar snacks.

Comments: Very British feel to this course ... Rich countryside in affluent area ... Very mature woodland site ... Grass bunkers give an old-fashioned feel ... Feels like a country retreat ... Holes wind their way down to the Thames ... Watch out for the chalk pit on the 12th ... Fine course.

The Lambourne Golf Club ★★★

Dropmore Road, Burnham, SL1 8NF
Website: www.gch.co.uk
Nearest main town: Burnham

Secretary: Mr D. Hart   Tel: 01628 666755
     Fax: 01628 663301
Professional: Mr D. Hart   Tel: 01628 662936

Playing: Midweek: round £40.00 (18 holes); day £45.00. Weekend: round £38.00; day £48.00.

Facilities: Bar: 11am–11pm. Food: Lunch and dinner from 10am–9pm. Bar snacks.

Comments: Perfect location ... Well worth visiting and some cracking courses nearby ... A course with big ambition ... Championship feel here and close to Burnham Beeches.

Stoke Park Golf Club ★★★★

Park Road, Stoke Poges, SL2 4PG
Website: www.stokeparkclub.com   E-mail: info@stokeparkclub.com
Nearest main town: Stoke Poges

Secretary: Ms K. Ford   Tel: 01753 717171
     Fax: 01753 717181
Professional: Mr S. Collier   Tel: 01753 717184
     Fax: 01753 717181

Playing: Midweek: round £125.00; day n/a. Weekend: round £200.00 (Saturday only); day n/a.

Facilities: Bar: 11am–9pm. Food: Lunch and dinner from 11am–9pm. Bar snacks.

Comments: A tough course that can be a long slog at times ... The clubhouse is almost a palace – a gorgeous course ... Well presented and always in cream condition ... Clever bunkering ... Once one of my favourite old-fashioned clubs, now a vulgar country club (but the condition's better) ... Superbly restored clubhouse and the course is becoming a real complement ... Follow in the footsteps of James Bond.

Weston Turville Golf Club ★★

New Road, Weston Turville, Aylesbury, HP22 5QT
E-mail: westonturvillego@btconnect.com
Nearest main town: Aylesbury

Secretary:	Mr D. Allen	Tel: 01296 424084
		Fax: 01296 397536
Professional:	Mr G. George	Tel: 01296 425949
		Fax: 01296 397536

Playing: Midweek: round £20.00; day n/a. Weekend: round £25.00; day n/a.

Facilities: Bar: 10am–9pm. Food: Bar snacks.

Comments: Easy walking ... Nothing special here ... Some interesting, natural holes ... Good value for a well-conditioned course ... Flat course with little definition ... Pretty good value for money.

Woburn Golf Club (Duchess) ★★★★

Bow Brickhill, Milton Keynes, MK17 9LJ
Website: www.woburngolf.com
Nearest main town: Milton Keynes

Secretary:	Mrs G. Beasley	Tel: 01908 370756
		Fax: 01908 378436
Professional:	Mr L. Blacklock	Tel: 01908 626600

Playing: Midweek: round prices on application; day n/a. Weekend: round n/a; day n/a.

Facilities: Bar: 10.30am–11pm. Food: Lunch from 12pm–2.30pm.

Comments: Looks great ... Excellent carvery meal ... Super day out ... Slightly easier than the Dukes but first class in its own right ... Give me the Duchess over the Dukes anyday.

Woburn Golf Club (Marquess)   ★★★★

Little Brickhill, Milton Keynes, MK17 9LJ
Website: www.woburngolf.com
Nearest main town: Milton Keynes

Secretary: Mrs G. Beasley   Tel: 01908 370756
                                       Fax: 01908 378436
Professional: Mr L. Blacklock   Tel: 01908 626600

Playing: Midweek: round prices on application; day n/a. Weekend: round n/a; day n/a.

Facilities: Bar: 10.30am–11pm. Food: Lunch from 12pm–2.30pm.

Comments: The Marquess is the jewel in Woburn's majestic crown ... It may be Woburn's newest course but it is certainly not overawed by the neighbouring Dukes and Duchess layouts ... It's expensive but even so it's worth every penny, a truly memorable golfing experience ... You'd be hard pushed to find a finer inland course.

Cambridgeshire

Gog Magog Golf Club ★★★★

Shelford Bottom, Cambridge, CB2 4AB
Website: www.gogmagog.co.uk   E-mail: secretary@gogmagog.co.uk
Nearest main town: Cambridge

With a name like Gog Magog you certainly expect something different from this course. In fact, it is very traditional and English, a hillside/parkland layout which has not changed much since its creation a hundred years ago.

Just 3½ miles south-west of the university city of Cambridge, Gog Magog is accustomed to entertaining some of the best amateur golfers in the country. The famous Lagonda Trophy has been played here many times and even the best amateurs have struggled to humiliate a course that celebrated its centenary in 2001.

Gog Magog is hilly in terms of Cambridgeshire's general relief, with the first two holes rising away and the last two holes descending to the clubhouse. In between you will find punishing rough, deep pot bunkers, hard and fast greens, and a mix of winds that makes it increasingly difficult throughout the round to stay on the straight and narrow.

It is a fine challenge for a par-70 and the members will tell you that the front nine, 330 yards shorter than the back, is the place to make your score. Certainly the 1st is as gentle an opening hole as you can find anywhere and the 2nd, despite sounding intimidating with an old quarry in front of the tee box, is anything but, and can be a fair birdie opportunity. Out of the open country the course gets progressively flatter and more straightforward. Protecting your score is dependent on accurate driving and scoring well on the simple holes.

The finishing trio of holes is tough. The 449-yard 16th is regarded as a signature hole with heavy-handed fairway bunkering, while the 17th is a tricky downhill par-3 of 165 yards with a difficult-to-hold green. As a finishing hole, the 18th is a cracker, a par-4 of 446 yards running downhill to a green that runs away from you.

Secretary: Mr I. Simpson   Tel: 01223 247626
                                      Fax: 01223 414990
Professional: Mr I. Bamborough   Tel: 01223 246058
                                      Fax: 01223 413644

Playing: Midweek: round £37.00 (18 holes); £44.00 (36 holes); day n/a. Weekend: round £60.00 (18 holes, weekends and bank holidays); day n/a.

Facilities: Bar: 11am–11pm. Food: Lunch and dinner from 10am–9pm.

Comments: Challenging, hilly course that leaves you wanting more ... Forget the Wandlebury, the one you want is the Old course ... Improves all the time ... Well-maintained pro shop ... The finest course in Cambridgeshire ... A must play for the traditionalist.

Abbotsley Golf & Country Club (Abbotsley)   ★★

Eynesbury, Hardwicke, St Neots, PE19 6XN
E-mail: abbotsley@americangolf.uk.com
Nearest main town: Cambridge

Secretary: Mr J. Tubb   Tel: 01480 474000
                                          Fax: 01480 403280
Professional: Mr S. Connolly   Tel: 01480 215153
                                          Fax: 01480 406463

Playing: Midweek: round £20.00; day n/a. Weekend: round £30.00; day n/a.

Facilities: Bar: 10am–12 midnight. Food: Bar snacks. Dinner from 7.30pm–9.30pm.

Comments: Value for the money ... Mature parkland with numerous water hazards ... In design terms, way ahead of the Cromwell ... Tough finish ... Course surrounds a moated country house.

Abbotsley Golf & Country Club (Cromwell)   ★★

Eynesbury, Hardwicke, St Neots, PE19 6XN
E-mail: abbotsley@americangolf.uk.com
Nearest main town: Cambridge

Secretary: Mr J. Tubb   Tel: 01480 474000
                                          Fax: 01480 403280
Professional: Mr S. Connolly   Tel: 01480 215153
                                          Fax: 01480 406463

Playing: Midweek: round £14.00; day n/a. Weekend: round £20.00; day n/a.

Facilities: Bar: 11am–11pm. Food: Bar snacks.

Comments: Very simple ... Less taxing than the main course ... Nice course to learn the game ... Average condition and challenge.

Brampton Park Golf Club   ★★★

Buckden Road, Brampton, Huntingdon, PE28 4NF
Nearest main town: Huntingdon

Secretary: Mr R. Oakes   Tel: 01480 434700
                                      Fax: 01480 411145
Professional: Mr A. Currie   Tel: 01480 434705

Playing: Midweek: round £20.00; day £25.00. Weekend: round n/a; day n/a.

Facilities: Bar: 11am–11pm. Food: Bar snacks.

Comments: Island green at the 4th ... Nice touches on this attractive course ... Solid club, very welcoming ... Good value for the area.

Cambridge National Golf   ★

Comberton Road, Toft, Cambridge, CB3 7RY
Website: www.golfsocieties.com   E-mail: meridian@golfsocieties.com
Nearest main town: Cambridge

Secretary: Mrs I. Van Rooyen   Tel: 01223 264700
                                      Fax: 01223 264701
Professional: Mr J. Saxon-Mills   Tel: 01223 264702

Playing: Midweek: round £16.00; day n/a. Weekend: round £25.00; day n/a.

Facilities: Bar: 10.30am–9pm. Food: Bar snacks.

Comments: Can think of better places to be ... Very long ... A little unnatural ... Bold, sweeping parkland.

Elton Furze Golf Club

Bullock Road, Haddon, Peterborough, PE7 3TT
Website: www.eltonfurzegolfclub.co.uk
E-mail: secretary@eltonfurzegolfclub.co.uk
Nearest main town: Peterborough

Secretary:	Mrs H. Barrow	Tel: 01832 280189
		Fax: 01832 280299
Professional:	None	Tel: 01832 280614

Playing: Midweek: round £22.00; day £30.00. Weekend: round £32.00; day n/a.

Facilities: Bar: 11am–11pm. Food: Lunch from 12.30pm–2pm. Dinner from 6pm–8.45pm. Bar snacks.

Comments: Can only get better ... Not one for the notebook ... Parkland without much character.

Lakeside Lodge Golf Centre ★★★

Fen Road, Pidley, Huntingdon, PE28 3DF
Website: www.lakeside-lodge.co.uk
E-mail: info@lakeside-lodge.co.uk
Nearest main town: Huntingdon

Secretary:	Mrs J. Hopkins	Tel: 01487 740540
		Fax: 01487 740852
Professional:	Mr S. Waterman	Tel: 01487 741541
		Fax: 01487 740852

Playing: Midweek: round £14.00 (9 holes £7.50); day n/a. Weekend: round £22.00 (9 holes £11.00); day n/a.

Facilities: Bar: 11am–11pm. Food: Lunch and dinner from 12pm–9pm. Closed Monday and Tuesday evenings.

Comments: Pay-and-play with excellent practice facilities ... Training ground for new players – can't be bettered in its field ... Open, kind course ... 9th and 18th around the lake are the best holes.

Peterborough Milton Golf Club ★★★

Milton Ferry, Peterborough, PE6 7AG
Website: www.club-noticeboard.co.uk
E-mail: miltongolfclub@aol.com
Nearest main town: Peterborough

Secretary:	Mr A. Izod	Tel: 01733 380489
		Fax: 01733 380489
Professional:	Mr M. Gallagher	Tel: 01733 380793

Playing: Midweek: round £30.00; day £40.00. Weekend: round £30.00; day £40.00.

Facilities: Bar: 11am–11pm. Food: Bar and restaurant.

Comments: Parkland course ... Practice ground ... Friendly club ... Best in Peterborough.

Thorpe Wood Golf Course   ★★★

Thorpe Wood, Peterborough, PE3 6SE
Website: www.thorpewoodgolfcourse.co.uk
E-mail: enquiries@thorpewoodgolfcourse.co.uk
Nearest main town: Peterborough

Secretary: Mr R. Palmer
Professional: Mr R. Fitton   Tel: 01733 267701
                                       Fax: 01733 332774

Playing: Midweek: round £11.90; day n/a. Weekend: round £15.70; day n/a.

Facilities: Bar: 11am–11pm. Food: Lunch and dinner from 10am–9pm.

Comments: Excellent greens and layout for a municipal ... Alliss/Thomas turn their hands to municipals ... Over 7000 yards, so best value for money in the country ... Well presented, an absolute pleasure to play whatever your handicap ... Superb municipal with excellent service.

Channel Islands

Royal Jersey Golf Club ★★★★

Le Chemin Au Greves, Grouville, JE3 9BD
Website: www.royaljersey.com   E-mail: thesecretary@royaljersey.com
Nearest main town: St Helier

There is some great golf to be had on the Channel Islands, but the best golf is on Jersey, where there are two cracking links, the Royal course and La Moye. Royal Jersey is a flat links that runs at sea level along the exposed links turf of Grouville Bay. The bay was such a favourite with Queen Victoria that she insisted it be called the Royal Bay of Grouville. Close by is the little fishing village of Gorey, and above on the headland is a 13th-century fortress known as Mont Orgueil, which commands attention from every corner of the course.

The opening hole at the Royal Jersey is one of the toughest in the British Isles. Fresh from the changing rooms, you are asked to thread your new ball on this 468-yard monster between the old remains of Fort Henry and two German pillboxes (the Germans occupied the Channel Islands for five years from 1939 to 1944). Any slight push on any part of the hole goes over the wall, on to the sand and – depending on the tides, which vary hugely from day to day – into the sea.

The first nine holes run alongside the shore, while the second nine have a more inland feel, with more evidence of bracken and gorse. The layout actually takes up a remarkably small plot of land and it has been tweaked over the years in order to ease congestion and improve safety. Plateau greens are a feature, not least at the finish, where the 15th, 16th and 17th are notoriously slippery to stay on.

Harry Vardon, the greatest British golfer of all time who won the Open six times, was born just a duffed chip away from the 12th and his spirit lives on here. During the same period, stories tell of him driving in his afternoon round into the divot marks he had made in the morning.

The demand for golf in the Channel Islands well outstrips supply, so if you want to play Royal Jersey in the summer be prepared for a crowded course.

Secretary: Mr D. Attwood   Tel: 01534 854416
                                        Fax: 01534 854684
Professional: Mr D. Morgan   Tel: 01534 852234
                                        Fax: 01534 854684

Playing: Midweek: round £50.00; day n/a. Weekend: round £50.00; day n/a.

Facilities: Bar: 8am–midnight. Food: Breakfast, lunch and dinner from 8am–9pm. Bar snacks.

Comments: Harry Vardon was born here ... Short course but you always need to be good off the tee ... Seaside links on blessed piece of land ... Old club, a pleasure to play.

Alderney Golf Club ★★★

Route des Carrieres, Alderney, GY9 3YD
Nearest main town: St Anne's

Secretary: Mr K. Bithell   Tel: 01481 822835
Fax: 01481 823609

Professional: None

Playing: Midweek: round n/a; day £20.00. Weekend: round n/a; day £25.00.

Facilities: Bar: 8.30am–7pm. Food: Bar snacks.

Comments: Up in the clouds ... Nine holes at this neat seaside course ... Views are what makes it ... Come here for the views, not the golf.

La Moye Golf Club ★★★★

St Brelade, Jersey, JE3 8GQ
Nearest main town: St Helier

Secretary: Mr C. Greetham   Tel: 01534 743401
Fax: 01534 747289

Professional: Mr M. Deeley   Tel: 01534 743130

Playing: Midweek: round £45.00; day n/a. Weekend: round £50.00; day n/a.

Facilities: Bar: 10am–11pm. Food: Lunch from 12pm–2pm. Dinner from 7pm–8pm. Booking essential.

Comments: Stunning location ... Incredibly natural terrain ... Exciting blind shots ... You need years to understand this course ... Many memorable summer evenings here ... Cold and windy ... Wonderfully natural with dunes and gulleys.

Royal Guernsey Golf Club   ★★★

L'Ancresse, Guernsey, GY3 5BY
E-mail: r-g-g-c@lineone.net
Nearest main town: St Peter's Port

Secretary: Mr M. de Laune   Tel: 01481 247022
                                        Fax: 01481 243960
Professional: Mr N. Wood   Tel: 01481 245070

Playing: Midweek: round n/a; day £38.00. Weekend: round n/a;
                  day £38.00.

Facilities: Bar: 9.30am–11pm. Food: Lunch from 12pm–1.45pm.
                  Dinner from 7pm–9.30pm.

Comments: Can get very busy ... Impossible when the wind gets up
                  ... Use your imagination ... You'll never play another
                  like it ... Very unfair in the summer ... In the summer it's
                  like playing pinball ... Gets very busy ... Location
                  superb ... Riveting course.

Cheshire

Carden Park Golf Club ★★★★

Carden Park Hotel, Golf Resort & Spa, Chester, CH3 9DQ
Website: www.devereonline.co.uk
Nearest main town: Chester

Carden Park is a member of the Jack Nicklaus design stable and is also the first co-design in Britain with his son, Steve.

The first course at Carden Park has been open since 1993, but the addition of a Nicklaus course makes it a popular venue for visitors and societies. Essentially, this is a one-stop shop for golfers with the Nicklaus teaching facility, one of the best pro shops in the country, an excellent driving range and a luxury hotel.

But Carden Park has essentially received the accolades on account of the course, an innovative, imaginative layout, demanding the best from players, whether you're a scratch golfer or a high handicapper. Even though it can be relatively short off the front tees, the tiger tees transform the challenge to 7010 yards.

The course embodies the ethos of the Nicklaus design – golf should be fun, challenging and fair (some say this means easy). Everything is in front of the player with no blind shots, hidden obstacles or surprises. Two holes, the 7th and 15th, embody the characteristic Nicklaus double-fairway option with the emphasis purely on risk and reward.

An elevated tee with a dramatic drop to a fairway bordered by trees on the left is the start of the Nicklaus experience. Immediately from the 450-yard, par-4 1st, the emphasis is put on length and accuracy, qualities the Golden Bear had perhaps more than anyone.

After the short par-4 2nd, you face up to one of a tough selection of par-3s; the 205-yard 3rd is perhaps the pick. The 12th is another strong par-3 at 231 yards with water on the right and a well-guarded green. Two par-5s on the back nine at the 13th and 18th make a tough closing loop, but those who can drive the ball will really enjoy the test.

Secretary:	Ms G. Burgess	Tel: 01829 731600
		Fax: 01829 731629
Professional:	Mr P. Hodgson	Tel: 01829 731500
		Fax: 01829 731629
Playing:	Midweek: round £40.00 (Cheshire), £60.00 (Nicklaus); day n/a. Weekend: round £40.00 (Cheshire), £60.00 (Nicklaus); day n/a.	

Facilities: Bar: 11am–11pm. Food: Bar snacks.

Comments: Beautifully presented course with excellent facilities ... Fair to all handicaps ... Young course but a club with the right attitude ... Best course played since St Andrews ... Top-class practice facilities ... Very good driving range for practice ... Nicklaus boys have excelled themselves ... Progressive club going the right way with this parkland layout – keep it up.

Birchwood Golf Club   ★★★

Kelvin Close, Birchwood, Warrington, WA3 7PB
Nearest main town: Warrington

Secretary: Mrs A. Harper   Tel: 01925 818819
                                          Fax: 01925 822403
Professional: Mr P. McEwan   Tel: 01925 816574
                                          Fax: 01925 816574

Playing: Midweek: round £18.00; day £26.00. Weekend: round £34.00; day £34.00.

Facilities: Bar: 11am–11pm. Food: Lunch and dinner from 12pm–6pm. Bar snacks.

Comments: Excellent facilities all round ... Just under 7000 yards but still a fair test ... Moorland marvel ... 612-yard par-5 a novelty ... Bit of everything on this underrated, undulating layout.

Delamere Forest Golf Club   ★★★★

Station Road, Delamere, Northwich, CW8 2JE
Website: www.delameregolf.co.uk   E-mail: delamere@btconnect.com
Nearest main town: Northwich

Secretary: Mr J. Mulder   Tel: 01606 883800
                                          Fax: 01606 889444
Professional: Mr E. Jones   Tel: 01606 883307
                                          Fax: 01606 889444

Playing: Midweek: round £35.00; day £50.00. Weekend: round £60.00; day n/a.

Facilities: Bar: 11am–11pm. Food: Bar snacks.

Comments: One of England's hidden gems – a Herbert Fowler layout with excellent long par-4s ... Take advantage of the day rate – exceptional value ... Challenging, well presented and scenic ... Undulating heathland, something different for Cheshire ... Heathland, then pine forests – what a course!

Disley Golf Club   ★

Stanley Hall Lane, Disley, Stockport, SK12 2JX
Nearest main town: Stockport

Secretary: Ms D. Bradley   Tel: 01663 762071
                                       Fax: 01663 762678
Professional: Mr A. Esplin   Tel: 01663 762884

Playing: Midweek: round £25.00; day £25.00. Weekend: round £30.00; day £30.00.

Facilities: Bar: 12pm–11pm. Food: Lunch from 12pm–2pm. Bar snacks. Dinner from 7pm–9.30pm. Closed on Mondays.

Comments: Worth seeking out ... Cheap golf on refined course ... Moorland/parkland combination ... Sloping lies and high winds make this a challenge ... Cracking value.

Dunham Forest Golf & Country Club   ★★

Oldfield Lane, Altrincham, WA14 4TY
Nearest main town: Altrincham

Secretary: Mrs S. Klaus   Tel: 0161 928 2605
                                       Fax: 0161 929 8975
Professional: Mr I. Wrigley   Tel: 0161 928 2727

Playing: Midweek: round £40.00; day £45.00. Weekend: round £45.00; day n/a.

Facilities: Bar: 11am–11pm. Food: Lunch from 12pm–2.30pm.

Comments: Fine woodland course ... Invariably well presented ... Facilities don't cater for visitors ... Magnificent beech trees frame this clever track ... Unknown outside Manchester ... Very long and penal.

Eaton Golf Club ★★★

Guy Lane, Waverton, Chester, CH3 7PH
Website: www.eatongolfclub.co.uk
E-mail: office@eatongolfclub.co.uk
Nearest main town: Chester

Secretary:	Mrs K. Brown	Tel: 01244 335885
		Fax: 01244 335782
Professional:	Mr B. Tye	Tel: 01244 335826
		Fax: 01244 335782

Playing: Midweek: round £30.00–£35.00; day n/a. Weekend: round £35.00–£40.00; day n/a.

Facilities: Bar: 11am–11pm. Food: Lunch and dinner from 10am–9pm. Bar snacks.

Comments: Long course with plenty going for it ... Mature trees give this course an established feel ... Not as gaudy as many new clubs ... Preferred the old venue ... Better value than some of the new clubs in Cheshire.

Frodsham Golf Club ★★★

Simons Lane, Frodsham, WA6 6HE
Website: www.frodshamgolfclub.co.uk
Nearest main town: Cheshire

Secretary:	Mr E. Roylance	Tel: 01928 732159
		Fax: 01928 734070
Professional:	Mr G. Tonge	Tel: 01928 739442

Playing: Midweek: round £30.00; day n/a. Weekend: round n/a; day n/a.

Facilities: Bar: 11am–11pm. Food: Lunch and dinner from 11am–9pm. Bar snacks.

Comments: Very picturesque and in fair condition ... A tough nut to crack but not impossible ... Top condition on each visit ... Parkland course with few significant characteristics ... There's a lot better in Cheshire.

Heyrose Golf Club ★★

Budworth Road, Tabley, Knutsford, WA16 0HZ
Website: www.heyrosegolfclub.com
E-mail: info@heyrosegolfclub.com
Nearest main town: Knutsford

Secretary:	Mrs E. Bridge	Tel: 01565 733664
		Fax: 01565 734578
Professional:	Mr P. Affleck	Tel: 01565 734267

Playing: Midweek: round £25.00; day n/a. Weekend: round £30.00; day n/a.

Facilities: Bar: 12pm–10.30pm. Food: Lunch and dinner from 12pm–10.30pm. Bar snacks.

Comments: Attractive club in wooded valley ... Quaint course ... A little overlong for some ... Nice welcome from the pro ... Very relaxed feel to this parkland course.

Leigh Golf Club ★★

Kenyon Hall, Culcheth, Warrington, WA3 4BG
Website: www.leighgolf.co.uk   E-mail: golf@leighgolf.fsnet.co.uk
Nearest main town: Warrington

Secretary:	Mr D. Taylor	Tel: 01925 762943
		Fax: 01925 765097
Professional:	Mr A. Baguley	Tel: 01925 762013

Playing: Midweek: round £30.00; day n/a. Weekend: round £40.00; day n/a.

Facilities: Bar: 12pm–10.30pm. Food: Lunch and dinner from 12pm–8.30pm. Bar snacks.

Comments: Well regarded in Cheshire ... Doesn't live up to its billing – too short ... Short but undeniably sweet ... Nice woodland gives boring design a lift ... Something a bit different for the area.

Mere Golf and Country Club

Chester Road, Knutsford, WA16 6LJ
Website: www.meregolf.co.uk   E-mail: enquiries@meregolf.co.uk
Nearest main town: Knutsford

Secretary:	Mr S. Janvier	Tel: 01565 830155
		Fax: 01565 830713
Professional:	Mr P. Eyre	Tel: 01565 830219

Playing: Midweek: round n/a; day £70.00 (summer), £50.00 (winter). Weekend: round n/a; day n/a.

Facilities: Bar: 11am–11pm. Food: Breakfast, lunch and dinner from 9am–11pm. Bar snacks.

Comments: Gorgeous parkland course ... Very friendly to visitors ... Great water hazards at the 7th and 8th ... Multi-tiered greens protected by deep bunkers ... Modern feel.

Mottram Hall Golf Centre ★★★

Wilmslow Road, Mottram St Andrews, Prestbury, SK10 4QT
Nearest main town: Prestbury

Secretary:	Mr D. Goodwin	Tel: 01625 828135
		Fax: 01625 829284
Professional:	Mr T. Rastall	Tel: 01625 820064

Playing: Midweek: round £39.00; day n/a. Weekend: round £44.00; day n/a.

Facilities: Bar: 7am–10pm. Food: Bar snacks.

Comments: Decent challenge although greens poor on visit ... Condition not what you would expect for hotel course ... Not up to its five-star rating ... Flat, meadowland course with few distinguishing features.

Portal Golf & Country Club ★★★

Cobblers Cross Lane, Tarporley, CW6 0DJ
Nearest main town: Chester

Secretary:	Mrs J. Kite	Tel: 01829 733884
	(Operations Manager)	Fax: 01829 733666
Professional:	Miss J. Statham	Tel: 01829 733933

Playing: Midweek: round £30.00; day £45.00. Weekend: round £30.00; day n/a.

Facilities: Bar: 12pm–11pm. Food: Lunch from 12pm–2.30pm. Dinner from 6pm–9pm.

Comments: Very hilly, take a buggy if you can ... Exhilarating course with plunging approaches ... Amazing construction on the side of a hill ... Heady golf ... An epic encounter with Donald Steel ... Facilities some of the best in country.

Portal Premier Golf & Country Club   ★★★

Forest Road, Tarporley, CW6 0JA
Website: www.portalpremier.co.uk
E-mail: julie@portalpremier.totalserve.co.uk
Nearest main town: Chester

Secretary: Mrs J. Kite   Tel: 01829 733884
                                           Fax: 01829 733666
Professional: Miss J. Statham   Tel: 01829 733884

Playing: Midweek: round £30.00; day £45.00. Weekend: round £35.00; day n/a.

Facilities: Bar: 11am–11pm. Food: Lunch and dinner from 11.30am–9.30pm. Closed Sunday and Monday evenings.

Comments: Not far behind the main course ... Prefer it to the over-long Championship course ... Difficult for high handicappers.

Prestbury Golf Club   ★★★

The Clubhouse, Macclesfield Road, Prestbury, SK10 4BJ
Website: www.prestburygolfclub.com
E-mail: office@prestburygolfclub.com
Nearest main town: Macclesfield

Secretary: Mr N. Young   Tel: 01625 828241
                                           Fax: 01625 828241
Professional: Mr N. Summerfield

Playing: Midweek: round n/a; day £45.00. Weekend: round n/a; day £45.00.

Facilities: Bar: 12pm–2pm and 4pm–10.30pm. Food: Lunch from 11.30am–2.30pm. Dinner from 5pm–9pm.

Comments: In good condition with challenging holes ... Lovely clubhouse ... Looked after by a Master Greenkeeper ... Real slog, so many undulations ... I thought you didn't get fit playing golf?

Reddish Vale Golf Club ★★★

The Golf House, Southcliffe Road, South Reddish, Stockport, SK5 7EE
Website: www.reddishvalegolfclub.co.uk
E-mail: admin@reddishvalegolfclub.co.uk
Nearest main town: Stockport

Secretary: Mr B. Rendell JP   Tel: 0161 480 2359
    Fax: 0161 477 8242
Professional: Mr B. Freeman   Tel: 0161 480 3824
    Fax: 0161 477 8242

Playing: Midweek: round n/a; day £25.00. Weekend: round n/a; day n/a.

Facilities: Bar: 11am–11pm. Food: Lunch from 12pm–2.30pm. Dinner by arrangement.

Comments: An Alister Mackenzie gem of a course in the least fashionable part of Stockport – great value for money ... Situated in the River Tame valley ... One of the best examples of heathland golf around.

Romiley Golf Club ★

Goosehouse Green, Romiley, SK6 4LJ
Website: www.romileygolfclub.org
E-mail: office@romileygolfclub.org
Nearest main town: Stockport

Secretary: Mr P. Trafford   Tel: 0161 430 2392
    Fax: 0161 430 7258
Professional: Mr L. Sullivan   Tel: 0161 430 7122

Playing: Midweek: round £30.00; day £40.00. Weekend: round £40.00; day £50.00.

Facilities: Bar: 11am–11pm. Food: Lunch and dinner from 10am–8pm. Bar snacks.

Comments: Some nice individual holes ... Overall a bit of a disappointment ... Nestles at the foot of the Derbyshire hills ... Liked the back nine ... Not in the top rank in the area.

Sandiway Golf Club   ★★★★

Chester Road, Sandiway, CW8 2DJ
Website: www.sandiwaygolf.co.uk
E-mail: info@sandiwaygolf.fsnet.co.uk
Nearest main town: Chester

Secretary: Mr R. Owens   Tel: 01606 883247
                                         Fax: 01606 888548
Professional: Mr W. Laird   Tel: 01606 883180

Playing: Midweek: round n/a; day £50.00. Weekend: round n/a;
                    day £60.00.

Facilities: Bar: 11am–11pm. Food: Breakfast and lunch from
                    9am–3pm. Dinner by arrangement.

Comments: Strong, beautiful amateur course that deserves more
                    recognition ... Par-3 finish lets down an otherwise pleas-
                    ant experience ... Classic design that has no tricks or
                    twists ... Very pretty parkland ... Too many sloping lies
                    ... Clear strategy needed here ... Fell in love with it.

Shrigley Hall Hotel, Golf & Country Club   ★★

Shrigley Park, Pott Shrigley, Macclesfield, SK10 5SB
E-mail: shrigleyhallgolf@paramount-hotels.co.uk
Nearest main town: Macclesfield

Secretary: Miss L. Lawton   Tel: 01625 576681
                                         Fax: 01625 575437
Professional: Mr T. Stevens   Tel: 01625 575626

Playing: Midweek: round prices on application; day n/a.
                    Weekend: round n/a; day n/a.

Facilities: Bar: 8am–8.30pm. Food: Breakfast and lunch served
                    from 8am–6pm.

Comments: Undulating and very enjoyable ... Another Donald Steel
                    disappointment ... Views over Peak District make up for
                    what course lacks ... Preferred the hotel to the course.

Stockport Golf Club   ★★★

Offerton Road, Offerton, Stockport, SK2 5HL
E-mail: info@stockportgolf.co.uk
Nearest main town: Stockport

Secretary:	Mr J. Flanagan	Tel: 0161 427 8369
		Fax: 0161 449 8293
Professional:	Mr M. Peel	Tel: 0161 427 2421

Playing: Midweek: round £40.00; day n/a. Weekend: round £50.00; day n/a.

Facilities: Bar: 11am–9pm. Food: Bar snacks. Lunch and dinner by arrangement.

Comments: Superb greens ... Bites you if you stop concentrating ... Open course of little standing ... Tough opener that really sets the standard on this parkland treasure.

The Tytherington Club ★★★★

Dorchester Way, Tytherington, Macclesfield, SK10 2JP
Website: www.clubhaus.com
Nearest main town: Macclesfield

Secretary:	None	Tel: 01625 506000
		Fax: 01625 506040
Professional:	Mr M. McCleod	Tel: 01625 434562

Playing: Midweek: round £32.00; day £45.00. Weekend: round £40.00; day £68.00.

Facilities: Bar: 8am–11pm. Food: Lunch from 12pm–2.30pm. Dinner from 6.30pm–10pm. Closed Sunday and Monday.

Comments: Excellent off-course facilities ... Course requires pure, strong hitting ... Good quality mature parkland course that plays tough and fair ... Always have good offers on ... Can get very busy ... Improving and a variety of holes ... Exceptional clubhouse and food ... Excellent course spoilt by too many society days ... Signature hole is the 12th, a genuine three-shotter par-5.

The Wilmslow Golf Club ★★

Great Warford, Mobberley, Knutsford, WA16 7AY
Website: www.wilmslowgolfclub.ukf.net
E-mail: wilmslowgolfclub@ukf.net
Nearest main town: Wilmslow

Secretary:	Mrs M. Padfield	Tel: 01565 872148
		Fax: 01565 872172

Professional: Mr L. Nowicki   Tel: 01565 873620
                                         Fax: 01565 873620

Playing: Midweek: round £45.00; day £55.00. Weekend: round
                 £55.00; day £65.00.

Facilities: Bar: 12pm–2pm and 4.30pm–10pm. Food: Lunch
                 from 12pm–2pm. Dinner from 5pm–8.30pm. Bar
                 snacks.

Comments: Far better than nearby Mottram Hall ... Nice condition
                 ... Long parkland course with much character ... Very
                 expensive but worth it ... Gulped at the price ... Perfect
                 condition ... Never a bad lie.

Cornwall

St Enodoc Golf Club ★★★★

Rock, Wadebridge, PL27 6LD
E-mail: stenodocgolfclub@tiscali.co.uk
Nearest main town: Wadebridge

Like so much of the natural beauty adorning the rugged coastline of Cornwall, the small yachting village of Rock and the nearby golf course at St Enodoc are little known north of the border or, as the Cornish would say, in England. But to the many discerning golfers of this proud county, the stretch of links that separates the Camel Estuary from Daymer Bay is the finest natural golf they know.

In his introduction to the official handbook on the history of St Enodoc, the poet laureate Sir John Betjeman, who lived at Trebetherick and died there in 1984, wrote that 'golf is a solitary game even if you are playing in a foursome. It makes you aware of the lie of the land, of the hills, outline, grass, flowers and sky.' At St Enodoc, you have it all.

It is by no means a long course – measuring 6027 yards – but its skilful design dictates that it will not surrender easily to just a brash, powerful game. Nowhere is this more apparent than at the 1st hole, a rolling 518-yard par-5 with a fairway of erratic folds and undulations. Your drive and lay-up are not threatened, but the green is set on a natural plateau, curved at the edges, and frustrating to hit no matter how short your third shot is.

Very few courses can shock you visually, but at the 6th you will be shocked. Known as the 'Himalayas' hole, what is believed to be the largest sandhill on any course in Britain rises some 80 feet above the fairways, totally eclipsing your view of the green, which lies amid dunes about 100 yards beyond. And at the 10th you encounter a little church dug out of the sand sixty years ago which stands as the centrepiece for a magnificent stretch of holes that ends at the 15th.

You'll spend plenty of time in the dunes at St Enodoc, and you'll probably have more than a few encounters with the thick rough. Throw in an overgrown marsh, blind greens and a pond, and you'll come away from St Enodoc wanting to play it again.

Secretary: Mr T. Clagett Tel: 01208 863216
Fax: 01208 862976
Professional: Mr N. Williams Tel: 01208 862402

Playing: Midweek: round £40.00; day n/a. Weekend: round £50.00; day n/a.

Facilities: Bar: 8am–11pm. Food: Lunch and dinner from 11.30am–10pm. Bar snacks.

Comments: Unmissable course for the serious golfer ... Not for the beginner ... Great fun – some very unusual holes and bizarre challenges ... Good variety of holes and superb facilities ... 10th hole is a beauty ... Marvellous surroundings and variety on this unforgettable links ... Could play every day and not get bored ... Last three holes give a great finish ... Sand dunes like ocean liners and the one on the 6th like the *Titanic* ... A super course but spoilt by the attitude of some of the members.

Bude & North Cornwall Golf Club   ★★★

Burn View, Bude, EX23 8DA
Website: www.budeandnorthcornwall.golfclub.20m.com
Nearest main town: Bude

Secretary: Mrs P. Ralph   Tel: 01288 352006
                                        Fax: 01288 356855
Professional: Mr J. Yeo   Tel: 01288 352006

Playing: Midweek: round £20.00; day n/a. Weekend: round £25.00; day n/a.

Facilities: Bar: 11am–8.30pm. Food: Bar snacks.

Comments: Warm welcome inside ... Not the best example of a natural links ... Top-class local course.

Cape Cornwall Golf & Country Club   ★

St Just, Penzance, TR19 7NL
Nearest main town: Penzance

Secretary: Mr M. Waters   Tel: 01736 788611
                                        Fax: 01736 788611
Professional: None

Playing: Midweek: round £20.00; day £25.00. Weekend: round £20.00; day £25.00.

Facilities: Bar: 11am–11pm. Food: Lunch from 10am–5pm.

Comments: Very scenic but poor condition ... Natural course with walls part of the old design ... Superb facilities overshadow the course ... Not your average country club ... Course rather out of place with spanking new country club ... Good value for a very natural game.

Carlyon Bay Golf Club   ★★★★

Sea Road, Carlyon Bay, St Austell, PL25 3RD
Website: www.carlyonbay.com
Nearest main town: St Austell

Secretary: Mr P. Clemo   Tel: 01726 814250
                                    Fax: 01726 814250
Professional: Mr M. Rowe   Tel: 01726 814250
                                    Fax: 01726 815604

Playing: Midweek: round n/a; day £39.00 (high season). Weekend: round n/a; day £39.00 (high season).

Facilities: Bar: 9am–11pm. Food: Lunch and dinner from 10am–9pm. Bar snacks.

Comments: Fair course for holiday golf ... A real slog ... Don't send your worst enemy there ... Prevailing wind makes course so tough ... Much improved due to excellent hotel ... With the hotel, this is a good package.

China Fleet Country Club   ★★★

Saltash, PL12 6LJ
Website: www.china-fleet.co.uk   E-mail: golf@china-fleet.co.uk
Nearest main town: Plymouth

Secretary: Mrs L. Goddard   Tel: 01752 854657
                                    Fax: 01752 848456
Professional: Mr N. Cook   Tel: 01752 854665
                                    Fax: 01752 848456

Playing: Midweek: round £25.00; day n/a. Weekend: round £30.00; day n/a.

Facilities: Bar: 11am–11pm. Food: Bar snacks all day. Dinner from 7pm–9pm.

Comments: Course and greens good ... Basic country club facilities ... Not the best course in Cornwall, but nice attitude.

Falmouth Golf Club   ★★

Swanpool Road, Falmouth, TR11 5BQ
Website: www.falmouthgolfclub.co.uk
E-mail: falmouthgolfclub@freezone.co.uk
Nearest main town: Falmouth

Secretary:	Mr R. Wooldridge	Tel: 01326 311262
		Fax: 01326 317783
Professional:	Mr B. Patterson	Tel: 01326 311262

Playing: Midweek: round £25.00; day £35.00. Weekend: round
£25.00; day £35.00.

Facilities: Bar: 11am–11pm. Food: Lunch from 11am–5pm.
Dinner by arrangement.

Comments: Outstanding coastal views ... Beautiful course overlooking the harbour ... Well bunkered and can be a tough
challenge ... Anyone know of a better practice ground?
I mean, five acres.

Lanhydrock Golf Club   ★★★★

Lostwithiel Road, Bodmin, PL30 5AQ
Website: www.lanhydrock-golf.co.uk
E-mail: golfing@lanhydrock-golf.co.uk
Nearest main town: Bodmin

Secretary:	Mr G. Bond	Tel: 01208 73600
	(Director)	Fax: 01208 77325
Professional:	Mr J. Broadway	Tel: 01208 73600
		Fax: 01208 77325

Playing: Midweek: round £22.00–£45.00; day n/a. Weekend:
round £22.00–£45.00; day n/a.

Facilities: Bar: 11am–9pm. Food: Lunch and dinner from
8am–9pm. Bar snacks.

Comments: The real beast of Bodmin ... Scenic course in wooded
valley ... A real pleasure to play ... Understated and
underrated.

Launceston Golf Club   ★★

St Stephens, Launceston, PL15 8HF
Website: www.launcestongolfclub.com
Nearest main town: Bude

Secretary:	Mr B. Grant	Tel: 01566 773442
		Fax: 01566 777506
Professional:	Mr J. Tozer	Tel: 01566 775359

Playing: Midweek: round £20.00; day £24.00. Weekend: round n/a; day n/a.

Facilities: Bar: 11.30am–11pm. Food: Members only.

Comments: Great cardiac-arrest course ... Excellent facilities and friendly members ... Undulating with four greens sitting on a hill ... Is this really how the game was meant to be played?

Looe Golf Club

Bindown, Looe, PL13 1PX
Nearest main town: Looe

Secretary:	Mr T. Day	Tel: 01503 240239
		Fax: 01503 240864
Professional:	Mr A. MacDonald	Tel: 01503 240239
		Fax: 01503 240864

Playing: Midweek: round £24.00; day n/a. Weekend: round £24.00; day n/a.

Facilities: Bar: 10.30am–11pm. Food: Lunch from 11am–6pm. Bar snacks.

Comments: Proud club ... Views of the Cornwall coast ... Established course and excellent design ... Not the best condition ... Views more impressive than the course ... Holiday golf at fair price.

Mullion Golf Club ★★

Cury, Helston, TR12 7BP
Nearest main town: Helston

Secretary:	Mr G. Fitter	Tel: 01326 240685
		Fax: 01326 240685
Professional:	Mr P. Blundell	Tel: 01326 241176

Playing: Midweek: round £20.00; day £20.00. Weekend: round £20.00; day £20.00.

Facilities: Bar: 12pm–11pm. Food: Lunch from 12pm–3pm. Dinner from 6pm–9.30pm. Bar snacks.

Comments: Catches the spirit of golf in Cornwall ... Spectacular setting ... Perching on a cliff top, this is a treat ... Special and exhilarating ... Not as famous as St Enodoc but gives the player a real rush.

Newquay Golf Club   ★

Tower Road, Newquay, TR7 1LT
Website: www.newquay-golf-club.com
E-mail: newquaygolfclub@smartone.co.uk
Nearest main town: Newquay

Secretary: Mr G. Binney   Tel: 01637 874354
                              Fax: 01637 874066
Professional: Mr M. Bevan   Tel: 01637 874830
                                Fax: 01637 874830

Playing: Midweek: round £25.00; day n/a. Weekend: round £25.00; day n/a.

Facilities: Bar: 11am–11pm. Food: Lunch and dinner from 11am–11pm. Bar snacks.

Comments: Exciting course to play ... Exposed layout, not well known, but value nonetheless ... One of my favourite courses in Cornwall.

Perranporth Golf Club

Budnic Hill, Perranporth, TR6 0AB
Website: www.perranporthgolfclub.com
E-mail: perranporth@golfclub92.fsnet.co.uk
Nearest main town: Perranporth

Secretary: Mr D. Mugford   Tel: 01872 573701
                               Fax: 01872 573701
Professional: Mr D. Michell   Tel: 01872 572317

Playing: Midweek: round £25.00; day £30.00. Weekend: round £30.00; day £35.00.

Facilities: Bar: 11.30am–11pm. Food: Breakfast, lunch and dinner from 7.30am–10pm. Bar snacks.

Comments: A brilliant layout, hardly ever talked about or advertised ... You have to feel very strong for this course ... Par-5s make this one.

Roserrow Golf & Country Club ★★★

St Minver, Wadebridge, PL27 6QT
Website: www.roserrow.co.uk   E-mail: roserrow@aol.com
Nearest main town: Wadebridge

Secretary:	Mr W. Blewitt	Tel: 01208 863000
		Fax: 01208 863002
Professional:	Mr N. Sears	Tel: 01208 863000
		Fax: 01208 863002

Playing: Midweek: round £20.00 (off season), £30.00 (on season); day n/a. Weekend: round n/a; day n/a.

Facilities: Bar: 11am–11pm. Food: Lunch and dinner from 10am–9pm. Bar snacks.

Comments: Well established with excellent facilities ... Seems as though it has been around for years ... Facilities overshadow the course ... An excellent addition to golf in Cornwall ... Another bloody country club.

St Austell Golf Club ★★

Tregongeeves, St Austell, PL26 7DS
Nearest main town: St Austell

Secretary:	Mr K. Trahair	Tel: 01726 74756
		Fax: 01726 71978
Professional:	Mr T. Pitts	Tel: 01726 68621

Playing: Midweek: round £20.00; day £20.00. Weekend: round n/a; day n/a.

Facilities: Bar: 11.30am–11pm. Food: Lunch from 12pm–2.30pm. Dinner from 6pm–8.30pm. Bar snacks.

Comments: What views! ... Fairly unknown course and good value ... Very interesting and fun ... Would come again.

St Mellion Hotel Golf & Country Club (Nicklaus) ★★★★

St Mellion, Saltash, PL12 6SD
Website: www.st-mellion.co.uk
E-mail: stmellion@americangolf.uk.com
Nearest main town: Saltash

Secretary:	None	Tel: 01579 351351
		Fax: 01579 350537

Professional: Mr D. Moon   Tel: 01579 352002
                                      Fax: 01579 350537

Playing: Midweek: round £55.00 (Nicklaus), £38.00 (Old); day
                  n/a. Weekend: round £58.00 (Nicklaus), £40.00 (Old);
                  day n/a.

Facilities: Bar: 11am–11pm. Food: Breakfast, lunch and dinner
                  from 7am–9pm. Bar snacks.

Comments: Very testing and in excellent condition ... .Course gets
                  very boggy after a little rain ... Difficult tee shots with
                  trouble seemingly everywhere ... Too long for the
                  average player ... A real masterpiece of design ...
                  Tough and exhilarating ... The toughest course in the
                  country ... Rather hilly so consider a buggy.

Trevose Golf & Country Club   ★★★★

Constantine Bay, Padstow, PL28 8JB
Website: www.trevose-gc.co.uk   E-mail: info@trevose-gc.co.uk
Nearest main town: Padstow

Secretary: Mr N. Gammon   Tel: 01841 520208
                                      Fax: 01841 521057
Professional: Mr G. Alliss   Tel: 01841 520261

Playing: Midweek: round £25.00–£40.00 (depending on
                  season); day n/a. Weekend: round £25.00–£40.00
                  (depending on season); day n/a.

Facilities: Bar: 11am–11pm. Food: Lunch and dinner from
                  10am–9pm. Bar snacks.

Comments: Excellent links and friendly club ... Exhilarating links ...
                  Brilliant links course in fantastic setting ... Trevose or St
                  Enodoc? – I can't decide ... Wonderful golf on a links of
                  real mystery and excitement ... A memorable afternoon
                  ... Links legend that just gets better and better.

West Cornwall Golf Club   ★★★★

Church Lane, Lelant, St Ives, TR26 3DZ
Website: www.westcornwallgolfclub.fsnet.co.uk
E-mail: ian@westcornwallgolfclub.fsnet.co.uk
Nearest main town: St Ives

Secretary: Mr I. Veale   Tel: 01736 753401
                                      Fax: 01736 753401

Professional: Mr J. Broadway   Tel: 01736 753177

Playing: Midweek: round £25.00; day n/a. Weekend: round £30.00; day n/a.

Facilities: Bar: 11am–11pm. Food: Bar snacks.

Comments: Overlooked by many ... One of Cornwall's best but few go here ... Great 'Calamity Corner' from the 5th–7th ... A little exposed ... Great thought in the design ... A short course that has never been mastered ... Can be unfair with sloping fairways ... Recommended ... Include it with St Enodoc, Trevose and Perranporth in a golfing break – can't be bettered.

Whitsand Bay Hotel Golf Club   ★

Portwrinkle, Torpoint, PL11 3BU
Website: www.cornish-golf-hotels.co.uk
Nearest main town: Plymouth

Secretary: Mr G. Dwyer   Tel: 01503 230276
                                    Fax: 01503 230329
Professional: Mr S. Poole   Tel: 01503 230778

Playing: Midweek: round £25.00; day n/a. Weekend: round £25.00; day n/a.

Facilities: Bar: 11am–11pm. Food: Bar snacks. Dinner from 7.30pm–8.15pm.

Comments: Interesting cliff-top course linked to country club ... Unusual par-3s ... Facilities poor for country club ... Very bracing.

Cumbria

Silloth-on-Solway Golf Club ★★★★★

The Clubhouse, Silloth, Wigton, CA7 4BL
Website: sillothgolfclub.co.uk   E-mail: sillothgolfclub@lineone.net
Nearest main town: Carlisle

Silloth-on-Solway's isolated location on the north-west coast of England has been a boon for the golfers of Cumbria for many years. The presence of such a magnificent links in an industrial and soulless area of England has meant empty fairways and time to get to understand and appreciate the intricacies of this form of undiluted golf.

The benefits have also been felt in the condition of the course, which is consistently excellent, the fairways like silk, accentuating every natural contour of the land. The greens, too, have a wonderful feel; the ball clinging to the subtle borrows of each and every putting surface. Silloth-on-Solway is that rare beast – an outstanding course that no one knows about.

It is a very flat, exposed course. The wind is not tunnelled through the dunes as on so many links; rather it belligerently rushes in from the south-west and the holes rarely change character, which is a blessing because otherwise Silloth would be as stern a test of golf as you will find. The problems start off the tee where the ball is placed on delicate contoured fairways, which run off in places or channel your ball into depressions. From there, normally a sloping lie, you are invariably asked to find tight greens with very small approach areas. Silloth's individuality is further enhanced by the fact that the fairway bunkers have been replaced with wiry gorse and heather.

The attraction of Silloth, ignoring the obvious, such as the condition of the course and its peace and tranquillity, is its price. In a period when green fees are rising all the time, you will not find better value anywhere in Britain and Ireland.

Secretary:	Mr J. Hill	Tel: 01697 331304
		Fax: 01697 331782
Professional:	Mr J. Graham	Tel: 01697 332404
Playing:	Midweek: round n/a; day £32.00. Weekend: round £43.00; day n/a.	
Facilities:	Bar: 12pm–11pm. Food: Bar snacks.	

Comments: Tremendous links course – everything as it should be ... Good, contrasting nines ... Championship links that is tough in wind ... A fabulous links in tip-top condition ... An undervalued and underused course ... Fantastic links.

Appleby Golf Club ★★

Brackenber Moor, Appleby, CA16 6LP
Website: www.applebygolfclub.org.uk
E-mail: mail@applebygolfclub.org.uk
Nearest main town: Appleby

Secretary: Mr J. Doig   Tel: 01768 351432
    Fax: 01768 352773
Professional: Mr J. Taylor   Tel: 01768 352922

Playing: Midweek: round £19.00; day £21.00. Weekend: round £23.00; day £26.00.

Facilities: Bar: 7.45am–11pm. Food: Breakfast, lunch and dinner from 7.45am–7.30pm. Closed for dinner on Tuesdays.

Comments: One of the best-value courses in the country ... Very remote ... Fine heather and moorland at sale prices ... Cracking welcome ... Great golf at a snip ... Really strong course at crazy price.

Barrow Golf Club ★★

Rakesmoor Lane, Hawcoat, Barrow-in-Furness, LA14 4QB
Nearest main town: Barrow-in-Furness

Secretary: Mr J. Slater   Tel: 01229 825444
Professional: Mr A. Whitehall   Tel: 01229 832121

Playing: Midweek: round £20.00; day £20.00. Weekend: round £20.00; day £20.00.

Facilities: Bar: 4pm–11pm (weekends 12pm–11pm). Food: Bar snacks.

Comments: On a wet, windy day it can feel very lonely here ... Views of Lakeland Fells ... Wonderful on a tortured, windswept day ... A real test in this bleak landscape.

Brampton Golf Club (Talkin Tarn)   ★★★

Tarn Road, Brampton, CA8 1HN
Website: www.bramptongolfclub.com
E-mail: secretary@bramptongolfclub.com
Nearest main town: Brampton

Secretary: Mr I. Meldrum   Tel: 01900 827985
                                        Fax: 01900 827852
Professional: Mr S. Wilkinson   Tel: 01697 72000
                                        Fax: 01697 741487

Playing: Midweek: round n/a; day £22.00. Weekend: round n/a; day £30.00.

Facilities: Bar: 11am–11pm. Food: Bar snacks.

Comments: Pleasant but tricky ... Has propensity to get wet underfoot ... Fell country course that plays long ... Course rarely dries out.

Carlisle Golf Club   ★★★★

Allonby, Carlisle, CA4 8AG
Website: www.carlislegolfclub.org
E-mail: secretary@carlislegolfclub.org
Nearest main town: Carlisle

Secretary: Mr R. Johnson   Tel: 01228 513029
                                        Fax: 01228 513303
Professional: Mr G. Lisle   Tel: 01228 513241
                                        Fax: 01228 513303

Playing: Midweek: round £30.00; day £45.00. Weekend: round £45.00; day n/a.

Facilities: Bar: 11am–11pm. Food: Lunch and dinner from 11am–11pm. Bar snacks.

Comments: Superb course, great facilities ... A very well-respected and friendly club ... Good location and some tricky holes ... Stands out in an otherwise barren corner of golfing country ... Parkland course with fine turf that hosts Open qualifying.

Cockermouth Golf Club   ★

The Clubhouse, Embleton, Cockermouth, CA13 9SG
Website: www.cockermouthgolf.co.uk/login.htm
E-mail: secretary@cockermouthgolf.co.uk
Nearest main town: Cockermouth

Secretary: Mr D. Pollard   Tel: 01768 776223
                                           Fax: 01768 776941

Professional: None

Playing: Midweek: round n/a; day £18.00. Weekend: round n/a;
                    day £22.00.

Facilities: Bar: 12pm–2pm and 4pm–8pm. Food: Snacks avail-
                    able.

Comments: Too hilly ... As much a fitness test as a round of golf ...
                    Gets better each year ... Very typical Cumbria course ...
                    Fell walking ... Not great in winter.

Eden Golf Course

Crosby-on-Eden, Carlisle, CA6 4RA
Website: www.edengolf.co.uk   E-mail: edengolf1@aol.com
Nearest main town: Carlisle

Secretary: None   Tel: 01228 573003
Professional: Mr S. Harrison   Tel: 01228 573003

Playing: Midweek: round £28.00; day n/a. Weekend: round
                    £32.00; day n/a.

Facilities: Bar: 9.30am–11pm. Food: Breakfast, lunch and dinner
                    from 9.30am–9pm. Bar snacks.

Comments: Nice little course, very pretty and good fun ... Club facil-
                    ities are rather better than the course ... Boring parkland
                    course that offers few exciting challenges.

Furness Golf Club

Walney Island, Barrow-in-Furness, LA14 6HB
Nearest main town: Barrow-in-Furness

Secretary: Mr W. French   Tel: 01229 471232
Professional: Mr A. Crook

Playing: Midweek: round £17.00; day £17.00. Weekend: round
                    £17.00; day £17.00.

Facilities: Bar: 12pm–11pm. Food: Lunch from 12pm–3pm.

Comments: One of the better courses in Cumbria ... Housing estate makes some holes unattractive ... Unusual links ... Rugged second nine ... Links of indefinable character ... Fairly isolated.

Grange Fell Golf Club

Fell Road, Grange-over-Sands, LA11 6HB
Nearest main town: Grange-over-Sands

Secretary: Mr M. Higginson   Tel: 01539 532536
Professional: None

Playing: Midweek: round n/a; day £15.00. Weekend: round n/a; day £20.00.

Facilities: Bar: 11am–11pm. Food: None.

Comments: Great, fun holiday golf, but it's not in the league of other courses in the area ... Hard work, not for the over 50s ... Good par-5 8th with terrific views ... Hillside course with outstanding views on a clear day.

Grange-over-Sands Golf Club   ★

Meathop Road, Grange-over-Sands, LA11 6QX
Nearest main town: Grange-over-Sands

Secretary: Mr J. Green   Tel: 01539 533180
                                    Fax: 01539 533754
Professional: Mr S. Summer-Roberts   Tel: 01539 535937

Playing: Midweek: round £18.00; day £24.00. Weekend: round £24.00; day £28.00.

Facilities: Bar: 11am–11pm. Food: Lunch from 11am–5pm.

Comments: Not up to much ... Can be fun on a warm day ... Nothing you haven't seen before ... Poor condition ... Not worth the effort ... Pleasant enough parkland course.

Kendal Golf Club

The Heights, High Tenterfell, Kendal, LA9 4PQ
Website: www.cumbria.com/kendalgc
Nearest main town: Kendal

Secretary:	Mr I. Clancy	Tel: 01539 733708 Fax: 01539 733708
Professional:	Mr P. Scott	Tel: 01539 723499 Fax: 01539 733708

Playing: Midweek: round £22.00; day £26.00. Weekend: round £27.50; day £32.00.

Facilities: Bar: 11.30am–11pm. Food: Breakfast, lunch and dinner from 9am–9pm. Bar snacks.

Comments: Go here for the views, not much else ... Fell golf ... Have done well with what they have got ... Nice example of a fell-land course ... Not highly rated by pros in the area.

Keswick Golf Club Ltd ★★★

Tyrelkeld Hall, Tyrelkeld, Keswick, CA12 4SX
Website: www.keswickgolfclub.com
E-mail: secretary@keswickgolfclub.com
Nearest main town: Keswick

Secretary:	Mr R. Jackson	Tel: 01768 779324 Fax: 01768 779861
Professional:	Mr G. Watson	Tel: 01768 779010 Fax: 01768 779861

Playing: Midweek: round £20.00; day n/a. Weekend: round £25.00; day n/a. Prices may increase in 2004.

Facilities: Bar: 11am–11pm. Food: Lunch and dinner from 11.30am–8pm (11.30am–4pm in winter).

Comments: Pray for a dry day because it can get depressing out there ... Set in the magnificent scenery of the Lake District ... Challenging.

Penrith Golf Club ★★★

Salkeld Road, Penrith, CA11 8SG
Nearest main town: Penrith

Secretary:	Mr D. Noble	Tel: 01768 891919 Fax: 01768 891919
Professional:	Mr G. Key	Tel: 01768 891919

Playing: Midweek: round £20.00; day £25.00. Weekend: round £25.00; day £30.00.

Facilities: Bar: 11am–11pm. Food: Breakfast and lunch from 8am–6pm.

Comments: Spectacular views on the edge of the Lake District ... Good course, views and welcome ... Short track on rolling moorland ... Good condition and one of the better cheaper courses in Cumbria.

Seascale Golf Club ★★★

The Banks, Seascale, CA20 1QL
Website: www.seascalegolfclub.org
E-mail: seascalegolfclub@aol.com
Nearest main town: Whitehaven

Secretary: Mr J. Stobart   Tel: 01946 728202
Fax: 01946 728202
Professional: Mr S. Rudd   Tel: 01946 721779

Playing: Midweek: round £24.00; day £29.00. Weekend: round £27.00; day £32.00 (discounts for parties).

Facilities: Bar: 11am–11pm. Food: Bar snacks.

Comments: A real test of golf to be enjoyed by all handicaps ... Course quality matches quality of the views over the Irish Sea ... Old-fashioned golf in unfettered club environment ... Refreshing, simple course ... Clear your mind at Seascale.

Silecroft Golf Club ★★★

Silecroft, Millom, LA18 4NX
Nearest main town: Millom

Secretary: Mr D. MacLardie   Tel: 01229 774342
Fax: 01229 774342
Professional: None

Playing: Midweek: round n/a; day £15.00. Weekend: round n/a; day £20.00.

Facilities: Bar: By prior arrangement for groups of 16-plus. Food: None.

Comments: Just nine holes but nine excellent links holes ... Best greens in county ... Better links course nearby – and with 18 holes ... Nothing manufactured here, just nine natural golf holes ... Very basic ... Not exactly great holiday golf.

Ulverston Golf Club ★★★

Bardsea Park, Ulverston, LA12 9QJ
Nearest main town: Ulverston

Secretary:	Mr J. Wood	Tel: 01229 582824
		Fax: 01229 588910
Professional:	Mr M. Smith	Tel: 01229 582806

Playing: Midweek: round £14.00–£22.00; day £18.00–£35.00. Weekend: round £30.00; day £35.00.

Facilities: Bar: 11am–11pm. Food: Lunch and dinner from 11am–9pm.

Comments: Inhaler was required for the 17th ... Beautiful part of the country ... Excellent course but hilly ... Great course in lovely part of the world.

Windermere Golf Club ★★

Cleabarrow, Windermere, LA23 3NB
Website: www.windermere-golf-club.org.uk
E-mail: windermeregc@btconnect.com
Nearest main town: Windermere

Secretary:	Mr K. Moffat	Tel: 01539 443123
		Fax: 01539 443123
Professional:	Mr S. Rooke	Tel: 01539 443550

Playing: Midweek: round £25.00; day £40.00. Weekend: round £30.00; day £45.00.

Facilities: Bar: 11am–11pm. Food: Lunch from 12pm–2pm. Dinner from 6pm–9pm. Bar snacks.

Comments: Play here and die ... Everything about this place is excellent ... Short and very sweet ... Stupendous scenery ... Blind shots to narrow landings among heather – just perfect.

Workington Golf Club ★★★

Branthwaite Road, Workington, CA14 4SS
Nearest main town: Workington

Secretary:	Mr T. Stout	Tel: 01900 603460
Professional:	Mr A. Drabble	Tel: 01900 67828
		Fax: 01900 67828

Playing: Midweek: round £15.00; day £19.00. Weekend: round £18.00; day £25.00.

Facilities: Bar: 11am–11pm. Food: Lunch and dinner from 11am–9pm. Bar snacks.

Comments: Nice condition ... Ordinary setting ... Kept in good condition ... Not championship stuff ... Parkland/meadowland ... Back nine can put the wind up you.

Derbyshire

Cavendish Golf Club ★★★★

Gadley Lane, Buxton, SK17 6XD
Website: www.cavendishgolfcourse.com
E-mail: admin@cavendishgolfcourse.com
Nearest main town: Derby

Alister Mackenzie's influence on golf in England is often underrated, much like Cavendish, one of his designs set in the heart of Derbyshire. From the man who crafted Augusta, the home of the Masters, this is England's answer to the 'Cathedral in the Pines'.

No one would ever claim that Cavendish, near Buxton, is as immaculately kept as its Georgia counterpart, but its prime condition and the quality of its High Peak turf is impressive. This parkland/downland course is also exceptional value for money. Founded in 1925, it has become a firm favourite among golfers in the area, and at 5800-plus yards, it presents a challenge that is not too daunting for the average player. It is one of those courses that you would be happy to recommend to anyone who enjoys fair golf in a wonderful setting.

The hallmarks of Mackenzie design are evident wherever you look – huge swales in front of the greens, tees set in shoots of trees and putting surfaces that meander and dip with a vengeance worthy of its American sister. It is a generous course, like Augusta, in that the fairways are accommodating and there is no punishing rough. It gets its own back by placing a premium on shotmaking – land in the wrong part of the fairway and the shot to the green is always tough, but get the tee shot right and you are presented with a birdie opportunity.

The course really begins to bite at the 8th, the start of a loop of five holes which are seen by members as the biggest card-wreckers – three of the par-4s in this stretch are over 400 yards long and the 9th is a tricky par-3 with a small green.

An added bonus at Cavendish is that for visitors to the Peak District it is particularly well placed, especially if you are staying in Buxton, less than a mile away.

Secretary:	Mr J. Rushton	Tel: 01298 79708
		Fax: 01298 79708
Professional:	Mr P. Hunstone	Tel: 01298 25052
Playing:	Midweek: round £30.00; day n/a. Weekend: round £40.00; day n/a.	

Facilities: Bar: 11am–11pm. Food: Lunch and dinner from 12pm–9pm. Bar snacks.

Comments: You really need a short game on these greens ... Friendly atmosphere at this parkland/moorland course ... Fantastic day, fantastic course ... Subtle greens – a tribute to Alister Mackenzie.

Birch Hall Golf Club   ★★

Sheffield Road, Unstone, Chesterfield, S18 5DH
Nearest main town: Chesterfield

Secretary: Mr F. Parker   Tel: 01246 291979
Professional: None

Playing: Midweek: round prices on application; day n/a. Weekend: round n/a; day n/a.

Facilities: Bar: 11am–11pm. Food: Lunch and dinner from 12pm–9pm. Bar snacks.

Comments: For the price, this is good stuff ... Poor facilities for the visitor ... Can't fault the value ... Really nasty and challenging ... Rough, raw and ready.

Bondhay Golf Club   ★

Bondhay Lane, Whitwell, Worksop, S80 3EH
Nearest main town: Worksop

Secretary: Mr H. Hardisty   Tel: 01909 723608
                                      Fax: 01909 720226
Professional: Mr M. Ramsden

Playing: Midweek: round £16.00; day £21.00. Weekend: round £21.00; day n/a.

Facilities: Bar: 11am–11pm. Food: Lunch and dinner from 11am–9pm. Bar snacks.

Comments: New course with basic facilities you would expect ... Course caters for all players – not a compliment ... What I'd call an early learning centre for golfers ... Some exciting water holes but not much substance ... Kept in good order despite popularity.

Breadsall Priory Hotel Golf & Country Club (Priory)   ★★

Moor Road, Morley, Derby, DE7 6DL
Nearest main town: Derby

Secretary:	Mr P. Le Roi	Tel: 01332 832235
	(General Manager)	Fax: 01332 833509
Professional:	Mr D. Steels	Tel: 01332 834425

Playing: Midweek: round £25.00; day £38.00. Weekend: round n/a; day n/a.

Facilities: Bar: 11am–11pm. Food: Breakfast, lunch and dinner from 9am–9pm. Bar snacks.

Comments: Overpriced for standard of course ... Looks great ... A bit of fun.

Burton-on-Trent Golf Club   ★

43 Ashby Road East, Burton-on-Trent, DE15 0PS
E-mail: burtongolfclub@talk21.com
Nearest main town: Burton

Secretary:	Mr D. Hartley	Tel: 01283 544551
		Fax: 01283 544551
Professional:	Mr G. Stafford	Tel: 01283 562240

Playing: Midweek: round £28.00; day £38.00. Weekend: round £32.00; day £40.00.

Facilities: Bar: 11am–11pm. Food: Lunch and dinner from 11am–9pm. Bar snacks.

Comments: Long and tiring ... Improves on the back nine ... Well worth the money ... Very long and difficult.

Buxton & High Peak Golf Club   ★★

Waterwallows Road, Buxton, SK17 7EN
Website: www.buxtonandhighpeakgolfclub.co.uk
E-mail: sec@bhpgc.fsnet.co.uk
Nearest main town: Derby

Secretary:	Mr H. Smith	Tel: 01298 26263
		Fax: 01298 26333
Professional:	Mr G. Brown	Tel: 01298 23112

Playing: Midweek: round £24.00 (18 holes), £30.00 (18+); day n/a. Weekend: round £30.00 (18 holes), £36.00 (18+); day n/a.

Facilities: Bar: 11am–11pm. Food: Lunch from 11am–6pm. Bar snacks. Dinner by arrangement.

Comments: As tough as they come ... Course can eat you alive ... Blind shots to small undulating greens – enough said ... If you forget the condition, this is great fun ... Highest course in Derbyshire ... Plenty of blind driving and second shots.

Chapel-en-le-Frith Golf Club   ★★

Manchester Road, Chapel-en-le-Frith, SK23 9UH
Website: www.chapelgolf.co.uk   E-mail: info@chapelgolf.co.uk
Nearest main town: Stockport

Secretary: Mr J. Hilton   Tel: 01298 813943
                                       Fax: 01298 814990
Professional: Mr D. Cullen   Tel: 01298 812118
                                       Fax: 01298 814990

Playing: Midweek: round £28.00; day £38.00. Weekend: round £38.00; day n/a.

Facilities: Bar: 11am–11pm. Food: Lunch and dinner served from 11am–9pm. Bar snacks.

Comments: Value for money here ... Design a little lacking but scenery exceptional ... Easy on your pocket ... Very scenic ... Views best in the area.

Chesterfield Golf Club   ★★★

Walton, Chesterfield, S42 7LA
Nearest main town: Chesterfield

Secretary: Mr B. Broughton   Tel: 01246 279256
                                       Fax: 01246 276622
Professional: Mr M. McLean   Tel: 01246 276297

Playing: Midweek: round £26.00; day n/a. Weekend: round £35.00; day n/a.

Facilities: Bar: 11am–11pm. Food: Lunch from 12pm–2pm. Dinner from 7pm–9pm. Bookings required.

Comments: Traditional club, one of the best in Derbyshire ...
Pleasant parkland golf with good 19th ... Nice reception
... Course not known for its condition.

Horsley Lodge Golf Club   ★★★

Smalley Mill Road, Horsley, DE21 5BL
Nearest main town: Derby

Secretary: Mr G. Johnson   Tel: 01332 780838
                                         Fax: 01332 781118
Professional: Mr G. Lyall   Tel: 01332 780838

Playing: Midweek: round £25.00; day £37.00. Weekend: round
                    £25.00; day £37.00.

Facilities: Bar: 11am–11pm. Food: Lunch from 12pm–3pm.
                    Dinner from 6pm–9pm. Bar snacks.

Comments: First-class driving range ... Good place to practise ...
                    Very open ... Tasty food.

Kedleston Park Golf Club   ★★★

Kedleston Road, Quarndon, DE22 5JD
Website: www.kedlestonparkgolf.co.uk
E-mail: kedlestonparkgolf.fsnet.co.uk
Nearest main town: Derby

Secretary: Mr G. Duckmanton   Tel: 01332 841685
                                        Fax: 01332 840035
Professional: Mr P. Wesselingh   Tel: 01332 840035

Playing: Midweek: round £35.00; day n/a. Weekend: round
                    £35.00; day n/a.

Facilities: Bar: 11am–11pm. Food: Lunch and dinner from
                    11am–11pm.

Comments: New clubhouse ... Fine course with views of Kedleston
                    Hall ... Condition not what it should be ... Course
                    management severely tested.

Shirland Golf Club

Lower Delves, Shirland, DE5 6AU
Nearest main town: Alfreton

Secretary: Mr G. Brassington   Tel: 01773 834935
Professional: Mr N. Hallam   Tel: 01773 834935

Playing: Midweek: round £15.00; day £25.00. Weekend: round £20.00; day £30.00.

Facilities: Bar: 10am–11pm. Food: Lunch and dinner from 10am–9pm. Bar snacks.

Comments: Parkland course with good welcome ... Fairly open with little definition ... Always very welcoming.

Sickleholme Golf Club   ★★

Bamford, Sheffield, S33 0BH
Nearest main town: Sheffield

Secretary: Mr P. Taylor   Tel: 01433 651306
                                Fax: 01433 651306
Professional: Mr P. Taylor   Tel: 01433 651306

Playing: Midweek: round £27.00; day £27.00. Weekend: round £30.00; day £30.00.

Facilities: Bar: 10am–11pm. Food: Lunch and dinner from 10am–9pm. Bar snacks.

Comments: Right in the middle of the Peak District ... Very rough and rugged ... You can get lost out there ... Deep ravines and outstanding views ... Very pure, clean air.

Devon

Saunton Golf Club (East)　　★★★★★

Saunton, Braunton, EX33 1LG
Website: www.sauntongolf.co.uk　　E-mail: info@sauntongolf.co.uk
Nearest main town: Barnstaple

It has been said that if ever the Open Championship had to be staged in the West Country, the East course at Saunton would be the only true candidate.

The course is set amid a sea of sand dunes on the northern crest of Devon's engaging Bideford Bay, almost directly opposite the famous links at Westward Ho!, and quite frankly, links golf does not come much better than this. It charms and captures you with a surreal, mystical ambience. Each and every fairway winds its way about what can only be described as God-given property, and once you set off, you're rarely aware of anything but the hole at hand, located in a natural tunnel of dunes.

Saunton, designed by the great Herbert Fowler, who crafted the Berkshire and Walton Heath but only worked on one other links course, Royal Lytham & St Annes, is a wonderfully balanced course, with survival the name of the game for the first four and final four holes. Players who know the East course will temper their games to fit this design, taking caution early on before opening their shoulders and being a little more aggressive around the turn. Unlike a lot of links courses, this policy is not so dependent on the wind because each hole at Saunton is well protected and the greens nestle in the bosoms of the dunes. There are exceptions, of course, like the 5th where you could be hitting a wedge or a long iron depending on the wind.

Saunton may not have the exhilarating nature of other links courses, where the wind burns your cheeks and shots are played across bays or rocks, but it has its own discreet nature, and if you're greedy, it will turn the screw on you.

Secretary:　　Mr T. Reynolds　　　　Tel: 01271 812436
　　　　　　　　　　　　　　　　　　　　Fax: 01271 814241
Professional: Mr A. Mackenzie　　　 Tel: 01271 812013
　　　　　　　　　　　　　　　　　　　　Fax: 01271 812126

Playing:　　Midweek: round £50.00 (18 holes), £70.00 (36 holes inc. meal voucher); day n/a. Weekend: round £50.00 (18 holes), £70.00 (36 holes inc. meal voucher); day n/a.

Facilities: Bar: 11am–10.30pm. Food: Breakfast, lunch and dinner 11am–9pm. Bar snacks.

Comments: Quite simply the best in the West ... A course worthy of the Open at half the price ... Golf in traditional links setting ... True raw links ... Not cheap, but a superior course ... Great golf club, course and facilities first class ... Great welcome, fascinating course – well worth the drive ... Encompasses all that is best about links golf ... An Open venue in the making, surely ... If you want a new Open course, try here ... An absolute belter!

Bigbury Golf Club   ★★★

Bigbury on Sea, Kingsbridge, TQ7 4BB
Nearest main town: Plymouth

Secretary: Mr M. Lowry   Tel: 01548 810557
                                      Fax: 01548 810207
Professional: Mr S. Lloyd   Tel: 01548 810412

Playing: Midweek: round £27.00; day n/a. Weekend: round £30.00; day n/a.

Facilities: Bar: 11am–11pm. Food: Breakfast and lunch from 9am–6pm.

Comments: Beautiful coastal course that proves a friendly day out ... Views over the River Avon ... Impressive setting for short, tricky course ... Something a little bit different.

Churston Golf Club   ★★★

Dartmouth Road, Brixham, TQ5 0LA
Website: www.churstongolfclublimited.co.uk
E-mail: manager@churstongc.freeserve.co.uk
Nearest main town: Brixham

Secretary: Mr S. Banden   Tel: 01803 842751
                                      Fax: 01803 845738
Professional: Mr N. Holman   Tel: 01803 843442

Playing: Midweek: round £30.00; day n/a. Weekend: round £35.00; day n/a.

Facilities: Bar: 11am–11pm. Food: Breakfast, lunch and dinner from 8am–7pm. Bar snacks.

Comments: Excellent clubhouse ... Cliff-top course that needs all the shots ... Course that hugs the cliff tops ... Real cliffhanger ... Tangly gorse.

Dainton Park Golf Club ★★

Ipplepen, Newton Abbot, TQ12 5TN
Nearest main town: Newton Abbot

Secretary: Mr M. Penlington   Tel: 01803 815000
Professional: Mr M. Tyson   Tel: 01803 815000

Playing: Midweek: round n/a; day n/a. Weekend: round £25.00; day n/a.

Facilities: Bar: 11am–11pm. Food: Bar snacks.

Comments: Up-and-coming club ... Course can get heavy underfoot, so watch out ... Well thought out ... Blind shots make for accurate club selection ... Interesting course that gets better each year ... Great par-3s ... Cracking value in the Devon countryside.

Dartmouth Golf & Country Club ★★★★

Blackawton, Dartmouth, TQ9 7DE
Website: www.dgcc.co.uk   E-mail: info@dgcc.co.uk
Nearest main town: Totnes

Secretary: Mr B. Clark   Tel: 01803 712016
                                Fax: 01803 712628
Professional: Mr S. Dougan   Tel: 01803 712650
                                Fax: 01803 712628

Playing: Midweek: round £30.00 (18 Championship), £13.00 (9 Club); day n/a. Weekend: round £40.00 (18 Chamionship), £14.00 (9 Club); day n/a.

Facilities: Bar: 11am–11pm. Food: Breakfast, lunch and dinner from 7.30am–9.30pm. Bar snacks.

Comments: Best to have a buggy ... No two holes the same on this thinking man's golf course ... Very difficult, excellent course ... Difficult but satisfying course ... 4th hole sums up everything about Dartmouth ... No bailing out on this tough-as-old-boots layout ... West Country woe on this parkland monster.

East Devon ★★★

Links Road, Budleigh Salterton, EX9 6DG
Website: www.edgc.co.uk   E-mail: secretary@edgc.co.uk
Nearest main town: Budleigh Salterton

Secretary: Mr R. Burley   Tel: 01395 443370
Professional: Mr T. Underwood   Tel: 01395 445195

Playing: Midweek: round £30.00; day £40.00. Weekend: round
£30.00; day £40.00.

Facilities: Bar: 11am–7pm. Food: Bar snacks.

Comments: Best in the area without doubt … Very fair test of golf on
attractive downland turf … Need high levels of skill …
Cliff-top beauty … On a clear day so refreshing.

Exeter Golf & Country Club ★★★

Countess Wear, Exeter, EX2 7AE
Nearest main town: Exeter

Secretary: Mr K. Ham   Tel: 01392 874139
                                       Fax: 01392 874139
Professional: Mr M. Rowett   Tel: 01392 875028

Playing: Midweek: round £26.00; day £26.00. Weekend: round
£26.00; day £26.00.

Facilities: Bar: 11am–11pm. Food: Lunch and dinner served from
10am–9pm. Bar snacks.

Comments: Very flat … Popular layout that can get busy … Basic
country club course … Mature and full of character.

Ilfracombe Golf Club ★★★

Hele Bay, Ilfracombe, EX34 9RT
Website: www.ilfracombegolfclub.com
E-mail: ilfracombe.golfclub@virgin.net
Nearest main town: Ilfracombe

Secretary: Mr J. Hoskings   Tel: 01271 862176
                                       Fax: 01271 867731
Professional: Mr M. Davies   Tel: 01271 863328
                                       Fax: 01271 867731

Playing: Midweek: round £22.00; day £27.00. Weekend: round
£27.00; day £32.00.

Facilities: Bar: 11am–11pm. Food: Breakfast, lunch and dinner from 9am–9pm. Bar snacks.

Comments: Unusual, breathtaking views and great welcome ... Bristol Channel the backdrop for this supreme test ... Devon delight in heathland setting.

Royal North Devon Golf Club   ★★★★

Golf Links Road, Westward Ho!, Bideford, EX39 1HD
Website: www.royalnorthdevongolfclub.co.uk
E-mail: info@royalnorthdevongolfclub.co.uk
Nearest main town: Bideford

Secretary: Mr R. Fowler   Tel: 01237 473817
                                      Fax: 01237 423456
Professional: Mr R. Herring   Tel: 01237 477598

Playing: Midweek: round £34.00; day £40.00. Weekend: round £40.00; day £44.00.

Facilities: Bar: 11am–11pm. Food: Breakfast, lunch and dinner from 9am–7pm. Bar snacks.

Comments: A unique golf experience ... From the 3rd hole things get very interesting ... No better place to play ... Links legend that never fails to surprise or disappoint ... What golf is all about ... Heavenly links that catches spirit of bygone days.

Saunton Golf Club (West)   ★★★★

Saunton, Braunton, EX33 1LG
Nearest main town: Barnstaple

Secretary: Mr T. Reynolds   Tel: 01271 812436
                                      Fax: 01271 814241
Professional: Mr A. Mackenzie   Tel: 01271 812013
                                      Fax: 01271 812126

Playing: Midweek: round £30.00; day £45.00. Weekend: round £40.00; day £55.00.

Facilities: Bar: 11am–10.30pm. Food: Lunch and dinner from 11am–9pm. Bar snacks.

Comments: Wonderful links (although not as good as the East) with outstanding practice facilities ... Great test for all abilities ... I don't know which I prefer ... Shorter than the East but more interesting ... What lucky members to have two such sublime links.

Tavistock Golf Club   ★★

Down Road, Tavistock, PL18 9BH
Website: www.tavistockgolfclub.org.uk
E-mail: tavygolf@hotmail.com
Nearest main town: Tavistock

Secretary:	Mr J. Cole	Tel: 01822 612344
		Fax: 01822 612344
Professional:	Mr D. Rehaag	Tel: 01822 612316

Playing: Midweek: round £26.00; day n/a. Weekend: round £32.00; day n/a.

Facilities: Bar: 11am–11pm. Food: Lunch and dinner from 10am–9pm. Bar snacks.

Comments: The better of the two courses in Tavistock ... Superb setting ... Springy turf ... Rarified atmosphere here ... Don't let your guard down.

Teignmouth Golf Club   ★★

Haldon Moor, Teignmouth, TQ14 9NY
Website: www.teignmouthgolfclubltd.co.uk
E-mail: tgc@btconnect.com
Nearest main town: Teignmouth

Secretary:	Mr W. Hendry	Tel: 01626 777070
		Fax: 01626 777304
Professional:	Mr R. Selley	Tel: 01626 772894

Playing: Midweek: round £27.00; day n/a. Weekend: round £29.50; day n/a.

Facilities: Bar: Members only. Food: Members only.

Comments: Good, tough course ... Windswept ... Good challenge for low handicaps ... Greens excellent ... The day spoiled by reception at this exclusive club ... Holiday golf but without the welcome ... Heathland course spoilt by club's exclusivity.

Thurlestone Golf Club   ★★★★

Thurlestone, Kingsbridge, TQ7 3NZ
Website: www.thurlestonegc.co.uk
Nearest main town: Kingsbridge

Secretary: Mr J. Scott   Tel: 01548 560405
           Fax: 01548 562149
Professional: Mr P. Laugher   Tel: 01548 560715
           Fax: 01548 560715

Playing: Midweek: round n/a; day £32.00. Weekend: round n/a; day £32.00.

Facilities: Bar: 11.15am–2.15pm and 5pm–7.30pm. Food: Lunch from 10am–5.30pm. Bar snacks.

Comments: Lovely links course ... Presentation without fault all year round ... Harsh test of golf ... Fine finish to this cliffhanger ... Downland course on edge of cliffs ... Typical Devon course and always in fine nick.

Tiverton Golf Club ★★

Post Hill, Tiverton, EX16 4NE
Nearest main town: Tiverton

Secretary: Mrs R. Perry   Tel: 01884 252187
           Fax: 01884 252187
Professional: Mr D. Sheppard   Tel: 01884 254836

Playing: Midweek: round £25.50; day £25.50. Weekend: round £33.00; day £33.00.

Facilities: Bar: 11am–11pm. Food: Lunch and dinner from 10.30am–9pm. Bar snacks.

Comments: Excellent condition ... Fairways always finely cut ... Diverse parkland ... Not that exciting ... A slightly unusual Devon course ... Always well kept.

Torquay Golf Club ★★★

Petitor Road, St Marychurch, Torquay, TQ1 4QF
Nearest main town: Torquay

Secretary: Mr B. Long   Tel: 01803 314591
           Fax: 01803 316116
Professional: Mr M. Ruth   Tel: 01803 329113

Playing: Midweek: round £24.00; day £24.00. Weekend: round £28.00; day £28.00.

Facilities: Bar: 11am–11pm. Food: Lunch and dinner from 10am–9pm. Bar snacks.

Comments: Well-laid-out course with a few difficult holes ... Views over Dartmoor best part of otherwise taciturn course.

Warren Golf Club

Dawlish Warren, EX7 0NF
Website: www.dwgc.co.uk   E-mail: secretary@dwgc.co.uk
Nearest main town: Dawlish

Secretary: Mr T. Aggett   Tel: 01626 862255
                                        Fax: 01626 888005
Professional: Mr D. Prowse   Tel: 01626 864002

Playing: Midweek: round £25.00; day n/a. Weekend: round £26.00; day n/a.

Facilities: Bar: 11am–11pm. Food: Lunch from 10.30am–4pm. Dinner from 5.30–7.30pm. Bar snacks.

Comments: Links with much personality ... Treasured location ... Cute links on Exe estuary ... Railway runs along 18th ... Located on a spit between estuary and sea ... A little bleak and exposed ... Condition lets it down.

Woodbury Park Hotel, Golf & Country Club   ★★★

Woodbury Castle, Woodbury, EX5 1JJ
Website: www.woodburypark.co.uk
E-mail: golfbookings@woodburypark.co.uk
Nearest main town: Exmouth

Secretary: Mr A. Richards   Tel: 01395 233500
                                        Fax: 01395 233384
Professional: Mr A. Richards   Tel: 01395 233500
                                        Fax: 01395 233384

Playing: Midweek: round £35.00; day n/a. Weekend: round £45.00; day n/a.

Facilities: Bar: 11am–11pm. Food: Breakfast, lunch and dinner from 9am–11pm. Bar snacks.

Comments: Progressive club with nice attitude ... Nicely balanced course with woodland and parkland ... Great variety with beautiful woodland ... Super resort course ... Crater-sized bunkers make life a misery ... A US-style course that blends with the countryside ... An excellent addition to golf in Devon ... Will improve with age.

Yelverton Golf Club ★★

Golf Links Road, Yelverton, PL20 6BN
Website: www.yelvertongc.co.uk   E-mail: secretary@yelvertongc.co.uk
Nearest main town: Plymouth

Secretary:	Mr S. Barnes	Tel: 01822 852824
		Fax: 01822 854869
Professional:	Mr T. McSherry	Tel: 01822 853593
		Fax: 01822 854869

Playing: Midweek: round £30.00; day n/a. Weekend: round £40.00 (not Saturday); day n/a.

Facilities: Bar: 11am–11pm. Food: Lunch from 11am–5pm. Bar snacks.

Comments: Welcoming, good food and excellent value for money ... Another typical Devon course with good welcome ... Will be back again for the views and quality back nine ... Well worth the money for interesting golf in pleasant atmosphere.

Dorset

Ferndown Golf Club (Old) ★★★★

119 Golf Links Road, Ferndown, BH22 8BU
Website: www.ferndown-golf-club.co.uk
E-mail: ferndowngc@lineone.net
Nearest main town: Ferndown

If you are looking for the best golf in Dorset then you have come to the right place. Everything about Ferndown exudes quality and on a clear, sunny day, when the views from the clubhouse extend to the Isle of Wight, there are few nicer places to be. Although just 6 miles north of Bournemouth, there is much about the layout that is reminiscent of the more famous Surrey heathlands. Ferndown, with its rhododendrons, heather, pines and fir trees, has a good deal of history dating back to the days of double Open champion Harold Hilton, who designed the Old course in 1912.

In keeping with the designs of that time, the course is not long, measuring just under 6500 yards, but you will find it an intriguing challenge nonetheless. There are a good number of doglegs, which place a premium on intelligent course management, the toughest of which come at the 9th and the 11th. The uphill 6th, generally played into the breeze, is also among the more difficult obstacles to a pleasing score. There are a good set of par-3s, the rhododendrons on the 5th making a colourful scene during the spring, while the 16th is named 'Hilton's Hole' in recognition of the architect.

The gentle mounds and swales give the fairways both definition and character on a layout that is made up of two loops, the inner one containing the first eight holes, while the journey home is played around the outside. It is also worth noting that Ferndown has a reputation for being in excellent condition. The sandy sub-soil means it rarely gets waterlogged and you are usually guaranteed some of the best-kept fairways and greens on which to play.

Secretary:	Mr M. Davies	Tel: 01202 874602
Professional:	None	Tel: 01202 873825

Playing: Midweek: round £50.00; day n/a. Weekend: round £60.00; day n/a.

Facilities: Bar: 11am–10pm. Food: Lunch from 10am–5pm. Dinner by arrangement.

Comments: Best course in Dorset and splendid, friendly clubhouse
                  ... Gorse, pine trees, numerous doglegs ... One of the
                  most interesting courses around ... Solid reputation and
                  wasn't disappointed ... Matches some of the best inland
                  courses in Surrey ... One of the best-kept courses in the
                  country ... In fine nick but a rather boring layout that is
                  vastly overrated ... Views across the Isle of Wight ...
                  I wish I knew a member!

Bridport & West Dorset Golf Club   ★

Burton Road, Bridport, DT6 4PS
Website: www.bridportgolfclub.org.uk
E-mail: b_wdgc@btinternet.com
Nearest main town: Bridport

Secretary: Mr P. Ridler   Tel: 01308 421095
                                           Fax: 01308 421095
Professional: Mr D. Parsons   Tel: 01308 421491
                                           Fax: 01308 421491

Playing: Midweek: round n/a; day £22.00 (£16.00 after 12 noon).
                   Weekend: round n/a; day £22.00 (£16.00 after 2pm).

Facilities: Bar: 11am–11pm. Food: Lunch and dinner from
                   11am–10pm. Bar snacks.

Comments: Typical cliff-top course ... Very in tune with natural
                   surroundings ... Clever design for this subtle course ...
                   Par-3 14th an instant classic.

Broadstone (Dorset) Golf Club   ★★★★

Wentworth Drive, Broadstone, BH18 8DQ
Website: www.broadstonegolfclub.com
E-mail: admin@broadstonegolfclub.com
Nearest main town: Poole

Secretary: Mr C. Robinson   Tel: 01202 692595
                                           Fax: 01202 642520
Professional: Mr N. Tokely   Tel: 01202 692835
                                           Fax: 01202 692835

Playing: Midweek: round £40.00; day £60.00. Weekend: round
                   £45.00 (one round only – after 2.30pm); day n/a.

Facilities: Bar: 11am–11pm. Food: Lunch and dinner from
                   11am–9pm. Bar snacks.

Comments: Tight and difficult course in excellent condition ... Certainly in the top three in Dorset, but not for welcome ... Good clubhouse but members don't exactly welcome you with open arms ... Value, quality course although there's better in Dorset ... A peach of a golf experience – will be back ... Heathland heaven for us links haters.

Came Down Golf Club   ★★★

Came Down, Dorchester, DT2 8NR
Nearest main town: Dorchester

Secretary:	Mr R. Kelly	Tel: 01305 813494
		Fax: 01305 813494
Professional:	Mr N. Rodgers	Tel: 01305 812670

Playing: Midweek: round £24.00; day n/a. Weekend: round £28.00; day n/a.

Facilities: Bar: 11am–11pm. Food: Lunch from 10am–6pm. Bar snacks.

Comments: Venue for many local championships ... Honest and tough ... Exceptional value ... Wonderful downland course with lush feel ... Best value for money in Dorset.

The Dorset Golf & Country Club   ★★★★

Bere Regis, Poole, BH20 7NT
Website: www.dorsetgolfresort.com
E-mail: admin@dorsetgolfresort.com
Nearest main town: Wool

Secretary:	Mr N. Carruthers	Tel: 01929 472244
	(Corporate Manager)	Fax: 01929 471294
Professional:	Mr S. Porter	Tel: 01929 472244
		Fax: 01929 471294

Playing: Midweek: round £35.00 (Lakeland), £24.00 (Woodland); day £40.00 (27/36 holes). Weekend: round £39.00 (Lakeland), £28.00 (Woodland); day £45.00 (27/36 holes).

Facilities: Bar: 11am–11pm. Food: Lunch from 11.30am–2.30pm. Dinner from 6pm–9.30pm.

Comments: Underrated course and improving all the time ...
Presentation could not be faulted ... Established course
with decent practice facilities ... Nice attitude at this
parkland pearl.

Dudsbury Golf Club ★★

64 Christchurch Road, Ferndown, BH22 8ST
Website: www.thedudsbury.co.uk
E-mail: golf@dudsbury.demon.co.uk
Nearest main town: Bournemouth

Secretary:	Mr G. Legg	Tel: 01202 593499	
		Fax: 01202 594555	
Professional:	Mr K. Spurgeon	Tel: 01202 594488	

Playing: Midweek: round £34.00 (18 holes), £44.00 (36 holes);
day n/a. Weekend: round £39.00 (18 holes), £49.00
(36 holes); day n/a.

Facilities: Bar: 11am–11pm. Food: Lunch and dinner from
10am–9pm. Bar snacks.

Comments: Well presented but can be a brutal course in the winter
... Not as busy as some of the clubs in Devon and well
worth the trip.

Isle of Purbeck Golf Club ★★★★

Studland, Swanage, BH19 3AB
Website: www.purbeckgolf.co.uk
Nearest main town: Studland

Secretary: Mrs J. Robinson   Tel: 01929 450361
             (Managing Director)   Fax: 01929 450501
Professional: Mr I. Brake   Tel: 01929 450354

Playing: Midweek: round £35.00; day £45.00. Weekend: round
£40.00; day £47.50.

Facilities: Bar: 11am–10pm. Food: Lunch from 12.30pm–
5.30pm except Mondays.

Comments: Views. Oh, what views! ... Play Purbeck and die a happy
man ... Set on the Purbeck Hills ... Gorse and heather
everywhere ... The natural selection ... Most spectacular views anywhere in Britain ... Best in the county and
in fantastic, natural condition ... Wonderful turf and
views ... Simply unique.

Parkstone Golf Club   ★★★★

49A Links Road, Poole, BH14 9QS
E-mail: admin@parkstonegolfclub.co.uk
Nearest main town: Bournemouth

Secretary:	Ms C. Radford	Tel: 01202 707138
	(General Manager)	Fax: 01202 706027
Professional:	Mr M. Thompson	Tel: 01202 708092
		Fax: 01202 706027

Playing: Midweek: round £40.00; day £60.00. Weekend: round
£50.00; day £70.00.

Facilities: Bar: 11am–11pm. Food: Lunch from 11am–5.30pm.
Bar snacks. Dinner on Fridays only from 8pm–10pm.

Comments: Golf in its purest and finest form ... Old club with set-in-
stone attitude ... Not as good as Purbeck or Ferndown
but a good third string ... Heathland masterpiece that I
can't help going back to again and again ...
Mesmerising course.

Sherborne Golf Club   ★★★

Higher Clatcombe, Sherborne, DT9 4RN
E-mail: enquiries@sherbornegolfclub.fsnet.co.uk
Nearest main town: Sherborne

Secretary:	Mr M. Betteridge	Tel: 01935 814431
		Fax: 01935 814218
Professional:	Mr S. Wright	Tel: 01935 812274

Playing: Midweek: round £22.00; day £28.00. Weekend: round
£30.00; day £36.00.

Facilities: Bar: 11am–10.30pm. Food: Lunch and dinner from
10am–8pm except Mondays. Bar snacks.

Comments: Delightful part of the country ... Don't really want to let
this cat out of the bag ... Natural course relying on slope
of the land for its defence ... You can never really fully
understand the greens ... Protected greens ... One of
the best parkland courses in Dorset ... Charming course
and same goes for nearby village.

Weymouth Golf Club   ★★

Links Road, Weymouth, DT4 0PF
Website: www.weymouthgolfclub.co.uk
E-mail: weymouthgolfclub@aol.com
Nearest main town: Weymouth

Secretary:	Mr B. Chatham	Tel: 01305 773981
		Fax: 01305 788029
Professional:	Mr D. Lochrie	Tel: 01305 773997
		Fax: 01305 788029

Playing: Midweek: round n/a; day £26.00. Weekend: round n/a; day £34.00.

Facilities: Bar: 11am–7pm. Food: Breakfast and lunch from 9.30am–5pm. Bar snacks.

Comments: Pleasing course near the seaside ... Not much style here ... Fairly straightforward and simple ... Cheap holiday golf.

County Durham

Brancepeth Castle Golf Club ★★★★

The Clubhouse, Brancepeth, Durham, DH7 8EA
Website: www.brancepeth-castle-golf.co.uk
E-mail: brancepeth-castle@btclick.com
Nearest main town: Durham

Brancepeth Castle is tucked away in the Durham countryside down a leafy lane from Brancepeth village, a former best-kept village in England. The golf club is also a best-kept secret: never too crowded and usually in good condition.

This parkland course is very exposed and is apt to be very windy, even to the admission of a linksman. You will find that it is essentially a strategic course with the exception of some of the closing holes, and the bunkering will generally direct you in the right areas to find the one line for the approach shot. Your strategy will also be directed by the mature trees that have separated themselves from the wooded surrounds.

The course's architect, Harry Colt, was not a man impressed with immaculately kept courses, and for him a nasty lie now and again was to be accepted with a rueful smile rather than an expletive directed at the greenkeeper. Consequently, in keeping with Colt's philosophy, the fairways are rippled, a drainage effect, and you should be prepared to hit approach shots off downslopes. The greens are also humpy, true and very quick, and they peak in midsummer, the best time to visit the club.

Much of the enjoyment of playing Brancepeth Castle is not derived from the beauty of the parkland but the historic surrounds that include the twelfth-century castle and the church of St Brandon, which flanks the castle and sits behind the 18th green. There's also a deep ravine that has to be crossed three times over a wobbling bridge constructed by the Royal Engineers. The drive at the 18th is straight over the ravine and it requires a solid strike if you don't want to be delving for more balls. The best hole, though, is probably the 9th, a par-3 through a chute of trees and then it's all carry to a small green that drops sharply away to the right and rises equally sharply to the left. The green is positioned at the foot of the castle, but only a monstrous hook will cause damage.

Secretary: None

Professional: Mr D. Howden

Tel: 0191 378 0075
Fax: 0191 378 3835
Tel: 0191 378 0183

Playing: Midweek: round £30.00; day £35.00. Weekend: round £40.00; day n/a.

Facilities: Bar: 11am–11pm. Food: Lunch and dinner from 11am–9.30pm. Bar snacks.

Comments: Rolling fairways in parkland setting ... Great selection of par-3s ... Difficult par-3s ... What do you expect from the man who designed Pine Valley? ... Cracking 1st hole and doesn't let up ... Colourful club with proud tradition ... Best par-3s on any course plus splendid views ... Always a great challenge and in excellent condition.

Barnard Castle Golf Club ★★★

Harmire Road, Barnard Castle, DL12 8QN
Website: www.barnardcastlegolfclub.org.uk
E-mail: sec@barnardcastlegolfclub.org.uk
Nearest main town: Barnard Castle

Secretary: Mr J. Kilgarriff   Tel: 01833 638355
                                     Fax: 01833 695551
Professional: Mr D. Pearce   Tel: 01883 631980
                                     Fax: 01883 631980

Playing: Midweek: round £20.00 (18 holes), £24.00 (27 holes); day n/a. Weekend: round £30.00 (18 holes), £35.00 (27 holes); day n/a.

Facilities: Bar: 11am–11pm. Food: Lunch and dinner from 11am–10.30pm. Bar snacks.

Comments: Improved since the course was extended in mid-1990s ... Full of character ... Enjoyable, simple course ... Views up Teesdale ... Water in play on almost all the holes with natural becks.

Beamish Park Golf Club ★★

Beamish, DH9 0RH
Nearest main town: Stanley

Secretary: Mr B. Bradley   Tel: 0191 370 1382
                                  Fax: 0191 370 2937
Professional: Mr C. Cole   Tel: 0191 370 1984

Playing: Midweek: round £16.00; day £24.00. Weekend: round £24.00; day £30.00.

Facilities: Bar: 11am–11pm. Food: Lunch and dinner from 10am–9pm. Bar snacks.

Comments: Parkland course with value food and drink ... Henry Cotton design ... Nice club attitude, but course average.

Bishop Auckland Golf Club   ★

High Plains, Durham Road, Bishop Auckland, DL14 8DL
Website: www.bagc.co.uk   E-mail: enquiries@bagc.co.uk
Nearest main town: Bishop Auckland

Secretary: Mr A. Milne   Tel: 01388 661618
                                        Fax: 01388 607005
Professional: Mr D. Skiffington   Tel: 01388 661618
                                        Fax: 01388 607005

Playing: Midweek: round £24.00; day £30.00. Weekend: round £30.00; day n/a.

Facilities: Bar: 11am–11pm. Food: Lunch and dinner from 11am–10pm. Bar snacks.

Comments: In good condition and clubhouse lacks nothing ... Pleasant parkland, manicured fairways and fast greens ... Views over the Wear Valley ... Only two par-4s in first 12 holes ... Club that bleeds tradition ... 7th hole is the highlight.

Castle Eden & Peterlee Golf Club   ★★

Castle Eden, Hartlepool, TS27 4SS
Nearest main town: Peterlee

Secretary: Mr D. Livingston   Tel: 01429 836510
                                        Fax: 01429 836689
Professional: Mr G. Laidlaw   Tel: 01429 836510

Playing: Midweek: round £18.00; day £22.00. Weekend: round £30.00; day £30.00.

Facilities: Bar: 11am–11pm. Food: Lunch and dinner (booking recommended) from 11am–9.30pm. Bar snacks.

Comments: Site of Cotton's infamous 620-yard par-5, now thankfully shortened ... Dogged opening with three killer par-4s ... Charming course, so testing ... Attractive course with little spinneys ... One of the best in the area, give it a go ... Easy walking.

Dinsdale Spa Golf Club ★★

Middleton St George, Darlington, DL12 1DW
Nearest main town: Darlington

Secretary:	Mr P. Davison	Tel: 01325 332297
		Fax: 01325 332297
Professional:	Mr N. Metcalfe	Tel: 01325 332515

Playing: Midweek: round £25.00 (non-members), £12.50 (with member); day n/a. Weekend: round with member only; day n/a.

Facilities: Bar: 11am–11pm. Food: Breakfast, lunch and dinner from 8am–9pm.

Comments: A bit straightforward for the demanding player ... Gentle course but fairly bland ... Bleak, short course ... Toughest stretch from the start ... Fair condition through the year.

Eaglescliffe Golf Club ★★★

Yarm Road, Eaglescliffe, Stockton-on-Tees, TS16 0DQ
E-mail: eaglescliffegcsec@tiscali.co.uk
Nearest main town: Stockton-on-Tees

Secretary:	Mr M. Sample	Tel: 01642 780238
		Fax: 01642 780238
Professional:	Mr G. Bell	Tel: 01642 790122
		Fax: 01642 780238

Playing: Midweek: round £27.00; day £37.00. Weekend: round £36.00; day £50.00.

Facilities: Bar: 11am–11pm. Food: Lunch and dinner from 11am–9pm. Bar snacks.

Comments: Club that enjoys having visitors ... Club's history lends the club a rather noble air ... Super par-5 14th ... Endless fun on this cheery course ... Not much better in the area ... Hilly course with views to the Cleveland Hills.

Hartlepool Golf Club ★★★

Hart Warren, Hartlepool, TS24 9QF
Website: www.hartlepoolgolfclub.co.uk
Nearest main town: Hartlepool

Secretary: Mr L. Gordon   Tel: 01429 274398
                                        Fax: 01429 274129
Professional: Mr M. Cole   Tel: 01429 267473

Playing: Midweek: round n/a; day £25.00. Weekend: round n/a;
                  day £36.00.

Facilities: Bar: 11am–11pm. Food: Lunch from 12pm–2.30pm.
                  Dinner from 6pm–9pm.

Comments: Better than Seaton Carew … Underrated … Links for
                  which you need a strong heart … Refined club with
                  course to match … Highlight of the back nine is the
                  par-3 11th … Unique links played along the North Sea
                  … Not a classic design but a raw test … Highly recom-
                  mended by those in the area.

Ramside Hall Golf Club   ★★

Ramside Hall Hotel, Carville, Durham, DH1 1TD
Nearest main town: Durham

Secretary: Mr T. Flowers   Tel: 0191 386 9514
                                        Fax: 0191 386 9519
Professional: Mr R. Lister   Tel: 0191 386 9514

Playing: Midweek: round £27.00; day £33.00. Weekend: round
                  £33.00; day £40.00.

Facilities: Bar: 11am–11pm. Food: Lunch from 12pm–2.30pm.
                  Dinner from 7pm–9.30pm. Bar snacks.

Comments: Average facilities and greens could be better … Recently
                  opened 'super-course' with three nines … Golf
                  academy and driving range … Courses don't match the
                  facilities or hotel.

Seaton Carew Golf Club   ★★★★

Tees Road, Seaton Carew, Hartlepool, TS25 1DE
Website: www.seatoncarewgolfclub.org.uk
Nearest main town: Hartlepool

Secretary: Mr J. Hall   Tel: 01429 261040
                                        Fax: 01429 261040
Professional: Mr M. Rogers   Tel: 01429 890660
                                        Fax: 01429 261040

Playing: Midweek: round £28.00; day n/a. Weekend: round £35.00; day n/a.

Facilities: Bar: 11am–11pm. Food: Lunch and dinner from 10am–9pm. Bar snacks.

Comments: Links test of all the shots ... Most enjoyable day out ... Dignified club, surely underrated ... This wild, tortured links is always in good condition ... Exposed with un-appealing views, but what a sensual feast.

South Moor Golf Club ★★

The Middles, Craghead, Stanley, DH9 6AG
Website: www.southmoorgolfclub.com
E-mail: bryandavison@southmoorgc.freeserve.co.uk
Nearest main town: Durham

Secretary: Mr B. Davison   Tel: 01207 232848
                                     Fax: 01207 284616
Professional: Mr S. Cowell   Tel: 01207 283525
                                     Fax: 01207 284616

Playing: Midweek: round £15.00 (without member); day £22.00. Weekend: round £18.00 (without member); day £26.00.

Facilities: Bar: 11am–11pm. Food: Lunch and dinner from 11am–9pm. Bar snacks.

Comments: Testing course and superb welcome in the clubhouse ... Fair test of golf on well-presented course ... Moor and heathland which never lets up ... Golfing outpost that like many courses in area feels exposed ... 12th a terrific hole ... Open course that complements many courses in the area.

Woodham Golf & Country Club ★★

Burnhill Way, Newton Aycliffe, DL5 4PN
Nearest main town: Newton Aycliffe

Secretary: Mr J. Jenkinson   Tel: 01325 320574
                                     Fax: 01325 315254
Professional: Mr E. Wilson   Tel: 01325 315257

Playing: Midweek: round £16.50 (one round), £22.00 (two rounds); day n/a. Weekend: round £26.50 (one round), £33.00 (two rounds); day n/a.

Facilities: Bar: 11am–11pm. Food: Lunch from 12pm–2.30pm. Dinner from 7pm–9.30pm.

Comments: Brute of a course ... Fairly unnatural ... Easily missable ... Very tough for the beginner ... Nice facilities but course lacks character.

Essex

Thorndon Park Golf Club ★★★

Ingrave, Brentwood, CM13 3RH
Website: www.thorndonparkgolfclub.com   E-mail: tpgc@btclick.com
Nearest main town: Brentwood

If anyone refers to Essex as a golfing wasteland, don't take a blind bit of notice. Londoners head in all directions but east to find golfing fulfilment, which is a pity because they are missing out on courses of the pedigree of Thorndon Park. Set in the grounds of a former hunting estate, dominated by an impressive neo-classical mansion, Thorndon Park is a charming course.

Designed by Harry Colt, who counts on his CV courses like Royal Portrush and the Alwoodley, Thorndon Park is ostensibly a members' club, and the benefits of not being overplayed are very clear. The conditions of fairways and greens is consistently excellent, and even the wilder parts of the course on the front nine are well manicured.

The contrast between the two nines is subtle but influences the way you play the course. The front nine is more open and in the summer has a baked appearance, requiring thought and planning to cope with the variable bounces. But as you make the turn, the course, running through tall stands of mature trees, has a lush feel and rewards strong, accurate hitting. Indeed, as you walk down to the lowest part of the course, it is so well watered that it has a Continental appearance.

This variety is traditionally the hallmark of a great course and provides much of the entertainment in planning and executing shots. Of course, you would be hard pressed to agree after playing the 1st, a wishy-washy par-4 where you can hit an enormous hook off the tee and still be well placed to reach the green. But don't give up – it gets better.

There's an enormous lake to carry at the 3rd, a short par-4 over a gully at the 4th and a brutish par-4 at the 6th. On the back nine, fine holes include the huge dogleg at the par-4 11th and a par-4 over the corner of the lake at the 17th. In between, you can get up to all sorts of scrapes escaping from the trees. Thorndon Park is a quality layout that constantly challenges you visually and technically.

Secretary: Lt Col R. Estcourt   Tel: 01277 810345
                                     Fax: 01277 810645
Professional: Mr B. White   Tel: 01277 810736

Playing: Midweek: round £45.00; day £60.00. Weekend: round £50 (after 1pm in summer); day n/a.

Facilities: Bar: 11am–7pm. Food: Lunch from 11am–2pm. Bar snacks.

Comments: The 3rd over the lake is a joy ... Beautiful course – greens exceptional ... Value for money not bad ... Expensive, but in superb condition, especially the greens ... Difficult-to-judge approach shots make this a difficult course ... Lovely variety of holes with no holes running in the same direction ... Unknown club that manages to feel unstuffy and welcoming ... Weak 1st hole but it just gets better and better ... Clever course with interesting selection of holes.

Abridge Golf & Country Club   ★★★

Epping Lane, Stapleford Tawney, RW14 1ST
Website: www.abridgegolf.com   E-mail: info@abridgegolf.com
Nearest main town: Romford

Secretary: Mr M. Gottlieb   Tel: 01708 688396
                                       Fax: 01708 688550
Professional: Mr S. Layton   Tel: 01708 688333
                                       Fax: 01708 688550

Playing: Midweek: round £35.00; day n/a. Weekend: round £45.00; day n/a.

Facilities: Bar: 11am–11pm. Food: Lunch from 11am–5pm.

Comments: Very good facilities ... Many holes crossing valleys ... Mature and very challenging ... Can play very long ... A monster off the back tees ... Strong par-4s ... First-rate par-4s ... Genuine par-4s.

Braintree Golf Club   ★★

Kings Lane, Stisted, Braintree, CM7 8DA
Website: www.braintreegolfclub.freeserve.co.uk
E-mail: manager@braintreegolfclub.freeserve.co.uk
Nearest main town: Braintree

Secretary: Mr J. Ball   Tel: 01376 346079
                                       Fax: 01376 348677
Professional: Mr T. Parcell   Tel: 01376 343465

Playing: Midweek: round £25.00; day £32.00. Weekend: round £42.00; day £42.00.

Facilities: Bar: 11am–11pm. Food: Lunch from 12pm–2.30pm. Dinner from 7pm–9.30pm on Friday and Saturday only.

Comments: 17th plays right next to a church ... Not the best condition ... Heavily bunkered ... Condition variable ... Decent design ... A bit flat.

The Burstead Golf Club   ★★

Tye Common Road, Little Burstead, Billericay, CM12 9SS
Nearest main town: Billericay

Secretary: Mr L. Mence   Tel: 01277 631171
                                            Fax: 01277 632766
Professional: Mr K. Bridges   Tel: 01277 631171

Playing: Midweek: round £19.00; day £25.00. Weekend: round n/a; day n/a.

Facilities: Bar: 11am–11pm. Food: Bar snacks. Dinner from 7pm–9.30pm on Thursday, Friday and Saturday.

Comments: Food first class ... If only the course was as good as the food ... Welcoming clubhouse ... Better courses to be had in Essex ... Very fair ... Not particularly difficult.

Channels Golf Club Limited   ★

Belsteads Farm Lane, Little Waltham, Chelmsford, CM3 3PT
Website: www.channelsgolf.co.uk   E-mail: info@channelsgolf.co.uk
Nearest main town: Chelmsford

Secretary: Mr T. Squire   Tel: 01245 440005
                                            Fax: 01245 442032
Professional: Mr I. Sinclair   Tel: 01245 441056

Playing: Midweek: round £32.00; day £45.00. Weekend: round Belsteads course only £14.00 (9 holes), £20.00 (18 holes); day n/a.

Facilities: Bar: 11am–11pm. Food: Lunch and dinner from 11am–10pm. Bar snacks.

Comments: Old gravel works, making maximum use of lakes and mounds ... Lush rough with undulating fairways ... Unfamiliar, unfashionable course that asks a lot of questions from the player ... Flattish, exciting course.

Chelmsford Golf Club   ★★

Widford Road, Chelmsford, CM2 9AP
Website: www.chelmsfordgc.co.uk
E-mail: office@chelmsfordgc.co.uk
Nearest main town: Chelmsford

Secretary:	Mr G. Winckless	Tel: 01245 256483
		Fax: 01245 256483
Professional:	Mr M. Welch	Tel: 01245 257079
		Fax: 01245 256483

Playing: Midweek: round £37.00; day £47.00. Weekend: round n/a; day n/a.

Facilities: Bar: 11am–9pm. Food: Lunch from 11am–6pm. Bar snacks.

Comments: Club with a colourful history ... Very good condition ... Very taxing par-68 ... Never had a bad time here ... Good value ... A little short ... Facilities a little sub-standard.

Chigwell Golf Club   ★★

High Road, Chigwell, IG7 5BH
Website: www.chigwellgolfclub.co.uk
E-mail: info@chigwellgolfclub.co.uk
Nearest main town: London

Secretary:	Mr R. Danzey	Tel: 020 8500 2059
		Fax: 020 8501 3410
Professional:	Mr R. Beard	Tel: 020 8500 2384
		Fax: 020 8501 3410

Playing: Midweek: round £35.00; day n/a. Weekend: round only with a member; day n/a.

Facilities: Bar: 11am–11pm. Food: Lunch from 11am–5pm. Bar snacks.

Comments: A good course, tucked away in sparse golfing country ... Quality greens on visit ... Surprisingly undulating for Essex ... Meadowland but don't let that put you off.

The Essex Golf & Country Club (County)   ★★

Earls Colne, Colchester, CO6 2NS
Website: www.clubhaus.com   E-mail: retail@clubhaus.com
Nearest main town: Colchester

Secretary: Mr J. Gathercole   Tel: 01787 224466
                   (Golf Manager)   Fax: 01787 224410
Professional: Mr L. Cocker   Tel: 01787 224466
                                           Fax: 01787 224410

Playing: Midweek: round £25.00; day n/a. Weekend: round
                   £30.00; day n/a.

Facilities: Bar: 11am–11pm. Food: Lunch and dinner from
                   10am–9pm. Bar snacks.

Comments: Premier new course in Essex ... Target golf ... US-style
                   course with water everywhere ... A course for the
                   average punter ... Too long ... Huge complex bring-
                   ing golf to the masses ... Go there to practise, not play
                   ... Practise there all the time ... Overblown ...
                   Exciting.

Five Lakes Hotel Golf & Country Club (Lakes)   ★★★

Colchester Road, Tolleshunt Knights, Maldon, CM9 8HX
E-mail: enquiries@fivelakes.co.uk
Nearest main town: Colchester

Secretary: Mr M. Tucker   Tel: 01621 868888
                                           Fax: 01621 869696
Professional: Mr G. Carter   Tel: 01621 862326
                                           Fax: 01621 862320

Playing: Midweek: round £25.00; day £37.50. Weekend: round
                   £33.00; day £44.00.

Facilities: Bar: 11am–11pm. Food: Lunch from 12pm–2.30pm.
                   Dinner from 7pm–10pm. Bar snacks.

Comments: Out in the wilds ... Plenty of other things to do at this
                   country club ... US-style course, very unnatural with
                   lakes and huge moundings ... There's better in Essex,
                   believe me ... Good for the beginner.

Five Lakes Hotel Golf & Country Club (Links)   ★★

Colchester Road, Tolleshunt Knights, Maldon, CM9 8HX
E-mail: enquiries@fivelakes.co.uk
Nearest main town: Colchester

Secretary:	Mr M. Tucker	Tel: 01621 868888
		Fax: 01621 869696
Professional:	Mr G. Carter	Tel: 01621 862326
		Fax: 01621 862320

Playing: Midweek: round n/a; day £20.00. Weekend: round n/a; day £28.00.

Facilities: Bar: 11am–11pm. Food: Lunch from 12pm–2.30pm. Dinner from 7pm–10pm. Bar snacks.

Comments: Not as good as the Lakes course ... Preferred the Lakes ... Very flat and boring ... Not a patch on the Lakes ... As far from a links as you could get ... Facilities good but poor course.

Frinton Golf Club (Long)   ★★

1 The Esplanade, Frinton-on-Sea, CO13 9EP
Website: www.frintongolfclub.com   E-mail: frintongolf@lineone.net
Nearest main town: Colchester

Secretary:	Lt Col R. Attrill	Tel: 01255 674618
		Fax: 01255 682450
Professional:	Mr P. Taggart	Tel: 01255 671618
		Fax: 01255 671618

Playing: Midweek: round £32.00; day n/a. Weekend: round £35.00; day n/a.

Facilities: Bar: 11am–11pm. Food: Lunch and dinner from 11am–10pm. Bar snacks.

Comments: The only true links in Essex ... Interesting Zulu hut by the 10th ... Condition variable ... Nice design but not blessed with great land ... Very generous fairways and greens ... Wide fairways as rough can get very unruly ... The only links in Essex – thank goodness!

Langdon Hills Golf Centre   ★★★

Lower Dunton Road, Bulphan, RM14 3TY
Nearest main town: Basildon

Secretary:	Mr B. Hardie	Tel: 01268 548444
		Fax: 01268 490084

Professional: Mr T. Moncur   Tel: 01268 544300

Playing: Midweek: round £14.85; day n/a. Weekend: round £19.75; day n/a.

Facilities: Bar: 11am–11pm. Food: Lunch and dinner from 11am–9.30pm. Bar snacks.

Comments: Great value-for-money for course in fairly good condition ... Three nines of varying standard ... Nice practice facilities for beginner ... A bit of a donkey track ... Fun golf with friends.

Orsett Golf Club   ★★

Brentwood Road, Orsett, RM16 3DS
Website: www.club-noticeboard.co.uk   E-mail: orsettgc@aol.com
Nearest main town: Orsett

Secretary: Mr C. Smith   Tel: 01375 891352
                                 Fax: 01375 892471

Professional: Mr P. Joiner

Playing: Midweek: round £30.00; day n/a. Weekend: round by arrangement; day n/a.

Facilities: Bar: 11am–variable. Food: Bar snacks from 11am–2pm.

Comments: One of the best in Essex ... Regional Open qualifying course ... Lovely pines, silver birch and hawthorn ... Really natural with plenty of gorse and hawthorn ... Undoubtedly one of the top dogs in Essex ... Be accurate ... Quality par-4s ... Nice variety of long and short par-4s.

Romford Golf Club   ★★★

Heath Drive, Gidea Park, Romford, RM2 5QB
Nearest main town: Romford

Secretary:	Mrs H. Robinson	Tel: 01708 740986
		Fax: 01708 752157

Professional: Mr H. Flatman   Tel: 01708 749393

Playing: Midweek: round £25.00; day £35.00. Weekend: round n/a; day n/a.

Facilities: Bar: 11am–11pm. Food: Lunch from 10am–5pm.

Comments: Historic course ... Wasn't looking forward to playing but loved it ... Loads of sand ... Almost has a 'Surrey' feel to it ... Perhaps the best in Essex ... Top notch.

Royal Epping Forest Golf Club   ★★★

Forest Approach, Chingford, London, E4 7AZ
Nearest main town: London

Secretary:	Mrs P. Runciman	Tel: 020 8529 6407
		Fax: 020 8559 4664
Professional:	Mr A. Traynor	Tel: 020 8529 5708

Playing: Midweek: round £10.70; day n/a. Weekend: round £14.80; day n/a.

Facilities: Bar: 11am–11pm. Food: Bar snacks.

Comments: The course where you must wear red clothes ... Eccentric club ... Not a great course but an interesting one that has to be played ... Loved it ... Unusual ... Very cheap.

Stapleford Abbotts Golf Club (Abbotts)   ★★

Horseman Side, Tysea Hill, Stapleford Abbotts, RM4 1JU
E-mail: staplefordabbottsessex@americangolf.uk.com
Nearest main town: Romford

Secretary:	None	Tel: 01708 381108
		Fax: 01708 386345
Professional:	Mr D. Vickerman	Tel: 01708 381278
		Fax: 01708 386345

Playing: Midweek: round £30.00 (Abbotts), £14.00 (Priors); day n/a. Weekend: round £40.00 (Abbotts), £19.00 (Priors); day n/a.

Facilities: Bar: 11am–11pm. Food: Lunch and dinner from 11am–10pm. Bar snacks.

Comments: 47 holes at this fair golf centre ... Getting better but still not in top condition ... Abbotts is best of three courses ... Great facilities for beginner.

Stock Brook Manor Golf Club   ★★★

Queen's Park Avenue, Billericay, CM12 0SP
Nearest main town: Chelmsford

Secretary:	Mr K. Roe	Tel: 01277 653616
		Fax: 01277 633063
Professional:	Mr K. Merry	Tel: 01277 653616

Playing: Midweek: round n/a; day £25.00. Weekend: round n/a; day £30.00.

Facilities: Bar: 11am–11pm. Food: Lunch and dinner from 11am–10pm. Bar snacks.

Comments: First-class clubhouse ... Really treat the visitor well here ... Impressive society day ... Magnificent clubhouse ... Good for beginners with training holes ... Treats everyone well ... Par-5 9th has two lakes ... Exciting holes for the novice.

Theydon Bois Golf Club   ★★

Theydon Road, Epping, CM16 4EH
Website: www.theydongolf.co.uk   E-mail: theydonbois@btconnect.co.uk
Nearest main town: Epping

Secretary:	Mr M. Slatter	Tel: 01992 813054
		Fax: 01992 815602
Professional:	Mr R. Hall	Tel: 01992 812460
		Fax: 01992 812460

Playing: Midweek: round £26.00; day n/a. Weekend: round £26.00; day n/a.

Facilities: Bar: 11am–11pm. Food: Lunch from 12pm–2.30pm.

Comments: Testing golf at an affordable price ... Original nine holes in Epping Forest a treat ... Club with good tradition and nice welcome.

Three Rivers Golf Club (Kings)   ★★★

Stow Road, Cold Norton, Chelmsford, CM3 6RR
E-mail: d.evers@clubhaus.com
Nearest main town: Maldon

Secretary:	Ms D. Evers	Tel: 01621 828631
		Fax: 01621 828060
Professional:	Mr S. Clark	Tel: 01621 829781

Playing: Midweek: round £20.00 (Kings), £10.00 (Jubilee); day £25.00. Weekend: round £25.00 (Kings), £12.50 (Jubilee); day £35.00.

Facilities:	Bar: 11am–11pm. Food: Lunch and dinner from 10am–9pm. Bar snacks.
Comments:	You would have to go a long way to find a more enjoyable course ... Clubhouse is second to none ... Good challenge ... Interesting course with ponds, doglegs and natural hazards ... Wooded parkland ... Value for money.

Upminster Golf Club   ★★

114 Hall Lane, Upminster, RM14 1AU
Nearest main town: Upminster

Secretary:	Mr W. Collantine	Tel: 01708 222788
		Fax: 01708 222788
Professional:	Mr N. Carr	Tel: 01708 220000

Playing:	Midweek: round £25.00; day £30.00. Weekend: round n/a; day n/a.
Facilities:	Bar: 11am–11pm. Food: Lunch from 12pm–2.30pm.
Comments:	Very attractive clubhouse ... A bit of old world charm ... Liked it ... Riverside course ... Best holes probably the 6th and 11th ... Greens consistently good.

West Essex Golf Club   ★★★

Bury Road, Sewardstonebury, Chingford, London, E4 7QL
Website: www.westessexgolfclub.co.uk
E-mail: sec@westessexgolfclub.co.uk
Nearest main town: Chingford

Secretary:	Mr D. Wilson	Tel: 020 8529 7558
		Fax: 020 8524 7870
Professional:	Mr R. Joyce	Tel: 020 8529 4367
		Fax: 020 8524 7870

Playing:	Midweek: round £35.00; day £40.00. Weekend: round n/a; day n/a.
Facilities:	Bar: 11am–11pm. Food: Lunch from 12pm–3pm.
Comments:	Very admirable course ... Epping Forest setting ... Too hilly ... Tiring in sections ... Hogs-back fairways, pulpit greens, rich forest – not too shabby ... A diverse challenge ... Real variety ... Club that really tries hard ... Club very proud of its course.

Gloucestershire

Long Ashton Golf Club ★★★

Clarken Coombe, Long Ashton, BS41 9DW
Website: www.longashtongolfclub.co.uk
E-mail: secretary@longashtongolfclub.co.uk
Nearest main town: Bristol

Gloucestershire is not renowned for the depth and variety of its courses, and no discussion of the best course would find universal agreement. One of the contenders, situated on the western outskirts of Bristol, would surely be Long Ashton, a wooded parkland course that you'll generally find in excellent order.

Long Ashton is a very traditional course bar one welcome eccentricity – a par-3, played over a road to a green nestled in an old quarry. It's worth the price of admission alone. But Long Ashton has more to offer than just its signature hole: two very distinctive nines that will test your patience and only reward good golf.

The preferred nine is on the front side, with the holes sweeping along a plateau with views of Bristol at the eastern extent of the course (if you're lucky, you'll spot one of the hot air balloons that take off from Ashton Park throughout the year and soar above the course). The fairways hug every contour of the land and taper towards fairly open but subtle undulating greens. The back nine is flatter, with a few holes you would willingly chuck out. It is here that you make your score, with the par-4s fairly short and the par-3 without much trouble.

Long Ashton is unusual for an old, provincial course in that it houses a practice range worthy of an Open venue.

Secretary: Mr R. Williams
Tel: 01275 392229
Fax: 01275 394395

Professional: Mr M. Hart
Tel: 01275 392229
Fax: 01275 394395

Playing: Midweek: round £30.00; day n/a. Weekend: round £35.00; day n/a.

Facilities: Bar: 11am–11pm. Food: Breakfast and lunch from 9.30am–6pm. Bar snacks.

Comments: Fascinating par-3 over the road marks this out as something special ... A little exposed in places although the course makes good use of the land ... Nice selection of secluded and open holes at this friendly club ... Value golf and excellent practice ground.

The Players Golf Club   ★★★★

Codrington, Bristol, BS37 6RX
Website: www.theplayersgolfclub.com
E-mail: paul@theplayersgolfclub.com
Nearest main town: Bristol

It took three years to create the Players Golf Club, which finally opened in May 2000, but golfers lucky and wise enough to have paid it a visit unanimously agree the wait has been more than worthwhile.

Little-known course designer Adrian Stiff has somehow carved out a 'magical monster' – it's an incredible 7600 yards off the back tips, making it one of the longest in the land – just a 15-minute drive from bustling Bristol and 1 mile from Junction 18 on the M4. Stiff's idea was to create '18 very different holes, some resembling classic links land and some US-style', and he's definitely succeeded in that goal.

The key to enjoying your round at the Players Golf Club is to ensure you play off the right tees (there's six sets of them!) for your game. Whatever you do, don't bite off more than you can chew, otherwise you'll be in for a torrid time. You certainly need to carefully negotiate the trees, water, gorse and bunkering that act as the course's defences along with its sheer length (off the tiger tees).

The biggest compliment you can pay this quality venue is that although it's only been open a short while, it looks as though it's been around forever. There are several outstanding holes, but the par-4 4th, where you need to avoid two lots of water, is arguably the pick of a very impressive bunch.

Secretary:	Mr P. Barrington	Tel: 01454 313029
	(Director of Golf)	Fax: 01454 323446
Professional:	Mr M. Brookes	Tel: 01454 311818
		Fax: 01454 323446

Playing: Midweek: round £70.00; day n/a. Weekend: round £70.00; day n/a.

Facilities: New clubhouse opens April 2004; no details available at time of going to press.

Comments: One of the best new courses I've seen and played ... It can be long and tough so make sure you play off the right tees ... A bit pricey but it is a class act ... I'd heard good things about this new venue near Bristol and it fully lived up to expectations.

Bristol & Clifton Golf Club ★★★

Beggar Bush Lane, Failand, Bristol, BS8 3TH
Website: www.bristolgolf.co.uk   E-mail: mansec@bristolgolf.co.uk
Nearest main town: Bristol

Secretary:	Mr C. Percy	Tel: 01275 393474
		Fax: 01275 394611
Professional:	Mr P. Dawson	Tel: 01275 393031
		Fax: 01275 393031

Playing: Midweek: round n/a; day £32.00. Weekend: round n/a; day £35.00.

Facilities: Bar: 11am–11pm. Food: Breakfast and lunch from 8am–6pm. Bar snacks.

Comments: Setting what makes this course ... Rather ungroomed ... Make a beeline for this one ... Stand-out par-3s ... Make sure you don't miss it.

Broadway Golf Club ★★★

Willersey Hill, Broadway, WR12 7LG
E-mail: beta.broadwaygolfclub@care4free.net
Nearest main town: Broadway

Secretary:	Mr B. Carnie	Tel: 01386 853683
		Fax: 01386 858643
Professional:	Mr M. Freeman	Tel: 01386 853275
		Fax: 01386 859392

Playing: Midweek: round £30.00; day £38.00. Weekend: round £38.00 (price also applies on bank holidays); day n/a.

Facilities: Bar: 11am–11pm. Food: Lunch and dinner from 11am–9pm. Bar snacks.

Comments: Interesting course with views over the Vale of Evesham ... 800ft above sea level – not worth the climb! ... For a downland course, fairly unnatural.

Chipping Sodbury Golf Club ★★

Chipping Sodbury, BS37 6PU
Website: www.chippingsodburygolfclub.co.uk
E-mail: info@chippingsodburygolfclub.co.uk
Nearest main town: Bristol

Secretary:	Mr S. Mowbray	Tel: 01454 319042
		Fax: 01454 320052
Professional:	Mr M. Watts	Tel: 01454 314087

Playing: Midweek: round £25.00; day n/a. Weekend: round £30.00; day n/a.

Facilities: Bar: 11am–11pm. Food: Lunch and dinner from 11am–7pm.

Comments: After major surgery, this course is easily the best presented in the Bristol area ... Much improved and a nice challenge ... Drainage dyke the main hazard ... Changes are best decision the club ever made.

Cleeve Hill Golf Club ★★

Cleeve Hill, Cheltenham, GL52 3PW
Website: www.cleevehill.com   E-mail: golf@cleevehill.com
Nearest main town: Cheltenham

Secretary:	Mr S. Gilman	Tel: 01242 672025
		Fax: 01242 678444
Professional:	Mr D. Finch	Tel: 01242 672592
		Fax: 01242 678444

Playing: Midweek: round £15.00; day n/a. Weekend: round £18.00; day n/a.

Facilities: Bar: 11am–11pm. Food: Lunch and dinner from 11am–9pm. Bar snacks.

Comments: Course deficiencies nullified by fine views ... Great day out ... Inland course with spectacular views.

Filton Golf Club ★

Golf Course Lane, Filton, Bristol, BS34 7QS
Website: www.filtongolfclub.co.uk
E-mail: thesecretary@filtongolfclub.co.uk
Nearest main town: Bristol

Secretary: Mrs E. Mannering   Tel: 0117 969 4169
                                       Fax: 0117 931 4359
Professional: Mr D. Robinson   Tel: 0117 969 6968
                                       Fax: 0117 969 6968

Playing: Midweek: round £22.00; day £27.00. Weekend: round with member only; day n/a.

Facilities: Bar: 11am–11pm. Food: Lunch from 11am–6pm. Bar snacks.

Comments: One of the weaker courses in Bristol ... On a clear day look for the Brecon Beacons ... Very challenging.

Forest Hills Golf Club   ★

Mile End Road, Coleford, GL16 7BY
Nearest main town: Coleford

Secretary: Mr P. Burston   Tel: 01594 810620
Professional: Mr J. Nicol   Tel: 01594 810620

Playing: Midweek: round £13.00; day £18.00. Weekend: round £15.00; day £20.00.

Facilities: Bar: 11am–11pm. Food: Lunch from 11am–6pm. Bar snacks.

Comments: Unimaginative ... Spectacular finish ... One of the cheapest courses around ... Good facilities for visitors.

Henbury Golf Club

Henbury Road, Westbury-on-Trym, Bristol, BS10 7QB
Website: www.henburygolfclub.co.uk
E-mail: thesecretary@henburygolfclub.co.uk
Nearest main town: Bristol

Secretary: Mr J. Keight   Tel: 0117 950 0044
                                 Fax: 0117 959 1928
Professional: Mr N. Riley   Tel: 0117 950 2121

Playing: Midweek: round £25.00; day n/a. Weekend: round £30.00; day n/a. Handicap certificate required.

Facilities: Bar: 11am–11pm. Food: Lunch and dinner from 11am–9pm. Bar snacks.

Comments: Much improved now alterations complete ... Best to have a member as guide ... Parkland course with attractive woodland ... Short track but good value.

Jarvis Gloucester Hotel Golf Club

Matson Lane, Gloucester, GL4 9EA
Website: www.gloucestergolf.com
Nearest main town: Gloucester

Secretary:	Mr G. Osborne	Tel: 01452 411311
		Fax: 01452 307212
Professional:	Messrs J. & C. Whiddon & Gillick	Tel: 01452 411311

Playing: Midweek: round £19.50; day n/a. Weekend: round £25.50; day n/a.

Facilities: Bar: 11am–11pm. Food: Breakfast, lunch and dinner from 7am–10pm.

Comments: Sheer value for money and very accommodating to large groups ... Two very different nines, one very flat, one very undulating ... Pro shop extremely well informed and helpful ... One hole named Coronary Hill – enough said ... Undulating with vistas to the Cotswolds.

The Kendleshire Golf Club ★★★★

Henfield Road, Coalpit Heath, Bristol, BS36 2UY
Website: www.kendleshire.co.uk   E-mail: info@kendleshire.co.uk
Nearest main town: Bristol

Secretary:	Mr P. Murphy	Tel: 0117 956 7007
		Fax: 0117 957 3433
Professional:	Mr M. Bessell	Tel: 0117 956 7000

Playing: Midweek: round £29.00; day n/a. Weekend: round £35.00; day n/a.

Facilities: Bar: 11am–11pm. Food: Lunch and dinner from 12pm–9pm. Bar snacks.

Comments: A fun course ... Very welcoming ... Water hazards intelligently used ... 10 hazards on 18 holes is too much ... Island green 11th a dead-ringer for Sawgrass ... For learners a very exciting course ... Never played anything like it ... Target golf but well thought out and planned.

Knowle Golf Club ★★

Fairway, West Town Lane, Brislington, BS4 5DF
Nearest main town: Bristol

Secretary:	Mr M. Harrington	Tel: 0117 977 0660
		Fax: 0117 972 0615
Professional:	Mr G. Brand	Tel: 0117 977 9193

Playing: Midweek: round £22.00; day £27.00. Weekend: round £27.00; day £32.00.

Facilities: Bar: 11am–11pm. Food: Lunch from 12pm–2pm. Bar snacks.

Comments: Lovely greens ... Interesting par-3s ... Don't be put off by the strenuous start – it gets easier ... Attractive course, if a little easy.

Minchinhampton Golf Club (Avening) ★★

New Course, Minchinhampton, Stroud, GL6 9AW
Website: www.mgcnew.co.uk   E-mail: sec@mgcnew.co.uk
Nearest main town: Stroud

Secretary:	Mr P. Keeling	Tel: 01453 833866
		Fax: 01453 837360
Professional:	Mr C. Steele	Tel: 01453 837351

Playing: Midweek: round n/a; day £30.00. Weekend: round n/a; day £34.00.

Facilities: Bar: 11am–11pm. Food: Lunch from 11am–6pm. Dinner by arrangement.

Comments: A well-kept straightforward course with a variety of pleasant holes ... Excellent catering ... Cotswold views ... Better than the Cherington and unbeatable value.

Minchinhampton Golf Club (Cherington) ★★

Minchinhampton, Stroud, GL6 9BE
Nearest main town: Stroud

Secretary:	Mr P. Keeling	Tel: 01453 833866
		Fax: 01453 835703
Professional:	Mr C. Steele	Tel: 01453 833860

Playing: Midweek: round n/a; day £25.00. Weekend: round n/a; day £30.00.

Facilities: Bar: 11am–11pm. Food: Lunch from 11am–6pm. Dinner by arrangement.

Comments: Excellent clubhouse ... Exciting course with plenty of startling features ... Pot bunkers, sloping greens – great test for a relatively new course.

Hilton Puckrup Hall Hotel Golf Club ★★

Puckrup, Tewkesbury, GL20 6EL
Nearest main town: Tewkesbury

Secretary: Mrs C. Sandyford-Sykes   Tel: 01684 271591
Fax: 01684 271550
Professional: Mr K. Pickett   Tel: 01684 271591

Playing: Midweek: round £25.00; day n/a. Weekend: round £30.00; day n/a.

Facilities: Bar: 11am–11pm. Food: Breakfast, lunch and dinner from 7am–10pm. Bar snacks.

Comments: Expensive food and drink ... A little over-priced for standard of course ... Undulating parkland layout which makes good use of land ... Nice course with good back-up facilities – will go again.

Shirehampton Park Golf Club ★

Park Hill, Shirehampton, Bristol, BS11 0UL
Website: shirehamptonparkgolfclub.co.uk
E-mail: info@shirehamptonparkgolfclub.co.uk
Nearest main town: Bristol

Secretary: Mr A. Hobbs   Tel: 0117 982 2083
Fax: 0117 982 5280
Professional: Mr B. Ellis   Tel: 0117 982 2488

Playing: Midweek: round £20.00; day n/a. Weekend: round £17.00 (playing with a member only); day n/a.

Facilities: Bar: 11am–11pm. Food: Lunch from 12pm–2.30pm. Dinner from 5pm–8pm.

Comments: Weak for the Bristol area ... Don't slice it at the 1st! ... Some attractive features but overall poor ... Could be better.

Stinchcombe Hill Golf Club   ★★

Stinchcombe Hill, Dursley, GL11 6BA
Website: www.stinchcombehillgolfclub.com
E-mail: stinchcombehill@golfers.net
Nearest main town: Dursley

Secretary:	Mr P. Jones	Tel: 01453 542015
		Fax: 01453 549545
Professional:	Mr P. Bushell	Tel: 01453 541094
		Fax: 01453 549545

Playing: Midweek: round £25.00 (18 holes); day n/a. Weekend: round £35.00 (18 holes); day n/a.

Facilities: Bar: 11am–11pm. Food: Lunch from 10am–6pm. Bar snacks.

Comments: Lofty location ... Looks out over the Cotswolds ... Views make it ... At its best when the wind is up ... Downland course with personality.

Tewkesbury Park Hotel Golf Club   ★★

Lincoln Green Lane, Tewkesbury, GL20 7DN
Nearest main town: Tewkesbury

Secretary:	Mr R. Nichol	Tel: 01684 272322
		Fax: 01684 292386
Professional:	Mr C. Boast	Tel: 01684 294892

Playing: Midweek: round £25.00; day n/a. Weekend: round £30.00; day n/a.

Facilities: Bar: 11am–11pm. Food: Lunch from 12pm–2.30pm. Dinner from 6pm–9.30pm.

Comments: Peaceful course with good greens and lovely views ... Can feel pretty depressing on a wet day ... Best holes are on the back nine ... In variable condition but hotel makes up for it ... Good, open course that lends itself to practice before tackling better courses ... Open, bleak course on undulating ground that did nothing for me ... Good value for standard of facilities.

Tracy Park Golf Club ★★

Tracy Park, Bath Road, Wick, BS30 5RN
Website: www.tracypark.com   E-mail: golf@tracypark.com
Nearest main town: Bath

Secretary:	Mr D. Knipe	Tel: 0117 937 2251
		Fax: 0117 937 4288
Professional:	Mr T. Thompson-Green	Tel: 0117 937 3521

Playing: Midweek: round £30.00; day £36.00. Weekend: round £36.00; day £40.00.

Facilities: Bar: 11am–11pm. Food: Lunch and dinner from 10am–9.30pm.

Comments: Clubhouse the best part about this club ... 17th-century clubhouse ... Quite natural ... Condition needs improving ... Couldn't call it value for money ... 27 holes of fairly average golf.

Woodlands Golf & Country Club ★★

Trench Lane, Almondsbury, Bristol, BS12 4JZ
Nearest main town: Bristol

Secretary:	Mr I. Knipe	Tel: 01454 619319
		Fax: 01454 619397
Professional:	Messrs N. & A. Warburton & Lowen	

Playing: Midweek: round £12.00; day n/a. Weekend: round £14.00; day n/a.

Facilities: Bar: 11am–11pm. Food: Bar snacks.

Comments: In good condition even during the winter months ... Five par-3s set around lakes are best feature of otherwise bland course ... Classic case of overuse of water ... Good value for interesting course.

Woodspring Golf Club

Woodlands Lane, Almondsbury, BS18 9LR
Nearest main town: Bristol

Secretary:	Mr M. Pierce	Tel: 01275 394378
		Fax: 01275 394473
Professional:	Mr N. Beer	

Playing: Midweek: round £20.00; day £20.00. Weekend: round £28.50; day £28.50.

Facilities: Bar: 11am–11pm. Food: Lunch and dinner from 12pm–9pm. Bar snacks.

Comments: Superb site for a fairly new course ... Heathland setting ... Will get better with time ... Natural course by Alliss/Clark ... Very tough.

Greater Manchester

Manchester Golf Club ★★★★

Hopwood Cottage, Rochdale Road, Middleton, Manchester, M24 6QP
Website: www.mangc.co.uk   E-mail: mgc@zen.co.uk
Nearest main town: Manchester

Unlike London, which has many fine courses in its suburbs, Manchester is not well blessed, and its best courses are located to the north of the city, where the moorland landscape provides excellent drainage. For many, the best in the area is Bolton Old Links; a venerable course set on the side of a hill with ravines and grand trees. Others choose Manchester, a fine parkland/moorland course located just 10 miles north of the city centre.

Manchester is a very user-friendly course as it is never too busy (peculiar for a course next to such a large urban centre) and has excellent practice facilities. Once you tee off, it won't take you long to realise that the course is not so accommodating, with the wind whipping across the rugged moorland landscape and accentuating badly struck shots, particularly so with the proliferation of sloping lies you can get on these undulating fairways.

Despite the temptation to try and overwhelm the course with brute strength, Manchester embraces intelligent play, and the members generally cite the 12th as a good example. At this par-4 a driver off the tee will leave you with a longer approach shot but a flat lie. These trade-offs are classic Colt design traits and if you bear this in mind throughout you should have few problems with the course.

As you would expect in this area of the country, the reception at the club is always first class and you always feel as if you are a member of the club, if only for a day. Recommended.

Secretary:	Mr K. Flett	Tel: 0161 643 3202
		Fax: 0161 643 9174
Professional:	Mr B. Connor	Tel: 0161 643 2638
Playing:	Midweek: round £25.00; day n/a. Weekend: round £40.00; day n/a.	
Facilities:	Bar: 11am–11pm. Food: Lunch from 12pm–2.30pm. Dinner by arrangement.	
Comments:	A course that puts golfers first and not profit ... High-class moorland golf at an affordable price ... Characters at this club make it a pleasure to play ... Good finish.	

Chorlton-cum-Hardy Golf Club ★★★

Barlow Hall, Barlow Hall Road, Manchester, M21 7JJ
E-mail: chorltongolf@hotmail.com
Nearest main town: Manchester

Secretary:	Mrs K. Poole	Tel: 0161 881 5830
		Fax: 0161 881 4532
Professional:	Mr D. Valentine	Tel: 0161 881 9911

Playing: Midweek: round n/a; day £25.00. Weekend: round n/a; day £30.00.

Facilities: Bar: 12pm–11pm. Food: Lunch and dinner from 11am–9pm. Bar snacks.

Comments: Average meadowland course ... Keep clear of the streams and ditches ... Fair condition but nothing special ... Good matchplay course.

Northenden Golf Club ★★

Palatine Road, Manchester, M22 4FR
Website: www.northendengolfclub.com
E-mail: northenden.golfclub@btopenworld.com
Nearest main town: Manchester

Secretary:	Ms F. Woodwoan	Tel: 0161 998 4738
		Fax: 0161 945 5592
Professional:	Mr J. Curtis	Tel: 0161 945 3386

Playing: Midweek: round n/a; day £28.00. Weekend: round n/a; day £32.00.

Facilities: Bar: 11am–11pm. Food: Bar snacks. Lunch and dinner by arrangement.

Comments: Parkland course next to the River Mersey ... Cheap, fun golf on a championship-length course ... Nothing special ... Not great value for money.

Stand Golf Club

Ashbourne Grove, Whitefield, Manchester, M45 7NL
Nearest main town: Manchester

Secretary:	Mr T. Thacker	Tel: 0161 766 3197
		Fax: 0161 796 3234
Professional:	Mr M. Dance	Tel: 0161 766 2214

Playing: Midweek: round £25.50; day n/a. Weekend: round n/a; day £25.50.

Facilities: Bar: 11am–11pm. Food: Lunch and dinner from 10am–9pm. Bar snacks.

Comments: It's all about the finish here ... Devilish climax to a fairly average layout ... Parkland/moorland ... Reasonable value.

Swinton Park Golf Club   ★★

East Lancs Road, Swinton, M27 5LX
Website: www.spgc.com   E-mail: gm@spgc.com
Nearest main town: Manchester

Secretary: Mr T. Glover   Tel: 0161 794 0861
                                          Fax: 0161 281 0698
Professional: Mr J. Wilson   Tel: 0161 793 8077
                                          Fax: 0161 281 0698

Playing: Midweek: round £28.00; day n/a. Weekend: round no visitors; day n/a.

Facilities: Bar: 11am–11pm. Food: Lunch from 12pm–6pm.

Comments: Fascinating course ... Bit of a trek ... One of the longest in Lancashire ... Worth a long, lingering look.

Whitefield Golf Club   ★★

Higher Lane, Whitefield, M45 7EZ
E-mail: golfclub@whitefield.u-net.com
Nearest main town: Manchester

Secretary: Mrs A. Schofield   Tel: 0161 351 2700
                                          Fax: 0161 351 2712
Professional: Mr P. Reeves   Tel: 0161 766 3096

Playing: Midweek: round £25.00; day £25.00. Weekend: round £35.00; day n/a.

Facilities: Bar: 12pm–3pm. Food: Lunch and dinner from 12pm–2.30pm. Dinner on Tuesday and Thursday by arrangement.

Comments: Fantastic landscape ... Unbelievable par-3s ... Sporting, welcoming course ... Golf without the snobbery of a members' club ... Never had a bad experience here.

Worsley Golf Club   ★

Stableford Avenue, Monton Green, Eccles, M30 8AP
Nearest main town: Manchester

Secretary:	Mr R. Pizzey MBE	Tel: 0161 789 4202
		Fax: 0161 789 3200
Professional:	Mr C. Cousins	Tel: 0161 789 4202

Playing: Midweek: round £20.00; day £25.00. Weekend: round £30.00; day n/a.

Facilities: Bar: 11am–11pm. Food: Lunch and dinner from 10am–6pm. Bar snacks.

Comments: Open woodland track ... Plenty of birdie chances ... Woodland but enough room for wayward shots ... Good value for money.

Hampshire

North Hants Golf Club ★★★★

Minley Road, Fleet, GU51 1RF
E-mail: secretary@north-hants-fleetgc.co.uk
Nearest main town: Farnborough

North Hants' star has recently risen with the emergence of one of its favourite sons, Justin Rose. There is no greater testament to a course than the player it breeds, and on that basis North Hants is very good, although a little uncultured around the edges.

But, ironically, North Hants is a very protected course, designed intelligently through dense woods where you will find it very easy to concentrate on your game. The most difficult part of the course is the tee shots, which have to be cleverly placed to facilitate an easy line into the flag. The greens are generally large and approach shots tend to hold the ball well. Indeed, the condition of the course is a tribute to the greenkeeping staff.

Like the Berkshire, located close by, North Hants is heathland in type and like that gem it has a great variety of holes that keeps the player consistently interested. There are blind shots which make club selection exceptionally difficult at times and holes where the shape of the fairways dictates the flight of shot you should hit. It is perhaps not a course to experiment on, however, as the trees, heather and gorse gobble up anything off line.

Golfers in Hampshire are spoilt for choice and there are those that prefer the nearby charms of Blackmoor and Liphook. But for the welcome and experience, North Hants is hard to beat, as a visit will testify.

Secretary:	Mr G. Hogg	Tel: 01252 616443
		Fax: 01252 811627
Professional:	Mr S. Porter	Tel: 01252 616655
Playing:	Midweek: round £35.00; day £48.00. Weekend: round n/a; day n/a.	
Facilities:	Bar: 11am–11pm. Food: Bar snacks.	
Comments:	Super course and obviously a good training ground for Justin Rose ... Blind holes, undulating ground ... Tough task to select clubs with confidence ... Tree-lined course, a real marvel.	

Army Golf Club ★★★

Laffans Road, Aldershot, GU11 2HF
Website: www.whichgolfclub.com/army   E-mail: agc@is24.net
Nearest main town: Aldershot

Secretary: Maj J. Douglass   Tel: 01252 337272
                                         Fax: 01252 337562
Professional: Mr G. Cowley   Tel: 01252 336722
                                         Fax: 01252 336686

Playing: Midweek: round £26.00 (18 holes), £36.00 (36 holes);
                  day n/a. Weekend: round members only; day n/a.

Facilities: Bar: 11am–11pm. Food: Lunch from 11.30am–7pm.

Comments: Respected club ... Very traditional ... One of the oldest
                  in the area ... Nice touches on this subtle course ...
                  Plenty of room for expression ... Not very welcoming.

Barton-on-Sea Golf Club ★★★★

Milford Lane, New Milton, BH25 5PP
Website: www.barton-on-sea-golf.co.uk
Nearest main town: New Milton

Secretary: Mr G. Prince   Tel: 01425 615308
                                         Fax: 01425 621457
Professional: Mr P. Rodgers   Tel: 01425 611210
                                         Fax: 01425 621457

Playing: Midweek: round n/a; day £38.00. Weekend: round n/a;
                  day £43.00.

Facilities: Bar: 11am–11pm. Food: Lunch from 12pm–2pm.
                  Dinner by arrangement.

Comments: Welcoming and friendly links golf ... Excellent course,
                  very friendly and food superb ... Good day out with
                  three nines ... Good golfing experience ... Provided a
                  fabulous day out with tasty bar snacks ... Golf slightly
                  pricey.

Basingstoke Golf Club ★★

Kempshott Park, Basingstoke, RG23 7LL
Website: www.basingstokegolfclub.co.uk
E-mail: enquiries@basingstokegolfclub.co.uk
Nearest main town: Basingstoke

Secretary:	Mr W. Jefford	Tel: 01256 465990
		Fax: 01256 331793
Professional:	Mr G. Shoesmith	Tel: 01256 351332
		Fax: 01256 331793

Playing: Midweek: round £35.00; day n/a. Weekend: round only with a member; day n/a.

Facilities: Bar: 11am–11pm. Food: Lunch and dinner from 11am–7pm.

Comments: Challenging, well presented and good value ... Attractive course in rolling countryside ... Scenic and a round to savour.

Blackmoor Golf Club   ★★★★

Firgrove Road, Whitehill, GU35 9EH
Website: www.blackmoorgolf.co.uk
E-mail: admin@blackmoorgolf.co.uk
Nearest main town: Bordon

Secretary:	Mr A. Harris	Tel: 01420 472775
		Fax: 01420 487666
Professional:	Mr S. Clay	Tel: 01420 472345
		Fax: 01420 472345

Playing: Midweek: round n/a; day £35.00 (18 holes), £47.00 (36 holes). Weekend: round n/a; day members' guests only.

Facilities: Bar: 11am–11pm. Food: Lunch from 11am–6pm. Bar snacks.

Comments: Very attractive, some great holes and good greens ... A real gem ... A smaller Wentworth West course ... Snobby clubhouse but good society venue.

Botley Park Hotel Golf & Country Club   ★

Winchester Road, Boorley Green, Botley, SO3 2UA
E-mail: info@botleypark.macdonald-hotels.co.uk
Nearest main town: Southampton

Secretary:	Mr T. Barter	Tel: 01489 789771
	(Director of Golf)	Fax: 01489 789242
Professional:	Mr T. Barter	Tel: 01489 789771

Playing: Midweek: round £30.00; day £45.00. Weekend: round £30.00; day £45.00.

Facilities: Bar: 11am–11pm. Food: Breakfast, lunch and dinner from 7am–10pm.

Comments: Attractive course, although not in same echelon as many of its neighbours ... Typical country club where the course isn't the star.

Bramshaw Golf Club (Manor) ★★

Brook, Lyndhurst, SO43 7HE
Website: www.bramshaw.co.uk E-mail: golf@bramshaw.co.uk
Nearest main town: Southampton

Secretary: Mr R. Tingey Tel: 023 8081 3433
Fax: 023 8081 3460
Professional: Mr C. Bonner Tel: 023 8081 3434
Fax: 023 8081 2131

Playing: Midweek: round £33.00 (Manor); £28.00 (Forest); day n/a. Weekend: round £36.00 (Manor), £32.00 (Forest); day n/a.

Facilities: Bar: 11am–11pm. Food: Breakfast, lunch and dinner from 7am–10pm. Bar snacks.

Comments: Why can't all courses be as natural as this? ... Mature trees and greens at this lovely course.

Brockenhurst Manor Golf Club ★★★

Sway Road, Brockenhurst, SO42 7SG
Nearest main town: Brockenhurst

Secretary: Mr P. Clifford Tel: 01590 623332
Fax: 01590 624140
Professional: Mr B. Parker Tel: 01590 623092

Playing: Midweek: round £35.00; day £45.00. Weekend: round n/a; day £60.00.

Facilities: Bar: 11am–9pm. Food: Bar snacks.

Comments: Nice course in summer with much game in evidence ... Very friendly club and course ... Food and drink very good ... Prime location on the edge of the New Forest ... A new, intriguing challenge at every turn.

Cams Hall Estate Golf Club (Creek) ★★

Cams Hall Estate, Fareham, PO16 8UP
E-mail: camshall@americangolf
Nearest main town: Portsmouth

Secretary:	Mr S. Wright	Tel:	01329 827222
	(General Manager)	Fax:	01329 827111
Professional:	Mr J. Neve	Tel:	01329 827732
		Fax:	01329 827111

Playing: Midweek: round £24.00 (18 holes), £9.00 (9 holes); day n/a. Weekend: round £32.00 (18 holes), £9.00 (9 holes); day n/a.

Facilities: Bar: 11am–11pm. Food: Lunch and dinner by arrangement.

Comments: Modern club with course to match ... Manufactured course with some idiosyncrasies ... Plenty of lakes and mounding ... One of the best new courses in Hampshire of recent years ... Excellent ... Fair value.

Corhampton Golf Club ★★★

Sheep's Pond Lane, Corhampton, SO32 3LP
Nearest main town: Winchester

Secretary:	Mrs L. Collins	Tel:	01489 877279
		Fax:	01489 877680
Professional:	Mr I. Roper	Tel:	01489 877638

Playing: Midweek: round £24.00; day £34.00. Weekend: round n/a; day n/a.

Facilities: Bar: 11am–11pm. Food: Lunch from 10am–3pm. Dinner by arrangement.

Comments: Very picturesque ... Downland course that makes you think ... Fine setting in the Meon Valley.

Dummer Golf Club ★★★

Dummer, RG25 2AR
Website: www.dummergc.co.uk
Nearest main town: Basingstoke

Secretary:	Mr R. Corkhill	Tel:	01256 397888
		Fax:	01256 397889

Professional: Messrs A. & A. Fannon & Wain Tel: 01256 397950

Playing: Midweek: round £27.00; day £30.00. Weekend: round n/a; day n/a.

Facilities: Bar: 11am–11pm. Food: Lunch and dinner from 12pm–8pm. Bar snacks.

Comments: The 10th is a superb design … Alliss/Clark course of variable quality … Two nine-hole loops of character.

Freshwater Bay Golf Club   ★★★

Afton Down, Freshwater, PO40 9TZ
Nearest main town: Freshwater

Secretary: Mr J. Copleston   Tel: 01983 752955
                                     Fax: 01983 756704

Professional: None

Playing: Midweek: round n/a; day £20.00. Weekend: round n/a; day £24.00.

Facilities: Bar: 11am–11pm. Food: Lunch and dinner served from 9am–9pm. Bar snacks.

Comments: Well-named club … You feel so fresh and alive here … Views all around of the English Channel … Glorious air here.

Hayling Golf Club   ★★★★

Links Lane, Hayling Island, PO11 0BX
Website: www.haylinggolf.co.uk   E-mail: hgcltd@aol.com
Nearest main town: Havant

Secretary: Mr C. Cavill   Tel: 023 9246 4446
                                    Fax: 023 9246 1119
Professional: Mr R. Gadd   Tel: 023 9246 4491
                                    Fax: 023 9246 1119

Playing: Midweek: round £40.00; day £50.00. Weekend: round £55.00; day n/a.

Facilities: Bar: 11am–11pm. Food: Breakfast, lunch and dinner from 8am–9pm. Bar snacks.

Comments: A joy to play ... Lovely springy turf ... When the wind blows this is proper golf ... Excellent value, very friendly and links golf to boot ... Views to the Isle of Wight mark this out as special ... Most interesting course in Hants.

Hockley Golf Club   ★★★

Twyford, Winchester, SO21 1PL
Website: www.hockleygolfclub.com
E-mail: secretary@hockleygolfclub.com
Nearest main town: Winchester

Secretary:	Mrs L. Dyer	Tel: 01962 713165
		Fax: 01962 713612
Professional:	Mr G. Stubbington	Tel: 01962 713678

Playing: Midweek: round £35.00; day n/a. Weekend: round £50.00; day n/a.

Facilities: Bar: 11am–11pm. Food: Breakfast, lunch and dinner from 9am–9pm. Bar snacks.

Comments: High quality downland course ... One of the best in Hampshire ... Excellent views.

Liphook Golf Club   ★★★★

Wheatsheaf Enclosure, Liphook, GU33 7QB
E-mail: liphookgolfclub@btconnect.com
Nearest main town: Petersfield

Secretary:	Maj J. Morgan MBE	Tel: 01428 723785
		Fax: 01428 724853
Professional:	Mr I. Mowbray	Tel: 01428 723785
		Fax: 01428 724853

Playing: Midweek: round £39.00; day £47.00. Weekend: round £45.00; day £55.00.

Facilities: Bar: 11am–11pm. Food: Bar snacks.

Comments: An ideal course for the middle-handicapper ... Heather plays its part ... Course has got everything in a beautifully understated way ... Made to feel very welcome ... Easy heathland course in class golfing country.

Marriott Meon Valley Hotel and Country Club ★★★

Sandy Lane, Shedfield, Southampton, SO32 2HQ
Nearest main town: Southampton

Secretary:	Mr G. McMenemy	Tel: 01329 833455
		Fax: 01329 834411
Professional:	Mr R. Cameron	Tel: 01329 832184
		Fax: 01329 834411

Playing: Midweek: round £38.00; day n/a. Weekend: round £45.00; day n/a.

Facilities: Bar: 11am–11pm. Food: Breakfast, lunch and dinner from 7am–10pm.

Comments: Well-known course connected to country club ... Feels as though it's been around for years ... Exciting ... Well presented ... No complaints ... Lovely design making full use of parkland.

New Forest Golf Club ★

Southampton Road, Lyndhurst, SO43 7BU
Nearest main town: Southampton

Secretary:	Mrs B. Shaw	Tel: 023 8028 2484
		Fax: 023 8028 2484
Professional:	Mr D. Harris	Tel: 023 8028 2752

Playing: Midweek: round £12.00; day £18.00. Weekend: round £15.00; day £25.00.

Facilities: Bar: 11am–11pm. Food: Lunch from 11am–3.30pm. Bar snacks.

Comments: Heathland setting ... Something of a mixed bag ... High class feel ... A little short ... You don't need to be a big hitter ... Tricky.

Old Thorns Golf and Country Club ★★

Griggs Green, Liphook, GU30 7PE
Website: www.oldthorns.com   E-mail: info@oldthorns.com
Nearest main town: Petersfield

Secretary:	None	Tel: 01428 724555
		Fax: 01428 725036

Professional: Mr R. Hyder   Tel: 01428 722183
(Director of Golf)

Playing: Midweek: round £40.00; day n/a. Weekend: round £60.00; day n/a.

Facilities: Bar: 11am–11pm. Food: Dinner from 6.30pm–9pm. Bar snacks.

Comments: Very expensive ... Great facilities for non-golfer ... Course not worthy of its high prices ... Condition good, but it should be at that price ... Sumptuous setting.

Rowlands Castle Golf Club   ★★

31 Links Lane, Rowlands Castle, PO9 6AE
Website: www.rowlandscastlegolfclub.co.uk
E-mail: manager@rowlandscastlegolfclub.co.uk
Nearest main town: Petersfield

Secretary: Mr K. Fisher   Tel: 023 9241 2784
                                     Fax: 023 9241 3649
Professional: Mr P. Klepacz   Tel: 023 9241 2785

Playing: Midweek: round n/a; day £34.00. Weekend: round n/a; day £38.00.

Facilities: Bar: 11am–11pm. Food: Bar snacks.

Comments: Excellent clubhouse and well-tended course ... Armchair green at the 7th ... Open all year round for fine golf ... Not the most well-known course in Hants – keep it that way ... Doglegs the course's primary protection.

Royal Winchester Golf Club   ★★★

Sarum Road, Winchester, SO22 5QE
Website: www.royalwinchestergolfclub.com
E-mail: manager@royalwinchestergolfclub.com
Nearest main town: Winchester

Secretary: Mr A. Buck   Tel: 01962 852462
                                   Fax: 01962 865048
Professional: Mr S. Hunter   Tel: 01962 862473

Playing: Midweek: round £33.00 (18 holes); day £46.00. Weekend: round n/a; day with member only.

Facilities: Bar: 12pm–8pm. Food: Lunch from 11am–5pm. Bar snacks.

Comments: Friendly course with beautiful vistas ... Surprising course with handful of fine, attractive holes ... Can be tough at times although the finish is a little weak ... Nice opening nine but tails off towards the end ... Was getting a little bored near the death ... Be on your game quick here or you will never get your score back.

Sandford Springs Golf Club ★★★

Wolverton, Tadley, RG26 5RT
Nearest main town: Basingstoke

Secretary: Mr G. Tipple   Tel: 01635 297881
                                         Fax: 01635 298065

Professional: Mr G. Edmunds   Tel: 01635 297883

Playing: Midweek: round £23.00; day £29.00. Weekend: round n/a; day n/a.

Facilities: Bar: 11am–11pm. Food: Bar snacks.

Comments: Three loops of nine for what is a memorable day's golf ... Take lots of balls ... Great views from highest point ... Something for every player here ... Consistently surprising course.

Shanklin & Sandown Golf Club ★★★★

The Fairway, Lake, Sandown, PO36 9PR
Nearest main town: Sandown

Secretary: Mr A. Creed   Tel: 01983 403217
                                         Fax: 01983 403007

Professional: Mr P. Hammond   Tel: 01983 404424

Playing: Midweek: round £27.50; day n/a. Weekend: round £33.00; day n/a.

Facilities: Bar: 11am–11pm. Food: Lunch and dinner from 10am–6pm. Bar snacks.

Comments: A very good feel to the whole club – welcoming, relaxing and appealing ... Always interesting course ... Heathland in jaw-dropping location ... Simply superb day's golf ... Will be going again.

South Winchester Golf Club ★★★

Romsey Road, Pitt, Winchester, SO22 5QX
Website: www.crown-golf.co.uk
E-mail: winchester-sales@crown-golf.co.uk
Nearest main town: Winchester

Secretary:	Mr L. Ross (General Manager)	Tel: 01962 877800 Fax: 01962 877900
Professional:	Mr R. Adams	Tel: 01962 840469 Fax: 01962 877900

Playing: Midweek: round £25.00; day n/a. Weekend: round £40.00; day n/a.

Facilities: Bar: Members only. Food: Members only.

Comments: Fair condition and enjoyable to play ... Should mature into a great test of golf ... Excellent par-5s ... Carved from ancient woodland, this is an exercise in ball placement.

Southampton Golf Club ★★

Golf Course Road, Bassett, Southampton, SO16 7AY
Nearest main town: Southampton

Secretary:	Mr B. Gibson	Tel: 023 8076 8407 Fax: 023 8076 0412
Professional:	Mr J. Cave	

Playing: Midweek: round £8.60; day n/a. Weekend: round £11.90; day n/a.

Facilities: Bar: 6am–10pm. Food: Breakfast, lunch and dinner from 6am–10pm. Bar snacks.

Comments: One of the best municipals in the country ... Exceptional muni where you feel very welcome ... Knocks spots off many private clubs ... A real people's course ... Value all the way.

Stoneham Golf Club

Monks Wood Close, Bassett, Southampton, SO16 3TT
Website: www.stonehamgolfclub.org.uk
E-mail: richard.penley-martin@stonehamgolfclub.org.uk
Nearest main town: Southampton

Secretary:	Mr R. Penley-Martin	Tel: 023 8076 9272
		Fax: 023 8076 6320
Professional:	Mr I. Young	Tel: 023 8076 8397
		Fax: 023 8076 6320

Playing: Midweek: round £35.00; day £40.00. Weekend: round £45.00; day £57.00.

Facilities: Bar: 11am–11pm. Food: Lunch from 11am–5pm. Bar snacks.

Comments: Excellent greens ... Always a rewarding challenge ... Always made very welcome ... Excellent, hilly course with sprinkling of heather ... Cross bunkers can make life difficult.

Test Valley Golf Club ★

Micheldever Road, Overton, RG25 3DS
Website: www.testvalleygolf.com   E-mail: pro@testvalleygolf.com
Nearest main town: Basingstoke

Secretary:	Mr A. Briggs	Tel: 01256 771737
		Fax: 01256 771285
Professional:	Mr A. Briggs	Tel: 01256 771737

Playing: Midweek: round £20.00; day n/a. Weekend: round £28.00; day n/a.

Facilities: Bar: 11am–11pm. Food: Breakfast, lunch and dinner from 9am–9pm. Bar snacks.

Comments: Hosted many events but can't see why ... Extremely long ... Highly rated in the area ... Wasn't that impressed ... Fun for the high handicapper with lakes and prominent bunkers.

Waterlooville Golf Club ★★★

Cherry Tree Avenue, Waterlooville, PO8 8AP
Website: www.waterloovillegolfclub.com
Nearest main town: Portsmouth

Secretary:	Mr D. Nairne	Tel: 023 9226 3388
		Fax: 023 9234 7513
Professional:	Mr J. Hay	Tel: 023 9225 6911
		Fax: 023 9225 6911

Playing: Midweek: round £30.00; day £35.00. Weekend: round n/a; day n/a.

Facilities: Bar: 11am–11pm. Food: Lunch from 11am–5pm. Bar snacks.

Comments: Highly thought of in the area ... Excellent variety ... Very challenging ... Par-5s genuine three-shotters.

Hereford & Worcester

Ross-on-Wye Golf Club ★★★★

Two Park, Gorsley, Ross-on-Wye, HR9 7UT
Website: www.therossonwyegolfclub.co.uk
E-mail: secretary@therossonwyegolfclub.co.uk
Nearest main town: Ross-on-Wye

Just before they enter the grey, industrial corridor of South Wales where golfers head to play some great links courses, travellers from the north pass through the beautiful Wye Valley. The only stop-off point for golfers here is Ross-on-Wye, a fairly new course that is cut through a verdant forest and provides some exciting golf.

Keeping the ball in play is the secret at Ross-on-Wye, although if you do land in the trees, there is always an escape route – the greenkeepers are instructed to keep the undergrowth at a minimum. The course's other protection are the bunkers, which were reconstructed a few years back and have added a new dimension to the course.

Some golfers find this sort of golf unappealing, but it is not all a matter of accurate hitting. Indeed, at the 5th and 6th, you are faced with consecutive par-5s where the trees open out and the player is allowed to hit freely. There's also a strong selection of par-3s, including the 9th and the 12th, a par-3 played over a pond, the only one on the course.

With a standard scratch score of 73, there is no denying that Ross-on-Wye is hard, but the steady stream of visitors suggest its difficulty does not take away from the experience. Off-course the feel is good also, with a lively bar and a genial atmosphere through the club.

Secretary:	Mr P. Plumb	Tel: 01989 720267
		Fax: 01989 720212
Professional:	Mr N. Catchpole	Tel: 01989 720439

Playing: Midweek: round £34.00 (18 holes), £40.00 (27 holes), £44.00 (36 holes); day n/a. Weekend: round n/a; day n/a.

Facilities: Bar: 11am–11pm. Food: Lunch from 11am–5pm. Bar snacks. Dinner by arrangement.

Comments: Gracious members and well-kept course ... Tree-lined, you really need to know where to drive ... Undulating parkland through silver birch forest – fine stuff ... Greens always good.

The Bank House Hotel Golf & Country Club ★

Bransford, Worcester, WR4 9NN
Website: www.bankhousehotel.co.uk
E-mail: info@bransfordgolfclub.co.uk
Nearest main town: Worcester

Secretary:	Ms M. Roberts	Tel: 01886 833545
		Fax: 01886 833545
Professional:	Mr S. Fordyce	Tel: 01886 833621
		Fax: 01886 833545

Playing: Midweek: round £20.00; day n/a. Weekend: round £30.00; day n/a.

Facilities: Bar: 11am–11pm. Food: Breakfast, lunch and dinner from 7am–10pm.

Comments: American-style course with lots of water and tough finishing holes ... Enjoyable day out ... Poor use of water hazards ... Very unnatural use of water ... Island greens and sculptured fairways.

Belmont Lodge and Golf Club ★★★

Belmont, Hereford, HR2 9SA
Website: www.belmontlodge.co.uk   E-mail: info@belmontlodge.co.uk
Nearest main town: Hereford

Secretary:	Mr I. Lewis	Tel: 01432 352666
		Fax: 01432 358090
Professional:	Mr M. Welsh	Tel: 01432 352717

Playing: Midweek: round £19.00; day n/a. Weekend: round £26.00; day n/a.

Facilities: Bar: 11am–11pm. Food: Lunch and dinner from 11am–11pm. Bar snacks.

Comments: Nice variety ... Two nines with a very different flavour ... Outstanding views over Herefordshire ... Best holes run alongside the River Wye ... Felt very contented walking off the 18th.

Burghill Valley Golf Club ★★

Tillington Road, Burghill, HR4 7RW
Nearest main town: Hereford

Secretary:	Mr K. Smith	Tel: 01432 760456
		Fax: 01432 761654
Professional:	Mr N. Clarke	Tel: 01432 760808

Playing: Midweek: round £17.00; day £25.00. Weekend: round £25.00; day n/a.

Facilities: Bar: 11am–11pm. Food: Lunch and dinner from 10am–10pm. Bar snacks.

Comments: Fairly unoriginal … Very easy walking … Condition not in the top bracket … Cuts through a cider orchard at one point … A course that suits all standards … Not on my 'wish' list.

Churchill & Blakedown Golf Club ★

Churchill Lane, Blakedown, DY10 3NB
Nearest main town: Kidderminster

Secretary:	Mr M. Taylor	Tel: 01562 700018
Professional:	Mr K. Wheeler	Tel: 01562 700454

Playing: Midweek: round £20.00; day n/a. Weekend: round n/a; day n/a.

Facilities: Bar: 11am–11pm. Food: Lunch and dinner from 11am–9pm. Bar snacks.

Comments: Nine-hole hilltop course … Nothing special apart from views … Nine-holer with character … Condition not great.

Fulford Heath Golf Club ★★★★

Tanners Green Lane, Wythall, B47 6BH
Website: www.fulfordheath.co.uk
E-mail: secretary@fulfordheath.co.uk
Nearest main town: Birmingham

Secretary:	Mrs M. Tuckett	Tel: 01564 824758
		Fax: 01564 822629
Professional:	Mr R. Dunbar	Tel: 01564 822930

Playing: Midweek: round £12.00 (with member), £35.00 (casual rate); day n/a. Weekend: round n/a; day n/a.

Facilities: Bar: 11am–2pm and 6pm–10pm. Food: Lunch from 12pm–2.30pm. Dinner from 7pm–10pm. Snacks 2.30pm–7pm.

Comments: Such magnificent condition, every hole is just so different ... Imaginative course, still a pleasure to play ... Mature parkland ... Two stunning par-3s.

Hagley Country Club   ★

Wassell Grove, Hagley, Stourbridge, DY9 9JW
Nearest main town: Birmingham

Secretary:	Mr G. Yardley	Tel: 01562 883701
		Fax: 01562 887518
Professional:	Mr I. Clark	Tel: 01562 883852

Playing: Midweek: round £22.00; day £28.00. Weekend: round n/a; day n/a.

Facilities: Bar: 11am–11pm. Food: Lunch from 12pm–3pm. Dinner from 6pm–9pm. Food not served on Mondays.

Comments: Very good value ... Course nothing special but good value ... Thoroughly enjoyed this undulating course ... Value.

Herefordshire Golf Club   ★

Raven's Causeway, Wormsley, Hereford, HR4 8LY
Website: www.golf.sagehost.co.uk
E-mail: herefordshire@golf.sagehost.co.uk
Nearest main town: Hereford

Secretary:	Mr T. Horobin	Tel: 01432 830219
		Fax: 01432 830095
Professional:	Mr D. Hemming	Tel: 01432 830465

Playing: Midweek: round £20.00; day £25.00. Weekend: round £25.00; day £32.00.

Facilities: Bar: 11am–11pm. Food: Bar snacks.

Comments: Parkland of variable character ... Plenty of birdie chances ... Course gives you a clear strategy ... Average condition.

Kings Norton Golf Club

Brockhill Lane, Weatheroak, Alvechurch, B48 7ED
Nearest main town: Birmingham

Secretary: Mr T. Webb (Manager)   Tel: 01564 826789
Fax: 01564 826955
Professional: Mr K. Hayward   Tel: 01564 822635

Playing: Midweek: round £31.00; day £37.00. Weekend: round n/a; day n/a.

Facilities: Bar: 11am–11pm. Food: Lunch and dinner from 12pm–9pm. Bar snacks.

Comments: Traditional design ... Condition not what it used to be ... Respected course ... Long and exacting ... If you like a challenge ... One for the big hitters ... Need to bomb it off the tee ... Don't be put off by the length.

Kington Golf Club ★★★

Bradnor Hill, Kington, HR5 3RE
Nearest main town: Kington

Secretary: Mr G. Wictome   Tel: 01544 340270
Fax: 01544 340270
Professional: Mr D. Oliver   Tel: 01544 231320

Playing: Midweek: round £14.00; day £18.00. Weekend: round £18.00; day £22.00.

Facilities: Bar: 11am–11pm. Food: Lunch from 11am–4pm. Dinner by arrangement.

Comments: Links-type course ... Difficult to master in the wind ... Highest 18-hole course in England and worth the climb ... Natural course with no bunkers ... Fascinating course that plays very tough despite lack of man-made hazards.

Leominster Golf Club ★

Ford Bridge, Leominster, HR6 0LE
E-mail: leominstergolf@freeuk.com
Nearest main town: Leominster

Secretary: Mr L. Green   Tel: 01568 610055
Fax: 01568 610055
Professional: Mr A. Ferriday   Tel: 01568 611402
Fax: 01568 610055

Playing: Midweek: round £15.50; day £19.00. Weekend: round £22.00; day £25.00.

Facilities: Bar: 11am–11pm. Food: Lunch from 11.30am–2pm. Dinner from 6pm–9pm.

Comments: Short and hilly, not everyone's choice ... A day you won't forget and you can fish too ... Best holes run alongside the River Lugg ... Exceptional value and fun as well.

Moseley Golf Club   ★

Springfield Road, Kings Heath, Birmingham, B14 7DX
Website: www.wugc.co.uk/moseley
E-mail: admin@mosgolf.freeserve.co.uk
Nearest main town: Birmingham

Secretary: Mr A. Sanders   Tel: 0121 444 4957
                                       Fax: 0121 441 4662
Professional: Mr M. Griffin   Tel: 0121 444 2063
                                       Fax: 0121 444 2063

Playing: Midweek: round £37.00; day n/a. Weekend: round with a member only; day n/a.

Facilities: Bar: 11am–11pm. Food: Lunch and dinner from 11am–9pm. Bar snacks.

Comments: Didn't do it for me ... Welcome and facilities a little lacking ... Not the best in the area ... Couple of nice holes ... Wasn't bowled over.

North Worcestershire Golf Club Ltd   ★

Frankley Beeches Road, Northfield, Birmingham, B31 5LP
Nearest main town: Birmingham

Secretary: Mr D. Wilson   Tel: 0121 475 1047
                                       Fax: 0121 476 8681
Professional: Mr F. Clark   Tel: 0121 475 5721
                                       Fax: 0121 476 8681

Playing: Midweek: round £12.50 (with a member), £25.00; day n/a. Weekend: round £15.00 (with a member; no unaccompanied visitors); day n/a.

Facilities: Bar: 11am–11pm. Food: Lunch and dinner from 11am–9pm. Bar snacks.

Comments: Well worth a visit ... Old established course with very fair standards ... Well-designed, testing course ... Obviously a well-run club and greens were first rate.

The Vale Golf Club   ★

Hill Furze Road, Bishampton, Pershore, WR10 2LZ
Website: www.crown-golf.co.uk   E-mail: vale-sales@crown-golf.co.uk
Nearest main town: Evesham

Secretary:	Mr R. Griffiths (General Manager)	Tel: 01386 462781 Fax: 01386 462597
Professional:	Mrs C. Griffiths	Tel: 01386 462520

Playing: Midweek: round £25.00; day n/a. Weekend: round £35.00; day n/a.

Facilities: Bar: 11am–11pm. Food: Restaurant.

Comments: Young course ... Extensive practice facilities ... American-style course – fairly unimaginative ... Big greens look receptive, but are protected by lots of water and sand ... Good society venue.

Wharton Park Golf Club   ★★

Long Bank, Bewdley, DY12 2QW
Website: www.whartonpark.co.uk   E-mail: golf@whartonpark.co.uk
Nearest main town: Bewdley

Secretary:	Mr P. Dougan	Tel: 01299 405163 Fax: 01299 405121
Professional:	Mr A. Hoare	Tel: 01299 405163 Fax: 01299 405121

Playing: Midweek: round £30.00; day n/a. Weekend: round £35.00; day n/a.

Facilities: Bar: 11am–11pm. Food: Bar snacks.

Comments: Protected by its length ... Long and tiring ... Par-73 that plays every inch ... Genuine three-shot par-5s ... Overrated in the area ... Can try the patience ... Wide open ... Predominantly a driver's course.

Worcester Golf & Country Club   ★★

Boughton Park, Worcester, WR2 4EZ
Nearest main town: Worcester

Secretary:	Mr D. Bettsworth	Tel: 01905 422555 Fax: 01905 749090
Professional:	Mr C. Colenso	Tel: 01905 422044

Playing: Midweek: round £25.00; day £25.00. Weekend: round n/a; day n/a.

Facilities: Bar: 11am–11pm. Food: Bar snacks. Dinner from 7pm–9pm.

Comments: Pretty tough ... A stern test ... Doesn't look too tricky ... Country club course that has retained an identity ... Get to know it ... Mature parkland ... Views of the Malvern Hills ... A stiff challenge.

Hertfordshire

The Grove ★★★★

Chandlers Cross, Rickmansworth, WD3 4TG
Website: www.thegrove.co.uk
Nearest main town: Rickmansworth

American course designer Kyle Phillips created a links classic at Kingsbarns in the kingdom of Fife a few years back, and now he's produced another class act – this time just off the M25!

Construction at the multi-talented architect's latest high-profile UK layout started in June 2000, though the course itself didn't officially open until the end of summer 2003. Phillips wanted to make absolutely certain that everything was in place and just right, and the wait has truly been worthwhile. He's produced a stunning 7170-yard, par-72 layout in 300 acres of mature parkland on the former estate of the Earls of Clarendon. It simply looks as though it's been around forever, rather than just a matter of months. It's that good and it's going to get a whole lot better too.

The people at the Grove may seem a tad biased when they claim their venue is 'one of the most exciting golfing developments in the UK for many years', but, to be fair, they're not too far off the mark. The course is an absolute belter with a host of superb holes, of which the par-4 3rd, where the green is guarded by the appropriately named Hell's Lake, is arguably the most demanding and memorable of them all. But what you'll probably remember most are the greens, which are incredibly fast and true.

So the next time you're stuck in traffic on the dreaded M25 with your clubs in the boot, you know where to head for!

Secretary: Ms M. Twyman (Administration)   Tel: 01923 296103
Fax: 01923 221008
Professional: Mr B. Reid   Tel: 01923 296100

Playing: Midweek: round £65.00–£95.00; day n/a. Weekend: round n/a; day n/a.

Facilities: Bar: Mon–Thurs 11am–11pm, Fri/Sat 11am–12 midnight, Sun 11am–10.30pm. Food: Mon–Thurs 11.30am–10.30pm, Fri 11.30am–11pm, Sat 7am–11pm, Sun 7am–4.30pm.

Comments: Just as good as the designer's Kingsbarns classic ... Hard to believe you're just a booming driver away from the dreaded M25 ... A new course with a rosy future ... It's one of those courses you've just got to play – and play ... It's expensive but well worth the outlay ... The greens were *magnifique* ... Also has three swimming pools and a 30,000-square-foot luxury spa.

Hanbury Manor Golf Club   ★★★★

Funridge, Ware, SG12 0SD
Website: www.marriott.com
Nearest main town: Ware

Creating the perfect country-house retreat is a tricky business. Sometimes the quest for authenticity clouds the issue and often does the opposite, making for a feeling of falseness – almost a film-set atmosphere rather than the real thing. Hanbury Manor was an ambitious project, turning a former convent into a luxury hotel with a championship golf course in its grounds, but it has been more successful than most.

There is no doubting the expertise that has shaped the golf course. It may not have been Jack Nicklaus himself who crafted the beautifully lush and intriguing holes, but his son Jack Jnr has done an excellent job, under the guidance of the great man. It is tough, uncompromising, yet picturesque, mixing an open and undulating front nine played on the edge of a valley with a wooded and winding back half. Its conditioning is first class, far superior to a glut of excellent new courses nearby including Hadley Wood and the Hertfordshire.

The tone for the round is set at the 1st, a driveable par-4, protected by a ravine in front of the green. There are plenty of other do-or-die holes on the layout, and some excellent par-5s, specifically the 9th, a long three-shotter that snakes up to the clubhouse, and the 17th, where you must be careful of the lake on your approach to the green.

Hanbury Manor has an excellent reputation, having hosted the English Open in the past, and the hotel more than matches it – an exquisite restaurant and superb off-course facilities. It is probably Hanbury's stone's-throw location from London that keeps the cost on the highish side, but if you do have the clout, you cannot deny that a lot of life's pleasures are here to be indulged in, and thoroughly indulged.

Secretary:	Mr I. McInally	Tel: 01920 487722
	(Director of Golf)	Fax: 01920 487692
Professional:	Mr I. McInally	Tel: 01920 463474

Playing: Midweek: round prices on application; day n/a. Weekend: round n/a; day n/a.

Facilities: Bar: Hotel guests and members only. Food: Hotel guests and members only.

Comments: Not as good value for money as you would expect ... Fantastic around the English Open ... Two contrasting nines ... Beautifully manicured course ... Fairways better than some club greens ... Great course in a lovely setting ... Five holes with water and two with greens on the edge of water ... Refreshment at halfway was welcome ... Jack Nicklaus II design of great character ... Some holes based on original Harry Vardon design ... Book a room at the hotel to play this course ... Greens fast and true each time I go back.

Aldenham Golf & Country Club (Old)   ★★

Church Lane, Aldenham, WD25 8NN
E-mail: info@aldenhamgolfclub.co.uk
Nearest main town: Watford

Secretary: Mrs J. Phillips   Tel: 01923 853929
   Fax: 01923 858472
Professional: Mr T. Dunstan   Tel: 01923 857889
   Fax: 01923 858472

Playing: Midweek: round £26.00 (18 holes), £10.00 (9 holes); day n/a. Weekend: round £35.00 (18 holes), £12.00 (9 holes); day n/a.

Facilities: Bar: 11am–11pm. Food: Bar snacks. Sunday lunch by arrangement.

Comments: The 13th should be a par-6 – I'd hate to play it from the back tees ... Facilities for visitors are a little basic ... Parkland course but there are better examples around.

Ashridge Golf Club   ★★★★

Little Gaddesden, Berkhamsted, HP4 1LY
Website: www.ashridgegolfclub.ltd.uk
E-mail: info@ashridgegolfclub.ltd.uk
Nearest main town: Berkhamsted

Secretary: Mr M. Silver   Tel: 01442 842244
   Fax: 01442 843770

Professional: Mr A. Ainsworth   Tel: 01442 842307

Playing: Midweek: round prices on application; day n/a. Weekend: round n/a; day n/a.

Facilities: Bar: 11am–11pm. Food: Lunch from 12pm–2pm. Bar snacks.

Comments: Where Henry Cotton used to be club professional ... Fairly straightforward course with rough the primary defence ... A real good-looker ... Very captivating ... Relaxing venue ... You feel completely untroubled on this little beauty ... Keep it straight.

Berkhamsted Golf Club   ★★★

The Common, Berkhamsted, HP4 2QB
Nearest main town: Berkhamsted

Secretary: Mr C. Hextall   Tel: 01442 865832
                                          Fax: 01442 863730
Professional: Mr B. Proudfoot   Tel: 01442 865851

Playing: Midweek: round £25.00; day £35.00. Weekend: round £35.00; day £35.00.

Facilities: Bar: 11am–11pm. Food: Lunch from 11am–2.30pm. Dinner by arrangement.

Comments: Still fairly unknown, thank goodness ... High quality golf in nice surroundings ... Some long carries over heather ... No bunkers ... Bunkers – who needs them when it's this tough ... Would willingly trade my membership for this club.

Brookmans Park Golf Club   ★★★★

Brookmans Park, Hatfield, AL9 7AT
Nearest main town: Hatfield

Secretary: Mr P. Gill   Tel: 01707 652487
                                          Fax: 01707 661851
Professional: Mr I. Jelley   Tel: 01707 652468

Playing: Midweek: round £30.00; day £30.00. Weekend: round n/a; day n/a.

Facilities: Bar: 11am–11pm. Food: Bar snacks.

Comments: Generally kept in fine condition ... Clever, tricky holes
                 ... Value in buckets ... Makes the visitor welcome ...
                 Can play long depending on tees ... Not too intimidat-
                 ing.

Chesfield Downs Golf Club   ★★★

Jack's Hill, Graveley, SG4 7EQ
Nearest main town: Graveley

Secretary: Mr D. Burridge   Tel: 01462 482929
                                            Fax: 01462 482930
Professional: Ms J. Fernley   Tel: 01462 482929

Playing: Midweek: round £14.75; day £20.00. Weekend: round
                    £21.00; day £30.00.

Facilities: Bar: 11am–11pm. Food: Breakfast, lunch and dinner
                    from 8am–10pm. Bar snacks.

Comments: Course that is aimed at beginners ... Nice place to learn
                    the game ... Facilities second to none ... Excellent golf
                    centre catering to learners ... Natural downland ...
                    Couldn't get excited about this rather bleak course.

East Herts Golf Club   ★★

Hamels Park, Buntingford, SG9 9NA
Nearest main town: Puckeridge

Secretary: Mr C. Wilkinson   Tel: 01920 821978
                                            Fax: 01920 823700
Professional: Mr G. Culmer   Tel: 01920 821922

Playing: Midweek: round £35.00; day £35.00. Weekend: round
                    n/a; day n/a.

Facilities: Bar: 11am–11pm. Food: Lunch from 12pm–2.30pm.
                    Dinner by arrangement.

Comments: A beautiful parkland course ... Worth a visit but not the
                    best in Herts by any measure ... Fair value for course in
                    good condition.

Great Hadham Golf & Country Club   ★★

Great Hadham Road, Much Hadham, SG10 6JE
E-mail: info@ghgcc.co.uk
Nearest main town: Bishop's Stortford

Secretary:	Mr I. Bailey	Tel: 01279 843558
		Fax: 01279 842122
Professional:	Mr K. Lunt	Tel: 01279 843888
		Fax: 01279 843884

Playing: Midweek: round £20.00; day n/a. Weekend: round £27.00; day n/a.

Facilities: Bar: 11am–11pm. Food: Lunch from 12pm–2.30pm. Dinner by arrangement.

Comments: Bent over backwards to make sure you enjoyed yourself ... Open course with varying difficulty of holes ... Undulating meadowland/links with fair facilities and welcome.

Hadley Wood Golf Club   ★★★★

Beech Hill, Hadley Wood, Barnet, EN4 0JJ
Website: www.hadleywoodgc.com
E-mail: gen.mgr@hadleywoodgc.com
Nearest main town: Barnet

Secretary:	Mr C. Silcox	Tel: 020 8449 4328
	(General Manager)	Fax: 020 8364 8633
Professional:	Mr P. Jones	Tel: 020 8449 3285

Playing: Midweek: round £50.00; day £65.00. Weekend: round £65.00 (Sunday afternoon only); day n/a.

Facilities: Bar: 11am–11pm. Food: Bar snacks. Dinner by arrangement.

Comments: An absolute gem ... Food is fabulous ... Appealing course for big hitter although there is severe rough ... As golf should be played ... Many nice features at this progressive club ... Give me the keys to the club ... Everything right about this attractive club.

Letchworth Golf Club

Letchworth Lane, Letchworth Garden City, SG6 3NQ
E-mail: letchworthgolfclub@uk2.net
Nearest main town: Letchworth

Secretary:	Mr C. Allen	Tel: 01462 683203
		Fax: 01462 484567
Professional:	Mr K. Teschner	Tel: 01462 682713
		Fax: 01462 682713

Playing: Midweek: round £17.00 (Monday), £30.00 (Tuesday to Friday); day n/a. Weekend: round with member only; day n/a.

Facilities: Bar: 11am–11pm. Food: Lunch from 11am–2pm. Dinner from 6pm–9pm. Bar snacks.

Comments: Mixed course with good and bad holes ... Wouldn't rank it that highly ... Peaceful ... Tranquil setting but golf rather weak ... Had many great rounds here ... Tough par-70 ... Doesn't give you birdies.

Manor of Groves Golf Club

High Wych, Sawbridgeworth, CM21 0LA
Nearest main town: Harlow

Secretary:	Mrs S. Hughes	Tel: 01279 722333
		Fax: 01279 726972
Professional:	Mr C. Laurence	Tel: 01279 721986

Playing: Midweek: round £20.00; day £30.00. Weekend: round £25.00; day n/a.

Facilities: Bar: 11am–11pm. Food: Lunch from 11.30am–2pm. Dinner from 6pm–10pm. Bar snacks.

Comments: Varied holes in wood/farmland setting ... Interesting course ... Average quality all round ... Fair value for unimposing course.

Mill Green Golf Club ★

Gypsy Lane, Mill Green, Welwyn Garden City, AL7 4TY
Website: www.americangolf.com
E-mail: millgreen@americangolf.uk.com
Nearest main town: Welwyn Garden City

Secretary:	Mr T. Hudson	Tel: 01707 276900
		Fax: 01707 276898
Professional:	Mr I. Parker	Tel: 01707 270542

Playing: Midweek: round £25.00; day n/a. Weekend: round £32.00; day n/a.

Facilities: Bar: 11am–11pm. Food: Breakfast, lunch and dinner from 10am–9pm. Bar snacks.

Comments: What you'd expect from an Alliss/Clark creation ... New course for all levels ... One of a good collection of courses in Welwyn Garden City ... Won't produce a Nick Faldo ... Wooded holes better than the meadowland section.

Moor Park Golf Club (High)   ★★★★

Rickmansworth, WD3 1QN
Website: www.moorparkgc.co.uk
E-mail: enquiries@moorparkgc.co.uk
Nearest main town: Rickmansworth

Secretary:	Mr J. Moore	Tel: 01923 773146
		Fax: 01923 777109
Professional:	Mr L. Farmer	Tel: 01923 773146
		Fax: 01923 777109

Playing: Midweek: round £69.00 (High), £42.50 (West); day £99.50. Weekend: round members only; day n/a.

Facilities: Bar: 11am–11pm. Food: Lunch from 12pm–2.30pm.

Comments: Attractive, well-kept course although very expensive ... Surprisingly friendly and good golf facilities ... High course is far superior to the West ... Well worth the rather pricey green fee.

Panshanger Golf Club   ★★

Old Herns Lane, Welwyn Garden City, AL7 2ED
E-mail: rpreece@welhat.gov.co.uk
Nearest main town: Welwyn Garden City

Secretary:	Ms S. Ryan	Tel: 01707 332837
		Fax: 01707 390010
Professional:	Messrs M. & B. Corlass & Lewis	Tel: 01707 323443

Playing: Midweek: round £14.50; day n/a. Weekend: round £18.50; day n/a.

Facilities: Bar: 11am–11pm. Food: Lunch and dinner from 11am–11pm. Bar snacks.

Comments: A real value course ... If you object to high green fees, this is the one for you ... Recommended to all.

Porters Park Golf Club

Shenley Hill, Radlett, WD7 7AZ
Nearest main town: Radlett

Secretary: Mr P. Phillips   Tel: 01923 854127
Fax: 01923 575992

Professional: Mr D. Gleeson   Tel: 01923 854366

Playing: Midweek: round £29.00; day £44.00. Weekend: round n/a; day n/a.

Facilities: Bar: Members only. Food: Members only.

Comments: Rather exclusive club ... Well worth the money ... Fantastic presentation ... Benefits from restricted play ... Excellent condition ... A real good-looker ... Very lush ... Can't go in the bar but you only come here for the course ... Super layout ... Very difficult to get to know.

Sandy Lodge Golf Club   ★★

Sandy Lodge Lane, Northwood, HA6 2JD
Website: www.sandylodge.co.uk
E-mail: lesleydiamond@sandylodge.co.uk
Nearest main town: Northwood

Secretary: Mr J. Coombes   Tel: 01923 825429
Fax: 01923 824319

Professional: Mr J. Pinsent   Tel: 01923 825321
Fax: 01923 825321

Playing: Midweek: round £35.00 (society rates on request); day n/a. Weekend: round with member only; day n/a.

Facilities: Bar: 11am–11pm. Food: Bar snacks.

Comments: Sandy soil perfect for golf ... Heathland-type course – not out of place ... Very enjoyable ... Linksy feel.

South Herts Golf Club

Links Drive, Totteridge, N20 8QU
Website: www.southhertsgolfclub.co.uk
E-mail: secretary@southhertsgolfclub.co.uk
Nearest main town: London

Secretary:	Mr K. Bravant	Tel: 020 8445 2035
		Fax: 020 8445 7569
Professional:	Mr B. Mitchell	Tel: 020 8445 4633

Playing: Midweek: round £30.00; day n/a. Weekend: round £40.00; day n/a.

Facilities: Bar: 11am–11pm. Food: Lunch from 11am–4pm. Bar snacks.

Comments: Harry Vardon and Dai Rees were professionals here ... Well worth the visit ... One of the best in London ... Would go again ... Greens exceptional ... Find time to play here.

Stocks Hotel Golf Club   ★★★

Stocks Road, Aldbury, Tring, HP23 5RX
Website: www.stocksgolf.co.uk   E-mail: rdarling@stocksgolf.co.uk
Nearest main town: Tring

Secretary:	Mr R. Darling	Tel: 01442 852504
		Fax: 01442 851253
Professional:	Mr P. Lane	Tel: 01442 852511
		Fax: 01442 851253

Playing: Midweek: round £35.00 (non-members); day n/a. Weekend: round £45.00 (non-members); day n/a.

Facilities: Bar: 11am–11pm. Food: Breakfast, lunch and dinner from 7am–10pm.

Comments: Well-managed course and country club ... How a resort course should be ... First-class facilities and course ... Not a 'name' course but well worth playing ... Really tries hard ... Very difficult (standard scratch 73) ... They treat you well here.

Verulam Golf Club ★★★

London Road, St Albans, AL1 1JG
Website: www.verulamgolf.co.uk   E-mail: genman@verulamgolf.co.uk
Nearest main town: St Albans

Secretary:	Mr J. Maguire	Tel: 01727 853327
		Fax: 01727 812201
Professional:	Mr N. Burch	Tel: 01727 861401

Playing: Midweek: round £15.00 (Mon), £25.00 (Tues, Thurs, Fri); day £25.00 (Mon), £35.00 (Tues, Thurs, Fri). Weekend: round n/a; day n/a.

Facilities: Bar: 11am–11pm. Food: Lunch and dinner from 10am–9pm. Bar snacks.

Comments: Home of Sam Ryder ... Greens are not so hot but course is a spirited test of any player ... Course could be better maintained and welcome not so good ... Fourteen holes with out-of-bounds ... Good stretch of holes near the turn.

West Herts Golf Club ★★

Cassiobury Park, Rousebarn Lane, Croxley Green, Rickmansworth, WD3 3GG
Nearest main town: Watford

Secretary:	Mr C. Dodman	Tel: 01923 236484
		Fax: 01923 222300
Professional:	Mr C. Gough	Tel: 01923 220352

Playing: Midweek: round £38.00; day n/a. Weekend: round £48.00; day n/a.

Facilities: Bar: 11am–11pm. Food: Breakfast, lunch and dinner from 7.30am–6pm. Bar snacks.

Comments: A welcome smile whether in the pro shop or at the bar ... Open all year round ... Rarely gets boggy ... Well-established club with mind-boggling tradition ... Go play, it's a treat ... A memorable round in the late afternoon sun.

Whipsnade Park Golf Club   ★★

Studham Lane, Dagnall, HP4 1RH
Website: www.whipsnadeparkgolf.co.uk
E-mail: whipsnadeparkgolfc@btopenworld.com
Nearest main town: Hemel Hempstead

Secretary:	Ms A. King	Tel: 01442 842330
		Fax: 01442 842090
Professional:	Mr D. Turner	Tel: 01442 842310

Playing: Midweek: round £29.00; day £40.00. Weekend: round £24.00 (with member only); day n/a.

Facilities: Bar: 12pm–9pm. Food: Lunch from 12pm–3pm.

Comments: Very long track right near the zoo ... Poor facilities for visitors ... Not value for money ... Bit of a bore ... Nice views ... Average course in the Chilterns.

Isle of Man

Castletown Golf Links   ★★★★

Golf Office, Derbyhaven, IM9 1UA
Website: www.golfiom.com   E-mail: 1sttee@manx.net
Nearest main town: Castletown

Step outside the front of the Links Hotel and you are straight on the 1st tee at Castletown – but just pray the wind is not blowing too hard.

The Castletown Links is set on a rocky peninsula on the south of the Isle of Man and, as such, is completely exposed. When squalls race in off the Irish Sea, players rush in all directions for shelter as the course is just too difficult to play – as you hit, you feel as if the ball is going to come back over your head. It is an extremely elemental golf experience – rocks jut out from the fairways as natural hazards and you must drive over the Irish Sea itself (at the 17th), certainly the highlight of any round.

There are other high points too, particularly the challenging 5th that the hotel manager is always happy to have a bet with you about. The wager is straightforward: a bottle of champagne for anyone who pars the hole, and if you fail, you buy the champagne for the manager. He says he has rarely lost his money over this hole, which has a habit of enticing a push or a slice. When Greg Norman played here he managed a par, but not many do, especially when the wind is up. Tug your tee shot left and you hit a rugged bank.

As befits a links, the wind will always play a pivotal role on a layout that offers an intriguing mix of long and short holes. The course can look deceptively easy, as it is not a monster in length, but be prepared to be surprised. The course is undoubtedly the best on the island and there is no shortage of competition. Those in the know always make sure to visit during a quiet period when Castletown is at its toughest and most satisfying.

Secretary:	Ms D. Barron	Tel: 01624 822220
		Fax: 01624 829661
Professional:	Mr M. Crowe	Tel: 01624 822211
Playing:	Midweek: round £35.00; day n/a. Weekend: round £40.00; day n/a.	
Facilities:	Bar: 10am–11pm. Food: Lunch from 12pm–2pm. Dinner from 7pm–10pm. Bar snacks.	

Comments: A very tricky course on the Langness Peninsula ... Plenty of Manx charm here ... Sea covers the course on three sides ... So tough, so beautiful, so wild ... Hard to master even in calm conditions.

Mount Murray Golf & Country Club   ★★

Santon, IM4 2HT
Nearest main town: Douglas

Secretary: Mr A. Dyson   Tel: 01624 661111
                                        Fax: 01624 611116
Professional: Mr A. Dyson   Tel: 01624 661111

Playing: Midweek: round £18.00; day £18.00. Weekend: round £24.00; day £24.00.

Facilities: Bar: 11am–11pm. Food: Breakfast, lunch and dinner from 8am–11pm. Bar snacks.

Comments: Really underrated ... Views out of this world ... Lovely outlook over the Isle of Man ... Moorland beauty ... Very exposed on moorland outcrop ... Massive par-5s ... A real behemoth of a course at 6600+ yards.

Kent

Royal St George's Golf Club ★★★★★

Sandwich, CT13 9PB
Nearest main town: Sandwich

In 1894 the Open Championship moved out of Scotland for the first time. It headed south to a links course that was barely seven years old, but had already built up a reputation as a test every bit the equal of those north of the border.

Royal St George's hosted the first Open to be held in England and since then it has welcomed the world's greatest tournament on twelve occasions, probably the most exciting being in 1993 when Greg Norman, Nick Faldo, Payne Stewart and Bernhard Langer conspired to make it one of the best Open Championships in recent memory.

Norman won the day with an outstanding final round of 64, taming a course that is full of awkward twists and turns, each liable to derail an overconfident approach. Take the bunker on the 4th, for example, a towering, cavernous hole that gawps at you off the tee like some giant open-mouthed alligator. It is named Reg Glading's bunker after the poor soul who got gobbled up by it in the Amateur Championship. The 5th hole is a 421-yard dogleg that was driven by John Daly in a practice round in 1993; this is followed by a par-3 with a tight, thin green.

The back nine is equally treacherous, opening with a stiff par-4 that is uphill all the way to a green that is buffeted by the wind and sits like an impregnable fortress. Suez is the par-5 14th, a straightforward enough challenge if it wasn't for the fact that out-of-bounds borders the right-hand side off the tee.

Of course, the added bonus of a trip to Sandwich is that Royal St George's need not be your only port of call. The course is sandwiched, if you'll excuse the pun, between two other links, the creditable Princes, and the excellent Royal Cinque Ports.

Secretary:	Mr G. Watts	Tel: 01304 613090
		Fax: 01304 611245
Professional:	Mr A. Brooks	Tel: 01304 615236
		Fax: 01304 615236
Playing:	Midweek: round £70.00; day £100.00. Weekend: round n/a; day n/a.	

Facilities: Bar: 11am–11pm. Food: Lunch from 12pm–2.30pm. Dinner from 7pm–9.30pm.

Comments: Probably the best in the world ... Don't forget your bucket and spade – you can get lost in the bunkers ... In the footsteps of heroes – what a course ... History, tradition, windy, interesting and the chance to pretend you are playing in the Open ... Always enjoy tackling this giant ... Untouched by human hands, the natural way to play golf ... Open venue at reasonable price – if only they were all like this ... Warmth of welcome unsurpassed ... Didn't want to leave.

Austin Lodge Golf Club   ★★

Eynsford, Swanley, DA4 0HU
Nearest main town: Swanley

Secretary: Mr S. Bevan   Tel: 01322 863000
                                     Fax: 01322 862406
Professional: Mr P. Edwards

Playing: Midweek: round £16.00; day £28.00. Weekend: round £25.00; day n/a.

Facilities: Bar: 11am–11pm. Food: Breakfast, lunch and dinner from 7am–7pm. Bar snacks.

Comments: Long and hilly, a buggy may be required ... Idyllic setting ... Well drained ... Very challenging and quite difficult ... Demanding course, tranquil setting, requiring all the shots ... Picturesque surroundings, very challenging ... Quiet, long course offering value and interest ... Good welcome.

Broome Park Golf Club   ★

Broome Park Estate, Barham, Canterbury, CT4 6QX
Website: www.broomepark.co.uk   E-mail: broomepark@o2.co.uk
Nearest main town: Canterbury

Secretary: Mr G. Robins   Tel: 01227 830728
                                     Fax: 01227 832591
Professional: Mr T. Britz   Tel: 01227 831126
                                     Fax: 01227 832546

Playing: Midweek: round £40.00; day n/a. Weekend: round £50.00; day n/a.

Facilities: Bar: 11am–11pm. Food: Breakfast, lunch and dinner from 7am–10pm.

Comments: Nice parkland course ... Kitchener's House makes a fabulous clubhouse ... Absolutely wonderful setting ... Championship course I'll visit again.

Canterbury Golf Club   ★★

Scotland Hills, Littlebourne Road, Canterbury, CT1 1TW
E-mail: cgc@freeola.com
Nearest main town: Canterbury

Secretary:	Mr J. Morgan	Tel: 01227 453532
		Fax: 01227 784277
Professional:	Mr P. Everard	Tel: 01227 462865

Playing: Midweek: round £30.00 (at restricted times); day £36.00. Weekend: round £30.00; day £36.00.

Facilities: Bar: 11am–11pm. Food: Lunch and dinner from 11am–9pm. Bar snacks.

Comments: All the trouble is off the tee ... Heavily wooded ... Peace and seclusion ... Very tight driving ... You need a game plan.

Chart Hills Golf Club   ★★★★

Weeks Lane, Biddenden, TN27 8JX
Website: www.charthills.co.uk   E-mail: info@charthills.co.uk
Nearest main town: Ashford

Secretary:	Mr D. Walls	Tel: 01580 292222
	(Operations Manager)	Fax: 01580 292233
Professional:	Mr S. Cranfield	Tel: 01580 291444

Playing: Midweek: round £50.00 (18 holes); day n/a. Weekend: round £60.00 (18 holes); day n/a.

Facilities: Bar: 11am–11pm. Food: Lunch and dinner by arrangement.

Comments: Daunting first impression ... Need a good short game
... A golfer's dream ... Immaculate, class shows from
arrival to the moment the last putt drops ... Best food
ever tasted at a golf club ... Par-4s and 5s well
designed, shame about the 3s ... Top-notch venue,
though expensive worth every penny ... Unusual course
with challenging tee shots ... If God played golf he
would play here ... Fabulous test and for a young course
it is an instant classic ... A fantastic course but overpriced ... Take advantage of the twilight fees ...
Designed by Nick Faldo ... Knockout ... Unbeatable.

Cherry Lodge Golf Club ★★

Jail Lane, Biggin Hill, Westerham, TN16 3AX
Website: www.cherrylodgegc.co.uk
E-mail: info@cherrylodgegc.co.uk
Nearest main town: Bromley

Secretary: Mr W. Tambling   Tel: 01959 572250
Fax: 01959 540672
Professional: Mr N. Child   Tel: 01959 572989
Fax: 01959 540672

Playing: Midweek: round £35.00; day n/a. Weekend: round n/a;
day n/a.

Facilities: Bar: 11am–11pm. Food: Lunch from 10am–6pm. Bar
snacks.

Comments: High up with strong winds a persistent factor ...
Presentation always first class ... Greens consistently
good ... Looks good ... Not everyone's favourite.

Executive Golf Club of Cranbrook ★

Golford Road, Cranbrook, TN17 4AL
Website: www.executivemembership.co.uk
Nearest main town: Tunbridge Wells

Secretary: Mr K. Stevenson   Tel: 01580 712833
Fax: 01580 714274
Professional: Mr G. Kay

Playing: Midweek: round £27.50; day n/a. Weekend: round
£32.50; day n/a.

Facilities: Bar: 11am–11pm. Food: Bar snacks.

Comments: Well thought of in Kent ... Keeps you interested ... Wonderful countryside ... Not well known but great test of golf ... Make sure to make a visit.

Faversham Golf Club ★★★

Belmont Park, Faversham, ME13 0HB
Website: www.favershamgolf.co.uk
E-mail: manager@favershamgolf.co.uk
Nearest main town: Faversham

Secretary:	Mr J. Edgington	Tel: 01795 890561
		Fax: 01795 890760
Professional:	Mr S. Rokes	Tel: 01795 890275
		Fax: 01795 890760

Playing: Midweek: round £30.00; day n/a. Weekend: round members' guests only; day n/a.

Facilities: Bar: 10.30am–11pm. Food: Lunch and dinner from 11am–7pm. Bar snacks.

Comments: A testing course with fastish greens ... Could have had a better welcome ... Inland masterpiece ... Go find your game on this straightforward and welcoming course.

Hever Castle Golf Club ★★★

Hever Road, Edenbridge, Hever, TN8 7NP
Website: www.hevercastlegolfclub.co.uk
E-mail: mail@hevercastlegolfclub.co.uk
Nearest main town: Edenbridge

Secretary:	Mr M. Hickson	Tel: 01732 700771
	(General Manager)	Fax: 01732 700775
Professional:	Mr P. Parks	Tel: 01732 700771
		Fax: 01732 700775

Playing: Midweek: round £35.00 (18 holes), £45.00 (27 holes); day n/a. Weekend: round £55.00 (18 holes after 11am); day n/a.

Facilities: Bar: 7am–11pm. Food: Breakfast, lunch and dinner from 7am–9pm. Bar snacks.

Comments: Pricey but well-run club ... Very modern and very long ... One of the best new courses in Britain ... Bit of a monster ... Has a wonderful feel ... American-style new course ... Worth the wait.

Knole Park Golf Club   ★★★

Seal Hollow Road, Sevenoaks, TN15 0HJ
Website: www.knoleparkgolfclub.co.uk
E-mail: secretary@knolepark.fsnet.co.uk
Nearest main town: Sevenoaks

Secretary:	Mr P. Mitchell	Tel: 01732 452150
		Fax: 01732 463159
Professional:	Mr P. Sykes	Tel: 01732 451740

Playing: Midweek: round £35.00; day n/a. Weekend: round n/a; day n/a.

Facilities: Bar: 11am–11pm. Food: Lunch and dinner from 10am–6pm. Bar snacks.

Comments: Beautiful parkland course with some tricky holes – mind the deer! ... Deer running loose ... Well kept with views of the North Downs ... Greens to putt on all year ... Superb greens ... Exclusive feel to this welcoming club.

Langley Park Golf Club   ★★★

Barnfield Wood Road, Beckenham, BR3 6SZ
Website: www.langleyparkgolf.co.uk
E-mail: manager@langleyparkgolf.co.uk
Nearest main town: Bromley

Secretary:	Mr R. Pollard	Tel: 020 8658 6849
		Fax: 020 8658 6310
Professional:	Mr C. Staff	Tel: 020 8650 1663
		Fax: 020 8658 6310

Playing: Midweek: round £30.00; day £40.00. Weekend: round n/a; day n/a.

Facilities: Bar: 11am–11pm. Food: Lunch from 12pm–2.30pm. Dinner from 7pm–9.30pm.

Comments: Well wooded ... Cracking finishing hole ... One of the best in the area ... Tough, long par-4s ... Always a pleasure to play here ... Regional Open qualifying course ... Never get bored of it.

Littlestone Golf Club ★★★★

St Andrews Road, Littlestone, New Romney, TN28 8RB
Website: www.littlestonegolfclub.org.uk
E-mail: secretary@littlestonegolfclub.org.uk
Nearest main town: Romsey

Secretary:	Col C. Moorhouse	Tel: 01797 363355
		Fax: 01797 362740
Professional:	Mr A. Jones	

Playing: Midweek: round £38.00; day £55.00. Weekend: round £50.00; day £65.00.

Facilities: Bar: 11am–11pm. Food: Lunch from 12pm–2.30pm. Bar snacks.

Comments: Fantastic links with immaculate greens ... An absolute classic ... Design-wise there is very little to touch it ... Located on Romney Marshes ... Exceptional, interesting course ... Now for something a little bit different.

The London Golf Club (Heritage) ★★★★

South Ash Manor Estate, Ash, Sevenoaks, TN15 7EN
Website: www.londongolf.co.uk   E-mail: london@londongolf.co.uk
Nearest main town: Sevenoaks

Secretary:	None	Tel: 01474 879899
		Fax: 01474 879912
Professional:	Mr B. Longmuir	Tel: 01474 879899

Playing: Midweek: round prices on application; day n/a. Weekend: round n/a; day n/a.

Facilities: Bar: Members only. Food: Members only

Comments: More than you should pay but worth double ... Can only play with a member ... Outstanding condition ... A very unnatural course, not for links lovers ... Had a great time, but couldn't wait to get away ... Conditioning second to none ... Not Nicklaus' finest moment.

The London Golf Club (International)

South Ash Manor Estate, Ash, Sevenoaks, TN15 7EN
Website: www.londongolf.co.uk   E-mail: london@londongolf.co.uk
Nearest main town: Sevenoaks

Secretary:	None	Tel: 01474 879899
		Fax: 01474 879912
Professional:	Mr B. Longmuir	Tel: 01474 879899

Playing: Midweek: round £70.00; day n/a. Weekend: round n/a; day n/a.

Facilities: Bar: Members only. Food: Members only

Comments: Still the best greens around ... Find a member and play it ... Little to choose between two courses ... Lakes and generous fairways – designed for all standards but no-one can play it ... Delight to play, but club lacks character.

Lullingstone Park Golf Club   ★★★

Parkgate Road, Chelsfield, Orpington, BR6 7PX
Nearest main town: Orpington

Secretary:	Mr B. Vallance	Tel: 01959 533793
		Fax: 01959 533795
Professional:	Mr M. Watt	Tel: 01959 533793

Playing: Midweek: round £10.00; day n/a. Weekend: round £15.00; day n/a.

Facilities: Bar: 11am–11pm. Food: Lunch from 10am–4pm. Bar snacks.

Comments: Very welcoming ... For price, you won't get a better round of golf – superb ... Popular course and rightly so with facilities ... Good set-up.

Lydd Golf Club   ★

Romney Road, Lydd, Romney Marsh, TN29 9LS
Website: www.lyddgolfclub.co.uk   E-mail: info@lyddgolfclub.co.uk
Nearest main town: Ashford

Secretary:	Mr B. Evans	Tel: 01797 320808
		Fax: 01797 321482
Professional:	Mr R. Perkins	Tel: 01797 321201

Playing: Midweek: round £17.00 (18 holes); day n/a. Weekend: round £25.00 (18 holes); day n/a.

Facilities: Bar: 11am–11pm. Food: Lunch from 12pm–3pm. Dinner by arrangement.

Comments: Links-style course ... Wide open linksy course ... Not strictly a links but many of its features ... Golfer's course ... Course that is fair to all categories of player.

Mid Kent Golf Club   ★

Singlewell Road, Gravesend, DA11 7RB
E-mail: sarahgreenwell@aol.com
Nearest main town: Gravesend

Secretary:	Mr P. Gleeson	Tel: 01474 746069
		Fax: 01474 564218
Professional:	Mr M. Foreman	Tel: 01474 332810
		Fax: 01474 332810

Playing: Midweek: round £25.00; day £35.00. Weekend: round n/a; day n/a.

Facilities: Bar: 11am–11pm. Food: Lunch and dinner from 11am–8pm. Bar snacks.

Comments: Stiff opening stretch but gets easier ... Popular course in fair condition ... Downland with plenty of challenge ... Well established.

Moatlands Golf Club

Watermans Lane, Brenchley, Tonbridge, TN12 6ND
Website: www.moatlands.com
E-mail: moatlandsgolf@btconnect.com
Nearest main town: Matfield

Secretary:	Mr K. Wiley	Tel: 01892 724400
		Fax: 01892 723300
Professional:	Mr S. Wood	Tel: 01892 724252

Playing: Midweek: round £29.00; day £45.00. Weekend: round £39.00; day £55.00.

Facilities: Bar: 11am–11pm. Food: Dinner from 6pm–9.30pm Thursday–Saturday. Bar snacks.

Comments: Built to high standards ... Lovely clubhouse ... Friendly club with special off-course facilities ... Watch out for the Victorian bath-house on the back nine ... Long course making clever use of natural setting ... Rolling parkland course.

Nizels Golf Club ★★★★

Nizels Lane, Hildenborough, Tonbridge, TN11 8NX
E-mail: nizels@clubhaus.com
Nearest main town: Tonbridge

Secretary:	Mr W. Tambling	Tel: 01732 838926
		Fax: 01732 835492
Professional:	Mr B. Wynne	Tel: 01732 838926

Playing: Midweek: round £45.00; day n/a. Weekend: round £50.00; day n/a.

Facilities: Bar: 11am–11pm. Food: Lunch and dinner from 11am–9pm.

Comments: Water features and natural landscape are sources of interest and challenge ... Unusually named club and course ... Fascinating woodland course ... One for the notebook ... Outstanding wildlife and nature's blessing makes this a course to treasure.

North Foreland Golf Club ★★★★

Convent Road, Thanet, CT10 3PU
Nearest main town: Broadstairs

Secretary:	Mr B. Preston	Tel: 01843 862140
		Fax: 01843 862663
Professional:	Mr N. Hanson	Tel: 01843 604471

Playing: Midweek: round £30.00; day £40.00. Weekend: round £40.00; day n/a.

Facilities: Bar: 11am–11pm. Food: Breakfast, lunch and dinner from 9am–6pm. Bar snacks.

Comments: Very exposed and bracing ... Very few hazards and yet it's so difficult ... Played it in a gale – super ... Real triumph for the designers ... Not in great condition but that's how it is supposed to be.

Prince's Golf Club ★★★★

Prince's Drive, Sandwich Bay, Sandwich, CT13 9QB
Website: www.princes-leisure.co.uk
E-mail: golf@princes-leisure.co.uk
Nearest main town: Sandwich

Secretary:	Mr B. Howie	Tel: 01304 611118
		Fax: 01304 612000
Professional:	Mr D. Barbour	Tel: 01304 613797
		Fax: 01304 612000

Playing: Midweek: round £60.00, £70.00 (27 holes); day n/a. Weekend: round £70.00, £80.00 (27 holes); day n/a.

Facilities: Bar: 11am–11pm. Food: Lunch and dinner from 11am–9pm. Bar snacks.

Comments: Everyone here makes you feel so welcome ... Friendly classic links in tremendous location ... Great day out on a championship links ... Refreshing links golf ... Sea breezes can mean changing your driver for a wedge ... Worth travelling to from afar ... Always a great welcome for visitors ... Fabulous in every respect ... Watch out for chapping on this exposed links ... A natural beauty.

Redlibbets Golf Club   ★★★

Manor Lane, West Yoke, Nr Sevenoaks, TN15 7HT
Website: www.golfandsport.co.uk
E-mail: redlibbets@golfandsport.com
Nearest main town: Sevenoaks

Secretary:	Mr J. Potter	Tel: 01474 879190
		Fax: 01474 879290
Professional:	Mr R. Taylor	Tel: 01474 872278
		Fax: 01474 879290

Playing: Midweek: round £40.00; day n/a. Weekend: round n/a; day n/a.

Facilities: Bar: 11am–11pm. Food: Lunch and dinner from 10am–6pm. Dinner by arrangement.

Comments: Fine new course ... Shot-maker's course ... Take your time to plot your way around this course ... Condition excellent ... This course's stock is set to rise.

Rochester & Cobham Park Golf Club   ★★

Park Pale, By Rochester, ME2 3UL
Website: www.rochesterandcobhamgc.co.uk
E-mail: rcpgc@talk21.com
Nearest main town: Gravesend

Secretary:	Mr D. Smith	Tel: 01474 823411
Professional:	Mr I. Higgins	Fax: 01474 824446
		Tel: 01474 823658
		Fax: 01474 824446

Playing: Midweek: round £35.00; day £45.00. Weekend: round only with a member; day n/a.

Facilities: Bar: 11am–11pm. Food: Lunch and dinner from 10.30am–6.30pm. Bar snacks.

Comments: Long and difficult ... Very narrow so watch your driving ... Keep it straight, John ... Very varied and interesting ... Excellent value for such a fascinating course.

Royal Blackheath Golf Club   ★★★

Court Road, Eltham, London, SE9 5AF
Website: www.rbgc.com   E-mail: info@rbgc.com
Nearest main town: London

Secretary:	Mr T. Dunlop	Tel: 020 8850 1795
Professional:	Mr R. Harrison	Fax: 020 8859 0150
		Tel: 020 8850 1763
		Fax: 020 8859 0150

Playing: Midweek: round £45.00 (18 holes), £60.00 (36 holes); day n/a. Weekend: round members only; day n/a.

Facilities: Bar: 11am–11pm. Food: Lunch and dinner from 11am–9pm.

Comments: Steeped in history and just a few miles from Marble Arch ... A club bathed in history and tradition ... The best trophy room in golf? ... Parkland golf at its best.

Royal Cinque Ports Golf Club Ltd   ★★★★★

Golf Road, Deal, CT14 6RF
Website: www.royalcinqueports.com   E-mail: rcpgcsec@aol.com
Nearest main town: Deal

Secretary:	Mr N. Symington	Tel: 01304 374007
Professional:	Mr A. Reynolds	Fax: 01304 379530
		Tel: 01304 374170

Playing: Midweek: round £75.00; day n/a. Weekend: round £85.00; day n/a.

Facilities: Bar: 11am–8pm. Food: Bar snacks. Dinner by arrangement.

Comments: Friendly staff and members ... Never had so much fun playing golf ... Really tough course ... 16th is a classic ... Refreshingly warm welcome ... Blustery course but easy on your legs ... One of the top 100 in the British Isles ... So many stories and memories ... Nothing but the best here.

St Augustines Golf Club ★★

Cottington Road, Cliffsend, Ramsgate, CT12 5JN
Nearest main town: Ramsgate

Secretary: Mr L. Dyke Tel: 01843 590333
Fax: 01843 590444
Professional: Mr D. Scott Tel: 01843 590222

Playing: Midweek: round £21.50; day £21.50. Weekend: round £23.50; day £23.50.

Facilities: Bar: 11am–11pm. Food: Lunch from 11am–4pm.

Comments: Close to some more illustrious neighbours ... Too short to take seriously ... Very short but it's good ... Very low standard scratch ... Play it for fun.

Sundridge Park Golf Club (East) ★★★

Garden Road, Bromley, BR1 3NE
Website: www.spgc.co.uk   E-mail: secretary@spgc.co.uk
Nearest main town: Bromley

Secretary: Mr C. Winning Tel: 020 8460 0278
Fax: 020 8289 3050
Professional: Mr S. Dowsett Tel: 020 8460 5540

Playing: Midweek: round n/a; day £55.00. Weekend: round n/a; day n/a.

Facilities: Bar: 11am–11pm. Food: Lunch from 12pm–2.30pm.

Comments: Open qualifying course ... Test of genuine quality ... Tough finish ... Many holes played through a valley ... 16th weakest hole on the course ... 18th is a cracking finish with massive elevated tee on long dogleg right.

Sundridge Park Golf Club (West)   ★★★

Garden Road, Bromley, BR1 3NE
Website: www.spgc.co.uk   E-mail: secretary@spgc.co.uk
Nearest main town: Bromley

Secretary:	Mr C. Winning	Tel: 020 8460 0278
		Fax: 020 8289 3050
Professional:	Mr S. Dowsett	Tel: 020 8460 5540

Playing: Midweek: round n/a; day £55.00. Weekend: round n/a; day n/a.

Facilities: Bar: 11am–11pm. Food: Lunch from 12pm–2.30pm.

Comments: Pleasant woodland ... 4th is a bit of a joke ... Easy finish with driveable par-4 and simple par-5 ... Views over London.

Tudor Park Hotel Golf Club   ★★

Ashford Road, Bearstead, Maidstone, ME14 4NQ
Nearest main town: Maidstone

Secretary:	Mr J. Ladbrook	Tel: 01622 734334
		Fax: 01622 735360
Professional:	Mr N. MacNally	Tel: 01622 739412

Playing: Midweek: round £25.00; day £30.00. Weekend: round £35.00; day n/a.

Facilities: Bar: 11am–11pm. Food: Breakfast, lunch and dinner served from 7am–10pm. Bar snacks.

Comments: Great facilities – should do more with the course ... A little overplayed but facilities are first class ... Little ragged around the edges but a nice day out ... Good society venue ... Undulating course but not particularly challenging between the ears.

Walmer & Kingsdown Golf Club

The Leas, Kingsdown, Deal, CT14 8EP
E-mail: kingsdown.golf@gtwiz.co.uk
Nearest main town: Deal

Secretary:	Mr R. Harrison	Tel: 01304 373256
		Fax: 01304 382336
Professional:	Mr M. Paget	Tel: 01304 363017

Playing: Midweek: round £25.00; day £30.00. Weekend: round £24.00; day £30.00.

Facilities: Bar: 11am–11pm. Food: Breakfast, lunch and dinner from 7.30am–9pm. Bar snacks.

Comments: Cliff-top thrills ... A real adventure ... Not given recognition it deserves ... Views of the North Sea ... Nicely presented ... Facilities lacking ... Overall very good scenic course.

Weald of Kent Golf Club   ★

Maidstone Road, Headcorn, TN27 9PT
Nearest main town: Maidstone

Secretary: Mr S. Doran   Tel: 01622 890866
                                         Fax: 01622 891793

Professional: None

Playing: Midweek: round £15.50; day £30.00. Weekend: round £19.00; day £37.00.

Facilities: Bar: 11am–11pm. Food: Lunch and dinner from 11am–9pm.

Comments: Good value ... For the money, very reasonable ... Course uses natural defences ... Parkland ... Lots of streams and ditches.

Woodlands Manor Golf Club   ★★

Woodlands, Tinkerpot Lane, Otford, Sevenoaks, TN15 6AB
E-mail: woodlandsgolfclub@hotmail.com
Nearest main town: Sevenoaks

Secretary: Mr C. Robins   Tel: 01959 523806
                                         Fax: 01959 524398
Professional: Mr P. Womack   Tel: 01959 524161

Playing: Midweek: round £21.00; day £31.50. Weekend: round £27.00 (after 1pm); day n/a.

Facilities: Bar: 11am–11pm. Food: Lunch and dinner from 10am–10pm.

Comments: Facile parkland course ... One of the cheaper quality courses in Kent ... Progressive club ... Always turned out well.

Lancashire

Royal Lytham & St Annes Golf Club ★★★★★

Links Gate, Lytham St Annes, FY8 3LQ
Website: www.royallytham.org   E-mail: bookings@royallytham.org
Nearest main town: St Annes

Royal Lytham & St Annes is a different breed to most links, set in an urban landscape and lacking most of the distinguishing features of that type of course – no sandhills between the fairways and no dramatic landscapes. Neither is there any sign that the course, situated just south of the gaudy holiday town of Blackpool, is near the sea.

This confusing picture does not make it one of the favoured Open Championship courses with amateurs, but it is still highly rated for the diversity of the holes, achieved on a rather unremarkable piece of land. Uniquely for an Open venue, Lytham starts with a 206-yard par-3 and a mighty tough one at that, the green being thoroughly protected by four bunkers on the left side with another trio of traps on the right. It is also liked for the difficulty of its finish, certainly on a level with that at Royal Troon – the back nine has, in the past, played four shots harder than the front nine in the same weather conditions for players in the Open.

The great golf writer Bernard Darwin once described some of the closing holes as 'unpleasantly difficult'. Jack Nicklaus was more straightforward, describing the 15th as one of the hardest holes he had ever played when, in the 1974 Open Championship, the average score for this 468-yard monster was an almost unprecedented stroke average of a full shot over par.

The 11th is the only par-5 coming back, but at 542 yards, it is normally out of reach in two shots. Meanwhile, the lone par-3 on the back nine, the 12th, is equally uncompromising. With its shallow, narrow green, protected by six bunkers and unkempt grassy ridges (not forgetting the out-of-bounds perilously close down the right) and you have the most exacting shot of the whole round. Seve Ballesteros voted this hole the best par-3 in the British Isles in a *Golf World* survey, while Tom Watson was similarly full of praise.

The prevailing wind is from the north-west at Royal Lytham, which helps most of the way on the outward nine. It is here that the course has more of a links feel; the dunes are wild and owe nothing to any sculpting or moulding. The 8th green is a superb example, an exposed target from the fairway below, as is the 9th, a pure target nestling among bunkers.

The 18th is a short finishing hole and not exactly the climax you expect. The only problems come from the possibility of overclubbing, which might leave you hitting your recovery shot backhanded, like Gary Player, from the walls of the magnificent redbrick Victorian clubhouse.

Secretary:	Mr R. Cochrane	Tel: 01253 724206
		Fax: 01253 780946
Professional:	Mr E. Birchenough	Tel: 01253 720094
		Fax: 01253 720094

Playing: Midweek: Prices on application. Weekend: Limited availability.

Facilities: Bar: 11am–11pm. Food: Breakfast, lunch and dinner from 7am–10pm. Bar snacks.

Comments: Worth playing at least once ... Good value for an Open course ... So many memorable holes ... Great atmosphere ... Back nine is outstanding ... Extremely trying on the patience ... Apart from the course, very poor and disappointing ... Great experience for the traditionalist ... A must for links lovers ... Never liked a par-3 start – like it even less now ... One of the worst Open courses ... Lacks atmosphere ... Worthy Open venue and the best attitude towards visitors.

Beacon Park Golf Club   ★

Beacon Lane, Up Holland, Dalton, WN8 7RU
Nearest main town: Dalton

Secretary:	Mr T. Harris	Tel: 01695 627500
		Fax: 01695 633066
Professional:	Mr R. Peters	Tel: 01695 622700

Playing: Midweek: round prices on application; day n/a. Weekend: round n/a; day n/a.

Facilities: Bar: 11am–11pm. Food: Lunch from 11.30am–2.30pm.

Comments: Outstanding practice facilities ... Topography not ideal for beginners ... Very hilly ... Condition not great ... Everything you need to practise with purpose.

Blackburn Golf Club ★

Beardwood Brow, Blackburn, BB2 7AX
E-mail: customer@blackburngolfclub.com
Nearest main town: Blackburn

Secretary: Mr G. Readett   Tel: 01254 51122
                                      Fax: 01254 665578
Professional: Mr A. Rodwell   Tel: 01254 55942

Playing: Midweek: round £24.00; day £24.00. Weekend: round
             £28.00; day £28.00.

Facilities: Bar: 11am–11pm. Food: Breakfast, lunch and dinner
                from 7am–9pm. Bar snacks.

Comments: Looking out over the Pennines ... Set on a plateau ...
              Not the best condition ... High up and exposed.

Bolton Golf Club ★★★★

Lostock Park, Bolton, BL6 4AJ
E-mail: bostongolf@lostockpark.fsbusiness.co.uk
Nearest main town: Bolton

Secretary: Mrs H. Stuart   Tel: 01204 843067
                                     Fax: 01204 843067
Professional: Mr B. Longworth   Tel: 01204 843073

Playing: Midweek: round prices on application; day n/a.
             Weekend: round n/a; day n/a.

Facilities: Bar: 11am–11pm. Food: Dinner from 6pm–9.30pm
                Thursday–Saturday. Bar snacks.

Comments: Overshadowed by the Old Links ... Heathland ... Not
              always in top condition ... A brutal finish to a traditional
              course ... If you're in the area, pop in.

Bolton Old Links Golf Club ★★★★

Chorley Old Road, Montserrat, Bolton, BL1 5SU
Nearest main town: Bolton

Secretary: Mrs J. Boardman   Tel: 01204 842307
                                      Fax: 01204 842307
Professional: Mr P. Horridge   Tel: 01204 843089
                                      Fax: 01204 843089

Playing: Midweek: round £30.00; day £30.00. Weekend: round £40.00; day £40.00.

Facilities: Bar: 11am–11pm. Food: Breakfast, lunch and dinner from 9.30am–9pm.

Comments: Certainly worth a visit but not in the winter … Moorland course with great character and history.

Chorley Golf Club ★★

Hall o' th' Hill, Heath Charnock, Chorley, PR6 9HX
Website: www.chorleygolfclub.co.uk
E-mail: secretary@chorleygolfclub.freeserve.co.uk
Nearest main town: Chorley

Secretary: Mrs A. Green   Tel: 01257 480263
                             Fax: 01257 480722
Professional: Mr M. Bradley   Tel: 01257 481245

Playing: Midweek: round prices on application; day n/a. Weekend: round n/a; day n/a.

Facilities: Bar: 11am–9pm. Food: Lunch from 11.30am–2.30pm.

Comments: Good condition for moorland … Clean air and well-kept course – perfect … As nature intended … Very amiable members … Worth the drive.

Clitheroe Golf Club ★★★

Whalley Road, Pendleton, Clitheroe, BB7 4PP
Website: www.clitheroegolfclub.com
E-mail: secretary@clitheroegolfclub.com
Nearest main town: Clitheroe

Secretary: Mr T. Ashton   Tel: 01200 422292
                             Fax: 01200 422292
Professional: Mr J. Twissell   Tel: 01200 424242
                             Fax: 01200 424242

Playing: Midweek: round £32.00–£37.00; day n/a. Weekend: round £45.00; day n/a.

Facilities: Bar: 11am–11pm. Food: Lunch from 11am–5pm. Bar snacks. Dinner by arrangement.

Comments: Worth the visit ... A thinking course demanding different shots ... Excellent course with friendly atmosphere and good welcome ... Unknown course that must be one of the finest inland tracks in the country ... Absolute delight ... Not a name course, but who cares if it keeps the visitors down?

Dean Wood Golf Club   ★★

Lafford Lane, Up Holland, Skelmersdale, WN8 0QZ
E-mail: office@dwgc.fsnet.co.uk
Nearest main town: Wigan

Secretary:	Mr A. McGregor	Tel: 01695 622219
		Fax: 01695 622245
Professional:	Mr S. Danchin	Tel: 01695 627480

Playing: Midweek: round n/a; day £30.00. Weekend: round n/a; day £33.00.

Facilities: Bar: 12pm–11pm. Food: Lunch and dinner from 10.30am–9.30pm.

Comments: Nice condition, fairly unremarkable course ... Front nine boring but back nine spices it up ... Two courses in one ... Good greenkeeping ... Condition usually good ... Challenging holes on back nine.

Dunscar Golf Limited   ★

Longworth Lane, Bromley Cross, Bolton, BL7 9QY
E-mail: secretary@dunscargolfclub.fsnet.co.uk
Nearest main town: Bolton

Secretary:	Mr J. Jennings	Tel: 01204 303321
Professional:	Mr G. Treadgold	Tel: 01204 592992

Playing: Midweek: round n/a; day £25.00. Weekend: round n/a; day £35.00.

Facilities: Bar: 11am–11pm. Food: Lunch from 12pm–2.30pm. Dinner from 7pm–9pm.

Comments: Fine value at this picturesque moorland course ... Many good days' golfing here ... Presentation sometimes lacking ... Conditioning not perfect ... Very natural and not for moaners.

Fairhaven Golf Club ★★★

Lytham Hall Park, Ansdell, Lytham St Annes, FY8 4JU
Nearest main town: St Annes

Secretary:	Mr H. Fielding	Tel: 01253 736741
		Fax: 01253 731461
Professional:	Mr B. Blucknett	Tel: 01253 736976

Playing: Midweek: round £33.00; day n/a. Weekend: round £40.00; day n/a.

Facilities: Bar: 11am–11pm. Food: Lunch and dinner from 11am–9pm. Bar snacks.

Comments: Memorable holes and bunkers ... Lovely parkland course ... Long and hard with lots of bunkers ... Very long and difficult ... One bunker for every day of the year here ... Good facilities and particularly liked the reading room.

Fleetwood Golf Club ★★★

Golf House, Princes Way, Fleetwood, FY7 8AF
Nearest main town: Fleetwood

Secretary:	Mr R. Yates	Tel: 01253 773573
		Fax: 01253 773573
Professional:	Mr S. McLaughlin	Tel: 01253 873661

Playing: Midweek: round £30.00; day £30.00. Weekend: round £34.00; day £34.00.

Facilities: Bar: 11am–11pm. Food: Lunch and dinner from 10am–9pm. Bar snacks.

Comments: Wind makes it very difficult ... Wind dictates how the course plays ... An interesting course that is made wonderful by strong winds ... Flat, long track but a place to enjoy and contemplate ... Good food ... Nice unpretentious club.

De Vere Herons Reach Hotel & Golf Club ★★

East Park Drive, Blackpool, FY3 8LL
E-mail: richard.bowman@devere-hotels.com
Nearest main town: Blackpool

Secretary:	None	Tel: 01253 766156
		Fax: 01253 798800
Professional:	Mr R. Bowman	Tel: 01253 766156
		Fax: 01253 798800

Playing: Midweek: round £40.00; day n/a. Weekend: round £45.00; day n/a.

Facilities: Bar: 11am–11pm. Food: Breakfast, lunch and dinner from 7am–10pm. Bar snacks.

Comments: Tough course with greens extremely hard to read ... Difficult due to the water ... Not set up for the high handicapper ... Very difficult course with greens tricky to judge.

Kirkby Lonsdale Golf Club ★★

Scaleber Lane, Barbon, Kirkby Lonsdale, LA6 2LJ
Website: www.klgolf.dial.pipex.com   E-mail: klgolf@dial.pipex.com
Nearest main town: Carnforth

Secretary:	Mr G. Hall	Tel: 01524 276365
		Fax: 01524 276503
Professional:	Mr J. Barrett	Tel: 01524 276366
		Fax: 01524 276566

Playing: Midweek: round £26.00; day n/a. Weekend: round £32.00; day n/a.

Facilities: Bar: 11am–11pm. Food: Lunch from 11am–6pm. Dinner by arrangement.

Comments: Cheap course that does everything well ... Very natural ... Water hazards cleverly placed ... A fine, unpretentious layout.

Lancaster Golf Club Ltd ★★★

Ashton Hall, Ashton-with-Stodday, Lancaster, LA2 0AJ
Website: www.lancastergc.co.uk
Nearest main town: Lancaster

Secretary:	Mr P. Irvine	Tel: 01524 751247
		Fax: 01524 752742
Professional:	Mr D. Sutcliffe	Tel: 01524 751802

Playing: Midweek: round £30.00; day £25.00. Weekend: round n/a; day n/a.

Facilities: Bar: 11am–11pm. Food: Lunch and dinner from 10am–10pm. Bar snacks.

Comments: An attractively set-out course – well worth playing ... Extremely friendly, helpful staff with a superb course ... Situated on the Lune Estuary ... Old club with grand tradition ... Welcoming club ... Flattish course, not difficult by any yardstick.

Longridge Golf Club ★★

Fell Barn, Jeffrey Hill, Longridge, Preston, PR3 2TU
Website: www.longridgegolfclub.co.uk
E-mail: secretary@longridgegolfclub.fsnet.co.uk
Nearest main town: Preston

Secretary: Mr D. Simpson   Tel: 01772 783291
                           Fax: 01772 783022
Professional: Mr S. Taylor   Tel: 01772 783291
                           Fax: 01772 783022

Playing: Midweek: round £21.00 (includes bar meal); day n/a. Weekend: round £26.00 (includes bar meal); day n/a.

Facilities: Bar: 11am–11pm. Food: Lunch and dinner served from 11am–9pm. Bar snacks.

Comments: Old course that's seen better days ... Moorland walking ... Views can't be bettered in Lancashire ... Variable condition.

Lytham Green Drive Golf Club ★★★★

Ballam Road, Lytham St Annes, FY8 4LE
Website: www.ukgolfer.org   E-mail: sec@greendrive.fsnet.co.uk
Nearest main town: Lytham St Annes

Secretary: Mr S. Higham   Tel: 01253 737390
                           Fax: 01253 731350
Professional: Mr A. Lancaster   Tel: 01253 737379

Playing: Midweek: round £32.00; day n/a. Weekend: round £40.00; day n/a.

Facilities: Bar: 11am–11pm. Food: Lunch and dinner served from 11am–8pm. Bar snacks.

Comments: A joy to play and captain made a point of welcoming us ... Nice, true greens ... Holiday parkland course, nothing serious ... If you find yourself here, you're at the wrong Lytham.

Morecambe Golf Club   ★

Bare, Morecambe, LA4 6AJ
Nearest main town: Morecambe

Secretary: Mrs J. Atkinson   Tel: 01524 412841
                                         Fax: 01524 412841
Professional: Mr S. Fletcher   Tel: 01524 415596

Playing: Midweek: round £22.00; day £27.00. Weekend: round £27.00; day £32.00.

Facilities: Bar: 11am–11pm. Food: Lunch from 10am–4pm. Dinner by arrangement.

Comments: Holiday course ... Best course for miles around ... Very welcoming to holiday golfers ... Go there every year ... Very fair seaside parkland course.

Ormskirk Golf Club   ★★★

Cranes Lane, Lathom, Ormskirk, L40 5UJ
Website: www.ukgolfer.org   E-mail: ormskirk@ukgolfer.org
Nearest main town: Ormskirk

Secretary: Mr R. Lawrence   Tel: 01695 572227
Professional: Mr J. Hammond   Tel: 01695 572074

Playing: Midweek: round £40.00; day £50.00. Weekend: round £45.00; day £55.00.

Facilities: Bar: 11.30am–11pm. Food: Bar snacks. Dinner from 6pm–8.30pm.

Comments: In immaculate condition and secretary's welcome very pleasing ... Flat, parkland course – like many in the area ... Welcoming sort of club ... Easy course ... Worth a detour for 18 peaceful holes.

Penwortham Golf Club   ★

Blundell Lane, Penwortham, Preston, PR1 0AX
E-mail: penworthamgolfclub@supanet.com
Nearest main town: Preston

Secretary:	Mr N. Annandale	Tel: 01772 744630
		Fax: 01772 740172
Professional:	Mr S. Holden	Tel: 01772 742345

Playing: Midweek: round £25.00; day £30.00. Weekend: round £33.00; day £33.00.

Facilities: Bar: 11am–11pm. Food: Lunch and dinner served from 11am–8pm.

Comments: Reasonable value ... Poor by Lancashire standards ... Tree-lined fairways ... Good individual holes ... Very fair but not the best.

Pleasington Golf Club   ★

Pleasington Lane, Blackburn, BB2 5JF
Website: www.pleasington-golf.co.uk
E-mail: jean@pleasington-golf.co.uk
Nearest main town: Blackburn

Secretary:	Mr M. Trickett	Tel: 01254 202177
		Fax: 01254 201028
Professional:	Mr G. Furey	Tel: 01254 201630

Playing: Midweek: round £36.00 (one round), £42.00 (two rounds); day n/a. Weekend: round £46.00 (one round only); day n/a.

Facilities: Bar: 11am–11pm. Food: Lunch and dinner served from 11am–9pm.

Comments: Not for the faint-hearted ... Good clubhouse and tasty food ... Demanding but enjoyable course ... Always well presented and beautifully scenic ... Please, please let me play ... The pleasure was all mine at this up-and-down moorland masterpiece ... Back nine is where it all starts happening.

St Annes Old Links Golf Club ★★★

Highbury Road East, Lytham St Annes, FY8 2LD
Website: www.coastalgolf.co.uk   E-mail: secretary@coastalgolf.co.uk
Nearest main town: Blackpool

Secretary:	None	Tel: 01253 723597	
		Fax: 01253 781506	
Professional:	Mr D. Webster	Tel: 01253 722432	
		Fax: 01253 781506	

Playing: Midweek: round £30.00; day £45.00. Weekend: round £50.00; day £50.00.

Facilities: Bar: 11am–11pm. Food: Breakfast and lunch from 9am–5pm.

Comments: Open qualifying course of some repute ... Extremely long and tiring ... Memorable links ... Par-3 9th a legend in these parts ... Worth it just for the 9th ... An unknown links that deserves more acclaim ... Real test if you want to make it to the Open.

Shaw Hill Hotel Golf & Country Club ★★★

Preston Road, Whittle-le-Woods, Chorley, PR6 7PP
E-mail: info@shaw-hill.co.uk
Nearest main town: Chorley

Secretary:	Mr P. Quibell	Tel: 01257 269221	
		Fax: 01257 261223	
Professional:	Mr D. Clarke	Tel: 01257 279222	

Playing: Midweek: round £30.00; day n/a. Weekend: round n/a; day n/a.

Facilities: Bar: 11am–11pm. Food: Lunch from 12pm–2.30pm. Dinner from 7pm–9.30pm. Bar snacks.

Comments: Poor condition of tees and greens ... Great layout in scenic location ... Watery graves lurk everywhere ... Peaceful and scenic ... Fairly simple course but nice tranquil atmosphere.

Standish Court Golf Club ★★★

Rectory Lane, Standish, WN6 0XD
Website: www.standishgolf.co.uk   E-mail: info@standishgolf.co.uk
Nearest main town: Wigan

Secretary: Mr S. Dawson   Tel: 01257 425777
                                   Fax: 01257 425888
Professional: Mr T. Kershaw   Tel: 01257 425777

Playing: Midweek: round £10.00; day £20.00. Weekend: round £15.00; day £30.00.

Facilities: Bar: 11am–11pm. Food: Lunch and dinner from 11am–9pm. Bar snacks.

Comments: Short but well worth a look ... Back nine cuts through woodland ... Much admired little course ... Very popular in the area ... Basic facilities but course makes up for it.

Leicestershire

Longcliffe Golf Club ★★★★

Snells Nook Lane, Nanpantan, Loughborough, LE11 3YA
E-mail: longcliffegolf@btconnect.com
Nearest main town: Loughborough

To be fair, Longcliffe suffers from a little bit of an identity problem. It is labelled a heathland course but over the years the heather has receded and you have to be incredibly unlucky nowadays to find your ball buried in heather. It now resembles parkland, but do not be put off into thinking that it is in any way dull. Longcliffe is a refreshing course that constantly surprises.

Indeed, almost every hole here is tree-lined, which gives the course a splendidly isolated feel. Along each avenue of trees the fairways undulate gently, and as you would expect, placement of your tee shot is the first and most important thing you need to do here to score well. Go off line and you are likely to run up a big score once in the trees.

The course's feature hole is probably the 15th, a par-3 played from an elevated tee to a green surrounded by a pond and dangerous bunkers. It's a gamble to go for the flag but there are a lot of such dilemmas at Longcliffe.

Much of the pleasure of playing here is the atmosphere created by the members, which is always jolly and laughter can often be heard on different holes as you pass through the avenues of trees. They are an active bunch and it really does give the course a very homely feel.

Secretary:	Mr P. Keeling	Tel: 01509 239129
		Fax: 01509 231286
Professional:	Mr D. Mee	Tel: 01509 231450

Playing: Midweek: round £29.00; day £39.00. Weekend: round n/a; day n/a.

Facilities: Bar: 11am–11pm. Food: Lunch and dinner from 11.30am–8.45pm. Bar snacks.

Comments: Absolute blinder ... Trouble everywhere with granite outcrops, heather and tangly gorse ... Real test of man versus course ... Could not ask for more, especially at the bargain price ... A perfect golf experience.

Cosby Golf Club   ★

Chapel Lane, Broughton Road, Cosby, LE9 1RG
E-mail: secretary@cosby-golf-club.co.uk
Nearest main town: Leicester

Secretary:	Mr G. Kirkpatrick	Tel: 0116 286 4759
		Fax: 0116 286 4484
Professional:	Mr M. Wing	Tel: 0116 284 8275

Playing: Midweek: round £18.00; day £26.00. Weekend: round n/a; day n/a.

Facilities: Bar: 11am–11pm. Food: Bar snacks.

Comments: Friendly welcome and good value for visitors ... Narrow course but little trouble around the greens ... Best value golf in Leicestershire ... Parkland course with right attitude.

Greetham Valley Golf Club   ★★

Wood Lane, Greetham, Oakham, LE15 7NP
Website: www.gvgc.co.uk   E-mail: info@gvgc.co.uk
Nearest main town: Oakham

Secretary:	Mr F. Hinch	Tel: 01780 460004
		Fax: 01780 460623
Professional:	Mr J. Pengelly	Tel: 01780 460666
		Fax: 01780 460623

Playing: Midweek: round £32.00; day n/a. Weekend: round £36.00; day n/a.

Facilities: Bar: 11am–11pm. Food: Lunch from 12pm–4pm. Dinner by arrangement.

Comments: Mixture of good and bad holes ... Golf centre with good facilities ... Condition variable.

Kilworth Springs Golf Club

South Kilworth Road, North Kilworth, Lutterworth, LE17 6HJ
Nearest main town: Lutterworth

Secretary:	Mrs A. Vickers	Tel: 01858 575082
		Fax: 01858 575078
Professional:	Mr N. Melvin	Tel: 01858 575082

Playing: Midweek: round £17.00; day £30.00. Weekend: round £21.00; day £30.00.

Facilities: Bar: 7.30am–10pm. Food: Breakfast, lunch and dinner from 7.30am–8pm. Bar snacks.

Comments: Always open for play ... Two contrasting nines ... Fair course but low down the pecking order in the county rankings.

Market Harborough Golf Club   ★★

Great Oxendon Road, Market Harborough, LE16 8NB
Nearest main town: Market Harborough

Secretary: Mr A. Price-Jones   Tel: 01858 463684
                                       Fax: 01858 432906
Professional: Mr F. Baxter   Tel: 01858 463684
                                       Fax: 01858 432906

Playing: Midweek: round £25.00 (18 holes); day n/a. Weekend: round n/a; day n/a.

Facilities: Bar: 11am–11pm. Food: Lunch and dinner from 11am–9pm. Bar snacks.

Comments: Not in the same league as others in the county ... Club with welcoming attitude ... Best holes towards the end ... Average greens and condition ... Numerous lakes and streams.

Park Hill Golf Club   ★

Seagrave, Loughborough, LE12 7NG
Website: www.parkhillgolf.co.uk   E-mail: mail@parkhillgolf.co.uk
Nearest main town: Leicester

Secretary: Mr J. Hutson   Tel: 01509 815454
                                    Fax: 01509 816062
Professional: Mr M. Ulyett   Tel: 01509 815775

Playing: Midweek: round £22.00; day n/a. Weekend: round £26.00; day n/a.

Facilities: Bar: 11am–11pm. Food: Bar snacks.

Comments: Course getting better all the time ... Views over Charnwood Forest ... Unusual finish with two par-5s ... Over 7000 yards of parkland golf.

Ullesthorpe Court Hotel & Golf Club   ★★

Frolesworth Road, Ullesthorpe, LE17 5BZ
Website: www.ullesthorpecourt.co.uk
E-mail: bookings@ullesthorpecourt.co.uk
Nearest main town: Lutterworth

Secretary:	Mr G. Woolley	Tel: 01455 209023
		Fax: 01455 202537
Professional:	Mr D. Bowring	Tel: 01455 209150
		Fax: 01455 202537

Playing: Midweek: round prices on application; day n/a. Weekend: round n/a; day n/a.

Facilities: Bar: 11am–11pm. Food: Breakfast, lunch and dinner from 7am–10pm.

Comments: Tricky course but they are forgiven because of the best BLT in golf ... Parkland course set around 17th-century manor house ... A lovely place to spend three or four days golfing.

Western Park Golf Club   ★★

Scudamore Road, Leicester, LE3 1UQ
Nearest main town: Leicester

Secretary:	Mr I. Nicholson	Tel: 0116 287 2339
		Fax: 0116 287 2339
Professional:	Mr D. Butler	Tel: 0116 287 2339

Playing: Midweek: round £8.75; day n/a. Weekend: round £10.25; day n/a.

Facilities: Bar: 11am–11pm. Food: Lunch and dinner from 11am–10pm. Bar snacks.

Comments: Quite simple parkland course ... Small club with decent facilities ... Nothing striking ... Fair upkeep ... Not one to go out of your way for.

Lincolnshire

Woodhall Spa Golf Club (Hotchkin) ★★★★★

Woodhall Spa, LN10 0DD
Website: www.englishgolfunion.org
E-mail: bookings@englishgolfunion.org
Nearest main town: Woodhall Spa

Golf has some quite famous bridges – the Swilcan Bridge at St Andrews and the Hogan Bridge at Augusta to name but two – but there are few that I would look forward to crossing more than the Kirkstead Bridge on the B1191, just to the west of Woodhall Spa. The bridge itself is nothing to look at. Indeed, it is almost ramshackle in appearance, but those who have used it to visit the little town on whose border it lies will be familiar with the tingle of excitement and anticipation that dances up the spine.

Woodhall Spa is an oasis in an otherwise bland landscape and amid the riches of heather and gorse is the golf course. It vies with Sunningdale and Ganton as the best inland course in the British Isles.

To try and say something new about the Hotchkin course would be an almost impossible task. To the best of my knowledge it has no detractors and the list of admirers seems endless. Henry Cotton chose the 8th as his favourite; Henry Longhurst was a fan of the three short holes, of which the 12th has been voted the best 12th in the world. Perhaps now you begin to get the picture. As I walked off, having been coaxed, cajoled and truly smitten by its charms, I declared that the back nine was the most enjoyable homeward stretch I could ever remember playing. If you like the tree-lined style of Sunningdale then you might be apt to agree, but if the more open, heather-clad nature of Walton Heath is your cup of tea then the front nine might have the edge.

Lastly, you cannot talk about the Woodhall Spa experience without mentioning the bunkers. I don't care where you have played, you will not have come across traps that are as huge and as deep. These are not bunkers, they are quarries, and to that end, my sand save from the left of the 12th will forever remain in my golfing memory.

Secretary:	Mr R. Latham	Tel: 01526 352511
	(Director of Golf)	Fax: 01526 352778
Professional:	Mr C. Elliot	Tel: 01526 353229
Playing:	Midweek: round £55.00; day £95.00. Weekend: round £55.00; day £95.00.	

Facilities: Bar: 11am–11pm. Food: Lunch from 10am–6pm. Bar snacks.

Comments: Very fair course and well worth the journey … Very hard and demanding … You really want to play here – then go round again … Exceptional value with an EGU discount … Tremendous condition and facilities thanks to EGU – sensational now … Very challenging with good bunkering … Very high standard club without airs and graces … Wish it was easier to get there … UK's finest inland course.

Belton Park Golf Club   ★★

Londonthorpe Road, Grantham, NG31 9SH
Website: www.beltonpark.co.uk   E-mail: greatgolf@beltonpark.co.uk
Nearest main town: Grantham

Secretary: Mr T. Ireland   Tel: 01476 567399
                                             Fax: 01476 592078
Professional: Mr B. McKee   Tel: 01476 563911
                                             Fax: 01476 592078

Playing: Midweek: round £30.00; day £36.00. Weekend: round £36.00; day £42.00.

Facilities: Bar: 11am–11pm. Food: Lunch and dinner from 11am–9pm.

Comments: Well-established, difficult-to-master course … Three loops of nine at this undulating parkland venue … Progressive club, well worth the visit … Mature parkland course.

De Vere Belton Woods Hotel & Golf Club (Lakes)   ★★★

Belton, Grantham, NG32 2LN
Website: www.devereonline.com
E-mail: rina.ozolins@devere-hotels.com
Nearest main town: Grantham

Secretary: Mr C. Stevens   Tel: 01476 593200
                                             Fax: 01476 514399
Professional: Mr S. Sayers   Tel: 01476 514332
                                             Fax: 01476 514399

Playing: Midweek: round £35.00 (Lakes), £30.00 (Woodside); day n/a. Weekend: round £45.00 (Lakes), £40.00 (Woodside); day n/a.

Facilities: Bar: 11am–11pm. Food: Breakfast, lunch and dinner from 7am–10pm. Bar snacks.

Comments: Testing course in spacious surroundings ... Course okay but condition subject to weather ... Spike bar is excellent although food and drink is a little overpriced ... Needs to mature ... Two 18-hole courses and knockout practice facilities ... Very user-friendly club ... Woodside course has third longest hole in Europe – a whopping 613 yards.

Boston Golf Club   ★

Cowbridge, Horncastle Road, Boston, PE22 7EL
Nearest main town: Boston

Secretary: Mr D. Smith   Tel: 01205 350589
                                    Fax: 01205 350589
Professional: Mr T. Squires   Tel: 01205 362306

Playing: Midweek: round £18.00; day £24.00. Weekend: round £24.00; day £30.00.

Facilities: Bar: 11am–11pm. Food: Lunch from 12pm–2.30pm. Dinner from 7pm–9pm.

Comments: Plenty of watery graves ... Unimaginative ... Always a great welcome ... Very welcoming ... Course not great but plenty of fun to be had.

Carholme Golf Club

Carholme Road, Lincoln, LN1 1SE
Website: www.carholme-golf-club.co.uk
E-mail: info@carholme-golf-club.co.uk
Nearest main town: Lincoln

Secretary: Mr J. Lammin   Tel: 01522 523725
                                    Fax: 01522 533733
Professional: Mr M. Ross   Tel: 01522 536811

Playing: Midweek: round £10.00 (summer), £9.00 (winter); day n/a. Weekend: round £10.00 (after 2.30pm summer), £9.00 (after 12.30pm winter); day n/a.

Facilities: Bar: 11am–11pm. Food: Lunch from 12pm–2pm. Dinner from 6pm–9pm.

Comments: Adequate condition ... Played better for the money ... Fairly dour parkland course.

Forest Pines Hotel, Golf Course & Spa   ★★★★

Ermine Street, Broughton, Brigg, DN20 0AQ
Website: www.forestpines.co.uk   E-mail: enquiries@forestpines.co.uk
Nearest main town: Scunthorpe

Secretary:	Mr D. Edwards	Tel: 01652 650756
	(Director of Golf)	Fax: 01652 650495
Professional:	Mr D. Edwards	Tel: 01652 650756
		Fax: 01652 650495

Playing: Midweek: round £35.00 (18 holes), £45.00 (27/36 holes); day n/a. Weekend: round £35.00 (18 holes), £45.00 (27/36 holes); day n/a.

Facilities: Bar: 11am–11pm. Food: Bar snacks.

Comments: Swarming with visitors from Yorkshire ... Good course with friendly welcome ... Extremely good greens and fairways ... Great facilities ... Course very well laid out ... New, emerging course that deserves its plaudits ... It really is good ... Attractive course undoubtedly going the right way ... Parkland/heathland mix of subtle, intriguing holes ... One for the notebook if you're in the area.

Gainsborough Golf Club (Karsten)   ★★★★

Thonock, Gainsborough, DN21 1PZ
E-mail: liz@gainsboroughgc.co.uk
Nearest main town: Gainsborough

Secretary:	Mr D. Bowers	Tel: 01427 613088
		Fax: 01427 810172
Professional:	Mr S. Cooper	

Playing: Midweek: round £25.00; day £35.00. Weekend: round n/a; day n/a.

Facilities: Bar: Members only. Food: Lunch from 12pm–2.30pm.

Comments: Loads of water and trees – very interesting ... One of the best clubhouses in the country ... Club owned by Ping ... Off the back tees this is a monster ... Facilities first class ... Not for the faint hearted.

Gainsborough Golf Club (Thonock)   ★

Thonock, Gainsborough, DN21 1PZ
Email: liz@gainsboroughgc.co.uk
Nearest main town: Gainsborough

Secretary: Mr D. Bowers   Tel: 01427 613088
                                   Fax: 01427 810172

Professional: Mr S. Cooper

Playing: Midweek: round £18.00; day £35.00. Weekend: round n/a; day n/a.

Facilities: Bar: Members only. Food: Lunch from 12pm–2.30pm.

Comments: Less of a challenge than Karsten Lakes ... Shorter than the Lakes and far less impressive ... Not as good as the Lakes but facilities still the best around.

Luffenham Heath Golf Club   ★★★★

Ketton, Stamford, PE9 3UU
Website: www.luffenhamheath.co.uk
E-mail: jingleby@theluffenhamheathgc.co.uk
Nearest main town: Stamford

Secretary: Mr J. Ingleby   Tel: 01780 720205
                                   Fax: 01780 722146

Professional: Mr I. Burnett   Tel: 01780 720298
                                   Fax: 01780 720298

Playing: Midweek: round £40.00; day £50.00. Weekend: round £40.00; day £50.00.

Facilities: Bar: 11am–11pm. Food: Lunch and dinner from 11am–9pm. Bar snacks.

Comments: Very enchanting ... Gripping stuff ... In good condition ... No manicuring here, just fine golf in scenic surroundings ... One of the county's best.

North Shore Hotel Golf Club   ★★★

North Shore Road, Skegness, PE25 1DN
Nearest main town: Skegness

Secretary: Mr B. Howard   Tel: 01754 763298
                                   Fax: 01754 761902

Professional: Mr J. Cornelius   Tel: 01754 764822

Playing: Midweek: round £19.00; day £29.00. Weekend: round £29.00; day £39.00.

Facilities: Bar: 11am–11pm. Food: Lunch from 12pm–2.30pm. Bar snacks. Dinner from 6pm–9.30pm.

Comments: Wonderful combination of links and parkland ... Rip-roaring value on reasonable course with sea views ... Most welcoming ... First class in nearly all respects ... James Braid bruiser – well worth the drive ... Not heard of it, but can't get it out my head now ... Links/parkland hybrid – and pulls it off ... Unfashionable course but we don't mind.

Seacroft Golf Club   ★★★★

Drummond Road, Skegness, PE25 3AU
Website: www.seacroft-golfclub.co.uk
E-mail: enquiries@seacroft-golfclub.co.uk
Nearest main town: Skegness

Secretary: Mr R. England   Tel: 01754 763020
                                       Fax: 01754 763020
Professional: Mr R. Lawie   Tel: 01754 769624
                                       Fax: 01754 763020

Playing: Midweek: round £32.50; day £42.50. Weekend: round £37.50; day £47.50.

Facilities: Bar: 11am–11pm. Food: Lunch and dinner from 10am–9pm. Bar snacks.

Comments: Very good links – deserves a major! ... Flat links, nothing to get excited about ... Nothing brash about this club, just good, honest golf ... Reading the subtle undulations is the key to good scoring.

South Kyme Golf Club   ★★

Skinners Lane, South Kyme, Lincoln, LN4 4AT
Website: www.skgc.co.uk   E-mail: southkymegc@hotmail.com
Nearest main town: Lincoln

Secretary: Mr P. Chamberlain   Tel: 01526 861113
                  (Director of Golf)   Fax: 01526 861080
Professional: Mr P. Chamberlain   Tel: 01526 861113
                                       Fax: 01526 861080

Playing: Midweek: round £20.00; day n/a. Weekend: round £24.00; day n/a.

Facilities: Bar: 11am–11pm (weekends only). Food: Bar snacks.

Comments: Course is exceptional value ... Hospitality second to none ... Course is difficult due to the wind ... Improving ... Food very cheap and good value ... Unheralded course which does everything the right way ... Don't shout too loud about this one – it's our secret ... Fenland course.

Spalding Golf Club   ★★

Surfleet, Spalding, PE11 4EA
Nearest main town: Spalding

Secretary: Mr B. Walker   Tel: 01775 680386
                                      Fax: 01775 680988
Professional: Mr J. Spencer   Tel: 01775 680474
                                      Fax: 01775 680474

Playing: Midweek: round £25.00 (societies £20.00); day £30.00 (societies £25.00). Weekend: round £30.00; day n/a.

Facilities: Bar: 11am–11pm. Food: Lunch from 11am–2pm. Dinner from 5pm–9pm. Closed on Tuesdays.

Comments: All sorts of rivers, lakes and ponds here ... Fairly one-dimensional course but good value ... Bundles of fun ... Very long and very stern.

Woodhall Spa Golf Club (Bracken)   ★★★

Woodhall Spa, LN10 6PU
Website: www.englishgolfunion.org
E-mail: bookings@englishgolfunion.org
Nearest main town: Woodhall Spa

Secretary: Mr R. Latham   Tel: 01526 352511
                   (Director of Golf) Fax: 01526 352778
Professional: Mr C. Elliot   Tel: 01526 353229

Playing: Midweek: round £40.00; day £65.00. Weekend: round £40.00; day £65.00.

Facilities: Bar: 11am–11pm. Food: Lunch and dinner from 10am–6pm. Bar snacks.

Comments: Only two memorable holes on what could have been a great course ... Very good when a bit more mature.

Merseyside

Royal Birkdale Golf Club ★★★★★

Waterloo Road, Birkdale, Southport, PR8 2LX
Nearest main town: Southport

In 1998 Royal Birkdale was voted the No.1 course in the British Isles by *Golf World*. For an Open Championship venue, it could be considered a fairly unremarkable achievement. But if you consider that some years before the world's top players were slating Birkdale for the quality of its greens, suddenly it becomes quite a feat.

Birkdale has always been regarded as a pure example of links golf, but now it is even better. Massive improvements were made prior to the 1998 Open that have given the course some solid foundations for the future.

Seven years ago the club decided to take serious action in the battle against meadow grass, thatching and compaction on the greens that caused uproar at the Open. They removed the surfaces, replaced the subsoil with one that encouraged a deeper root base and then replaced the turf. Greens were overseeded with fescue grass and some of them were recontoured. The result: greens that are regarded as some of the best ever for an Open Championship.

Birkdale is very tough to master. From the 1st it demands the very best of all who play here. Your game must be plotted from tee to green, and as you would expect the wind plays a major part in how you score, particularly as the dunes which follow the fairways protect the player from it – you'll find that distances are very difficult to judge here.

Holes to watch out for are the 6th, a dogleg right to a green protected in the sandhills, the 12th, one of the finest par-3s in the country, and the 17th, a par-5 where the drive must be threaded through a gap in the sandhills.

It's a tough start and tough finish with not too many forgiving holes in between. Cherish the moment when you stand on the 18th tee – this is a wonderful vista after what should be a memorable round. If you get time, take tea in the clubhouse and you can sit down by the massive windows and look out on the 18th green and this wonderful, evocative place to play golf.

Secretary: Mr M. Gilyeat   Tel: 01704 567920
Fax: 01704 562327
Professional: Mr R. Bradbeer   Tel: 01704 568857
Fax: 01704 562615

Playing: Midweek: round £98.00; day £125.00. Weekend: round £125.00; day n/a.

Facilities: Bar: 11am–11pm. Food: Breakfast, lunch and dinner from 8am–9pm. Bar snacks. Green fee price includes lunch.

Comments: Excellent, if a little expensive ... The best Merseyside course ... Best course in England, very hard to beat ... A cracking course with so much history ... Wonderful, the time of my life ... A previous No.1 rated course in the *Golf World* Top 100 – still one of the best courses in the country.

Caldy Golf Club   ★★

Links Hay Road, Caldy, Wirral, L48 1NB
Website: www.caldygolfclub.co.uk
E-mail: gail@caldygolfclub.fsnet.co.uk
Nearest main town: West Kirby

Secretary: Ms G. Copple   Tel: 0151 625 5660
                                       Fax: 0151 625 7394
Professional: Mr K. Jones   Tel: 0151 625 1818

Playing: Midweek: round £37.00; day £42.00. Weekend: round n/a; day n/a.

Facilities: Bar: 11am–11pm. Food: Lunch and dinner from 11am–5pm. Bar snacks.

Comments: A marvellous parkland test ... Very long and not without difficulty ... Always worth a game ... Never seen it in bad condition ... Surprises you when you least expect it ... Very tidy.

The Childwall Golf Club   ★★★

Naylor's Road, Gateacre, Liverpool, L27 2YB
Nearest main town: Liverpool

Secretary: Mr K. Jennions   Tel: 0151 487 0654
                                       Fax: 0151 487 0882
Professional: Mr N. Parr   Tel: 0151 487 9871

Playing: Midweek: round £26.00; day £26.00. Weekend: round £35.00; day £35.00.

Facilities: Bar: 11am–11pm. Food: Lunch from 12pm–2pm. Dinner from 6pm–9pm. Bar snacks.

Comments: Very good course with tree-lined fairways ... James Braid design ... Parkland pearl ... Accuracy the watchword ... For the price, it does not get much better.

Formby Golf Club ★★★★

Golf Road, Formby, L37 1LQ
Website: www.formbygolfclub.co.uk
E-mail: info@formbygolfclub.co.uk
Nearest main town: Liverpool

Secretary: Mr C. Barker   Tel: 01704 872164
                              Fax: 01704 833028
Professional: Mr G. Butler   Tel: 01704 873090
                                  Fax: 01704 833028

Playing: Midweek: round n/a; day £90.00. Weekend: round £95.00 (Sat after 3.30pm, Sun after 2.30pm); day n/a.

Facilities: Bar: 11am–11pm. Food: Lunch from 12pm–2.30pm.

Comments: Played the second round of my life here and never looked back ... Such a hard course ... Tough course ... Made welcome ... Well-drained course open all year ... Classic links, so much history between these sand dunes.

Grange Park Golf Club ★★★

Prescot Road, St Helens, WA10 3AD
E-mail: gpgc@ic24.net
Nearest main town: St Helens

Secretary: Mr C. Hadley   Tel: 01744 26318
                              Fax: 01744 26318
Professional: Mr P. Roberts   Tel: 01744 28785

Playing: Midweek: round £28.00; day £36.00. Weekend: round £36.00; day n/a.

Facilities: Bar: 11am–11pm. Food: Breakfast and lunch from 10.30am–6pm. Bar snacks.

Comments: Excellent greens ... Great course in bleak surroundings ... Class course with long par-3s – clue is they're all in the same direction.

Haydock Park Golf Club ★★

Golborne Park, Newton Lane, Newton-le-Willows, WA12 0HX
E-mail: haydockparkgc@onetel.net.uk
Nearest main town: Liverpool

Secretary:	Mrs V. Wiseman	Tel: 01925 228525
		Fax: 01925 224984
Professional:	Mr P. Kenwright	Tel: 01925 226944
		Fax: 01925 226944

Playing: Midweek: round £30.00; day n/a. Weekend: round n/a; day n/a.

Facilities: Bar: 11am–11pm. Food: Bar snacks.

Comments: Made welcome by members ... Close to racecourse ... Undulating parkland ... Cheap, value course with interesting members ... Generally in good condition.

Hesketh Golf Club ★★★★

Cockle Dicks Lane, Southport, PR9 9QQ
Website: www.ukgolfer.org/clubs/hesketh
E-mail: hesketh@ukgolfer.org
Nearest main town: Merseyside

Secretary:	Mr M. Senior	Tel: 01704 536897
		Fax: 01704 539250
Professional:	Mr J. Donoghue	Tel: 01704 530050
		Fax: 01704 539250

Playing: Midweek: round £50.00; day £60.00. Weekend: round £60.00; day n/a.

Facilities: Bar: 11am–11pm. Food: Lunch and dinner from 11am–9pm, except Mondays.

Comments: Pretty, links-type course ... Behind Hillside and Birkdale in Southport ... Superb clubhouse ... Historic club.

Heswall Golf Club

Cottage Lane, Gayton, Chester, Wirral, L60 8PB
Nearest main town: Chester

Secretary:	Mr R. Butler	Tel: 0151 342 1237
		Fax: 0151 342 1237

Professional: Mr A. Thompson   Tel: 0151 342 7431
                                       Fax: 0151 342 7431

Playing: Midweek: round £35.00; day £35.00. Weekend: round
                  £40.00; day £40.00.

Facilities: Bar: 11am–11pm. Food: Lunch and dinner from
                  11am–6pm.

Comments: 'Mary, call the cattle home across the sands of Dee' ...
                  Idyllic setting on salt marshes and site of first RAF para-
                  chute jump ... Overlooks the River Dee with views into
                  Wales ... Spectacular setting for a course where you
                  need plenty of guile.

Hillside Golf Club   ★★★★

Hastings Road, Hillside, Southport, PR8 2LU
Nearest main town: Southport

Secretary: Mr J. Graham   Tel: 01704 567169
                                      Fax: 01704 563192
Professional: Mr B. Seddon   Tel: 01704 568360

Playing: Midweek: round £40.00; day £50.00. Weekend: round
                  £50.00; day n/a.

Facilities: Bar: 11am–11pm. Food: Breakfast, lunch and dinner
                  from 7am–9pm.

Comments: Absolutely gorgeous ... Very memorable ... Best back
                  nine in England ... The best course that I have played
                  anywhere in the world ... Nice variety of holes ... Not to
                  be underrated alongside its illustrious neighbour
                  (Birkdale) ... Beautifully manicured fairways and greens
                  – a test of any player ... Lovely clubhouse and pro shop
                  ... Wonderful greens ... A natural beauty ... Greens like
                  silk.

Hoylake Municipal Golf Club   ★★

Carr Lane, Hoylake, L47 4BQ
Nearest main town: Birkenhead

Secretary: Mr A. Peacock   Tel: 0151 632 2956
Professional: Mr S. Hooton

Playing: Midweek: round £7.00; day n/a. Weekend: round
                  £7.00; day n/a.

Facilities: Bar: Club meetings only. Food: Breakfast and lunch from 9am–4pm.

Comments: Great course for a muni ... Windy links-type course ... Good value, knocks spots off municipals in the South ... Cheap, fun, value golf.

Royal Liverpool Golf Club   ★★★★★

Meols Drive, Hoylake, CH47 4AL
Website: www.royal-liverpool-golf.com
E-mail: sec@royal-liverpool-golf.com
Nearest main town: Liverpool

Secretary: Gp Capt C. Moore CBE   Tel: 0151 632 3101
                                                 Fax: 0151 632 6737
Professional: Mr J. Heggarty   Tel: 0151 632 5868

Playing: Midweek: round £100.00; day £130.00 (inc. lunch). Weekend: round £130.00 (limited availability); day n/a.

Facilities: Bar: 11am–9pm. Food: Lunch from 12pm–2.30pm.

Comments: Flat, uninteresting with no definition ... Didn't like the internal out-of-bounds ... Well presented and they let us use the medal tees – nice touch ... Quite simply the best greens I have ever seen ... Links legend.

Southport & Ainsdale Golf Club   ★★★★

Bradshaws Lane, Ainsdale, Southport, PR8 3LG
Website: www.sandagolfclub.co.uk
E-mail: secretary@sandagolfclub.co.uk
Nearest main town: Southport

Secretary: Ms C. Birrell   Tel: 01704 578000
                                                 Fax: 01704 570896
Professional: Mr J. Payne   Tel: 01704 578000
                                                 Fax: 01704 576298

Playing: Midweek: round £60.00; day £75.00. Weekend: round £75.00; day n/a.

Facilities: Bar: 11am–11pm. Food: Lunch by arrangement.

Comments: Very good test with tricky greens ... Unusual par-3 start ... Historic course ... Where golf should be played.

Southport Old Links Golf Club ★★★

Moss Lane, Southport, PR9 7QS
Nearest main town: Churchtown

Secretary:	Mr B. Kenyon	Tel: 01704 228207
Professional:	None	

Playing: Midweek: round £18.50; day £25.50. Weekend: round £25.50; day n/a.

Facilities: Bar: 11am–11pm. Food: Lunch from 11am–4pm, except Mondays.

Comments: Nine holes, two sets of tees – really nice course ... As tough as they come for a nine-hole ... One of the most respected clubs in Southport ... A brilliant, brilliant experience.

Wallasey Golf Club ★★★★

Bayswater Road, Wallasey, CH45 8LA
Website: www.wallaseygolfclub.com   E-mail: wallaseygc@aol.com
Nearest main town: New Brighton

Secretary:	Mr J. Barraclough	Tel: 0151 691 1024
		Fax: 0151 638 8988
Professional:	Mr M. Adams	Tel: 0151 691 1024

Playing: Midweek: round £50.00 (18 holes), £60.00 (18+ holes); day n/a. Weekend: round £65.00 (18 holes), £75.00 (18+ holes); day n/a.

Facilities: Bar: 11am–11pm. Food: Bar snacks from 10am–6pm.

Comments: Condition of course top class ... Pro shop high standard ... Gorgeous ... Very native course yet beautiful ... Quite exceptional ... So much trouble off the tee ... Fairly unknown ... Next to Hoylake so combine the two.

West Derby Golf Club ★★★★

Yew Tree Lane, Liverpool, L12 9HQ
Website: www.ukgolfer.org
E-mail: pmilne@westderbygc.freeserve.co.uk
Nearest main town: Liverpool

Secretary:	Mr A. Milne	Tel: 0151 254 1034
		Fax: 0151 259 0505

Professional: Mr A. Witherup   Tel: 0151 220 5478
                                       Fax: 0151 259 0505

Playing: Midweek: round £28.50; day n/a. Weekend: round £37.00; day n/a.

Facilities: Bar: 11am–11pm. Food: Lunch from 11.30am–2.30pm. Dinner by arrangement.

Comments: Tempting mixture of parkland and woodland ... Condition top notch ... Very underrated ... Great clubhouse ... Nothing but praise for this course ... Shortish but enjoyable ... Front nine widely regarded as better.

The West Lancashire Golf Club   ★★★★

Hall Road West, Liverpool, L23 8SZ
Website: www.westlancashiregolf.co.uk
E-mail: golf@westlancashiregolf.co.uk
Nearest main town: Liverpool

Secretary: Mr S. King   Tel: 0151 924 1076
                                       Fax: 0151 931 4448
Professional: Mr G. Edge   Tel: 0151 924 5662

Playing: Midweek: round £60.00; day £75.00. Weekend: round £80.00; day £95.00.

Facilities: Bar: 11am–11pm. Food: Lunch from 11am–4pm. Dinner by arrangement.

Comments: Good welcome, good food ... Fair golf course, well maintained ... A cracker, and open most of the year ... For all your golfing delights.

Middlesex

Mill Hill Golf Club   ★★★

100 Barnet Way, Mill Hill, London, NW7 3AL
Website: www.millhillgolfclub.co.uk
E-mail: dcromie.millhillgc@virgin.net
Nearest main town: London

Dashing across a dual carriageway in your spikes may not be the greatest preparation for a round of golf, but at Mill Hill it works. That could be because the opening hole there is a bit of a bruiser and should not be played while still either half asleep or groggy from a long drive. Dicing with traffic prepares you mentally for this long par-4 that gently doglegs to the left and always seems to play longer than its yardage. Indeed, in winter it can take two lusty blows to get up.

Founded in 1925, the place has a comforting maturity and an expertise in design that was probably instilled by the great Harry Colt, who had a hand in its development. The course is not all that long, but with a par of 69, it can be quite a tough challenge.

After that stern start, the 2nd is a par-3 over water which might be hazardous for some, but really shouldn't cause too many problems with only a very short iron. The 3rd is perhaps the weakest hole on the course, but once it has been negotiated the rest are all of genuine quality. The par-4s are the main strengths, with three holes on the back nine, the 12th, 15th and 17th, being the pick of the bunch.

Mill Hill, like most courses in the North London area, can get a little boggy in the winter, but in the right conditions it is definitely worth a visit.

Secretary:	Mr D. Cromie	Tel: 020 8959 2889
		Fax: 020 8959 0731
Professional:	Mr D. Beal	
Playing:	Midweek: round £25.00; day n/a. Weekend: round £30.00; day n/a.	
Facilities:	Bar: 11am–11.30pm. Food: Lunch and dinner served. Bar snacks.	
Comments:	A mature, tree-lined course so watch out for the timber … The course is next to the busy A1 but you'd barely know it … There's some difficult par-3s requiring accurate tee shots … A good mix of long and short holes.	

Fulwell Golf Club   ★★★

Wellington Road, Hampton Hill, TW12 1JY
Nearest main town: Fulwell

Secretary: Mr P. Butcher   Tel: 020 8977 2733
                                          Fax: 020 8977 7732
Professional: Mr N. Turner   Tel: 020 8977 3844

Playing: Midweek: round £30.00; day n/a. Weekend: round
                  £35.00; day n/a.

Facilities: Bar: Members only. Food: Members only.

Comments: Nicely kept course ... Long but not too taxing ... Stylish
                  and a fair price ... Too long for some at over 6500 yards
                  ... Worth paying a visit.

North Middlesex Golf Club   ★★

The Manor House, Friern Barnet Lane, Whetstone, N20 0NL
Website: www.northmiddlesexgc.co.uk
E-mail: manager@northmiddlesexgc.co.uk
Nearest main town: London

Secretary: Miss A. McDonald   Tel: 020 8445 1604
                                          Fax: 020 8445 5023
Professional: Mr F. George   Tel: 020 8445 3060
                                          Fax: 020 8445 5023

Playing: Midweek: round £25.00 (summer), £20.00 (winter); day
                  n/a. Weekend: round £30.00 (summer), £25.00
                  (winter); day n/a.

Facilities: Bar: 11am–11pm. Food: Bar snacks.

Comments: Neat and tidy parkland ... Great par-3 finish towards
                  clubhouse ... Good condition ... Great greens.

The Northwood Golf Club   ★

Rickmansworth Road, Northwood, HA6 2QW
Website: www.northwoodgolf.co.uk
E-mail: secretary@northwoodgolf.co.uk
Nearest main town: Rickmansworth

Secretary: Mr T. Collingwood   Tel: 01923 821384
                                          Fax: 01923 840150
Professional: Mr C. Holdsworth   Tel: 01923 820112

Playing: Midweek: round £36.00; day n/a. Weekend: round n/a; day n/a.

Facilities: Bar: 11am–11pm. Food: Lunch from 10am–6pm. Bar snacks.

Comments: Traditional club ... Fairly flat ... Course in good order ... A little unfriendly ... Better to be had near London.

Stockley Park Golf Club   ★★★

The Clubhouse, Stockley Park, Uxbridge, UB11 1AQ
Website: www.stockleyparkgolf.com
Nearest main town: Uxbridge

Secretary: Mr N. Munro   Tel: 020 8813 5700
                                        Fax: 020 8813 5655
Professional: Mr A. Knox   Tel: 020 8813 5700

Playing: Midweek: round £24.00; day n/a. Weekend: round £34.00; day n/a.

Facilities: Bar: 11am–11pm. Food: Breakfast, lunch and dinner from 7.30am–9pm.

Comments: Planes rather distracting ... Set right by Heathrow ... A new course with much character ... A little hilly for my liking.

Norfolk

Hunstanton Golf Club ★★★★★

Golf Course Road, Old Hunstanton, PE36 6JQ
E-mail: hunstanton.golf@eidosnet.co.uk
Nearest main town: Hunstanton

For years, Hunstanton was known primarily for the quality of its greens. It was as if the smoothness and hard-to-read borrows of its putting surfaces overshadowed everything that went before them. The wild grasses, the camber fairways, the scratchy bushes speckling the course and, most importantly, the timeless course designs were eclipsed by the fact that balls on Hunstanton greens held their line better than any other in the country.

This traditional club still prides itself on its greens, but there is much more to discover. Hunstanton is located just a short drive from the holiday town at the western end of a magnificent stretch of golf courses including Royal West Norfolk, Sheringham and Royal Cromer. There are those that prefer the incredibly natural setting of Royal West Norfolk, but the majority of golfers in the area plump for Hunstanton, a traditional out-and-back links with no end of difficulties for the average player.

Once you've got over a 1st tee shot in front of the clubhouse over dunes, for the first three holes there is nothing to suggest this is a special golf course. But from the 4th onwards, every hole presents an individual challenge. It is not only from the dunes, which in the context of links golf are merely dressing, pinstripe fairways and an extremely penal design. There are angled greens, blind par-3s and drives to angled fairways, contriving to create a very knotty problem. You also need to watch the holidaymakers crossing the fairway at the 10th on their way to the beach.

In the pecking order of golf courses in Britain and Ireland, Hunstanton is not ranked in the top league, but do not let that put you off. This is an exhilarating adventure and one you won't forget.

Secretary:	Mr D. Thomson	Tel: 01485 532811
		Fax: 01485 532319
Professional:	Mr J. Dodds	Tel: 01485 532751
Playing:	Midweek: round n/a; day £60.00. Weekend: round n/a; day £70.00.	
Facilities:	Bar: 11am–11pm. Food: Lunch from 11.30am–2.30pm. Bar snacks. Dinner by arrangement.	

Comments: Magnificent greens – large and receptive ... Very under-rated, so do go ... Absolutely top-class links with superb greens and beautiful scenery.

Barnham Broom Hotel Golf Club (Valley) ★

Honingham, Barnham Broom, Norwich, NR9 4DD
Website: www.barnham-broom.co.uk
E-mail: enquiry@barnhambroomhotel.co.uk
Nearest main town: Norwich

Secretary:	Mr R. Brooks	Tel: 01603 759393
		Fax: 01603 758224
Professional:	Mr P. Ballingall	Tel: 01603 759552

Playing: Midweek: round £30.00; day n/a. Weekend: round £40.00; day n/a.

Facilities: Bar: 11am–11pm. Food: Breakfast, lunch and dinner from 7am–9pm.

Comments: Overrated, featureless slug over average terrain ... Unfriendly pro shop and hotel ... Nothing better for a winter break ... Two quality courses and comfortable hotel.

Bawburgh Golf Club ★

Glen Lodge, Marlingford Road, Bawburgh, NR9 3LU
Website: www.bawburgh.com E-mail: info@bawburgh.com
Nearest main town: Norwich

Secretary:	Mr J. Barnard	Tel: 01603 740404
		Fax: 01603 740403
Professional:	Mr C. Potter	Tel: 01603 742323
		Fax: 01603 742323

Playing: Midweek: round £25.00; day n/a. Weekend: round £28.00; day n/a.

Facilities: Bar: 11am–11pm. Food: Lunch from 12pm–4pm.

Comments: Interesting course that will mature into a fine one ... Parkland/heathland mix ... Cheap at the price ... Not one to go out of your way for, but still good.

Eaton Golf Club ★★★

Newmarket Road, Norwich, NR4 6SF
E-mail: lizbovill@eatongolfclub.fsnet.co.uk
Nearest main town: Norwich

Secretary: Mrs L. Bovill   Tel: 01603 451686
                                    Fax: 01603 451686
Professional: Mr M. Allen   Tel: 01603 452478

Playing: Midweek: round £30.00; day £30.00. Weekend: round £40.00; day £40.00.

Facilities: Bar: 11am–11pm. Food: Lunch from 12pm–2.30pm. Dinner by arrangement.

Comments: Hidden gem, superb greens and interesting holes ... Small greens and heavy rough make this a toughie ... Affordable golf in nice surroundings.

Gorleston Golf Club ★★

Warren Road, Gorleston, NR31 6JT
Website: www.gorlestongolfclub.co.uk
E-mail: manager@gorlestongolfclub.co.uk
Nearest main town: Great Yarmouth

Secretary: Mr J. Woodhouse   Tel: 01493 661911
                                    Fax: 01493 661911
Professional: Mr N. Brown   Tel: 01493 662103

Playing: Midweek: round £25.00; day n/a. Weekend: round £30.00; day n/a.

Facilities: Bar: 11am–11pm. Food: Lunch and dinner from 11am–7pm. Bar snacks.

Comments: Presentation not up to scratch ... Holiday course ... Standard seaside course ... Better examples of seaside golf around.

Great Yarmouth & Caister Golf Club ★★★

Beach House, Caister-on-Sea, Great Yarmouth, NR30 5TD
Website: www.caistergolf.co.uk   E-mail: office@caistergolf.co.uk
Nearest main town: Great Yarmouth

Secretary: Mr R. Peck   Tel: 01493 728699
                                    Fax: 01493 728831

Professional: Mr M. Clarke   Tel: 01493 720421
Fax: 01493 728831

Playing: Midweek: round n/a; day £30.00. Weekend: round n/a; day £35.00.

Facilities: Bar: 11am–11pm. Food: Lunch from 12pm–2.30pm. Dinner from 6pm–9.30pm in summer (winter by arrangement).

Comments: Old club with colourful history ... Condition not what it once was ... Fine links ... A links to really get your teeth into ... Links with attitude.

King's Lynn Golf Club   ★★★

Castle Rising, King's Lynn, PE31 6BD
Website: www.club-noticeboard.co.uk   E-mail: klgc@eidosnet.co.uk
Nearest main town: King's Lynn

Secretary: Mr M. Sackree   Tel: 01553 631654
(General Manager)   Fax: 01553 631036
Professional: Mr J. Reynolds   Tel: 01553 631655
Fax: 01553 631036

Playing: Midweek: round n/a; day £40.00. Weekend: round n/a; day £50.00.

Facilities: Bar: 11am–11pm. Food: Lunch from 11.30am–2.30pm. Bar snacks. Dinner from 6pm–9pm Thursday, Friday and Saturday.

Comments: An absolute joy to play and a clubhouse to match ... If you go to Norfolk this is a must visit ... Surprisingly good ... A real pleasure ... In top condition on visit ... Set up in a US Open style with narrow fairways and heavy rough ... Has the feel of a top-class club.

The Norfolk Golf & Country Club   ★

Hingham Road, Reymerston, Norwich, NR9 4QQ
Nearest main town: Norwich

Secretary: Mr M. Aho   Tel: 01362 850297
Fax: 01362 850614
Professional: Mr T. Varney

Playing: Midweek: round £24.00; day n/a. Weekend: round £20.00; day n/a.

Facilities: Bar: 11am–11pm. Food: Breakfast, lunch and dinner from 9am–9pm. Bar snacks.

Comments: Soulless course created from farmland ... Flat and not very interesting ... Fairly good value ... Very open ... Nice condition – open all year.

Royal Cromer Golf Club   ★★★

145 Overstrand Road, Cromer, NR27 0JH
Website: www.royalcromergolfclub.com
E-mail: general.manager@royal-cromer.com
Nearest main town: Cromer

Secretary: Mrs D. Hopkins   Tel: 01263 512884
                                          Fax: 01263 512430
Professional: Mr L. Patterson   Tel: 01263 512267

Playing: Midweek: round n/a; day £37.00. Weekend: round n/a; day £50.00.

Facilities: Bar: 11am–11pm. Food: Lunch and dinner from 11am–7pm. Bar snacks.

Comments: Always a pleasure to play ... Very tough in the wind ... Can get very windy ... Set on a cliff edge, Cromer is an experience not to be missed ... Awaken your senses at Cromer.

Royal Norwich Golf Club   ★★★

Drayton High Road, Hellesdon, Norwich, NR6 5AH
Website: www.royalnorwichgolf.co.uk
E-mail: mail@royalnorwichgolf.co.uk
Nearest main town: Norwich

Secretary: Mr J. Meggy   Tel: 01603 429928
                    (Manager)   Fax: 01603 417945
Professional: Mr D. Futter   Tel: 01603 408459

Playing: Midweek: round £24.00 (single round after 2pm); day £38.00. Weekend: round £30.00 (single round after 3pm); day £46.00.

Facilities: Bar: 11am–10.30pm. Food: Lunch from 10am–6pm.

Comments: One of the weakest Royal courses around ... Mixed selection of holes ... Parkland course ... Get tangled in the gorse ... Blasted gorse can make things tough here.

Royal West Norfolk Golf Club ★★★★★

Beach Road, Brancaster, PE31 8AX
E-mail: rwngc@btinternet.com
Nearest main town: Hunstanton

Secretary:	Maj N. Carrington-Smith	Tel: 01485 210087
		Fax: 01485 210087
Professional:	Mr S. Raynes	Tel: 01485 210616

Playing: Midweek: round n/a; day £65.00. Weekend: round n/a; day £75.00.

Facilities: Bar: 11am–11pm. Food: Lunch and dinner from 11am–7pm.

Comments: Great course and history, but not keen on visitors ... Old-fashioned links where the sea has an influence ... Stepping back in time 100 years to this traditional, rugged links ... Epitome of traditional links golf ... Nothing to match it.

Sheringham Golf Club ★★★

Weybourne Road, Sheringham, NR26 8HG
Website: www.sheringhamgolfclub.co.uk
E-mail: sgc.sec@care4free.net
Nearest main town: Sheringham

Secretary:	Mr P. Mounfield	Tel: 01263 823488
		Fax: 01263 826129
Professional:	Mr M. Jubb	Tel: 01263 822980

Playing: Midweek: round n/a; day £45.00 (Sunday to Friday). Weekend: round n/a; day £60.00 (Saturday).

Facilities: Bar: 9am–11pm. Food: Bar snacks.

Comments: Go there for the views ... Watch out for the walkers, especially if you slice ... Don't forget this course when you are in Norfolk ... Pretty course, but don't be lulled into thinking it's easy.

Thetford Golf Club ★★★

Brandon Road, Thetford, IP24 3NE
Nearest main town: Thetford

Secretary:	Mrs S. Redpath	Tel: 01842 752169
Professional:	Mr G. Kitley	Fax: 01842 766212
		Tel: 01842 752662
		Fax: 01842 752662

Playing: Midweek: round £34.00; day n/a. Weekend: round £34.00; day n/a.

Facilities: Bar: 11am–8pm. Food: Lunch from 12pm–2.30pm.

Comments: Superb setting and condition throughout ... Not the best practice facilities ... Touched by many hands of greatness ... Unusual course with intimidating reputation.

Wensum Valley Golf Club (Valley)   ★★

Beech Avenue, Taverham, NR8 6HP
E-mail: enqs@wensum.valley.co.uk
Nearest main town: Norwich

Secretary:	Mrs B. Hall	Tel: 01603 261012
Professional:	Mr P. Whittle	Fax: 01603 261664
		Tel: 01603 261012

Playing: Midweek: round £18.00; day £18.00. Weekend: round £18.00; day £18.00.

Facilities: Bar: 11am–11pm. Food: Lunch and dinner from 11am–9pm. Bar snacks.

Comments: Good scoring ... Golf centre for all abilities ... Nice condition ... Course not up to much ... Built on the side of a valley ... Friendly club ... Course can get boggy in winter.

Northamptonshire

Northamptonshire County Golf Club ★★★★

Golf Lane, Church Brampton, Northampton, NN6 8AZ
Nearest main town: Northampton

Northamptonshire County has hosted county events for many years and such is its quality that it is now an Open Championship regional qualifying course. The condition of the course is always top class, and with the addition of a special fairway watering system, it is now even better.

Located just 4 miles outside Northampton itself, tucked away in the quiet village of Church Brampton, the course is heathland, sculpted by the hand of Harry Colt. The master designer had fine raw materials with which to fashion the course, an advantageous mixture of peat/sand base for the fairways and undulating positions on which to place the greens.

The members will tell you it is very easy to run up a big score on some of the holes here. But, in truth, it is not a particularly difficult heathland course, the gorse that lines the fairways is not as tough as some of the Surrey courses and the sturdy fir trees rarely block your sight of the fairways and greens. All the hazards here are laid out clearly before you and are completely natural – a stream comes into play for some on the 9th and 15th.

Rather than easing the golfer into the round, Northamptonshire County starts fiercely with a 450-yard par-4, followed by a par-5 of 520 yards. For many amateurs, it is a disillusioning start. But if you crack it, things get easier – that is, until the 10th, 11th and 12th. The 10th looks an innocuous medium-length par-4 but it is anything but, while the 11th is another par-4 with out-of-bounds over the back and to the right of the green. It may look a tiddler, but the 12th has a habit of catching out the unwary, a short par-3 of 136 yards protected by a very deep bunker at the front and a small bunker to the right.

No one would ever claim that Northamptonshire County is an exceptional course, but for the average player it is very fair and probably the finest all-round test for the player in the county.

Secretary:	Mrs M. Wadley	Tel: 01604 843025
		Fax: 01604 843463
Professional:	Mr T. Rouse	Tel: 01604 842226
Playing:	Midweek: round n/a; day £45.00. Weekend: round £45.00; day n/a.	

Facilities: Bar: 11am–9.30pm. Food: Bar snacks.

Comments: Very good Open regional qualifying course ... Excellent greens and course presentation ... Carpet fairways and slippery greens ... Good test, particularly the bunkers ... Loved this one.

Cold Ashby Golf Club   ★★

Stanford Road, Cold Ashby, NN6 6EP
Nearest main town: Northampton

Secretary: Mr D. Croxton   Tel: 01604 740548
                                        Fax: 01604 740548
Professional: Mr S. Rose   Tel: 01604 740099

Playing: Midweek: round £16.00; day £25.00. Weekend: round £19.00; day n/a.

Facilities: Bar: 11am–11pm. Food: Lunch and dinner from 11am–9pm. Bar snacks.

Comments: Nicely matured course with plenty of character ... Three loops of nine ... Nice individual holes, but as a whole average.

Collingtree Park Golf Club   ★★★

Windingbrook Lane, Northampton, NN4 0XN
Nearest main town: Northampton

Secretary: Mr J. Laidler   Tel: 01604 700000
                   (Gen Mgr)   Fax: 01604 702600
Professional: Mr G. Pook   Tel: 01604 700000

Playing: Midweek: round n/a; day £15.00. Weekend: round n/a; day £20.00.

Facilities: Bar: 11am–11pm. Food: Bar snacks.

Comments: It is as hard as you make it ... Exciting layout with lots of water holes ... Everything a championship course should be ... 10th is a cracking hole.

Hellidon Lakes Hotel Golf & Country Club   ★★★

Hellidon, Daventry, NN11 6LN
Nearest main town: Daventry

Secretary: Mr A. Thomas   Tel: 01327 262550
                                    Fax: 01327 262559

Professional: Mr G. Wills   Tel: 01327 262551

Playing: Midweek: round £20.00; day n/a. Weekend: round £30.00; day n/a.

Facilities: Bar: 11am–11pm. Food: Breakfast, lunch and dinner from 7am–9pm.

Comments: I never knew that they could breed greens this fast ... Excellent value for money and enjoyed every hole ... Very stuffy atmosphere ... 27-hole course with plenty of variation.

Kingsthorpe Golf Club

Kingsley Road, Northampton, NN2 7BU
Website: www.kingsthorpe-golf.co.uk
E-mail: secretary@kingsthorpe-golf.co.uk
Nearest main town: Northampton

Secretary: Mr J. Harris   Tel: 01604 710610
                                    Fax: 01604 710610

Professional: Mr P. Armstrong   Tel: 01604 719602

Playing: Midweek: round n/a; day £25.00. Weekend: round n/a; day n/a.

Facilities: Bar: 11am–11pm. Food: Bar snacks.

Comments: Friendly club ... Course usually in good upkeep ... Short but competitive ... Parkland ... Value day rate.

Oundle Golf Club   ★

Benefield Road, Oundle, PE8 4EZ
Website: www.oundlegolfclub.com
E-mail: oundlegc@btopenworld.com
Nearest main town: Oundle

Secretary: Mr D. Foley   Tel: 01832 273267
                                    Fax: 01832 273267

Professional: Mr R. Keys   Tel: 01832 272273
                                    Fax: 01832 273267

Playing: Midweek: round £23.00; day £30.00. Weekend: round £40.00 (after 10.30am); day n/a.

Facilities: Bar: 11am–11pm. Food: Breakfast, lunch and dinner from 11am–9pm.

Comments: Nothing to see here ... No problems off the tee ... Fair value in the week ... A parkland track with little definition.

Staverton Park Golf Club   ★★★

Staverton, Daventry, NN11 6JT
Nearest main town: Daventry

Secretary: Mr D. Entwhistle   Tel: 01327 302000
                                          Fax: 01327 311428
Professional: Mr R. Mudge   Tel: 01327 705506

Playing: Midweek: round £25.00; day n/a. Weekend: round £27.50; day n/a.

Facilities: Bar: 11am–11pm. Food: Breakfast from 7.30am–9am. Lunch from 12.30pm–1.45pm. Dinner from 7.30pm–9pm.

Comments: Fairly open and bleak ... Plenty of room for the driver ... Wayward shots go unpenalised ... Not great condition.

Wellingborough Golf Club   ★★★★

Harrowden Hall, Great Harrowden, Wellingborough, NN9 5AD
Website: www.wellingboroughgolfclub.org
E-mail: info@wellingboroughgolfclub.org
Nearest main town: Wellingborough

Secretary: Mr R. Tomlin   Tel: 01933 677234
                                          Fax: 01933 679379
Professional: Mr D. Clifford   Tel: 01933 678752

Playing: Midweek: round £40.00; day n/a. Weekend: round n/a; day n/a.

Facilities: Bar: 11am–11pm. Food: Lunch and dinner from 11am–9pm.

Comments: Magnificent clubhouse ... Excellent club course ... Right up there with the best in the county ... Condition always first class ... Rarely gets unplayable ... Nice provincial course.

Whittlebury Park Golf & Country Club ★★★

Whittlebury, Towcester, NN12 8WP
Website: www.whittlebury.com   E-mail: enquiries@whittlebury.com
Nearest main town: Towcester

Secretary:	None	Tel: 01327 858092
		Fax: 01327 858009
Professional:	Mr S. Harlock	Tel: 01327 858588
		Fax: 01327 858009

Playing: Midweek: round £20.00; day n/a. Weekend: round £30.00; day n/a.

Facilities: Bar: 11am–11pm. Food: Breakfast, lunch and dinner from 9am–9pm.

Comments: 36 holes at this parkland course ... Right next to Silverstone racetrack ... Interesting setting but course average ... Fair value for straightforward course ... Bland parkland.

Northumberland

De Vere Slaley Hall Golf Club ★★★★

Hexham, Newcastle-upon-Tyne, NE47 0BY
Website: www.deveregolf.co.uk
E-mail: slaley.hall@devere-hotels.com
Nearest main town: Corbridge

Just twenty minutes from Newcastle, Slaley Hall is a very striking course (opened in 1991) in an area not exactly famed for its courses. With a hotel on site, it has been designed with Tour events in mind and as such has hosted the European Masters.

While the players rate the course highly, the terrible weather that has afflicted these tournaments – wiping out one – has not exactly put Slaley Hall in the shop window. Many have labelled it a 'Woburn of the North', but in truth it has been like a 'Manchester of the North-East': every time a tournament goes there, a deluge has followed. This may have long-term benefits for the course, and players in the area are now certainly blessed with a course to be proud of, and one that is not over-busy.

Designer Dave Thomas wanted to make every hole individual as well as challenging, and to some extent he succeeded. The start at Slaley is tough, as is the finish, although it is fair to say that the opening holes are generally tighter, with much emphasis placed on accuracy off the tee. The back nine is more open and the place to open your shoulders.

The course stretches over 7000 yards off the back tees and is carved through a 1000-acre estate of impressive pine forests. The trees define the opening loop and golfers who can manoeuvre the ball will be the greatest beneficiaries of its layout. For many, the signature hole is the 450-yard par-4 9th, known as the 'Sleeping Giant', which is uphill all the way to a green surrounded by rhododendrons, magnificent when in summer bloom. With a pond and a ditch to the left, and towering pines to the right, it is quite a combination.

Secretary:	None	Tel: 01434 673154
		Fax: 01434 673152
Professional:	Mr G. Robinson	Tel: 01434 673154
		Fax: 01434 673152
Playing:	Midweek: round £45.00 (Hunting), £30.00 (Priestman); day n/a. Weekend: round n/a; day n/a.	

Facilities: Bar: 11am–11pm. Food: Breakfast, lunch and dinner from 7am–10pm. Bar snacks.

Comments: Costly but very good course ... Excellent – no other words to describe this one ... Excellent condition and a good challenge ... Great course and an exquisite restaurant ... A course that asks you many questions ... Products are just way too pricey ... Unquestionably one of the best new courses around ... Very well-managed and enjoyable club ... Straight tee shots required on a course that sparkles in the summer ... Has everything at a price.

Allendale Golf Club   ★

High Studdon, Allenheads Road, Allendale, NE47 9DH
Nearest main town: Allendale

Secretary: Mr P. Mason   Tel: 01434 632288
Professional: None

Playing: Midweek: round n/a; day £12.00. Weekend: round n/a; day £12.00.

Facilities: Bar: 11am–11pm Friday, Saturday and Sunday only. Food: Bar snacks.

Comments: Hilly parkland course extended to 18 holes ... Not up to much even with extension ... 1000ft up – wasn't worth the climb ... Cheap golf all that can be said.

Alnmouth Golf Club   ★★

Foxton Hall, Alnmouth, NE66 3BE
Website: www.alnmouthgolfclub.com
Nearest main town: Alnmouth

Secretary: Mr M. Tate   Tel: 01665 830231
                                        Fax: 01665 830922
Professional: Mrs L. Hardy   Tel: 01665 830043

Playing: Midweek: round n/a; day £30.00 (£25.00 after 2pm). Weekend: round n/a; day n/a.

Facilities: Bar: 11am–11pm. Food: Lunch and dinner from 11am–9pm. Bar snacks.

Comments: Hugs the Northumberland coastline ... Good, honest test at a fair price ... Popular course kept in decent nick ... Worth seeking out for something a bit different.

Bamburgh Castle Golf Club ★★★★

The Clubhouse, Bamburgh, NE69 7DE
Website: www.bamburghcastlegolfclub.org
E-mail: bamburghcastlegolf@hotmail.com
Nearest main town: Bamburgh

Secretary: Mr A. Patterson   Tel: 01668 214321
                                        Fax: 01668 214607

Professional: None

Playing: Midweek: round £30.00; day £40.00. Weekend: round
                  £35.00; day £45.00.

Facilities: Bar: 11am–11pm. Food: Bar snacks.

Comments: Views really make this course what it is ... Fabulous
                  views ... Don't miss it ... Be on your game early, two
                  par-3s to open ... Scenic wonder ... Short course but
                  stunningly beautiful ... Book early for this one ...
                  Unheralded masterpiece.

Bedlingtonshire Golf Club ★

Acorn Bank, Hartford Road, Bedlington, NE22 6AA
Website: www.bedlingtongolfclub.com
E-mail: secretary@bedlingtongolfclub.com
Nearest main town: Bedlington

Secretary: Mr F. Hanson   Tel: 01670 822457
                                        Fax: 01670 823048
Professional: Mr M. Webb   Tel: 01670 822457
                                        Fax: 01670 823048

Playing: Midweek: round £19.00; day £28.00. Weekend: round
                  £27.00; day £34.00.

Facilities: Bar: 11am–11pm. Food: Lunch and dinner from
                  11am–9pm. Bar snacks.

Comments: Facilities poor ... Too long for mere amateurs ... Very
                  flat ... Nothing that makes it stand out.

Bellingham Golf Club ★★

Boggle Hole, Bellingham, NE48 2DT
Website: www.bellinghamgolfclub.com
E-mail: admin@bellinghamgolfclub.com
Nearest main town: Hexham

Secretary: Mr P. Cordiner   Tel: 01434 220530
                   Mr I. Wilson (Club Manager)   Fax: 01434 220152
Professional: None

Playing: Midweek: round £22.00; day n/a. Weekend: round
                   £27.00; day n/a.

Facilities: Bar: 11am–11pm. Food: Lunch and dinner from
                   11am–9pm. Bar snacks.

Comments: A tiny club that tries really hard ... Great welcome, great
                   value ... Situated between Hadrian's Wall and the
                   Scottish border.

Berwick-upon-Tweed Golf Club (Goswick)   ★★★★

Goswick, Berwick-upon-Tweed, TD15 2RW
E-mail: goswickgc@btconnect.com
Nearest main town: Berwick-upon-Tweed

Secretary: Mr D. Wilkinson   Tel: 01289 387256
                                         Fax: 01289 387334
Professional: Mr P. Terras   Tel: 01289 387380

Playing: Midweek: round £28.00; day £35.00. Weekend: round
                   £35.00; day £45.00.

Facilities: Bar: 11am–10pm. Food: Lunch and dinner from
                   11am–9pm, except Mondays.

Comments: Ideal links for competitive holiday golf ... Good fair test
                   for a links and excellent greens ... Natural links.

Dunstanburgh Castle Golf Club   ★★

Alnwick, Embleton, NE66 3XQ
Nearest main town: Alnwick

Secretary: Mr E. Williams   Tel: 01665 576562
                                         Fax: 01665 576562
Professional: None

Playing: Midweek: round n/a; day £15.00. Weekend: round
                   £20.00; day £25.00.

Facilities: Bar: 11am–11pm. Food: Lunch and dinner from
                   11am–9pm. Bar snacks.

Comments: A romantic course as you approach the castle ... Great value ... A charming place, especially in the wind ... Variable condition but that's the beauty of this track ... Vintage course ... Bet they don't get this down South ... Ruins, rabbit scrape, howling gales, dunes, tidal burns, outstanding flora and fauna ... A real treat.

Hexham Golf Club   ★★

Spital Park, Hexham, NE46 3RZ
Website: www.hexhamgolfclub.ntb.org.uk
E-mail: hexhamgolfclub@btopenworld.com
Nearest main town: Hexham

Secretary:	Ms D. Wylie	Tel: 01434 603072
		Fax: 01434 601865
Professional:	Mr M. Forster	Tel: 01434 603072
		Fax: 01434 601865

Playing: Midweek: round £30.00; day £40.00. Weekend: round £40.00; day n/a.

Facilities: Bar: 11am–11pm. Food: Lunch and dinner from 11am–6pm. Bar snacks.

Comments: Excellent layout in good condition ... Harry Vardon layout ... Undulating parkland with a bit of fizz ... Wonderful views from this charmingly contoured gem.

Linden Hall   ★★★

Linden Hall Hotel, Longhorsley, Morpeth, NE65 8XF
Website: www.lindenhall.co.uk   E-mail: golf@lindenhall.co.uk
Nearest main town: Morpeth

Secretary:	Mr D. Curry	Tel: 01670 500011
		Fax: 01670 500001
Professional:	Mr D. Curry	Tel: 01670 500011
		Fax: 01670 500001

Playing: Midweek: round £30.00; day n/a. Weekend: round £35.00; day n/a.

Facilities: Bar: 11am–11pm. Food: Lunch and dinner from 11am–9pm. Dinner by arrangement.

Comments: Excellent short par-3s ... Nice balance of holes ... Very
promising course with nice feel ... Good condition ...
Signs are this is a course with a future ... Best I've felt on
a course for years ... Cultured design that keeps the
player on their toes.

Magdalene Fields Golf Club   ★

Magdalene Fields, Berwick-upon-Tweed, TD15 1NE
Website: www.magdalene-fields.co.uk
E-mail: mail@magdalene-fields.co.uk
Nearest main town: Berwick-upon-Tweed

Secretary: Mr M. Lynch   Tel: 01289 306130
                                       Fax: 01289 306384

Professional: None

Playing: Midweek: round £21.00; day n/a. Weekend: round
£23.00; day n/a.

Facilities: Bar: 11am–11pm. Food: Lunch from 12pm–2pm.
Dinner from 7pm–9pm. Bar snacks.

Comments: Very natural seaside course ... Exposed and some severe
wind chill ... Poor condition ... Gone to seed a bit.

Newbiggin-by-the-Sea Golf Club   ★

Newbiggin, Newbiggin-by-the-Sea, NE64 6DW
Nearest main town: Newbiggin

Secretary: Mr G. Beattie   Tel: 01670 852959
                                       Fax: 01670 520236

Professional: Mr M. Webb   Tel: 01670 817833

Playing: Midweek: round n/a; day £14.00. Weekend: round n/a;
day £19.00.

Facilities: Bar: 11am–11pm. Food: Bar snacks.

Comments: Average links ... Condition not what it was ... Not much
fun in the wind and rain.

Seahouses Golf Club   ★★★

Beadnell Road, Seahouses, NE68 7XT
Website: www.seahousesgolf.co.uk
E-mail: secretary@seahousesgolf.co.uk
Nearest main town: Alnwick

Secretary: Mr J. Gray   Tel: 01665 720794
                                        Fax: 01665 721994
Professional: None

Playing: Midweek: round £18.00; day £25.00 (juniors under 16
                   half rates). Weekend: round £25.00; day £30.00
                   (juniors under 16 half rates).

Facilities: Bar: 11am–11pm. Food: Lunch and dinner from
                   12pm–9pm, except Mondays. Bar snacks.

Comments: Very nice surrounding area and great fun to play the
                   holes next to the sea ... Epitome of golf in the North – a
                   rugged course across marshland ... Eccentric design
                   and a cracking par-3 at the 10th ... Natural, undiluted
                   golf ... Across coves and down dale – superb.

Wooler Golf Club   ★

Dod Law, Doddington, Wooler, NE71 6EA
Nearest main town: Wooler

Secretary: Mr S. Lowrey   Tel: 01668 281631
Professional: None

Playing: Midweek: round n/a; day £15.00. Weekend: round n/a;
                   day £20.00.

Facilities: Bar: 11am–3pm (by arrangement). Food: Snacks (by
                   arrangement).

Comments: A little gem ... Hilltop moorland course with nine holes
                   and 18 tees ... Can always get a game ... Eccentric
                   course for nine-holer with one par-5 of 580 yards.

Nottinghamshire

Notts Golf Club ★★★★★

Hollinwell, Derby Road, Kirby-in-Ashfield, NG17 7QR
Nearest main town: Mansfield

Notts, or Hollinwell as it is more commonly known, must rank as one of the finest inland courses in Britain. Set within the boundaries of Sherwood Forest, Notts is blessed with outstanding natural scenery and a colourful past – many golfers will be unaware that Notts held the Dunlop Masters and John Player Classic in 1970, when the first prize of £25,000 was a world record.

The course, which is predominantly heather and gorse, dates back to the turn of the last century with the original Willie Park design revised by John Henry Taylor. His revisions were primarily cosmetic, barely scratching the surface of the established layout apart from the addition of some bunkers. The silver birch and oak forest that framed the land was left untouched, as were the well-drained carpet fairways, which twist and turn through a lush valley.

You are reminded of the impressive location as early as the 2nd, where the rock behind the green is known as Robin Hood's Chair. It's a gentle start to the round with the longest hole on the course coming at the 6th, where its length is rather mitigated by being downhill.

The name of the course is derived from the 8th, named 'Holy Well'. Off the back tees, your drive needs to carry the lake some 180 yards to a fairway bordered by trees. As with many of the holes at Hollinwell, place your tee shot well and you are rewarded with a simple approach shot. The 205-yard 13th is another good hole, played from an elevated tee into a valley to a heavily bunkered green.

You will soon realise Notts is not a long course, but it is still very demanding. The shaping of the fairways (the 12th is a good example) means that a wrongly positioned ball meanders its way to the very edge of the playing surface. And when you have finished, Hollinwell boasts one of the finest and most homely clubhouses in the country. It is well worth lunching here as the surroundings and food match each other in quality.

Secretary:	Mr N. Symington	Tel: 01623 753225
		Fax: 01623 753655
Professional:	Mr A. Thomas	Tel: 01623 753087
Playing:	Midweek: round £45.00; day £65.00 (£10.00 with member). Weekend: round n/a; day n/a.	

Facilities: Bar: 11am–11pm. Food: Lunch and dinner from 11am–8pm. Bar snacks.

Comments: Did not feel that welcome at what is ostensibly a members club ... Golf as it should be ... Tough course in excellent condition ... Superb day out on a renowned course ... Don't leave this area without playing Notts – there is nothing else like it.

Cotgrave Place Golf & Country Club   ★★

Stragglethorpe, Nottingham, NG12 3HB
Nearest main town: Nottingham

Secretary:	Mr M. Hatch	Tel: 0115 933 3344
		Fax: 0115 933 4567
Professional:	None	Tel: 0115 933 3344

Playing: Midweek: round prices on application; day n/a. Weekend: round n/a; day n/a.

Facilities: Bar: 11am–11pm. Food: Breakfast, lunch and dinner from 7am–10pm.

Comments: Could develop into an excellent golf centre with some long, demanding holes ... Challenging par-3s .... Nice feel about the place ... Improving ... 36 different challenging holes.

Coxmoor Golf Club   ★★★

Coxmoor Road, Sutton-in-Ashfield, NG17 5LF
Website: www.coxmoor.freeuk.com   E-mail: coxmoor@freeuk.com
Nearest main town: Sutton-in-Ashfield

Secretary:	Mr P. Snow	Tel: 01623 557359
		Fax: 01623 557359
Professional:	Mr D. Ridley	Tel: 01623 559906

Playing: Midweek: round £40.00; day £50.00. Weekend: round £40.00; day £50.00. Prices may increase in 2004.

Facilities: Bar: 11am–11pm. Food: Breakfast and bar snacks from 10am–9pm.

Comments: Splendid value on a sparkling course ... Good quality course ... Undulating moorland track, generally in fine condition.

Mapperley Golf Club   ★★

Central Avenue, Plains Road, Mapperley, NG3 6RH
Website: www.mapperleygolfclub.org
E-mail: info@mapperleygolfclub.org
Nearest main town: Nottingham

Secretary: Mr A. Newton   Tel: 0115 955 6672
                                         Fax: 0115 955 6670
Professional: Mr J. Barker   Tel: 0115 955 6673
                                         Fax: 0115 955 6670

Playing: Midweek: round £20.00; day £25.00. Weekend: round
                   £25.00; day £30.00.

Facilities: Bar: 11am–11pm. Food: Lunch and dinner from
                   11am–7pm. Bar snacks.

Comments: Mature, hilly course ... Meadowland course ... Not the
                   best in Notts ... Don't bust a gut to get there.

Newark Golf Club   ★★

Coddington, NG24 2QX
Nearest main town: Newark

Secretary: Mr P. Snow   Tel: 01636 626282
                                         Fax: 01636 626497
Professional: Mr P. Lockley   Tel: 01636 626492
                                         Fax: 01636 626492

Playing: Midweek: round £23.00; day £28.00. Weekend: round
                   n/a; day n/a.

Facilities: Bar: 11am–11pm. Food: Lunch and dinner from
                   11am–7pm. Bar snacks.

Comments: Pleasant parkland course with excellent 19th ... Not bad
                   and good for the area ... Secluded, parkland course
                   with friendly members.

Oakmere Park Golf Club (Admirals)   ★

Oaks Lane, Oxton, NG25 0RH
Website: www.oakmerepark.co.uk
E-mail: enquiries@oakmerepark.co.uk
Nearest main town: Nottingham

Secretary: Mr B. Ward   Tel: 0115 965 3545
                                  Fax: 0115 965 5628

Professional: Mr D. St John Jones Tel: 0115 965 3545

Playing: Midweek: round £18.00; day n/a. Weekend: round £24.00; day n/a.

Facilities: Bar: 11am–11pm. Food: Lunch and dinner from 11am–9pm. Bar snacks.

Comments: Nice course but a bit untidy ... Complete golf centre where practice facilities overshadow the course ... Average parkland fare.

Ramsdale Park Golf Centre (High) ★★

Oxton Road, Calverton, NG14 6NU
Nearest main town: Nottingham

Secretary: Mr B. Jenkinson   Tel: 0115 965 5600
                                  Fax: 0115 965 4105

Professional: Mr R. Macey   Tel: 0115 965 5600

Playing: Midweek: round £14.00; day £23.00. Weekend: round £16.00; day £27.00.

Facilities: Bar: 11am–11pm. Food: Lunch and dinner from 11am–9pm. Bar snacks.

Comments: Nice course if a little tiring ... Hilly parkland course ... Extensive practice facilities ... Basic golf at value price ... Two courses in fair condition.

Ruddington Grange Golf Club ★★

Wilford Road, Nottingham, NG11 6NB
Website: www.ruddingtongrange.com
E-mail: info@ruddingtongrange.com
Nearest main town: Nottingham

Secretary: Mr A. Johnson   Tel: 0115 921 4139
                                  Fax: 0115 940 5165

Professional: Mr R. Simpson   Tel: 0115 921 1951
                                  Fax: 0115 940 5165

Playing: Midweek: round £19.00; day £28.00. Weekend: round £26.00; day £35.00.

Facilities: Bar: 11am–11pm. Food: Lunch and dinner from 11am–9pm. Bar snacks.

Comments: Superb greens ... Plenty of water hazards.

Rufford Park Golf & Country Club ★★

Rufford Lane, Newark, NG22 9DG
Website: www.ruffordpark.co.uk   E-mail: enquiries@ruffordpark.co.uk
Nearest main town: Newark

Secretary: Ms K. Whitehead   Tel: 01623 825253
                                 Fax: 01623 825254
Professional: Mr J. Vaughan

Playing: Midweek: round £19.00; day n/a. Weekend: round £25.00; day n/a.

Facilities: Bar: 11am–11pm. Food: Breakfast, lunch and dinner from 9am–9pm. Bar snacks.

Comments: Good course to learn the game ... Off-course facilities are improving ... Nice variety at this basic course.

Sherwood Forest Golf Club ★★★★

Eakring Road, Mansfield, NG18 3EW
Nearest main town: Mansfield

Secretary: Mr K. Hall   Tel: 01623 626689
                            Fax: 01623 420412
Professional: Mr K. Hall   Tel: 01623 627403

Playing: Midweek: round prices on application; day n/a. Weekend: round n/a; day n/a.

Facilities: Bar: 11am–11pm. Food: Lunch and dinner from 11am–9pm. Bar snacks.

Comments: Good course and club ... One of the best in the county and in lovely setting ... Delightful silver birch and pine trees ... Back nine the highlight.

Wollaton Park Golf Club ★★★

Lime Tree Avenue, Wollaton Park, Nottingham, NG8 1BT
Nearest main town: Nottingham

Secretary:	Mr M. Harvey	Tel: 0115 978 7574
		Fax: 0115 970 0736
Professional:	Mr J. Lower	Tel: 0115 978 4834

Playing: Midweek: round £28.50; day £39.00. Weekend: round £28.50; day £39.00.

Facilities: Bar: 11am–11pm. Food: Lunch and dinner from 11am–11pm. Bar snacks.

Comments: Interesting parkland with lively deer roaming the fairways ... Teasing course with teasing holes ... Very enticing course in public park ... Pleasant oasis just 3 miles from centre of Nottingham ... Top quality inner city course.

Worksop Golf Club ★★★★

Windmill Lane, Worksop, S80 2SQ
E-mail: worksopgolfclub@worksop.co.uk
Nearest main town: Worksop

Secretary:	Mr D. Dufall	Tel: 01909 477731
		Fax: 01909 477732
Professional:	Mr C. Weatherhead	Tel: 01909 477732
		Fax: 01909 477732

Playing: Midweek: round n/a; day £35.00. Weekend: round n/a; day £50.00.

Facilities: Bar: 11am–11pm. Food: Lunch and dinner from 11am–8pm. Bar snacks.

Comments: A wonderfully British course – immaculate ... Demanding course, I can see why Lee Westwood is so good ... Lee Westwood plays here – enough said ... Delightful parkland course with fast greens ... Fast greens – just as Lee likes them ... Top-notch course ... Right attitude at this friendly club.

Oxfordshire

Tadmarton Heath Golf Club ★★★★

Wigginton, Banbury, OX15 5HL
Website: www.thgc.btinternet.co.uk   E-mail: thgc@btinternet.co.uk
Nearest main town: Banbury

Before the construction of a golf course at Tadmarton Heath, Harry Vardon was consulted about the viability of a course on the top of Wigginton Hill. Without reservation he commented: 'God made it to be a golf course.' Seventy-six years on, Tadmarton Heath is a joy to play, a course that has stood the test of time and gets better with age.

Ironically for a heathland course, there is no heather, just gorse and broom which define all the fairways. There are plenty of other natural features, including the ravine at the 7th (originally a holy well where the water was reputed to have healing powers) and the natural plateaus which form the fairways for the 11th and 12th. There are very few trees, agronomy experts having recommended that they were of little use on a heathland course.

As you would expect of a course that measures just under 6000 yards, the fairways are very tight and much thought goes into each hole. The course is generally flat but visually it is very exciting, a genuine test despite its short length. The best holes are probably the 6th, where a 7-foot-deep bunker with railway sleepers guards the green, and the short 7th, played to a small green set in an embankment. It also finishes with a flourish: the 18th is a dogleg, but the bend in the fairways only starts at around 240 yards.

Like many heathland courses, Tadmarton Heath is blessed with excellent drainage, the sandy soil sitting above ironstone which means all-year-round play. The members of this club are generally welcoming and are happy to share their clubhouse, a delightful converted farmhouse, with visitors. There's a lovely lounge bar to sit in during the evening.

Secretary:	Mr J. Cox	Tel: 01608 737278
		Fax: 01608 730548
Professional:	Mr T. Jones	Tel: 01608 730047

Playing: Midweek: round n/a; day £39.00. Weekend: round n/a; day n/a. Prices may increase in 2004.

Facilities: Bar: 11am–2pm and 4pm–10pm. Food: Lunch from 8am–2pm. Dinner from 4pm–9.30pm. Bar snacks.

Comments: Excellent condition ... Tight, short course ... One mistake can be very costly ... Favourite hole is the 7th ... Course with colourful history ... Heathland track with excellent drainage for year-round play.

Badgemore Park Golf Club   ★★★

Badgemore, Henley-on-Thames, RG9 4NR
Website: www.badgemorepark.com
E-mail: info@badgemorepark.com
Nearest main town: Henley-on-Thames

Secretary: Mr J. Connell   Tel: 01491 637300
                                      Fax: 01491 576899
Professional: Mr J. Dunn   Tel: 01491 574175
                                      Fax: 01491 576899

Playing: Midweek: round £25.00; day n/a. Weekend: round £36.00 (£25.00 after 2pm); day n/a.

Facilities: Bar: 11am–11pm. Food: Lunch and dinner from 11am–10pm. Bar snacks.

Comments: Tricky ... Played it all my life and love it ... Trees in play on each hole.

Brailes Golf Club   ★

Sutton Lane, Lower Brailes, Banbury, OX15 5BB
Website: www.brailes-golf-club.co.uk
E-mail: office@brailes-golf-club.co.uk
Nearest main town: Shipston-on-Stour

Secretary: Mr R. Malir   Tel: 01608 685336
                                      Fax: 01608 685205
Professional: Mr A. Brown   Tel: 01608 685633
                                      Fax: 01608 685205

Playing: Midweek: round £25.00; day n/a. Weekend: round £35.00; day n/a.

Facilities: Bar: 11am–11pm. Food: Lunch and dinner from 11am–9pm. Bar snacks.

Comments: Magnificent links setting ... Views of three counties from the 17th tee ... In fair condition but don't go out of your way.

Chesterton Country Golf Club ★

Bicester, Chesterton, OX6 8TE
Nearest main town: Bicester

Secretary: Mr B. Carter   Tel: 01869 241204
Professional: Mr J. Wilkshire   Tel: 01869 242023

Playing: Midweek: round £12.00; day £16.00. Weekend: round £15.00; day £20.00.

Facilities: Bar: 11am–11pm. Food: Lunch from 11am–3pm.

Comments: Flat course on old farmland ... Standard new course ... Flat terrain, not very interesting.

Chipping Norton Golf Club ★

Southcombe, Chipping Norton, OX7 5QH
E-mail: chipping-nortongc@virgin.net
Nearest main town: Chipping Norton

Secretary: Mr S. Chislett   Tel: 01608 642383
    Fax: 01608 645422
Professional: Mr N. Rowlands   Tel: 01608 643356
    Fax: 01608 645422

Playing: Midweek: round £32.00; day n/a. Weekend: round n/a; day £16.00 (visitors with members only).

Facilities: Bar: 11am–11pm. Food: Lunch and dinner from 11am–9pm. Bar snacks.

Comments: Exposed downland course ... Not much to see ... Friendly club course ... Straightforward ... Well thought of in the area.

Drayton Park Golf Club ★★

Steventon Road, Drayton, OX14 4LA
Nearest main town: Abingdon

Secretary: Ms G. Masey   Tel: 01235 528989
    Fax: 01235 525731
Professional: Mr M. Morbey   Tel: 01235 550607

Playing: Midweek: round £16.50; day n/a. Weekend: round £19.50; day n/a.

Facilities: Bar: 11am–11pm. Food: Lunch and dinner from 11am–9pm.

Comments: Challenging but forgiving ... Hawtree design with interesting use of water hazards ... Facile parkland course.

Frilford Heath Golf Club (Blue)   ★★★

Frilford Heath, Abingdon, OX13 5NW
Website: www.frilfordheath.co.uk   E-mail: secretary@frilfordheath.co.uk
Nearest main town: Abingdon

Secretary: Mr S. Styles   Tel: 01865 390864
                                          Fax: 01865 390823
Professional: Mr D. Craik Jnr   Tel: 01865 390887

Playing: Midweek: round £34.00; day £60.00. Weekend: round £34.00; day £60.00.

Facilities: Bar: 8am–11pm. Food: Breakfast, lunch and dinner from 8am–9pm. Bar snacks.

Comments: Very open ... Modern design with large bunkers and water ... Thick rough and bunkers the hazards ... Tough start ... Par-3 3rd a cracker.

Frilford Heath Golf Club (Green)   ★★★

Frilford Heath, Abingdon, OX13 5NW
Website: www.frilfordheath.co.uk   E-mail: secretary@frilfordheath.co.uk
Nearest main town: Abingdon

Secretary: Mr S. Styles   Tel: 01865 390864
                                          Fax: 01865 390823
Professional: Mr D. Craik Jnr   Tel: 01865 390887

Playing: Midweek: round £34.00; day £60.00. Weekend: round £34.00; day £60.00.

Facilities: Bar: 8am–11pm. Food: Breakfast, lunch and dinner from 8am–9pm. Bar snacks.

Comments: Prettiest and shortest of three courses ... Some great long par-4s ... 7th and 16th very special ... Nice collection of par-3s.

Frilford Heath Golf Club (Red)   ★★★★

Frilford Heath, Abingdon, OX13 5NW
Website: www.frilfordheath.co.uk   E-mail: secretary@frilfordheath.co.uk
Nearest main town: Abingdon

Secretary: Mr S. Styles   Tel: 01865 390864
                                          Fax: 01865 390823
Professional: Mr D. Craik Jnr   Tel: 01865 390887

Playing: Midweek: round n/a; day £55.00. Weekend: round n/a;
                    day £65.00.

Facilities: Bar: 8am–11pm. Food: Breakfast, lunch and dinner
                    from 8am–9pm. Bar snacks.

Comments: Clubhouse grand and welcoming ... Building of Blue
                    course means some holes out of style with the rest ...
                    The best at Frilford Heath ... 8th the best hole, a long
                    tight par-4 ... Nice par-3 through a spinney ... Good
                    food in lovely clubhouse.

Henley Golf Club   ★★★

Harpsden, Henley-on-Thames, RG9 4HG
Website: www.henleygc.com   E-mail: henleygolfclub@btinternet.com
Nearest main town: Henley-on-Thames

Secretary: Mr A. Chaundy   Tel: 01491 575742
                                          Fax: 01491 412179
Professional: Mr M. Howell   Tel: 01491 575710
                                          Fax: 01491 575710

Playing: Midweek: round £33.00 (£21.00 after 4pm); day
                    £42.00. Weekend: round £18.50 (as member's guest);
                    day n/a.

Facilities: Bar: 11am–11pm. Food: Lunch and dinner from
                    11am–9pm. Bar snacks.

Comments: Short parkland course ... Basic facilities but quaint little
                    course ... Charming course in pretty area ... Good
                    golfing ... Never a problem to get a game.

Huntercombe Golf Club   ★★★

Nuffield, Henley-on-Thames, RG9 5SL
Website: www.huntercombegolfclub.co.uk
E-mail: office@huntercombegolfclub.co.uk
Nearest main town: Henley-on-Thames

Secretary:	Mr K. McCrea	Tel: 01491 641207
		Fax: 01491 642060
Professional:	Mr D. Reffin	Tel: 01491 641241

Playing: Midweek: round £32.00; day n/a. Weekend: round £48.00; day n/a.

Facilities: Bar: 8am–11pm. Food: Breakfast, lunch and dinner from 8am–8pm. Bar snacks.

Comments: Quaintly, quintessentially English ... A jewel in the Chilterns – keep it quiet ... Superb condition and can be tricky ... Medium difficulty and greens in superb condition.

The Oxfordshire Golf Club   ★★★

Rycote Lane, Milton Common, Thame, OX9 2PU
Nearest main town: Thame

Secretary:	Mr M. Obata	Tel: 01844 278300
		Fax: 01844 278003
Professional:	Mr N. Pike	Tel: 01844 278505

Playing: Midweek: round prices on application; day n/a. Weekend: round n/a; day n/a.

Facilities: Bar: Members only. Food: Members only.

Comments: Expensive, over-priced for an unnatural course ... Superb practice facilities ... Did the earth move for you? It certainly did for the designers ... Exciting, if unnatural course ... Links lovers steer a wide berth round this one.

Southfield Golf Club   ★★★

Hill Top Road, Oxford, OX4 1PF
Website: www.southfieldgolf.com
E-mail: southfieldgolfclub@btinternet.com
Nearest main town: Oxford

Secretary:	Mr C. Maxted	Tel: 01865 242158
		Fax: 01865 728544
Professional:	Mr T. Rees	Tel: 01865 244258

Playing: Midweek: round £25.00; day £35.00. Weekend: round n/a; day n/a.

Facilities: Bar: 11am–11pm. Food: Lunch from 12pm–2pm. Dinner from 4pm–8pm. Bar snacks.

Comments: Not too taxing ... Peaceful ... Course used by Oxford University ... Interesting course but there's better in the county.

Waterstock Golf Club ★★

Thame Road, Waterstock, OX33 1HT
Nearest main town: Oxford

Secretary:	Mr A. Wyatt	Tel: 01844 338093
		Fax: 01844 338036
Professional:	Mr J. Goodman	

Playing: Midweek: round £14.00; day £22.00. Weekend: round £17.00; day £30.00.

Facilities: Bar: 11am–11pm. Food: Lunch and dinner served from 11am–9pm. Bar snacks.

Comments: Very modern and interesting ... Donald Steel design ... Outstanding facilities for the visitor ... Course with character ... Clever design ... All the shots required.

The Wychwood Golf Club ★★★

Lyneham, Chipping Norton, OX7 6QQ
E-mail: golf@wychwoodgc.freeserve.co.uk
Nearest main town: Chipping Norton

Secretary:	Mr C. Howkins	Tel: 01993 831841
Professional:	Mr J. Fincher	Tel: 01993 831841

Playing: Midweek: round £23.00; day n/a. Weekend: round £28.00; day n/a.

Facilities: Bar: 11am–11pm. Food: Lunch and dinner from 11am–9pm. Bar snacks.

Comments: Tremendous value for money, good food and warm welcome ... Water in play on eight holes ... New course which looks natural for its age.

Shropshire

Llanymynech Golf Club ★★★★

Pant, Oswestry, SY10 8LB
Website: www.llanymynechgolfclub.co.uk
Nearest main town: Oswestry

Llanymynech, 6 miles north of Oswestry, is famed for its association with Ian Woosnam, who fashioned his skills here as a youngster. It is a spectacular layout, riding high on limestone outcrops and offering views extending for 50 miles. Famously, on the 4th you tee off in Wales, but putt out in England, and it is not until the 9th that you return.

The course is something of a throwback to the days when courses were built on high land so that the farmers could use the pastureland at lower levels. For years, the condition of the course was maintained by the sheep that roamed the site, but they left in 1973 and since then more traditional methods of greenkeeping have been used.

No one would ever claim that Llanymynech is in outstanding condition, and some would argue that there are better courses in the area, but the diversity of the holes creates much excitement for the player. The front nine is cut through a forest and requires clever placement of tee shots to maximise the scoring opportunities. On the back nine, the course is at its most scenic with views overlooking Shropshire and out to the Welsh Hills. It is also a more open and satisfying part of the course, where you really feel the uniqueness of the golf experience.

As you would expect from a course located in a fairly barren golfing region, green fees are very good value. You can pay more for, say, Hawkstone Park Hotel, a very popular stop-off for golfers, but Llanymynech offers a more varied experience.

Secretary:	Mr D. Thomas	Tel: 01691 830983
Professional:	Mr A. Griffiths	Tel: 01691 830879

Playing: Midweek: round £20.00; day £25.00 (reductions for parties). Weekend: round £25.00 (subject to availability); day n/a.

Facilities: Bar: 11am–11pm. Food: Lunch and dinner from 11am–11pm. Bar snacks.

Comments: Idiosyncratic mountain golf with fabulous views – a must for a clear spring or autumn day ... Most unusual course ... Scenic and invigorating ... A pilgrimage to this weird and wonderful course is highly recommended.

Arscott Golf Club ★

Arscott, Pomtesbury, SY5 0XP
E-mail: argc@tiscali.co.uk
Nearest main town: Shrewsbury

Secretary:	Maj B. Harper	Tel: 01743 860114
		Fax: 01743 860114
Professional:	None	

Playing: Midweek: round prices on application; day n/a. Weekend: round n/a; day n/a.

Facilities: Bar: 11am–11pm. Food: Lunch from 12pm–3pm. Dinner from 6pm–9pm at weekends only. Bar snacks.

Comments: Modern course with fine views over Wales ... Fairly hilly ... Can only get better ... Plenty of water hazards ... You can learn the game here.

Bridgnorth Golf Club ★

Stanley Lane, Bridgnorth, WV16 4SF
Website: www.bridgnorthgolfclub.co.uk
E-mail: bridgnorth-golf@supanet.com
Nearest main town: Bridgnorth

Secretary:	Mr G. Kelsall	Tel: 01746 763315
		Fax: 01746 761381
Professional:	Mr P. Hinton	Tel: 01746 762045

Playing: Midweek: round £24.00; day n/a. Weekend: round £30.00; day n/a.

Facilities: Bar: 11am–11pm. Food: Lunch and dinner from 11am–9pm. Bar snacks.

Comments: Good value ... Friendly club ... Fine if you're in the area, but otherwise no ... Friendly atmosphere ... Pro very helpful.

Church Stretton Golf Club ★★★

Hunters Moon, Trevor Hill, Church Stretton, SY6 6JH
Website: www.churchstrettongolfclub.co.uk
E-mail: secretary@churchstrettongolfclub.co.uk
Nearest main town: Church Stretton

Secretary:	Mr J. Povall	Tel: 01743 860679
		Fax: 01743 861917
Professional:	Mr J. Townsend	Tel: 01694 722281

Playing: Midweek: round £20.00; day n/a. Weekend: round £28.00; day n/a.

Facilities: Bar: 12pm–3pm and 5pm–9.30pm. Food: Lunch from 12pm–3pm. Dinner from 5pm–8pm. Bar snacks.

Comments: Good test for an inland course ... James Braid design ... Hilly course where wild things roam ... Unusual course but nice club attitude.

Hawkstone Park Hotel & Golf Club ★★★★

Weston-under-Redcastle, SY4 5UY
Website: www.hawkstone.co.uk   E-mail: info@hawkstone.co.uk
Nearest main town: Shrewsbury

Secretary:	None	Tel: 01939 200611
		Fax: 01939 200311
Professional:	Mr P. Wesselingh	Tel: 01939 200611

Playing: Midweek: round £30.00; day n/a. Weekend: round £38.00; day n/a.

Facilities: Bar: 11am–11pm. Food: Lunch and dinner from 11am–10pm. Bar snacks.

Comments: Very mature course in a lovely area ... Delightful golf experience with dramatic views ... A long weekend visit offered at a great value course ... Hotel and food both excellent ... Resort course that does the little things well.

Hill Valley Golf & Country Club (Emerald) ★★★

Terrick Road, Whitchurch, SY13 4JZ
Nearest main town: Whitchurch

Secretary:	None	Tel: 01948 663584
		Fax: 01948 665927
Professional:	Mr C. Burgess	Tel: 01948 663032

Playing: Midweek: round £20.00; day £26.00. Weekend: round £25.00; day £32.00.

Facilities: Bar: 11am–11pm. Food: Lunch and dinner from 10am–10pm. Bar snacks.

Comments: Could not fault the way our society day was handled ...
Two courses, one designed by Alliss/Thomas ... US-style
layout – very unnatural ... Even the lakes and streams
can't disguise a bland course.

Hill Valley Golf & Country Club (Sapphire)   ★★★

Terrick Road, Whitchurch, SY13 4JZ
Nearest main town: Whitchurch

Secretary: None   Tel: 01948 663584
                                          Fax: 01948 665927
Professional: Mr C. Burgess   Tel: 01948 663032

Playing: Midweek: round £20.00; day £26.00. Weekend: round
                  £25.00; day £32.00.

Facilities: Bar: 11am–11pm. Food: Lunch from 11am–6pm.
                  Dinner by arrangement.

Comments: US-style golf ... Very comfortable club ... Liked the
                  numerous water hazards ... Really blends in with the
                  landscape ... Nice course for a nice price.

Mile End Golf Club   ★

Old Shrewsbury Road, Oswestry, SY11 4JF
Website: www.mileendgolfclub.co.uk   E-mail: mileendgc@aol.com
Nearest main town: Oswestry

Secretary: Mr R. Thompson   Tel: 01691 671246
                                          Fax: 01691 670580
Professional: Mr S. Carpenter   Tel: 01691 671246
                                          Fax: 01691 670580

Playing: Midweek: round £16.00; day £22.00. Weekend: round
                  £22.00; day £30.00.

Facilities: Bar: 11am–11pm. Food: Lunch from 11.30am–3pm.
                  Dinner by arrangement.

Comments: Suitable for all standards ... Good facility for beginners
                  ... Not the best in the area.

Shifnal Golf Club   ★★★

Decker Hill, Shifnal, TF11 8QL
Website: www.shifnalgolfclub.co.uk
E-mail: secretary@shifnalgolfclub.co.uk
Nearest main town: Telford

Secretary:	Mr M. Vanner	Tel: 01952 460330
		Fax: 01952 461127
Professional:	Mr J. Flanagan	Tel: 01952 460457

Playing: Midweek: round £25.00; day n/a. Weekend: round £25.00; day n/a.

Facilities: Bar: 11am–11pm. Food: Lunch and dinner from 11am–8pm. Bar snacks.

Comments: Clubhouse the best thing about this course ... Woodland/ parkland course of variable standard ... Enjoyed it.

The Shropshire   ★★★

Muxton Lane, Muxton, TF2 8PQ
Website: www.theshropshire.co.uk   E-mail: golf@theshropshire.co.uk
Nearest main town: Telford

Secretary:	Ms T. May	Tel: 01952 677800
		Fax: 01952 677622
Professional:	Mr R. Grier	Tel: 01952 677866
		Fax: 01952 677622

Playing: Midweek: round £18.00; day n/a. Weekend: round £24.00; day n/a.

Facilities: Bar: 11am–11pm. Food: Lunch and dinner from 12pm–7pm. Bar snacks.

Comments: Ideal golf society venue with three loops of nine ... Gold/ Silver course is the best combination ... A fine golfing day out ... New golf centre providing affordable golf for everyone ... Not a top course but it does the job well.

Telford Golf & Country Club   ★★★

Great Hay Drive, Sutton Heights, Telford, TF7 4DT
E-mail: ibarlem@aol.com
Nearest main town: Telford

Secretary:	Mr I. Lucas	Tel: 01952 422960
		Fax: 01952 586602

Professional: Mr D. Bateman   Tel: 01952 586052
                                        Fax: 01952 586052

Playing: Midweek: round £25.00; day n/a. Weekend: round £35.00; day n/a.

Facilities: Bar: 11am–11pm. Food: Breakfast, lunch and dinner from 7am–10pm.

Comments: Enormous lakes and bunkers ... Not much thought in the design ... Fine facilities ... Try and keep out of the water!

Worfield Golf Club ★

Worfield, Bridgnorth, WV15 5HE
Nearest main town: Wolverhampton

Secretary: Mr W. Weaver   Tel: 01746 716372
                                        Fax: 01746 716302
Professional: Mr S. Russell   Tel: 01746 716541

Playing: Midweek: round £16.00; day £22.00. Weekend: round £25.00; day n/a.

Facilities: Bar: 11am–11pm. Food: Dinner from 6pm–9pm. Bar snacks.

Comments: Good standard course ... All you would expect from a relatively new course ... Undulating greens ... Looks easy but is anything but.

Wrekin Golf Club ★★

Ercall Woods, Wellington, Telford, TF6 5BX
E-mail: wrekingolfclub@lineone.net
Nearest main town: Telford

Secretary: Mr D. Briscoe   Tel: 01952 244032
                                        Fax: 01952 252906
Professional: Mr K. Housden   Tel: 01952 223101

Playing: Midweek: round £22.00; day £30.00. Weekend: round £30.00; day n/a.

Facilities: Bar: 11am–11pm. Food: Lunch and dinner from 11am–11pm. Bar snacks.

Comments: Very hilly but worth the effort ... Condition not always what you would expect.

Somerset

Burnham & Berrow Golf Club ★★★★

St Christopher's Way, Burnham-on-Sea, TA8 2PE
Nearest main town: Burnham-on-Sea

Some golfers find the out-and-back links an outdated layout, so they should be well warned off Burnham & Berrow, a very traditional course set on the North Somerset coast, with views of the Bristol Channel and the distant Glamorgan shore. Players who baulk at playing the course on this basis are, however, missing out, because Burnham & Berrrow delights in so many ways that the rigidness of the layout becomes a secondary consideration.

The out-and-back links was immortalised by St Andrews, a course that, when golf was first played, was essentially a fairway that stretched out for nine holes, then a fairway that stretched back for nine holes. Burnham & Berrow is just like this. A strip of coastal land that was left when the seas receded after the last Ice Age, it is sparsely vegetated with fine-bladed grass for fairways and wild, rough grasses forming the course's primary protection against good scoring.

The course has been altered many times in the twentieth century to cut out a lot of blind shots that existed and in particular to avoid hitting churchgoers who walked across the fairways to reach the church in the middle of the course. Steps have also been taken to preserve the plant life, which is abundant amid the wild grasses, particularly the orchids.

As befits a grand course, it is the finishing holes at Burnham & Berrow that prove the highlight of any round. The 15th is a long par-4, followed by the short par-4 16th, which requires a short pitch to a small, elevated green (a feature of Burnham & Berrow is the small greens, which slope in all directions). A long par-3 at the 17th that can require a driver at times precedes the finishing hole, a par-4 sculpted through small sandhills. The course will test all your shots and offers you some spectacular positions from which to play. If you're to score well, you'd better have your short game in good nick, as the chances are you will fail to hold many of the greens at your first attempt.

Secretary:	Mrs E. Sloman	Tel: 01278 783137
		Fax: 01278 795440
Professional:	Mr M. Crowther-Smith	Tel: 01278 784545
Playing:	Midweek: round £38.00; day n/a. Weekend: round £50.00; day £50.00.	

Facilities: Bar: 11am–11pm. Food: Lunch and dinner from 11am–9pm. Bar snacks.

Comments: Classic links with plenty of variety ... Lovely links ... Hard course when the wind is blowing ... Vicious rough ... Excellent, knowledgable staff ... Magnificent links with some of the best greens anywhere ... Not quite a traditional links but seaside golf at its best ... Tough links with the character of an old smooth malt whisky ... Best course in the UK for the price ... Twilight fee is unbeatable value.

Bath Golf Club   ★★★

Sham Castle, North Road, Bath, BA2 6JG
Website: www.bathgolfclub.org.uk
E-mail: enquiries@bathgolfclub.org.uk
Nearest main town: Bath

Secretary: Mr P. Ware   Tel: 01225 463834
                                          Fax: 01225 331027
Professional: Mr P. Hancox   Tel: 01225 466953

Playing: Midweek: round £28.00; day £32.00. Weekend: round £32.00; day £40.00.

Facilities: Bar: 11am–11pm. Food: Lunch and dinner from 11am–7pm. Bar snacks.

Comments: A lot of thought required here ... Accuracy rather than brute strength rewarded ... Best in Bath ... Ranks alongside some of Bristol's best ... Views over the city and countryside.

Clevedon Golf Club   ★★★

Castle Road, Clevedon, BS21 7AA
Website: www.clevedongolfclub.co.uk
E-mail: clevedongc.sec@virgin.net
Nearest main town: Clevedon

Secretary: Mr J. Cunning   Tel: 01275 874057
                                          Fax: 01275 341228
Professional: Mr R. Scanlan   Tel: 01275 874704
                                          Fax: 01275 341228

Playing: Midweek: round £28.00; day n/a. Weekend: round £40.00; day n/a.

Facilities: Bar: 11am–11pm. Food: Lunch and dinner from 11am–7pm. Bar snacks.

Comments: Long walks ... Variety and challenge in abundance ... Views over the Severn Estuary ... Exhilarating golf with a perfect backdrop.

Farrington Golf & Country Club (Main)   ★★★

Marsh Lane, Farrington Gurney, BS39 6TS
Website: www.farringtongolfclub.net
Nearest main town: Bath

Secretary: Mr S. Cook   Tel: 01761 451596
Fax: 01761 451021
Professional: Mr J. Cowgill   Tel: 01761 451046
Fax: 01761 451021

Playing: Midweek: round £20.00; day n/a. Weekend: round £30.00; day n/a.

Facilities: Bar: 11am–11pm. Food: Lunch and dinner from 11am–9pm. Bar snacks.

Comments: Not very pretty but excellent value ... Catering to every standard of golfer ... 27 holes of undiluted US-style golf ... Unimaginative design on unremarkable piece of land ... Valuable addition for area's golfers.

Isle of Wedmore Golf Club   ★★

Lineage, Lascotts Hill, Wedmore, BS28 4QT
Nearest main town: Wedmore

Secretary: Mr A. Edwards   Tel: 01934 713649
Fax: 01934 713696
Professional: Mr G. Coombe   Tel: 01934 712452

Playing: Midweek: round £18.00; day £22.00. Weekend: round £22.00; day £25.00.

Facilities: Bar: 11am–11pm. Food: Lunch and dinner from 11am–9pm. Bar snacks.

Comments: Natural course ... Views of Cheddar Valley make up for otherwise plain track ... Odd course, the 12th green cut at a 50-degree slope.

Mendip Golf Club ★

Gurney Slade, Radstock, Bath, BA3 4UT
Website: www.mendipgolfclub.co.uk   E-mail: mendipgc@lineone.net
Nearest main town: Bath

Secretary:	Mr B. Warren	Tel: 01749 840570
		Fax: 01749 841439
Professional:	Mr A. Marsh	Tel: 01749 841439

Playing: Midweek: round £21.00; day £26.00. Weekend: round £31.00; day n/a.

Facilities: Bar: 11am–11pm. Food: Lunch and dinner from 10am–10pm. Bar snacks.

Comments: Lovely springy turf ... Compact course ... Ordinary clubhouse ... Nice course, a little overrated in the area ... Above average condition ... Recommended at a fair price.

Mendip Spring Golf & Country Club ★★★

Honeyhall Lane, Congresbury, BS49 5JT
Website: www.mendipspring.co.uk
E-mail: mendipspringgolfclub@yahoo.co.uk
Nearest main town: Congresbury

Secretary:	Mr A. Melhuish	Tel: 01934 852322
Professional:	Messrs J. & R. Blackburn & Moss	Tel: 01934 852322
		Fax: 01934 853021

Playing: Midweek: round prices on application; day n/a. Weekend: round n/a; day n/a.

Facilities: Bar: 11am–11pm. Food: Lunch and dinner from 11am–9pm. Bar snacks.

Comments: Pleasant, friendly, well-laid-out course ... Best hole named Kin-el ... Good facilities, food and welcome ... Island green at the 12th ... Imaginative course kept in good order ... High-class golf facility.

Minehead & West Somerset Golf Club ★★

The Warren, Warren Road, Minehead, TA24 5SJ
Nearest main town: Minehead

Secretary:	Mr R. Raynor	Tel: 01643 702057
		Fax: 01643 705095

Professional: Mr I. Read   Tel: 01643 704378

Playing: Midweek: round n/a; day £24.50 (£19.00 after 12 noon). Weekend: round £27.50; day n/a.

Facilities: Bar: 11am–11pm. Food: Lunch and dinner from 10am–10pm. Bar snacks.

Comments: Links course set on a shingle spit ... Par-3 finish ... Can get windy ... Average condition ... Very flat and exposed.

Oake Manor Golf Club   ★★★

Oake, Taunton, TA4 1BA
Website: www.oakemanor.com   E-mail: russell@oakemanor.com
Nearest main town: Taunton

Secretary: Mr R. Gardner   Tel: 01823 461993
(Golf Operations Manager)   Fax: 01823 461995
Professional: Messrs R. & J. Gardner   Tel: 01823 461993
& Smallacombe   Fax: 01823 461995

Playing: Midweek: round £22.00; day £33.00. Weekend: round £25.00; day £44.00.

Facilities: Bar: 11am–11pm. Food: Lunch and dinner from 11am–10pm. Bar snacks.

Comments: Perfect parkland course at a bargain price ... Great condition for fairly new course ... Plenty of water hazards ... Flat course but difficult ... Great fun ... One of some high quality new courses in Somerset ... Surrounding countryside makes this course.

Orchardleigh Golf Club   ★★★

Frome, BA11 2PH
E-mail: info@orchardleighgolfclub.co.uk
Nearest main town: Frome

Secretary: Mr T. Atkinson   Tel: 01373 454200
Fax: 01373 454202
Professional: Mr I. Ridsdale   Tel: 01373 454206
Fax: 01373 454202

Playing: Midweek: round £30.00; day n/a. Weekend: round £40.00; day n/a.

Facilities: Bar: 11am–11pm. Food: Lunch and dinner from 11am–9pm. Bar snacks.

Comments: Been there every season and course always in good condition ... Superb new course in established parkland ... Feels as if it has been around for a long time ... Hats off to Brian Huggett for a fine design ... Another quality course in the West Country.

Weston-super-Mare Golf Club   ★★

Uphill Road North, Weston-super-Mare, BS23 4NQ
Website: www.westonsupermaregolfclub.com
E-mail: karen@wsmgolfclub.fsnet.co.uk
Nearest main town: Weston-super-Mare

Secretary: Mrs K. Drake   Tel: 01934 626968
                                          Fax: 01934 621360
Professional: Mr M. La Band   Tel: 01934 633360

Playing: Midweek: round £36.00; day £48.00. Weekend: round £54.00; day £60.00.

Facilities: Bar: 11am–11pm. Food: Lunch and dinner from 11am–10pm. Bar snacks.

Comments: Great opening hole right next to the beach ... Historic course that's part of the town ... Great condition ... Fine test ... So hard on the first try ... Never stop loving it.

Windwhistle Golf Club   ★

Cricket St Thomas, Chard, TA20 4DG
Website: www.windwhistlegolf.co.uk
Nearest main town: Chard

Secretary: Mr I. Dodd   Tel: 01460 30231
                                          Fax: 01460 30055
Professional: Mr P. Deeprose   Tel: 01460 30231

Playing: Midweek: round £20.00; day n/a. Weekend: round £25.00; day n/a.

Facilities: Bar: 11am–11pm. Food: Lunch and dinner from 10am–9pm. Bar snacks.

Comments: Relatively new course ... Great views at this course in the clouds ... Respected country club with eccentric course.

Yeovil Golf Club (Old)   ★★★

Sherborne Road, Yeovil, BA21 5BW
Website: www.yeovilgolfclub.co.uk
E-mail: yeovilgolfclub@yeovilgc.fsnet.co.uk
Nearest main town: Yeovil

Secretary:	Mr G. Dodd	Tel: 01935 422965
		Fax: 01935 411283
Professional:	Mr G. Kite	Tel: 01935 473763

Playing: Midweek: round £30.00 (Old); day £18.00 (Newton).
Weekend: round £40.00 (Old); day £20.00 (Newton).

Facilities: Bar: 11am–11pm. Food: Lunch from 11am–4pm.
Dinner by arrangement.

Comments: Mature, interesting course ... Attractive layout ... Not
too punishing ... Best holes on the back nine ... Good
value for condition of course ... Variable catering.

Staffordshire

Little Aston Golf Club ★★★★★

Roman Road, Streetly, B74 3AN
Website: www.littleastongolf.co.uk
E-mail: manager@littleastongolf.co.uk
Nearest main town: Birmingham

One feels that this little gem, tucked away in a corner of Staffordshire, known to many as the West Midlands, has to be one of the most unheralded courses in the British Isles. By that I mean that most golfers will have heard of it, but very few have played there or even know exactly where it is.

That is not to say that the club has made a particular effort to remain undiscovered. A number of major tournaments, particularly on the amateur circuit, have been held there and it is a venue that never fails to impress the visitor expecting 'just another parkland layout'.

This is to parkland golf what the Woodhall Spas and Sunningdales are to the heathland code. There are a number of excellent two-shot holes and the greens have great variety. Some are elevated onto plateaus, which are then protected by strong bunkering, while others are kept at ground level, allowing greater choice for the approach.

The course was originally laid down by the great Harry Vardon in 1908, although certain revisions were made by Harry Colt in the 1920s.

Secretary:	Mr G. Ridley	Tel: 0121 353 2942
		Fax: 0121 580 8387
Professional:	Mr B. Rimmer	Tel: 0121 353 0330
		Fax: 0121 580 8387
Playing:	Midweek: round £55.00; day £70.00. Weekend: round £55.00; day £70.00.	
Facilities:	Bar: 11am–11pm. Food: Lunch and dinner from 11am–8pm. Bar snacks.	
Comments:	Exceptional parkland course ... Vardon masterpiece ... Bunkering is lethal ... Sand everywhere ... A special place for golfers ... Blasted sand traps ... The best in Birmingham ... Some fine short par-4s ... Held some memorable Dunlop Masters here ... Exemplary condition and course ... Play it as soon as you can.	

Beau Desert Golf Club ★★★★

Rubeley Road, Hazel Slade, Cannock, WS12 0PJ
Website: www.bdgc.co.uk   E-mail: bdgc@btconnect.com
Nearest main town: Cannock

Secretary:	Mr J. Bradbury	Tel: 01543 422626
		Fax: 01543 451137
Professional:	Mr B. Stevens	Tel: 01543 422492
		Fax: 01543 451137

Playing: Midweek: round £40.00; day n/a. Weekend: round £50.00; day n/a.

Facilities: Bar: 8am–11pm. Food: Breakfast, lunch and dinner from 8am–9pm.

Comments: A hidden gem for the average player ... Heathland cut into pine forest ... Little gem in the Midlands ... Real test of golf ... Long carries off many tees and punishing rough ... A Herbert Fowler gem, always making you think ... Wicked heather, fascinating greens and lovely situation ... Every hole a pleasure ... What a charming course with great condition throughout.

Branston Golf & Country Club ★★★

Burton Road, Branston, Burton-on-Trent, DE14 3DP
Website: www.branston-golf-club.co.uk
E-mail: sales@branston-golf-club.co.uk
Nearest main town: Burton

Secretary:	None	Tel: 01283 543207
		Fax: 01283 566984
Professional:	Mr R. Odell	Tel: 01283 543207
		Fax: 01283 566984

Playing: Midweek: round £32.00; day n/a. Weekend: round £40.00; day n/a.

Facilities: Bar: 11am–11pm. Food: Breakfast, lunch and dinner from 7am–10pm.

Comments: Testing course that requires accurate irons ... A lot of golf clubs could learn from this one ... Flat course with natural water hazards ... Water torture ... Next to the River Trent.

Brocton Hall Golf Club   ★★★

Brocton, Stafford, ST17 0TH
E-mail: broctonsec@aol.com
Nearest main town: Stafford

Secretary: Mr G. Nicholls   Tel: 01785 661901
                                           Fax: 01785 661591
Professional: Mr N. Bland   Tel: 01785 661485

Playing: Midweek: round n/a; day £33.00. Weekend: round n/a;
                  day £40.00.

Facilities: Bar: 11am–11pm. Food: Lunch and dinner from
                  11am–11pm. Bar snacks.

Comments: Parkland course, kept in fine condition ... Greens
                  consistently good for this type of course ... Will go back
                  ... Not well known but excellent value.

Druids Heath Golf Club   ★★★★

Stonnall Road, Aldridge, WS9 8JZ
Nearest main town: Sutton Coldfield

Secretary: Mr K. Taylor   Tel: 01922 455595
                                           Fax: 01922 452887
Professional: Mr G. Williams   Tel: 01922 459523
                                           Fax: 01922 459523

Playing: Midweek: round £30.00; day £30.00. Weekend: round
                  £38.00 (after 2pm); day £38.00 (after 2pm).

Facilities: Bar: 11am–11pm. Food: Lunch and dinner from
                  11am–3pm. Bar snacks.

Comments: Nice course but very pretentious clubhouse ... Felt a bit
                  unwelcoming ... Some cracking holes ... Heathland
                  course.

Enville Golf Club (Highgate)   ★★★

Highgate Common, Enville, Stourbridge, DY7 5BN
Website: www.envillegolfclub.com
E-mail: secretary@envillegolfclub.com
Nearest main town: Stourbridge

Secretary: Mr J. Bishop   Tel: 01384 872074
                                           Fax: 01384 873396

Professional: Mr S. Power   Tel: 01384 872585

Playing: Midweek: round £30.00; day £40.00. Weekend: round n/a; day no visitors.

Facilities: Bar: 11am–7.30pm. Food: Lunch and dinner from 11am–7.30pm. Bar snacks.

Comments: Excellent greens and fairways surrounded by heather and trees ... Flat moorland course ... Far superior to the Lodge ... Overpriced.

Enville Golf Club (Lodge)   ★★★

Highgate Common, Enville, Stourbridge, DY7 5BN
Website: www.envillegolfclub.com
E-mail: secretary@envillegolfclub.com
Nearest main town: Stourbridge

Secretary: Mr J. Bishop   Tel: 01384 872074
                                      Fax: 01384 873396
Professional: Mr S. Power   Tel: 01384 872585

Playing: Midweek: round £30.00; day £40.00. Weekend: round n/a; day n/a.

Facilities: Bar: 11am–7.30pm. Food: Lunch and dinner from 11am–7.30pm. Bar snacks.

Comments: Not far behind the Highgate course ... Similar style to the main course ... Emphasis on accuracy ... Nicely balanced.

Leek Golf Club

Cheddleton Road, Leek, ST13 5RE
Nearest main town: Leek

Secretary: Mr J. Cooper   Tel: 01538 384779
                                      Fax: 01538 384535
Professional: None   Tel: 01538 384767
                                      Fax: 01538 384535

Playing: Midweek: round £26.00; day n/a. Weekend: round £32.00; day n/a.

Facilities: Bar: 11am–11pm. Food: Bar snacks. Dinner by arrangement.

Comments: Excellent condition ... Very challenging ... Always enjoy it here ... One for the notebook if you're around.

Patshull Park Hotel Golf & Country Club ★★

Pattingham, Wolverhampton, WV6 7HR
Website: www.patshull-park.co.uk   E-mail: sales@patshull-park.co.uk
Nearest main town: Wolverhampton

Secretary: None   Tel: 01902 700100
                                        Fax: 01902 700874
Professional: Mr R. Bissell   Tel: 01902 700342

Playing: Midweek: round £40.00; day n/a. Weekend: round £40.00; day n/a.

Facilities: Bar: 11am–11pm. Food: Breakfast, lunch and dinner from 7am–10pm. Bar snacks.

Comments: A natural course in tune with the landscape ... Very expensive for what you get ... Not in the same league as other Jacobs designs ... Good facilities.

Sandwell Park Golf Club ★★

Birmingham Road, West Bromwich, B71 4JJ
Website: www.sandwellparkgolfclub.co.uk
E-mail: secretary@sandwellparkgolfclub.co.uk
Nearest main town: West Bromwich

Secretary: Mr D. Paterson   Tel: 0121 553 4637
                                        Fax: 0121 525 1651
Professional: Mr N. Wylie   Tel: 0121 553 4384
                                        Fax: 0121 525 1651

Playing: Midweek: round £36.00 (18 holes), £42.00 (27/36 holes); day from £31.00 for society and company days. Weekend: round n/a; day n/a.

Facilities: Bar: 11am–11pm. Food: Lunch and dinner from 11am–9pm. Bar snacks.

Comments: Tight tree-lined course with fast greens the norm ... Heathland course in the Sandwell Valley ... Excellent value course – an oasis in a concrete jungle.

Seedy Mill Golf Club ★★

Elmhurst, Lichfield, WS13 3HE
Website: www.clubhaus.com
Nearest main town: Lichfield

Secretary:	Mr S. Dixon	Tel: 01543 417333
	(General Manager)	Fax: 01543 418098
Professional:	Mr C. Stanley	Tel: 01543 417333

Playing: Midweek: round £21.00; day n/a. Weekend: round £26.00; day n/a.

Facilities: Bar: 11am–11pm. Food: Bar snacks.

Comments: Simple course protected by heavy rough ... Greens not always in best shape ... New course with lakes, sculpted bunkers and excessive contouring ... Rolling parkland.

Swindon Golf Club   ★★★

Bridgnorth Road, Swindon, Dudley, DY3 4PH
Nearest main town: Dudley

Secretary:	Mrs R. Pope	Tel: 01902 897031
		Fax: 01902 326219
Professional:	Mr P. Tester	Tel: 01902 896191

Playing: Midweek: round £18.00; day £28.00. Weekend: round £27.00; day £40.00.

Facilities: Bar: 11am–10.30pm. Food: Breakfast and lunch from 8am–3pm. Dinner by arrangement.

Comments: Very fine layout on moorland ... Views make up for course deficiencies ... Right in the middle of the Black Country ... Not much room for error ... A very severe test ... One for the notebook.

Trentham Park Golf Club   ★

Trentham Park, Stoke-on-Trent, ST4 8AE
E-mail: trevor.berrisford@barbox.net
Nearest main town: Newcastle

Secretary:	Mr T. Berrisford	Tel: 01782 658800
		Fax: 01782 658800
Professional:	Mr S. Lynn	Tel: 01782 642125
		Fax: 01782 658800

Playing: Midweek: round n/a; day £30.00. Weekend: round n/a; day £35.00.

Facilities: Bar: 11am–11pm. Food: Lunch and dinner from 11am–9pm, except Mondays.

Comments: Woodland course that constantly surprises ... Condition not all it should be ... Very helpful pro and staff.

Westwood Golf Club (Leek) ★★

Newcastle Road, Leek, ST13 7AA
Nearest main town: Leek

Secretary: Mr C. Reid   Tel: 01538 398385
    Fax: 01538 382485

Professional: Mr D. Squire

Playing: Midweek: round £20.00 (unaccompanied visitors); day n/a. Weekend: round £20.00 (unaccompanied visitors); day n/a.

Facilities: Bar: 11am–11pm. Food: Lunch and dinner from 11am–9pm. Bar snacks.

Comments: A great welcome and interesting course ... Moorland course, nice and natural ... Value price for above-average course.

Whittington Heath Golf Club ★★★

Tamworth Road, Lichfield, WS14 9UN
E-mail: info@whgcgolf.freeserve.co.uk
Nearest main town: Lichfield

Secretary: Mrs J. Burton   Tel: 01543 432317
    Fax: 01543 433962

Professional: Mr A. Sadler   Tel: 01543 432261

Playing: Midweek: round £25.00 (18 holes), £42.00 (27 holes), £50.00 (36 holes); day n/a. Weekend: round no visitors; day n/a.

Facilities: Bar: 11am–9pm. Food: Breakfast, lunch and dinner from 8am–9pm. Bar snacks.

Comments: Heathland in woods ... Difficult well-guarded greens make up for lack of length ... Course in good condition and company excellent ... Peaceful, calm course ... Great doglegs ... Views of Lichfield Cathedral.

Suffolk

Royal Worlington & Newmarket Golf Club ★★★★

Golf Links Road, Worlington, Bury St Edmunds, IP28 8SD
E-mail: pinkjug@lineone.net
Nearest main town: Newmarket

Nine-hole courses are traditionally regarded with a certain amount of suspicion by golfers, who rather blithely dismiss them as 'fun' courses, lacking sufficient variety and length to provide a discernible challenge. Players who visit Royal Worlington generally have these illusions shattered by what is a very challenging and picturesque course, and almost certainly one of the best nine-hole courses in the world.

Suffolk is blessed with an excellent variety of courses, including the fiendishly difficult Aldeburgh, Purdis Heath, Woodbridge and Thorpeness, which prove excellent for holiday golfers to this quiet corner of England. Royal Worlington is situated some way away in the racing town of Newmarket, but is well worth the trip, particularly if you take in Gog Magog, on the southern side of the university town of Cambridge.

Royal Worlington, inaugurated in 1890, has a very linksy feel for an inland course, an impression which can in part be put down to the rather haphazard arrangement of holes, with a couple of par-3s crossing fairways, and drives being played almost straight over greens. This calls for a certain amount of courtesy to fellow players and a great deal of concentration to cope with the unusual layout. The links feel is also on account of the sandy soil, which provides excellent drainage.

The best holes come halfway, starting with the 5th, a stunning, bunkerless short hole, where an overlong shot is punished by the trees behind the green. The 7th is another fine par-3, with a classic saucer green leaving only the top of the pin visible from the tee.

It is hard not to come away from here impressed, and the plaudits heaped upon the course, particularly by journalists who have been known to get it wrong, in this case are completely justified.

Secretary:	Mr K. Weston	Tel: 01638 712216
Professional:	Mr M. Hawkins	Tel: 01638 715224

Playing: Midweek: round n/a; day £40.00–£55.00. Weekend: round n/a; day no visitors.

Facilities: Bar: 11am–11pm. Food: Lunch from 12pm–2.30pm. Bar snacks.

Comments: How did they design such a great nine holes in a large field? ... A real treat and will return soon ... The best nine-hole course in the world? ... Wonderfully traditional ... Who needs 18 when you've got nine of this quality? ... Will be back ... Stunning short course.

Aldeburgh Golf Club ★★★★

Saxmundham Road, Aldeburgh, IP15 5PE
E-mail: info@aldeburghgolfclub.co.uk
Nearest main town: Aldeburgh

Secretary:	Mr I. Simpson	Tel: 01728 452890
		Fax: 01728 452937
Professional:	Mr K. Preston	Tel: 01728 453309

Playing: Midweek: round n/a; day £45.00. Weekend: round n/a; day £60.00.

Facilities: Bar: 11am–11pm. Food: Lunch from 11am–4pm.

Comments: A hard course to play to your handicap ... Terrific collection of par-4s, bunkers and gorse ... Tight and difficult ... Hard-running at times ... Real tough cookie ... Standard scratch says it all.

Brett Vale Golf Club ★

Noakes Road, Raydon, Ipswich, IP7 5LR
Website: www.brettvalegolf.com   E-mail: info@brettvalegolf.com
Nearest main town: Ipswich

Secretary:	Mr J. Reid	Tel: 01473 310718
Professional:	Mr R. Taylor	Tel: 01473 310718

Playing: Midweek: round £20.00; day n/a. Weekend: round £25.00; day n/a.

Facilities: Bar: 11am–11pm. Food: Bar snacks.

Comments: Well-fashioned course that runs through a nature reserve ... A course completely in tune with the surroundings ... Condition generally good ... Will always have affection for this place.

Bury St Edmunds Golf Club   ★★★

Tut Hill, Bury St Edmunds, IP28 6LG
Nearest main town: Bury St Edmunds

Secretary: Mr J. Sayer   Tel: 01284 755979
                                     Fax: 01284 763288
Professional: Mr M. Jillings   Tel: 01284 755978

Playing: Midweek: round £24.00; day £26.00. Weekend: round
                  n/a; day n/a.

Facilities: Bar: 11am–11pm. Food: Bar snacks. Dinner by
                  arrangement.

Comments: Welcoming members' course ... Parkland with a few
                  twists along the way ... Heartily recommended ...
                  Another quality Suffolk course.

Felixstowe Ferry Golf Club   ★★★

Ferry Road, Felixstowe, IP11 9RY
Website: www.felixstowegolf.co.uk
E-mail: secretary@felixstowegolf.co.uk
Nearest main town: Felixstowe

Secretary: Mr R. Tibbs   Tel: 01394 286834
                                     Fax: 01394 273679
Professional: Mr I. Macpherson   Tel: 01394 283975

Playing: Midweek: round n/a; day £35.00 (before 1pm), £25.00
                  (after 1pm). Weekend: round n/a; day £40.00 (after 2pm).

Facilities: Bar: 11am–9pm. Food: Bar snacks. Catering
                  11am–3pm (evenings on request).

Comments: Links for the purist ... Bleak but warming landscape ...
                  Feels very fresh and exciting here ... Very unusual course
                  for Suffolk ... Plays like a dream.

Hintlesham Hall Golf Club   ★

Hintlesham, Ipswich, IP8 3NS
Website: www.hintleshamhallgolfclub.com
E-mail: office@hintleshamhallgolfclub.com
Nearest main town: Ipswich

Secretary: Mr I. Procter   Tel: 01473 652761
                                     Fax: 01473 652750

Professional: Mr A. Spink   Tel: 01473 656006
Fax: 01473 652750

Playing: Midweek: round £36.00; day n/a. Weekend: round £44.00; day n/a.

Facilities: Bar: 11am–11pm. Food: Lunch and dinner from 11am–9pm. Bar snacks.

Comments: Mature parkland course in grounds of sumptuous hotel ... Very regal atmosphere ... Quality through and through ... Very established and inviting.

Ipswich Golf Club (Purdis Heath)   ★★★

Purdis Heath, Bucklesham Road, Ipswich, IP3 8UQ
Website: www.ipswichgolfclub.com
E-mail: mail@ipswichgolfclub.com
Nearest main town: Ipswich

Secretary: Mr N. Ellice   Tel: 01473 728941
Fax: 01473 715236
Professional: Mr S. Whymark   Tel: 01473 724017
Fax: 01473 715236

Playing: Midweek: round n/a; day £45.00 (£35.00 after 12pm). Weekend: round n/a; day £50.00 (£45.00 after 12pm).

Facilities: Bar: 11am–11pm. Food: Breakfast, lunch and dinner from 8am–7pm. Bar snacks.

Comments: A hidden gem in Suffolk ... Heathland beauty, well worth the visit ... Nothing else like it in Suffolk ... As good as it gets.

Rushmere Golf Club   ★★★

Rushmere Heath, Ipswich, IP4 5QQ
Website: www.club-noticeboard.co.uk/rushmere
E-mail: rushmeregolfclub@talk21.com
Nearest main town: Ipswich

Secretary: Mr R. Tawell   Tel: 01473 725648
Fax: 01473 273852
Professional: None   Tel: 01473 728076

Playing: Midweek: round £30.00; day n/a. Weekend: round £30.00; day n/a.

Facilities: Bar: 11am–11pm. Food: Lunch from 12pm–2.30pm. Bar snacks. Dinner by arrangement.

Comments: Rather ragged heathland course ... At the mercy of the wind ... Watch out you don't get blown away.

Seckford Golf Club   ★★★

Seckford Hall Road, Woodbridge, IP13 6NT
Website: www.seckfordgolf.co.uk   E-mail: info@seckfordgolf.co.uk
Nearest main town: Woodbridge

Secretary:	Mr N. Grundtvig	Tel: 01394 446193
		Fax: 01394 382818
Professional:	Messrs S. & N. Jay & Grundtvig	Tel: 01394 388000
		Fax: 01394 382818

Playing: Midweek: round £13.00 (9 holes), £20.00 (18 holes); day n/a. Weekend: round £15.00 (9 holes), £30.00 (18 holes before 12pm), £20.00 (18 holes after 12pm); day n/a.

Facilities: Bar: 11am–11pm. Food: Lunch and dinner from 11am–8pm. Bar snacks.

Comments: Short course but not without charm ... Keeps getting better ... Riveting stretch of finishing holes ... A little open ... Too easy.

Stoke-by-Nayland Golf Club (Constable)   ★★

Keepers Lane, Leavenheath, Colchester, CO6 4PZ
Website: www.stokebynaylandclub.co.uk
E-mail: info@golf-club.co.uk
Nearest main town: Colchester

Secretary:	Mr P. Barfield	Tel: 01206 262836
		Fax: 01206 263356
Professional:	Mr K. Lovelock	Tel: 01206 262769

Playing: Midweek: round £22.00; day £35.00. Weekend: round £27.50; day n/a.

Facilities: Bar: 11am–11pm. Food: Bar snacks.

Comments: Just shorter than the Gainsborough but just as good ... Not great condition but fun ... Very similar to the Gainsborough ... Parkland of very little character.

Stoke-by-Nayland Golf Club (Gainsborough) ★★★

Keepers Lane, Leavenheath, Colchester, CO6 4PZ
Website: www.stokebynaylandclub.co.uk
E-mail: info@golf-club.co.uk
Nearest main town: Colchester

Secretary:	Mr P. Barfield	Tel: 01206 262836
		Fax: 01206 263356
Professional:	Mr K. Lovelock	Tel: 01206 262769

Playing: Midweek: round £25.00; day £40.00. Weekend: round £35.00; day £50.00 (after 12pm).

Facilities: Bar: 11am–11pm. Food: Bar snacks.

Comments: Playing both courses in a day gives better value ... Great value for societies ... It's got everything for a day's golf including the best value ... Undulating course with water and plenty of natural hazards ... Not bad for a golf centre.

The Suffolk Golf & Country Club ★★★

Fornham Street, Genevieve, Bury St Edmunds, IP28 6JQ
Website: www.the-suffolk.co.uk E-mail: thelodge@the-suffolk.co.uk
Nearest main town: Bury St Edmunds

Secretary:	Mr P. Thorpe	Tel: 01284 706777
		Fax: 01284 706721
Professional:	Mr S. Hall	Tel: 01284 706777
		Fax: 01284 706721

Playing: Midweek: round £25.00; day n/a. Weekend: round £30.00; day n/a.

Facilities: Bar: 11am–11pm. Food: Breakfast, lunch and dinner from 7am–9pm. Bar snacks.

Comments: A country club course that's very boring ... Flat and rather dull ... Condition good ... Smattering of water hazards ... Tough for beginners.

Thorpeness Hotel & Golf Club ★★★★

Lakeside Avenue, Thorpeness, Leiston, IP16 4NH
Website: www.thorpeness.co.uk E-mail: charlie@thorpeness.co.uk
Nearest main town: Aldeburgh

Secretary:	Mr C. Damonsing	Tel: 01728 452176
	(Golf Manager)	Fax: 01728 453868
Professional:	Mr F. Hill	Tel: 01728 454926
		Fax: 01728 453868

Playing: Midweek: round £35.00; day £35.00. Weekend: round £40.00; day £40.00.

Facilities: Bar: 11am–11pm. Food: Breakfast, lunch and dinner from 7am–10pm. Bar snacks.

Comments: This course has it all – especially gorse ... Takes golf to the next level ... Excellent society venue and good value for money ... Tough, interesting track with super practice facilities and catering ... James Braid design of classic brilliance.

Best Western Ufford Park Hotel, Golf & Leisure   ★★

Yarmouth Road, Ufford, Woodbridge, IP12 1QW
Website: www.uffordpark.co.uk   E-mail: mail@uffordpark.co.uk
Nearest main town: Ipswich

Secretary:	Mr R. Tidy	Tel: 01394 382836
		Fax: 01394 383582
Professional:	Mr S. Robertson	Tel: 01394 383480
		Fax: 01394 383480

Playing: Midweek: round from £18.00; day n/a. Weekend: round from £20.00; day n/a.

Facilities: Bar: 11am–11pm. Food: Breakfast, lunch and dinner from 7am–10pm. Bar snacks.

Comments: Good feel about place ... Natural parkland track making good use of unremarkable land ... Leisure complex more than a golf club ... Facility for beginners.

Woodbridge Golf Club   ★★★

Bromeswell Heath, Woodbridge, IP12 2PF
E-mail: woodbridgegc@anglianet.co.uk
Nearest main town: Woodbridge

Secretary:	Mr A. Theunissen	Tel: 01394 382038
		Fax: 01394 382392
Professional:	Mr A. Hubbert	Tel: 01394 383213

Playing: Midweek: round n/a; day £33.00 (Main), £16.00 (Forest – 9 holes). Weekend: round n/a; day n/a.

Facilities: Bar: 11am–11pm. Food: Breakfast, lunch and dinner from 9am–9pm. Bar snacks.

Comments: Old-fashioned atmosphere ... One of the best courses in East Anglia ... Heavenly place on high ground ... At its best in the autumn ... A magical place – the best in Suffolk.

Surrey

St George's Hill Golf Club ★★★★★

Golf Club Road, St George's Hill, Weybridge, KT13 0NL
Website: www.stgeorgeshillgolfclub.co.uk
E-mail: admin@stgeorgeshillgolfclub.co.uk
Nearest main town: Weybridge

Shots rang out through the trees on St George's Hill long before any golfers were set loose on the land. The sounds emanated from the pond that is now flanked by the 9th fairway. Dead man's pond to be exact, for it was here that the last duel to be fought on British soil is believed to have taken place.

Today the only shots to be heard echoing through the trees are those from golfers as they plot their way round one of the most scenically beautiful courses that the heathlands of Surrey have to offer. St George's Hill, near Weybridge, has long been regarded in high esteem and is, frankly, a gem.

The estate of St George's Hill exudes exclusivity. The fairways roll past properties that sit amid meticulously mown lawns, but that was the way it was always meant to be when a local builder, a Mr Tarrant, acquired the land in the 1900s. He engaged Harry Colt to design the course, but due to a shortage of funds he sold the site to concentrate on another course sited at Virginia Water, which came to be known as Wentworth.

While many of Surrey's heath and heather courses appear to be clones of each other, St George's Hill stands apart. There is the profusion of heather and gorse that you would expect from a course in this part of the country, but, unlike its neighbours, St George's Hill is played over very undulating, spectacular terrain, making for exhilarating golf with deep drops and blind drives. There are no weak holes here. From the 1st, where you drive over a valley, it's one classic after another.

The beauty of St George's Hill goes unchallenged. As Bernard Darwin once wrote: 'The prettiest courses are also the best and certainly one of the best is St George's Hill.'

Secretary: Mr J. Robinson   Tel: 01932 847758
                               Fax: 01932 821564
Professional: Mr A. Rattue   Tel: 01932 843523
                               Fax: 01932 843523

Playing: Midweek: round £80.00 (Visitors only accepted Wed, Thurs, Fri); day £105.00 (Visitors only accepted Wed, Thurs, Fri). Weekend: round n/a; day n/a.

Facilities: Bar: 11am–11pm. Food: Lunch from 11am–3pm. Bar snacks. Dinner by arrangement.

Comments: Wonderful tall pines ... Tee shots very intimidating ... A match for any course in the country ... Better than Wentworth and without the attitude ... Grandeur nestled in beauty ... Very old, very traditional, but welcoming ... Wooded course with spilling heather.

Sunningdale Golf Club (Old)   ★★★★★

Ridgemount Road, Sunningdale, SL5 9RR
Website: www.sunningdale-golfclub.co.uk
Nearest main town: Sunningdale

Seve Ballesteros knew what he was doing when he helped put Sunningdale back on the professional golf map by taking the Seve Trophy, a team event between Great Britain and Ireland and the rest of Europe, there in the spring of 2000.

Sunningdale's Old course is steeped in history, whether it's the famous 66 of Bobby Jones, 33 out and 33 back, or the European Open tournaments that used to be held there in the early 1990s. It is only recently that the club has slipped off the regular fixture list of the European Tour, which is partly due to the fact that the course may now be considered a little short by today's long-hitting standards.

The fact that the Seve Trophy was such a success, however, tends to prove that Sunningdale can still have a part to play and there is no doubt that if you were to poll the professional Tour players of today many of them would welcome a return there.

There are, of course, two layouts at Sunningdale and it is a perpetual argument as to which is the best. The Old, designed by Willie Park in 1901, gets all the acclaim and can boast the best holes on the estate, particularly the stretches from the 5th to the 7th and those holes just after the turn. But it has a couple of slightly weaker holes, something that the New, designed by Harry Colt in 1922, does not. The New course is tougher and maintains a high standard from start to finish without producing a hole that is 'stand alone' stunning.

At the end of the day, the advice is to try both; that way you are guaranteed just about the best that heathland golf has to offer.

Secretary: Mr S. Zuill   Tel: 01344 621681
                                        Fax: 01344 624154
Professional: Mr K. Maxwell   Tel: 01344 620128
                                        Fax: 01344 874903

Playing: Midweek: round £135.00; day n/a. Weekend: round n/a; day n/a.

Facilities: Bar: 11am–8pm. Food: Lunch and dinner from 10am–6pm.

Comments: Magical heathland course ... What golf is all about ... Requires real thought ... Wonderful course and club ... Lovely course, requiring straight-hitting ... Expensive but just has to be played ... As good as you can get – at a price ... Traditional course – always enjoyable but too expensive ... My choice for the final round of my life ... The blueprint for all courses ... Not bad, but overpriced and surely an easy course ... No better place to play an inland course than at Sunningdale ... Stand on the 10th tee and just take a deep breath – magic.

Walton Heath Golf Club (Old)   ★★★★★

Deans Lane, Walton-on-the-Hill, Tadworth, KT20 7TP
Website: www.whgc.co.uk   E-mail: secretary@whgc.co.uk
Nearest main town: Tadworth

So many of Surrey's heathland courses can, to the uninitiated eye, appear very similar. Fairways clad in heather and gorse and flanked on both sides by deep woodland of pines and silver birch. Walton Heath, while retaining much of the flavour, has a unique charm about it, possibly because it is much more wild and open than its close cousins.

There are two courses, the Old and the New, and for the professional tournaments that have been held there, a composite of the two has been used. It is difficult to distinguish which is the best, although it is the Old course, which began as nine holes in 1907, which generally gets the vote. That could be because of its mighty finish, which was once described by Tom Weiskopf as among the best he had seen. A cracking par-4 to a tough raised green, which has a cavernous bunker chewing into its right corner, is followed by a par-3 over a small valley. Then there's a finishing hole that has a bunker short of the green stretching from one side of the fairway to the other.

Walton Heath is steeped in a fascinating history. Five times Open champion James Braid was the first professional there and the great cricketer W. G. Grace was a member. It was rumoured that he made almost as many hundreds on the heath as he did at the Oval.

The club, which has one of the best putting greens you'll find anywhere, has also had plenty of MPs on its books. Just prior to the First World War, no less than twenty-four Members played there, including a young Winston Churchill and David Lloyd George.

Secretary: Mr M. Bawden   Tel: 01737 812380
                                 Fax: 01737 814225
Professional: Mr K. Macpherson   Tel: 01737 812152
                                 Fax: 01737 814225

Playing: Midweek: round £80.00; day n/a. Weekend: round £90.00; day n/a.

Facilities: Bar: 11am–9pm. Food: Lunch from 11.30am–2.30pm. Afternoon tea.

Comments: Make use of the caddies – most helpful ... Suffers from ludicrously high heather ... Best course near London ... Fantastic course in very good condition ... Hard but fair ... Bloody heather ... Superb food after damn difficult game ... Will be back again and again.

The Wentworth Golf Club (West)   ★★★★★

Wentworth Drive, Virginia Water, GU25 4LS
Website: www.wentworthclub.com
E-mail: reception@wentworthclub.com
Nearest main town: Guildford

Even before the European Tour moved their offices there from the Oval, Wentworth had long been the home of professional golf in this country. The West course, or Burma Road as it is often known, has become hallowed turf through its long familiarity with the greatest names in the history of the game.

The Tour's flagship PGA Championship is the real prestige event to be held there, but many of the biggest names head to the West course to compete in the World Matchplay Championship each autumn. Tiger Woods, Seve Ballesteros and Arnold Palmer mark the generations that have tackled one of the severest tests to be had for inland golf in Britain.

It's a big course, measuring well over 7000 yards from the back, and it has a delicious balance of holes that mixes birdie opportunities with some treacherous turns that you can bogey just as easily. The opening hole is a long par-4 with a huge swell short of the green, and the 3rd, with its three-tiered green, can also trip you up. The 4th, though, is a very birdieable par-5 and the 6th is a driver, wedge par-4. And so it goes on, weaving its way out into the heathland country throwing challenges down at every turn. It is a classic course with a classic double par-5 finish that has been the scene of so many 72-hole tournament dramas.

The East course, by contrast, is much shorter and far less severe. Nevertheless, it's a gem to play and possesses what many feel is the best hole on the estate, the par-4 11th.

The South, or Edinburgh course, is not quite in the same league as its two sisters and was a comparatively recent addition to the estate. Gary Player and John Jacobs were behind the design, which has too many doglegs and not enough moments of real inspiration to join the other two in the top 100 listings.

Secretary:	Mr S. Christie	Tel: 01344 842201
		Fax: 01344 842804
Professional:	Mr D. Rennie	Tel: 01344 846306
		Fax: 01344 842804

Playing: Midweek: round in summer £220.00 (West), £45.00 (Edinburgh), £115.00 (East); day n/a. Weekend: round n/a; day n/a.

Facilities: Bar: 11am–11pm. Food: Lunch from 12pm–2.30pm. Dinner from 6pm–9.30pm. Bar snacks.

Comments: Course always in excellent condition … Any serious golfers must play this course … Exceptional course, well laid out … Truly a championship course … Corporate membership has proved exceptional value for money … Wonderful, peaceful setting … Front tees can mess up this course and take driver out of your hands … Not as hard as it looks but still good quality … For the money, is it really worth it? … Good condition but what should you expect for the price?

The Addington Golf Club   ★★★★

205 Shirley Church Road, Croydon, CR0 5AB
E-mail: theaddgc@dialstart.net
Nearest main town: Croydon

Secretary:	Mr B. Hill	Tel: 020 8777 1055
		Fax: 020 8777 1701
Professional:	None	

Playing: Midweek: round £55.00; day n/a. Weekend: round £80.00; day n/a.

Facilities: Bar: 11am–11pm. Food: Lunch from 12pm–2.30pm.

Comments: Very good course tucked away in suburbia ... A forgotten gem in London – beautiful ... Some stunning holes, but course lacked condition ... A wonderful course, forgotten by golfers everywhere ... Just the best experience in 10 years of golf – will be back.

Burhill Golf Club   ★★★

Burwood Road, Walton-on-Thames, KT12 4BL
Website: www.burghillgolf-club.co.uk
E-mail: sally@burhillgolf-club.co.uk
Nearest main town: Walton-on-Thames

Secretary: Mr D. Cook   Tel: 01932 227345
                  (General Manager)   Fax: 01932 267159
Professional: Mr L. Johnson   Tel: 01932 221729

Playing: Midweek: round n/a; day £62.50. Weekend: round n/a; day n/a.

Facilities: Bar: 11am–11pm. Food: Lunch from 11.30am–2.30pm. Bar snacks.

Comments: Lots of long par-4s and a great clubhouse ... Never known it in anything but immaculate condition ... True greens ... Welcoming clubhouse ... One of the friendlier clubs in Surrey ... Short and difficult ... Give me the keys to this place!

Camberley Heath Golf Club Ltd   ★★★

Golf Drive, Camberley, GU15 1JG
Website: www.camberleyheathgolfclub.co.uk
E-mail: info@camberleyheathgolfclub.co.uk
Nearest main town: Camberley

Secretary: Mr M. Harris   Tel: 01276 23258
                                        Fax: 01276 692505
Professional: Mr G. Ralph   Tel: 01276 27905
                                        Fax: 01276 692505

Playing: Midweek: round £52.00; day n/a. Weekend: round £68.00; day n/a.

Facilities: Bar: 11am–9pm. Food: Bar snacks. English and Japanese cuisine.

Comments: Good quality of service ... Odd course with tight fairways and a lot of heather ... Heath and heather – what a treat ... One of Harry Colt's best ... A delight ... Typical Surrey course – heather and gorse spilling everywhere.

Coombe Hill Golf Club

Golf Club Drive, off Coombe Lane West, Kingston, KT2 7DF
Website: www.coombehillgolfclub.com
E-mail: thesecretary@coombehillgolf.demon.co.uk
Nearest main town: New Maldon

Secretary: Mrs C. DeFoy   Tel: 020 8336 7600
                                                  Fax: 020 8336 7601
Professional: Mr C. DeFoy   Tel: 020 8336 7615
                                                  Fax: 020 8336 7601

Playing: Midweek: round £80.00 (18 holes), £100.00 (36 holes); day n/a. Weekend: round n/a; day n/a.

Facilities: Bar: 11am–11pm. Food: Lunch from 11am–6pm. Bar snacks.

Comments: Conditioning always top class ... Far too pricey ... Charming course but not at that price ... At its best during spring and early summer.

Drift Golf Club   ★★★

Drift Road, East Horsley, KT24 5HD
Website: www.driftgolfclub.com   E-mail: info@driftgolfclub.com
Nearest main town: East Horsley

Secretary: Mr L. Greasley   Tel: 01483 284641
                          (General Manager)   Fax: 01483 284642
Professional: Mr M. Smith   Tel: 01483 284772
                                                  Fax: 01483 284642

Playing: Midweek: round £35.00; day £45.00. Weekend: round £45.00 (after 12pm), £25.00 (after 3pm); day n/a.

Facilities: Bar: 11am–11pm. Food: Lunch from 11.30am–2.30pm. Bar snacks.

Comments: Tight, tree-lined course with very fast greens ... Long
woodland course ... Par-73 and feels it ... Get away
from it all here ... A great place to contemplate.

Duke's Dene Golf Club   ★★

Slines New Road, Woldingham, CR3 7HA
Website: www.clubhaus.com
Nearest main town: Woldingham

Secretary: Mr T. Del Sol   Tel: 01883 653501
                                            Fax: 01883 653502
Professional: Mr P. Thornley   Tel: 01883 653541

Playing: Midweek: round £25.00; day £45.00. Weekend: round
£30.00; day n/a.

Facilities: Bar: 11am–11pm. Food: Bar snacks. Sunday lunch
only.

Comments: Great layout with some difficult holes ... Excellent clubhouse and food ... Valley course ... A little bit different
to normal Surrey fare ... Food excellent ... A pleasure to
play.

Effingham Golf Club   ★★★

Guildford Road, Effingham, KT24 5PZ
Website: www.effinghamgolfclub.com
E-mail: secretary@effinghamgolfclub.com
Nearest main town: Guildford

Secretary: Mr S. Sheppard   Tel: 01372 452203
                                            Fax: 01372 459959
Professional: Mr S. Hoatson   Tel: 01372 452606

Playing: Midweek: round £45.00; day n/a. Weekend: round n/a;
day n/a.

Facilities: Bar: 11am–11pm. Food: Lunch from 11.30am–
2.30pm. Bar snacks.

Comments: A treat to play ... Well presented all year round ...
Exhausting long course ... Downland track ... A warm
reception at this mature club.

Epsom Golf Club   ★★

Longdown Lane South, Epsom Downs, Epsom, KT17 4JR
Website: www.epsomgolfclub.co.uk
E-mail: enquiries@epsomgolfclub.co.uk
Nearest main town: Epsom

Secretary: Mr L. Anderson   Tel: 01372 721666
                                        Fax: 01372 817183
Professional: Mr R. Goudie   Tel: 01372 741867

Playing: Midweek: round £26.00; day £36.00. Weekend: round
                  £30.00; day £40.00.

Facilities: Bar: 11am–11pm. Food: Bar snacks.

Comments: A short course with quality holes on the back nine ...
                  Right next to the racecourse ... Consistently good
                  greens throughout the year ... Undulating turf ...
                  Something about the grandstands that makes this
                  course special.

Farnham Golf Club   ★★

The Sands, Farnham, GU10 1PX
Website: www.farnhamgolfclub.com
E-mail: info@farnhamgolfclub.com
Nearest main town: Farnham

Secretary: Mrs J. Elliott   Tel: 01252 782109
                                        Fax: 01252 781185
Professional: Mr G. Cowlishaw   Tel: 01252 782198

Playing: Midweek: round £40.00; day n/a. Weekend: round n/a;
                  day n/a.

Facilities: Bar: 11am–11pm. Food: Bar snacks.

Comments: Good front nine, full of character ... Worth a look ...
                  Opening nine far superior ... Longish course worth
                  playing once or twice ... Enjoyed every minute.

Foxhills Golf Club (Chertsey)   ★★★★

Stonehill Road, Ottershaw, KT16 0EL
Nearest main town: Chertsey

Secretary: Mr A. Laking   Tel: 01932 872050
                                        Fax: 01932 874762

Professional: Mr A. Good   Tel: 01932 873961
                                      Fax: 01932 872913

Playing: Midweek: round £50.00; day £70.00. Weekend: round
                  £65.00; day n/a.

Facilities: Bar: 11am–11pm. Food: Lunch from 11am–3pm.
                  Dinner from 7pm–9.30pm. Bar snacks.

Comments: Tree-lined treasure ... Excellent golf club ... Courses
                  both have distinctive character ... Chertsey almost un-
                  animously preferred to the Longcross.

Gatton Manor Hotel Golf & Country Club   ★★

Standon Lane, Ockley, RH5 5PQ
Website: www.gattonmanor.co.uk
E-mail: gattonmanor@enterprise.net
Nearest main town: Dorking

Secretary: Mrs L. Heath   Tel: 01306 627555
                  (Managing Director)   Fax: 01306 627713
Professional: Mr R. Sargent   Tel: 01306 627557
                                        Fax: 01306 627713

Playing: Midweek: round £25.00 (summer), £20.00 (winter); day
                  n/a. Weekend: round £35.00 (summer), £25.00
                  (winter); day n/a.

Facilities: Bar: 11am–11pm. Food: Lunch and dinner from
                  11am–10pm. Bar snacks.

Comments: Sprawling country-club course ... Standard country-club
                  fare ... A little soulless ... Water hazards will test your
                  nerves.

Guildford Golf Club   ★★★

High Path Road, Merrow, Guildford, GU1 2HL
Website: www.guildfordgolfclub.co.uk
E-mail: secretary@guildfordgolfclub.co.uk
Nearest main town: Guildford

Secretary: Mr B. Green   Tel: 01483 563941
                                       Fax: 01483 453228
Professional: Mr P. Hollington   Tel: 01483 566765

Playing: Midweek: round £36.00; day n/a. Weekend: round n/a;
                  day n/a.

Facilities: Bar: 11am–11pm. Food: Lunch and dinner from 11am–9pm. Bar snacks.

Comments: Unusual course but pleasant ... Excellent greens ... Setting ensures all-year-round play ... Clear away the cobwebs on this invigorating course ... One for the notebook ... Easily missed but you will regret it.

Hankley Common Golf Club   ★★★★

The Clubhouse, Tilford, Farnham, GU10 2DD
Website: www.hankley.co.uk   E-mail: jhay@hankley-commongc.co.uk
Nearest main town: Farnham

Secretary: Mr J. Scott   Tel: 01252 792493
                                    Fax: 01252 795699
Professional: Mr P. Stow   Tel: 01252 793761
                                    Fax: 01252 795699

Playing: Midweek: round £55.00; day £70.00. Weekend: round £70.00; day n/a.

Facilities: Bar: 11am–11pm. Food: Lunch from 11.20am–3pm. Bar snacks. Dinner by arrangement.

Comments: Excellent course – better than Sunningdale ... Superb greens ... Unexpected links character in places ... Greens first class ... Many memorable holes on this heathland masterpiece ... Give me this anyday ... Highly rated course that matches its billing ... Oh, to live in Surrey.

The Hindhead Golf Club   ★★★★

Churt Road, Hindhead, GU26 6HX
Website: www.the-hindhead-golf-club.co.uk
E-mail: secretary@the-hindhead-golf-club.co.uk
Nearest main town: Hindhead

Secretary: Mr J. Davies   Tel: 01428 604614
                                    Fax: 01428 608508
Professional: Mr I. Benson   Tel: 01428 604458
                                    Fax: 01428 608508

Playing: Midweek: round £40.00; day £50.00. Weekend: round £65.00; day n/a.

Facilities: Bar: 11am–11pm. Food: Bar snacks.

Comments: Elevated tees looking down on heather – magnificent ...
Made very welcome ... Visually preferred the first nine in
the valley ... Great view from the bar onto the 18th ...
Two different nines but heath and heather all the way ...
Take this any day over links golf ... One of the best in
Surrey.

Merrist Wood Golf Club   ★★★

Coombe Lane, Worplesdon, Guildford, GU3 3PE
Website: www.merristwood-golfclub.co.uk
E-mail: mwgc@merristwood-golfclub.co.uk
Nearest main town: Worplesdon

Secretary: Mr P. Flavin   Tel: 01483 238890
                                     Fax: 01483 238896
Professional: Mr C. Connell   Tel: 01483 238897

Playing: Midweek: round from £20.00 (please ring for up-to-
date packages); day n/a. Weekend: round from £25.00;
day n/a.

Facilities: Bar: 11am–11pm. Food: Breakfast, lunch and dinner
from 10am–10pm.

Comments: Course, pro shop, welcome and food all very good ...
Good day's golf ... Unusual Surrey course with little
heather ... Relaxed atmosphere at this private members'
club ... Good fun, if a little open ... Rather play nearby
Worplesdon and Woking ... As if Surrey needed another
course.

New Zealand Golf Club   ★★★★

Woodham Lane, Addlestone, KT15 3QD
E-mail: roger.marrett@nzgc.org
Nearest main town: Woking

Secretary: Mr R. Marrett   Tel: 01932 345049
                                      Fax: 01932 342891
Professional: Mr V. Elvidge   Tel: 01932 349619

Playing: Midweek: round £50.00; day £65.00. Weekend: round
n/a; day n/a.

Facilities: Bar: 11am–7pm. Food: Lunch from 12pm–2.30pm.
Bar snacks.

Comments: Never have a bad time here ... Riveting course ... Heathland with bags of style ... Up there with the best.

Pyrford Golf Club   ★★★

Warren Lane, Pyrford, GU22 8XR
E-mail: pyrford@americangolf.uk.com
Nearest main town: Ripley

Secretary:	Mr P. Dawson	Tel: 01483 723555
		Fax: 01483 729777
Professional:	Mr D. Brewer	Tel: 01483 751070

Playing: Midweek: round £40.00; day n/a. Weekend: round £60.00; day n/a.

Facilities: Bar: 11am–11pm. Food: Bar snacks.

Comments: Don't count your chickens until you've played the final two holes – tough ... Nice attempt to recreate links feel in middle of Surrey ... 25 acres of water ... Try the Pyrford experience ... Water fun that you will remember.

Reigate Heath Golf Club   ★★

The Club House, Reigate Heath, RH2 8QR
Website: www.reigateheathgolfclub.co.uk
E-mail: reigateheath@surreygolf.co.uk
Nearest main town: Reigate

Secretary:	Mr R. Perkins	Tel: 01737 226793
		Fax: 01737 249226
Professional:	Mr B. Davies	

Playing: Midweek: round £25.00; day n/a. Weekend: round members' guests only; day n/a.

Facilities: Bar: 11am–11pm. Food: Lunch from 11.30am–2.30pm. Bar snacks.

Comments: The best nine-hole course in Surrey ... Real heath and heather course of charm ... Not the best condition but good fun ... Members very proud of their course ... Pine and birch trees the backdrop for shots.

The Richmond Golf Club ★

Sudbrook Park, Richmond, TW9 7AS
Website: www.therichmondgolfclub.streamline.co.uk
E-mail: generalmanager.rgc@tiscali.co.uk
Nearest main town: Richmond

Secretary: Mr D. Cromie   Tel: 020 8940 4351
(General Manager)   Fax: 020 8332 7914
Professional: Mr N. Job   Tel: 020 8940 7792
Fax: 020 8332 6694

Playing: Midweek: round £40.00; day n/a. Weekend: round £45.00 (after 3.30pm); day n/a.

Facilities: Bar: 11am–11pm. Food: Lunch from 12pm–2.30pm. Bar snacks.

Comments: Lovely Georgian clubhouse ... Great collection of six par-3s ... One to treasure ... You need a strategy ... Par-3s are course's trademark.

Richmond Park Golf Club ★

Roehampton Gate, London, SW15 5JR
Nearest main town: London

Secretary: Mr A. Gourvish   Tel: 020 8876 3205
Fax: 020 8878 1354
Professional: Mr D. Brown   Tel: 020 8876 3205

Playing: Midweek: round £13.50; day n/a. Weekend: round £16.80; day n/a.

Facilities: Bar: None. Food: None.

Comments: Decent value ... Presentation could be improved ... Well-worn course ... Better than average for the price.

Royal Mid-Surrey Golf Club (Outer) ★★★

Old Deer Park, Twickenham Road, Richmond, TW9 2SB
Website: www.rmsgc.co.uk   E-mail: secretary@rmsgc.co.uk
Nearest main town: Richmond

Secretary: Mr J. Harper   Tel: 020 8940 1894
Fax: 020 8332 2957
Professional: Mr P. Talbot   Tel: 020 8940 1894
Fax: 020 8939 0149

Playing: Midweek: round n/a; day £70.00 (all day), £46.50 (afternoon). Weekend: round n/a; day members and their guests only.

Facilities: Bar: 11am–11pm. Food: Lunch from 12pm–2.30pm. Dinner on Thursdays only.

Comments: Was looking forward to it and wasn't disappointed ... One of the best in London ... Bunkers cunningly placed ... Flat course protected by bunkers.

Royal Wimbledon Golf Club   ★★

29 Camp Road, Wimbledon, London, SW19 4UW
Website: www.rwgc.co.uk   E-mail: secretary@rwgc.co.uk
Nearest main town: London

Secretary: Mr N. Smith   Tel: 020 8946 2125
                                        Fax: 020 8944 8652
Professional: Mr D. Jones   Tel: 020 8946 4606

Playing: Midweek: round £60.00 (by prior arrangement); day n/a. Weekend: round no visitors; day n/a.

Facilities: Bar: Members only. Food: Members only.

Comments: Classic Surrey course with sandy loam soil and heather ... Always in good condition ... How does Surrey have so many great courses? ... Tradition through and through ... Very traditional, a litte staid ... Course that has aged wonderfully.

Selsdon Park Hotel Golf Club   ★★★

Addington Road, Sanderstead, South Croydon, CR2 8YA
Nearest main town: Croydon

Secretary: Mrs C. Screene   Tel: 020 8657 8811
                                          Fax: 020 8651 3401
Professional: Mr M. Churchill   Tel: 020 8657 4129

Playing: Midweek: round £22.50; day £40.00. Weekend: round £27.50; day £50.00.

Facilities: Bar: 11am–11pm. Food: Lunch from 12pm–2pm. Dinner from 7pm–10pm.

Comments: A visually attractive course ... Always a pleasure to play ... Parkland with unbelievable facilities ... One of the best welcomes anywhere ... Great welcome to a beginner with no handicap.

Shirley Park Golf Club ★★

194 Addiscombe Road, Croydon, CR0 7LB
Website: www.shirleyparkgolfclub.co.uk
E-mail: secretary@shirleyparkgolfclub.co.uk
Nearest main town: Croydon

Secretary:	Mr D. Roy	Tel: 020 8654 1143
		Fax: 020 8654 6733
Professional:	Mr M. Taylor	Tel: 020 8654 8767

Playing: Midweek: round £38.00; day n/a. Weekend: round £45.00; day n/a.

Facilities: Bar: 11am–11pm. Food: Lunch and dinner from 10am–7pm. Bar snacks.

Comments: Very good society course ... Good value ... Felt very welcome ... 7th a cracking par-3 ... Short holes make this ... Can't think of a better day out.

Sunningdale Golf Club (New) ★★★★★

Ridgemount Road, Sunningdale, SL5 9RW
Nearest main town: Sunningdale

Secretary:	Mr S. Zuill	Tel: 01344 621681
		Fax: 01344 624154
Professional:	Mr K. Maxwell	Tel: 01344 620128
		Fax: 01344 874903

Playing: Midweek: round £75.00; day £125.00. Weekend: round n/a; day n/a.

Facilities: Bar: 11am–8pm. Food: Lunch and dinner from 10am–6pm.

Comments: Simply perfect condition for a traditional golf club ... Has a real championship feel to it now ... Old course? Give me the New anyday ... Cheaper than the Old in the week and worth the saving.

Tandridge Golf Club   ★★★★

Oxted, RH8 9NQ
Website: www.tandridgegolfclub.com
E-mail: secretary@tandridgegolfclub.com
Nearest main town: Redhill

Secretary:	Lt Cdr S. Kennard RN	Tel: 01883 712274
		Fax: 01883 730537
Professional:	Mr C. Evans	Tel: 01883 713701

Playing: Midweek: round n/a; day in summer £52.00 (all day), £40.00 (after 12pm), in winter £40.00 (all day), £30.00 (single round). Weekend: round n/a; day no visitors.

Facilities: Bar: 11am–11pm. Food: Snack bar from 11am–3pm. Dinner by arrangement.

Comments: Two distinct halves – very tidy course ... Mature, tight and enjoyable course ... Well-established layout ... Harry Colt design ... Underrated course.

Walton Heath Golf Club (New)   ★★★

Deans Lane, Walton-on-Thames, Tadworth, KT20 7TP
Nearest main town: Tadworth

Secretary:	Mr N. Lomas	Tel: 01737 812380
		Fax: 01737 814225
Professional:	Mr K. Macpherson	Tel: 01737 812152

Playing: Midweek: round £68.00; day n/a. Weekend: round n/a; day n/a.

Facilities: Bar: 11am–9pm. Food: Lunch from 11.30am–2.30pm. Afternoon tea.

Comments: Easy start (1st and 2nd), but great par-4s later on, notably the 9th, 12th, 14th and 18th ... Not far behind the Old course and better than the Bracken ... A treat to play.

The Wentworth Golf Club (East)   ★★★★★

Wentworth Drive, Virginia Water, GU25 4LS
Website: www.wentworthclub.com
E-mail: reception@wentworthclub.com
Nearest main town: Guildford

Secretary:	Mr S. Christie	Tel: 01344 842201
		Fax: 01344 842804
Professional:	Mr D. Rennie	Tel: 01344 846306
		Fax: 01344 842804

Playing: Midweek: round £115.00; day n/a. Weekend: round n/a; day n/a.

Facilities: Bar: 11am–11pm. Food: Lunch from 12pm–2.30pm. Dinner from 6pm–9.30pm. Bar snacks.

Comments: Some good, challenging par-4s and par-3s, notably the 2nd, 6th and 7th ... Always in A1 condition ... Good test of golf ... Prefer it to the West – and I'm not alone ... More fun than the West ... A cracking day out ... Was thinking about the West all the time I was playing here.

West Byfleet Golf Club   ★★★

Sheerwater Road, West Byfleet, KT14 6AA
Nearest main town: West Byfleet

Secretary:	Mr D. Lee	Tel: 01932 343433
		Fax: 01932 340667
Professional:	Mr D. Regan	Tel: 01932 346584

Playing: Midweek: round £32.00; day n/a. Weekend: round n/a; day n/a.

Facilities: Bar: 11am–variable. Food: Bar snacks.

Comments: Traditional club, pretty and challenging ... A difficult par-70 with attractive woodland ... Nice club and fair value in area of high green fees ... Not as celebrated as many of Surrey's greats, but worth a visit.

West Hill Golf Club   ★★★★

Bagshot Road, Brookwood, GU24 0BH
Website: www.westhill-golfclub.co.uk
E-mail: secretary@westhill-golfclub.co.uk
Nearest main town: Woking

Secretary:	Mr I. McColl	Tel: 01483 474365
		Fax: 01483 474252
Professional:	Mr J. Clements	Tel: 01483 473172

Playing: Midweek: round £55.00; day n/a. Weekend: round n/a; day n/a.

Facilities: Bar: 11am–9pm. Food: Lunch and dinner by arrangement.

Comments: A great course to test your outer limits ... Charming course ... Better than Woking and Worplesdon ... Narrow, twisty course with smallish greens ... Long carries to the fairways ... Champion course ... Right next door to Worplesdon ... Heath and heather monster.

West Surrey Golf Club   ★★★★

Enton Green, Godalming, GU8 5AF
Website: www.wsgc.co.uk   E-mail: westsurreygolfclub@btinternet.com
Nearest main town: Milford

Secretary: Mr R. Crabb   Tel: 01483 421275
Fax: 01483 415419

Professional: Mr A. Tawse   Tel: 01483 417278

Playing: Midweek: round £35.00; day n/a. Weekend: round £45.00; day n/a.

Facilities: Bar: 11am–11pm. Food: Bar snacks.

Comments: Real struggle in the summer with running fairways ... Best time to play is in autumn ... Good facilities for traditional club ... Short course with birdie opportunities ... Rather underrated in Surrey.

Wildwood Country Club

Horsham Road, Alford, GU6 8JE
Website: www.wildwoodgolf.co.uk
Nearest main town: Guildford

Secretary: None   Tel: 01403 753255
Fax: 01403 752005

Professional: Mr M. Dowdell

Playing: Midweek: round £35.00; day n/a. Weekend: round £50.00; day n/a.

Facilities: Bar: 11am–11pm. Food: Lunch from 10am–5pm. Bar snacks.

Comments: Serious golf ... Difficult course and excellent greens ... Facilities for the visitor are first class ... Old oak trees dominate this homely club ... True, fast greens.

Wimbledon Common Golf Club ★

19 Camp Road, London, SW19 4UW
Website: www.wcgc.co.uk   E-mail: secretary@wcgc.co.uk
Nearest main town: London

Secretary: Mr R. Pierce   Tel: 020 8946 7571
                                                Fax: 020 8947 8697
Professional: Mr J. Jukes

Playing: Midweek: round prices on application; day n/a.
                    Weekend: round n/a; day n/a.

Facilities: Bar: 11am–11pm. Food: Lunch and dinner from
                    11am–8.30pm. Bar snacks.

Comments: Another with the red clothing rule ... Nice woodland in
                    parts ... Special aura about this short, challenging
                    course ... Good value.

Windlesham Golf Club ★★

Grove End, Bagshot, GU19 5HY
Website: www.windleshamgolf.com
Nearest main town: Bagshot

Secretary: Mr C. Lumley   Tel: 01276 452220
                                                Fax: 01276 452290
Professional: Mr L. Mucklow   Tel: 01276 472323

Playing: Midweek: round £25.00; day n/a. Weekend: round
                    £35.00; day n/a.

Facilities: Bar: 11am–11pm. Food: Lunch from 11.30am–3pm.
                    Bar snacks. Dinner by arrangement.

Comments: Very long course by Tommy Horton ... Charming course
                    but not without difficulty ... Some rather long, boring
                    par-4s ... Fine facilities ... Uninteresting parkland track.

The Wisley Golf Club ★★★★

Mill Lane, Ripley, Woking, GU23 6QU
Website: www.wisleygc.com   E-mail: reception@wisleygc.com
Nearest main town: Woking

Secretary: Mr A. Lawrence   Tel: 01483 211022
                                                Fax: 01483 211662

| Professional: | Mr D. Pugh | Tel: 01483 211213 |
| | | Fax: 01483 211662 |

Playing: Midweek: round £35.00 (with a member only); day n/a. Weekend: round £65.00 (with a member only); day n/a.

Facilities: Bar: Members only. Food: Members only

Comments: Very impressive – trusting and sophisticated ... Robert Trent Jones Jnr design to a high calibre ... Undeniably good course, but who wants to be in the club? ... No-one is missing much here.

Woking Golf Club   ★★★★

Pond Road, Hook Heath, Woking, GU22 0JZ
Nearest main town: Woking

Secretary:	Lt Col I. Holmes	Tel: 01483 760053
		Fax: 01483 772441
Professional:	Mr J. Thorne	Tel: 01483 769582

Playing: Midweek: round £40.00; day £50.00. Weekend: round n/a; day n/a.

Facilities: Bar: 11am–7.30pm. Food: Lunch from 11.30am–3pm. Bar snacks. Dinner by arrangement.

Comments: The spilling heather can be a real struggle ... You can forget about balls landing in the heather ... Touch of class here ... Very traditional place ... Choice course ... On a par with the best in Surrey ... What heathland golf is all about ... Rather stuffy atmosphere ... Super ... Value golf.

Worplesdon Golf Club   ★★★★

Heath House Road, Woking, GU22 0RA
Nearest main town: Woking

Secretary:	Mr J. Christine	Tel: 01483 472277
		Fax: 01483 473303
Professional:	Mr J. Christine	Tel: 01483 473287

Playing: Midweek: round £44.00; day £57.00. Weekend: round n/a; day n/a.

Facilities: Bar: 11am–3pm and 5pm–10pm. Food: Lunch from 11.30am–3pm. Bar snacks.

Comments: Just like playing Augusta ... A course of privilege ...
Quick greens ... Very tight course, perhaps the toughest
in Surrey ... Short 10th the highlight ... Narrow, twisty
course.

East Sussex

Royal Ashdown Forest Golf Club (Old)   ★★★★

Chapel Lane, Forest Row, RH18 5LR
Website: www.royalashdown.co.uk
E-mail: office@royalashdown.co.uk
Nearest main town: East Grinstead

The absence of a single bunker means that Royal Ashdown holds an immediate fascination. It is difficult to imagine an entire course without any sand at all. Bunkers add a dimension to golf, whether it's in their purest form as a hazard or, in a more architectural role, where they can define the hole. For a course to be devoid of such an animal would appear detrimental to its character. Not at Royal Ashdown.

The club was ranked 94th in *Golf World*'s most recent ranking of courses in the British Isles, which tends to suggest that it gets along very nicely without the need for its visitors to carry deep flanges on the bottom of their sand irons. For the record, the club was prevented long ago by the Forestry Commission from creating bunkers and it has to be said that it doesn't really miss them.

Formed in 1888, the club is now well into its second century and it is a testament to the layout that it has changed little since those early days. Four sub-400-yard par-4s get you under way, but don't be fooled because this is no easy test. Some of the carries from the back tees to the fairways are quite significant and, as a test of golf, Royal Ashdown has a reputation of being among the most demanding in the South East.

With tight tree-lined fairways, it is a thinker's course and therein lies the irony, because it was in these woods that one of Britain's best-loved bears was said to roam. Winnie the Pooh and his friends were created nearby by the author A. A. Milne, adding a certain charm to a course that already has great tranquillity and some magnificent views.

Secretary:	Mr D. Scrivens	Tel: 01342 822018
		Fax: 01342 825211
Professional:	Mr M. Landsborough	Tel: 01342 822247
Playing:	Midweek: round £45.00; day £55.00. Weekend: round £60.00; day £60.00.	
Facilities:	Bar: 11am–8pm. Food: Bar snacks.	

Comments: What about all that heather and gorse – just brilliant ... A challenging, heathery, rugged course requiring great accuracy ... Pines and birches ... Quick greens in the summer ... As natural a course as you will find ... Well worth the visit.

Ashdown Forest Golf Hotel (Hotel) ★★★

Chapel Lane, Forest Row, RH18 5LR
Nearest main town: East Grinstead

Secretary: Mr S. Maguire   Tel: 01342 824866
Fax: 01342 824869
Professional: Mr M. Landsborough   Tel: 01342 822247

Playing: Midweek: round £30.00; day £40.00. Weekend: round £40.00; day £45.00.

Facilities: Bar: 11am–8pm. Food: Bar snacks.

Comments: Not a single bunker on this course ... Carries over heather ... One of East Sussex's best ... Keep coming back time and time again ... Very natural ... Imaginative and intriguing ... A complete delight.

Ashdown Forest Golf Hotel (Old) ★★★

Chapel Lane, Forest Row, RH18 5BB
Nearest main town: East Grinstead

Secretary: Mr S. Maguire   Tel: 01342 824866
Fax: 01342 824869
Professional: Mr M. Landsborough   Tel: 01342 822247

Playing: Midweek: round £16.00; day £21.00. Weekend: round £21.00; day £26.00.

Facilities: Bar: 11am–8pm. Food: Bar snacks.

Comments: Typical Sussex course with heather and undulating, quick-drying ground ... No bunkers ... Nice layout but nothing special ... Testing dunes.

Cooden Beach Golf Club ★★★

Cooden Sea Road, Bexhill-on-Sea, TN39 4TR
Website: www.coodenbeachgc.com
E-mail: enquiries@coodenbeachgc.force9.co.uk
Nearest main town: Bexhill

Secretary:	Mr K. Wiley	Tel: 01424 842040
		Fax: 01424 842040
Professional:	Mr J. Sim	Tel: 01424 843938
		Fax: 01424 842040

Playing: Midweek: round £32.00; day n/a. Weekend: round £35.00; day n/a.

Facilities: Bar: 11am–11pm. Food: Lunch from 12pm–3pm.

Comments: Always welcoming at this great club ... Must keep on the fairways ... Pro shop is consistently helpful ... Playable throughout the year.

Crowborough Beacon Golf Club ★★★

Beacon Road, Crowborough, TN6 1UJ
Website: www.cbgc.co.uk or www.crowboroughbeacongolfclub.co.uk
E-mail: cbgc@eastsx.fsnet.co.uk
Nearest main town: Tunbridge Wells

Secretary:	Mrs V. Harwood	Tel: 01892 661511
		Fax: 01892 667339
Professional:	Mr D. Newnham	Tel: 01892 653877
		Fax: 01892 667339

Playing: Midweek: round £32.00; day £44.00. Weekend: round £40.00 (one round only after 2.30pm); day n/a.

Facilities: Bar: 11am–11pm. Food: Breakfast, lunch and dinner from 8am–9pm. Bar snacks.

Comments: Beautiful course with great views ... A gem in God's country – please keep it that way ... Heathland masterpiece.

The Dyke Golf Club ★

Devil's Dyke, Dyke Road, Brighton, BN1 8YJ
Nearest main town: Brighton

Secretary:	Mr M. Harrity	Tel: 01273 857296
		Fax: 01273 857078
Professional:	Mr R. Arnold	Tel: 01273 857260
		Fax: 01273 857564

Playing: Midweek: round £28.00; day £38.00. Weekend: round £40.00; day n/a.

Facilities: Bar: 11am–11pm. Food: Lunch from 11.30am–3pm. Bar snacks. Dinner by arrangement.

Comments: Greens are always good and so is scoring ... Too many poor holes – badly defined, blind with average greens ... Great views but didn't enjoy the course ... You either love it or hate it – I loved it.

East Sussex National Golf Club   ★★★★

Little Horsted, Uckfield, TN22 5ES
Website: www.eastsussexnational.co.uk
E-mail: golf@eastsussexnational.co.uk
Nearest main town: Uckfield

Secretary:	Mr D. Howe M.Inst.GCM	Tel: 01825 880088
	(General Manager)	Fax: 01825 880066
Professional:	Ms S. Maclennan	Tel: 01825 880088
		Fax: 01825 880066

Playing: Midweek: round £50.00; day n/a. Weekend: round £60.00; day n/a.

Facilities: Bar: 11am–11pm. Food: Lunch from 12pm–3pm. Bar snacks.

Comments: Service and course presentation excellent ... An inspiring course ... A superb facility every club player should enjoy ... Superb course design, lovely tees and greens, great off-course facilities ... Sussex hills put to excellent use ... A Tour course ... They make you feel like a pro here – everything you could hope from a golf club ... Great condition ... Service and facilities are the best ever ... Members' course is the better ... Shame about US-type grasses ... East Sussex – the top dog ... Excellent course condition and practice facilities ... A little expensive ... They treat you as though you have won the lottery here ... Need one say more, the best so far ... Course is just superb ... US-style courses but in many cases you can play bump-and-run shots ... West course for members is more intimate.

Eastbourne Downs Golf Club ★★

East Dean Road, Eastbourne, BN20 8ES
Nearest main town: Eastbourne

Secretary:	Mr A. Reeves	Tel: 01323 720827
		Fax: 01323 412506
Professional:	Mr T. Marshall	Tel: 01323 732264

Playing: Midweek: round £18.00 (18 holes); day n/a. Weekend: round £25.00 (18 holes); day n/a.

Facilities: Bar: 11am–11pm. Food: Lunch and dinner from 11am–9pm. Bar snacks.

Comments: Could be my least favourite course despite the views ... Interesting course on South Downs, not many flat lies ... Excellent food here ... Open gorseland on top of Beachy Head, rough to get lost in, greens that hold, horizontal trees – simple! ... A cracker.

Mid Sussex Golf Club ★★

Spatham Lane, Ditchling, BN6 8XJ
Website: www.midsussexgolfclub.co.uk
E-mail: admin@midsussexgolfclub.co.uk
Nearest main town: Eastbourne

Secretary:	Mr A. McNiven	Tel: 01273 841835
		Fax: 01273 847815
Professional:	Mr N. Plimmer	Tel: 01273 846567
		Fax: 01273 847815

Playing: Midweek: round £28.00; day n/a. Weekend: round £30.00; day n/a.

Facilities: Bar: 11am–11pm. Food: Lunch and dinner from 11am–9pm. Bar snacks.

Comments: A little parkland jewel ... Tight driving holes to small, well-guarded greens ... Wanted to play the 14th again and again ... Mature course ... Driving key to making a good score.

Nevill Golf Club ★★★

Benhall Mill Road, Tunbridge Wells, TN2 5JW
Website: www.nevillgolfclub.co.uk
E-mail: manager@nevillgolfclub.co.uk
Nearest main town: Tunbridge Wells

Secretary: Mr T. Fensom   Tel: 01892 525818
                                        Fax: 01892 517861
Professional: Mr P. Huggett   Tel: 01892 532941

Playing: Midweek: round £30.00; day £45.00. Weekend: round
                  £40.00; day n/a.

Facilities: Bar: 11am–11pm. Food: Bar snacks. Sunday lunch.

Comments: Interesting front nine, tails off a bit ... Course always
                  well maintained ... Excellent clubhouse ... Nice mixture
                  of heathland and woodland ... Open in places, not too
                  claustrophobic.

Piltdown Golf Club ★★★★

Piltdown, Uckfield, TN22 3XB
E-mail: piltdowngolf@lineone.net
Nearest main town: Uckfield

Secretary: Mr P. De Pinna   Tel: 01825 722033
                                        Fax: 01825 724192
Professional: Mr J. Partridge   Tel: 01825 722389
                                        Fax: 01825 723330

Playing: Midweek: round £32.00, £25.00 (after 1.30pm),
                  £16.00 (after 4pm); day £42.00. Weekend: round
                  £32.00, £25.00 (after 1.30pm), £16.00 (after 4pm);
                  day £42.00.

Facilities: Bar: 11am–11pm. Food: Bar snacks. Dinner by
                  arrangement.

Comments: Well designed with excellent greens ... Charming club-
                  house and good-value day's golf ... Natural heathland
                  ... Charming course but brutal.

Royal Eastbourne Golf Club (Devonshire)   ★★★

Paradise Drive, Eastbourne, BN20 8BP
Website: www.regc.co.uk   E-mail: sec@regc.co.uk
Nearest main town: Eastbourne

Secretary: Mr D. Lockyer   Tel: 01323 729738
                                  Fax: 01323 729738
Professional: Mr A. Harrison   Tel: 01323 736986
                                  Fax: 01323 736986

Playing: Midweek: round £26.00; day £42.00. Weekend: round
               £32.00; day £52.00.

Facilities: Bar: 11am–11pm. Food: Lunch from 10am–5.30pm.
                  Bar snacks.

Comments: Two different nines, first fairly flat, second in the dunes
                ... Four classic par-3s make this a fine course ... Short,
                easy course ... Par-3s the highlight.

Rye Golf Club   ★★★★★

New Lydd Road, Camber, Rye, TN31 7QS
E-mail: ryelinks@btclick.com
Nearest main town: Rye

Secretary: Mr J. Smith   Tel: 01797 225241
                                Fax: 01797 225460
Professional: Mr M. Lee   Tel: 01797 225218

Playing: Midweek: round members and guests only; day n/a.
               Weekend: round n/a; day n/a.

Facilities: Bar: Members only. Food: Members only.

Comments: One of the most difficult courses around – and it wasn't
                even windy ... Classic links golf ... Lots of character and
                tradition ... Dream to eventually play it.

Seaford Golf Club   ★★★★

East Blatchington, Seaford, BN25 2JD
Website: www.seafordgolfclub.co.uk
E-mail: manager@seafordgolfclub.co.uk
Nearest main town: Seaford

Secretary: Mr P. Court   Tel: 01323 892442
                                Fax: 01323 894113

Professional: Mr D. Mills   Tel: 01323 894160

Playing: Midweek: round £27.00; day n/a. Weekend: round n/a; day n/a.

Facilities: Bar: 11am–11pm. Food: Lunch and dinner from 10am–9pm. Bar snacks.

Comments: Very good value for the money, warm welcome ... Massively underrated ... Brilliant links with excellent views – simply great value ... Tricky in the wind ... Welcoming dormy house ... Finest inland course in the south.

Seaford Head Golf Club   ★★

Southdown Road, Seaford, BN25 4JS
Nearest main town: Eastbourne

Secretary: Mr J. Wass   Tel: 01323 890139
Professional: Mr A. Lowies   Tel: 01323 890139

Playing: Midweek: round £13.00; day £19.00. Weekend: round £15.50; day £21.00.

Facilities: Bar: 11am–11pm. Food: Lunch from 11.30am–5pm. Bar snacks.

Comments: Great views ... Like Seaford, good quality ... Highlight is the 'Hell Hole' ... Quality layout with interesting and diverse challenges ... Cliff-top jinks of the highest order.

Sedlescombe Golf Club   ★★

Kent Street, Sedlescombe, TN33 0SD
Website: www.golfschool.co.uk   E-mail: golf@golfschool.co.uk
Nearest main town: Hastings

Secretary: Mr J. Gail   Tel: 01424 871700
                                        Fax: 01424 871712
Professional: Mr J. Andrews   Tel: 01424 871700
                                        Fax: 01424 871712

Playing: Midweek: round £20.00; day n/a. Weekend: round £25.00; day n/a.

Facilities: Bar: 11am–11pm. Food: Lunch from 10am–2pm. Bar snacks.

Comments: Simple but fun ... Needs to mature ... Recently established parkland but going the right way ... Fairly exposed.

West Hove Golf Club   ★★

Church Farm, Hangleton, Hove, BN3 8AN
Nearest main town: Hove

Secretary:	Mr K. Haste	Tel: 01273 419738
		Fax: 01273 439988
Professional:	Mr D. Cook	Tel: 01273 413494

Playing: Midweek: round £14.00; day n/a. Weekend: round £18.00; day n/a.

Facilities: Bar: 11am–11pm. Food: Lunch and dinner from 10am–9pm. Bar snacks.

Comments: Hawtree-designed downland course with nice variety of holes ... Built on chalk so in play most of the year.

West Sussex

West Sussex Golf Club ★★★★★

Golf Club Lane, Wiggonholt, Pulborough, RH20 2EN
Website: www.westsussexgolf.co.uk
E-mail: secretary@westsussexgolf.co.uk
Nearest main town: Pulborough

It comes as quite a relief to visit West Sussex. As modern course design gets to grips with the improvements in golf-club technology, so courses are getting longer and longer, pushing the 7000-yard barrier and over. West Sussex, situated in a luxuriant basin of pines, heather and sandy turf just below Chanctonbury Ring, stands as an example of classic design, its total length of 6156 yards no reflection of the perils that lurk on every hole.

That said, long, accurate driving is the game you want here, setting up mid-to-short iron approaches to fairly defenceless greens. Sounds easy, but standing on the tee, the fairways are not what catches your eye. Rather, it's the heather, vast expanses of deep purple, hugging the fairways and edging up to the bases of the indigenous pines and silver birches. Not only will you struggle to find your ball in there, but you'll be forced to play out sideways, the roots of the heather twisting the club face as you muster all your strength to escape.

Although this challenge exists on almost every hole, West Sussex is also marked for greatness by the variety and excitement of its par-3s. There are five in total, three coming in the space of four holes. The 6th plays over 200 yards from an elevated tee over a lake, while the 12th is a long iron over a heather-filled gully with out-of-bounds all the way down the left. The course's most attractive hole is the 15th; a par-3 played through a funnel of mature trees over a lake to a back-to-front sloping green. All three are memorable.

You'll be hynotised by the lush beauty of West Sussex, especially if you get the chance to visit in the autumn when the heather blooms and the leaves take on their tawny colours. Also, make sure to have a meal here after your round – the food is consistently good.

Secretary:	Mr C. Simpson	Tel: 01798 872563
		Fax: 01798 872033
Professional:	Mr T. Packham	Tel: 01798 872426
		Fax: 01798 872033

Playing: Midweek: round £60.00 (18 holes), £75.00 (36 holes); day n/a. Weekend: round £65.00 (18 holes), £80.00 (36 holes); day n/a.

Facilities: Bar: 11am–11pm. Food: Lunch from 11am–3pm. Bar snacks.

Comments: Kept in superb condition ... Clubhouse outstanding ... Members a little overprotective of their beautiful course ... Charming and an excellent test ... Nearest to a classic links inland ... Tougher than it looks.

Bognor Regis Golf Club   ★★

Downview Road, Felpham, Bognor Regis, PO22 8JD
Website: www.bognorgolfclub.co.uk
E-mail: sec@bognorgolfclub.co.uk
Nearest main town: Bognor Regis

Secretary: Mr P. Badger   Tel: 01243 821929
    Fax: 01243 860719
Professional: Mr S. Bassil   Tel: 01243 865209
    Fax: 01243 860719

Playing: Midweek: round £25.00; day n/a. Weekend: round £30.00; day n/a.

Facilities: Bar: 11am–11pm. Food: Bar snacks.

Comments: A fine day out ... Holidaying golfers give this course a special atmosphere ... They don't take the game too seriously here ... Flat but certainly not dull.

Chichester Golf Club (Cathedral)   ★★

Hunston Village, Chichester, PO20 6AX
Website: www.chichestergolf.com
E-mail: enquiries@chichestergolf.com
Nearest main town: Chichester

Secretary: Mr R. Haygarth   Tel: 01243 533833
    Fax: 01243 539922
Professional: Mr R. Kirby   Tel: 01243 528999

Playing: Midweek: round £15.00; day £20.00. Weekend: round £19.50; day £27.00.

Facilities: Bar: 11am–11pm. Food: Lunch from 11am–3pm.

Comments: New course protected by too many water hazards ... Tried to recreate Florida in West Sussex – doesn't work.

Chichester Golf Club (Tower)   ★★

Hunston Village, Chichester, PO20 6AX
Website: www.chichestergolf.com
E-mail: enquiries@chichestergolf.com
Nearest main town: Chichester

Secretary:	Mr R. Haygarth	Tel: 01243 533833
		Fax: 01243 539922
Professional:	Mr R. Kirby	Tel: 01243 528999

Playing: Midweek: round £16.00; day n/a. Weekend: round £21.00; day n/a.

Facilities: Bar: 11am–11pm. Food: Lunch from 11am–3pm.

Comments: More established than the Cathedral but not much better ... Condition not up to much ... Cheap golf for the family.

Copthorne Golf Club   ★★★

Borers Arm Road, Copthorne, RH10 3LL
Nearest main town: Copthorne

Secretary:	Mr J. Pyne	Tel: 01342 712033
		Fax: 01342 717682
Professional:	Mr J. Burrell	Tel: 01342 712405

Playing: Midweek: round £32.00; day n/a. Weekend: round £34.00; day n/a.

Facilities: Bar: 11am–11pm. Food: Lunch from 11am–5pm. Dinner by arrangement.

Comments: Excellent wooded heathland course ... A good test of golf ... Very attractive course unknown outside Sussex ... Mystery why this course is so underrated.

Cottesmore Golf & Country Club (Griffin)   ★

Pease Pottage, Crawley, RH12 3SD
E-mail: cottesmore@americangolf.com
Nearest main town: Crawley

Secretary:	Mr R. Nipper	Tel: 01293 528256
		Fax: 01293 522819
Professional:	Mr C. Callan	Tel: 01293 535399
		Fax: 01293 522819

Playing: Midweek: round £26.00 (Mon–Thurs), £30.00 (Fri); day n/a. Weekend: round £35.00; day n/a.

Facilities: Bar: 11am–11pm. Food: Breakfast and lunch from 8am–3pm. Dinner from 6pm–9.30pm.

Comments: Newish course, a little overpriced ... Fairly pretty but triumph of style over substance ... Nice to look at ... Appealing simple course ... Too expensive for what you get.

Goodwood Golf Club   ★★

Goodwood, PO18 0PN
Nearest main town: Chichester

Secretary:	Mr J. Stevens	Tel: 01243 774968
		Fax: 01243 781741
Professional:	Mr K. MacDonald	Tel: 01243 774994

Playing: Midweek: round £32.00; day £32.00. Weekend: round £42.00; day £42.00.

Facilities: Bar: 11am–11pm. Food: Lunch from 11am–6pm.

Comments: Tough downland course ... Very entertaining ... Braid design ... Marvellous beech trees frame each hole at this pleasant course ... Views across the Downs.

Ham Manor Golf Club   ★★

West Drive, Angmering, BN16 4JE
Website: www.hammanor.co.uk   E-mail: secretary@hammanor.co.uk
Nearest main town: Littlehampton

Secretary:	Maj V. Chaszczewski	Tel: 01903 783288
		Fax: 01903 850886
Professional:	Mr S. Buckley	Tel: 01903 783732
		Fax: 01903 783732

Playing: Midweek: round £30.00; day n/a. Weekend: round £40.00; day n/a.

Facilities: Bar: 11am–2.30pm and 5pm–10pm (all day Saturday). Food: Lunch from 11.30am–3pm. Dinner from 6pm–9pm. No food on Mondays.

Comments: Look out for Des Lynam, this is his course ... Fairly uninteresting design but nice feel to the club ... Nice course with soft turf, but better around.

Littlehampton Golf Club ★★★

170 Rope Walk, Littlehampton, BN17 5DL
Nearest main town: Littlehampton

Secretary: Mr A. Sapsed   Tel: 01903 717170
                              Fax: 01903 726629
Professional: Mr G. McQuitty   Tel: 01903 716369

Playing: Midweek: round £28.00; day £28.00. Weekend: round £35.00; day £35.00.

Facilities: Bar: 11am–9pm. Food: Breakfast and lunch from 8am–5.30pm. Bar snacks.

Comments: Part links, part parkland ... Excellent club ... Links is very hard in the wind ... Links with great par-3s ... Nice, fast greens ... One to treasure.

Mannings Heath Golf Club (Kingfisher) ★★★

Fullers, Hammerpond Road, Mannings Heath, RH13 6PG
Website: www.manningsheath.com
E-mail: enquiries@manningsheath.com
Nearest main town: Horsham

Secretary: Mr N. Parfrement   Tel: 01403 210228
                              Fax: 01403 270974
Professional: Mr C. Tucker   Tel: 01403 210228
                              Fax: 01403 270974

Playing: Midweek: round £40.00; day n/a. Weekend: round £45.00; day n/a.

Facilities: Bar: 11am–11pm. Food: Breakfast, lunch and dinner from 7am–8pm. Bar snacks.

Comments: Tradition makes this course appear timeless ... Pleasant but not as testing as the Waterfall course ... Not a good-value course.

Mannings Heath Golf Club (Waterfall)   ★★★★

Fullers, Hammerpond Road, Mannings Heath, RH13 6PG
Website: www.manningsheath.com
E-mail: enquiries@manningsheath.com
Nearest main town: Horsham

Secretary:	Mr N. Parfrement	Tel: 01403 210228
		Fax: 01403 270974
Professional:	Mr C. Tucker	Tel: 01403 210228
		Fax: 01403 270974

Playing: Midweek: round £50.00; day n/a. Weekend: round £60.00; day n/a.

Facilities: Bar: 11am–11pm. Food: Breakfast, lunch and dinner from 7am–8pm. Bar snacks.

Comments: Value for money ... Pleasure to play ... Outstanding facilities ... Best in the South – value and quality in spades ... Improvement to two holes and this would be unbeatable ... Tiring course ... 10th and 11th fabulous back-to-back holes ... Lovely clubhouse.

Pyecombe Golf Club   ★

Clayton Hill, Pyecombe, BN45 7FF
E-mail: pyecombegc@btopenworld.com
Nearest main town: Brighton

Secretary:	Mr I. Bradbery	Tel: 01273 845372
		Fax: 01273 843338
Professional:	Mr C. White	Tel: 01273 845398

Playing: Midweek: round £25.00; day n/a. Weekend: round £30.00; day n/a.

Facilities: Bar: 11am–11pm. Food: Lunch and dinner from 11am–6pm.

Comments: Views were the highlight of this round ... Course lacks a little pizzazz ... Course doesn't match the views ... In the heart of the South Downs ... Natural setting for this typical downland course.

Singing Hills Golf Course Ltd ★

Off B2117, Albourne, BN6 9EB
Website: www.singinghills.co.uk   E-mail: info@singinghills.co.uk
Nearest main town: Brighton

Secretary:	Mr D. Weston	Tel: 01273 835353
		Fax: 01273 835444
Professional:	Mr W. Street	Tel: 01273 835353
		Fax: 01273 835444

Playing: Midweek: round £24.00 (18 holes), £34.00 (27–36 holes); day n/a. Weekend: round £32.00 (18 holes), £42.00 (27–36 holes); day n/a.

Facilities: Bar: 11am–10pm. Food: Lunch and dinner from 12pm–9pm, Bar snacks.

Comments: No special feeling here ... Island green a little different ... Lots of water, very unnatural ... Seen it all before and done better.

Slinford Park Golf Club ★

Stane Street, Slinford, RH13 7RE
Nearest main town: Horsham

Secretary:	None	Tel: 01403 791154
		Fax: 01403 791465
Professional:	Mr G. McKay	Tel: 01403 791555

Playing: Midweek: round £25.00; day n/a. Weekend: round n/a; day n/a.

Facilities: Bar: 11am–11pm. Food: Lunch from 11.30am–3pm. Dinner from 6pm–9pm. Bar snacks.

Comments: Quite dramatic for a relatively new course ... Maturing well ... Will be better in ten years ... Condition variable ... Can get a little wet ... Two large lakes form focus of many holes.

Tilgate Forest Golf Club

Titmus Drive, Tilgate, Crawley, RH10 5EU
Nearest main town: Crawley

Secretary:	Mr S. Priest	Tel: 01293 530103
		Fax: 01293 523478

Professional: Mr S. Trussell   Tel: 01293 530103

Playing: Midweek: round £12.30; day £21.30. Weekend: round £17.00; day n/a.

Facilities: Bar: 11am–11pm. Food: Lunch from 12pm–3pm. Dinner from 6pm–9pm. Bar snacks.

Comments: One drawback to this lovely course was a five-hour round ... Left me feeling completely at one with the world – smashing course ... Magical splendour guarantees a dream golf day fulfilled ... Absolutely sublime golfing pleasure.

Worthing Golf Club (Lower)   ★★★

Links Road, Worthing, BN14 9QZ
E-mail: worthinggolf@pavilion.co.uk
Nearest main town: Worthing

Secretary: Mr I. Evans   Tel: 01903 260801
                                       Fax: 01903 694664
Professional: Mr S. Rolley   Tel: 01903 260718

Playing: Midweek: round £32.00 (Lower), £22.00 (Upper); day £38.00. Weekend: round £40.00; day £50.00.

Facilities: Bar: 11am–9pm. Food: Lunch from 11am–3pm. Bar snacks. Dinner from 6pm–9pm (Wed–Fri).

Comments: Very enjoyable downland course ... Entertaining ... Would go back ... Better to be had in West Sussex ... Easy walking.

Tyne & Wear

Boldon Golf Club ★★

Dipe Lane, East Boldon, NE36 0PQ
Website: www.boldongolfclub.co.uk
Nearest main town: Newcastle

Secretary: Mr R. Benton   Tel: 0191 536 5360
    Fax: 0191 537 2270
Professional: Phipps Golf   Tel: 0191 536 5835

Playing: Midweek: round prices on application; day n/a. Weekend: round n/a; day n/a.

Facilities: Bar: 11am–11pm. Food: Lunch from 11am–2pm.

Comments: Pleasant course with some difficult holes ... Excellent pro shop ... Pro-shop staff very knowledgable ... Rugged course with interesting features ... A tough course and horrific in a gale ... Exposed but exciting value course.

Garesfield Golf Club ★★

Chopwell, NE17 7AP
E-mail: garesfield@onetel.co.uk
Nearest main town: Newcastle

Secretary: Mrs J. Barclay   Tel: 01207 561309
    Fax: 01207 561309
Professional: Mr D. Race

Playing: Midweek: round £19.00; day £25.00. Weekend: round n/a; day packages available for parties of 12–24 after 10.30am Sundays.

Facilities: Bar: 11am–11pm. Food: Lunch and dinner from 11am–9pm. Bar snacks.

Comments: Stonking value for money ... Really good for the price ... Woodland surroundings ... Won't make a point of going back ... Price neglects the course's shortcomings.

George Washington Golf & Country Club ★★

Stone Cellar Road, High Usworth, District 12, Washington, NE37 1PH
Website: www.regalhotels.co.uk/georgewashington
Nearest main town: Newcastle

Secretary: Mr M. Godfrey   Tel: 0191 402 9988
                                         Fax: 0191 415 1166
Professional: Mr D. Patterson   Tel: 0191 417 8346

Playing: Midweek: round £20.00; day £30.00. Weekend: round
                   £20.00; day £30.00.

Facilities: Bar: 11am–11pm. Food: Breakfast, lunch and dinner
                   from 8am–10pm. Bar snacks.

Comments: Facilities good ... Course and facilities fairly middle of
                   the road ... Rather overplayed ... Not known for its
                   condition.

Northumberland Golf Club ★

High Gosforth Park, Newcastle-upon-Tyne, NE3 5HT
E-mail: gun2446@aol.com
Nearest main town: Newcastle

Secretary: Mr J. Forteath   Tel: 0191 236 2498
                                         Fax: 0191 236 2036
Professional: None

Playing: Midweek: round £40.00; day £50.00. Weekend: round
                   with member only; day n/a.

Facilities: Bar: 11am–11pm. Food: Lunch from 12pm–2pm.
                   Dinner from 6pm–9pm. Bar snacks.

Comments: Shortish course with plenty of heather ... Narrow fair-
                   ways ... Situated in the middle of a racecourse ...
                   Course affects play on eight holes ... Some drives over
                   racecourse rails ... Unique course.

Parklands Golf Club ★

High Gosforth Park, Newcastle-upon-Tyne, NE3 5HQ
Nearest main town: Newcastle

Secretary: Mr B. Woof   Tel: 0191 236 4480
                                         Fax: 0191 236 3322
Professional: Mr B. Rumney   Tel: 0191 236 4480

Playing: Midweek: round £15.00; day n/a. Weekend: round £18.00; day n/a.

Facilities: Bar: 11am–11pm. Food: Lunch from 11am–4pm.

Comments: Fairly mundane ... Couldn't get my enthusiasm up for this one ... Easily missable.

South Shields Golf Club   ★

Hillcrest, Cleadon Hills, South Shields, NE34 8EG
Website: www.ssgc.co.uk
E-mail: thesecretary@south-shields-golf.freeserve.co.uk
Nearest main town: Newcastle

Secretary: Mr R. Stanness   Tel: 0191 456 8942
                                        Fax: 0191 456 8942
Professional: Mr G. Parsons   Tel: 0191 456 0110

Playing: Midweek: round £22.00; day £30.00. Weekend: round £27.00; day £36.00.

Facilities: Bar: 11am–11pm. Food: Lunch and dinner from 11am–9pm.

Comments: Opens with a par-3 ... True greens and marvellous views ... Rough can transform this course ... Blasted boundary wall affects many of the holes ... Good fun ... Nice matchplay course.

Wearside Golf Club   ★★

Coxgreen, Sunderland, SR4 9JT
Website: www.wearsidegolf.com
E-mail: wearsidegolfclub@yahoo.co.uk
Nearest main town: Sunderland

Secretary: Mr M. Gowland   Tel: 0191 534 2518
                                        Fax: 0191 534 6186
Professional: Mr D. Brolls   Tel: 0191 534 4269
                                        Fax: 0191 534 6186

Playing: Midweek: round £20.00; day n/a. Weekend: round £26.00; day n/a.

Facilities: Bar: 11am–11pm. Food: Lunch and dinner from 11am–9pm, except Mondays.

Comments: Lovely layout ... Opens with a par-3 ... Watch out for Penshaw Monument ... Fair condition ... Interesting, historic course.

Whitley Bay Golf Club   ★

Claremont Road, Whitley Bay, NE26 3UF
Website: www.whitleybaygolfclub.co.uk
E-mail: secretary@whitleybaygolfclub.co.uk
Nearest main town: Newcastle

Secretary: Mr H. Hanover   Tel: 0191 252 0180
                                       Fax: 0191 297 0030
Professional: Mr G. Shipley   Tel: 0191 252 5688

Playing: Midweek: round £24.00; day £33.00. Weekend: round £35.00 (Sunday after 12pm); day n/a.

Facilities: Bar: 11am–11pm. Food: Lunch and dinner from 11am–9pm. Bar snacks.

Comments: Not up to much ... Bracing ... Not really a visitor's course ... Basic facilities ... One to avoid for visitors.

Warwickshire

The Belfry (Brabazon) ★★★

Lichfield Road, Wishaw, B76 9PR
Nearest main town: Wishaw

Prior to the 2001 Ryder Cup, the Belfry's Brabazon course underwent some major surgery. The most significant change since the previous visit of America's best golfers is the 3rd hole, which is now a par-5 with a green tucked behind a lake that bites into the left-hand side. You can go for it in two, but, as with the approaches to some of the Belfry's more famous holes, you are dicing with serious danger.

The facelift cost £2.4 million, with other changes to the 4th, the 12th and the 14th combining to make this a greatly improved parkland test compared with the course that marked the return of Ryder Cup spoils to this country way back in 1985.

Much of the fun of playing the Belfry comes from its familiarity. Holes that you have watched on the TV come to life standing on the tee, and you track your progress down each one comparing your own shots to those of the professionals. The 10th and the 18th are the most famous examples, the former a short par-4 where it is possible to drive the green depending on the position of the tee and wind conditions, and the latter a dogleg par-4 where you can cross the water twice.

What's for certain is that you won't find the course set up in the same way as it was for the Ryder Cup. The thick rough will certainly be shorter and the course will not play as long. That's good news for amateurs, because the Belfry is no pushover, despite the professional scores that have been shot here in the past. Neither will the fairways and greens be in the same excellent condition. The Belfry is fairly exposed to the wind and you will need to take it into account on most days. Otherwise, everything is laid out in front of you and any difficulties you get into will be entirely of your own making. A very fair test.

Secretary:	Mr R. Maxfield	Tel: 01675 470301
		Fax: 01675 470178
Professional:	Mr P. McGovern	Tel: 01675 470301
Playing:	Midweek: round n/a; day £90.00 (Brabazon), £30.00 (Derby). Weekend: round n/a; day n/a.	
Facilities:	Bar: 11am–11pm. Food: Breakfast, lunch and dinner from 10am–10pm.	

Comments: Everyone knows it but playing experience is top class ... Redesign has improved course dramatically ... 18th is still one of the memorable holes in British golf ... Its light may be fading but for average punter still a magic experience ... One of the top courses and hospitality to match ... As challenging as the TV suggests.

The Belfry (PGA National)   ★★★

Lichfield Road, Wishaw, B76 9PR
Nearest main town: Wishaw

Secretary: Mr R. Maxfield   Tel: 01675 470301
                                     Fax: 01675 470178
Professional: Mr P. McGovern   Tel: 01675 470301

Playing: Midweek: round £50.00; day n/a. Weekend: round £50.00; day n/a.

Facilities: Bar: 11am–11pm. Food: Breakfast, lunch and dinner from 10am–10pm.

Comments: Completely artificial course ... Unimpressive site with mounds everywhere ... Exciting golf on a course for the pros ... Designed purely for tournament golf ... Could not get excited about it ... Very unnatural but will appeal to lovers of modern design ... Walked off a happy man.

Bidford Grange Golf Club   ★

Stratford Road, Bidford-on-Avon, B50 4LY
Website: www.ukgolfer.com/bidfordgrange
E-mail: bidfordgrange@ukgolfer.com
Nearest main town: Stratford-upon-Avon

Secretary: None   Tel: 01789 490319
                                 Fax: 01789 490998
Professional: Mr S. Leahy

Playing: Midweek: round £10.00 (9 holes), £15.00 (18 holes); day n/a. Weekend: round £12.00 (9 holes), £18.00 (18 holes); day n/a.

Facilities: Bar: 11am–11pm. Food: Lunch by arrangement.

Comments: A water sports venue ... Very testing and sometimes too long ... Meant to feel like a links ... Too long at almost 7300 yards ... Good-value society location ... Not for those afraid of water.

Copt Heath Golf Club ★★

1220 Warwick Road, Knowle, Solihull, B93 9LN
Website: www.coptheathgolf.co.uk   E-mail: golf@copt-heath.co.uk
Nearest main town: Solihull

Secretary: Mr C. Hadley   Tel: 01564 772650
                                        Fax: 01564 771022
Professional: Mr B. Barton   Tel: 01564 776155
                                        Fax: 01564 771022

Playing: Midweek: round £40.00; day £50.00. Weekend: round
                  £40.00; day n/a.

Facilities: Bar: 11am–11pm. Food: Lunch from 11.30am–2.30pm.

Comments: Easy walking course with hundreds of bunkers – great
                  fun! ... Designed by Harry Vardon ... Parkland beauty
                  ... Homely club.

Coventry Golf Club ★★★

Finham Park, Coventry, CV3 6PJ
Nearest main town: Coventry

Secretary: Mr B. Fox   Tel: 01203 414152
                                        Fax: 01203 690131
Professional: Mr P. Weaver   Tel: 01203 411298

Playing: Midweek: round £30.00; day £30.00. Weekend: round
                  n/a; day n/a.

Facilities: Bar: 11am–11pm. Food: Lunch and dinner from
                  11am–9pm. Bar snacks.

Comments: Hard course in fine fettle ... Why the segregation of
                  sexes – come on! ... Extremely tough course, well worth
                  seeking out ... Go for the course, not the club.

Edgbaston Golf Club ★★★

Edgbaston Hall, Church Road, Edgbaston, B15 3TB
Website: www.edgbastongc.co.uk
E-mail: secretary@edgbastongc.co.uk
Nearest main town: Birmingham

Secretary: Mr P. Heath   Tel: 0121 454 1736
                                        Fax: 0121 454 2395
Professional: Mr J. Cundy   Tel: 0121 454 3226

Playing: Midweek: round £40.00; day n/a. Weekend: round £50.00; day n/a.

Facilities: Bar: 11am–2pm and 6pm–10pm. Food: Lunch from 12pm–2pm. Dinner from 6pm–9pm.

Comments: Honest track ... Sublime woodland/parkland setting ... Gorgeous parkland with Georgian clubhouse ... Overpriced but such a perfect setting ... Deserves more recognition ... Not a hit-and-hope course, you need a brain ... Just what a golfing day out should be ... .Only 3 miles out of the city but you feel very at one with nature ... Kept in exceptional condition ... If someone offers, go ... Play it every year and it just gets better.

Marriott Forest of Arden Golf Club   ★★★★

Maxstoke Lane, Meriden, Coventry, CV7 7HR
Nearest main town: Coventry

Secretary: Mr A. Salmon   Tel: 01676 522335
             (Director of Golf)   Fax: 01676 523711
Professional: Mr D. Tudor

Playing: Midweek: round prices on application; day n/a. Weekend: round n/a; day n/a.

Facilities: Bar: 11am–11pm. Food: Breakfast, lunch and dinner from 8am–9.30pm. Bar snacks.

Comments: Quiet atmosphere – loved it ... Disappointing for club of supposed standing ... Interesting course on the right day ... Technically interesting ... Thick rough ... Can get wet ... Extremely tricky for amateurs and pros.

Leamington & County Golf Club   ★

Golf Lane, Whitnash, Leamington Spa, CV31 2QA
Website: www.leamingtongolf.co.uk
E-mail: secretary@leamingtongolf.co.uk
Nearest main town: Leamington Spa

Secretary: Mr D. Beck   Tel: 01926 425961
                Fax: 01926 425961
Professional: Mr J. Mellor   Tel: 01926 428014

Playing: Midweek: round £35.00; day n/a. Weekend: round £40.00; day n/a.

Facilities: Bar: 11am–11pm. Food: Lunch and dinner from 11am–6pm. Bar snacks.

Comments: A course with a good pedigree ... Many dull holes ... Rather barren and windswept ... Bleak clubhouse.

Oakridge Golf Club ★★

Arley Lane, Ansley Village, Nuneaton, CV10 9PH
Nearest main town: Nuneaton

Secretary: Mrs S. Lovric   Tel: 01676 541389
Professional: Mr T. Harper   Tel: 01676 540542

Playing: Midweek: round £16.00; day n/a. Weekend: round £20.00; day n/a.

Facilities: Bar: 11am–11pm. Food: Lunch and dinner from 12pm–9pm. Bar snacks.

Comments: A bit of a walkover ... Water hazards, but nothing too frightening ... Little protection for this open course ... Facilities don't cater for beginner.

Pype Hayes Golf Club ★★

Eachelhurst Road, Walmley, Sutton Coldfield, B76 8EP
Nearest main town: Sutton Coldfield

Secretary: Mr L. Brogan   Tel: 0121 351 1014
                                       Fax: 0121 313 0206
Professional: Mr J. Bayliss   Tel: 0121 351 1014

Playing: Midweek: round £9.00; day n/a. Weekend: round £10.00; day n/a.

Facilities: Bar: 11am–11pm. Food: Breakfast, lunch and dinner from 10am–7pm. Bar snacks.

Comments: Cracking pay-and-play ... Best value in the country ... How can they do it so cheap? ... Municipal course in better-than-average condition ... Very accessible.

Robin Hood Golf Club

St Bernards Road, Solihull, B92 7DJ
E-mail: robin.hood.golf.club@dial.pipex.com
Nearest main town: Birmingham

Secretary: Ms P. Hollingsworth   Tel: 0121 706 0061
                                         Fax: 0121 706 0061
Professional: Mr A. Harvey   Tel: 0121 706 0806

Playing: Midweek: round £30 (18 holes); day n/a. Weekend: round n/a; day £35.00.

Facilities: Bar: 11am–11pm. Food: Bar snacks.

Comments: Riveting course with much variety ... Difficulty factor very high ... A little long for the novice ... You need to give it a belt here ... Not a chance of matching your handicap ... Really stiff finish.

Stratford-upon-Avon Golf Club   ★★★

Tiddington Road, Stratford-upon-Avon, CV37 7BA
Website: www.stratfordgolf.co.uk   E-mail: sec@stratfordgolf.co.uk
Nearest main town: Stratford-upon-Avon

Secretary: Mr S. Dodd   Tel: 01789 205749
                                      Fax: 01789 414909
Professional: Mr D. Sutherland   Tel: 01789 205677
                                      Fax: 01789 292608

Playing: Midweek: round £35.00; day £40.00 (£15.00 with member). Weekend: round £40.00 (£15.00 with member); day £50.00.

Facilities: Bar: 11am–11pm. Food: Breakfast, lunch and dinner from 8am–9pm. Bar snacks.

Comments: Presentation can't be faulted ... Best finishing holes in the county ... Highly rated in the area ... Always ruin my card at the finish.

Sutton Coldfield Golf Club   ★★★

110 Thornhill Road, Sutton Coldfield, B74 3ER
Website: www.suttoncoldfieldgc.com   E-mail: sc.golfclub@virgin.net
Nearest main town: Birmingham

Secretary: Mr R. Mitchell   Tel: 0121 353 9633
                                       Fax: 0121 353 5503
Professional: Mr J. Hayes   Tel: 0121 580 7878
                                       Fax: 0121 353 5503

Playing: Midweek: round £30.00; day £40.00. Weekend: round £40.00; day n/a.

Facilities: Bar: 11am–11pm. Food: Bar snacks.

Comments: Gorse everywhere ... Enjoyable course with good facilities ... Made very welcome on this tricky layout.

The Warwickshire (NW)   ★★

Leek Wootton, Warwick, CV35 7QT
Nearest main town: Warwick

Secretary: Mr G. Ivory   Tel: 01926 409409
                                            Fax: 01926 408409
Professional: Mr J. Cook   Tel: 01926 409409

Playing: Midweek: round £45.00; day £75.00. Weekend: round £45.00; day £75.00.

Facilities: Bar: 11am–11pm. Food: Bar snacks.

Comments: Corporate golf at its best ... Good course and food ... Great challenge and how golf should be played ... Great facilities but golf could be better.

The Warwickshire (SE)   ★★★

Leek Wootton, Warwick, CV35 7QT
Nearest main town: Warwick

Secretary: Mr B. Fotheringham   Tel: 01926 409409
                  (Golf Operations Manager) Fax: 01926 408409
Professional: Mr D. Peck   Tel: 01926 409409

Playing: Midweek: round £35.00; day n/a. Weekend: round £45.00; day n/a.

Facilities: Bar: 11am–11pm. Food: Bar snacks.

Comments: Play a pro's course ... A joy to play ... Tight holes making for accurate drives ... No soul at this new US-style course ... Get me back to a links.

Welcombe Hotel & Golf Club   ★★★★

Warwick Road, Stratford-upon-Avon, CV37 0NR
Website: www.welcombe.co.uk
Nearest main town: Stratford-upon-Avon

Secretary: Mr C. Mason   Tel: 01789 262665
                  (Director of Golf)   Fax: 01789 262028

Professional: Mr K. Hayler   Tel: 01789 299012

Playing: Midweek: round £40.00; day n/a. Weekend: round £50.00; day n/a.

Facilities: Bar: 11am–11pm. Food: Breakfast, lunch and dinner from 8am–9.30pm. Bar snacks.

Comments: Can't fault its presentation ... Overpriced but money should go to greenkeepers ... Visually very attractive ... Woodland course in terrific nick.

Whitefields Hotel Golf and Country Club   ★

Coventry Road, Thurlaston, Rugby, CV23 9JR
Website: www.whitefields-hotel.co.uk
Nearest main town: Rugby

Secretary: Mr B. Coleman   Tel: 01788 815555
                                 Fax: 01788 817777
Professional: Mr D. Price   Tel: 01788 817777
                                 Fax: 01788 817777

Playing: Midweek: round £24.00; day £30.00. Weekend: round £24.00; day £30.00.

Facilities: Bar: 11am–11pm. Food: Breakfast, lunch and dinner from 7am–10pm. Bar snacks.

Comments: Fairly unimaginative ... Practice facilities deserve a better course ... Always enjoy society days here ... A course for the higher handicappers ... Caters for the learner.

Windmill Village Golf Club   ★

Birmingham Road, Allesley, CV5 9AL
Website: www.windmillvillagehotel.co.uk
E-mail: leisure@windmillvillagehotel.co.uk
Nearest main town: Coventry

Secretary: Mr N. Hartland   Tel: 02476 404041
                                 Fax: 02476 407016
Professional: Mr R. Hunter   Tel: 02476 404041

Playing: Midweek: round £10.95; day n/a. Weekend: round £15.95; day n/a.

Facilities: Bar: 11am–11pm. Food: Breakfast, lunch and dinner from 10am–10pm. Bar snacks.

Comments: Redesigned and improving in all aspects ... Very short course ... Fun for beginners with water hazards ... Better places to play in the West Midlands.

Wiltshire

Bowood Golf & Country Club ★★★

Derry Hill, Calne, SN11 9PQ
Website: www.bowood.org   E-mail: golfclub@bowood.org
Nearest main town: Chippenham

The early 1990s saw a trend towards a new breed of 'luxury' golf resorts as developers attempted to match the standards set by the likes of Turnberry and Gleneagles, far-flung but long-established favourites in Britain. Many of these big-dollar, high-maintenance country clubs failed, but some flourished, like Bowood, which even today remains a popular West Country retreat.

On what is essentially a flat site, although majestic in its own way with mature woodland encasing the Bowood estate, the course is a fair test of golf, blending 18 holes with the property's 2000-acre Great Park, originally the creation of Capability Brown in the late 1700s. The cavernous, moulded bunkers, skilfully planned hillocks that skirt and define the fairways, vast greens, and the occasional lake or stream are in complete harmony with the surroundings.

From the very back tees, Bowood weighs in at 7317 yards, which includes a 600-yard par-5. Anyone with any sanity will settle for the more under-friendly, although still long, 6890 yards from the whites. Given its length, you could be forgiven for thinking this is some US Open-style course with pencil-thin fairways and punishing rough. In fact, the rough is loose knit and relatively benign, but, by and large, like so many quintessentially English designs, it begs you to think on every hole.

Pick of the holes are the 13th, Wyatt's Spire, the green framed by dense woodland and a towering old church spire, and the 15th, The Moors, a scenic dogleg with a couple of huge dominant oak trees. The 18th, Home Farm, with water all the way down the right and another small lake sitting just short and left of the green, is a bit of a cliché, but these designers like to finish with a flourish.

Secretary:	Ms K. Elson	Tel: 01249 822228
	(Sales & Marketing Manager)	Fax: 01249 822218
Professional:	Mr M. Taylor	Tel: 01249 822228
		Fax: 01249 822218
Playing:	Midweek: round £39.00; day n/a. Weekend: round £41.00; day n/a.	

Facilities: Bar: 11am–11pm. Food: Breakfast, lunch and dinner from 8am–10pm. Bar snacks.

Comments: Long and demanding ... Well-thought-out course ... Hazard warning ... Gets wet in winter ... Excellent course but poor drainage so avoid in winter.

Cumberwell Park Golf Club   ★★★★

Bradford-on-Avon, BA15 2PQ
Nearest main town: Bath

Secretary: Mr J. Jacobs   Tel: 01225 863322
                  (Golf Director)   Fax: 01225 868160
Professional: Mr J. Jacobs   Tel: 01255 863322

Playing: Midweek: round £20.00; day £35.00. Weekend: round £25.00; day £40.00.

Facilities: Bar: 11am–11pm. Food: Sunday lunch. Bar snacks.

Comments: One of the best new courses around ... No excessive contouring, just natural golf ... What golf clubs should be all about – friendly and accessible ... Best in Wiltshire ... Very long from the tiger tees.

High Post Golf Club   ★★★

Great Durnford, Salisbury, SP4 6AT
Website: www.highpostgolfclub.co.uk
E-mail: highpostgolfclub@lineone.net
Nearest main town: Salisbury

Secretary: Mr P. Grimes   Tel: 01722 782356
                                          Fax: 01722 782674
Professional: Mr T. Isaacs   Tel: 01722 782219
                                          Fax: 01722 782674

Playing: Midweek: round £30.00; day £40.00. Weekend: round £40.00; day £50.00.

Facilities: Bar: 11am–10pm. Food: Lunch and dinner from 11am–9pm.

Comments: Very open course on Salisbury Plain ... Watch out for jet fighters overhead ... A treat ... Very English and traditional ... One of the best in Wiltshire ... Great value ... Tremendous ... Facilities a little basic.

Manor House Golf Club   ★★★★

Castle Combe, Chippenham, SN14 7JW
Website: www.exclusivehotels.co.uk
E-mail: manorhousegolfclubatcastlecombe@msn.com
Nearest main town: Chippenham

Secretary:	Mrs S. Auld	Tel: 01249 782982
	(General Manager)	Fax: 01249 782992
Professional:	Mr P. Green	Tel: 01249 783101
		Fax: 01249 783103

Playing: Midweek: round £40.00 (Mon–Thurs); day £60.00
              (Mon–Thurs). Weekend: round £50.00 (Fri–Sun); day
              £80.00 (Fri–Sun).

Facilities: Bar: 11am–11pm. Food: Lunch and dinner from
              11am–9pm. Bar snacks.

Comments: The best Alliss/Clark layout ... You have to plot your
              way round here ... Rather hilly and exhausting ... A
              cracker ... Expensive ... Get a strategy ready ...
              Modern club with excellent facilities ... Complete
              course with pot bunkers, loads of water and roller-
              coaster greens.

Marlborough Golf Club   ★★

The Common, Marlborough, SN8 1DU
Website: www.marlboroughgolfclub.co.uk
E-mail: contactus@marlboroughgolfclub.co.uk
Nearest main town: Marlborough

Secretary:	Mr J. Sullivan	Tel: 01672 512147
		Fax: 01672 513164
Professional:	Mr S. Amor	Tel: 01672 512493
		Fax: 01672 513164

Playing: Midweek: round £27.00; day £36.00. Weekend: round
              £33.00; day £45.00.

Facilities: Bar: 11am–11pm. Food: Restaurant open all day, every
              day.

Comments: Good reputation ... Decent value ... Smart club ...
              Tranquil and attractive ... Could come here more often
              ... Have a day out at the course and town.

North Wilts Golf Club ★★

Bishop's Cannings, Devizes, SN10 2LP
Website: www.northwiltsgolf.com
E-mail: secretary@northwiltsgolf.com
Nearest main town: Devizes

Secretary:	Mrs P. Stephenson	Tel: 01380 860627
		Fax: 01380 860877
Professional:	Mr G. Laing	Tel: 01380 860330

Playing: Midweek: round n/a; day £30.00. Weekend: round £35.00; day n/a.

Facilities: Bar: 11am–11pm. Food: Lunch and dinner from 11am–10pm. Bar snacks.

Comments: Well-presented course and a very friendly welcome ... Downland course with fine views.

Ogbourne Downs Golf Club ★

Ogbourne St George, Marlborough, SN8 1TB
Website: www.ogdgc.co.uk   E-mail: clubsecretary@ogdgc.co.uk
Nearest main town: Marlborough

Secretary:	Miss M. Green	Tel: 01672 841327
		Fax: 01672 841101
Professional:	Mr A. Kirk	Tel: 01672 841287
		Fax: 01672 841287

Playing: Midweek: round £20.00 (Mon), £25.00 (Tues–Fri); day n/a. Weekend: round £30.00 (after 3.30pm); day n/a.

Facilities: Bar: 11am–11pm. Food: Lunch and dinner from 11am–6pm.

Comments: Nice welcome ... Course a little down the pecking order ... Better examples of downland golf elsewhere ... Missable ... A little tiresome.

Salisbury & South Wilts Golf Club ★★★

Netherhampton, Salisbury, SP2 8PR
Website: www.sswgc.com   E-mail: mail@salisburygolf.com
Nearest main town: Salisbury

Secretary:	Mr P. Clash	Tel: 01722 742645
	(General Manager)	Fax: 01722 742676

Professional: Mr G. Teschner   Tel: 01722 742929

Playing: Midweek: round £25.00 (main), £12.00 (9-hole course – 18 holes); day n/a. Weekend: round £40.00 (£30.00 after 2.30pm), £15.00 (9-hole course – 18 holes); day n/a.

Facilities: Bar: 11am–11pm. Food: Lunch and dinner from 11am–9pm.

Comments: Excellent presentation ... Kept in mint condition ... Really had fun ... Not too busy like a lot of courses in the area ... Large and welcoming membership ... Have grown to love it over the years.

Tidworth Garrison Golf Club   ★★★

Bulford Road, Tidworth, SP9 7AF
Website: www.tidworthgolfclub.co.uk
E-mail: tidworth@garrison-golfclub.fsnet.co.uk
Nearest main town: Tidworth

Secretary: Mr T. Harris   Tel: 01980 842301
                                     Fax: 01980 842301
Professional: Mr T. Gosden   Tel: 01980 842393
                                     Fax: 01980 842393

Playing: Midweek: round £33.00; day £33.00. Weekend: round £33.00; day £33.00.

Facilities: Bar: 11am–11pm. Food: Lunch from 11am–4pm.

Comments: Views of Salisbury Plain ... Perhaps overrated ... Always in neat order ... Very dry in the summer ... Bouncy course when dry ... Downland – best in the spring or autumn ... Exciting par-5s.

Upavon Golf Club   ★★

Douglas Avenue, Upavon, SN9 6BQ
Website: www.upavongolfclub.co.uk
E-mail: play@upavongolfclub.co.uk
Nearest main town: Upavon

Secretary: Mr L. Mitchell   Tel: 01980 630787
                                     Fax: 01980 635419
Professional: Mr R. Blake   Tel: 01980 630281

Playing: Midweek: round £26.00; day n/a. Weekend: round £36.00; day n/a.

Facilities: Bar: 11am–11pm. Food: Lunch from 11am–4pm.

Comments: Nice example of downland course ... Can always get a game ... Never busy ... Straightforward ... Plenty of birdie chances ... Great welcome at this uncrowded course.

West Wilts Golf Club ★★

Elm Hill, Warminster, BA12 0AU
Website: www.westwiltsgolfclub.co.uk
E-mail: westwiltsgc@btopenworld.com
Nearest main town: Westbury

Secretary: Mr G. Morgan   Tel: 01985 213133
                                     Fax: 01985 219809
Professional: Mr S. Swales   Tel: 01985 212110

Playing: Midweek: round £25.00; day £35.00. Weekend: round £30.00; day £40.00 (no visitors Sat).

Facilities: Bar: 11am–9pm. Food: Lunch from 11am–3pm.

Comments: Short course with tight fairways ... Well thought out ... Good all-round club ... Downland course with excellent drainage ... Condition tip-top.

The Wiltshire Golf & Country Club ★★

Vastern, Wootton Bassett, SN4 7PB
Nearest main town: Wootton Bassett

Secretary: Mrs T. Lee   Tel: 01793 849999
                                 Fax: 01793 849988
Professional: Mr K. Picket

Playing: Midweek: round n/a; day £30.00. Weekend: round n/a; day n/a.

Facilities: Bar: 11am–11pm. Food: Lunch and dinner from 11am–6pm.

Comments: Tight fairways with many lakes and ponds ... Nothing special ... Water hazards the primary defence to this average course.

East Yorkshire

Beverley & East Riding Golf Club ★★

Westwood, Beverley, HU17 8RG
Nearest main town: Beverley

Secretary:	Mr M. Drew	Tel: 01482 868757	
		Fax: 01482 868757	
Professional:	Mr A. Ashby	Tel: 01482 869519	

Playing: Midweek: round £13.00; day £17.00. Weekend: round £17.00; day £22.00.

Facilities: Bar: 11am–11pm. Food: Lunch from 12pm–3pm. Dinner by arrangement.

Comments: Outstanding greens for a commonland course ... Watch out for the sheep ... Natural layout – not everyone's choice ... Rugged ... Gorse the main defence.

Bridlington Golf Club ★

Belvedere Road, Bridlington, YO15 3NA
Website: www.bridlingtongolfclub.co.uk
E-mail: enquiries@bridlingtongolfclub.co.uk
Nearest main town: Bridlington

Secretary:	Mr C. Rhodes	Tel: 01262 606367	
		Fax: 01262 606367	
Professional:	Mr A. Howarth	Tel: 01262 674721	

Playing: Midweek: round £20.00; day £30.00. Weekend: round £35.00; day n/a. Prices may increase in 2004.

Facilities: Bar: 11am–11pm. Food: Lunch and dinner from 11am–9pm. Bar snacks.

Comments: Excellent and unusual club – beautiful waitresses ... Seaside course ... Unmanicured, wild course on top of cliffs ... On a cold day can be brutal ... Enjoyable, natural course.

Cave Castle Golf Hotel ★

South Cave, Hull, HU15 2EU
Nearest main town: Hull

Secretary:	Mr J. Pattison	Tel: 01430 421286
		Fax: 01430 421118
Professional:	Mr S. Mackinder	Tel: 01430 421286

Playing: Midweek: round £14.00; day n/a. Weekend: round £20.00; day n/a.

Facilities: Bar: 11am–11pm. Food: Breakfast, lunch and dinner from 7am–10pm. Bar snacks.

Comments: Young course with improving standards ... Great value course where beginners are welcome ... Enjoyed every minute of it ... Some way to go, but good future.

Flamborough Head Golf Club ★

Lighthouse Road, Flamborough, YO15 1AR
Website: www.flamboroughheadgolfclub.co.uk
E-mail: secretary@flamboroughheadgolfclub.co.uk
Nearest main town: Bridlington

Secretary:	Mr G. Thornton	Tel: 01262 850333
		Fax: 01262 850279
Professional:	None	Tel: 01262 850222

Playing: Midweek: round £22.00; day n/a. Weekend: round £27.00; day n/a.

Facilities: Bar: 11am–9pm. Food: Lunch and dinner by arrangement. Bar snacks.

Comments: Unusual links ... Could be better ... Old-style club with remarkable course ... Very English.

Hornsea Golf Club ★★

Rolston Road, Hornsea, HU18 1XG
Website: www.hornseagolfclub.com   E-mail: hornseagolfclub@aol.com
Nearest main town: Hornsea

Secretary:	Mr D. Crossley	Tel: 01964 532020
		Fax: 01964 532080
Professional:	Mr S. Wright	Tel: 01964 534989
		Fax: 01964 532080

Playing: Midweek: round £26.00; day £34.00. Weekend: round £34.00 Saturdays, £26.00 Sundays (time restrictions apply at weekends); day n/a.

Facilities: Bar: 11am–11pm. Food: Lunch from 11am–5pm. Bar snacks.

Comments: Members only before 3pm at weekends ... Parkland course ... Greens exceptional on visit ... Nothing special ... Homely club.

North Yorkshire

Ganton Golf Club ★★★★★

Ganton, Scarborough, YO12 4PA
Website: www.gantongolfclub.com
E-mail: secretary@gantongolfclub.com
Nearest main town: Scarborough

All that is missing from Ganton is the sea. The course feels as if it should have been moulded by the crushing of waves against cliffs, but despite the freshness of the air and the sea shells that can be found in some of the bunkers, it remains indelibly moorland with gorse and heather carpeting the edges of the fairways. Links lovers might snobbishly label it inadequate on this count, but any honest golfer would agree that Ganton is a magnificent course.

It has been likened to some of the great courses in Surrey in character, but the similarity is very tenuous, with trees only affecting play on four holes. There are no great avenues of woodland and only occasionally, where great banks of gorse can threaten, is there not an awareness of space. In truth, it bears a similarity to Woodhall Spa in Lincolnshire, another heathland course.

Situated in the Vale of Pickering not far from Scarborough, Ganton is a terrific challenge on a windy day and a good one on a calm day. The gorse and heather dictate the style and pace of play, but so do the bunkers, which are expansive (none more so than the huge bunker on the 16th, in which you could get two coaches and still have room for a car) on the fairways and deeply potted around the greens.

Ganton is unique for a course of such standing in that it has only two par-3s and two par-5s to make a par of 72. The monotony of the par-4s is thankfully broken with some excellent examples of the short par-4, and few walk off the 18th green bored or nonplussed with the examination that they have just sat.

Memorable holes include the 4th, a 397-yard par-4 which is played over a gully to a plateau green with a water hazard guarding the left-hand side, and the 17th with a carry over a road and across a bunker to a far green, closely trapped and exposed to all the winds. In some ways the best is saved until last, a dogleg where if you drive too far to the left, you will find your second shot, requiring a long iron, screened by a copse of pines.

Secretary:	Maj R. Woolsey	Tel: 01944 710329
		Fax: 01944 710922
Professional:	Mr G. Brown	Tel: 01944 710260

Playing: Midweek: round £60.00; day £60.00. Weekend: round £70.00; day £70.00.

Facilities: Bar: 11am–11pm. Food: Lunch and dinner by arrangement.

Comments: Secretary and members could not have been more friendly ... A real thinking man's course ... Very tough track in the wind ... Terrific course, and what bunkers! ... Get the European Tour to play here in the wind ... Interesting and varied ... Genuine course ... Shame it can't hold Tour events any more ... Many links characteristics but essentially moorland.

Catterick Golf Club   ★

Leyburn Road, Catterick Garrison, DL9 3QE
Website: www.catterickgolfclub.co.uk
E-mail: grant@catterickgolfclub.co.uk
Nearest main town: Scotch Corner

Secretary:	Mr G. McDonnell	Tel: 01748 833268
		Fax: 01748 833268
Professional:	Mr A. Marshall	Tel: 01748 833671
		Fax: 01748 833268

Playing: Midweek: round £24.00; day £27.00. Weekend: round £33.00; day n/a.

Facilities: Bar: 11am–11pm. Food: Lunch and dinner from 11am–9pm. Bar snacks.

Comments: Played here many times and always a new set of problems ... Watch out for Heartbreak Hill ... Opens as it means to go on – tough ... Fairly unkempt course but interesting ... Plenty of out-of-bounds.

Cleveland Golf Club   ★★

Queen Street, Redcar, TS10 1BT
Website: www.clevelandgolfclub.co.uk
Nearest main town: Redcar

| Secretary: | Mr P. Fletcher | Tel: 01642 471798 |
| | | Fax: 01642 471798 |

Professional: Mr S. Wynn   Tel: 01642 483462

Playing: Midweek: round £20.00; day £22.00. Weekend: round £22.00; day £26.00.

Facilities: Bar: 11am–11pm. Food: Lunch and dinner from 11am–7pm. Bar snacks.

Comments: A potentially fine links spoiled by its dreadfully industrial surroundings ... A spirited club ... Only links in Yorkshire ... Polluted air spoils otherwise fine course ... Steelworks a blot on the landscape ... A monster on a windy day ... Very long for the amateur.

Cocksford Golf Club   ★★

Stutton, Tadcaster, LS24 9NG
Nearest main town: Tadcaster

Secretary: Mrs G. Coxon   Tel: 01937 834253
                                      Fax: 01937 834253
Professional: Mr G. Thompson   Tel: 01937 834253

Playing: Midweek: round £18.00; day £21.00. Weekend: round £24.00; day £26.00.

Facilities: Bar: 11am–11pm. Food: Lunch from 12pm–2pm. Dinner from 6pm–9pm. Bar snacks.

Comments: Caters for all standards ... Slightly poor condition ... Historic setting on scene of battle ... Main hazard a beck that affects half the 27 holes ... Won't be going again ... Cheap, fun golf.

Forest Park Golf Club (Old Foss)   ★★

Stockton-on-the-Forest, York, YO32 9UW
Website: www.forestparkgolfclub.co.uk
E-mail: admin@forestparkgolfclub.co.uk
Nearest main town: York

Secretary: Miss F. Crossley   Tel: 01904 400425
Professional: Mr M. Winterburn   Tel: 01900 400425

Playing: Midweek: round £20.00 (Old Foss), £9.00 (West 9-hole), £16.00 (9 holes x 2); day n/a. Weekend: round £25.00 (Old Foss), £11.00 (West 9-hole), £20.00 (9 holes x 2); day n/a.

Facilities: Bar: 11am–11pm. Food: Bar snacks.

Comments: Improving all the time ... Parkland setting with mature trees and strategic design ... Very average ... 27 holes ... Improving ... Some way to go.

Fulford (York) Golf Club   ★★★★

Heslington Lane, York, YO10 5DY
Website: www.fulfordgolfclub.co.uk
E-mail: info@fulfordgolfclub.co.uk
Nearest main town: York

Secretary:	Mr I. Mackland	Tel: 01904 413579
		Fax: 01904 416918
Professional:	Mr M. Brown	Tel: 01904 412882

Playing: Midweek: round £45.00; day £55.00. Weekend: round £55.00; day n/a.

Facilities: Bar: 11am–11pm. Food: Lunch and dinner from 11am–9pm.

Comments: Excellent all round and good value ... Nice memories of Bernhard Langer and Peter Baker ... Traditional and superb ... Excellent facilities ... Nice, peaceful with good greens, fairways and beer ... It may have been easy for the pros, but great for 15-handicapper ... Condition always superb, too easy for the pros but just about perfect for us ... Par-4s make this course super all round ... Welcomed with open arms ... Surely could be used for a Tour event ... Oozes nostalgia.

Harrogate Golf Club   ★★★★

Forest Lane Head, Harrogate, HG2 7TF
Website: www.harrogate-gc.co.uk
E-mail: hon.secretary@harrogate-gc.co.uk
Nearest main town: Harrogate

Secretary:	Mr P. Banks	Tel: 01423 862999
		Fax: 01423 860073
Professional:	Mr P. Johnson	Tel: 01423 862547

Playing: Midweek: round £30.00; day £35.00. Weekend: round £40.00; day n/a.

Facilities: Bar: 11am–11pm. Food: Lunch and dinner from 11am–9pm. Bar snacks.

Comments: Very mature ... Delightful in every way ... One of the finest in Yorkshire ... 14th overlooked by Knaresborough Castle ... Straightforward and honest ... Quality in spades.

Kirkbymoorside Golf Club ★★★

Manor Vale, Kirkbymoorside, YO62 6EG
Website: www.kirkbymoorsidegolf.co.uk
E-mail: enqs@kirkbymoorsidegolf.co.uk
Nearest main town: Pickering

Secretary:	Ms R. Rivis	Tel: 01751 431525
Professional:	Mr J. Hinchliffe	Tel: 01751 430402

Playing: Midweek: round £22.00; day £28.00. Weekend: round £32.00; day n/a.

Facilities: Bar: 11am–11pm. Food: Lunch from 12pm–3pm. Dinner by arrangement.

Comments: A wonderful welcome ... Every hole a potential card-killer ... A nice test with imagination in the design ... Well-kept greens.

Malton & Norton Golf Club ★★

Welham Park, Norton, Malton, YO17 9QE
Website: www.maltonandnortongolfclub.co.uk
E-mail: maltonandnorton@btconnect.com
Nearest main town: York

Secretary:	Mr E. Harrison	Tel: 01653 697912
		Fax: 01653 697912
Professional:	Mr S. Robinson	Tel: 01653 693882
		Fax: 01653 693882

Playing: Midweek: round £27.00; day £27.00. Weekend: round £32.00; day £32.00.

Facilities: Bar: 11am–11pm. Food: Lunch from 12pm–3pm. Dinner by arrangement.

Comments: Average course with 27 holes ... Holes work in all directions ... Mixed quality ... A mixture of flat and sloping parkland ... Nothing out of the ordinary ... Pretty decent value.

Oakdale Golf Club ★★

Oakdale Glen, Harrogate, HG1 2LN
Website: www.oakdale-golfclub.com
E-mail: mikecross@oakdale-golfclub.com
Nearest main town: Harrogate

Secretary:	Mr M. Cross	Tel: 01423 567162	
		Fax: 01423 536030	
Professional:	Mr C. Dell	Tel: 01423 560510	

Playing: Midweek: round £30.00; day n/a. Weekend: round £40.00; day n/a.

Facilities: Bar: 11am–11pm. Food: Lunch from 12pm–3pm. Dinner from 7pm–9.30pm. No food on Mondays.

Comments: High quality ... Another touch of Mackenzie in Yorkshire ... Subtle ... Makes you think ... Not a great, but bubbling under ... You never have the course licked.

Pannal Golf Club ★★★

Follifoot Road, Pannal, HG3 1ES
Website: www.pannalgc.co.uk   E-mail: secretary@pannalgc.co.uk
Nearest main town: Harrogate

Secretary:	Mr R. Braddon	Tel: 01423 872628	
		Fax: 01423 870043	
Professional:	Mr D. Padgett	Tel: 01423 872620	

Playing: Midweek: round £41.00; day £51.00. Weekend: round £51.00; day n/a.

Facilities: Bar: 11am–11pm. Food: Lunch and dinner from 12pm–9pm.

Comments: Very exposed ... Fascinating moorland course ... Rather barren and bleak ... Overpriced ... A driver's course ... Natural course where you have to feel the layout ... Greens of the highest order ... Presentation an absolute dream.

Romanby Golf Club ★★★

Yafforth Road, Northallerton, DL7 0PE
Website: www.romanbygolf.co.uk   E-mail: grant@romanbygolf.co.uk
Nearest main town: Northallerton

Secretary: Mr G. McDonnell   Tel: 01609 778855
                                       Fax: 01609 779084

Professional: Mr T. Jenkins

Playing: Midweek: round £20.00; day £30.00. Weekend: round
                  £25.00; day £37.50.

Facilities: Bar: 11am–11pm. Food: Lunch and dinner from
                  10am–9pm. Bar snacks.

Comments: Still a young course but the best is yet to come …
                  Excellent course and catering … Outstanding pay-as-
                  you-play … Water in play on seven holes …
                  Considerate design … Makes full use of natural terrain
                  … Everything a new course should be … First-class
                  facilities.

Rudding Park Golf Club   ★★★

Rudding Park, Follifoot, Harrogate, HG3 1DJ
E-mail: sales@ruddingpark.com
Nearest main town: Harrogate

Secretary: Ms L. Nicholls   Tel: 01423 872100
                                       Fax: 01423 873011

Professional: Mr M. Moore   Tel: 01423 873400

Playing: Midweek: round £19.50; day n/a. Weekend: round
                  £23.50; day n/a.

Facilities: Bar: 11am–11pm. Food: Lunch and dinner from
                  11am–8pm. Bar snacks.

Comments: Skill needed on these slick greens … No problems off
                  the tee … Nice complex with hotel site … Much imagi-
                  nation needed to interpret these sloping greens …
                  Course has an 'old' feel for a modern layout …
                  Excellent covered driving range – a place to learn the
                  game.

Scarborough North Cliff Golf Club   ★★★

North Cliff Avenue, Burniston Road, Scarborough, YO12 6PP
Website: www.ncgc.co.uk   E-mail: info@ncgc.co.uk
Nearest main town: Scarborough

Secretary: Mrs J. Lloyd   Tel: 01723 360786
Professional: Mr S. Deller   Tel: 01723 365920

Playing: Midweek: round £24.00; day £30.00. Weekend: round £28.00; day £34.00. Prices may increase in 2004.

Facilities: Bar: 11am–11pm. Food: Lunch from 12pm–2pm.

Comments: A stunning location ... Views over the North Sea ... A very natural course with spectacular views ... Views over choice countryside ... Superior to South Cliff.

Scarborough South Cliff Golf Club   ★★★

Deepdale Avenue, Scarborough, YO11 2UE
Website: www.scarboroughgolfclub.co.uk
Nearest main town: Scarborough

Secretary: Mr D. Roberts   Tel: 01723 374737
                                         Fax: 01723 374737
Professional: Mr T. Skingle   Tel: 01723 365150

Playing: Midweek: round £25.00; day £30.00. Weekend: round £30.00; day £35.00.

Facilities: Bar: 11am–11pm. Food: Lunch and dinner from 12pm–8pm.

Comments: Very different feel to the North Cliff ... Course has its own 'Amen Corner' at the 15th, 16th and 17th ... Ian Woosnam has won here ... Problems start on the green ... Multi-tiered greens ... Tricky, hard-to-read greens.

York Golf Club   ★★★★

Lords Moor Lane, Strensall, York, YO32 5XF
Nearest main town: York

Secretary: Mr S. Watson   Tel: 01904 491840
                                         Fax: 01904 491852
Professional: Mr A. Hoyles   Tel: 01904 490304

Playing: Midweek: round £30.00 (18 holes), £35.00 (27 holes), £40.00 (36 holes); day n/a. Weekend: round £45.00; day n/a.

Facilities: Bar: 11am–11pm. Food: Lunch from 12pm–2pm. Dinner from 7pm–9pm. Bar snacks.

Comments: Overshadowed by Ganton and Fulford but a great day's golf nonetheless ... Friendly, enjoyable place to play ... Heathland gem ... Felt like a member for the day ... Not too tiring ... Bar meals out of this world.

South Yorkshire

Rotherham Golf Club ★★★★

Thrybergh Park, Doncaster Road, Thrybergh, Rotherham, S65 4NU
Nearest main town: Rotherham

Rotherham Golf Club could not be more removed from the typical picture people might have of the area – one of industrial bleakness. Indeed, only standing on the 17th tee can you see any evidence that this is the industrial heartland of England, such is the protection that the mature deciduous trees give the course.

Only 3 miles out of the city centre, you approach the course on a road that gives you the impression that Rotherham could be a mini-Sunningdale or Wentworth in the heart of Yorkshire. Indeed, the impression is confirmed when you reach the clubhouse, a country mansion that was once owned by the Rearsby family. In front of the clubhouse is a massive beech tree, and standing by the first tee an intimidating oak that you feel you will see more of once you are out on the course.

But, some might say disappointingly, that is not the case, as you will find that Rotherham is an open and undulating course, the trees not really interfering with play but simply forming the boundaries of the course.

A par-70 with two par-5s and four par-3s, Rotherham is not particularly difficult in terms of losing balls, but rather in scoring. For sheer difficulty, Hallamshire or nearby Lindrick (Derbyshire) come out tops, but Rotherham makes you think, particularly when you are playing approach shots to small undulating greens protected by deep bunkers. The par-3s are excellent examples of this: with the exception of the 9th, all are played to raised and elevated greens on banks.

Rotherham is a friendly and compact course that is very popular with societies. There's a lively atmosphere in the impressive clubhouse and the course weathers well in the winter.

Secretary: Mr G. Smalley Tel: 01709 850466
Fax: 01709 859517

Professional: Mr S. Thornhill Tel: 01709 850480

Playing: Midweek: round £30.00; day £35.00. Weekend: round £30.00; day £35.00.

Facilities: Bar: 11am–11pm. Food: Lunch and dinner from 11am–9pm.

Comments: Tests your skills to the limit ... Great value for money on this mature course ... Fairly straightforward established course ... Enjoyed it ... Will be back.

Doncaster Golf Club ★★

Bawtry Road, Bessacarr, Doncaster, DN4 7PD
Website: www.doncastergolfclub.org.uk
E-mail: doncastergolf@aol.com
Nearest main town: Doncaster

Secretary:	Mr G. Needham	Tel: 01302 865632
		Fax: 01302 860869
Professional:	Mr G. Bailey	Tel: 01302 868404
		Fax: 01302 860869

Playing: Midweek: round £19.00; day £26.00. Weekend: round £36.00; day n/a.

Facilities: Bar: 11am–11pm. Food: Bar snacks. Sunday lunch by arrangement.

Comments: Parkland/heathland with nice feel ... Wouldn't return in a hurry ... A few too many parallel fairways ... Well bunkered ... One for the long hitters with plenty of room ... Undulating with well-placed bunkers.

Hallamshire Golf Club ★★★

Sandygate, Sheffield, S10 4LA
Nearest main town: Sheffield

Secretary:	Mrs K. Redshaw	Tel: 0114 230 2153
		Fax: 0114 230 2153
Professional:	Mr G. Tickell	Tel: 0114 230 5222

Playing: Midweek: round £38.00; day n/a. Weekend: round £43.00; day n/a.

Facilities: Bar: 11am–10pm. Food: Lunch from 11.30am–3pm.

Comments: Very difficult front nine due to the wind ... Greens hard and fast on visit ... Superbly natural course at 800ft ... Excellent condition ... Can always get a game here ... A cracker of a moorland course.

Hallowes Golf Club   ★★

Dronfield, Sheffield, S18 6UR
Nearest main town: Sheffield

Secretary: Mr T. Stuart   Tel: 01246 413734
                                                   Fax: 01246 413734
Professional: Mr P. Dunn   Tel: 01246 411196

Playing: Midweek: round £30.00; day n/a. Weekend: round
                   £30.00; day n/a.

Facilities: Bar: 11am–11pm. Food: Breakfast, lunch and dinner
                   from 7am–9pm. Closed on Mondays.

Comments: A favourite course in the area ... Good layout and
                   always friendly ... Moorland course with good atmos-
                   phere ... Unlikely to be on a must-play list.

Hillsborough Golf Club   ★★★

Worrall Road, Sheffield, S6 4BE
E-mail: admin@hillsboroughgolfclub.co.uk
Nearest main town: Sheffield

Secretary: Mr T. Pigott   Tel: 0114 234 9151
                                                   Fax: 0114 229 4105
Professional: Mr L. Horsman   Tel: 0114 229 4100

Playing: Midweek: round £30.00; day n/a. Weekend: round
                   £35.00; day n/a.

Facilities: Bar: 11am–11pm. Food: Lunch from 11.30am–3pm.

Comments: Not a bunker to be seen ... Mature parkland of some
                   reputation ... Hard to beat in Yorkshire ... Opening hole
                   an absolute cracker ... Very stiff test ... Pick of the bunch
                   the par-3 3rd.

Lindrick Golf Club   ★★★★

Lindrick Common, Worksop, S81 8BH
Website: www.lindrickgolf.com
Nearest main town: Worksop

Secretary: Lt Cdr R. Jack RN   Tel: 01909 475282
                                                   Fax: 01909 488685
Professional: Mr J. King   Tel: 01909 475820

Playing: Midweek: round n/a; day £35.00–£45.00. Weekend: round n/a; day n/a.

Facilities: Bar: 11am–11pm. Food: Lunch and dinner from 11am–9pm. Bar snacks.

Comments: Excellent course but could be friendlier ... Just pop off the M1 to find this great course ... Course not as good as I was led to believe ... Overrated – only three or four good holes and not very friendly ... Expected more from this heathland course.

Silkstone Golf Club   ★

Field Head, Elmhirst Lane, Silkstone, S75 4LD
Nearest main town: Barnsley

Secretary: None   Tel: 01226 790328
Fax: 01226 792653
Professional: Mr K. Guy   Tel: 01226 790128

Playing: Midweek: round £24.00 (2 for 1 offers); day n/a. Weekend: round only with a member; day n/a.

Facilities: Bar: 11am–11pm. Food: Bar snacks.

Comments: A little too hilly for my liking ... Extremely tough walking ... Can be a struggle ... Heavily sloping fairways approaching small greens ... Very stiff test with terrible par-3 finish.

Tankersley Park Golf Club Ltd   ★

Park Lane, High Green, Sheffield, S35 1UR
Nearest main town: Sheffield

Secretary: Mr A. Brownhill   Tel: 0114 246 8247
Fax: 0114 245 7818
Professional: Mr I. Kirk   Tel: 0114 245 5583

Playing: Midweek: round £27.00; day £36.00. Weekend: round £36.00; day n/a.

Facilities: Bar: 11am–11pm. Food: Lunch and dinner from 11am–9.30pm.

Comments: Good condition with some tough holes, especially the 18th ... Nice course to play ... Nice welcome ... Views over the Pennines.

West Yorkshire

The Alwoodley Golf Club ★★★★

Wigton Lane, Leeds, LS17 8SA
Website: www.alwoodley.co.uk   E-mail: info@alwoodley.co.uk
Nearest main town: Leeds

With Moor Allerton, Sand Moor, Ilkley and Moortown in close proximity, the Alwoodley is the centrepiece of an outstanding selection of courses just north of Leeds. For golf lovers, it is sheer heaven, and it's never too busy – the area is not exactly known for its tourism, with holidaying golfers few and far between.

Perhaps it is not surprising that the Alwoodley should be such a superb golf course, given the quality of the men who have fashioned it through the years. Harry Colt and Alister Mackenzie supervised its birth and formative years and Mackenzie liked the product so much that he became the first club secretary. Minor alterations have been implemented down the years, and the greens and tees have recently been upgraded, while keeping the spirit of the original layout.

The layout of the course is the Alwoodley's best feature, with each hole being very individual. The danger comes not from the mature stands of trees, but from the heather, which must be avoided at all costs. The course's bunkering is fairly sparse, but what there is is cleverly placed and designed.

An indication of the Alwoodley's challenge comes as early as the 2nd, where the tee shot must carry 150 yards over gorse and heather to an unseen fairway, before twisting left to an angled green which is completely unprotected. The run from the 5th to the 8th is a particularly strong stretch of holes, while there are a number of devious doglegs, particularly the 15th and 16th which form half of a wonderful finishing stretch running back to the clubhouse, with each hole over 400 yards.

With only two par-5s and three of the four par-3s requiring long irons, the Alwoodley has a reputation for being one of the hardest courses in the country. Once you've experienced it, you'll find it hard to disagree. This really is a challenge.

Secretary:	Mr C. Wilcher	Tel: 0113 268 1680
		Fax: 0113 293 9458
Professional:	Mr J. Green	Tel: 0113 268 9603
		Fax: 0113 293 9458

Playing: Midweek: round £60.00; day £60.00. Weekend: round £75.00; day £75.00. Prices may increase in 2004.

Facilities: Bar: 11am–11pm. Food: Lunch and dinner from 11am–9pm. Bar snacks.

Comments: Quality course in excellent condition ... Lovely clubhouse ... Just five minutes outside Leeds – unbelievable ... Mackenzie masterpiece ... Play the designer who worked on Augusta ... Wonderful ... Exclusive club but possible to play ... Best in Yorkshire by far.

Bingley St Ives Golf Club Ltd   ★★★★

St Ives Estate, Harden, Bingley, BD16 1AT
Website: www.bingleystivesgc.co.uk
E-mail: bingleyst-ives@harden.freeserve.co.uk
Nearest main town: Bradford

Secretary:	Mr S. Axford	Tel: 01274 562436
		Fax: 01274 511788
Professional:	Mr R. Firth	Tel: 01274 562506
		Fax: 01274 511788

Playing: Midweek: round £25.00; day £30.00. Weekend: round £30.00; day n/a.

Facilities: Bar: 11am–11pm. Food: Lunch from 11am–5.30pm. Dinner by arrangement. Bar snacks.

Comments: Used to be municipal, now private ... Three courses in one with moorland, woodland and parkland ... Touched by the great Bobby Jones and Alister Mackenzie ... Hallowed fairways ... Much improved ... Sleeping giant reawakened ... Cracking finish .... Deserves more recognition ... Quality new clubhouse.

Garforth Golf Club

Long Lane, Garforth, Leeds, LS25 2DS
Website: www.garforthgolfclub.co.uk
E-mail: garforthgcltd@lineone.net
Nearest main town: Leeds

Secretary:	Mr N. Douglas	Tel: 0113 286 3308
		Fax: 0113 286 3308
Professional:	Mr K. Findlater	Tel: 0113 286 2063
		Fax: 0113 286 2063

Playing: Midweek: round £34.00; day £40.00. Weekend: round members' guests only; day n/a.

Facilities: Bar: 11am–11pm. Food: Bar snacks.

Comments: Wouldn't mind being a member here ... Practice ground one of the best around ... Course really sets the pulse racing ... So natural, so enjoyable ... Great location with Cock Beck providing natural water hazards ... Beck comes into play on ten holes.

Halifax Bradley Hall Golf Club ★

Holywell Green, Halifax, HX4 9AN
E-mail: hbhgc@freeuk.com
Nearest main town: Halifax

Secretary: Mr M. Dredge   Tel: 01422 374108
Professional: Mr P. Wood   Tel: 01422 370231

Playing: Midweek: round £25.00 (special offers available); day n/a. Weekend: round £30.00; day n/a.

Facilities: Bar: 11am–11pm. Food: Lunch from 11am–2pm. Dinner from 6pm–9pm.

Comments: Super closing holes ... Not particularly memorable ... Far superior front nine ... Moorland with plenty of heather ... Lovely setting but course doesn't match it.

The Halifax Golf Club Ltd ★★★

Union Lane, Ogden, Halifax, HX2 8XR
Nearest main town: Halifax

Secretary: Mr J. Abson   Tel: 01422 244849
Professional: Mr M. Allison   Tel: 01422 240047

Playing: Midweek: round £25.00; day n/a. Weekend: round £30.00; day n/a.

Facilities: Bar: 11am–11pm. Food: Lunch and dinner from 11am–9pm. Bar snacks.

Comments: Fascinating course with holes spilling in all directions ... Great design with wind a huge factor ... Design that has stood the test of time ... Excellent short par-4s ... Sprawling moorland ... Clever course ... Not one you can overpower ... Excellent variation.

Headingley Golf Club   ★★

Back Church Lane, Adel, Leeds, LS16 8DW
E-mail: headingley-golf@talk.21.com
Nearest main town: Leeds

Secretary:	Mr J. Burns	Tel: 0113 267 9573
		Fax: 0113 281 7334
Professional:	Mr N. Harvey	Tel: 0113 267 5100

Playing: Midweek: round £30.00; day n/a. Weekend: round £40.00; day n/a.

Facilities: Bar: 11am–11pm. Food: Lunch and dinner from 11am–9pm. Bar snacks.

Comments: Another Mackenzie special ... One of the best in Leeds ... Trademark Mackenzie layout ... Fantastic blend of heathland and woodland ... Enjoyed every minute of it ... Loved it ... Some nice Augusta touches ... A real tribute to the members.

Huddersfield Golf Club   ★★★

Fixby Hall, Lightridge Road, Huddersfield, HD2 2EP
Website: www.huddersfield-golf.co.uk
E-mail: secretary@huddersfield-golf.co.uk
Nearest main town: Huddersfield

Secretary:	Mrs S. Dennis	Tel: 01484 426203
		Fax: 01484 424623
Professional:	Mr P. Carman	Tel: 01484 426463

Playing: Midweek: round £37.00; day £47.00. Weekend: round £47.00; day £57.00.

Facilities: Bar: 11am–11pm. Food: Bar snacks. Dinner by arrangement (jackets required).

Comments: One of Yorkshire's finest and most respected clubs ... Very imaginative layout ... Fine golf in exulted setting ... Makes full use of natural contours of the land ... Hilly in parts ... Condition top class ... A very fair and rewarding course.

Ilkley Golf Club

Myddleton, Ilkley, LS29 0BE
Nearest main town: Ilkley

Secretary:	Mr A. Hatfield	Tel: 01943 600214
		Fax: 01943 816130
Professional:	Mr J. Hammond	Tel: 01943 607463
		Fax: 01943 607463

Playing: Midweek: round £37.00; day £37.00. Weekend: round £42.00; day £42.00.

Facilities: Bar: 11am–11pm. Food: Bar snacks or lunch by arrangement.

Comments: Maintained to perfection ... Pork pies at lunch were the best ever ... Immaculate fairways ... Nice greens and great scenery ... Unusual and consistently rewarding course ... Front nine gets my vote ... Had a great time.

Keighley Golf Club ★★

Howden Park, Utley, Keighley, BD20 6DH
Website: www.keighleygolfclub.com
E-mail: manager@keighleygolfclub.com
Nearest main town: Keighley

Secretary:	Mr C. Dawson	Tel: 01535 604778
		Fax: 01535 604833
Professional:	Mr M. Bradley	Tel: 01535 665370

Playing: Midweek: round £32.00; day £40.00. Weekend: round £36.00; day £44.00.

Facilities: Bar: 11am–11pm. Food: Lunch and dinner from 10am–9pm. Bar snacks.

Comments: Nightmare finish ... Nothing special ... Nestling in the Aire Valley ... Fairly tight with good finish.

Leeds Golf Club ★★

Elmete Road, Leeds, LS8 2LJ
Website: www.leedsgolfclub.com
Nearest main town: Leeds

| Secretary: | Mr S. Clarkson | Tel: 0113 265 9203 |
| Professional: | Mr S. Longster | Tel: 0113 265 8786 |

Playing: Midweek: round £30.00; day n/a. Weekend: round £35.00; day n/a.

Facilities: Bar: 11am–11pm. Food: Lunch and dinner from 10am–10pm. Bar snacks.

Comments: Unusual finish with a par-3 ... Very rural feel to this parkland course ... The oldest club in Leeds ... Very picturesque ... 11th hole a terror ... Traditional ... Well worth the money.

Mid Yorkshire Golf Club ★

Havercroft Lane, Darrington, Pontefract, WF8 3BP
E-mail: lindr23@hotmail-com
Nearest main town: Pontefract

Secretary:	Ms L. Darwood	Tel: 01977 704522
		Fax: 01977 600823
Professional:	Mr A. Corbett	Tel: 01977 600844
		Fax: 01977 600844

Playing: Midweek: round £12.00 (Mon/Tues), £18.00 (Thurs/Fri); day n/a. Weekend: round £25.00; day n/a.

Facilities: Bar: 11am–11pm. Food: Lunch from 11am–5pm. Dinner by arrangement.

Comments: Ideal society venue ... Extensive facilities for the beginner ... What you would expect from a new venue ... Course doesn't quite match the facilities ... Sweeping, well-maintained fairways.

Moor Allerton Golf Club ★★★★

Coal Road, Wike, Leeds, LS17 9NH
Website: www.magc@moorallerton.demon.co.uk
Nearest main town: Leeds

Secretary:	Mr J. Denton (Hon)	Tel: 0113 266 1154
		Fax: 0113 237 1124
Professional:	Mr R. Lane	Tel: 0113 266 5209

Playing: Midweek: round £45.00; day £50.00. Weekend: round n/a; day n/a.

Facilities: Bar: 11am–11pm. Food: Lunch and dinner from 10am–9pm.

Comments: Quiet, beautifully presented ... A serious challenge ... Relaxed atmosphere ... First Robert Trent Jones design in the UK ... Views across Vale of York ... Clever course with good, imaginative use of water hazards ... Thoroughly enjoyed it.

Moortown Golf Club   ★★★★

Harrogate Road, Alwoodley, Leeds, LS17 7DB
Website: www.moortown-gc.co.uk
E-mail: secretary@moortown-gc.co.uk
Nearest main town: Leeds

Secretary: Mr K. Bradley   Tel: 0113 268 6521
                                           Fax: 0113 268 0986
Professional: Mr M. Heggie   Tel: 0113 268 3636

Playing: Midweek: round £65.00; day £65.00. Weekend: round
                    £75.00; day £75.00.

Facilities: Bar: 11am–11pm. Food: Lunch from 11am–3pm.

Comments: Mackenzie masterpiece – top class … Wonderful old
                    clubhouse dominates a very tough course … Springy turf
                    … Written into Ryder Cup legend … Gorse, heather,
                    streams, hollows – has it all.

Northcliffe Golf Club   ★★★

High Bank Lane, Shipley, BD18 4LJ
Website: www.northcliffegolfclubshipley.co.uk
E-mail: northcliffe@bigfoot.com
Nearest main town: Bradford

Secretary: Mr I. Collins   Tel: 01274 596731
                                           Fax: 01274 584148
Professional: Mr M. Hillas   Tel: 01274 587193
                                           Fax: 01274 584148

Playing: Midweek: round £25.00; day £30.00. Weekend: round
                    n/a; day n/a.

Facilities: Bar: 11am–11pm. Food: Lunch and dinner from
                    11am–10pm. Bar snacks.

Comments: A homely club, stamina is a prerequisite … Great 1st
                    and 18th … Very welcoming … 18th green is 110ft
                    below tee … Go for the views.

Otley Golf Club

West Busk Lane, Otley, LS21 3NG
Website: www.otley-golfclub.co.uk   E-mail: office@otley-golfclub.co.uk
Nearest main town: Leeds

Secretary: Mr P. Clarke   Tel: 01943 465329
                                        Fax: 01943 850387

Professional: Mr S. Tomkinson   Tel: 01943 465329
                                        Fax: 01943 850387

Playing: Midweek: round £30.00; day n/a. Weekend: round
                 £37.00; day n/a.

Facilities: Bar: 11am–11pm. Food: Bar snacks.

Comments: Attractive club course with views to match ... Traditional
                 woodland course ... Rather basic facilities ... Definitely
                 worth the money ... A woodland special ... Really felt
                 away from it all here ... My kind of golf course.

Sand Moor Golf Club Ltd   ★★★★

Alwoodley Lane, Leeds, LS17 7DJ
Website: www.sandmoorgolfclub.co.uk
E-mail: sandmoorgolf@btclick.com
Nearest main town: Leeds

Secretary: Mr I. Kerr   Tel: 0113 268 5180
                                        Fax: 0113 266 1105

Professional: None   Tel: 0113 268 3925

Playing: Midweek: round £40.00; day £50.00. Weekend: round
                 £50.00; day n/a.

Facilities: Bar: 11am–11pm. Food: Lunch and dinner from
                 11am–9pm.

Comments: A bit on the short side ... Classic Mackenzie course with
                 natural hazards used ingeniously ... Excellent pro shop
                 ... Facilities first class for visitors – it wasn't always that
                 way here ... Very hilly ... A fine second-string course ...
                 Spacious course with notable par-3s.

Scarcroft Golf Club   ★★★★

Syke Lane, Scarcroft, Leeds, LS14 3BQ
Website: www.scarcroftgc.co.uk   E-mail: scarcroftgc@btconnect.com
Nearest main town: Leeds

Secretary: Mr D. Tear   Tel: 0113 289 2311
                                        Fax: 0113 289 3835

Professional: Mr D. Tear   Tel: 0113 289 2780
                                        Fax: 0113 289 3835

Playing: Midweek: round £32.00; day £40.00. Weekend: round £40.00 (restrictions apply); day n/a.

Facilities: Bar: 11am–11pm. Food: Lunch and dinner from 10am–9pm. Bar snacks.

Comments: Friendly atmosphere ... Well-cut fairways and greens ... Lovely course – peaceful, modern and good fun ... Popular course for visitors ... Well worth the visit.

The Shipley Golf Club ★★★

Beckfoot Lane, Bingley, BD16 1LX
Website: www.office@shipleygc.co.uk
E-mail: office@shipleygc.co.uk
Nearest main town: Bradford

Secretary: Mrs M. Bryan   Tel: 01274 568652
                              Fax: 01274 567739
Professional: Mr B. Parry Tel: 01274 563674
                              Fax: 01274 567739

Playing: Midweek: round n/a; day £37.00. Weekend: round n/a; day £42.00.

Facilities: Bar: 11am–11pm. Food: Breakfast, lunch and dinner from 9am–9pm. Bar snacks.

Comments: Superb examples of the Mackenzie green ... Situated in a verdant valley bottom ... Good condition ... Trees just keep getting in the way.

Wakefield Golf Club ★★★

28 Woodthorpe Lane, Sandal, Wakefield, WF2 6JH
E-mail: wakefieldgolfclub@woodthorpelane.freeserve.co.uk
Nearest main town: Wakefield

Secretary: Mr A. McVicar   Tel: 01924 258778
                              Fax: 01924 242752
Professional: Mr I. Wright Tel: 01924 255380
                              Fax: 01924 242752

Playing: Midweek: round £30.00; day £35.00. Weekend: round £40.00; day n/a.

Facilities: Bar: 11am–11pm. Food: Lunch and dinner from 12pm–9pm. Bar snacks.

Comments: Fairly straightforward with the exception of the left-hand dogleg at the 13th ... A few too many parallel holes ... Good par-3s ... Condition not consistent ... Plenty of bunkers.

West Bowling Golf Club ★

Newall Hall, Rooley Lane, Bradford, BD5 8LB
Nearest main town: Bradford

Secretary: Mr I. Brogden   Tel: 01274 393207
                                     Fax: 01274 393207
Professional: Mr I. Marshall   Tel: 01274 728036

Playing: Midweek: round £24.00; day £30.00. Weekend: round n/a; day n/a.

Facilities: Bar: 11am–11pm. Food: Lunch from 10am–5pm. Bar snacks. Dinner by arrangement.

Comments: Beautiful small course in urban surroundings ... Unheralded course ... Short but very good fun ... Recommended.

Woodsome Hall Golf Club

Woodsome Hall, Fenay Bridge, Huddersfield, HD8 0LQ
Website: www.woodsomehall.co.uk
Nearest main town: Huddersfield

Secretary: Mr A. Guest   Tel: 01484 602739
                                   Fax: 01484 608260
Professional: Mr M. Higginbottom Tel: 01484 602034

Playing: Midweek: round £30.00; day £40.00. Weekend: round £50.00; day £60.00.

Facilities: Bar: 11am–11pm. Food: Breakfast, lunch and dinner from 9am–10pm.

Comments: Tradition, style, one of the best in Yorkshire ... Quality ... Clubhouse makes the course ... Good, old-fashioned values at this club ... Real treat.

SCOTLAND

Strathclyde

Loch Lomond Golf Club ★★★★★

Rossdhu House, Alexandria, G83 8NT
Website: www.lochlomond.com   E-mail: info@lochlomond.com
Nearest main town: Glasgow

It has been impossible to resist the charm of Loch Lomond, just as it is scarcely believable that a course as young as this could have such an impact on the rankings of top courses in the British Isles. The UK, with its Open venues and historical heathland gems, is a tough league in which to survive. Yet Loch Lomond has done more than just survive. From being ranked as the best new course in the country by *Golf World* in 1994, it has progressed up the charts in unstoppable fashion, coming in at a remarkable No.6 in the latest rankings published in November 2002.

For anyone who has been to this corner of Scotland, you would have to believe that the stunning scenery around the loch plays a big part in the impression that this project has made. But you can't rely solely on location; the design of the course needs to be out of the top drawer and in this case it most certainly is. Tom Weiskopf, winner of the Open at Troon in 1973, teamed up with Jay Morrish to create a master-piece that blends in beautifully along the bonnie banks. Such is the overall quality that it is difficult to pull out key holes, although the 5th, a wonderful par-3 with the loch behind the green, kicks off a section along the shore that is most memorable.

Loch Lomond has added to its reputation through the professional tours, being home to an invitational tournament just before the Open and hosting the Solheim Cup in 2000. It remains, however, extremely exclusive which means that it is very difficult for a green-fee-paying member of the public to get a game there.

Secretary: None   Tel: 01436 655555
                                     Fax: 01436 655500
Professional: Mr C. Campbell

Playing: Midweek: round £175 (with member only); day n/a. Weekend: round n/a; day n/a.

Facilities: Bar: 11am–11pm. Food: Breakfast, lunch and dinner from 7am–10pm. Bar snacks.

Comments: Wonderful layout but very expensive ... Too wet and
fragile for extensive playing ... Great practice facilities
... Worth the cost if you get the chance.

Royal Troon Golf Club ★★★★★

Craigend Road, Troon, KA10 6EP
Website: www.royaltroon.com   E-mail: bookings@royaltroon.com
Nearest main town: Troon

Royal Troon is the centrepiece of a magnificent stretch of courses on the
coast of the Firth of Clyde that includes Prestwick and Western Gailes.
Unlike, say, the other Open venues like Muirfield or Turnberry, which are
showered with praise by almost all who play there, Troon is a links that
suffers from the imbalance of its two halves. They are not that different
in length, but the prevailing wind from the south-west makes the back
nine very harrowing. On the first day of the 1997 Open Championship,
only two players could match the par of 36 on the back nine.

This impression is not helped by the fact that Troon is essentially an
out-and-back links, so by the time you step into the teeth of the gale on
the 13th, the batteries are already running low. By the time you have
reached the 18th, you can feel thoroughly disillusioned with the game
and swear never to return to Troon.

Whether you label this a design fault, or merely package it as the
slings-and-arrows of playing a championship course, you can't fail to
be impressed with some of the holes at Troon. The best holes are at the
farthest extreme of the course, starting with the 7th, a sharp dogleg
protected by a conical sandhill on the right. They say the next, the
'Postage Stamp' 8th, a par-3 of just 126 yards, is the most difficult
stamp in the world to lick, played from an elevated tee into the prevailing wind to a green just 25 feet across at its widest point. The green is
protected by a gully, a sandhill and crater bunkers. The 9th runs round
the back of the Postage Stamp, a par-4 of 419 yards where the bunkers
on the left protect the best line in – if you're too far right there's no sight
of the green, which, unusually, is completely unprotected.

The 10th and 11th are Troon's best two holes. On both occasions,
you drive over sandhills to unreceptive, bumpy fairways, from where it's
uphill into the wind with a long iron. The 11th, with the railway running
just over the stone wall, plays as a par-5 for the members but is one of
the most difficult par-4s in the world for the pros.

Troon does not have the dramatic landscapes of other links courses;
its definition is confined to long wispy grasses and watchtower sandhills.
The compensation comes in the form of dramatic views over the Firth of
Clyde to the Isle of Arran and the Mull of Kintyre.

Secretary: Mr J. Chandler   Tel: 01292 311555
                                          Fax: 01292 318204
Professional: Mr R. Anderson   Tel: 01292 313281

Playing: Midweek: round £170.00 (Mon, Tues, Thurs only); day
                     n/a. Weekend: round n/a; day n/a. Prices may increase
                     in 2004.

Facilities: Bar: 11am–11pm. Food: Lunch for visitors on Mon,
                     Tues and Thurs only. Price includes buffet lunch.

Comments: Visitors Monday, Tuesday and Thursday only. Price
                     includes Old course round as well ... Have not played it
                     but walked it and reckon the Postage Stamp is one of the
                     best holes in the world ... Overpriced ... Back nine is
                     too tough ... Into the wind on the back nine is toughest
                     experience I've had on any course ... A long, hard slog
                     back ... Best holes are at far end of course ... Best holes
                     from 9th to 13th ... Hard to fault ... Still one of the best
                     around ... For the money, not worth it ... Loved it and
                     will be back.

The Westin Turnberry Resort (Ailsa)   ★★★★★

Maidens Road, Turnberry, KA26 9LT
Website: www.westin.com/turnberry   E-mail: turnberry@westin.com
Nearest main town: Girvan

Turnberry is arguably the most scenically stunning course on the Open
Championship rota. The views across to the Isle of Arran and Mull of
Kintyre are wondrous, and on a clear day you can sometimes see all the
way to Ireland. And looming out of the mid-Atlantic swell is the sinister
and primeval Ailsa Craig, a 1208-foot bulging hunk of rock, which
lends its name to Turnberry's famous links.

   The course, unusually for a links, is run entirely as a commercial
operation. There are none of the Rottweiler secretaries you associate
with the top private courses, so you should be able to play, although the
waiting list is growing. Guests of the first-class hotel, which looms over
the course, get preference, so if you really want to treat yourself, book
in. If not, you'll just have to wait, but it's worth it.

   Turnberry is maintained in absolutely stunning condition. The warts-
and-all nature of links golf doesn't seem to apply here, where the fairways
rarely get dry and the greens are always holding. It would have been
hard to imagine there could be a first-class links here in 1945 after the
course had been used as an airstrip in the war, a transformation that

destroyed many of its natural features. But, under the guidance of Mackenzie Ross, it was revived and stands as a monument to that architect's brilliance.

Turnberry is also blessed with a pleasant microclimate, the warm air of the Gulf Stream making for pleasant golfing conditions. There are all the perils you associate with Open courses, such as wiry rough, protected greens and sandhills, but it is not particularly wild and many of the tee shots are attractive from elevated tees to valley fairways. It truly is a very fair test of golf.

For many, the experience of playing Turnberry is purely to stand on the 9th tee, with the waves bludgeoning the rocky outcrop, with a drive across cliffs to a camber fairway marked by a stone cairn. But you wouldn't label it Turnberry's best hole. The 16th, a short par-4 called 'Wee Burn', could lay claim to that; so could any of the eight holes along the coast. The course truly will appeal to all and is the most accessible links for those who prefer the inland game.

Secretary:	Mr P. Burley	Tel: 01655 334000
	(Director of Golf)	Fax: 01655 331069
Professional:	Mr R. Hall	Tel: 01655 334062

Playing: Midweek: round £130.00 (Ailsa), £105.00 (Kintyre); day n/a. Weekend: round £175.00 (Ailsa), £105.00 (Kintyre); day n/a.

Facilities: Bar: 11am–11pm. Food: Breakfast, lunch and dinner from 7am–10pm. Bar snacks.

Comments: An experience that will live in the memory forever ... Just a wonderful place to play and forget about the world ... Forget the cost, you must play it at least once ... Not to be missed ... Playing the final hole towards the hotel is just a bit special ... Very beautiful ... History, tradition and a superb hotel ... Worth every penny.

Western Gailes Golf Club   ★★★★★

Gailes, Irvine, KA11 5AE
Website: www.westerngailes.com
E-mail: secretary@westerngailes.com
Nearest main town: Troon

Western Gailes is not the type of links where the scenery distracts you from your game, neither is there a great deal of variety. The attraction of Western Gailes lies in staying mentally strong enough to combat the ferocious winds that can pick up here. In fact, the second name of the club could not be more appropriate.

The course is completely exposed to the winds that race in from the south-west, much like neighbouring Royal Troon. The winds that make the incoming holes at Troon such a contest are the same ones that will send your ball ballooning in the air from the 6th to the 13th at Western Gailes. It is here that you must protect your score before the comparatively easy finishing holes.

The unusual layout of the course, with the clubhouse set in the middle of a narrow piece of tortured, bumpy land, and the holes spreading out in both directions, is intriguing. With the toughest part of the course in the middle, you can completely lose your appetite for the game if things are going badly, and the sorry golfers trudging off the 18th are testament to that. The impression is further confirmed by looking at the faces of the members in the bar, carved completely by the strong winds, and more akin to North Sea shrimp fishermen than golfers.

One of the club's most distinguished members, Lord Brabazon, once said: 'If you have the time, play just three courses – Western Gailes, Prestwick and Turnberry.' Advice to be taken with a pinch of salt, although you should play Western Gailes.

Secretary: Mr A. McBean   Tel: 0141 354 0354
                                     Fax: 0141 354 0355

Professional: None

Playing: Midweek: round £90.00 (including lunch); day n/a. Weekend: round £90.00 (Sunday afternoon only – no lunch included); day n/a. Prices may increase in 2004.

Facilities: Bar: 11am–11pm. Food: Lunch and dinner from 11am–10pm.

Comments: Beautifully maintained and managed course ... Excellent facilities ... What a wonderful traditional course with a warm Scottish welcome ... Warm and friendly clubhouse.

Ballochmyle Golf Club   ★★

Ballochmyle, Mauchline, KA5 6LE
Nearest main town: Mauchline

Secretary: Mr A. Williams   Tel: 01290 550469
                                     Fax: 01290 550469

Professional: None

Playing: Midweek: round £18.00; day £25.00. Weekend: round n/a; day £30.00.

Facilities: Bar: 11am–11pm. Food: Bar snacks.

Comments: Small greens, plenty of trees … Greens give this course protection against good scoring … Friendly attitude … Will go back for the welcome … Unpretentious club … Course honest, if somewhat unspectacular.

Belleisle Golf Club   ★★★★

Belleisle Park, Doonfoot Road, Ayr, KA7 4DU
Nearest main town: Ayr

Secretary: Mr T. Culter   Tel: 01292 441258
                   (Manager)   Fax: 01292 442632
Professional: Mr D. Gemmell   Tel: 01292 441314
                                       Fax: 01292 441314

Playing: Midweek: round £19.00; day £27.00. Weekend: round £31.00; day £31.00.

Facilities: Bar: 11am–11pm. Food: Breakfast, lunch and dinner from 7am–10pm. Bar snacks.

Comments: One of the best kept and presented public courses … Always in excellent condition – summer or winter … True and fast greens on visit … Tough and pretty.

Bothwell Castle Golf Club   ★★★

Blantyre Road, Bothwell, Glasgow, G71 8PJ
Nearest main town: Glasgow

Secretary: Mr D. McNaught   Tel: 01698 854052
                                       Fax: 01698 854052
Professional: Mr A. McCloskey   Tel: 01698 852052

Playing: Midweek: round £24.00; day £32.00. Weekend: round n/a; day n/a.

Facilities: Bar: 11am–11pm (seasonal). Food: Bar snacks, lunches, high teas, dinners on request. Food at weekends for members.

Comments: Quite short but enjoyable and fun to play. Basically flat parkland layout – no hills! ... Not difficult to score well on if you are hitting the ball reasonably straight ... Tough finish with a decision to be made about trying to carry the ditch that runs across the fairway at the 510-yard, par-5 16th. Final hole is also a testing 430-yard four played uphill to the green.

Brunston Castle Golf Club   ★★

Golf Course Road, Dailly, KA26 9GD
Website: www.brunstoncastle.co.uk
E-mail: golf@brunstoncastle.co.uk
Nearest main town: Girvan

Secretary:	Mr P. Muirhead	Tel: 01465 811471
		Fax: 01465 811545
Professional:	Mr L. Dowman	Tel: 01465 811477
		Fax: 01465 811545

Playing: Midweek: round £28.00; day n/a. Weekend: round £32.00; day n/a.

Facilities: Bar: 11am–11pm. Food: Lunch and dinner from 10am–10pm. Bar snacks.

Comments: Nice new course ... Tends to get boggy in wet conditions ... New Donald Steel course ... Praiseworthy design but course can get wet ... Perfect golf facility for novice.

Cardross Golf Club   ★★★

Main Road, Cardross, G82 5LB
Website: www.cardross.com   E-mail: golf@cardross.com
Nearest main town: Dumbarton

Secretary:	Mr I. Waugh	Tel: 01389 841754
		Fax: 01389 842162
Professional:	Mr R. Farrell	Tel: 01389 841350

Playing: Midweek: round £30.00; day £45.00. Weekend: round members only; day n/a.

Facilities: Bar: 11am–11pm (Apr 1–Sept 30). Food: 11.30am–3pm Mon, 11.30am–6pm Tues–Sun (Apr 1–Sept 30).

Comments: Inspiring view across the River Clyde from some of the higher vantage points on the course, especially the 2nd and 18th tees ... Mature parkland setting with moderately tight, tree-lined fairways ... Excellent fairways and greens which drain extremely well ... I'm taking a chainsaw on my next visit to chop down the lovely tree that sits right in the middle of the 14th fairway! ... Expected the wind to be a bigger factor but the holes are mainly well protected by the trees.

Carradale Golf Club   ★

The Arch, Torrisdale, Carradale, PA28 6QT
Nearest main town: Campbeltown

Secretary: Dr R. Abernethy   Tel: 01583 431321
Professional: None

Playing: Midweek: round n/a; day £12.00. Weekend: round n/a; day £12.00.

Facilities: Food: Hotels next to the course open for catering.

Comments: Nine-holer overlooking the Isle of Arran ... Good reviews ... So difficult ... Rough terrain and Lilliputian greens – very uncomfortable ... Pay it a visit.

Cathcart Castle Golf Club   ★★

Mearns Road, Clarkston, G76 7YL
Nearest main town: Clarkston

Secretary: Mr I. Sutherland   Tel: 0141 638 9449
Professional: Mr S. Duncan   Tel: 0141 638 3436

Playing: Midweek: round £28.00; day £40.00. Weekend: round n/a; day n/a.

Facilities: Bar: 11am–11pm. Food: Lunch and dinner from 10am–9pm. Bar snacks.

Comments: Straightforward course with few tricks ... Mature tree-lined course ... Excellent value for money ... Rather short and unmemorable.

Cathkin Braes Golf Club ★★★

Cathkin Road, Rutherglen, G73 4SE
Website: golf@cathkinbraes.freeserve.co.uk
E-mail: golf@cathkinbraes.freeserve.co.uk
Nearest main town: Glasgow

Secretary:	Mr D. Moir	Tel: 0141 634 6605
		Fax: 0141 630 9186
Professional:	Mr S. Bree	Tel: 0141 634 0650

Playing: Midweek: round £25.00; day £35.00. Weekend: round members only; day n/a.

Facilities: Bar: 11am–11pm. Food: Lunch and dinner from 10am–9pm.

Comments: Magnificent course prone to waterlogging and midges ... Wonderful layout but exclusivity should give it a minus rating ... Demanding but expensive ... Absolute luxury ... Fantastic service ... Wonderful course with fantastic scenery ... A dream whether wet or dry ... Moorland treat.

Cawder Golf Club ★★★

Cadder Road, Bishopbriggs, G64 3QD
Website: www.cawdergolfclub.org.uk
E-mail: secretary@cawdergolfclub.org.uk
Nearest main town: Glasgow

Secretary:	Mr A. Jones	Tel: 0141 761 1282
		Fax: 0141 761 1285
Professional:	Mr K. Stevely	Tel: 0141 772 7102

Playing: Midweek: round £30.00; day n/a. Weekend: round n/a; day n/a.

Facilities: Bar: 11am–11pm. Food: 11am–11pm.

Comments: Fair challenge but you have to be able to hit the ball reasonably well from the tee ... Course gets progressively tougher over the back nine – especially the 13th and 16th holes.

Cochrane Castle

Scott Avenue, Craigstone, Johnstone, PA5 0HF
E-mail: secretary@cochranecastle.scottishgolf.com
Nearest main town: Johnstone

Secretary:	Mrs P. Quin	Tel: 01505 320146
		Fax: 01505 325338
Professional:	Mr A. Logan	Tel: 01505 328465
		Fax: 01505 328465

Playing: Midweek: round £22.00; day £30.00. Weekend: round n/a; day n/a.

Facilities: Bar: 11am–11pm. Food: Lunch and dinner from 10am–10pm.

Comments: One of the toughest opening holes you'll ever play and it's a par-3! ... Nice setting, undulating springy fairways lined with mature trees ... Inspiring view from 4th tee towards Ben Lomond ... Look out for the burn that runs through the course, especially where it passes in front of the green at the par-5 5th ... Good catering and friendly helpful staff.

Cowglen Golf Club

301 Barrhead Road, Glasgow, G46 1AU
Nearest main town: Glasgow

Secretary:	Mr R. Jamieson	Tel: 01505 503000
Professional:	Mr S. Payne	Tel: 0141 649 9401

Playing: Midweek: round £25.00; day £35.00. Weekend: round n/a; day no visitors.

Facilities: Bar: 11am–11pm. Food: Lunch and dinner from 10am–10pm.

Comments: There's better around Glasgow ... A club course, not really worth it for visitors ... Views of the Campsie Hills ... You're not missing much if you swerve it.

Crow Wood ★★★

Cumbernauld Road, Muirhead, Glasgow, G69 9JF
Nearest main town: Glasgow

Secretary:	Mr I. McInnes	Tel: 0141 779 4954
		Fax: 0141 779 9148
Professional:	Mr B. Moffat	Tel: 0141 779 1943

Playing: Midweek: round £23.00; day £34.00. Weekend: round n/a; day n/a.

Facilities: Bar: None. Food: None.

Comments: Laid out over the Garnkirk estate, this is a well-established parkland layout ... Fairways are fairly flat but also pretty tight ... There are 63 bunkers on the course, so it might be a good idea to brush up on your sand play before you pay this course a visit ... Hardest hole on the course is definitely the par-4 13th: it's a 453-yard two-shotter with the approach played to an elevated green. If that's not enough you also have to avoid a large oak tree that is positioned in the middle of the fairway ... Par-3 5th is the strongest of the three short holes – plays downhill to a slightly elevated green.

Dalmilling Golf Course ★★

Westwood Avenue, Ayr, KA8 0QY
Nearest main town: Ayr

Secretary:	None	
Professional:	Mr P. Cheyney	Tel: 01292 263893
		Fax: 01292 610543

Playing: Midweek: round £14.00; day £21.00. Weekend: round £15.00; day £27.00.

Facilities: Bar: 11am–8pm. Food: 10am–8pm.

Comments: Flat parkland layout but enjoyable to play ... 6th is a really good short hole; only 120 yards but with water all round the green ... Greens were a little on the slow side ... Everyone welcoming and friendly.

Drumpellier Golf Club

Drumpellier Avenue, Coatbridge, ML5 1RX
Website: www.drumpellier.com
E-mail: administrator@drumpelliergc.freeserve.co.uk
Nearest main town: Coatbridge

Secretary:	Mr J. Craig	Tel: 01236 424139
		Fax: 01236 428723
Professional:	Mr J. Carver	Tel: 01236 432971
		Fax: 01236 428723

Playing: Midweek: round £30.00; day £40.00. Weekend: round n/a; day no visitors Saturday or Sunday.

Facilities: Bar: 11.30am–12 midnight. Food: All day – last orders 9.30pm.

Comments: All three short holes have approximately the same yardage but the wind can make a big difference to the length each of them play ... Scenic parkland layout with the trees only coming into play from a fairly wayward stroke ... Many of the bunkers on the course have been recently upgraded but you won't find them too difficult to escape from ... First and last holes are two of the best on the course. The first is a long par-4, while the 18th is a very strong dogleg par-4 finishing hole ... Excellent challenge for the low-to-middle handicapper without being too tough a test for the less experienced player.

Dullatur Golf Club   ★★

1A Glen Douglas Drive, Craigmarloch, Cumbernauld, G68 0DW
Website: www.dullaturgolf.com
E-mail: carol.millar@dullaturgolf.com
Nearest main town: Cumbernauld

Secretary:	Ms C. Millar	Tel: 01236 723230
		Fax: 01236 727271
Professional:	Mr D. Sinclair	Tel: 01236 723230
		Fax: 01236 727271

Playing: Midweek: round £20.00 (plus insurance); day n/a. Weekend: round £25.00 (plus insurance); day n/a.

Facilities: Bar: 11am–11pm. Food: Lunch and dinner from 10am–9pm.

Comments: Poor holes to get up and down from on lower part of course but otherwise pretty good ... New course designed by Dave Thomas ... Depressing name, depressing course ... Two courses and fair facilities for novice.

The East Renfrewshire Golf Club ★★★

Loganswell, Pilmuir, Ayr Road, Newton Mearns, G77 6RT
E-mail: david@eastrengolfclub.demon.co.uk
Nearest main town: Newton Mearns

Secretary:	None	Tel: 01355 500256
		Fax: 01355 500323
Professional:	Mr S. Russell	Tel: 01355 500206

Playing: Midweek: round £40.00; day £50.00. Weekend: round £50.00; day £60.00.

Facilities: Bar: 11am–11pm. Food: Lunch and dinner from 10am–9pm. Bar snacks.

Comments: Superbly laid out and challenging course ... Very busy ... Holiday course that can get crowded ... Flattish course with plenty of intrigue.

Elderslie Golf Club ★

63 Main Road, Elderslie, G77 6RX
Nearest main town: Glasgow

Secretary:	Mrs A. Anderson	Tel: 01505 323956
Professional:	Mr R. Bowman	Tel: 01505 320032
		Fax: 01505 320032

Playing: Midweek: round £21.00; day £32.00. Weekend: round n/a; day n/a.

Facilities: Bar: 11am–11pm. Food: Lunch and dinner from 10am–8pm. Bar snacks.

Comments: Fairly easy ... Drop in if you are near Glasgow ... Simple parkland course with little trouble ... Not great value ... Large and welcoming membership.

Erskine Golf Club ★★★

Golf Road, Bishopton, PA7 5PH
E-mail: secretary.egc@beeb.net
Nearest main town: Glasgow

Secretary:	Mr T. McKillop	Tel: 01505 862302
		Fax: 01505 862898
Professional:	Mr P. Thomson	Tel: 01505 862108
		Fax: 01505 862898

Playing: Midweek: round £31.00; day £42.00. Weekend: round n/a; day n/a.

Facilities: Bar: 11am–6pm   (Sun–Thurs),   11am–7pm   (Fri), 11am–11pm   (Sat). Food: 11am–5pm (Sun–Thurs), 11am–6.30pm (Fri).

Comments: Very visually attractive golf course with no fewer than eight holes running directly alongside the River Clyde, with the Pentland Hills forming a stunning backdrop ... A course of two halves. First nine is usually the easiest, while the back nine is normally played directly into the prevailing wind ... This is an excellent challenge for the good player, while the fairness of the layout enables the medium-to-high handicapper to also enjoy the course, not to mention the stunning views ... We enjoyed a warm welcome and a memorable day's golf.

Girvan Golf Course   ★★

Golf Course Road, Girvan, KA26 9HW
Nearest main town: Ayr

Secretary: None   Tel: 01465 714272/714346 (Starters)
                                        Fax: 01465 714346
Professional: None

Playing: Midweek: round £13.00; day £25.00. Weekend: round £16.00; day n/a.

Facilities: Bar: None. Food: None.

Comments: Enjoyable public course features an interesting layout where the opening eight holes play out alongside the beach and the remaining ten holes are played on parkland terrain ... Pretty short by modern standards but still great fun to play ... Designed by James Braid ... Main hazard on the back nine is the River Girvan, where it comes into play on the 15th hole ... For a comparatively short track it has four of the toughest par-3 holes I've played, with three of the four featured on the course coming into play on the last nine ... Wind off the sea can make the opening holes tough.

Glasgow Golf Club ★★★

Killermont, Glasgow, G61 2TW
Nearest main town: Glasgow

Secretary: Mr D. Deas   Tel: 0141 942 2011
                                          Fax: 0141 942 0770
Professional: Mr J. Steven   Tel: 0141 942 8507

Playing: Midweek: round prices on application; day n/a.
                    Weekend: round n/a; day n/a.

Facilities: Bar: Members only. Food: Members only.

Comments: One of the oldest clubs in the world ... Course a little
                    outdated ... Absolutely superb clubhouse ... Wonderful
                    club which also owns Glasgow Gailes ... Very fine park-
                    land course ... Get your driver out here.

Glasgow Gailes Golf Club ★★★★

Gailes, Irvine, KA11 5AE
Website: www.glasgowgailes-golf.com
E-mail: secretary@glasgowgailes-golf.com
Nearest main town: Irvine

Secretary: Mr D. Deas   Tel: 0141 942 2011
                                          Fax: 0141 942 0770
Professional: Mr J. Steven   Tel: 01294 311561

Playing: Midweek: round £42.00; day £50.00. Weekend: round
                    n/a; day £55.00 (afternoons only).

Facilities: Bar: 11am–11pm. Food: Lunch from 11am–4pm. Bar
                    snacks all day.

Comments: Beguiling course, just heavenly when the sun shines ...
                    Heather-lined course of infinite character ... Ninth-
                    oldest course in the world ... Qualifying course for the
                    Open ... Championship-standard links with interesting
                    and varied holes ... A real beauty tucked away on some
                    precious turf ... Always in good order ... Make sure you
                    play it.

Gleddoch Golf Club   ★★★

Langbank, PA14 6YE
Nearest main town: Glasgow

Secretary:	Mr D. Tierney	Tel: 01475 540304
Professional:	Mr K. Campbell	Tel: 01475 540304

Playing: Midweek: round £30.00; day £40.00. Weekend: round £40.00; day £50.00.

Facilities: Bar: 11am–11pm. Food: 11am–11pm.

Comments: Stunning setting overlooking the Clyde Estuary ... Be prepared for a few ups and downs but well worth the effort ... Terrain on some holes can make it almost impossible to keep the ball on the fairway ... The short holes are outstanding ... Clubhouse is pretty small, but the locals were very friendly.

Glencruitten Golf Club   ★

Glencruitten Road, Oban, PA34 4PU
Nearest main town: Oban

Secretary:	Mr A. Brown	Tel: 01631 562868
Professional:	Mr G. Clark	Tel: 01631 564115

Playing: Midweek: round £16.00; day £16.00. Weekend: round £19.00; day £19.00.

Facilities: Bar: 11am–11pm. Food: Lunch and dinner from 10am–9pm.

Comments: Very short and isolated ... Fun to play ... Don't take it too seriously ... A picture ... Hard walking ... Loads of blind shots.

Gourock Golf Club   ★★

Cowal View, Gourock, PA19 1HD
Nearest main town: Greenock

Secretary:	Mr A. Taylor	Tel: 01475 631001
		Fax: 01475 631001
Professional:	Mr G. Coyle	Tel: 01475 636834

Playing: Midweek: round £18.00; day £25.00. Weekend: round £22.00; day £27.00.

Facilities: Bar: 11am–11pm. Food: Lunch from 12pm–2pm. Dinner from 5pm–7pm.

Comments: Rather hilly moorland track ... Nice facilities at this friendly club ... Views over the Firth of Clyde ... Nothing special for the area.

Haggs Castle Golf Club   ★★★

70 Dumbreck Road, Glasgow, G41 4SN
E-mail: haggscastlegc@lineone.net
Nearest main town: Glasgow

Secretary: Mr A. Williams   Tel: 0141 427 1157
                                     Fax: 0141 427 1157
Professional: Mr C. Elliott   Tel: 0141 427 3355

Playing: Midweek: round £40.00; day £50.00. Weekend: round n/a; day n/a.

Facilities: Bar: 11am–11pm. Food: Lunch from 11am–4pm. Dinner by arrangement.

Comments: Mature course which has hosted the Scottish Open ... High, lofted shots needed to elevated greens ... Welcoming private club ... Thoroughly enjoyed it ... Will be back one day ... Well maintained.

Hayston Golf Club   ★

Campsie Road, Kirkintilloch, Glasgow, G66 1RN
Website: www.haystongolf.com   E-mail: secretary@haystongolf.com
Nearest main town: Glasgow

Secretary: Mr J. Carmichael   Tel: 0141 775 0723
Professional: Mr S. Barnett   Tel: 0141 775 0882

Playing: Midweek: round £27.00 (introduced by a member); day n/a. Weekend: round n/a; day n/a.

Facilities: Bar: 11am–11pm. Food: Lunch and dinner from 10am–9pm.

Comments: Very undulating parkland course ... Fair test with good facilities ... By no means a classic but fair to the average player ... Not in great condition.

Hilton Park Golf Club (Hilton)   ★★★

Stockiemuir Road, Milngavie, G62 7HB
E-mail: info@hiltonparkgolfclub.fsnet.co.uk
Nearest main town: Glasgow

Secretary:	Mrs J. Dawson	Tel: 0141 956 4657
		Fax: 0141 956 4657
Professional:	Mr W. McCondichie	Tel: 0141 956 5125
		Fax: 0141 956 5125

Playing: Midweek: round £25.00; day £35.00. Weekend: round no visitors at weekends; day n/a.

Facilities: Bar: 11am–11pm. Food: Members and guests only.

Comments: Very scenic ... Interesting moorland course with trouble at every turn ... The Hilton far superior to the Allander course ... Good quality course.

The Irvine Golf Club   ★★★★

Bogside, Irvine, KA12 8SN
E-mail: secretary@theirvinegolfclub.co.uk
Nearest main town: Irvine

Secretary:	Mr W. McMahon	Tel: 01294 275979
		Fax: 01294 278209
Professional:	Mr J. McKinnon	Tel: 01294 275626
		Fax: 01294 275626

Playing: Midweek: round £50.00; day £60.00. Weekend: round £60.00; day n/a.

Facilities: Bar: 11am–11pm. Food: Lunch and dinner from 10am–9pm. Bar snacks.

Comments: Very tricky course with good variety of holes ... Excellent variation ... Good welcome ... Interesting parkland course ... Will go again ... Just the ticket for holiday golf.

Kilmacolm Golf Club   ★★★

Porterfield Road, Kilmacolm, PA13 4PD
Nearest main town: Paisley

Secretary:	Mr D. Tinton	Tel: 01505 872139
		Fax: 01505 874007
Professional:	Mr I. Nicholson	Tel: 01505 872695

Playing: Midweek: round £20.50; day £30.50. Weekend: round £20.50; day £30.50.

Facilities: Bar: 11am–11pm. Food: Lunch and dinner from 12pm–9pm. Bar snacks.

Comments: One of the best value smaller courses ... 7th is a bit special ... Moorland course of character.

Kilmarnock Golf Club (Barassie)   ★★★★

29 Hillhouse Road, Barassie, Troon, KA10 6SY
Website: www.kbgc.co.uk   E-mail: barassiegc@lineone.net
Nearest main town: Troon

Secretary: Mr D. Wilson   Tel: 01292 313920
                                      Fax: 01292 318300
Professional: Mr G. Howie   Tel: 01292 311322
                                      Fax: 01292 311322

Playing: Midweek: round n/a; day £58.00. Weekend: round £60.00; day n/a.

Facilities: Bar: 11am–11pm. Food: Lunch and dinner from 11am–9pm. Bar snacks.

Comments: Beautifully presented ... Hard test ... Open qualifying course ... Some blind shots ... A must play in the area ... Better than Troon ... New nine holes a little out of character with the rest ... Sensational seaside links ... Heather-lined fairways and small greens – it's awesome.

Kirkhill Golf Club   ★

Greenlees Road, Cambuslang, Glasgow, G72 8YN
Nearest main town: Glasgow

Secretary: Ms C. Downes   Tel: 0141 641 8499
                                      Fax: 0141 641 8499
Professional: Mr D. Williamson   Tel: 0141 641 7972
                                      Fax: 0141 641 8499

Playing: Midweek: round £20.00; day n/a. Weekend: round n/a; day n/a.

Facilities: Bar: 11am–11pm. Food: Lunch and dinner from 10am–9pm. Bar snacks.

Comments: Designed by the master craftsman, James Braid ... Hard walking ... Need to be fit ... Blasted 1st hole a good indication of what's to come.

Lanark Golf Club   ★★

The Moor, Whitelees Road, Lanark, ML11 7RX
E-mail: lanarkgolfclub@talk21.com
Nearest main town: Glasgow

Secretary: Mr G. Cuthill   Tel: 01555 663219
                                 Fax: 01555 663219
Professional: Mr A. White   Tel: 01555 661456
                                 Fax: 01555 661456

Playing: Midweek: round £30.00; day £40.00. Weekend: round no visitors at weekends; day n/a.

Facilities: Bar: 11am–11pm. Food: Lunch and dinner from 10am–9pm. Bar snacks.

Comments: Difficult-to-read greens made this a struggle ... Superb condition ... Always in good nick and a varied challenge ... A few blind shots ... Short and hilly ... Something different from the norm ... Heathland golf at its best.

Largs Golf Club   ★★

Irvine Road, Largs, KA30 8EU
Website: www.largsgolfclub.co.uk
E-mail: secretary@largsgolfclub.co.uk
Nearest main town: Largs

Secretary: Mr J. Callaghan   Tel: 01475 673594
                                   Fax: 01475 673594
Professional: Mr K. Docherty   Tel: 01475 686192
                                   Fax: 01475 686192

Playing: Midweek: round £30.00 (deals inclusive of catering for 12 players or more Tues and Thurs); day n/a. Weekend: round £40.00; day n/a.

Facilities: Bar: 11am–11pm. Food: Lunch and dinner from 11am–9pm. Bar snacks.

Comments: Very good club with lovely welcome ... Parkland course of some stature ... Great parkland course with streams affecting several holes ... Good hospitality ... Scotland not known for its parkland golf, but this is an exception ... Homely club ... Made very welcome.

Lochranza Golf Club ★★

Lochranza, Isle of Arran, KA27 8HL
Website: www.lochranzagolf.com
E-mail: office@lochgolf.demon.co.uk
Nearest main town: Brodick

Secretary: Mr I. Robertson Tel: 01770 830273
Fax: 01770 830600

Professional: None

Playing: Midweek: round £15.00; day £20.00. Weekend: round £15.00; day £20.00.

Facilities: Bar: None. Food: None.

Comments: Closed from late October until late April ... Worth playing if you're going to Machrie ... Very tough and windy ... Double nine layout where second nine holes are played from different tees to different landing areas to different flags, in some cases on separate greens ... Great fun.

Lochwinnoch Golf Club ★

Burnfoot Road, Lochwinnoch, PA12 4AN
Nearest main town: Paisley

Secretary: Mrs E. Wilson Tel: 01505 842153
Fax: 01505 843668

Professional: Mr G. Reilly Tel: 01505 843029

Playing: Midweek: round £15.00; day £20.00. Weekend: round £15.00; day £20.00.

Facilities: Bar: 11am–11pm. Food: Lunch and dinner from 10am–9pm.

Comments: Well kept but not a difficult course ... Useful practice for the high handicapper ... Rather hilly parkland course.

Loudoun Gowf Golf Club ★★

Galston, KA4 8PA
E-mail: secretary@loudgowf.sol.co.uk
Nearest main town: Kilmarnock

Secretary:	Mr W. Dougan	Tel: 01563 821993
		Fax: 01563 820011
Professional:	None	

Playing: Midweek: round £20.00; day £30.00. Weekend: round n/a; day n/a.

Facilities: Bar: 11am–11pm. Food: Lunch and dinner from 11am–10pm. Bar snacks.

Comments: Very difficult parkland course ... Short but designed to high order ... Nothing you won't find elsewhere ... Worthy of note ... Delightfully named, charming short course.

Machrie Hotel Golf Club ★★★★

Port Ellen, Isle of Islay, PA42 7AN
Nearest main town: Port Ellen

Secretary:	Mr T. Dunn	Tel: 01496 302310
		Fax: 01496 302404
Professional:	None	

Playing: Midweek: round £20.00; day £30.00. Weekend: round £20.00; day £30.00.

Facilities: Bar: 11am–11pm. Food: Breakfast, lunch and dinner from 7am–10pm. Bar snacks.

Comments: Unique atmosphere and incredibly challenging ... Almost unplayable in really bad weather ... Enjoy the whisky and peat fire in the clubhouse ... Surprising course design but very interesting ... Condition excellent ... Incredibly natural course ... Thrilling from start to finish.

Machrihanish Golf Club ★★★★

Machrihanish, PA28 6PT
Website: www.machgolf.com   E-mail: secretary@machgolf.com
Nearest main town: Campbeltown

Secretary: Mrs A. Anderson   Tel: 01586 810213
                                       Fax: 01586 810221
Professional: Mr K. Campbell   Tel: 01586 810277
                                       Fax: 01586 810221

Playing: Midweek: round £35.00 (Sun–Fri); day £55.00.
                   Weekend: round £45.00 (Sat); day £70.00.

Facilities: Bar: 11am–11pm. Food: Breakfast, lunch and dinner
                   from 9am–9pm. Bar snacks.

Comments: Natural setting offering stiff test of golf … Great links
                   course that is open to the elements … A wild, windswept
                   course … Great malt and fantastic people … Brilliant
                   and what a nice welcome and people … A mini
                   Turnberry despite its modest facilities … Tremendous
                   opening hole to a fantastic links course … Undulating,
                   wonderful greens … Cracking opening par-4 over the
                   sea.

Millport Golf Club   ★★★

Golf Road, Millport, Isle of Cumbrae, KA28 0HB
Website: www.millportgolfclub.co.uk
E-mail: secretary@millportgolfclub.co.uk
Nearest main town: Millport

Secretary: Mrs J. Frazer   Tel: 01475 530306
                                       Fax: 01475 530306
Professional: None

Playing: Midweek: round £20.00; day £25.00. Weekend: round
                   £25.00; day £31.00.

Facilities: Bar: 11am–11pm. Food: Lunch and dinner from
                   10am–9pm. Bar snacks.

Comments: Superb views to Bute, Arran and Kintyre … Moorland
                   course that can get windy … Felt very alive here.

Milngavie Golf Club   ★★

Laighpark, Glasgow, G62 8EP
Nearest main town: Glasgow

Secretary: Ms S. McGuinness   Tel: 0141 956 1619
                                       Fax: 0141 956 4252
Professional: None

Playing: Midweek: round £20.00; day £30.00. Weekend: round n/a; day n/a.

Facilities: Bar: 11am–11pm. Food: Bar snacks. Dinner by arrangement.

Comments: You need to hit the fairways running here ... 1st is a bit special ... Drive over the burn at the 1st is a great way to start ... Scenic course with elements of moorland golf ... Less than 6000 yards.

Paisley Golf Club ★★

The Bushes, Braehead Road, Paisley, PA2 8TZ
E-mail: paisleygc@onetel.net.uk
Nearest main town: Paisley

Secretary: Mr J. Hillis   Tel: 0141 884 3903
                                       Fax: 0141 884 3903
Professional: Mr G. Stewart   Tel: 0141 884 4114

Playing: Midweek: round £24.00; day n/a. Weekend: round n/a; day n/a.

Facilities: Bar: 11am–11pm. Food: Lunch and dinner from 10am–9pm. Bar snacks.

Comments: Terrific views and some fine hilly holes ... Good course and interesting greens ... Very windy at times ... Wind the main challenge.

Pollok Golf Club ★★★

90 Barrhead Road, Glasgow, G43 1BG
Website: www.pollokgolf.com   E-mail: pollok.gc@lineone.net
Nearest main town: Glasgow

Secretary: Mr I. Cumming   Tel: 0141 632 4351
                                       Fax: 0141 649 1398
Professional: None

Playing: Midweek: round £35.00; day £45.00. Weekend: round £40.00; day £50.00.

Facilities: Bar: 11am–11pm. Food: Full lunches, snacks, other meals by arrangement.

Comments: Wonderful secluded setting within the grounds of the Pollok Estate ... Great layout with some magnificent mature trees to contend with should you stray too far from the middle of the fairways ... 14th hole is a real challenge where you have to decide just how much of the River Cart you are brave enough to bite off with your tee shot ... Short 6th offers one of the most scenic tee shots on the course ... Nice people who obviously enjoy their golf.

Port Glasgow Golf Club   ★

Devol Farm, Port Glasgow, PA14 5XE
Nearest main town: Port Glasgow

Secretary: Mr N. Mitchell   Tel: 01475 700334
Professional: None   Tel: 01475 705671

Playing: Midweek: round £15.00; day £20.00. Weekend: round n/a; day n/a.

Facilities: Bar: 11am–11pm. Food: Lunch and dinner from 12pm–9pm. Bar snacks.

Comments: Views of the Clyde ... Cheap course primarily for beginners ... Short course with basic facilities ... Moorland track open most of the year.

Prestwick Golf Club

2 Links Road, Prestwick, KA9 1QG
Website: www.prestwickgc.co.uk
E-mail: secretary@prestwickgc.co.uk
Nearest main town: Prestwick

Secretary: Mr I. Bunch   Tel: 01292 477404
                    Fax: 01292 477255
Professional: Mr F. Rennie   Tel: 01292 479483
                    Fax: 01292 477255

Playing: Midweek: round £95.00; day £135.00. Weekend: round £110.00 (Sundays); day n/a.

Facilities: Bar: 11am–11pm. Food: Lunch from 11am–3pm.

Comments: 1st is just so tough, you feel disillusioned before you've got going ... Good fun ... Plenty of blind holes ... History and tradition with terrific holes next to the Firth ... Great value ... So difficult ... Walking in the footsteps of the greats ... An intoxicating experience.

Prestwick St Cuthbert Golf Club   ★★★

East Road, Prestwick, KA9 2SX
Website: www.stcuthbertgc.co.uk
E-mail: secretary@stcuthbertgc.co.uk
Nearest main town: Prestwick

Secretary: Mr J. Rutherford   Tel: 01292 477101
Fax: 01292 671730
Professional: None

Playing: Midweek: round £29.00; day £38.00. Weekend: round
no visitors at weekends; day n/a.

Facilities: Bar: 11am–11pm. Food: Lunch and dinner from
11am–9pm.

Comments: Good test ... Only minus point is flatness of course ...
Flat and exposed ... Little attractive to the eye ... Fun on
an historic course.

Prestwick St Nicholas Golf Club   ★★

Grangemuir Road, Prestwick, KA9 1SN
Website: www.prestwickstnicholas.com
E-mail: secretary@prestwickstnicholas.com
Nearest main town: Prestwick

Secretary: Mr T. Hepburn   Tel: 01292 477608
Fax: 01292 473900
Professional: Mr D. Barbour   Tel: 01292 473904
(Starters)   Fax: 01292 473900

Playing: Midweek: round £36.00; day £56.00 (under review).
Weekend: round £41.00 (under review); day n/a.

Facilities: Bar: 11am–11pm. Food: Lunch from 12pm–4pm.
Dinner by arrangement.

Comments: Weekend play Sunday only ... Laid out between the sea
and the railway line ... A very honest links ... One to
savour ... Enormous greens ... Don't leave Prestwick
without playing here ... Won't forget it in a hurry.

Ralston Golf Club   ★★

Strathmore Avenue, Paisley, PA1 2DT
Nearest main town: Paisley

Secretary:	Mr J. Pearson	Tel: 0141 882 1349
		Fax: 0141 883 9837
Professional:	Mr C. Munro	Tel: 0141 810 4925

Playing: Midweek: round £18.00 (visiting parties only); day £28.00 (visiting parties only). Weekend: round n/a; day no visitors.

Facilities: Bar: 12pm–11pm (Mon–Fri), 11am–11pm (weekends). Food: Kitchen open 12pm–9.30pm Mon–Fri (coffee and biscuits before noon). Weekends 11am–9.30pm. Bar snacks and restaurant.

Comments: At least one bunker to avoid on every hole ... Mature parkland but the fairways are tight enough in places to threaten some of the tee shots ... Look out for the ditches that tend to pop up in all the wrong places ... Par-4 2nd, which measures 448 yards and plays uphill, is by far the toughest on the course ... Really enjoyed the closing hole. It may measure only 330 yards, but I'm sure the pond that guards the front of the green collects a fair number of golf balls during the season ... Friendly welcome assured.

Ranfurly Castle Golf Club ★

Golf Road, Bridge of Weir, PA11 3HN
Website: www.ranfurlycastle.com   E-mail: secranfur@aol.com
Nearest main town: Paisley

Secretary:	Mr J. King	Tel: 01505 612609
		Fax: 01505 610406
Professional:	Mr T. Eckford	Tel: 01505 614795

Playing: Midweek: round £25.00; day £35.00. Weekend: round n/a; day n/a.

Facilities: Bar: 11am–11pm. Food: Lunch and dinner from 10am–9pm. Bar snacks.

Comments: Good Scottish inland golf ... Very challenging and visually attractive ... Not out the top drawer but good value ... Hard walking ... Tough.

Shiskine Golf Club

Shore Road, Blackwaterfoot, Isle of Arran, KA27 8HA
Website: www.shiskinegolf.com   E-mail: info@shiskinegolf.com
Nearest main town: Brodick

Secretary:	Mrs F. Crawford	Tel: 01770 860226
		Fax: 01770 860205
Professional:	None	

Playing: Midweek: round £13.00; day £20.00. Weekend: round £16.00; day £24.00.

Facilities: Bar: 11am–11pm. Food: Tea room and snacks all day.

Comments: Wonderful views but course did not match them ... Plenty of blind shots ... Could be best value in Britain ... Good greens, great setting and great fun although can get congested ... More boys and girls have learned golf here than at all the private Glasgow and Edinburgh clubs combined ... A gem ... 12 holes only ... Great value ... Great views to Mull of Kintyre ... A pilgrimage to repeat again and again ... You will either love it or hate it.

Strathaven Golf Club ★★★

Glasgow Road, Strathaven, ML10 6NL
Website: www.strathavengc.com   E-mail: info@strathavengc.com
Nearest main town: Glasgow

Secretary:	Mr A. Wallace	Tel: 01357 520421
		Fax: 01357 520539
Professional:	Mr S. Kerr	Tel: 01357 521812

Playing: Midweek: round £26.00; day £36.00. Weekend: round n/a; day n/a.

Facilities: Bar: 11am–11pm. Food: Lunch and dinner from 10am–9pm.

Comments: Tree-lined course with oodles of character ... One to note ... A respite from the surfeit of links golf in Scotland ... Tight driving and tricky greens ... Always in good condition.

Troon Portland Golf Club ★★★

1 Crosbie Road, Troon, KA10 6EP
Nearest main town: Troon

Secretary:	Mr J. Irving	Tel: 01292 313488
		Fax: 01292 318204
Professional:	Mr R. Anderson	

Playing: Midweek: round n/a; day £35.00. Weekend: round n/a; day £45.00.

Facilities: Bar: 11am–11pm. Food: Lunch and dinner by arrangement. Bar snacks.

Comments: You don't go to Troon to play here ... Enjoyed it but only a warm-up to the main challenge ... Good fun.

Vale of Leven Golf Club ★

Northfield Road, Bonhill, Alexandria, G83 9ET
Website: www.valeoflevengolfclub.org.uk
E-mail: secretary@valegc.com
Nearest main town: Dumbarton

Secretary:	Mr R. Barclay	Tel: 01389 752351
		Fax: 0870 749 8950
Professional:	Mr B. Campbell	Tel: 0870 749 8930
		Fax: 0870 749 8950

Playing: Midweek: round £16.00; day £24.00. Weekend: round £20.00; day £30.00.

Facilities: Bar: 12pm–11pm. Food: Breakfast, lunch and dinner from 8am–9pm.

Comments: Holes overlook Loch Lomond ... Not in the same league as nearby Loch Lomond ... Very short but unbelievably tricky ... Can get very wet.

West Kilbride Golf Club ★★

33–35 Fullerton Drive, West Kilbride, KA23 9HT
E-mail: golf@westkilbridegolfclub.com
Nearest main town: West Kilbride

Secretary:	Mr H. Armour	Tel: 01294 823911
		Fax: 01294 823911
Professional:	Mr G. Ross	Tel: 01294 823042

Playing: Midweek: round £27.00; day £38.00. Weekend: round n/a; day n/a.

Facilities: Bar: 11am–11pm. Food: Lunch and dinner from 11am–10pm.

Comments: A really strong test off blue tees ... Invariably in great condition ... Warm welcome at a beautiful setting ... Views of the Isle of Arran ... Unheralded but excellent ... Good value compared to a lot of Scottish courses.

Westerwood Hotel Golf & Country Club   ★★

St Andrews Drive, Cumbernauld, G68 1RN
Nearest main town: Glasgow

Secretary:	Mr S. Killin	Tel: 01236 452772
		Fax: 01236 738478
Professional:	Mr S. Killin	Tel: 01236 725281

Playing: Midweek: round £22.50; day £35.00. Weekend: round £27.50; day £45.00.

Facilities: Bar: 11am–11pm. Food: Breakfast, lunch and dinner from 7am–10pm. Bar snacks.

Comments: Need to be long and straight, unlike its designer, Mr Ballesteros ... Will get better ... Imaginative course, what you would expect from Seve ... Beautiful location which course does not live up to ... Ambitious course ... Maybe Seve should stick to his day job.

The Westin Turnberry Resort (Arran)   ★★★

Turnberry, KA26 9LT
Nearest main town: Girvan

Secretary:	Mr P. Burley	Tel: 01655 334000
	(Director of Golf)	Fax: 01655 331069
Professional:	Mr R. Hall	Tel: 01655 334062

Playing: Midweek: round £55.00; day n/a. Weekend: round £55.00; day n/a.

Facilities: Bar: 11am–11pm. Food: Breakfast, lunch and dinner from 7am–10pm. Bar snacks.

Comments: Wonderful foil to the Ailsa ... Not easy and sometimes in better condition than the Ailsa ... Top-class second-string course at this luxurious hotel ... Very technical course, very rewarding.

Windyhill Golf Club ★★★

Windyhill, Bearsden, G61 4QQ
Nearest main town: Glasgow

Secretary: Mr B. Davidson   Tel: 0141 942 2349
                                  Fax: 0141 942 5874
Professional: Mr G. Collinson   Tel: 0141 942 7157

Playing: Midweek: round n/a; day £20.00. Weekend: round n/a; day n/a.

Facilities: Bar: 11am–11pm. Food: Lunch and dinner from 10am–9pm.

Comments: Not the best near Glasgow but worth a shout ... Nice feel to this open parkland course ... Some good technical holes on the back nine ... Front nine much harder.

Borders and Dumfries & Galloway

Southerness Golf Club ★★★★

Southerness, DG2 8AZ
Website: www.southernessgolfclub.com
E-mail: admin@southernessgc.sol.co.uk
Nearest main town: Dumfries

When you mention the Solway Firth as an area of outstanding natural golf, Silloth-on-Solway springs immediately to mind. But located almost directly opposite Silloth, across the calm of the Firth in Scotland, is a course few have heard of. Mention its name, Southerness, and you might still be corrected and told that you must mean Southerndown, the fine Welsh course. On the map of Britain's golf courses, someone's left a crumb of cake over Southerness.

The course's low profile is possibly because it is something of a rarity, a links course that was opened only in 1947, a second-generation course without the traditional feel and established nature of many of Scotland's great links; it may be because it is not blessed with the same outstanding natural scenery that one expects from a links; or it may be because it was designed by Mackenzie Ross, almost as an afterthought while he was working on the exceptional Ailsa course at Turnberry. Whatever it is, Southerness does not get the credit it deserves.

In design terms it is first class. There are no blind holes, where you hit your ball and scamper over a dune or hill to see which trap it has fallen into. Neither do balls bounce off the fairways after a good drive. Situated on a flat piece of land by the Solway Firth, and covered in gorse, heather and bracken, Southerness is very fair, the scores on each day governed by the wind that rushes in off the sea.

With the character of each hole at the mercy of the wind, Southerness is in constant flux. One thing that never changes is the quality of the par-4s, particularly the 12th, played to a green nestling precariously on the edge of the beach. Neither does the welcome, which is warm and hearty on arrival and in the clubhouse afterwards.

Secretary: Mr I. Robin   Tel: 01387 880677
                                Fax: 01387 880644
Professional: None

Playing:	Midweek: round n/a; day £38.00. Weekend: round n/a; day £48.00.
Facilities:	Bar: 11am–11pm. Food: Lunch and dinner from 11am–9pm. Bar snacks.
Comments:	Not a well-known course so invariably in good condition … Long and windy … A gem of a course, well worth the visit … Greens very good … People just superb.

Macdonald Cardrona Hotel, Golf & Country Club   ★★★

Cardrona, Peebles, EH45 9HX
Website: www.macdonaldhotels.co.uk
Nearest main town: Peebles

Secretary:	Ms M. Waddell (Administration)	Tel: 01896 833730 Fax: 01896 831166
Professional:	Mr F. Hall	Tel: 01896 833701
Playing:	Midweek: round £50.00 (Mon–Thurs); day n/a. Weekend: round £70.00 (Fri–Sun); day n/a.	
Facilities:	Bar: 7.30am–10pm. Food: 7.30am–10pm (Spike Bar and Restaurant).	
Comments:	It reminds me of Gleneagles … Stroke index one for the opening hole, you've got to be having a laugh! … Another Dave Thomas cracker … A beautiful course but an ugly-looking hotel … A super, very handy course guide … There's also a quality hotel with leisure club and spa, small practice ground and the new practice putting green should now be open.	

Dumfries & County Golf Club   ★★★

Nunfield, Edinburgh Road, Dumfries, DG1 1JX
Website: www.dumfriesandcounty-gc.fsnet.co.uk
E-mail: dumfriesc@aol.com
Nearest main town: Dumfries

Secretary:	Mr B. Duguia	Tel: 01387 253585 Fax: 01387 253585
Professional:	Mr S. Syme	Tel: 01387 268918 Fax: 01387 268918
Playing:	Midweek: round £27.50; day £33.50. Weekend: round £27.50; day £33.50.	

Facilities: Bar: 11am–11pm. Food: Lunch and dinner from 11am–9pm. Bar snacks.

Comments: Runs alongside River Nith ... A long journey to find it but worth the effort ... Parkland beauty sculpted by Willie Fernie ... One of the best examples of Scottish parkland golf ... An unforgettable par-3 14th ... Informative pro shop ... Off the beaten track but good for visitors.

Duns Golf Club   ★

Hardens Road, Duns, TD11 3NR
Website: www.dunsgolfclub.com
E-mail: secretary@dunsgolfclub.com
Nearest main town: Duns

Secretary: Mr A. Preston   Tel: 01361 882194
                                     Fax: 01361 883599

Professional: None

Playing: Midweek: round £22.00; day n/a. Weekend: round £25.00; day n/a.

Facilities: Bar: 11am–11pm. Food: Bar snacks.

Comments: Need to be fit here ... Odd course for an oddly named club ... Burn runs through middle of the course ... Burn dominates the 15th ... A warm welcome guaranteed ... A real Braveheart of a course.

Hawick Golf Club   ★★★

Vertish Hill, Hawick, TD9 0NY
Nearest main town: Carlisle (44 miles) or Edinburgh (52 miles)

Secretary: Mr J. Harley   Tel: 01450 372293
Professional: None

Playing: Midweek: round £20.00; day £25.00. Weekend: round £20.00; day £25.00.

Facilities: Bar: 12pm–11pm. Food: 12pm–9pm.

Comments: Hilly layout means you have to be fit to really enjoy playing here ... Wonderfully peaceful setting, even if some of the holes are a bit of a slog ... Great fun to play ... Greens a little slow but a great location.

Kelso Golf Club   ★★★

Abbotseat Road, Kelso, TD5 7SL
Nearest main town: Kelso

Secretary:	Mr D. Jack	Tel: 01573 223009
		Fax: 01573 228490

Professional: None

Playing: Midweek: round £16.00 (summer), £8.00 (winter); day £20.00 (summer), £12.00 (winter). Weekend: round £20.00 (summer), £10.00 (winter); day £28.00 (summer), £15.00 (winter).

Facilities: Bar: Normal hours. Food: Full catering.

Comments: The par-5s are long and demanding ... Great greens if you can find them – they're very well guarded ... A fair but challenging course which offers a test to all levels of golfer ... The greens are out of this world and the clubhouse food is pretty tasty too.

Moffat Golf Club   ★★★

Coatshill, Moffat, DG10 9SB
Website: www.moffatgolfclub.co.uk
E-mail: moffatgolfclub@onetel.net.uk
Nearest main town: Beattock

Secretary:	Mr J. Mein	Tel: 01683 220020
		Fax: 01683 221802

Professional: None

Playing: Midweek: round £19.50; day £24.00. Weekend: round £27.00; day £33.00.

Facilities: Bar: 11am–11pm. Food: Bar snacks.

Comments: Take your oxygen tank with you ... Up in the gods – you certainly need a head for heights ... Warm welcome but freezing-cold course ... Scenic course overlooking the town.

Newton Stewart Golf Club   ★★

Kirroughtree Avenue, Minnicaff, Newton Stewart, DG8 6PF
Nearest main town: Newton Stewart

Secretary: Mr M. Large   Tel: 01671 402172
                                     Fax: 01671 402172

Professional: None

Playing: Midweek: round £22.00; day £25.00. Weekend: round
                  £25.00; day £28.00.

Facilities: Bar: 11am–11pm (Easter until October 31, Friday
                  evenings, Saturday and Sunday). Food: 11am–11pm
                  (Easter until October 31, Friday evenings, Saturday and
                  Sunday).

Comments: A true hidden gem ... Ideal place to enjoy golf in a less
                  demanding guise ... Spray the ball about and you can
                  easily run up a bunch of bogeys ... Plenty of room from
                  the tee ... Greens receptive all year ... Five very individ-
                  ual par-3s a speciality ... Visitors welcome ... Buggies
                  available ... Pre-booking suggested in summer ...
                  Golf/food packages available.

Peebles Golf Club   ★★★

Kirkland Street, Peebles, EH45 8EU
Website: www.peeblesgolfclub.co.uk
E-mail: secretary@peeblesgolfclub.co.uk
Nearest main town: 23 miles due south of Edinburgh

Secretary: Mr H. Gilmore   Tel: 01721 720197
                                      Fax: 01721 724441

Professional: Mr C. Imlah   Tel: 01721 720197

Playing: Midweek: round £32.00 (group discounts available);
                  day n/a. Weekend: round £39.00 (group discounts
                  available); day n/a.

Facilities: Bar: 11am–11pm (summer). Food: All day to 9pm.

Comments: Not too demanding but design always presents different
                  challenges ... Tough opening two holes, the 200-yard
                  par-3 1st is followed by an equally demanding par-4
                  2nd ... Flattering, provided you can keep the ball
                  straight ... Short 16th is the best hole on the course ...
                  Very attractive setting and friendly staff.

Portpatrick Dunskey Golf Club ★★★★

Golf Course Road, Portpatrick, DG9 8TB
Website: www.portpatrickgolfclub.com
E-mail: enquiries@portpatrickgolfclub.com
Nearest main town: Stranraer

Secretary:	Mr J. McPhail	Tel: 01776 810817
		Fax: 01776 810811
Professional:	None	
Playing:	Midweek: round £28.00; day £38.00. Weekend: round £35.00; day £45.00.	
Facilities:	Bar: 11am–11pm. Food: Lunch and dinner from 11am–9pm. Bar snacks.	
Comments:	Remote links with bundles of character ... Course defence entirely dictated by the wind ... Wonderfully old-fashioned links ... Will linger in the memory for a long time ... Village simply breathes golf ... Very exposed.	

Powfoot Golf Club ★★★★

Cummertrees, Annan, DG12 5QE
Nearest main town: Annan

Secretary:	Mr B. Sutherland (Manager)	Tel: 01461 700276
		Fax: 01461 700276
Professional:	Mr G. Dick	Tel: 01461 700327
		Fax: 01461 700327
Playing:	Midweek: round £24.00; day £31.00. Weekend: round £24.00; day £31.00.	
Facilities:	Bar: 11am–11pm. Food: Lunch and dinner from 11am–9pm. Bar snacks.	
Comments:	Superb condition and nice surroundings ... A classic links ... Good layout, difficult in the wind.	

The Roxburghe Hotel & Golf Course ★★★★

Heiton, By Kelso, TD5 8JZ
Website: www.roxburghe.net   E-mail: golf@roxburghe.net
Nearest main town: Kelso

Secretary:	None	Tel: 01573 450333
		Fax: 01573 450611

Professional: Mr C. Montgomerie   Tel: 01573 450333
                                      Fax: 01573 450611

Playing: Midweek: round £60.00; day £80.00. Weekend: round £60.00; day £80.00.

Facilities: Bar: 11am–11pm. Food: Breakfast, lunch and dinner from 9am–9pm. Bar snacks.

Comments: Excellent course ... The 5th and 6th are exceptional holes ... Shop and food a little pricey ... When fully mature this will be a bit special ... Was allowed to use championship tees so a great welcome ... Anyone know a better new course? ... Best course in Scotland since Loch Lomond.

Stranraer Golf Club   ★★★

Creachmore, Stranraer, DG9 0LF
Website: www.stranraergolfclub.net
E-mail: www.stranraergolf@btclick.com
Nearest main town: Stranraer

Secretary: Mr B. Kelly   Tel: 01776 870245
                                       Fax: 01776 870445

Professional: None

Playing: Midweek: round £25.00; day £35.00. Weekend: round £30.00; day £40.00.

Facilities: Bar: 11am–11pm. Food: Snacks, bar meals and full meals.

Comments: One of the best courses in the south-west of Scotland ... Great scenery, especially the views towards Loch Ryan ... Good test of golf, especially when the wind blows ... Another cracker by James Braid.

Fife and Clackmannan

Kingsbarns Golf Links ★★★★★

Kingsbarns, KY16 8QD
Website: www.kingsbarns.com   E-mail: info@kingsbarns.com
Nearest main town: St Andrews

Being just along the Fife coastline from the magical Old course and the other battery of great courses that St Andrews, the home of golf, has to offer, Kingsbarns really had to be good. And, make no mistake, it is.

Although it only opened just prior to the 2000 Open Championship at neighbouring St Andrews, Kingsbarns has already become a links legend. It has successfully co-hosted the Dunhill Links Championship (with Carnoustie and, of course, the Old Course) and has picked up more awards than Sir Alex Ferguson. And deservedly so.

American course designer Kyle Phillips has created a spectacular and stunning par-72 layout, possibly the UK's last true classical links. What a way to bow out!

Like the Old course itself, Kingsbarns is one of those golfing rarities: a course every golfer simply has to play at least once before he retires to that great golf course in the sky. Mind you, at £125 to tee up, that round to remember doesn't come cheap, but high-quality goods never do.

Always in pristine condition, Kingsbarns has a heady mix of holes – some good, some great and some that are out of this world. Without doubt the star of the show is the par-5 12th, a breathtaking left dogleg that hugs the shoreline from tee to green. The par-3 15th is another stunner, with its long but narrow rolling green perilously perched on the other side of an inlet – underhit and your ball will be dancing among the rocks. There's a pulsating finale too with an uphill-downhill par-4, where you're faced with a difficult second shot over an ancient burn to an elevated green.

Provided you've got the cash to spare, you'll want to go back to Kingsbarns again and again.

Secretary: Ms D. Clark   Tel: 01334 460860
                                        Fax: 01334 460877
Professional: Mr D. Scott   Tel: 01334 460865
                  (Director of Golf)   Fax: 01334 460877

Playing: Midweek: round £125.00 (Apr–May), £135.00 (Jun–Mar); day n/a. Weekend: round £125.00 (Apr–May), £135.00 (Jun–Mar); day n/a.

Facilities: Bar: Dependant on tee times. Food: Bar snacks.

Comments: Stunning design ... Destined to become one of the best links courses, not just in Scotland but anywhere in the world ... Superb views of the sea from every single hole on the course ... When the wind blows, you will hit every club in the bag ... Looks so natural I can't believe it hasn't been here for over 100 years ... Finishing stretch of holes is just fantastic ... Great variety of classic links holes and a layout every golfer from pro to rabbit will enjoy playing.

St Andrews Bay Golf Resort & Spa (Devlin Course)   ★★★★

St Andrews Bay, St Andrews, KY16 8PN
Website: www.standrewsbay.com
Nearest main town: St Andrews

Being up the road from some of the best sport on offer on Planet Golf was never going to be an easy task, but fair play to the captivating Devlin layout for pulling it off – certainly no mean feat.

Like neighbouring superstars such as the Old Course and Kingsbarns, the Devlin is a class act in its own right. It's very much a quality US-style linksy test, with plenty of gaping bunkers and water (on the front nine) to negotiate.

Even in its infancy it already oozes character, while the gently rolling greens are humongous, fast and true. There's a superb mix of holes, several breathtaking elevated tees and stunning views – of the Old Grey Toon of St Andrews (especially impressive from the delightful par-3 7th). The holes just after the turn will literally blow you away, with the green at the par-4 11th virtually hovering above the beach and the shortish par-4 12th hugging the coastline.

There's a bit of a Jekyll and Hyde climax to the round via an outstanding par-4 dogleg penultimate hole – you're firing an approach shot to a green surrounded by bunkers and the sea – only to be unusually followed by a rather ordinary par-3 18th.

Secretary:	Mr I. Knox	Tel: 01334 837438
	(Golf sales manager)	Fax: 01334 837099
Professional:	Mr J. Kerr	Tel: 01334 837056

Playing: Midweek: round £85.00 (Mon–Fri); day n/a. Weekend: Not available at weekends unless you're a hotel resident.

Facilities: Bar: 11am–11pm Sun–Thurs, 11am–12 midnight
              Fri/Sat. Food: 7am–10pm (summer), 8am–9pm (winter).

Comments: A class act on and off course ... Loved the Devlin but
              thought it was odd finishing with a par-3 ... Some stun-
              ning holes and the neighbouring Torrance is pretty good
              too ... A worthy addition to the St Andrews 'club'.

St Andrews Old Golf Course   ★★★★★

St Andrews Links Trust, Pilmour House, St Andrews, KY16 9SF
Website: www.standrews.org.uk   E-mail: pr@standrews.org.uk
Nearest main town: St Andrews

No more than a flat, vast open playing field. Made redundant by the
improvements in golf-club technology. These are just two of the criti-
cisms levelled at the Old course at St Andrews, the home of the Royal
and Ancient Golf Club and the most famous golf course in the world. It
has almost become fashionable to have a pop at the Old course: once,
they say, a venerable work of art, but now its colours are fading and its
brush strokes criticised for their broadness and depth.

It wasn't always like this. The bunkers were once praised for their
depth and singularity, the double greens for their design and surreal
appearance, the double fairways for their uniqueness. But opinions
change, and as the game of golf grows and players seek out virgin
territory, so the memories of the Old course fade. Why the stark barren-
ness of the Old course when you can have the deep colours and
exhilaration of a County Down or a Turnberry?

What the Old course will do is make you think. If the design is such
a joke, why is it so difficult? Huge greens and wide fairways are
normally associated with good scoring, and yet, with the exception of
the pros, who can make a mockery of the front nine at times, you'll
struggle to better your handicap. The answer lies in the illusions the
landscape offers. From the tee you are presented with huge fairways,
but you see only rutted, unreceptive ones. For your approaches, you are
presented with huge greens, but they are often blind and so contoured
that your ball runs off in all directions. Then there's the fickle wind,
which can grab your ball in mid-flight and deposit it in a scrape or burn.

The Old course will also make you nervous. First-tee nerves for
golfers are as normal as the common cold, but you'll never have
experienced anything like this – and the irony is the fairway you'll be
aiming at is the biggest anywhere in the world. Then there's the 17th, a
hole so difficult you'll treat it like walking on eggshells and leave with
an eight. That's the difficulty at St Andrews. Much like meeting your
favourite celebrity, you'll clam up and the right words won't come out!

Secretary: Mr A. McGregor   Tel: 01334 466666
(General Manager)   Fax: 01334 479555
Professional: None

Playing: Midweek: round £10.00–£110.00; day n/a. Weekend: round n/a; day n/a.

Facilities: Bar: 11am–11pm. Food: Breakfast, lunch and dinner from 7am–9pm.

Comments: Sheer magic ... Anyone who's ever professed to be a golfer must play ... Take a caddie ... So subtle ... Feel the nerves on the 1st tee ... The course and the people, the best anywhere ... Tee shot at the 1st is so special ... Take away the 1st, 17th and 18th and this is a very ordinary links ... Course not up to much but the special feeling makes up for it ... It can be both cruel and kind ... A wonderful and mystical venue – not to be missed ... Treasure the experience.

Aberdour Golf Club   ★★★

Seaside Place, Aberdour, KT3 0TX
E-mail: aberdourgc@aol.com
Nearest main town: Dunfermline

Secretary: Mr S. Laing   Tel: 01383 860080
Fax: 01383 860050
Professional: Mr D. Gemmell   Tel: 01383 860256

Playing: Midweek: round £20.00; day £30.00. Weekend: round £35.00 (Sunday only); day £35.00 (Sunday only).

Facilities: Bar: 11am–11pm. Food: Lunch and dinner from 11am–9pm. Bar snacks.

Comments: Short course on nice piece of coastline ... Good views ... Great wee seaside course with lovely views.

Alloa Golf Club   ★★★

Schawpark Golf Course, Sauchie, Alloa, FK10 3AX
E-mail: alloagolf@schawpark.fsbusiness.co.uk
Nearest main town: Alloa

Secretary: Ms F. Nichols   Tel: 01259 722745
Fax: 01259 218796

Professional: Mr W. Bennett   Tel: 01259 724476
                                         Fax: 01259 724476

Playing: Midweek: round £26.00; day £36.00. Weekend: round
                  £30.00; day £40.00. Prices may increase in 2004.

Facilities: Bar: 11am–11pm. Food: Lunch and dinner from
                  11am–9pm. Bar snacks.

Comments: Hilly course with plenty of blind shots ... Strategic
                  bunkering with sunken greens ... Nice stop-over in
                  otherwise barren golfing region ... Worth seeking out ...
                  Reasonable green fees.

Balbirnie Park Golf Club   ★★★

Balbirnie Park, Markinch, Glenrothes, KY7 6NR
Nearest main town: Glenrothes

Secretary: Mr P. Todhunter   Tel: 01592 612095
                                           Fax: 01592 612383
Professional: Mr C. Donnelly   Tel: 01592 752006
                                           Fax: 01592 752006

Playing: Midweek: round £25.00; day £33.00. Weekend: round
                  £30.00; day £40.00.

Facilities: Bar: 11am–11pm. Food: Lunch and dinner from
                  12pm–9pm. Bar snacks.

Comments: One of the best parkland courses around with a high
                  degree of difficulty ... Still young but great fairways,
                  and greens will improve ... Excellent and unusual club
                  ... Compact links with views of Isle of Man on a clear
                  day.

Camperdown Golf Course   ★★

Camperdown Park, Dundee, DD4 9BX
Nearest main town: Dundee

Secretary: Mr R. Gordon   Tel: 01382 814445
Professional: Mr R. Brown

Playing: Midweek: round £15.00; day n/a. Weekend: round n/a;
                  day n/a.

Facilities: Bar: None. Food: None.

Comments: Excellent parkland-style layout with fairways running through avenues of tall mature pine trees ... Grass on the greens was a little long but really enjoyed the variety of holes ... Must be one of Scotland's best-value pay-and-play courses ... Superb setting in the Camperdown Estate ... Clubhouse facilities could be improved ... Must be the smallest pro shop in the country ... Cracking short holes, especially enjoyed the 4th and the 17th, which is around 160 yards and played uphill ... Tee shot on the par-5 10th is the scariest on the course ... Fairly hilly but not overly tiring to walk.

Crail Golfing Society (Balcomie)   ★★★★

Balcomie Clubhouse, Fifeness, Crail, KY10 3XN
Website: www.crailgolfingsociety.co.uk   E-mail: crailgs@hotmail.com
Nearest main town: St Andrews

Secretary: Mr A. Busby   Tel: 01333 450686
                                   Fax: 01333 450416
Professional: Mr G. Lennie   Tel: 01333 450960
                                   Fax: 01333 450960

Playing: Midweek: round £35.00 (both courses); day n/a. Weekend: round £44.00 (both courses); day n/a.

Facilities: Bar: 11am–11pm. Food: Breakfast, lunch and dinner from 7am–10pm. Bar snacks.

Comments: Beautiful part of the world ... Course in excellent nick ... Best holes by the sea ... Very friendly ... One of the oldest clubs in the world ... Superb little links ... Very hospitable ... Friendly Scottish links of the highest quality ... Greens true and fast ... Good holiday golf.

Drumoig Golf Hotel   ★★

Drumoig, Leuchars, St Andrews, KY16 0BE
Nearest main town: Dundee

Secretary: Mr D. Sievwright   Tel: 01382 541800
Professional: None

Playing: Midweek: round £25.00; day n/a. Weekend: round n/a; day £30.00.

Facilities: Bar: 11am–11pm. Food: 12pm–9.30pm.

Comments: A long slog off the back tees ... Still fairly new but maturing nicely ... Water comes into play in the shape of two large ponds that guard the 5th and 13th greens ... Undulating layout but pretty open with generous landing areas from most of the trees ... Some interesting holes, especially the ones where the layout incorporates some of the old quarries that were on the original site ... 7000 yards Championship course.

Dunfermline Golf Club ★★

Pitfirrane, Crossford, Dunfermline, KY12 8QW
Nearest main town: Dunfermline

Secretary: Mr R. De Rose   Tel: 01383 723534
Professional: Mr S. Craig   Tel: 01383 729061

Playing: Midweek: round £20.00; day £30.00. Weekend: round £25.00; day £35.00.

Facilities: Bar: 11am–11pm. Food: Lunch and dinner from 11am–9pm. Bar snacks.

Comments: Weekend play on Sundays only ... Nice parkland course ... Have fun ... Course has stood the test of time ... Rough and semi-rough too punishing on visitors ... Internal out-of-bounds very frustrating.

Glenbervie Golf Club ★★★

Stirling Road, Larbert, FK5 4SJ
Nearest main town: Falkirk

Secretary: Dr S. Hartley   Tel: 01324 562605
    Fax: 01324 551054
Professional: Mr J. Chillas   Tel: 01324 562725

Playing: Midweek: round £30.00; day £40.00. Weekend: round n/a; day members' guests only.

Facilities: Bar: 11am–11pm (summer). Food: 10am–8pm (summer).

Comments: Mature parkland layout ... Look out for the ditch that comes into play on a number of holes ... Super condition with excellent greens and fairways ... You will die happy if you manage to par the 407-yard par-4 14th ... The short 4th is a beauty ... Moderate number of bunkers and not too tight or too long for the average golfer ... James Braid design.

The Golf House Club   ★★★

Elie, KY9 1AS
E-mail: sandy@golfhouseclub.freeserve.co.uk
Nearest main town: St Andrews

Secretary:	Mr A. Sneddon	Tel: 01333 330301
		Fax: 01333 330895
Professional:	Mr R. Wilson	Tel: 01333 330955

Playing: Midweek: round £40.00; day £55.00. Weekend: round £50.00; day £65.00.

Facilities: Bar: 11am–11pm. Food: Breakfast, lunch and dinner from 9am–9pm. Bar snacks.

Comments: With 16 par-4s and two par-3s this course is full of quirks ... Excellent holiday golf here ... James Braid grew up here ... Located virtually in the middle of the village ... Bump-and-run is a shot you need ... Eccentric course with numerous semi-blind shots.

Kirkcaldy Golf Club   ★★★

Balwearie Road, Kirkcaldy, KY2 5LT
Website: www.kirkcaldygolfclub.co.uk
E-mail: enquiries@kirkcaldygolfclub.co.uk
Nearest main town: Kirkcaldy

Secretary:	Mr A. Thomson	Tel: 01592 205240
		Fax: 01592 205240
Professional:	Mr A. Caira	Tel: 01592 203258
	(Director of Golf)	Fax: 01592 205240

Playing: Midweek: round £24.00; day £30.00. Weekend: round £30.00; day £36.00.

Facilities: Bar: 11am–11pm. Food: Lunch and dinner from 12pm–9pm. Bar snacks.

Comments: Challenging parkland course ... Nicely kept, simple course that is surprisingly challenging ... In play most of the year.

Ladybank Golf Club ★★★★

Annsmuir, Ladybank, KY15 7RA
Website: www.ladybankgolf.co.uk   E-mail: ladybankgc@aol.com
Nearest main town: Cupar

Secretary: Mr D. Allan   Tel: 01337 830814
                                  Fax: 01337 831505

Professional: Mr M. Gray   Tel: 01337 830725
                                  Fax: 01337 830558

Playing: Midweek: round £45.00; day £55.00. Weekend: round £50.00; day n/a.

Facilities: Bar: 11am–11pm. Food: Lunch and dinner from 10am–9pm. Bar snacks.

Comments: Excellent test of golf in beautiful surroundings ... Well prepared ... Good all-round test ... Gorse is the main hazard here ... Excellent practice facilities ... Best time to play is in the autumn ... Very nice experience – warm clubhouse and course in top nick ... Forget about St Andrews, this is the best in Fife ... A golfer's golf course ... Tough but rewarding ... Set in exquisite mature woodland ... Pine trees, heather and gorse – perfect ... Really is the business ... Very easy on the eye.

Leven Links Golf Course ★★★★

The Starters Hut, The Promenade, Leven, KY8 4HS
Website: www.leven-links.com   E-mail: secretary@leven-links.com
Nearest main town: Leven

Secretary: Mr R. Bissett   Tel: 01333 428859
                                  Fax: 01333 428859

Professional: None

Playing: Midweek: round £30.00; day £40.00. Weekend: round £35.00; day £50.00.

Facilities: Bar: 11am–11pm. Food: Breakfast, lunch and dinner from 8am–9pm. Bar snacks.

Comments: Short course but wind stiffens things up ... Right next to Lundin ... Pure links ... Finishes with a flourish ... Real appreciation of the game at this club ... Has stood the test of time ... Always beautifully prepared.

Lundin Golf Club   ★★★★

Golf Road, Lundin Links, KY8 6BA
Website: www.lundingolfclub.co.uk
E-mail: secretary@lundingolfclub.co.uk
Nearest main town: Leven

Secretary:	Mr D. Thomson	Tel: 01333 320202
		Fax: 01333 329743
Professional:	Mr D. Webster	Tel: 01333 320051
		Fax: 01333 329743

Playing: Midweek: round £40.00; day £50.00. Weekend: round £50.00; day n/a.

Facilities: Bar: 11am–11pm. Food: Lunch and dinner from 10am–9pm. Bar snacks.

Comments: Weekend play on Saturday afternoons only ... Very hard and interesting course ... Greens are exceptional, while fairways can be scrappy ... Superb welcome ... Unusual course with challenging tee shots ... A parkland/links hybrid that's fun to play ... Old railway runs through the middle ... Let creativity be your watchword.

Pitreavie (Dunfermline) Golf Club   ★★

Queensferry Road, Dunfermline, KY11 8PR
Nearest main town: Dunfermline

Secretary:	Mr E. Comerford	Tel: 01383 822591
		Fax: 01383 722591
Professional:	Mr C. Mitchell	Tel: 01383 723151
		Fax: 01383 723151

Playing: Midweek: round £26.00; day n/a. Weekend: round £38.00; day n/a.

Facilities: Bar: 11am–11pm. Food: All day.

Comments: Fun course, but not as easy as you might think when you consider it plays just over 6000 yards ... Well maintained. Friendly welcome ... Surprised to discover the course was designed by Dr Alister Mackenzie, the man who also created Augusta National ... Little gem.

St Andrews Dukes Golf Course ★★★★

Old Course Hotel Golf Resort & Spa, St Andrews, KY16 9NS
Website: www.oldcoursehotel.co.uk
E-mail: reservations@oldcoursehotel.co.uk
Nearest main town: St Andrews

Secretary: Mr S. Toon

Tel: 01334 474371
Fax: 01334 477668

Professional: Mr J. Kelly

Tel: 01334 470214

Playing: Midweek: round £60.00 (Mon–Thurs); day n/a. Weekend: round £75.00 (Fri–Sun); day n/a.

Facilities: Bar: 11am–11pm. Food: Breakfast, lunch and dinner from 7am–10pm. Bar snacks.

Comments: Quality course ... Panoramic views over the old town ... Can be extremely difficult when the wind blows ... Can tear your game apart ... If you like to be humbled, go here ... Harder than the Old course ... Who said St Andrews was just about the Old course?

St Andrews Eden Golf Course ★★★★

St Andrews Links Trust, Pilmour House, St Andrews, KY16 9SF
Website: www.standrews.org.uk   E-mail: pr@standrews.org.uk
Nearest main town: St Andrews

Secretary: Mr A. McGregor

Tel: 01334 466666
Fax: 01334 479555

Professional: None

Playing: Midweek: round £10.00–£110.00; day n/a. Weekend: round n/a; day n/a.

Facilities: Bar: 11am–11pm. Food: Breakfast, lunch and dinner from 7am–9pm.

Comments: Excellent condition of greens ... The flair of St Andrews also very nice ... A great course for winter golf ... Play it every year ... Much more fun than other St Andrews courses ... Outstanding group of par-3s ... Played it in a sea mist – excellent!

St Andrews Jubilee Golf Course   ★★★★

St Andrews Links Trust, Pilmour House, St Andrews, KY16 9SF
Website: www.standrews.org.uk   E-mail: pr@standrews.org.uk
Nearest main town: St Andrews

Secretary:	Mr A. McGregor	Tel: 01334 466666
	(General Manager)	Fax: 01334 479555
Professional:	None	

Playing: Midweek: round £10.00–£110.00; day n/a. Weekend: round n/a; day n/a.

Facilities: Bar: 11am–11pm. Food: Breakfast, lunch and dinner from 7am–9pm.

Comments: Tough cookie when the wind blows ... From the back tees this can be a real challenge ... Longest course at St Andrews ... Requires deep reserves of concentration ... The toughest of all the St Andrews courses ... Found it so tough in the wind ... Lacks a bit of atmosphere ... Hard in the wind.

St Andrews New Golf Course   ★★★★★

St Andrews Links Trust, Pilmour House, St Andrews, KY16 9SF
Website: www.standrews.org.uk   E-mail: pr@standrews.org.uk
Nearest main town: St Andrews

Secretary:	Mr A. McGregor	Tel: 01334 466666
	(General Manager)	Fax: 01334 479555
Professional:	None	

Playing: Midweek: round £10.00–£110.00; day n/a. Weekend: round n/a; day n/a.

Facilities: Bar: 11am–11pm. Food: Breakfast, lunch and dinner from 7am–9pm.

Comments: Better than the Old course with some very strong holes ... Similar demands to the Old course ... Preferred it to the Old ... Great experience but too expensive ... Surprisingly undulating – soak up the atmosphere and prepare for the Old course.

Scotscraig Golf Club   ★★★★

Golf Road, Tayport, DD6 9DZ
Website: www.scotscraig-golf-club.co.uk
E-mail: scotscraig@scottishgolf.com
Nearest main town: St Andrews

Secretary: Mr B. Liddle   Tel: 01382 552515
                                        Fax: 01382 553130
Professional: Mr S. Campbell   Tel: 01382 552855

Playing: Midweek: round £44.00; day £50.00. Weekend: round
                  £50.00; day £60.00.

Facilities: Bar: 11am–11pm. Food: Lunch and dinner from
                  10am–9pm. Bar snacks.

Comments: Almost as hard as Carnoustie but without the hype ...
                  Deep bunkers on this links/heathland track ... Enjoyed it
                  immensely ... Lives up to its brutal reputation ... Greens
                  hard to read.

Lothian

Muirfield Golf Club ★★★★★

Gullane, EH31 2EG
Nearest main town: Edinburgh

If you have managed to arrange a game at Muirfield, what you score on the course is largely of secondary importance. This, after all, is the course that not even the late Payne Stewart, the former US Open champion, could get on after being told it was a members' day.

Protocol has become more relaxed since those days. The club, the Honourable Company of Edinburgh Golfers, is more open to approaches from players wishing to play the course, for years considered the best course in Britain and Ireland.

Muirfield is an astonishing links. It consists of nine holes arranged in a circular shape around the boundaries of the club, with the back nine forming the inner circle. There are no dunes as such, just yawning bunkers, thick rough and eighteen subtly contoured greens. One of Muirfield's outstanding features is its turf, which is very fine and tends to dry out quickly, as it lies on top of pure sand. This can give the course a different character from one day to the next; on the Saturday, an American-style target-golf course, and on the Sunday, a typical links.

You get an early indication of what is to come at the 1st, a 449-yard par-4, where the pitfalls of missing the fairway will become immediately apparent. By the time you come off the par-3 4th, you will be doing better than average if you've yet to land in one of the bunkers, which seem to be depositaries for balls which land short of the green.

An unusual split-level fairway, situated on a dogleg, defines the 6th, before the final three holes on the front nine that will make or break your score. The 8th is probably the toughest of the trio, where 12 bunkers guard the right-hand side of the fairways, forcing you to the left and giving you a longer approach shot.

The back nine is not tough as, say, a Troon or a Carnoustie, with birdie chances at the 14th, 15th and 17th, but it finishes with a bang, a devilish par-4 18th that is a fitting climax. Jack Nicklaus once described Muirfield as the fairest Open course he knew, and there is no greater praise than that.

Secretary: Group Captain J. Prideaux Tel: 01620 842123
Fax: 01620 842977
Professional: None

Playing: Midweek: round £85.00 (Tues & Thurs only); day £110.00 (Tues & Thurs only). Weekend: round n/a; day n/a.

Facilities: Bar: 11am–11pm. Food: Lunch from 12pm–2pm.

Comments: The best course I have ever played which is what it is all about ... Sadly, strange rules if you want to play ... Died and gone to heaven ... Just heaven ... True sense of history ... Thick rough, deep bunkering.

Baberton Golf Club   ★★

50 Baberton Avenue, Edinburgh, EH14 5DU
Website: www.babertongolfclub@btinternet.com
E-mail: manager@baberton.co.uk
Nearest main town: Edinburgh

Secretary: Mr B. Flockhart   Tel: 0131 453 4911
                                    Fax: 0131 453 4678
Professional: Mr K. Kelly   Tel: 0131 453 4911

Playing: Midweek: round prices on application; day n/a. Weekend: round n/a; day n/a.

Facilities: Bar: 11am–11pm. Food: Available.

Comments: Well-established parkland layout ... Scenic views towards Edinburgh, some 5 miles away ... Some of the toughest par-3s you will find anywhere ... 16th is the toughest par-4 ... All uphill, 467 yards into the wind ... Staff and members very sociable and friendly.

Braid Hills Golf Club

Braid Hills Road, Edinburgh, EH10 6JY
Nearest main town: Edinburgh

Secretary: None   Tel: 0131 447 6666
Professional: None

Playing: Midweek: round £8.50; day n/a. Weekend: round £8.50; day n/a.

Facilities: Bar: None. Food: None.

Comments: One of the best public courses in the UK ... Tough, challenging with tight fairways and gorse ... Fun to play.

Broomieknowie Golf Club Limited ★★

36 Golf Course Road, Bonnyrigg, EH19 2HZ
Nearest main town: Dalkeith

Secretary:	Mr J. White	Tel: 0131 663 9317
		Fax: 0131 663 2152
Professional:	Mr M. Patchett	Tel: 0131 660 2035

Playing: Midweek: round £17.00; day £25.00. Weekend: round £20.00; day n/a.

Facilities: Bar: All day in season. Food: Available.

Comments: Established parkland layout with some climbs between the holes, but otherwise fairly flat ... Toughest hole is the dogleg par-4 7th ... Enjoyed the short par-3 5th which drops down some 50 feet from the tee and offers a nice view to the south ... Good general condition ... Refurbished clubhouse provides good-value food all day during the summer.

Bruntsfield Links Golfing Society ★★★

The Clubhouse, 32 Barnton Avenue, Edinburgh, EH4 6JH
E-mail: secretary@bruntsfield.sol.co.uk
Nearest main town: Edinburgh

Secretary:	Cdr D. Sandford	Tel: 0131 336 1479
		Fax: 0131 336 5538
Professional:	Mr B. Mackenzie	Tel: 0131 336 4050

Playing: Midweek: round £40.00; day £55.00. Weekend: round £45.00; day £60.00.

Facilities: Bar: 11am–11pm. Food: Lunch from 12.30pm–2.30pm.

Comments: Magnificent parkland ... Heavenly scenery ... Good course and best lunch to be had in Edinburgh ... Excellent restaurant ... Food better than the course.

Marriott Dalmahoy Hotel & Country Club ★★★★

Dalmahoy, Kirknewton, EH27 8EB
Nearest main town: Edinburgh

Secretary:	Mrs J. Bryans	Tel: 0131 333 8010
		Fax: 0131 335 3203

Professional: Mr N. Graham

Playing: Midweek: round £60.00 (East), £35.00 (West); day n/a.
Weekend: round £75.00 (East), £45.00 (West); day n/a.

Facilities: Bar: 11am–11pm. Food: Breakfast, lunch and dinner from 7am–10pm. Bar snacks.

Comments: Corporate venue ... Expensive pay-and-play ... Choice of two good courses with excellent country club attached ... Narrow fairways are difficult to play but lots of fun ... Requires concentration ... Two courses, the East has been used for the Solheim Cup.

Deer Park CC ★★

Knightsbridge, Livingston, EH54 9PG
Nearest main town: Edinburgh

Secretary: Mr I. Thomson   Tel: 01506 431037
                                   Fax: 01506 435608

Professional: Mr W. Yule

Playing: Midweek: round £16.00; day £22.00. Weekend: round £26.00; day £32.00.

Facilities: Bar: None. Food: None.

Comments: First nine fairly flat but you will have to be pretty fit to tackle the back nine which is more up and down ... Par-5 15th a real tester played uphill all the way, but the climb is worth making because the view from the top to Edinburgh and the Forth Bridge is stunning ... Superb off-course facilities which include – believe it or not – a 16-lane ten-pin bowling alley ... Par-3 10th makes an excellent start to the back nine.

Duddingston Golf Club ★★★

Duddington Road West, Edinburgh, EH15 3QD
Website: www.duddingston-golf-club.com
E-mail: generalmanager@duddingston-golf-club.com
Nearest main town: Edinburgh

Secretary: Mr I. Sproule   Tel: 0131 661 7688
                                   Fax: 0131 661 4301

Professional: Mr A. Mclean   Tel: 0131 661 4301
                                   Fax: 0131 661 4301

Playing: Midweek: round £35.00; day £45.00. Weekend: round £35.00; day £45.00.

Facilities: Bar: 11am–11pm. Food: Lunch from 12pm–2pm. Dinner by arrangement.

Comments: The most welcoming and challenging of the parkland courses around Edinburgh – underrated ... Braid's Burn the main hazard ... A course designed for the average player ... Sporting track very near centre of Edinburgh.

Dunbar Golf Club   ★★★★

East Links, Dunbar, EH42 1LL
Website: www.dunbar-golfclub.co.uk
E-mail: secretary@dunbargolfclub.sol.co.uk
Nearest main town: Dunbar

Secretary: Mrs L. Thom   Tel: 01368 862317
                                    Fax: 01368 865202
Professional: Mr J. Montgomery   Tel: 01368 862086
                                    Fax: 01368 862086

Playing: Midweek: round £40.00; day £55.00. Weekend: round £50.00; day £70.00.

Facilities: Bar: 11am–11pm. Food: Lunch and dinner from 10am–9pm.

Comments: Singular links character ... A cracking links and a great test in the wind ... Great hospitality and value ... Excellent links with tight fairways and slap-you-on-the-back welcome ... Classic East Lothian links ... Bracing ... On a rocky outcrop, this is marvellous ... Wind races around this links ... A lonely experience on a cold day ... Best holes around the turn.

Glen Golf Club   ★★★★

Tantallon Terrace, East Links, North Berwick, EH39 4LE
Website: www.glengolfclub.co.uk
E-mail: secretary@glengolfclub.co.uk
Nearest main town: North Berwick

Secretary: Mr K. Fish   Tel: 01620 892726
                                    Fax: 01620 895447
Professional: None

Playing: Midweek: round £28.00; day £38.00. Weekend: round £39.00; day £50.00.

Facilities: Bar: 11am–11pm. Food: Lunch and dinner from 10am–8pm.

Comments: Good old-fashioned golf club with no over-the-top features ... The East Links of North Berwick ... Views over the Firth of Forth ... Blind shots all over the place ... Highlight was the 18th, left me with great impression of the course.

Greenburn Golf Course ★★

6 Greenburn Road, Fauldhouse, Bathgate, Edinburgh, EH47 9HG
Nearest main town: Edinburgh

Secretary: Mr A. Harris   Tel: 01506 770292
(Club Administrator)
Professional: Mr S. Catlin   Tel: 01501 771187

Playing: Midweek: round £19.00; day n/a. Weekend: round £25.00; day n/a.

Facilities: Bar: 11am–11pm. Food: During bar hours, bar snacks and meals are available on request. Visiting parties please pre-book.

Comments: Very pleasant moorland layout ... The location is fairly high up but the course itself is comparatively flat in nature ... Easy walking course and ideal if you are the type of golfer who is keen to play two rounds in the one day ... Four short holes with the best being the 6th, which plays around 160 yards with a stream guarding the back of the green and bunkers in front ... Pick of the par-4 holes is the 18th, only 350 yards, but out-of-bounds all the way down the left side, bunkers on the right and trees around the green, making the second shot difficult if your tee shot finishes in the wrong place!

Gullane Golf Club (No.1) ★★★★

West Links Road, Gullane, EH31 2BB
Website: www.gullanegolfclub.com
E-mail: manager@gullanegolfclub.com
Nearest main town: Edinburgh

Secretary:	Mr S. Owram	Tel: 01620 842255
		Fax: 01620 842327
Professional:	Mr A. Good	Tel: 01620 843111
		Fax: 01620 843090

Playing: Midweek: round £75.00; day n/a. Weekend: round £90.00; day n/a.

Facilities: Bar: 11am–11pm. Food: Lunch from 12pm–2.30pm except Mon–Wed.

Comments: Beautiful links course ... .Excellent greens ... Bunkers are almost unfair ... Vastly underrated ... Greens as fast as anything played ... Great greens and view ... Wonderful greens and a windy course ... Austere-looking course ... Basic course but golf as it should be played ... Don't bother with No.2 or No.3, this is the one ... You can see Muirfield from the highest point here.

Gullane Golf Club (No.2) ★★★

West Links Road, Gullane, EH31 2BB
Website: www.gullanegolfclub.com
E-mail: manager@gullanegolfclub.com
Nearest main town: Edinburgh

Secretary:	Mr S. Owram	Tel: 01620 842255
		Fax: 01620 842327
Professional:	Mr A. Good	Tel: 01620 843111
		Fax: 01620 843090

Playing: Midweek: round £30.00; day n/a. Weekend: round £36.00; day n/a.

Facilities: Bar: 11am–11pm. Food: Lunch from 12pm–2.30pm except Mon–Wed.

Comments: Clearly the second best links at Gullane ... Fairly open ... Not far behind No.1 ... Lives in the shadow of No.1.

Gullane Golf Club (No.3) ★★★★

West Links Road, Gullane, EH31 2BB
Website: www.gullanegolfclub.com
E-mail: manager@gullanegolfclub.com
Nearest main town: Edinburgh

Secretary:	Mr S. Owram	Tel: 01620 842255
		Fax: 01620 842327
Professional:	Mr A. Good	Tel: 01620 843111
		Fax: 01620 843090

Playing: Midweek: round £19.00; day n/a. Weekend: round £25.00; day n/a.

Facilities: Bar: 11am–11pm. Food: Lunch from 12pm–2.30pm except Mon–Wed.

Comments: Very well presented and managed – businesslike approach ... Fair welcome from helpful staff ... Comfortable, modern clubhouse ... Excellent short links to play with friends.

Haddington Golf Club ★★

Amisfield Park, Haddington, EH41 4PT
Nearest main town: Haddington

Secretary:	Mr S. Wilson	Tel: 01620 823627
		Fax: 01620 826580
Professional:	Mr J. Sandilands	Tel: 01620 822727

Playing: Midweek: round £18.00; day £26.00. Weekend: round £23.00; day £32.00.

Facilities: Bar: 10.30am–11pm summer (or until dusk). Food: All day Mar–Oct.

Comments: Parkland course laid out in the grounds of an old country house ... Interesting – if rather flat ... Look out for the water hazards ... The par-4 15th is a card-wrecker with water running all the way down the left side ... The uphill par-3 8th is played virtually blind ... Clubhouse could be better.

Kilspindie Golf Club ★★★

The Clubhouse, Aberlady, Longniddry, EH32 0QD
Website: www.golfeastlothian.com   E-mail: kilspindie@btconnect.com
Nearest main town: Aberlady

| Secretary: | Mr P. Casely | Tel: 01875 870358 |
| Professional: | Mr G. Sked | Tel: 01875 870695 |

Playing: Midweek: round £28.50; day £45.00. Weekend: round £35.00; day £57.50.

Facilities: Bar: 11am–11pm. Food: Lunch from 10am–3pm.

Comments: Old course which has been overtaken by technology ... Short and tight ... Old links with superb bunkering ... Natural test of any golfer ... 8th is a stunner ... Everything links golf should be ... A little short ... Step back in time.

Kings Acre Golf Club   ★★★

Lasswade, Edinburgh, EH18 1AW
Nearest main town: Edinburgh

Secretary: Mrs E. King   Tel: 0131 663 3456
                                        Fax: 0131 663 7076
Professional: Mr A. Murdoch   Tel: 0131 663 3456
                                        Fax: 0131 663 7076

Playing: Midweek: round £15.00; day n/a. Weekend: round £21.00; day n/a.

Facilities: Bar: 11am–11pm. Food: 9am onwards.

Comments: New layout but superb design ... Watch out for the water ... First nine fairly open but then the layout gets a bit tighter on the homeward run ... Greens in great condition considering how young the course is ... If you make par at the 13th you can go home a happy golfer ... Excellent clubhouse and facilities ... Great value for money.

Liberton Golf Club   ★★

297 Gilmerton Road, Edinburgh, EH16 5UJ
Nearest main town: Edinburgh

Secretary: Mrs B. Giefer   Tel: 0131 664 3009
                                        Fax: 0131 666 0853
Professional: Mr I. Seath   Tel: 0131 664 1056
                                        Fax: 0131 658 1988

Playing: Midweek: round £17.00; day £30.00. Weekend: round £30.00; day n/a.

Facilities: Bar: 11am–11pm. Food: Lunch and dinner from 11am–10pm. Bar snacks.

Comments: A bit of everything at this short parkland course ... A little easy ... Nice routing ... Wooded in places.

Longniddry Golf Club ★★★

Links Road, Longniddry, EH32 0NL
Nearest main town: Edinburgh

Secretary:	Mr N. Robertson	Tel: 01875 852141
		Fax: 01875 853371
Professional:	Mr W. Gray	Tel: 01875 852228

Playing: Midweek: round £27.50; day £38.50. Weekend: round £35.50; day n/a.

Facilities: Bar: 11am–11pm. Food: Lunch from 10am–8pm. Bar snacks.

Comments: Pleasant mixture of parkland and links golf with better-than-average greens ... Well-presented course with many feature holes ... Fair value for parkland course.

Lothianburn Golf Club ★★

106a Biggar Road, Edinburgh, EH10 7DU
Nearest main town: Edinburgh

Secretary:	Mr W. Jardine	Tel: 0131 445 5067
		Fax: 0131 445 2288
Professional:	Mr K. Mungall	Tel: 0131 445 2288
		Fax: 0131 445 2288

Playing: Midweek: round £15.00; day £22.00. Weekend: round £21.00; day n/a.

Facilities: Bar: 11am–11pm. Food: Lunch from 11am–3pm. Dinner by arrangement.

Comments: Very traditional club ... Too hilly by far ... Sloping lies make scoring difficult ... Course to learn the vagaries of the game ... All those sloping lies can mess up your game ... Just as well this exhausting course is fairly short.

Luffness Golf Club (New) ★★★★

Aberlady, EH32 0QA
E-mail: secretary@luffnessnew.com
Nearest main town: Gullane

Secretary:	Mr A. Yeates	Tel: 01620 843336
		Fax: 01620 842933
Professional:	None	

Playing: Midweek: round £45.00; day £65.00. Weekend: No weekend visitors.

Facilities: Bar: 11am–11pm. Food: Lunch from 12pm–2pm.

Comments: Stop off on the way to Muirfield ... Holes go in all directions ... Wind plays havoc ... Combine with Gullane, Muirfield and North Berwick ... One of the toughest courses in Scotland.

Mortonhall Golf Club   ★★

231 Braid Road, Edinburgh, EH10 6PB
Website: www.mortonhall.co.uk
Nearest main town: Edinburgh

Secretary: Mrs B. Gigfer   Tel: 0131 447 6974
                    (Manager)   Fax: 0131 447 8712
Professional: Mr D. Horn   Tel: 0131 447 5185

Playing: Midweek: round £30.00; day £40.00. Weekend: round £30.00; day £40.00.

Facilities: Bar: 11am–11pm. Food: Lunch from 12pm–2.30pm.

Comments: Views of Edinburgh ... Best part of course are the views ... Welcoming club with simple course ... Very long but worth the walk.

The Musselburgh Golf Club   ★★★

Monktonhall, Musselburgh, EH21 6SA
Website: www.themusselburghgolfclub.com
E-mail: secretary@themusselburghgolfclub.com
Nearest main town: Musselburgh

Secretary: Mr P. Millar   Tel: 0131 665 2005
                                           Fax: 0131 665 4435
Professional: Mr F. Mann   Tel: 0131 665 7055
                                           Fax: 0131 665 7055

Playing: Midweek: round £25.00; day £35.00. Weekend: round £30.00; day £40.00.

Facilities: Bar: 11am–11pm. Food: Lunch and dinner from 10am–8pm. Bar snacks.

Comments: Really interesting course ... Not overly challenging until the 18th ... Course right next to an oil production plant ... The view has to be seen to be believed.

North Berwick Golf Club ★★★★

West Links, Beach Road, North Berwick, EH39 4BB
E-mail: bookingsnbgc@aol.com
Nearest main town: North Berwick

Secretary: Mr N. Wilson   Tel: 01620 892135 (Bookings)
Fax: 01620 893274

Professional: Mr D. Huish

Playing: Midweek: round £50.00; day £75.00. Weekend: round £70.00 (afternoon only); day n/a.

Facilities: Bar: 11am–11pm. Food: Lunch and dinner from 10am–10pm. Bar snacks.

Comments: Attractive, welcoming course ... Real links golf with roads, walls, burns, humps and hollows ... Knee-length rough a bit of a bind ... A course with everything ... Really fun course – what the game is all about ... The ideal place to be, not as busy as Gullane and twice as welcoming ... Great location and best course in the area ... Designed by the sands of time ... Watch out for the famous Redan ... Prepare to be humbled by the North Berwick experience ... We would die for something like this in the States.

Prestonfield Golf Club ★★

6 Priestfield Road North, Edinburgh, EH16 5HS
Nearest main town: Edinburgh

Secretary: Mr A. Robertson   Tel: 0131 667 9665
Fax: 0131 667 9665

Professional: Mr J. MacFarlane   Tel: 0131 667 8597
Fax: 0131 667 9665

Playing: Midweek: round £20.00; day £30.00. Weekend: round £30.00; day £40.00.

Facilities: Bar: 11am–11pm. Food: All day.

Comments: Pleasant parkland layout that is not too tight from the tee ... Some great panoramic views, especially from the first tee, which looks directly towards Arthur's Seat in Edinburgh ... Par-4 4th is probably the toughest hole on the course, especially if you tangle with the trees ... Decent off-course facilities.

Ratho Park Golf Club   ★★★

Ratho, Edinburgh, EH28 8NX
Website: www.rathoparkgolfclub.com
E-mail: secretary.rpgc@btconnect.com
Nearest main town: Edinburgh

Secretary: Mr C. Innes   Tel: 0131 335 0068
                                        Fax: 0131 333 1752
Professional: Mr A. Pate   Tel: 0131 333 1406
                                        Fax: 0131 333 1406

Playing: Midweek: round £25.00; day £35.00. Weekend: round £35.00; day n/a.

Facilities: Bar: 11am–11pm (seasonal). Food: 11am–4pm and 6pm–9pm (not Mondays).

Comments: Comparatively flat course that is easy on the legs ... Attractive layout runs through the Ratho Park estate with lots of flowers in bloom around the course during the summer months ... Didn't find the fairways all that wide at times, but they were never tight enough to make me feel really inhibited ... Pleasant, if not all that challenging ... The clubhouse is a beautiful 19th-century building ... Especially enjoyed the short 15th ... Measuring 161 yards and played downhill to a green that is almost completely surrounded with bunkers, it's not surprising to discover that the hole is named Sandy Hollow.

The Royal Burgess Golfing Society of Edinburgh   ★★★

181 Whitehouse Road, Edinburgh, EH4 6BU
Website: www.royalburgess.co.uk
E-mail: secretary@royalburgess.co.uk
Nearest main town: Edinburgh

Secretary: Mr G. Seeley   Tel: 0131 339 2075
                                        Fax: 0131 339 3712

Professional: Mr S. Brian   Tel: 0131 339 6474
                                       Fax: 0131 339 3712

Playing: Midweek: round £45.00; day £55.00. Weekend: round
                 £75.00; day n/a.

Facilities: Bar: 11am–11pm. Food: Bar snacks.

Comments: Highly conditioned ... Fairways like greens at some
                 clubs ... Magnificent ... Accuracy more important than
                 distance ... Historic course with many nice features ...
                 Greens superb.

Royal Musselburgh Golf Club   ★★★★

Prestongrange House, Prestonpans, EH32 9RP
Website: www.royalmusselburgh.co.uk
E-mail: royalmusselburgh@btinternet.com
Nearest main town: Edinburgh

Secretary: Mr T. Hardie   Tel: 01875 810276
                                       Fax: 01875 810276
Professional: Mr J. Henderson   Tel: 01875 810139
                                       Fax: 01875 810139

Playing: Midweek: round £25.00; day £35.00. Weekend: round
                 £35.00 (by arrangement only); day n/a.

Facilities: Bar: 11am–11pm. Food: Lunch from 10am–4pm.
                 Dinner by arrangement.

Comments: Rather unbalanced with just one par-5 ... Special feel to
                 this venerable parkland layout ... Spirit in which golf
                 should be played ... Very strategic bunkering ... Usually
                 can be found in fine condition.

West Linton Golf Club   ★★★

Medwyn Road, West Linton, Edinburgh, EH46 7HN
Website: www.wlgc.co.uk   E-mail: secretary.wlgc@btinternet.com
Nearest main town: Edinburgh

Secretary: Ms J. Macnab   Tel: 01968 660970
                                       Fax: 01968 660970
Professional: Mr I. Wright   Tel: 01968 660256

Playing: Midweek: round £25.00; day £40.00. Weekend: round
                 £40.00; day n/a.

Facilities: Bar: 11am–11pm. Food: All day weekends, 11am–9pm weekdays in summer.

Comments: Located around 1000 feet above sea level, the course offers some stunning views of the surrounding country-side ... Wind is nearly always a factor ... The layout may measure just over 6000 yards, but it usually plays every inch of that ... Lovely moorland layout ... Excellent condition ... One of the toughest closing holes in golf and it's a par-3!

West Lothian Golf Club   ★★★

Airngath Hill, Linlithgow, Edinburgh, EH49 7RH
Nearest main town: Edinburgh

Secretary: Mr M. Todd   Tel: 01506 825060
                                        Fax: 01506 826030
Professional: Mr N. Robertson   Tel: 01506 825060

Playing: Midweek: round prices on application; day n/a. Weekend: round n/a; day n/a.

Facilities: Bar: 11am–11pm in summer. In winter: 11am–4pm Mon, 11am–4pm and 7pm–11pm Tues/Thurs, 11am–5pm and 7pm–11pm Wed, 11am–11pm Fri–Sun. Food: Bar snacks and soup.

Comments: Wonderful scenery with stunning views down towards the mouth of the Firth of Forth, Linlithgow Palace and the distant hills beyond the Forth Valley ... Terrain a bit up and down but not all that difficult to get round ... Enjoyable parkland setting with mature trees and good fairways and greens ... Scary tee shot from the medal tee at the 9th where you have to carry the Quarry Pond to find the safety of the fairway ... Four short holes on the course with the 18th the pick of the bunch; measuring around 144 yards, this little gem is played downhill from an elevated tee to a green that also features out-of-bounds ... Warm welcome.

Whitekirk Golf & Country Club   ★★★

Whitekirk, North Berwick, EH39 5PR
Website: www.whitekirk.com   E-mail: countryclub@whitekirk.com
Nearest main town: North Berwick

Secretary: Mr D. Brodie   Tel: 01620 870300
                                           Fax: 01620 870330
Professional: Mr P. Wardell   Tel: 01620 870300
                                           Fax: 01620 870330

Playing: Midweek: round £25.00; day £35.00. Weekend: round
                  £35.00; day £50.00.

Facilities: Bar: 11am–11pm. Food: Lunch and dinner from
                  10am–9pm. Bar snacks.

Comments: Relatively new course with wonderful views from the hill-
                  tops ... First-class catering ... Excellent value for money
                  ... Practice facilities first class ... Outstanding golf.

Highland and Moray

Royal Dornoch Golf Club ★★★★★

Golf Road, Dornoch, IV25 3LW
Website: www.royaldornoch.com   E-mail: rdgc@royaldornoch.com
Nearest main town: Dornoch

If you're travelling north towards the Highlands to play Royal Dornoch, chances are you're also going to take in a great quartet of courses, including Tain, Golspie and Brora. A word of advice – make sure to leave Dornoch until last and leave on a high note.

This is one of the finest golfing outposts in Britain. Unburdened by the weight of holding an Open Championship (although it surely could) and handed an air of mystique by its isolation, Royal Dornoch is an exceptional course for visitors. The whole place is shrouded in peace and tranquillity, and only serious golfers with an appreciation of the history and elegance of the game head out this way, so you can be sure of a respectful and warm welcome.

The course itself is something of a conundrum. It's a straight-forward, fair links, with few blind shots and all the trouble laid out clearly before you. But the classic links shot, the bump-and-run, can feel slightly redundant; the greens are too well protected to allow you a straight line in, and they are often set on small plateaus. This is not a criticism, just the character of the course. You'll also find dramatic tee shots from elevated tees falling into basin fairways, gorse-covered dunes, and hills and greens nestled in the shadow of hills.

It is a timeless design, touched by the hands of Donald Ross and Tom Morris. (Ross emigrated to North America in 1898 and went on to become one of the greatest course designers of all time – trademark Dornoch traits can be found on most of Ross's courses throughout the world.) Highlights include the 5th, an exciting driving hole, and the 14th, called 'Foxy', appropriately so, including, as it does, an inventive double dogleg.

Secretary:	Mr J. Duncan	Tel: 01862 810219
		Fax: 01862 810792
Professional:	Mr A. Skinner	Tel: 01862 810902
		Fax: 01862 810902
Playing:	Midweek: round £66.00; day n/a. Weekend: round £76.00; day n/a.	

Facilities: Bar: 11am–11pm. Food: Breakfast, lunch and dinner from 7am–10pm. Bar snacks.

Comments: So many cherished memories ... Finest links anywhere ... Golf as it should be ... Magical Northern gem ... Course and facilities excellent ... Good test of golf and good facilities ... Only drawback is remoteness, but still worth the journey ... It's not a frightening course but it can put egg on your face quite easily ... Very hard but fair course ... Just about worth the price of the trip ... A magical, classical links of charm and beauty ... Donald Ross country ... Miles from anywhere, a haven of tranquillity ... The best experience in 40 years of golf ... A real tear jerker.

Boat of Garten Golf Club   ★★★★

Boat of Garten, PH24 3BQ
Website: www.boatgolf.com   E-mail: boatgolf@enterprise.net
Nearest main town: Inverness

Secretary: Mr P. Smyth   Tel: 01479 831282
                                          Fax: 01479 831523
Professional: Mr J. Ingram   Tel: 01479 831282
                    (Shop Manager)   Fax: 01479 831523
Playing: Midweek: round £29.00; day £34.00. Weekend: round £34.00; day £39.00.
Facilities: Bar: 11am–11pm. Food: Breakfast, lunch and dinner from 9.30am–8pm. Bar snacks.
Comments: Good food, not to be missed ... Magnificent surroundings ... How golf should be played ... Maybe overrated ... An unfair course in the summer when the ball bounces everywhere ... Great location – I want to die here ... They get everything right here ... Superb scenery, absolutely compelling golf ... A little too hilly in places to be considered a great ... Had a great day.

Brora Golf Club   ★★★

43 Golf Road, Brora, KW9 6QS
Website: www.broragolf.co.uk   E-mail: secretary@broragolf.co.uk
Nearest main town: Dornoch

Secretary:	Mr J. Fraser	Tel: 01408 621417
		Fax: 01408 622157
Professional:	None	Tel: 01408 621417

Playing: Midweek: round £28.00; day £35.00. Weekend: round £33.00; day £40.00.

Facilities: Bar: 11am–11pm. Food: Lunch and dinner from 12pm–9pm.

Comments: Excellent hospitality ... Nice links course with good holes ... Electric fences rather annoying ... Friendly sheep on the fairways ... Perfect hospitality ... Any weaknesses the course has are made up for at the 19th ... An experience ... Elevated tees.

The Carnegie Club (Skibo Castle)   ★★★★

Skibo Castle, Clashmore, Dornoch, IV25 3RQ
Nearest main town: Dornoch

Secretary:	Mr A. Grant	Tel: 01862 894600
		Fax: 01862 894601
Professional:	Mr D. Thomson	Tel: 01862 881260

Playing: Midweek: round £130.00; day n/a. Weekend: round n/a; day n/a.

Facilities: Bar: 11am–11pm. Food: Lunch from 12.30pm–3pm.

Comments: Some tight holes near Dornoch Firth, but excellent for a new course ... Not worth the cost but undoubted brilliance ... Gulped at the price and course.

Elgin Golf Club   ★★★

Hardhillock, Birnie Road, Elgin, IV30 8SX
Website: www.elgingolfclub.com
E-mail: secretary@elgingolfclub.com
Nearest main town: Elgin

Secretary:	Mr D. Black	Tel: 01343 542338
		Fax: 01343 542341
Professional:	Mr K. Stables	Tel: 01343 542884
		Fax: 01343 542341

Playing: Midweek: round £28.00; day £38.00. Weekend: round £28.00; day £38.00.

Facilities: Bar: 11am–11pm. Food: Lunch and dinner from 10am–9pm. Bar snacks.

Comments: Good course, useful driving range ... Pro shop is consistently helpful to visitors ... Short but don't be fooled ... One of the best inland courses in Scotland ... A nice change from the surfeit of links.

Forres Golf Club   ★★★

Muiryshade, Edgehill Road, Forres, Moray, IV36 2RD
Website: www.forresgolfclub.fsnet.co.uk
E-mail: sandy@forresgolfclub.fsnet.co.uk
Nearest main town: Forres

Secretary: Mr D. McIntosh   Tel: 01309 672949
Professional: Mr S. Aird   Tel: 01309 672250
                                      Fax: 01309 672250

Playing: Midweek: round £25.00; day £32.00. Weekend: round £25.00; day £32.00.

Facilities: Bar: 11am–11pm. Food: Lunch and dinner from 10am–9pm. Bar snacks.

Comments: People at club could not do enough for the visitors ... Very up and down but nicely run club with good reception ... Well drained ... Welcoming visitors' course.

Fortrose & Rosemarkie Golf Club   ★★★

Ness Road East, Fortrose, IV10 8SE
Website: www.fortrosegolfclub.co.uk
E-mail: secretary@fortrosegolfclub.co.uk
Nearest main town: Inverness

Secretary: Mr M. MacDonald   Tel: 01381 620529
                                      Fax: 01381 621328
Professional: None   Tel: 01381 620733
                                      Fax: 01381 621328

Playing: Midweek: round £25.00; day £35.00. Weekend: round £30.00; day £40.00 (subject to change for 2004).

Facilities: Bar: 11am–11pm. Food: Lunch from 12pm–2pm. Dinner by arrangement.

Comments: Tight and tricky, but excellent ... Good place to play and absorb the game ... Sited on Black Isle ... Brute force the main weapon here ... Value for money ... Sea often in play ... Tough nut to crack.

Golspie Golf Club ★★★

Ferry Road, Golspie, KW10 6ST
Nearest main town: Dornoch

Secretary: Mrs M. MacLeod   Tel: 01408 633266
Fax: 01408 633393

Professional: None

Playing: Midweek: round £18.00; day £20.00. Weekend: round £18.00; day £25.00.

Facilities: Bar: 11am–11pm. Food: Lunch from 12pm–3pm. Dinner by arrangement.

Comments: Part links, part heathland ... Good variety of golf in pretty surroundings ... The only course with six seaside holes, six heathland holes and six inland holes ... Well kept and visitors made very welcome ... Far from the crowds ... A must in conjunction with Brora and Royal Dornoch.

Grantown-on-Spey Golf Club ★★★

Golf Course Road, Grantown-on-Spey, PH26 3HY
Website: www.grantownonspeygolfclub.co.uk
E-mail: secretary@grantownonspeygolfclub.co.uk
Nearest main town: Aviemore

Secretary: Mr J. MacPherron   Tel: 01479 872079
Fax: 01479 873725

Professional: None

Playing: Midweek: round £20.00; day £25.00. Weekend: round £25.00; day £30.00.

Facilities: Bar: 11am–11pm (Apr–Oct). Food: Lunch and dinner from 11am–9pm. Bar snacks (Apr–Oct).

Comments: Play it along with Boat of Garten ... Enjoy the air up here ... Wonderfully fresh and exhilarating course ... A little easy but the scenery is just perfect ... A treasured location near the rambling centre of Aviemore ... Completely unknown so excellent value ... Who said short courses were boring? ... Very eccentric but had a ball.

Hopeman Golf Club

The Clubhouse, Hopeman, Moray, IV30 6EX
Website: www.hopeman-golf-club.co.uk
E-mail: hopemangc@aol.com
Nearest main town: Elgin

Secretary: Mr J. Fraser   Tel: 01343 830578
                                          Fax: 01343 830152

Professional: None

Playing: Midweek: round £16.00; day £21.00. Weekend: round
                    £21.00; day £26.00.

Facilities: Bar: 11am–11pm. Food: Lunch and dinner from
                    10am–3pm. Dinner by arrangement.

Comments: Cracking course ... The 12th one of the best par-3s in
                    all of golf ... Links near the Moray Firth ... You hit and
                    hope at the 12th ... Par-3 is so memorable ...
                    Unbelievable value for classic links experience.

Invergordon Golf Club   ★★

King George Street, Invergordon, IV18 0BD
Nearest main town: Invergordon

Secretary: None   Tel: 01349 852715
Professional: None

Playing: Midweek: round £15.00; day £20.00. Weekend: round
                    £15.00; day £20.00.

Facilities: Bar: Normal hours. Food: Bar meals.

Comments: The 11 new holes blend in nicely with the rest of the
                    course ... Fairly flat but scenic setting ... Enjoyed the 9th
                    with the huge rhododendron bushes around the tee ...
                    Watch out for the out-of-bounds all the way along the
                    railway line on the right side of the 17th and 18th holes
                    ... Very friendly welcome.

Inverness Golf Club

Culcabock Road, Inverness, IV2 3XQ
Nearest main town: Inverness

Secretary: Mr G. Thomson   Tel: 01463 239882
                                          Fax: 01463 239882

Professional: Mr A. Thomson   Tel: 01463 231989

Playing: Midweek: round £25.00; day n/a. Weekend: round £30.00; day n/a.

Facilities: Bar: 11am–11pm. Food: Lunch from 12pm–3pm. Dinner by arrangement.

Comments: Flattish with very little definition ... A little overpriced for what you get ... Enjoyed myself thoroughly at this perfect little venue ... Parkland track in prime golfing country.

Kingussie Golf Club   ★★★★

Gynack Road, Kingussie, PH21 1LR
Website: www.kingussie-golf.co.uk
Nearest main town: Kingussie

Secretary: Mr N. MacWilliam   Tel: 01540 661600
                                      Fax: 01540 662066

Professional: None

Playing: Midweek: round £16.00; day £20.00. Weekend: round £18.00; day £25.00.

Facilities: Bar: 11am–11pm. Food: Breakfast, lunch and dinner from 10am–8pm.

Comments: Short but has all the shots and wonderful greens ... Highlands course up in the sky ... Very soft fairways ... Course plays longer than length ... Epitome of golfing in Scotland – scenic and good welcome ... Good value but could do with a practice ground.

Moray Golf Club (New)   ★★★

Stotfield Road, Lossiemouth, IV31 6QS
Website: www.moraygolf.co.uk   E-mail: secretary@moraygolf.co.uk
Nearest main town: Elgin

Secretary: Mr S. Crane   Tel: 01343 812018
                                     Fax: 01343 815102
Professional: Mr A. Thomson   Tel: 01343 813330
                                     Fax: 01343 813330

Playing: Midweek: round £30.00; day n/a. Weekend: round £35.00; day n/a.

Facilities: Bar: 11am–11pm. Food: Breakfast, lunch and dinner from 9am–9pm. Bar snacks.

Comments: Designed by Henry Cotton ... Does not have the same special feel as the Old ... Very favourable climate for good golf ... Not a patch on the Old.

Moray Golf Club (Old)   ★★★★

Stotfield Road, Lossiemouth, IV31 6QS
Website: www.moraygolf.co.uk   E-mail: secretary@moraygolf.co.uk
Nearest main town: Elgin

Secretary:	Mr S. Crane	Tel: 01343 812018
		Fax: 01343 815102
Professional:	Mr A. Thomson	Tel: 01343 813330
		Fax: 01343 813330

Playing: Midweek: round £40.00; day n/a. Weekend: round £50.00; day n/a.

Facilities: Bar: 11am–11pm. Food: Breakfast, lunch and dinner from 9am–9pm. Bar snacks.

Comments: Finishing hole is a cracker ... Unknown links ... Starts and ends in the town ... Views over the Moray Firth.

Muir of Ord Golf Club

Great North Road, Muir of Ord, IV6 7SX
Website: www.golfhighland.co.uk   E-mail: muirgolf@supanet.com
Nearest main town: Inverness

Secretary:	Mrs J. Gibson	Tel: 01463 870825
		Fax: 01463 871867
Professional:	None (Shop only)	Tel: 01463 871311
		Fax: 01463 871867

Playing: Midweek: round £16.00; day £20.00. Weekend: round £18.00; day £25.00.

Facilities: Bar: 11am–11pm. Food: Bar snacks.

Comments: Very short, eccentric heathland course ... Will test your patience ... Fairways you can stick a cigarette paper between – very tight and suffocating.

The Nairn Golf Club   ★★★★★

Seabank Road, Nairn, IV12 4HB
Website: www.nairngolfclub.co.uk
E-mail: bookings@nairngolfclub.co.uk
Nearest main town: Nairn

Secretary: Mr D. Corstorphine   Tel: 01667 453208
                                        Fax: 01667 456328
Professional: Mr R. Fyfe   Tel: 01667 452787
                                        Fax: 01667 451315

Playing: Midweek: round £70.00 (May–Sept); day n/a.
                  Weekend: round £70.00; day n/a.

Facilities: Bar: 11am–11pm. Food: Lunch and dinner from
                  10am–9pm. Bar snacks.

Comments: Joy to play ... Long way north but well worth the trip ...
                  Memorable challenge you want to repeat again and
                  again ... Very reasonable course ... Wonderful course
                  presentation and greens ... Outstanding new clubhouse
                  ... A little expensive but well worth the treat ... One of
                  the truly great Scottish links ... Greens quick ... Silky,
                  fast greens ... Devoid of natural beauty but tough as old
                  boots ... Don't forget to take your game with you ...
                  Bunkering and greens exceptional.

Nairn Dunbar Golf Club   ★★★

Lochloy Road, Nairn, IV12 5AE
Website: www.nairndunbar.com   E-mail: secretary@nairndunbar.com
Nearest main town: Nairn

Secretary: Mr S. Falconer   Tel: 01667 452741
                                        Fax: 01667 456897
Professional: Mr D. Torrance   Tel: 01667 453964
                                        Fax: 01667 456897

Playing: Midweek: round £39.50; day £55.00. Weekend: round
                  £48.00; day £62.00.

Facilities: Bar: 11am–11pm. Food: Catering from 9am–8pm
                  (Apr–Sept).

Comments: Hard slog but technically good ... Three new holes are
                  poor and badly out of character ... Good new club-
                  house but the other Nairn has Scotland's best new
                  clubhouse ... 10th hole the best ... Unattractive course
                  devoid of a links feel.

Newtonmore Golf Club   ★★★

Golf Course Road, Newtonmore, PH20 1AT
Website: www.newtonmoregolf.com
E-mail: secretary@newtonmoregolf.com
Nearest main town: Inverness (45 miles) or Aviemore (15 miles)

Secretary:	None	Tel: 01540 673878
		Fax: 01540 670147
Professional:	Mr R. Henderson	Tel: 01540 673611

Playing: Midweek: round £20.00; day £28.00. Weekend: round £24.00; day £33.00.

Facilities: Bar: 11am–11pm. Food: Full catering except Tuesday.

Comments: Super setting alongside the River Spey ... Not long, but long enough! ... Tremendous value ... Very friendly club ... Setting too nice to worry about how I was scoring ... Everyone was so helpful and friendly.

Strathpeffer Spa Golf Club   ★★★

Golf Course Road, Strathpeffer, IV14 9AS
Website: www.strathpeffergolf.co.uk
E-mail: mail@strathpeffergolf.co.uk
Nearest main town: Dingwall

Secretary:	Ms G. Anderson	Tel: 01997 421011/421219
		Fax: 01997 421011
Professional:	None	

Playing: Midweek: round £18.00; day £23.00. Weekend: round £18.00; day £23.00. Prices may change in 2004.

Facilities: Bar: 11am–12 midnight (11am–11.30pm Sun). Food: During bar hours, package (food and golf) available.

Comments: Basically flat but wonderfully scenic ... Loved the firm springy turn on the fairways, 5th has to be one of the very best short holes on the planet ... Has an almost heathland look and feel ... Great value if you play midweek ... Pleasant clubhouse and reasonable facilities.

Tain Golf Club   ★★★★

Chapel Road, Tain, IV19 1JE
Website: www.tain-golfclub.co.uk   E-mail: info@tain-golfclub.co.uk
Nearest main town: Dornoch

Secretary:	Ms J. Bell	Tel: 01862 892314
		Fax: 01862 892099
Professional:	None	

Playing: Midweek: round £33.00; day £40.00. Weekend: round £40.00; day £50.00.

Facilities: Bar: 11am–11pm. Food: Lunch from 10am–3pm. Dinner by arrangement.

Comments: Dornoch is the top course in the area but you must visit this one too ... Heather and links, a great combination ... Exceptional value ... Very unfashionable course ... Playing here is like a chess match ... Have a clear game plan.

Traigh Golf Course ★★

Traigh, Arisaig, PH39 4NT
Nearest main town: Fort William

| **Secretary:** | Mr W. Henderson | Tel: 01687 450645 |
| **Professional:** | None | Tel: 01687 450337 |

Playing: Midweek: round £12.00; day £12.00. Weekend: round £12.00; day £12.00.

Facilities: Bar: None. Food: None.

Comments: Marvellous evocative course with vistas to the islands of Rhum and Skye ... Only nine holes but don't let that put you off ... A couple of memorable holes ... Views make up for what course so noticeably lacks.

Wick Golf Club ★★★

Reiss, Wick, KW1 4RW
Website: www.wickgolfclub.fsnet.co.uk
E-mail: wickgolfclub@hotmail.com
Nearest main town: Wick

| **Secretary:** | Mr D. Shearer | Tel: 01955 602935 |
| **Professional:** | None | |

Playing: Midweek: round n/a; day £20.00. Weekend: round n/a; day £20.00.

Facilities: Bar: None. Food: Bar snacks. Lunch and dinner by arrangement.

Comments: Not worth the trek ... Northernmost course in the British Isles ... Very rugged and a little unfair in places ... Wonderful people here ... Course a little eccentric.

Angus and Perth & Kinross

Carnoustie Golf Links ★★★★★

Links Parade, Carnoustie, DD7 7JE
Website: www.carnoustiegolflinks.co.uk
E-mail: administrator@carnoustiegolflinks.co.uk
Nearest main town: Dundee

Carnoustie's reputation as the toughest course in the British Isles was taken to the top of the scale and beyond by the Open Championship that was held there in 1999. So tough was the course that it brought many of the world's best golfers to their knees as over-fertilised rough made the layout virtually unplayable. Since then the R&A have admitted that the set-up of the course was too severe and we can only hope that Carnoustie will be forgiven by the game's elite, who did not take kindly to being humiliated on such a public stage. In truth, it is a cracking golf course whose return to the Open rota was eagerly anticipated by all those who have played it in more favourable circumstances.

Visually it could not be more intimidating. The land is very cheerless, furnished with scrubs, scrapes and ditches. There are none of the moon-scape dunes that you associate with the great Open courses, neither is it a traditional out-and-back links. Instead, the severity of the course is entirely governed by the strength of the wind and the height of the rough.

Players have to hit the ground running at Carnoustie, requiring a long iron to a hidden green at the 1st, and then having to avoid a bunker in the middle of the fairway at the long par-4 2nd. There is a brief respite until the 6th, a par-5 with out-of-bounds all the way up the left and, once again, strategic bunkers placed in the middle of the fairway. From there, you need to thread a line through the out-of-bounds and a burn to set up a pitch to the green.

But it's the closing holes for which Carnoustie is famed, starting with the 15th, a 460-yard par-4 swinging spectacularly around a rolling ridge. The 16th is, wait for it, a 248-yard par-3, followed by the 17th, where you face a drive to a fairway which is almost completely surrounded by a stream. Both the 17th and the 18th, which cross the stream twice, provide a very un-links-style finish but are excellent for matchplay.

Secretary: Mr G. Duncan   Tel: 01241 853789
           (General Manager)   Fax: 01241 852720

Professional: None

Playing: Midweek: round prices on application; day n/a. Weekend: round n/a; day n/a.

Facilities: Bar: 11am–11pm. Food: Lunch and dinner served.

Comments: Best in the country ... Ultimate test of golf overrides lack of facilities ... Course only lacks playability ... Need to cut back rough for amateurs ... Don't play this beast in any more than a breeze ... What a course, a must ... A real education although expensive ... The No.1 in Scotland ... If the wind blows in the Open watch out ... 18th is a classic finishing hole ... New clubhouse will improve this club no end ... Most difficult I've played ... Great test – in the Portmarnock class ... No dunes, no long rough – it's the design that is so punishing ... Greens are the killer ... Finish is the toughest anywhere.

The Gleneagles Hotel (King's) ★★★★★

Auchterarder, PH3 1NF
Website: www.gleneagles.com   E-mail: resort.sales@gleneagles.com
Nearest main town: Perth

If you think of Scottish golf courses as wild and unkempt, then think again. Gleneagles will blow away any preconceptions you might have. There are four courses at this exclusive golf and hotel bolthole, all beautifully manicured with a very modern feel. The King's is the best of them all, and few come away from it without falling in love with this very sensuous and natural course.

The King's lays claim to being the best inland course in Scotland, and the claim is founded on very solid arguments. It is kept in consistently superb condition, but not even the heather-clad Grampian Mountains, which form the backdrop to the course, or the silver birch and rowan can persuade you that this is a victory of style over content. There are eighteen very individual holes here, providing a varied technical test. There are drives from elevated tees to camber fairways, approach shots to elevated greens, sweeping plateau doglegs, angled greens, downhill approaches and more.

Many of the best holes come towards the end of the round. There's the driveable short par-4 15th, where you can gamble on setting up an eagle or birdie, the plunge approach to the par-4 15th and the par-3 16th in wild grasses. The 17th swings around the side of a hill to a sloping elevated green, and finally there's the par-5 18th, the first half of which is a very natural roller-coaster fairway.

What will strike you about the King's course is the shaping and artistry of the holes. The fairways and greens have very curvy lines, and even the bunkers seem to draw your vision. With the bushes and grassy hills teeming with wildlife, it's a riveting experience. And if you're staying at the Gleneagles Hotel, a standard bearer for service and welcome in Scotland, you will truly be the envy of your golfing compatriots.

Secretary:	None	Tel: 01764 662231
		Fax: 01764 662134
Professional:	Mr S. Smith	Tel: 01764 662231
		Fax: 01764 662134

Playing: Midweek: round £110.00; day n/a. Weekend: round £110.00; day n/a.

Facilities: Bar: 11am–11pm. Food: Breakfast, lunch and dinner from 7am–10pm. Bar snacks.

Comments: Famed Gleneagles quality ... Palatial course ... A haven for wildlife ... Sculpted masterpiece with elements of all the classics ... Can get windy ... A right royal experience ... On a fine spring morning it is paradise ... Fantastic ... Nothing better, but at a price ... Outstanding in every way, only the cost is off-putting ... Beautiful, natural layout with fabulous practice facilities ... Perfect in every way ... Played like a rabbit, would like to go back and play well ... Heaven in the Glens ... Everything is excellent ... Layout and course condition second to none.

Alyth Golf Club   ★★★

Pitcrocknie, Alyth, PH11 8HF
Website: www.alythgolfclub.co.uk
E-mail: mansec@alythgolf.freeserve.co.uk
Nearest main town: Dundee

Secretary:	Mr J. Docherty	Tel: 01828 632268
		Fax: 01828 633491
Professional:	Mr T. Melville	Tel: 01828 632411
		Fax: 01828 632411

Playing: Midweek: round £22.00; day £33.00. Weekend: round £30.00; day £45.00.

Facilities: Bar: 11am–11pm. Food: Bar snacks. Dinner by arrangement.

Comments: Beautifully looked after, hard-to-master course ... Well-protected greens ... Does not get recognition it deserves ... Variety in abundance ... Far from straightforward parkland course ... In the shadow of a nearby classic links.

Arbroath Golf Course   ★★

Elliott, Arbroath, PD11 2PE
Nearest main town: Arbroath

Secretary: Mr S. Milne   Tel: 01241 875837
                                     Fax: 01241 875837
Professional: Mr J. Stewart   Tel: 01241 875837
                                     Fax: 01241 875837

Playing: Midweek: round £16.00; day £20.00. Weekend: round £20.00; day £30.00.

Facilities: Bar: 11am–11pm. Food: 9am–8pm.

Comments: Short but testing, especially when the wind blows in from the North Sea ... Perfect introduction to Scottish links courses before you decide to take on some of the real monsters! ... Course really gets going from the 7th ... Practise your bunker shots before you play here ... Clubhouse facilities could be better.

Auchterarder Golf Club   ★★★

Orchil Road, Auchterarder, PH3 1LS
Website: www.auchterardergolf.co.uk
E-mail: secretary@auchterardergolf.co.uk
Nearest main town: Auchterarder

Secretary: Mr W. Campbell   Tel: 01764 662804
                                     Fax: 01764 664423
Professional: Mr G. Baxter   Tel: 01764 663711

Playing: Midweek: round £24.00; day £35.00. Weekend: round £29.00; day £45.00.

Facilities: Bar: 11am–11pm. Food: Lunch and dinner from 11am–9pm. Bar snacks.

Comments: Great holiday golf ... Not too long or demanding ... Made to feel very welcome ... A mini Gleneagles ... No par-5s but still very enjoyable ... Good bar.

Blairgowrie Golf Club (Lansdowne)   ★★

Rosemount, Blairgowrie, PH10 6LG
Website: www.blairgowrie-golf.co.uk
E-mail: admin@blairgowrie-golf.co.uk
Nearest main town: Perth

Secretary: Mr J. Simpson   Tel: 01250 872622
                                   Fax: 01250 875451
Professional: Mr C. Dernie   Tel: 01250 873116
                                   Fax: 01250 873116

Playing: Midweek: round £40.00; day £70.00. Weekend: round
                £45.00; day n/a.

Facilities: Bar: 11am–11pm. Food: Lunch and dinner from
                 10am–9pm. Bar snacks.

Comments: Like Rosemount, greatly overrated but even less fun to
                play ... Trademark Alliss/Thomas design ... Very narrow
                driving areas ... Couldn't pick which course I preferred
                ... Somewhat monotonous layout ... Great clubhouse.

Blairgowrie Golf Club (Rosemount)   ★★★★

Rosemount, Blairgowie, PH10 6LG
Website: www.blairgowrie-golf.co.uk
E-mail: admin@blairgowrie-golf.co.uk
Nearest main town: Perth

Secretary: Mr J. Simpson   Tel: 01250 872622
                                   Fax: 01250 875451
Professional: Mr C. Dernie   Tel: 01250 873116
                                   Fax: 01250 873116

Playing: Midweek: round £50.00; day n/a. Weekend: round
                £55.00; day n/a.

Facilities: Bar: 11am–11pm. Food: Lunch and dinner from
                 10am–9pm. Bar snacks.

Comments: Setting and presentation could not be bettered ...
                Greatly overrated ... Unique in Scotland but not a patch
                on Sunningdale, Liphook, Swinley Forest, West Sussex ...
                Expensive with poor facilities for visitors ... If I lived in
                Scotland this is the club I would join ... Visitors are not
                made to feel welcome ... Unique in Scotland ... Each
                hole separated from the others ... Great flora and
                fauna.

Braehead Golf Club ★★

Alloa Road, Cambus, By Alloa, FK10 2NT
Website: www.braehead.gc.btinternet.com
E-mail: braehead.gc@btinternet.com
Nearest main town: Alloa

Secretary:	Mrs A. Nash	Tel: 01259 725766
		Fax: 01259 214070
Professional:	Mr J. Stevenson	Tel: 01259 722078
		Fax: 01259 214070

Playing: Midweek: round £20.00; day £30.00. Weekend: round £30.00; day £40.00.

Facilities: Bar: 11am–11pm. Food: Lunch and dinner from 10am–9pm. Bar snacks.

Comments: Some testing par-3s, particularly the 14th ... Not much to look at ... Nice design, fair to all standards.

Brechin Golf & Squash Club ★★

Trinity, By Brechin, DD9 7PD
Nearest main town: Brechin

Secretary:	Mr I. Jardine (Manager)	Tel: 01356 622383
Professional:	Mr S. Rennie	Tel: 01356 625270
		Fax: 01356 625270

Playing: Midweek: round £22.00; day £30.00. Weekend: round £27.00; day £35.00.

Facilities: Bar: 11am–11pm. Food: 11am–9pm.

Comments: Greens are among the best I've played on ... Some of the holes have been there for over 100 years ... My pick of the bunch are the 10th and 17th ... Putting surfaces very quick and true, but difficult to read.

Buchanan Castle Golf Club ★★★

Drymen, G63 0HY
E-mail: buchanancastle@sol.co.uk
Nearest main town: Glasgow

Secretary:	Mr R. Kinsella	Tel: 01360 660307
		Fax: 01360 660993

Professional: Mr K. Baxter   Tel: 01360 660330

Playing: Midweek: round £34.00; day n/a. Weekend: round £34.00; day n/a.

Facilities: Bar: 11am–11pm. Food: Lunch and dinner from 10am–9pm. Bar snacks.

Comments: Very welcoming ... Loch Lomond is nearby ... Plenty of water in play ... Nice mix of natural hazards ... Conditioning out of the top drawer ... Shamefully underrated.

Callander Golf Club   ★★★

Aveland Road, Callander, FK17 8EN
E-mail: callandergc@nextcall.net
Nearest main town: Callander

Secretary: Mrs S. Smart   Tel: 01877 330090
                                        Fax: 01877 330062
Professional: Mr A. Martin   Tel: 01877 330975
                                        Fax: 01877 330062

Playing: Midweek: round £20.00; day £30.00. Weekend: round £28.00; day £40.00.

Facilities: Bar: 11am–11pm. Food: Lunch and dinner from 10am–9pm. Bar snacks.

Comments: Good course from back tees but visitors only play about 4000 yards from front tees or bits of fairway ... Nice test in the Trossachs ... Design by Tom Morris Snr ... Members too protective of course ... Very poor value for visitors.

Carnoustie Burnside   ★★★

Links Parade, Carnoustie, St Andrews, DD7 7JE
Nearest main town: Dundee

Secretary: Mr E. Smith   Tel: 01241 855344 (Starters)
                                        01241 853789 (Bookings)
                                        Fax: 01241 852720
Professional: None

Playing: Midweek: round £20.00; day £20.00. Weekend: round £20.00; day £20.00 (Sat after 2pm, Sun after 11.30am).

Facilities: Bar: None. Food: None.

Comments: Always in the shadow of the Championship course but a really good test of golf in its own right ... Every bit as good as the Open venue it runs alongside, only shorter ... Short 5th is a really testing hole which is almost completely surrounded by the famous Barry Burn ... Great finishing stretch with the Barry Burn a major threat in the final two holes ... General condition of the course was excellent ... Much cheaper to play than the big course and much more fun for the average player ... Outstanding par-3 holes.

Crieff Golf Club   ★★★★

Perth Road, Crieff, PH7 3LR
Nearest main town: Perth

Secretary:	Mr J. Miller	Tel: 01764 652397
		Fax: 01764 655096
Professional:	Mr D. Murchie	Tel: 01764 652909

Playing: Midweek: round £25.00; day £34.00. Weekend: round £28.00; day n/a.

Facilities: Bar: 11am–10pm. Food: Lunch and dinner from 10am–9pm.

Comments: Parkland course where every shot needs careful thought ... Built on the side of a hill ... People are what make the club ... Sloping lies ad nauseum ... Only one blind hole and long par-4s ... Best golf experience in Scotland ... Nine in the morning, 18 in the afternoon – perfect.

Downfield Golf Club   ★★★★

Turnberry Avenue, Dundee, DD2 3QP
Nearest main town: Dundee

Secretary:	Mrs M. Stewart	Tel: 01382 825595
		Fax: 01382 813111
Professional:	Mr K. Hutton	Tel: 01382 889246

Playing: Midweek: round £16.00–£31.00; day £26.00–£46.00. Weekend: round £31.00–£36.00; day n/a.

Facilities: Bar: 11am–11pm. Food: Lunch and dinner from 10am–9pm. Bar snacks.

Comments: Slightly disappointed at condition on last visit as it is normally top class ... Best inland course I have played ... A bit of everything here ... Bit pricey ... Good practice and pro facilities ... Not well known outside Scotland ... Heavily wooded inland course ... Not what you expect in Scotland ... Don't miss it.

The Edzell Golf Club   ★★★★

High Street, Edzell, DD9 7TF
Website: www.edzellgolfclub.net   E-mail: secretary@edzellgolfclub.net
Nearest main town: Brechin

Secretary: Mr I. Farquhar   Tel: 01356 647283
                                         Fax: 01356 648094
Professional: Mr A. Webster   Tel: 01356 648462
                                         Fax: 01356 648884

Playing: Midweek: round £25.00; day £35.00. Weekend: round £31.00; day £45.00.

Facilities: Bar: 11am–11pm. Food: Lunch and dinner from 10am–9pm. Bar snacks.

Comments: Highly regarded but not all it's made out to be ... Would not rush back ... A course that combines challenge and chasm ... Friendliest club in Scotland ... One of Scotland's best-kept secrets ... Gets wet in winter ... Outstanding finishing hole and great greens ... Picturesque, interesting and friendly ... Small, compact course with tiny greens and quaint holes ... A treat ... Hospitality first class.

Forfar Golf Club   ★★★

Cunninghill, Arbroath Road, Forfar, DD8 2RL
Website: www.forfargolf.com   E-mail: forfargolfclub@uku.co.uk
Nearest main town: Forfar

Secretary: Mr W. Baird   Tel: 01307 463773
                                         Fax: 01307 468495
Professional: Mr P. McNiven   Tel: 01307 465683

Playing: Midweek: round £24.00; day £30.00. Weekend: round £28.00; day £35.00.

Facilities: Bar: 11am–11pm. Food: Lunch and dinner from 12pm–8pm. Bar snacks.

Comments: Tree-lined course always in immaculate condition ... A joy to play ... First-class condition ... Layout suspect but condition superb ... A little short, but undeniably sweet.

The Gleneagles Hotel (PGA Centenary) ★★★★

Auchterarder, PH3 1NF
Website: www.gleneagles.com   E-mail: resort.sales@gleneagles.com
Nearest main town: Perth

Secretary:	None	Tel: 01764 662231
		Fax: 01764 662134
Professional:	Mr S. Smith	Tel: 01764 662231
		Fax: 01764 662134

Playing: Midweek: round £110.00; day n/a. Weekend: round £110.00; day n/a.

Facilities: Bar: 11am–11pm. Food: Breakfast, lunch and dinner from 7am–10pm. Bar snacks.

Comments: Formerly the Monarch course ... A fantastic set-up with course presentation out of this world ... Only snag way too pricey ... Some good holes but overall a bit of a let-down ... Poor ground in places and rather ordinary greens ... Stunning US-style course not normally associated with Scotland ... Excellent presentation and condition.

The Gleneagles Hotel (Queen's) ★★★★★

Auchterarder, PH3 1NF
Website: www.gleneagles.com   E-mail: resort.sales@gleneagles.com
Nearest main town: Perth

Secretary:	None	Tel: 01764 662231
		Fax: 01764 662134
Professional:	Mr S. Smith	Tel: 01764 662231
		Fax: 01764 662134

Playing: Midweek: round £110.00; day n/a. Weekend: round £110.00; day n/a.

Facilities: Bar: 11am–11pm. Food: Breakfast, lunch and dinner from 7am–10pm. Bar snacks.

Comments: A good course in its own right ... Inevitably overshadowed by neighbours ... Condition a match for anything around ... Easiest course here ... Facilities just out of this world ... Surprisingly good ... Enjoyed it immensely ... Not far behind the other two.

King James VI Golf Club   ★★★

Moncreiffe Island, Perth, PH2 8NR
Website: www.kingjamesvi.co.uk   E-mail: info@kjvigc.fsnet.co.uk
Nearest main town: Perth

Secretary: Ms H. Blair   Tel: 01738 445132
                                       Fax: 01738 445132
Professional: Mr A. Crerar   Tel: 01738 632460

Playing: Midweek: round £18.00; day £25.00. Weekend: round n/a; day £30.00.

Facilities: Bar: 11am–11pm. Food: All day.

Comments: Unique and attractive setting on what is virtually an island in the middle of the River Tay ... Very flat but still interesting ... A little daunting at first with all that water surrounding the course ... Fairways and tees in excellent condition.

Kirriemuir Golf Club   ★★

Northmuir, Kirriemuir, DD8 4PN
Nearest main town: Dundee

Secretary: Mr C. Garry   Tel: 01575 573317
                                       Fax: 01575 574608
Professional: Mrs K. Ellis   Tel: 01575 573317

Playing: Midweek: round £18.00; day £24.00. Weekend: round n/a; day n/a.

Facilities: Bar: 11am–11pm. Food: Bar snacks.

Comments: Interesting and enjoyable but not that difficult ... Views of the Angus glens ... Short but not that sweet ... Better to be found in the area.

Monifieth Golf Links (Ashludie)   ★★★

Medal Starter's Box, Princes Street, Monifieth, DD5 4AW
Website: www.monifiethgolf.co.uk   E-mail: monifiethgolf@freeuk.com
Nearest main town: Dundee

Secretary: Mr S. Fyffe   Tel: 01382 535553
                                                   Fax: 01382 535816
Professional: Mr I. McLeod   Tel: 01382 532945

Playing: Midweek: round £17.00; day £20.00. Weekend: round
                   n/a; day n/a.

Facilities: Bar: 11am–11pm. Food: Breakfast, lunch and dinner
                   from 7am–10pm. Bar snacks.

Comments: Don't come to Monifieth for this one ... Short links of
                   some character ... Ticket to play both is good value.

Monifieth Golf Links (Medal)   ★★★★

Medal Starter's Box, Princes Street, Monifieth, DD5 4AW
Website: www.monifiethgolf.co.uk   E-mail: monifiethgolf@freeuk.com
Nearest main town: Dundee

Secretary: Mr S. Fyffe   Tel: 01382 535553
                                                   Fax: 01382 535816
Professional: Mr I. McLeod   Tel: 01382 532945

Playing: Midweek: round £35.00; day n/a. Weekend: round
                   £45.00; day n/a.

Facilities: Bar: 11am–11pm. Food: Breakfast, lunch and dinner
                   from 7am–10pm. Bar snacks.

Comments: A links with a friendly membership, unfriendly wind and
                   lovely   well-tended   greens   and   fairways   ...
                   Straightforward links ... Near Carnoustie ... Very
                   exposed.

Montrose Links Trust (Medal)   ★★★★

Traill Drive, Montrose, DD10 8SW
Website: www.montroselinks.co.uk
E-mail: secretary@montroselinks.co.uk
Nearest main town: Montrose

Secretary: Mrs M. Stewart   Tel: 01674 672932
                                                   Fax: 01674 671800

Professional: Mr J. Boyd   Tel: 01674 672634
                                   Fax: 01674 671800

Playing: Midweek: round £36.00; day £46.00. Weekend: round £40.00; day £54.00.

Facilities: Bar: 11am–11pm. Food: Lunch from 12pm–8pm.

Comments: Forgotten stern links that is part of the life of the town ... Superb course ... Tricky – just what you would expect from a links ... Good value and a joy to play ... Golf played here since the 16th century ... Historic masterpiece ... A links legend ... Deep bunkers, springy turf, towering sand dunes.

Murrayshall House Hotel & Golf Courses   ★★★

Scone, Perth, PH2 7PH
Website: www.murrayshall.co.uk   E-mail: lin.murrayshall@virgin.net
Nearest main town: Perth

Secretary: None
Professional: Mr A. Reid   Tel: 01738 554804
                                   Fax: 01738 552595

Playing: Midweek: round £30.00 (Murrayshall), £20.00 (Lynedoch); day n/a. Weekend: round £35.00 (Murrayshall), £25.00 (Lynedoch); day n/a.

Facilities: Bar: 11am–11pm. Food: Breakfast, lunch and dinner from 7am–10pm.

Comments: Some uninteresting holes on a course in average condition ... Take three trees out of the middle of the fairways and this would be a great course ... Difficult to find any faults ... Greens well protected and pins difficult to attack.

Panmure Golf Club   ★★★

Burnside Road, Barry, Carnoustie, DD7 7RT
Website: www.panmuregolfclub.co.uk
E-mail: secretary@panmuregolfclub.co.uk
Nearest main town: Carnoustie

Secretary: Mr G. Paton   Tel: 01241 855120
                                   Fax: 01241 859737
Professional: Mr N. Mackintosh Tel: 01241 852460
                                   Fax: 01241 859737

Playing: Midweek: round £48.00; day £64.00. Weekend: round £48.00; day £64.00.

Facilities: Bar: 11am–11pm. Food: Lunch from 10am–9pm. Bar snacks.

Comments: Weekend play on Sundays only ... Members not keen on visitors playing their course or using their clubhouse – just like Elie ... Complements nearby Carnoustie and Monifieth ... Bump-and-run golf ... Awkward bounces, narrow fairways, rough devastating ... Short but feels like 7000 yards in the wind.

Pitlochry Golf Club   ★★★

Golf Course Road, Pitlochry, PH16 5QY
Nearest main town: Perth

Secretary: Mr D. McKenzie   Tel: 01796 472114
                                         Fax: 01796 473599
Professional: Mr G. Hampton   Tel: 01796 472792

Playing: Midweek: round £14.00; day £21.00. Weekend: round £18.00; day £27.00.

Facilities: Bar: 11am–11pm. Food: Lunch and dinner from 10am–9pm. Bar snacks.

Comments: Stunning setting and top value for money ... A delight to play ... First four holes go straight uphill and are exhausting. Meanders back down and is worth a visit ... Hard opener and gets easier ... Up hill and down dale at this course on the side of a mountain ... Second shot to the 4th is a thriller ... Plunging approach shots and driveable par-4s, great fun.

Stirling Golf Club   ★

Queen's Road, Stirling, FK8 3AA
Website: www.stirlinggolfclub.tv   E-mail: enquiries@stirlinggolfclub.tv
Nearest main town: Stirling

Secretary: Mr A. Rankin   Tel: 01786 464098
                                         Fax: 01786 460090
Professional: Mr I. Collins   Tel: 01786 471490
                                         Fax: 01786 471490

Playing: Midweek: round £28.00; day £40.00. Weekend: round £28.00; day £40.00.

Facilities: Bar: 11am–11pm. Food: Breakfast, lunch and dinner from 10am–9pm. Bar snacks.

Comments: Nondescript rolling parkland course ... Usually in good condition ... Stirling Castle broods over the course ... Surprisingly difficult.

Taymouth Castle Golf Course   ★★★

Taymouth Castle Estate, Kenmore, PH15 2NT
Nearest main town: Aberfeldy (5 miles)

Secretary: Mr R. Smith   Tel: 01887 829771
Professional: Mr A. Marshall   Tel: 01887 820910

Playing: Midweek: round £20.00; day £30.00. Weekend: round £24.00; day £38.00.

Facilities: Bar: 11am–late Mon–Sat, 12.30pm–late Sun. Food: All day.

Comments: Delight to play ... Loved the big wide fairways and flat greens ... Wonderful setting in great condition ... Hard to beat for a relaxed round of golf ... Some fine holes, especially on the homeward run ... Scottish golf at its very best ... Very friendly staff in the clubhouse ... Clubhouse available from 8am until late.

Aberdeen & Grampian

Royal Aberdeen Golf Club ★★★★★

Links Road, Bridge of Don, Aberdeen, AB23 8AT
Website: www.royalaberdeengolf.com
E-mail: admin@royalaberdeengolf.com
Nearest main town: Aberdeen

If you are looking for a baptism into links golf then this might be a suitable choice. It follows the traditional layout of nine holes away from the clubhouse followed by nine holes coming home, and for rugged, windswept duneland, this fits the bill nicely.

There can be a problem with the nine-out, nine-back mentality, though, especially when, as is the case here, another course is positioned in a similar manner just a little further down the coast. In this case it's Murcar, and it has been known for visitors to Royal Aberdeen to end up in Murcar's car park thinking that their car has been stolen.

For a sense of the historical, this spot on the east coast of Scotland is a good place to come because it is reputed that golf, in some shape or form, has been played here since 1589. The Royal Aberdeen club was formed in 1780 and the links, set out by Archie Simpson, took shape in 1888. It is the first nine that are blessed with the uncompromising presence of the huge seaside dunes along their flank. Many of the fairways are played along valleys between these dunes and the greens are elevated, much as we see with modern designs, to make them even more awkward to hit. Another modern element can be found on holes like the short 8th, where an array of bunkers on both sides of the green, sometimes three deep, means the iron selected has to be crisply and accurately struck.

Bernard Darwin described this as 'much more than good golf, a noble links', which, for information in a nutshell, sums it up pretty well.

Secretary:	Mr G. Webster	Tel: 01224 702571
		Fax: 01224 826591
Professional:	Mr R. MacAskill	Tel: 01224 702221
		Fax: 01224 826591
Playing:	Midweek: round £75.00; day £100.00. Weekend: round £85.00; day n/a.	
Facilities:	Bar: 11am–11pm. Food: Lunch from 12pm–3pm. Dinner by arrangement.	

Comments: A forgotten links that is a privilege to play ... Inaccessible course that is so natural ... Bodies lurk in the rough here ... A treat for overseas visitors ... There's nothing else like it ... A classic of its type ... So much history here ... Where the game was born.

Aboyne Golf Club   ★★

Formaston Park, Aboyne, AB34 5HP
E-mail: aboynegolf@btinternet.com
Nearest main town: Aberdeen

Secretary:	Mrs M. MacLean	Tel: 01339 887078
		Fax: 01339 887592
Professional:	Mr I. Wright	Tel: 01339 886328
		Fax: 01339 887592

Playing: Midweek: round £20.00; day £25.00. Weekend: round £25.00; day £30.00.

Facilities: Bar: 11am–11pm. Food: Lunch from 10am–3pm.

Comments: Good pro shop ... Was impressed with condition ... Very flat and little definition ... Not bad value for fair quality golf ... Shoot the lights out ... Accessible first-time course ... Very straightforward.

Ballater Golf Club   ★★★

Victoria Road, Ballater, AB35 5QX
Nearest main town: Aberdeen (40 miles)

Secretary:	Mr S. Barclay	Tel: 01339 755567
		Fax: 01339 755057
Professional:	Mr B. Yule	Tel: 01339 755658
		Fax: 01339 755057

Playing: Midweek: round £18.00; day £27.00. Weekend: round £21.00; day £31.00.

Facilities: Bar: 11am–12 midnight. Food: 10am–8pm (unless prior arrangements are made).

Comments: Super setting that must be among the most scenic in this part of the country ... Short 3rd takes some beating, it plays uphill to a well-bunkered green that falls away steeply on the left. I couldn't wait to play the course again in the afternoon ... Greens in good condition but not what you would call lightning-fast ... Not too long and really enjoyable for the less-talented golfer ... When the sun shines there is no finer or more tranquil spot to play golf ... Everyone was so friendly and helpful.

Braemar Golf Club   ★★★

Cluniebank Road, Braemar, AB35 5XX
Nearest main town: Ballater

Secretary: Mr C. McIntosh   Tel: 01339 741618
                                       Fax: 01339 741400

Professional: None

Playing: Midweek: round £20.00; day £25.00. Weekend: round £23.00; day £28.00.

Facilities: Bar: 11am–11pm. Food: Bar snacks.

Comments: Enchanting for many reasons ... Must have some of the most difficult par-3s and easiest par-4s anywhere ... Wonderful setting for great golf ... Beautiful scenery ... Short course with good par-3s.

Cruden Bay Golf Club   ★★★★

Aulton Road, Cruden Bay, Peterhead, AB42 0NN
Website: www.crudenbaygolfclub.co.uk   E-mail: cbaygc@aol.com
Nearest main town: Peterhead

Secretary: Mrs R. Pittendrigh   Tel: 01779 812285
                                        Fax: 01779 812945
Professional: Mr R. Stewart   Tel: 01779 812414

Playing: Midweek: round £55.00; day n/a. Weekend: round £65.00; day n/a. Prices may change in 2004.

Facilities: Bar: 11am–11pm. Food: Breakfast, lunch and dinner from 9am–10pm. Bar snacks.

Comments: Tough links between high sand dunes ... Lovely views over the bay ... Experience not to be forgotten ... Wonderful location ... A true rival to courses across the UK ... Full of surprises, every hole is memorable ... Wonderfully peaceful and natural place to play ... Holes 4 to 8 are great ... A real links course apart from one silly hole – magnificent ... View from 10th tee is the best in golf ... Who needs Pebble Beach? ... Outstanding scenery ... The most difficult links course around ... Everything you would want from a golf course ... Gobsmacked ... Unbelievable.

Cullen Golf Club ★★

The Links, Cullen, AB56 4UU
E-mail: cullengolf@btnet.com
Nearest main town: Buckie

Secretary: Mrs J. James   Tel: 01542 840685
Professional: None

Playing: Midweek: round £14.00; day £20.00. Weekend: round £18.00; day £24.00. Prices may increase in 2004.

Facilities: Bar: 11am–11pm. Food: Bar snacks.

Comments: Eccentric little links ... So natural, pity the course can't be extended ... Balls can bounce off the rocks ... Beach can come into play for wayward shots ... An unusual golfing day out.

Deeside Golf Club ★★★

Golf Road, Bieldside, Aberdeen, AB15 9DL
Website: www.deesidegolfclub.com
E-mail: admin@deesidegolfclub.com
Nearest main town: Aberdeen

Secretary: Mr J. Keepe   Tel: 01224 869457
                            Fax: 01224 869457
Professional: Mr F. Courts   Tel: 01224 861041

Playing: Midweek: round £45.00; day n/a. Weekend: round £60.00; day n/a.

Facilities: Bar: 11am–11pm. Food: Lunch and dinner from 10am–9pm. Bar snacks.

Comments: Quality club ... Riverside course with brooks and streams ... All sorts of dangers lurking here ... Not long but not short on interest.

Duff House Royal Golf Club   ★★★★

The Barnyards, Banff, AB45 3SX
Nearest main town: Buckie

Secretary: Mrs J. Corbett   Tel: 01261 812062
                                      Fax: 01261 812224
Professional: Mr R. Strachan   Tel: 01261 812075
                                      Fax: 01261 812075

Playing: Midweek: round £24.00; day £24.00. Weekend: round £30.00; day £30.00.

Facilities: Bar: 11am–11pm. Food: Lunch and dinner from 10am–9pm. Bar snacks.

Comments: Cracking value for an interesting, challenging and subtle course of substance ... Could not fault the course ... Greens like silk and food that says 'more please' and it's in Scotland! ... Never too busy ... Great condition ... Course protected by tricky greens ... Exceptional greens.

Fraserburgh Golf Club   ★★

Philorth, Fraserburgh, AB4 8TL
Website: www.fraserburghgolfclub.net   E-mail: fburghgolf@aol.com
Nearest main town: Peterhead

Secretary: Mr J. Mollison   Tel: 01346 516616
                                      Fax: 01346 516616
Professional: None

Playing: Midweek: round £20.00; day £25.00. Weekend: round £25.00; day £30.00.

Facilities: Bar: 11am–11pm. Food: Full catering facilities.

Comments: A different challenge on almost every hole ... Really testing even when the wind is not blowing ... Hit it on the fairways, or be sure you bring plenty of golf balls ... Golf at its most natural with fairways running between huge sandhills ... Excellent greens.

Hazelhead Golf Course   ★★

Hazelhead Park, Aberdeen, AB15 8BD
Nearest main town: Aberdeen

Secretary: Mr W. MacKay   Tel: 01224 315747
Professional: Mr A. Smith   Tel: 01224 321830

Playing: Midweek: round £9.00 (winter rates are lower); day n/a.
                  Weekend: round £11.25 (winter rates are lower); day n/a.

Facilities: Bar: 11am–2.30pm and 5pm–11pm. Food: Bar snacks
                  and meals available during opening time.

Comments: There are three public golf courses at Hazelhead with
                  No.1 being the best of the bunch ... An interesting park-
                  land layout running through a tree-lined estate ... Not
                  too tight and can flatter your game if you are playing
                  well ... Originally designed by the famous golf-course
                  architect Alister Mackenzie, who also created Augusta
                  National ... Good value for money ... Toughest hole on
                  the course is the 435-yard 14th with out-of-bounds on
                  the right and trees on the left ... Best of the four short
                  holes is the 177-yard 5th, where the tee shot has to carry
                  a deep valley directly in front of the green.

Huntly Golf Club   ★★

Cooper Park, Huntly, AB54 4SH
Website: www.huntlygc.co.uk   E-mail: huntlygc@tinyworld.co.uk
Nearest main town: Huntly

Secretary: Mr A. Donald   Tel: 01466 792643
                                      Fax: 01466 792643
Professional: None

Playing: Midweek: round £12.00; day £18.00. Weekend: round
                  £18.00; day £24.00.

Facilities: Bar: 10am–11pm in summer. In winter closed from
                  2pm–6pm Mon–Fri, open all day Sat and Sun. Food:
                  Bar snacks and meals available (seasonal).

Comments: Great combination of rolling fairways running through
                  wonderful stands of mature trees ... Look out for that
                  troublesome little burn that features on at least four
                  holes ... A slicer's delight because most of the trouble is
                  on the left side ... Glimpses of Huntly Castle through the
                  trees at the 2nd hole provide a memorable start to the
                  round ... Clubhouse and facilities are excellent.

Kemnay Golf Club

Monymusk Road, Kemnay, AB51 5RA
Website: www.kemnaygolfclub.co.uk
E-mail: administrator@kemnaygolfclub.co.uk
Nearest main town: Aberdeen

Secretary: Mr Y. Moir   Tel: 01467 643746
                                      Fax: 01467 643746
Professional: Mr R. MacDonald   Tel: 01467 642225
                                      Fax: 01467 643517

Playing: Midweek: round £20.00; day n/a. Weekend: round £24.00; day n/a.

Facilities: Bar: 11am–11pm. Food: Bar snacks. Dinner by arrangement.

Comments: Undulating and exciting ... Always easy to get a round ... Excellent views ... Fairly ordinary parkland.

King's Links Golf Course

Golf Road, King's Links, Aberdeen, AB24 5QB
Nearest main town: Aberdeen

Secretary: Mr B. Davidson   Tel: 01224 632269
Professional: None

Playing: Midweek: round £9.00; day £11.25. Weekend: round n/a; day n/a.

Facilities: Bar: None. Food: None.

Comments: Golf has been played on the ground where the course stands today from about the 16th century ... Good value for money ... Public course but in good condition with some really excellent holes ... Good opportunity to sort out your swing faults and pick up a few tips at the nearby King's Links Golf Centre, which is one of the best practice and teaching facilities in Scotland.

Kintore Golf Club ★★

Balbithan, Kintore, AB51 0UR
Website: www.kintoregolfclub.net
E-mail: kintoregolfclub@lineone.net
Nearest main town: Aberdeen

Secretary: Mr J. Black   Tel: 01467 632631
                                       Fax: 01467 632995
Professional: None

Playing: Midweek: round £15.00; day £20.00. Weekend: round
                  £20.00; day £25.00.

Facilities: Bar: 11am–11pm. Food: Lunch from 12pm–2pm.
                  Dinner from 6pm–9pm (full catering service Apr–Sept).

Comments: Moorland/woodland course of character ... Excellent
                  round rate for this charming club ... Nothing special ...
                  Made welcome.

Letham Grange Golf Club (Old)   ★★★

Letham Grange, Colliston, DD11 4RL
E-mail: golf@lethamgrange.sol.co.uk
Nearest main town: Arbroath

Secretary: Miss C. Grainger   Tel: 01241 890377
                                       Fax: 01241 890414
Professional: Mr S. Moir

Playing: Midweek: round £35.00; day n/a. Weekend: round
                  £40.00; day n/a.

Facilities: Bar: 11am–11pm. Food: Breakfast, lunch and dinner
                  from 9am–11pm. Bar snacks.

Comments: Meant to be a Scottish Augusta but far from it ... Very
                  un-Scottish course but good fun ... Target golf with a few
                  blind shots thrown in ... New course complements the
                  superior Old well ... Nice change from links golf ...
                  Tranquil setting for this US-style course ... Excellent facil-
                  ities and a course to match ... Felt very peaceful and
                  golf was fun ... Had a great laugh ... One of Donald
                  Steel's best courses ... Water hazards a constant peril ...
                  Prefer it to all those links.

Murcar Golf Club   ★★★★

Bridge of Don, Aberdeen, AB23 8BD
Website: www.murcar.co.uk   E-mail: golf@murcar.co.uk
Nearest main town: Aberdeen

Secretary: Mrs B. Rogerson   Tel: 01224 704354
                                       Fax: 01224 704354

Professional: Mr G. Forbes   Tel: 01224 704370

Playing: Midweek: round £50.00; day £70.00. Weekend: round
£60.00; day £80.00.

Facilities: Bar: 11am–11pm. Food: Lunch and dinner from
10am–10pm. Bar snacks.

Comments: The total package ... Fantastic setting ... Great fun
(avoid a windy day, though) ... Great short par-4s.

Newburgh-on-Ythan   ★★★

Beach Road, Newburgh, AB41 6BY
Website: www.newburghgolfclub.co.uk
E-mail: secretary@newburghgolfclub.co.uk
Nearest main town: Aberdeen

Secretary: Mr R. Bruce   Tel: 01358 789058
Fax: 01358 788104

Professional: None

Playing: Midweek: round £20.00; day £25.00. Weekend: round
£25.00; day £30.00.

Facilities: Bar: Seasonal opening hours. Food: Meals by arrangement.

Comments: Played every hole 100 times but still look forward to
seeing them ... Founded in the 19th century and reeks
of history ... Forgotten course ... Lovely club with course
to be proud of.

Newmachar Golf Club (Hawkshill)   ★★★

Swailend, Newmachar, AB21 7UU
Website: www.newmachargolfclub.co.uk
E-mail: info@newmachargolfclub.co.uk
Nearest main town: Aberdeen

Secretary: Mr S. Wade   Tel: 01651 863002
Fax: 01651 863055

Professional: Mr G. Simpson   Tel: 01651 863222

Playing: Midweek: round £30.00; day £45.00. Weekend: round
£40.00; day n/a.

Facilities: Bar: 11am–11pm. Food: Lunch and dinner by arrangement. Bar snacks.

Comments: Excellent layout and good mix of holes ... Superb home stretch ... Dave Thomas design of considerable flair.

Newmachar Golf Club (Swailend)   ★★

Swailend, Newmachar, AB21 7UU
Website: www.newmachargolfclub.co.uk
E-mail: info@newmachargolfclub.co.uk
Nearest main town: Aberdeen

Secretary:	Mr S. Wade	Tel: 01651 863002
		Fax: 01651 863055
Professional:	Mr G. Simpson	Tel: 01651 863222

Playing: Midweek: round £15.00; day £25.00. Weekend: round £20.00; day £30.00.

Facilities: Bar: 11am–11pm. Food: Lunch and dinner by arrangement. Bar snacks.

Comments: Top course for one fairly young ... Newer than the Hawkshill and it shows ... Nice variety but wouldn't hurry back.

Peterculter Golf Club   ★★

Burnside Road, Peterculter, AB14 0LN
Website: www.petercultergolfclub.co.uk
E-mail: info@petercultergolfclub.co.uk
Nearest main town: Aberdeen

Secretary:	Mr R. Burnett	Tel: 01224 735245
		Fax: 01224 735580
Professional:	Mr D. Vannet	Tel: 01224 734994

Playing: Midweek: round £20.00; day £27.00. Weekend: round £24.00; day £30.00.

Facilities: Bar: 11am–11pm. Food: Lunch and dinner from 10am–9pm, except Mondays.

Comments: Great greens – lots of birdies ... Lovely wildlife by the River Dee ... Narrow course and tough par ... Interesting holes, the pick is the 2nd.

Peterhead Golf Club

Craigewan Links, Riverside Drive, Peterhead, AB42 1TL
Website: www.peterheadgolfclub.co.uk
Nearest main town: Aberdeen

Secretary: Mr D. Wood   Tel: 01779 472149
                                          Fax: 01779 480725

Professional: None

Playing: Midweek: round £18.00; day n/a. Weekend: round
                   £22.00; day n/a.

Facilities: Bar: 11am–11pm. Food: Lunch from 10am–3pm.
                   Dinner by arrangement.

Comments: Very basic facilities but course is good … Natural delight
                   … Ditches, streams, bunkers and bushes … A design
                   that seems timeless … Very intimidating in the wind …
                   Near to Cruden Bay, so combine the two.

Portlethen Golf Club ★★★

Badentoy Road, Portlethen, AB12 4YA
Nearest main town: Aberdeen

Secretary: None   Tel: 01224 781090
                                          Fax: 01224 781090
Professional: Mrs M. Thomson   Tel: 01224 782571

Playing: Midweek: round £14.00; day £21.00. Weekend: round
                   £21.00; day £30.00.

Facilities: Bar: 11am–11pm. Food: Lunch and dinner from
                   10am–10pm. Bar snacks.

Comments: Longish parkland course … Worth popping in … Good
                   value … Back nine a little tougher than front … Four
                   par-4s over 420 yards … A long hitter's paradise.

Royal Tarlair Golf Club

Buchan Street, Macduff, AB44 1TA
E-mail: info@royaltarlair.co.uk
Nearest main town: Banff

Secretary: Mrs C. Davidson   Tel: 01261 832897
                                          Fax: 01261 833455

Professional: None

Playing: Midweek: round £10.00; day £15.00. Weekend: round £15.00; day £20.00.

Facilities: Bar: 11am–11pm. Food: Lunch and dinner from 10am–9pm.

Comments: Superb views over the Moray Firth ... Cliff-top course, very attractive ... One of the weakest Royal courses ... Views the highlight of otherwise humdrum course.

Stonehaven Golf Club   ★★★

Cowie, Stonehaven, AB39 3RH
Nearest main town: Stonehaven

Secretary: Mr W. Donald   Tel: 01569 762124
                                      Fax: 01569 765973
Professional: None

Playing: Midweek: round n/a; day £15.00. Weekend: round n/a; day £20.00.

Facilities: Bar: 11am–11pm. Food: Breakfast, lunch and dinner from 9am–9pm. Bar snacks.

Comments: Very remote ... Short but a real battle ... Wish I'd never turned up – too tough ... If you like a challenge ... Seven par-3s ... At the mercy of the elements, as golf should be.

Strathlene Golf Club   ★

Buckie, AB5 2DJ
Nearest main town: Buckie

Secretary: None   Tel: 01542 831798
Professional: None

Playing: Midweek: round £12.00; day £18.00. Weekend: round £16.00; day £20.00.

Facilities: Bar: 11am–11pm. Food: Bar snacks.

Comments: Excellent value seaside course ... Plenty of elevated greens ... Always felt part of the club, even as a visitor ... Didn't mind leaving ... Wind plays havoc here.

WALES

Mid Wales

Aberdovey Golf Club ★★★★

Aberdovey, LL35 0RT
Website: www.aberdoveygolf.co.uk
Nearest main town: Aberdovey

It took over a hundred years for the Welsh to start boasting about their golf courses – so long, in fact, that not even the Welsh themselves were aware of the fairway treasures hidden around the country's rugged coastline and amid its mountains and valleys. At the north of the Dovey Estuary, you will find two such cracking courses. Borth & Ynyslas is excellent value for money, while Aberdovey is a fabulous course, which the esteemed Bernard Darwin famously eulogised as the course 'that my soul loves best in the world'.

This is an historic course, and the railway that runs alongside it harks back to an era where gentlemen would travel to play golf by train. The train would also deliver the caddies to the course to carry the bags of the affluent golfers, who would choose to play the favoured form of the game in that day, matchplay, on this lovely links.

Aberdovey, like the Victorian seafront terraces of the town, can seem utterly forlorn in the winter. But in the summer, when the crowds make the town come alive, so does the course, as holidaying golfers enjoy the delights of this very individual test.

While the course runs straight out and straight back in the manner of a traditional links, there is a marvellous diversity to the two nines, and indeed the holes themselves. On the front nine, the drive between the dunes at the 2nd is particularly memorable, as is the blind drive of the 3rd. After posing such stern questions early on, there is a brief rest until the marsh-ridden 10th, and the problems intensify at the 12th, where the second shot is played to a green set high amid the dunes.

Various designers have amended Aberdovey, like many famous courses, with Colt, Fowler and Braid adding their expertise to the original design; it remains a spiritually uplifting and varied experience.

Secretary:	Mr J. Griffiths	Tel: 01654 767493
		Fax: 01654 767027
Professional:	Mr J. Davies	Tel: 01654 767602
		Fax: 01654 767027
Playing:	Midweek: round £36.00; day n/a. Weekend: round £41.50; day n/a.	

Facilities: Bar: 11am–11pm. Food: Lunch and dinner from 11am–9pm. Bar snacks.

Comments: A well-run links with new clubhouse of high standard ... Railway runs alongside the course ... Straight out, straight back ... The classic design ... Brilliant course in every way ... Company, course and welcome all in place ... Superb day out in scenic surroundings.

Aberystwyth Golf Club ★★

Brynymor Road, Ceredigion, Aberystwyth, SY23 2HY
Website: www.aberystwythgolfclub.com
E-mail: aberystwythgolf@talk21.com
Nearest main town: Aberystwyth

Secretary:	Mr J. McLeod	Tel: 01970 615104
		Fax: 01970 626622
Professional:	Mr J. McLeod	Tel: 01970 625301
		Fax: 01970 626622

Playing: Midweek: round £20.00; day £25.00. Weekend: round £25.00; day £30.00 (restricted times).

Facilities: Bar: 11am–11pm. Food: Lunch and dinner from 11am–9pm. Bar snacks.

Comments: Cracking finish ... On a clear day the views over Cardigan Bay are fabulous ... Great drive along the coastal road to the course ... Course matches the quality of views.

Borth & Ynyslas Golf Club

Aer y Mor, Borth, SY24 5JS
Website: www.borthgolf.co.uk   E-mail: secretary@borthgolf.co.uk
Nearest main town: Aberystwyth

Secretary:	Mr G. Pritchard	Tel: 01970 871202
		Fax: 01970 871202
Professional:	Mr J. Lewis	Tel: 01970 871557

Playing: Midweek: round £28.00; day n/a. Weekend: round £28.00; day n/a.

Facilities: Bar: 11am–11pm. Food: Lunch and dinner from 11am–9pm. Bar snacks.

Comments: Top value, condition and character ... An unknown course that should remain that way ... Friendly and fun ... Testing links course with basic facilities.

Cradoc Golf Club   ★★★

Penoyre Park, Cradoc, Brecon, LD3 9LP
Website: www.cradoc.co.uk   E-mail: secretary@cradoc.co.uk
Nearest main town: Brecon

Secretary:	Mrs E. Pryce	Tel: 01874 623658
		Fax: 01874 611711
Professional:	Mr R. Davies	Tel: 01874 625524

Playing: Midweek: round £22.00; day n/a. Weekend: round £28.00; day n/a. Prices may increase in 2004.

Facilities: Bar: 11am–11pm. Food: Lunch and dinner from 10am–9pm. Bar snacks.

Comments: You need a strategy for each hole ... Spectacular views of the Brecon Beacons ... Remote course worth finding.

Llandrindod Wells Golf Club

The Clubhouse, Golf Links Road, Llandrindod Wells, LD1 5NY
Website: www.lwgc.co.uk   E-mail: secretary@lwgc.co.uk
Nearest main town: Llandrindod Wells

Secretary:	Mr R. Southcott	Tel: 01597 823873
		Fax: 01597 823873
Professional:	Mr P. Davies	Tel: 01597 822247

Playing: Midweek: round £20.00; day £28.00. Weekend: round £25.00; day £32.00.

Facilities: Bar: 11am–11pm. Food: Lunch and dinner from 10am–9pm. Bar snacks.

Comments: Delightful club with stupendous views ... Views magnificent ... Quiet, lazy golf that's very enjoyable ... Nice feel about this club ... Relaxed atmosphere ... Stunning on a warm summer's day.

Penrhos Golf & Country Club   ★★

Llanrhystud, Ceredigion, Aberystwyth, SY23 5AY
Website: www.penrhosgolf.co.uk   E-mail: info@penrhosgolf.co.uk
Nearest main town: Aberystwyth

Secretary: Mr R. Rees-Evans   Tel: 01974 202999
                                            Fax: 01974 202100
Professional: Mr P. Diamond

Playing: Midweek: round £18.00; day n/a. Weekend: round
                    £24.00; day n/a.

Facilities: Bar: 11am–11pm. Food: Breakfast, lunch and dinner
                    from 9am–9pm. Bar snacks.

Comments: Country club with fine facilities ... Basic golf with a few
                    lakes and fine views ... Long course with high standard
                    scratch ... Deceptively difficult.

North Wales

Royal St David's Golf Club ★★★★★

Harlech, LL46 2UB
Website: www.royalstdavids.co.uk
E-mail: secretary@royalstdavids.co.uk
Nearest main town: Harlech

Between arriving at Royal St David's and teeing off, you will almost certainly meet someone who tells you this is the toughest par-69 in the world. Of course, you will not believe it and, until you reach the turn, will confidently dismiss the comments as humbug. Then it hits you, an astonishing stretch of holes, played against a backdrop of dunes the size of the *Titanic*, that eat away at your score and leave you yearning for the warmth and friendliness of the clubhouse.

This imbalance between the two nines may earn rancour from some players, but for the majority it's a great relief, allowing you to hone your game before the real test begins. Whether it's the toughest par-69 in the world is up for debate, and one can imagine it has been the subject of lengthy discussions in the bar at this historic and traditional club.

Set on flat terrain and overlooked by the medieval castle of Harlech (very imposing and somewhat eerie), Royal St David's is a true rival for Royal Porthcawl as the best course in Wales. It may not have the same feeling of space as Porthcawl, but what it lacks in length and openness, it more than makes up for in the intimacy it creates between the player and the course. This is achieved, to some extent, by the visual cloak the dunes present all along the western extent of the course – unless you clamber over the back of the 16th tee, you can never glimpse the sea.

Royal St David's feels like a natural stadium for golf, framed by the hills, the castle and the dunes, and the holes on the back nine mirror this effect, plunging into seemingly never-ending tunnels of sandhills. The 14th is a blind par-3 into a punchbowl green, then the 15th and 16th are resolute par-4s where the dunes funnel towards the green. The champagne has been well and truly drunk by the time you reach the 18th, a finish so flat you wish you'd packed up the hole before.

Although the dunes protect the course, it does not mean you will escape strong winds, and on some drives you can be pushed to reach the fairways. But on the hardest par-69 in the world, what did you expect?

Secretary: Mr D. Morkill

Tel: 01766 780361
Fax: 01766 781110

Professional: Mr J. Barnett

Tel: 01766 780857
Fax: 01766 781110

Playing: Midweek: round £40.00; day £50.00. Weekend: round £50.00; day £60.00.

Facilities: Bar: 11am–11pm. Food: Lunch and dinner from 11am–9pm. Bar snacks.

Comments: Not as interesting as most links but some super greens ... Excellent ... Some great individual holes – aura of a championship course ... Fantastic back nine ... Par-69 that plays to about 72 ... Different links that is a killer on the back nine ... Prevailing wind on the back nine makes it an absolute slog ... Weak par-3 finishing hole ... Super 15th and 16th – great holes anyday ... Back nine unbelievable.

Bull Bay Golf Club   ★★

Bull Bay Road, Amlwch, LL68 9RY
Website: www.bullbaygc.co.uk   E-mail: ian@bullbaygc.co.uk
Nearest main town: Amlwch

Secretary: Mr I. Furlong

Tel: 01407 830960
Fax: 01407 832612

Professional: Mr J. Burns

Tel: 01407 831188
Fax: 01407 832612

Playing: Midweek: round £22.00; day £22.00. Weekend: round £27.00; day £27.00.

Facilities: Bar: 11am–11pm. Food: Lunch and dinner from 11am–9pm. Bar snacks.

Comments: Superbly natural course covered in gorse ... An awesome location in North Wales with views of Isle of Man, Anglesey and Snowdonia ... You feel very alone up on this well-drained course.

Chirk Golf Club   ★

Chirk, Wrexham, LL14 5AD
Website: www.chirkgolfclub.com
Nearest main town: Wrexham

Secretary:	None	Tel: 01691 774407
		Fax: 01691 773878

Professional: Mr M. Maddison

Playing: Midweek: round £18.00; day n/a. Weekend: round £25.00; day n/a.

Facilities: Bar: 11am–11pm. Food: Lunch and dinner from 11am–9pm. Bar snacks.

Comments: One of the longest par-5s in Europe (664 yards) ... Blessed setting overlooked by Chirk Castle ... New centre for all standards of player ... Basic layout, not always in good condition.

Conwy (Caernarvonshire) Golf Club ★★★★

Beacons Way, The Morfa, LL32 8ER
Website: www.conwygolfclub.co.uk
E-mail: thesecretary@conwygolfclub.co.uk
Nearest main town: Conwy

Secretary:	Mr D. Brown	Tel: 01492 592423
		Fax: 01492 593363
Professional:	Mr P. Lees	Tel: 01492 593225
		Fax: 01492 593339

Playing: Midweek: round £35.00; day £40.00. Weekend: round £40.00; day £48.00.

Facilities: Bar: 11am–11pm. Food: Lunch and dinner from 11am–9pm. Bar snacks.

Comments: Easy walking ... Pleasurable links terrain ... Superbly respectful pro ... Staff very good ... Very flat ... Natural course which oozes character ... A course for all seasons.

Holyhead Golf Club ★★★

Trearddur Bay,, LL65 2YL
Website: www.holyheadgolfclub.co.uk   E-mail: mgrsec@aol.com
Nearest main town: Holyhead

Secretary:	Mr J. Williams	Tel: 01407 763229
		Fax: 01407 763279
Professional:	Mr S. Elliott	Tel: 01407 762022

Playing: Midweek: round n/a; day £22.00. Weekend: round n/a; day £29.00.

Facilities: Bar: 11am–11pm. Food: Lunch and dinner by arrangement. Bar snacks.

Comments: Very rugged links with some punishing rough in places … A good test for all golfers … Hilly with tight contoured fairways … Thick heather and true greens … Exciting in the summer.

Maesdu Golf Club   ★★★

Hospital Road, Llandudno, LL30 1HU
Website: www.golfnw.co.uk
E-mail: george@maesdugolfclub.freeserve.co.uk
Nearest main town: Llandudno

Secretary:	Mr G. Dean	Tel: 01492 876450
		Fax: 01492 871570
Professional:	Mr S. Boulden	Tel: 01492 875195

Playing: Midweek: round £25.00; day £30.00. Weekend: round £35.00; day n/a.

Facilities: Bar: 11am–11pm. Food: Lunch and dinner from 11am–9pm. Bar snacks.

Comments: Go when the gorse is blooming … Part links, part parkland … Nice welcome … A little expensive for facilities … Very varied and entertaining … Enjoyed myself but once is enough.

Nefyn & District Golf Club   ★★★★

Morfa Nefyn, Pwllheli, LL53 6LR
Website: www.nefyn-golf-club.com   E-mail: nefyngolf@tesco.net
Nearest main town: Caernafon

Secretary:	Mr J. Owens	Tel: 01758 720966
		Fax: 01758 720476
Professional:	Mr J. Froom	Tel: 01758 720102

Playing: Midweek: round £27.00; day £33.00. Weekend: round £32.00; day £38.00. Prices may increase in 2004.

Facilities: Bar: 11am–11pm. Food: Lunch and dinner by arrangement. Bar snacks.

Comments: Stunning views, warm welcome ... Good condition ... Outstanding views and a nice day's golf ... Tough course ... For scenic beauty the course could be mentioned in the same breath as Cypress Point ... The old nine should be a listed treasure ... Simply the best location in all of golf ... Perched on cliffs with outstanding views ... Great do-or-die course ... Maintenance can't be matched.

De Vere Northop Country Park Golf Club   ★★★

Northop, Chester, CH7 6WA
Website: www.devereonline.co.uk
E-mail: northop@stdavidshotels.com
Nearest main town: Flint

Secretary: Ms P. Messham   Tel: 01352 840440
                   (Golf Administrator)   Fax: 01352 840445
Professional: Mr N. Sweeney   Tel: 01352 840440

Playing: Midweek: round £40.00; day n/a. Weekend: round £40.00; day n/a.

Facilities: Bar: 11am–11pm. Food: Bar snacks. Dinner by arrangement.

Comments: New facility, does everything right ... This and Carden Park have put the area on the map ... Opening holes a little tiresome but gets better ... An outstanding new service for golfers in North Wales.

Porthmadog Golf Club   ★★★

Morfa Bychan, Porthmadog, LL49 9UU
Nearest main town: Porthmadog

Secretary: Mrs A. Richardson   Tel: 01766 514124
                                          Fax: 01766 514638
Professional: Mr P. Bright   Tel: 01766 513828

Playing: Midweek: round £25.00; day £25.00. Weekend: round £27.00; day £27.00.

Facilities: Bar: 11am–11pm. Food: Lunch and dinner from 9am–9pm. Bar snacks.

Comments: Ideal mix of links and heathland ... Links/parkland with great variety and food ... Sand dunes and more sand dunes ... Good links in beautiful surroundings ... Smashing.

Pwllheli Golf Club ★

Golf Road, Pwllheli, LL53 5PS
Website: www.pwllheligolfclub.co.uk
E-mail: admin@pwllheligolfclub.co.uk
Nearest main town: Pwllheli

Secretary: Mrs M. Nash   Tel: 01758 701644
               (General Manager)   Fax: 01758 701644
Professional: Mr S. Pilkington   Tel: 01758 612520
                                    Fax: 01758 701644

Playing: Midweek: round £25.00 (summer), £15.50 (winter); day
               n/a. Weekend: round £30.00 (summer), £15.50
               (winter); day n/a.

Facilities: Bar: 11am–11pm. Food: Lunch and dinner from
               11am–9pm. Bar snacks.

Comments: Another course with views of Cardigan Bay and
               Snowdon ... Scenery rather overshadows the course ...
               Poor condition ... Greens like shag carpets ... With
               Cader Idris and Snowdon in the background this is very
               evocative.

South Wales

Royal Porthcawl Golf Club ★★★★★

Rest Bay, Porthcawl, CF36 3UW
Website: www.royalporthcawl.com
Nearest main town: Cardiff

Links lovers face an embarrassment of riches along the southern coast of Wales, but none is better than Royal Porthcawl, the most famous course in the Principality. Visitors come back again and again, attracted by panoramic views of the Bristol Channel from every hole, and a unique mixture of classic links and heathland holes, played out on lush springy turf.

The excellence of Royal Porthcawl could easily pass you by. Much as you might appreciate the spectacle of a musical and miss the nuances of the songs, so the raw beauty of this links might distract from the technical brilliance of its design. The first seven holes form a circle around the extremities of the site before spiralling inwards, thereby keeping the player constantly on his or her guard against the fluctuating directions of the wind. There are holes that reward accuracy, others that reward brute strength, penal holes and simple birdie holes.

As befits such a revered course, the opening three holes are as exciting as you will find anywhere and, at the 3rd, the player is asked to gamble on driving across rocks to an angled fairway. From there, you travel inland, rising to a heathland plateau where a simple stone wall marks the course boundaries. The strength of the course from here in lies in the strength of the par-4s and par-5s, their character dictated by the ferocity of the wind. A mention should go to the 15th, a par-4 that is intimidating off the tee and has cracked the fragile concentration of many players.

While Royal Porthcawl has not won the cachet of having staged an Open Championship (although it has held Curtis and Walker Cups), it is undeniably a special course. The blandness and restrained feel of Porthcawl town, with its retirement bungalows spread in all directions, is not translated to the course or the club. Relaxing post-round in the warm, wood-panelled bar, you are alive to the conversations of the lively, elderly membership, and a night spent in the dormy house can make this a never-to-be-forgotten golf experience.

Secretary: Mr F. Prescott   Tel: 01656 782251
                                             Fax: 01656 771687
Professional: Mr P. Evans   Tel: 01656 773702

Playing: Midweek: round prices on application; day n/a. Weekend: round n/a; day n/a.

Facilities: Bar: 11am–11pm. Food: Lunch and dinner from 11am–9pm. Bar snacks.

Comments: Very good course and friendly welcome ... Wonderful place to play and great reception ... Tough and testing golf ... As tough as any course ... Perhaps too many blind holes to be considered among the best ... Staying at the dormy house makes the visit ... Classic and unmastered by the so-called experts ... Perfect golf experience, superb atmosphere ... Sitting in the bar in the late afternoon with the sun streaming in is the best experience I've had in golf ... I could play this course every day for the rest of my life ... A complete delight.

Ashburnham Golf Club   ★★★★

Cliff Terrace, Burry Port, SA16 0HN
Nearest main town: Llanelli

Secretary: Mr D. Williams   Tel: 01554 832269
                                      Fax: 01554 832269
Professional: Mr R. Ryder   Tel: 01554 833846
                                      Fax: 01554 833846

Playing: Midweek: round £27.50; day £32.50. Weekend: round £32.50; day £40.50.

Facilities: Bar: 11am–11pm. Food: Breakfast, lunch and dinner from 9am–9pm. Bar snacks.

Comments: Great links that is playable all year round ... Hard-to-read greens ... Straightforward, but persistent wind makes life difficult ... Evocative course ... A memorable day.

Caerphilly Golf Club   ★★

Pencapel, Mountain Road, Caerphilly, CF83 1HJ
Nearest main town: Cardiff

Secretary: Mr R. Neill   Tel: 029 2086 3441
                                      Fax: 029 2086 3441
Professional: Mr J. Hill   Tel: 029 2086 9104
                                      Fax: 029 2086 3441

Playing: Midweek: round £26.00 (£13.00 with a member); day
                  n/a. Weekend: round £16.00 (playing with a member
                  only); day n/a.

Facilities: Bar: 11am–11pm. Food: Lunch from 12pm–4pm.
                  Dinner from 6pm–9pm.

Comments: Mountainous course with many par-5s ... Hard walking
                  and poor facilities ... Undulating mountain course ...
                  Par-73 and it feels like it.

Celtic Manor Hotel Golf & Country Club (Coldra)   ★★

Coldra Woods, Newport, NP6 1JQ
Website: www.celtic-manor.com
E-mail: postbox@celtic-manor.com or golf@celtic-manor.com
Nearest main town: Newport

Secretary: Mr J. McKenzie   Tel: 01633 413000
                   (Director of Golf)   Fax: 01633 410309
Professional: Mr K. Carpenter   Tel: 01633 410312

Playing: Midweek: round prices on application; day n/a.
                  Weekend: round n/a; day n/a.

Facilities: Bar: 11am–11pm. Food: Breakfast, lunch and dinner
                  from 7am–10pm. Bar snacks.

Comments: Too many par-3s on this tight course ... Facilities are
                  probably second to none ... Very friendly staff.

Celtic Manor Hotel Golf & Country Club (Roman Road)   ★★

Coldra Woods, Newport, NP6 1JQ
Website: www.celtic-manor.com
E-mail: postbox@celtic-manor.com or golf@celtic-manor.com
Nearest main town: Newport

Secretary: Mr J. McKenzie   Tel: 01633 413000
                   (Director of Golf)   Fax: 01633 410309
Professional: Mr K. Carpenter   Tel: 01633 410312

Playing: Midweek: round £37.00; day n/a. Weekend: round
                  £55.00; day n/a.

Facilities: Bar: 11am–11pm. Food: Breakfast, lunch and dinner
                  from 7am–10pm. Bar snacks.

Comments: Excellent course, fine condition and facilities ... Very nice, pleasant people and worth the trip ... Course can get boggy and it's a bit of a slog ... Great facilities, but course just drags on and on ... Great, unbelievably tough course with many memorable holes.

Glamorganshire Golf Club ★

Lavernock Road, Penarth, CF64 5UP
Website: www.glamorganshiregolfclub.co.uk
E-mail: glamgolf@btconnect.com
Nearest main town: Cardiff

Secretary:	Mr B. Williams	Tel: 029 2070 1185
		Fax: 029 2070 1185
Professional:	Mr A. Kerr-Smith	Tel: 029 2070 7401

Playing: Midweek: round n/a; day £35.00. Weekend: round n/a; day £40.00.

Facilities: Bar: 11am–11pm. Food: Lunch and dinner from 11am–9pm. Bar snacks.

Comments: Rather expensive for what you get ... Reasonable facilities but course not up to much ... Friendly club that is always welcoming to visitors.

Monmouthshire Golf Club ★

Llanfoist, Abergavenny, NP7 9HE
Website: www.monmouthshiregolfclub.co.uk
E-mail: secretary@mgcabergavenny.fsnet.co.uk
Nearest main town: Abergavenny

Secretary:	Mr R. Bradley	Tel: 01873 852606
		Fax: 01873 850470
Professional:	Mr B. Edwards	Tel: 01873 852532
		Fax: 01873 852532

Playing: Midweek: round n/a; day £30.00. Weekend: round n/a; day £35.00.

Facilities: Bar: 11am–11pm. Food: Bar snacks.

Comments: Course running alongside the River Usk ... Parkland course in area devoid of good golf ... Better fish to fry elsewhere.

Morlais Castle Golf Club   ★

Pant, Merthyr Tydfil, CF48 2UY
Website: www.morlaiscastle-golfclub.co.uk
E-mail: info@mcgc.fsnet.co.uk
Nearest main town: Merthyr Tydfil

Secretary:	Mr M. Price	Tel: 01685 722822
Professional:	Mr H. Jarrett	Tel: 01685 388700

Playing: Midweek: round £16.00 (£10.00 with member); day n/a. Weekend: round £20.00 (£16.00 with member); day n/a.

Facilities: Bar: 11am–11pm. Food: Lunch and dinner from 11am–9pm. Bar snacks.

Comments: The second nine has added much to this course ... Poorly designed and not worth a second helping ... Parkland course with views of the Bristol Channel.

The Newport Golf Club   ★★★

Great Oak, Newport, NP1 9FX
Nearest main town: Newport

Secretary:	Mr J. Dinsdale	Tel: 01633 892643
		Fax: 01633 896676
Professional:	Mr P. Mayo	Tel: 01633 893271

Playing: Midweek: round n/a; day £30.00. Weekend: round n/a; day £40.00.

Facilities: Bar: 11am–11pm. Food: Lunch and dinner from 11am–9pm. Bar snacks.

Comments: Better than both nearby St Pierre and Celtic Manor ... Quality in buckets ... Greens in outstanding condition ... Warm welcome ... Club couldn't have been more helpful ... Fast, true greens.

Pennard Golf Club   ★★★★

2 Southgate Road, Swansea, SA3 2BT
E-mail: pigeon01@globalnet.co.uk
Nearest main town: Swansea

Secretary:	Mr E. Howell	Tel: 01792 233131
		Fax: 01792 234797

Professional: Mr M. Bennett   Tel: 01792 233451
                                       Fax: 01792 234886

Playing: Midweek: round £27.00; day n/a. Weekend: round
                 £35.00; day n/a.

Facilities: Bar: 11am–11pm. Food: Lunch and dinner from
                 11am–9pm. Bar snacks.

Comments: Rugged coastline frames a cracking, unusual links ...
                 Steep hills force uneven lies ... Sloping lies, howling
                 winds and chill factor make this tougher than any
                 Scottish links ... Condition excellent ... An incredibly
                 natural course with much charm ... It has everything.

Pontypridd Golf Club   ★

Ty Gwyn Road, Pontypridd, CF37 4DJ
Nearest main town: Pontypridd

Secretary: Mrs V. Hooley   Tel: 01443 409904
                                       Fax: 01443 491622
Professional: Mr W. Walters   Tel: 01443 491210

Playing: Midweek: round £20.00; day n/a. Weekend: round
                 £20.00; day n/a.

Facilities: Bar: 11am–11pm. Food: Lunch and dinner from
                 11am–9pm. Bar snacks.

Comments: Mature woodland at this fair-value layout ... Classy golf
                 in bleak area ... Views of Rhondda Valley excellent ...
                 Not one to go out of your way for.

Pyle & Kenfig Golf Club

Waun-y-Mer, Kenfig, CF33 4PU
Website: www.pyleandkenfiggolfclub.co.uk
E-mail: secretary@pyleandkenfiggolfclub.co.uk
Nearest main town: Porthcawl

Secretary: Mr D. Fellowes   Tel: 01656 783093
                                       Fax: 01656 772822
Professional: Mr R. Evans   Tel: 01656 772446
                                       Fax: 01656 772822

Playing: Midweek: round n/a; day £40.00. Weekend: round n/a;
                 day £60.00 (Sundays only). Prices may increase in 2004.

Facilities: Bar: 11am–11pm. Food: Lunch from 11am–3pm. Dinner by arrangement.

Comments: An absolutely astonishing back nine ... People say it's an epic course – I'd agree ... All the trouble is off the tee ... If the greens were better protected this would be a monster ... Completely unknown outside Wales so let's keep it that way ... Unusually, first-class facilities for an established club ... This and Porthcawl just blow your mind.

Radyr Golf Club   ★

Drysgol Road, Radyr, CF15 8BS
Website: www.radyrgolf.co.uk   E-mail: manager@radyrgolf.co.uk
Nearest main town: Cardiff

Secretary: Mr A. Edwards   Tel: 029 2084 2408
                                        Fax: 029 2084 3914
Professional: Mr R. Butterworth   Tel: 029 2084 2476
                                        Fax: 029 2084 3914

Playing: Midweek: round n/a; day £38.00. Weekend: round n/a; day £38.00.

Facilities: Bar: 11am–11pm. Food: Lunch and dinner from 11am–9pm. Bar snacks.

Comments: Always in good condition ... Small elevated greens make for some good shot-making ... Hillside, parkland course that gets windy ... Very variable condition.

The Rolls of Monmouth   ★★★

The Hendre, Monmouth, NP25 5HG
Website: www.therollsgolfclub.co.uk
E-mail: enquiries@therollsgolfclub.co.uk
Nearest main town: Monmouth

Secretary: Mrs S. Orton   Tel: 01600 715353
                                        Fax: 01600 713115
Professional: None

Playing: Midweek: round n/a; day £36.00. Weekend: round n/a; day £40.00. Prices may increase in 2004.

Facilities: Bar: 11am–11pm. Food: Lunch and dinner from 11am–9pm. Bar snacks.

Comments: Beautiful vistas ... Luxurious feel to this course ... Very good all round ... Peaceful, remote location with lovely mansion as centrepiece ... Greens just too fast for me ... Highlight is the 18th ... Natural parkland golf as it should be.

St David's City Golf Club   ★★

Whitesands Bay, St David's, SA62 6PT
E-mail: wjwilcox@hotmail.com
Nearest main town: St David's

Secretary: Mr J. Wilcox   Tel: 01437 720058
                                 Fax: 01437 720058

Professional: None

Playing: Midweek: round n/a; day £15.00. Weekend: round n/a; day £15.00.

Facilities: Bar: Hotel bar next door.

Comments: No clubhouse or bar but changing facilities ... Superb views and greens ... Never busy ... Greens exceptional ... Basic golf where the course is the star ... Unusual, remote course ... Didn't want to leave ... Back-to-basics golf.

St Mellons Golf Club   ★★

St Mellons, Cardiff, CF3 2XS
Website: www.stmellonsgolfclub.co.uk
E-mail: stmellons@golf2003.fsnet.co.uk
Nearest main town: Cardiff

Secretary: Mr R. Boyce   Tel: 01633 680408
                                 Fax: 01633 680219
Professional: Mr B. Thomas   Tel: 01633 680101
                                 Fax: 01633 680101

Playing: Midweek: round £30.00; day n/a. Weekend: round £30.00 (when available); day n/a.

Facilities: Bar: 11am–11pm. Food: Lunch and dinner from 11am–9pm. Bar snacks.

Comments: Demanding course with a tough finish ... Pleasant parkland course with good greens ... Varied selection of par-3s ... Careful at the 12th.

St Pierre Hotel Golf Club ★★★★

St Pierre Park, Chepstow, NP6 6YA
Nearest main town: Chepstow

Secretary:	Mr T. Cleary	Tel: 01291 625261
		Fax: 01291 629975
Professional:	Mr C. Dunn	Tel: 01291 635205

Playing: Midweek: round £30.00; day n/a. Weekend: round £30.00; day n/a.

Facilities: Bar: 11am–11pm. Food: Breakfast, lunch and dinner from 7am–10pm. Bar snacks.

Comments: Food and drink just great ... Everything you would expect from a resort course ... Well presented ... Great hospitality.

Southerndown Golf Club ★★★★

Ogmore-by-Sea, Bridgend, CF32 0QP
Website: www.southerndowngolfclub.com
E-mail: southerndowngolf@btconnect.com
Nearest main town: Bridgend

Secretary:	Mr A. Hughes	Tel: 01656 880476
		Fax: 01656 880317
Professional:	Mr D. McMonagle	Tel: 01656 880326
		Fax: 01656 880317

Playing: Midweek: round £40.00; day n/a. Weekend: round £50.00; day n/a.

Facilities: Bar: 11am–11pm. Food: Lunch and dinner from 11am–9pm. Bar snacks.

Comments: Excellent large greens ... A very stiff test when the wind blows ... Very hilly and great views ... Vardon, Braid, Colt and Steel have all worked on this course ... Fairway mowers are the sheep ... Need to hit it low on this windy, exposed downland gem.

Tenby Golf Club ★★★★

The Burrows, Tenby, SA70 7NP
E-mail: tenbygolfclub@uku.co.uk
Nearest main town: Tenby

Secretary: Mr D. Hancock   Tel: 01834 842978
Fax: 01834 842978
Professional: Mr M. Hawkey   Tel: 01834 844447

Playing: Midweek: round £30.00; day n/a. Weekend: round £35.00; day n/a.

Facilities: Bar: 11am–11pm. Food: Breakfast, lunch and dinner from 9am–9pm.

Comments: Welsh hospitality at its best ... Very tough, eccentric course that can test your patience ... A tortured piece of land that remains fresh in the eye years afterwards ... A fine golf course where real golfers come to satisfy their minds ... Very, very tough ... A beast.

The Wales National   ★★★

The Vale of Glamorgan Hotel Golf & Country Club, Hensol Park, Hensol, CF72 8JY
Website: www.vale-hotel.com
Nearest main town: Cardiff

Secretary: Mr A. Morrison   Tel: 01443 667856
(Golf Sales Operations Manager) Fax: 01443 222220
Professional: Mr C. Coombs   Tel: 01443 665899

Playing: Midweek: round £50.00; day n/a. Weekend: round £50.00; day n/a.

Facilities: Bar: 8am–11pm. Food: Breakfast and snacks 8am–7pm (summer), 8am–5pm (winter).

Comments: It took three years to make but it's been well worth the wait ... No wonder it's already been short-listed for the 2007 Solheim Cup ... At nearly 7400 yards off the back tees, it's bloody long and tough ... A terrific US-style layout – the designer has brought a touch of Florida to a traditional Welsh landscape ... There is also another 18-hole course (Lake) and excellent practice and teaching facilities.

West Monmouthshire Golf Club   ★

Golf Road, Pond Road, Nantyglo, NP23 4QT
Website: www.westmongolfclub.co.uk
E-mail: care@westmongolfclub.co.uk
Nearest main town: Winchestown

Secretary: Mr S. Williams   Tel: 01495 310233
Professional: None

Playing: Midweek: round £12.00; day n/a. Weekend: round £15.00 (call for details); day n/a.

Facilities: Bar: 11am–11pm. Food: Bar snacks.

Comments: Weekend play on Sundays only ... Course designed around coal tips, mountain climbs and valleys ... One to steer clear of.

IRELAND

Munster

Ballybunion Golf Club (Old)   ★★★★★

Sandhill Road, Ballybunion, County Kerry
Website: www.ballybuniongolfclub.ie   E-mail: bbgolfc@iol.ie
Nearest main town: Limerick

Ballybunion, literally translated as 'town of the sapling', is a small resort village on the southern side of the Shannon estuary. It is rightly on the itinerary for those mega-rich Americans who come on short golfing tours to these islands. They take in Turnberry, Gleneagles, St Andrews and then Ballybunion Old. Not surprisingly, the price of playing here has gone through the roof, and anyone wanting to pick up some commemorative merchandise of their visit to Ballybunion will have to dig deep to afford the prices in the pro shop.

Ballybunion's remoteness and the sheer size of its dunes make it a honeypot for all golfers. The dunes at Turnberry and St Andrews are bumps by comparison. Unlike, say, Royal Birkdale, where the dunes tend to flank the fairways, at Ballybunion they often run perpendicular to the line of play. You are driving over them, into them, up them, and onto them. In the words of Christy O'Connor Snr, 'When the wind blows, anyone who breaks 70 here is playing better than he is able to play.'

It is difficult to score well at Ballybunion, simply because the distractions (shiny beaches, crumbling cliffs and so forth) are so engaging. As early as the 1st tee you stand looking straight at a graveyard, hardly the uplifting encouragement you need at the start of the round.

By comparison with many other great links, it is a modest opening after the 1st, but things start to get better at the 7th, a par-4 laid out along the shore with a small plateau green clinging to the dunes above the Atlantic. The 10th, another par-4, doglegs its way left, back to the very edge of the ocean, and the 11th has the twin threat of sandhills on the left and the Atlantic to the right.

Some talk of playing Ballybunion as if their life has been changed completely by the experience. Don't listen to the hype: take the course for what it's really worth – an excellent links but one that is surely bettered elsewhere.

Secretary: Mr J. McKenna   Tel: 068 27146
                                      Fax: 068 27387
Professional: Mr B. O'Callaghan   Tel: 068 27842
                                      Fax: 068 27387

Playing: Midweek: round €125; day €160. Weekend: round €125; day €160.

Facilities: Bar: 10.30am–11pm. Food: Lunch and dinner from 10am–9pm. Bar snacks.

Comments: Day fee is round on each course ... Spectacularly beautiful, very enjoyable ... What an experience ... Super course when the wind blows ... Absolute must for all golfers with stunning views and unique holes ... An absolute masterpiece.

Doonbeg Golf Club   ★★★★

Doonbeg, County Clare
Website: www.doonbeggolfclub.com
E-mail: links@doonbeggolfclub.com
Nearest main town: Kilkee

Doonbeg, spectacularly located on the west coast of County Clare, opened to great acclaim in July 2002 and has since fully lived up to its sky-high expectations. Its designer, Greg Norman, has created a links masterpiece worthy of being mentioned in the same breath as other Irish links legends such as Ballybunion and Portmarnock. The Great White Shark summed up his work of art by saying: 'It may be under 7000 yards [6885 yards, par-72 to be precise] but it will test any player in the world under any conditions.'

He's not kidding. The layout dramatically weaves its way through huge sand dunes, and the rough is, well, extremely rough. If you miss the fairways you can forget it, although to be fair you get what you deserve as the fairways are fairly generous.

First-timers will need to pull out all the stops and turn up with their A-game to register a decent score. Either that or book yourself a caddie! As with all links courses, good course management is essential; there are so many potential pitfalls waiting to trip you up, such as the 15-foot-deep bunker guarding the 11th green and some elevated, so-difficult-to-hit greens.

The round gets off to a flying start with a superb par-5 opening hole, the green nestling in a natural amphitheatre and setting the tone for a memorable round of golf. You'll also be blown away by the stunning views: a third of the holes play directly against Doughmore Bay, and you can see the Atlantic from 16 holes. Breathtaking.

Secretary: Ms C. Browne   Tel: 065 905 5246
                                        Fax: 065 905 5247

Professional: Mr B. Shaw   Tel: 065 905 5246

Playing: Midweek: round €185 (all week); day n/a. Weekend: round n/a; day n/a.

Facilities: Bar: 7am–6pm. Food: 7am–6pm. Snacks.

Comments: Simply one of the best courses I've ever played ... Does golf get any better than this? I doubt it ... Some fantastic golf holes interspersed with one or two plain ones ... It lived up to all my expectations ... Greg Norman has worked wonders.

Lahinch Golf Club (Old)   ★★★★★

Lahinch, County Clare
Website: www.lahinchgolf.com   E-mail: info@lahinchgolf.com
Nearest main town: Ennis

The small town of Lahinch overlooks Lisconnor Bay and the Cliffs of Moher, and its fabric is inextricably interwoven with the life of the golf club – hence its nickname of the Irish St Andrews. It's traditional but very fair, imposing and rewarding, and so natural you'll even see the goats milling around the course. They will tell you the weather forecast – if the goats come off the dunes and are sheltering by the clubhouse, don't bother going out: the heavens are about to open.

The Scots introduced golf to Lahinch in 1893, but it was in 1928 that Dr Alister Mackenzie, who had recently completed work at Cypress Point and was soon after to collaborate with Bobby Jones on Augusta, revised the links. Mackenzie was not allowed to touch two holes, the 5th and the 6th. The former, known as Klondyke, is a long par-4 with a second shot that has to clear a mound very much in the fashion of the 16th hole at Southport & Ainsdale. The 6th, 'Dell', is a blind par-3, an anachronism that is not without charm.

The toughest holes at Lahinch are at the end. After the short par-4 13th where a birdie is up for grabs, it just gets better and better. The par-5 14th plays to a landing area that serves the 15th as well, before running up to a green guarded on both sides by treacherous hills and impenetrable rough. You'll need to land the ball on the front of the green at the short par-4 16th before facing up to two cracking finishing holes, with the 18th playing across the 5th fairway.

The course has been subject to modifications, but the many faces of Lahinch are the products of the wind off the Atlantic that whistles through the dunes and the huge rocks and the squalls that rush in on many occasions. Members will say you can never really work out the nature of this links, but the bottom line is that if you keep it straight and are familiar with bump-and-run shots, then you cannot go too far wrong.

Secretary: Mr A. Reardon   Tel: 065 708 1003
                                         Fax: 065 708 1592
Professional: Mr R. McCavery   Tel: 065 708 1408
                                         Fax: 065 708 1592

Playing: Midweek: round €120–€125; day n/a. Weekend: round €120–€125; day n/a.

Facilities: Bar: 10.30am–11pm. Food: Breakfast, lunch and dinner from 9am–9pm. Bar snacks.

Comments: True golfer's course … Classic links made even more enjoyable by the friendly atmosphere … The whole Irish experience is tasted on the par-3 6th … Great old-fashioned links with very springy turf … The village and course as a unit are completely committed to golf … A must for all links lovers … Wonderful links with peculiar par-3 … Great welcome, facilities and course … Intriguing, immensely enjoyable links and very friendly … Devilish course with best bunkering ever seen … Remarkable course on choice piece of land … Will never forget it.

Waterville Golf Links   ★★★★★

Waterville, County Kerry
Website: www.watervillegolflinks.ie   E-mail: wvgolf@iol.ie
Nearest main town: Waterville

If it wasn't so alphabetically challenged, Waterville would appear near the top of most lists rather than near the bottom of them. On a western Irish coastline that has brought us such unforgettable giants as Ballybunion and Lahinch, Waterville, located somewhere between the two, has much about it to admire.

Surprisingly, the course is much younger than its neighbours, being opened in 1972 as the realisation of a dream for its builder, Irish-American John Mulcahy. He has a hole named after him, the 17th, which is played from an elevated tee to a green that is set amid the sort of uninhabitable gorse and rough from which balls are rarely recovered. It is 153 yards from the white tees and, known as 'Mulcahy's Peak', it is the icing on the cake of a back nine that is both long and demanding.

Waterville has a reputation as a long-hitter's course, but it is interesting to note that from the back tees Royal County Down, Royal

Portrush, Portstewart, Donegal and even Enniscrone are all longer. With three par-5s, though, it is a long way home, especially when the wind comes buffeting in over the Atlantic Ocean.

There are few more tricky long holes than the 11th, which works its way through the dunes following a thin strip of a fairway before climbing to a green. The 12th, a par-3, is another signature hole. It is played over a chasm that is protected on all sides by vast dunes. It was here in the last century that the local priest would hold secret services at a time when the Roman Catholic faith had been banned.

Secretary:	Mr N. Cronin	Tel: 066 947 4102
		Fax: 066 947 4482
Professional:	Mr L. Higgins	Tel: 066 947 4102
		Fax: 066 947 4482

Playing: Midweek: round n/a; day prices on application. Weekend: round n/a; day n/a.

Facilities: Bar: 10.30am–11pm. Food: Lunch and dinner from 10am–9pm. Bar snacks.

Comments: One of the greatest courses in the world ... The best links in the world ... Remote, wild and big ... Fantastic greens ... Remote but worth the trip for some holes of great beauty and thought ... Back nine are as good as it gets ... Some breathtaking holes ... Long, cagey course ... Back nine a slog.

Adare Manor Golf Club ★★★★

Adare, County Limerick
E-mail: golf@adaremanor.com
Nearest main town: Limerick

Secretary:	Mr M. Feane	Tel: 061 605 260
		Fax: 061 396 987
Professional:	Mr B. Shaw	

Playing: Midweek: round €120; day n/a. Weekend: round €120; day n/a.

Facilities: Bar: 10.30am–11pm. Food: Bar snacks.

Comments: A Robert Trent Jones classic ... Huge moulding gives this a very un-Irish feel ... Not what you go to Ireland for ... Not your typical Irish course ... Very American, but who cares? ... Very hard going, like the K Club ... Superb course with good bunkers and plenty of water ... Greens soft spikes only.

Ballybunion Golf Club (Cashen)   ★★★★

Sandhill Road, Ballybunion, County Kerry
Website: www.ballybuniongolfclub.ie   E-mail: bbgolfc@iol.ie
Nearest main town: Limerick

Secretary:	Mr J. McKenna	Tel: 068 27146
		Fax: 068 27387
Professional:	Mr B. O'Callaghan	Tel: 068 27842

Playing: Midweek: round €125; day €160. Weekend: round €125; day €160.

Facilities: Bar: 10.30am–11pm. Food: Lunch and dinner from 10am–9pm. Bar snacks.

Comments: Day fee is round on each course ... Great job by Robert Trent Jones ... Even though it was designed by an American, there is a magically Irish feel to this course ... Old course knocks it into a cocked hat ... Enjoyed it but was thinking about the Old course ... More difficult than the Old ... A lot bleaker than the Old course but just as enjoyable ... Amazing that this course should feel so ancient.

Ballykisteen Golf & Country Club   ★★★

Monard, County Tipperary
Nearest main town: Tipperary

Secretary:	Mrs J. Ryan	Tel: 062 33333
Professional:	Mr D. Reddan	

Playing: Midweek: round €34; day n/a. Weekend: round €38; day n/a.

Facilities: Bar: 10.30am–11pm. Food: Lunch and dinner from 11am–9pm. Bar snacks.

Comments: Warm, Irish welcome ... Welcome, people, food and course top class ... Water in play on ten holes ... Great par-3 15th ... Seemingly unnatural course that rewards all types of shot ... 15th is the most difficult par-3 in the country according to Des Smyth ... Modern course in timeless landscape ... In ten years' time everyone will be talking about this course ... Young but fast greens.

Beaufort Golf Club

Churchtown, Beaufort, Killarney, County Kerry
Website: www.beaufortgolfclub.com   E-mail: beaufortgc@eircom.net
Nearest main town: Killarney

Secretary:	Mr C. Kelly	Tel: 064 44440
		Fax: 064 44752

Professional: Mr H. Duggan

Playing: Midweek: round €45; day n/a. Weekend: round €55; day n/a.

Facilities: Bar: 10.30am–11pm. Food: Lunch and dinner from 10am–9pm. Bar snacks.

Comments: Superb setting with the McGillicuddy Reeks forming an impressive backdrop ... Historic course with ruins, natural hazards, deep bunkers, impressive foliage and multi-tiered greens ... Blind shots make this so difficult.

Castletroy Golf Club

Golf Links Road, Castletroy, Limerick, County Limerick
Website: www.castletroygolfclub.ie   E-mail: cgc@iol.ie
Nearest main town: Limerick

Secretary:	Mr P. Keane	Tel: 061 335 753
		Fax: 061 335 373

Professional: None

Playing: Midweek: round €40; day n/a. Weekend: round €50; day n/a.

Facilities: Bar: 10.30am–11pm. Food: Lunch and dinner from 10am–9pm.

Comments: Very short course that can be very flattering on your score ... Don't play it to improve your game, just for fun ... Cheap and cheerful.

Dingle Links/Ceann Sibeal ★★★★

Ballyferriter, Tralee, County Kerry
Website: www.dinglelinks.com   E-mail: dinglegc@iol.ie
Nearest main town: Tralee

Secretary:	Mr S. Fahy	Tel: 066 915 6255
		Fax: 066 915 6409

Professional: None   Tel: 066 9156 255

Playing: Midweek: round n/a; day €50–€60. Weekend: round €65–€70; day n/a.

Facilities: Bar: 11am–11pm. Food: Lunch and dinner from 10am–6pm. Bar snacks.

Comments: Magical setting overlooking Dingle Bay ... New links that's so exciting ... Wind wreaks havoc here ... Keep the ball as low as you can ... Links that simply teases you at every turn ... Evocative ... Preferred it to more prestigious courses in the area ... Very welcoming ... Very sandy and difficult ... Love this place ... A natural course with fine character.

Charleville Golf Club   ★★★

Charleville, County Cork
Website: www.charlevillegolf.com   E-mail: charlevillegolf@eircom.net
Nearest main town: Charleville

Secretary: Mr J. Murphy   Tel: 063 81257
                                            Fax: 063 81274
Professional: Mr D. Keating   Tel: 063 21269

Playing: Midweek: round €30; day n/a. Weekend: round €35; day n/a.

Facilities: Bar: 11am–11pm. Food: Lunch and dinner from 11am–9pm. Bar snacks.

Comments: Busy parkland ... Short but really nice ... Not particularly well regarded in Cork.

Clonmel Golf Club   ★

Lyreanearla, Clonmel, County Tipperary
Website: www.clonmelgolfclub.com   E-mail: cgc@indigo.ie
Nearest main town: Clonmel

Secretary: Ms A. Myles-Keating Tel: 052 24050
                  (Manager)   Fax: 052 83349
Professional: Mr R. Hayes   Tel: 052 24050

Playing: Midweek: round €30; day n/a. Weekend: round €35; day n/a. Prices may increase in 2004.

Facilities: Bar: 10.30am–11pm. Food: Bar snacks.

Comments: Open, bland course ... Very short on length and interest ... Gives you the freedom to open your shoulders off the tee ... A real driver's course with room for error ... Inland course of little standing.

Cork Golf Club ★★★★

Little Island, Cork, County Cork
Nearest main town: Cork

Secretary:	Mr M. Sands	Tel: 021 435 3451
		Fax: 021 435 3410
Professional:	Mr P. Hickey	Tel: 021 435 3421

Playing: Midweek: round €80; day n/a. Weekend: round €90; day n/a.

Facilities: Bar: 10.30am–11pm. Food: Breakfast, lunch and dinner from 9am–9pm. Bar snacks.

Comments: Excellent condition and plenty of birdie chances ... Touched by the hand of Alister Mackenzie ... Great club with course to match ... Not very exhilarating, but a fair technical challenge ... Prime condition ... Play here on the way to the Old Head of Kinsale further south.

County Tipperary Golf & Country Club ★★★★

Dundrum House Hotel, Dundrum, Cashel, County Tipperary
Website: www.dundrumhousehotel.com   E-mail: dundrumh@iol.ie
Nearest main town: Cashel

Secretary:	Mr W. Crowe	Tel: 062 71116
		Fax: 062 71366
Professional:	None	

Playing: Midweek: round €45; day n/a. Weekend: round €55; day n/a.

Facilities: Bar: 10.30am–11pm. Food: Breakfast, lunch and dinner from 7am–10pm. Bar snacks.

Comments: Back nine is where course really impresses ... Good use of water on some holes ... Unique Irish course designed by Philip Walton ... You can feel the American influences here ... Nice use of man-made hazards ... Hotel, converted from 18th-century manor, makes this a quality weekend getaway destination.

Dooks Golf Club ★★★★

Glenbeigh, County Kerry
Website: www.dooks.com   E-mail: office@dooks.com
Nearest main town: Kerry

Secretary: Mr D. Mangan   Tel: 066 976 8205
                                       Fax: 066 976 8476

Professional: None

Playing: Midweek: round €48; day n/a. Weekend: round €48;
                   day n/a.

Facilities: Bar: 10.30am–11pm. Food: Lunch and dinner from
                   12pm–9pm. Bar snacks.

Comments: Not to be missed ... Tough links with friendly welcome
                   and good food ... Always easy to get a game, lovely
                   scenery and friendly members ... Gem of a course with
                   interesting holes and warm welcome.

Dromoland Golf & Country Club ★★★

Dromoland, Newmarket-on-Fergus, County Clare
Website: www.dromoland.ie   E-mail: golf@dromoland.ie
Nearest main town: Limerick

Secretary: Mr J. O'Halloran   Tel: 061 368 444
                                       Fax: 061 368 498
Professional: Mr D. Foley   Tel: 061 368 444
                                       Fax: 061 368 498

Playing: Midweek: round €100; day n/a. Weekend: round €100;
                   day n/a.

Facilities: Bar: 10.30am–11pm. Food: Lunch and dinner from
                   10.30am–9pm. Bar snacks.

Comments: Set in the grounds of a magnificent castle ... Subtle
                   greens with hard-to-read breaks ... Lack of length coun-
                   tered by blind tee shots and sculpted greens ... Not
                   given the recognition it deserves ... Played badly but
                   eyes were open to the quality of the course ... Rolling
                   fairways ... Greens a pleasure to putt on.

Dungarvan Golf Club ★★

Knocknagranagh, Dungarvan, County Waterford
Website: www.dungarvangolfclub.com
E-mail: dungarvangc@eircom.net
Nearest main town: Waterford

Secretary:	Ms I. Howell	Tel: 058 43310 (Ext 20)
		Fax: 058 44113
Professional:	Mr D. Hayes	Tel: 058 44707

Playing: Midweek: round €30; day n/a. Weekend: round €40; day n/a.

Facilities: Bar: 10.30am–11pm. Food: Lunch and dinner from 12pm–9pm. Bar snacks.

Comments: Excellent variety of holes on a course that is improving all the time ... Comeragh Mountains provide the backdrop ... Weak course where all the hazards are man-made ... Average standard on not-too-difficult course.

Ennis Golf Club ★

Drumbiggle, Ennis, County Clare
Website: www.ennisgolfclub.com   E-mail: egc@eircom.net
Nearest main town: Ennis

Secretary:	Mr N. O'Donnell	Tel: 065 682 4074
	(Club Manager)	Fax: 065 684 1848
Professional:	Mr M. Ward	Tel: 065 682 4074

Playing: Midweek: round €30; day n/a. Weekend: round €35; day n/a.

Facilities: Bar: 10.30am–11pm. Food: Bar snacks.

Comments: Basic course with few features ... Course can get heavy underfoot ... Enniscrone yes, Ennis no ... Very picturesque ... Part mature woodland, part downland ... Cheerful, straightforward layout ... Good for friendly and family golf.

Faithlegg Golf Club   ★★★

Faithlegg, County Waterford
E-mail: darraghtighe@hotmail.com
Nearest main town: Waterford

Secretary:	Mr D. Tighe	Tel: 051 382 241
		Fax: 051 382 664
Professional:	Mr D. Tighe	Tel: 051 382 241
		Fax: 051 382 664

Playing: Midweek: round €40; day n/a. Weekend: round €55; day n/a. Prices may increase in 2004.

Facilities: Bar: 11am–11pm. Food: Lunch from 12pm–5pm. Dinner by arrangement.

Comments: Mature trees give this course an established feel ... Not always in top condition but I always return ... A little tricked up with hazards not visible from the tee ... Be on your guard, this course will catch you.

Kenmare Golf Club   ★★★

Kenmare, County Kerry
Nearest main town: Killarney

Secretary:	Mr M. MacGearailt	Tel: 064 41291
		Fax: 064 42061
Professional:	None	

Playing: Midweek: round €42 (Mon–Sat); day n/a. Weekend: round €50 (Sun); day n/a.

Facilities: Bar: 10.30am–11pm. Food: Bar snacks.

Comments: Not a difficult course but overall craic makes it a pleasant walk ... Par-3 17th a fun hole ... Nine holes in the valley very charming ... Small course with a lot going for it ... Open course, very enjoyable for the higher handicapper.

Killarney Golf & Fishing Club (Killeen)   ★★★★

Mahoney's Point, Killarney, County Kerry
Website: www.killarney-golf.com
E-mail: reservations@killarney-golf.com
Nearest main town: Killarney

Secretary:	Mr T. Prendergast	Tel: 064 31034
		Fax: 064 33065
Professional:	Mr T. Coveney	Tel: 064 31615

Playing: Midweek: round €75–80; day n/a. Weekend: round €75–80; day n/a.

Facilities: Bar: 10.30am–11pm. Food: Lunch and dinner from 10am–9pm. Bar snacks.

Comments: Lovely surroundings to a very special course ... From the back tees fairways look very narrow ... An amazing challenge with trouble everywhere ... Wonderful, scenic course, not overlong for amateurs ... Great setting with course in superb condition ... Epitome of the idyllic – great courses, great people and great food and drink.

Killarney Golf & Fishing Club (Mahoney's Point) ★★★★

Mahoney's Point, Killarney, County Kerry
Website: www.killarney-golf.com
E-mail: reservations@killarney-golf.com
Nearest main town: Killarney

Secretary:	Mr T. Prendergast	Tel: 064 31034
		Fax: 064 33065
Professional:	Mr T. Coveney	Tel: 064 31615

Playing: Midweek: round €75–80; day n/a. Weekend: round €75–80; day n/a.

Facilities: Bar: 10.30am–11pm. Food: Lunch and dinner from 10am–9pm. Bar snacks.

Comments: Course in exceptional condition with great views everywhere ... Finishes with the toughest of tough par-3s ... Great finish ... Doesn't compare to the Killeen ... Play them both in the same day – an awesome, life-changing experience.

Killorglin Golf Course ★★★

Stealroe, Killorglin, County Kerry
Website: www.killorglingolf.ie   E-mail: kilgolf@iol.ie
Nearest main town: Killarney

Secretary:	Mr B. Dodd	Tel: 066 976 1979
		Fax: 066 976 1437

Professional: Mr H. Duggan

Playing: Midweek: round €25; day n/a. Weekend: round €30; day n/a.

Facilities: Bar: 10.30am–11pm. Food: Bar snacks.

Comments: Played it when first opened – great ... Fairly easy despite small greens ... Overlooking Dingle Bay, this is cheap and cheerful ... Homely place where staff will arrange anything for you ... Great welcome at this testing, enjoyable course.

Lahinch Golf Club (Castle)   ★★★★

Lahinch, County Clare
Website: www.lahinchgolf.com   E-mail: info@lahinchgolf.com
Nearest main town: Ennis

Secretary: Mr A. Reardon   Tel: 065 708 1003
                                       Fax: 065 708 1592
Professional: Mr R. McCavery   Tel: 065 708 1408
                                       Fax: 065 708 1592

Playing: Midweek: round €50; day n/a. Weekend: round €50; day n/a.

Facilities: Bar: 10.30am–11pm. Food: Breakfast, lunch and dinner from 9am–9pm. Bar snacks.

Comments: Classic links track which is worth a visit in its own right ... Loved it ... Perfect partner to the Old course ... Underrated with holes that would not be out of place on the Old ... Shorter and easier, but a nice test.

The Lee Valley Golf & Country Club   ★★★

Clashanure, Ovens, County Cork
Website: www.leevalleygc.ie   E-mail: leevalleygolfclub@eircom.net
Nearest main town: Cork

Secretary: Ms C. Nyhan   Tel: 021 733 1721
                                       Fax: 021 733 1695
Professional: Mr J. Savage   Tel: 021 733 1759
                                       Fax: 021 733 1695

Playing: Midweek: round €40; day n/a. Weekend: round €45; day n/a.

Facilities: Bar: 10.30am–11pm. Food: Breakfast, lunch and dinner from 9am–9pm. Bar snacks.

Comments: New course designed by Christy O'Connor Jnr ... Very busy ... A course that caters for every standard of player ... Not much substance ... Take your time over every shot – you will have to ... Crowded course, not what I wanted from golf in Ireland ... Hilly, parkland course ... Unspectacular site for unspectacular design ... Facilities second to none.

Limerick County Golf & Country Club ★★★

Ballyneety, County Limerick
Website: www.limerickcounty.com
Nearest main town: Limerick

Secretary:	Mr J. Heaton	Tel: 061 351 881
	(Manager)	Fax: 061 351 384
Professional:	Mr P. Murphy	Tel: 061 351 874

Playing: Midweek: round €40 (Mon–Thurs); day n/a. Weekend: round €60 (Fri–Sun); day n/a.

Facilities: Bar: 10.30am–11pm. Food: Lunch and dinner from 10am–9pm.

Comments: The bar is out of this world ... A Des Smyth design, fairly unusual for a modern course ... Blind drives and deep bunkers give an old-style feel to a relatively new course ... Unusual clubhouse ... Great venue for matchplay golf.

Mallow Golf Club ★★

Ballyellis, Mallow, County Cork
E-mail: golfmall@gofree.indigo.ie
Nearest main town: Mallow

Secretary:	Mr D. Curtin	Tel: 022 21145
	(Secretary/Manager)	Fax: 022 42501
Professional:	Mr S. Conway	Tel: 022 42434

Playing: Midweek: round €35; day n/a. Weekend: round €40; day n/a.

Facilities: Bar: 10.30am–11pm. Food: Breakfast, lunch and dinner from 11am–9pm. Bar snacks.

Comments: Tree-lined parkland beauty ... Nice condition for this friendly club ... Nothing spectacular, but good honest golf.

Monkstown Golf Club ★

Monkstown, County Cork
Website: www.monkstowngolfclub.com
E-mail: office@monkstowngolfclub.com
Nearest main town: Cork

Secretary:	Mr H. Madden	Tel: 021 486 3910
		Fax: 021 484 1722
Professional:	Mr B. Murphy	Tel: 021 486 3912
		Fax: 021 484 1722

Playing: Midweek: round €37; day n/a. Weekend: round €44; day n/a.

Facilities: Bar: 10.30am–11pm. Food: Lunch and dinner from 12pm–9pm.

Comments: Scenic views of Cork Harbour ... Bunkers absolutely everywhere ... Bizarre bunkering ... Parkland course where accuracy is your watchword ... Fair value on this testing track.

Muskerry Golf Club ★

Carrigrohane, County Cork
Nearest main town: Blarney

Secretary:	Mr H. Gallagher	Tel: 021 438 5297
		Fax: 021 451 6860
Professional:	Mr M. Lehane	Tel: 021 438 1445

Playing: Midweek: round €35; day n/a. Weekend: round €45; day n/a.

Facilities: Bar: 10.30am–11pm. Food: Bar snacks.

Comments: Epitome of golf in Ireland ... Good value course, good craic ... Great welcome ... Course is so-so but the bar is always buzzing ... 16th and 17th across the river are the best holes.

Old Head Golf Club ★★★★

Kinsale, County Cork
Website: www.oldheadgolf.ie
Nearest main town: Kinsale

Secretary: Mr J. O'Brien

Tel: 021 477 8444
Fax: 021 477 8022

Professional: Mr D. Murray

Playing: Midweek: round €250; day €250. Weekend: round €250; day €250.

Facilities: Bar: 10.30am–11pm. Food: Breakfast, lunch and dinner from 9am–9pm. Bar snacks.

Comments: Unbelievable location ... Destined to be a classic ... You feel on the edge of the world ... In places you simply hit the ball out to sea ... I've just played the best course in the world ... Gobsmacked ... Course shut half the year and on some days is simply unplayable ... The most amazing experience ... A little haphazard but no complaints about the scenery.

Parknasilla Golf Club ★★★

Great Southern Hotel, Parknasilla, County Kerry
Website: www.gshotels.com   E-mail: res@parknasilla-gsh.com
Nearest main town: Sneem

Secretary: Mr M. Walsh

Tel: 064 45122
Fax: 064 45323

Professional: None

Playing: Midweek: round n/a; day €30. Weekend: round €30; day n/a.

Facilities: Bar: 10.30am–11pm. Food: Breakfast, lunch and dinner from 9am–9pm. Bar snacks.

Comments: Best nine-hole course ever played ... Location, location, location ... Unique nine-hole course of beauty and tranquillity ... Overlooking Kenmare Bay.

Shannon Golf Club ★★★

Shannon, County Clare
E-mail: shannongolfclub@eircom.net
Nearest main town: Shannon

Secretary:	Mr M. Corry	Tel: 061 471 849
		Fax: 061 471 507
Professional:	Mr A. Pyke	Tel: 061 471 551

Playing: Midweek: round €40; day n/a. Weekend: round €50; day n/a.

Facilities: Bar: 10.30am–11pm. Food: Breakfast, lunch and dinner from 9am–9pm. Bar snacks.

Comments: A mix of links and parkland ... Highlight is the 216-yard par-3 over the estuary ... Very tight course with character ... Water hazards the primary defence ... Rough can get high ... Pop off the plane and onto the course ... Tight, but you are lost without the driver ... Site of Greg Norman's famous 370-yard drive ... Front nine a hellish challenge.

Tralee Golf Club ★★★★

West Barrow, Ardfert, County Kerry
Website: www.traleegolfclub.com
E-mail: info@traleegolfclub.com or reservations@traleegolfclub.com
Nearest main town: Tralee

Secretary:	Mr A. Byrne	Tel: 066 713 6379
	(General Manager)	Fax: 066 713 6008
Professional:	Mr D. Power	Tel: 066 713 6379
		Fax: 066 713 6008

Playing: Midweek: round €150; day n/a. Weekend: round €150; day n/a.

Facilities: Bar: 10.30am–11pm. Food: Lunch and dinner from 10am–11pm. Bar snacks.

Comments: Visually stunning ... Very exciting ... Best back nine in Ireland ... Memorable holes ... What views, what greens, what a privilege to play there ... Best-ever welcome ... Palmer really worked his magic here.

Tramore Golf Club ★★★★

Newtown Hill, Tramore, County Waterford
Website: www.tramoregolfclub.com   E-mail: tragolf@oil.ie
Nearest main town: Waterford

Secretary: Mr E. Power   Tel: 051 386 170
                                    Fax: 051 390 961
Professional: None

Playing: Midweek: round €40 (May–Sept), €35 (Apr & Oct), €30
                  (Nov–Mar); day n/a. Weekend: round €55 (May–Sept),
                  €45 (Apr & Oct), €30 (Nov–Mar); day n/a.

Facilities: Bar: 10.30am–11pm. Food: Breakfast, lunch and
                  dinner from 9am–9pm. Bar snacks.

Comments: Great experience both on and off the course ... Stormy
                  weather has been known ... Very exposed and cold ...
                  Welcoming club with well-groomed course ... Fair test
                  for club golfer ... Lovely set-up at this club with warm,
                  friendly members.

Waterford Golf Club ★★

Newrath, Waterford, County Waterford
Website: www.waterfordgolfclub.com
E-mail: info@waterfordgolfclub.com
Nearest main town: Waterford

Secretary: Mr J. Condon   Tel: 051 876 748
                  (Secretary/Manager) Fax: 051 853 405
Professional: Mr B. McDermott   Tel: 051 833 711

Playing: Midweek: round €35; day n/a. Weekend: round €45;
                  day n/a.

Facilities: Bar: 10.30am–11pm. Food: Lunch and dinner from
                  12pm–9pm. Bar snacks.

Comments: Fairly dour parkland course ... Had to wait until the 18th
                  for the best hole ... Overshadowed by the other
                  Waterford (Castle) ... Pleasant enough, but I like a chal-
                  lenge ... Humdrum parkland course ... Fine day out
                  and the company is excellent.

Waterford Castle Hotel & Golf Club ★★

The Island, Waterford, County Waterford
Website: www.waterfordcastle.com
E-mail: golf@waterfordcastle.com
Nearest main town: Waterford

Secretary:	Mr T. Browne	Tel: 051 871 633
		Fax: 051 871 634
Professional:	Mr M. Garland	Tel: 051 871 633
	(Director of Golf)	Fax: 051 871 634

Playing: Midweek: round €49 (other prices on application); day n/a. Weekend: round €59 (other prices on application); day n/a.

Facilities: Bar: 10.30am–11pm. Food: Bar snacks.

Comments: Des Smyth design ... On-site hotel a real treat, albeit expensive ... Large greens ... Unremarkable land on which to build a course ... Course sits on island in the River Suir ... A flat, featureless course ... Wide open – get your driver out ... Clever design ... With such flat, boring land it's a credit to Smyth for his design.

West Waterford Golf & Country Club ★★★

Dungarvan, County Waterford
Website: www.westwaterfordgolf.com
E-mail: info@westwaterfordgolf.com
Nearest main town: Waterford

Secretary:	Mr T. Whelan	Tel: 058 43216/41475
		Fax: 058 44343
Professional:	None	Tel: 058 43216/41475
		Fax: 058 44343

Playing: Midweek: round €30; day n/a. Weekend: round €40; day n/a.

Facilities: Bar: 10.30am–11pm. Food: Lunch and dinner from 10am–9pm. Bar snacks.

Comments: Excellent greens for what is a young course ... Most natural course ... Contrasting nines ... Set by the Brickey River ... Panoramic views of County Waterford ... Great Irish welcome.

Leinster

Carton House Golf Club ★★★★

Maynooth, County Kildare
Website: www.carton.ie
Nearest main town: Maynooth

Carton House is just a short drive away from the prestigious K Club, the venue for the 2006 Ryder Cup, and it makes a very worthy neighbour indeed. In fact, the biggest compliment you can pay this outstanding new golfing venue is that in no way is Carton House overshadowed by the special K Club.

The new star attraction at Carton is Colin Montgomerie's superb 7300-yard inland links-style layout, which opened in summer 2003. Monty has produced a real cracker of a course that is surely destined for great things and big tournaments.

It's so links-like that you expect to see and hear the waves lashing the walls of the 1100-acre estate of Carton Demesne, formerly the ancestral home of the Earls of Kildare. With strategically placed penal pot bunkers and rough, as well as run-offs into cavernous swales, you need to plot your way around this one carefully. Precision all-round play is the name of the game on the Montgomerie, with the emphasis firmly on deadly accurate approach shots to the giant rolling greens, which demand red-hot putting.

In comparison, the O'Meara layout – which was of course designed by 1998 Open and US Masters champion Mark O'Meara – is literally a stroll in the park, though that too needs to be treated with the utmost respect if you're to register a decent score. The 7006-yard, par-72 course really bursts into life on the back nine, the superb par-5 15th, with its green lying tantalisingly on the other side of the River Rye, being sandwiched in between a couple of cracking par-3s. Definitely two rounds to remember.

Secretary:	Mr J. Lawler	Tel: 062 86271
	(Golf operations)	Fax: 062 86555
Professional:	Mr D. Fleming	Tel: 062 86271
Playing:	Midweek: round €70 (winter), €125 (summer); day n/a. Weekend: round n/a; day n/a.	
Facilities:	Bar: 8am–8pm (winter), 7am–11.30pm (summer). Food: 9am–7pm (winter), 10am–9pm (summer).	

Comments: I much prefer the Montgomerie, it's a real class act ... The O'Meara course has some fantastic holes and some fairly ordinary ones too ... It's as good as if not better than the K Club ... It's just a top place to play golf ... When Monty eventually hangs up his clubs he should take up course design full-time ... A brand new clubhouse is due to open May 2004 while also set to open in the summer of 2004 is a National Golf Academy featuring a floodlit driving range ... There's also a large practice area and practice putting green.

County Louth Golf Club

Baltray, Drogheda, County Louth
Website: www.countylouthgolfclub.com
E-mail: reservations@countylouthgolfclub.com
Nearest main town: Drogheda

One of the beauties about books such as this is that attention can be drawn to some of those courses which, for some inexplicable reason, continue to be overlooked by many a discerning traveller. Here we can shout the name from the rooftops, or at least from the top of the page, and persuade golfers to dig out their maps and discover some unsung gems.

Like the little fishing port of Baltray, for example, which can be found roughly an hour's drive north of Dublin and is home to the invigorating links of County Louth. Tom Simpson, one of the great course architects of his time, redesigned much of the layout in 1938, giving it a subtlety and charm that is still evident today.

A couple of tough opening holes, a long par-4 followed by a none-too-easy par-5, get you off to a brisk start, but it is the coastal holes on the back nine, the 12th and 13th, that will be the most memorable.

Baltray's short holes are also exceptionally good and there are really only two areas that may not be up to scratch. The fields on the inland side of the property detract a little from the overall feel and the two finishing holes do not have quite the character of the 16 that went before. Those can be the only reasons that County Louth is not up there with the Portmarnocks and European Clubs, also found on the east coast.

Secretary: Mr M. Delany   Tel: 041 988 1530
                                        Fax: 041 988 1531
Professional: Mr P. McGuirk   Tel: 041 988 1530

Playing: Midweek: round €95; day n/a. Weekend: round €120; day n/a.

Facilities: Bar: 10.30am–11pm. Food: Lunch and dinner from 10am–9pm. Bar snacks.

Comments: One of the best in Ireland … Classic and very enjoyable … Food always good … A refined course, not as wild as some other renowned courses … Difficult to get on due to competitions.

The European Club   ★★★★★

Brittas Bay, Wicklow, County Wicklow
Website: www.theeuropeanclub.com
E-mail: info@theeuropeanclub.com
Nearest main town: Wicklow

You may never have the pleasure of meeting Pat Ruddy, which is something of a shame. The man is a character in the truest sense of the word. He is a writer, a designer of courses, the father of five children and a man capable of turning down £22.5 million in cash. Is he mad? Well, some might say quite possibly. Those who have visited the European Club, however, might begin to understand how money can fade into obscurity in the face of a proud and rugged links.

Ruddy was offered that money to part with the European, an inspirational place that was designed and built by him on the east coast of Ireland some 30 miles south of Dublin. A new traditional links is a rare animal indeed, but it has been achieved here with fabulous results. The course is right up there with the best of Ireland's many majestic seaside tests.

There are some cracking holes both for aesthetic appeal and for pure shot-making ability. The 7th, for example, which sneaks along the lowland at the bottom edge of the course and is sandwiched between the dunes and the fluffy tops of the reeds in the marshland. Anything right here and you're dead.

When *Golf World* first visited the site in the shape of our reporter at that time, Dominic Pedler, Ruddy was so pleased with the publicity that he offered to name a part of the course after him. So the huge dune to the left of the 12th has been christened 'Pedler's White Knuckle'.

Secretary: Mr S. Ruddy   Tel: 0404 47415
                                         Fax: 0404 47449
Professional: None

Playing: Midweek: round €125 (any day Apr–Oct), €75 (any day Nov–Mar); day n/a. Weekend: round n/a; day n/a.

Facilities: Bar: Wine bar open all day. Food: Breakfast, lunch and dinner from 9am–9pm. Bar snacks.

Comments: Each hole a classic ... Very difficult links ... What a place! ... Easy to get a game on a beautiful links ... Outstanding welcome, manager even joined us for lunch ... Very demanding and exciting ... 7th and 17th are great holes ... Tough course with excellent greens ... Wonderful charm and hospitality.

The K Club (South)   ★★★★

Kildare Hotel & Country Club, Straffan, County Kildare
Website: www.kclub.ie
Nearest main town: Dublin

The legendary Arnold Palmer has created a spectacular layout that is destined for great things, quickly being pencilled in to stage the 2004 Smurfit European Open. The 7277-yard, par-72 (off the back tees) layout opened last July and superbly complements the existing North course, the two courses combining to make the K Club one of the hottest golfing properties in Europe.

Veteran Palmer is justifiably thrilled to bits with his latest work of art, saying: 'It's a very unique course in Europe. The large undulating fairways and greens, with numerous well-placed bunkers, make for a truly exciting challenge.' That just about hits the nail bang on the head, especially as far as the par-5 signature 7th hole is concerned. Aesthetically it's a stunner, with a man-made rockface, featuring waterfalls and cascades, rising 60 feet out of the lake bordering the right side of the fairway.

Obviously it's a championship-standard course, so you expect a severe test of golf, and make no mistake: that's exactly what you get – there's rough, bunkers and water galore. And if you're fortunate enough to get the chance to play it, you really do need to concentrate until the bitter end, because the last six holes all feature water, culminating at the 578-yard, par-5 18th complete with island green. A dramatic finale to a memorable round.

Secretary: Mr P. Crowe   Tel: 01 601 7362
                 (Director of Golf)   Fax: 01 601 7399
Professional: Mr J. McHenry   Tel: 01 601 7321

Playing: Midweek: round €265 all week; day n/a. Weekend: round n/a; day n/a.

Facilities: Bar: 11am–11.30pm. Food: 12pm–9.45pm.

Comments: A golfer's paradise ... A once-in-a-lifetime golfing experience ... It was expensive but it is a special course and a special venue ... If and when I can afford it, I'll be back ... Not quite as good as the older North course, but give it time.

Mount Juliet Golf Club   ★★★★

Thomastown, County Kilkenny
Website: www.mountjuliet.com   E-mail: golfinfo@mountjuliet.com
Nearest main town: Kilkenny

Mount Juliet is blessed with some of the finest natural scenery Ireland has to offer: the outcroppings of the Kilkenny countryside, ancient trees, gullies, copses and the furious rushing of the River Nore, which is rich in salmon and trout. It is one of the best parkland courses in the country and was designed by none other than Jack Nicklaus.

That's not to say that it has been without criticism. Many say you could transplant this course to any country in the world and it would not look out of place. They claim the excessive moulding, shifting and manipulation of the landscape is completely out of place with the feel and look of this corner of Ireland – in short, that Mount Juliet is an artificial course with no soul.

Whether you take this view or not, you cannot fault its condition. One journalist noted that the fairways are made from the same material as the carpets laid down when Prince Charles attends movie premieres; and that, even in the dead of winter, is hard to argue with. There are regiments of maintenance workers grooming the course and you can see golfers almost embarrassed to take a divot out of the fairways.

It is also very fair, some might say easy. Off the tee there is little trouble with wide, generous fairways and even the greens are large. The majestic oak and lime trees that pepper the landscape rarely affect the line of shots into the greens. Nicklaus designs have become more lenient, but it seems there has been a policy that Mount Juliet should be fun and you should not walk off the course hanging your head like a tired dog.

Water is the main form of defence at Mount Juliet, fronting the par-3 3rd and the par-4 13th. It also protects the 18th, a climactic finish that sums up everything about this modern course.

Secretary:	Mr S. O'Neill	Tel: 056 777 3064
	(Golf Manager)	Fax: 056 777 3078
Professional:	Mr S. Cotter	Tel: 056 777 3071
		Fax: 056 777 3078

Playing: Midweek: round €115 (Apr), €140 (May–Sept); day n/a. Weekend: round €125 (Fri–Sun, Apr), €155 (Fri–Sun, May–Sept); day n/a.

Facilities: Bar: 10.30am–11pm. Food: Breakfast, lunch and dinner from 9am–9pm. Bar snacks.

Comments: What every golf course should aspire to … Best parkland course in Europe … One of the best new courses in Ireland … A Nicklaus cracker … Doesn't necessarily fit into the landscape but good nonetheless … Vast contoured greens … One of Jack's best … Didn't want to go home … Basic Nicklaus fare, very unnatural … Cracking par-3 3rd.

Portmarnock Golf Club (Old)   ★★★★★

Portmarnock, County Dublin
Website: www.portmarnockgolfclub.ie
Nearest main town: Dublin

Few courses are blessed with the natural magnificence of Portmarnock. Set on a long tongue of links land between the Irish Sea and an inland tidal bay, Portmarnock is magnificently cut off from the world, a private playground for golfers in search of hidden delights. The holes run through dune grasses and are completely at the mercy of the wind, which rushes in from the sea, quickly changing the moods and toughness of the challenge.

Portmarnock is relatively flat and devoid of any blind shots, but that does not mean the course is monotonous or boring. Instead, you will find a collection of holes that are very exciting, ranging from short holes that require great thought and clever execution of shots, to long holes where brute strength and a daredevil game plan will pay dividends.

Never is this more clearly evident than at the 6th, one of the best holes on the front nine but long at 586 yards. Along its dimpled fairways and valleys, it can be three woods to reach the green, so big hitters are at an advantage. But immediately, at the 7th, the emphasis changes with a short hole played into a dell, where you really need to get a feel for the shot.

This delicate balance continues around the turn with more good examples at the 14th, a shortish par-4 with a second shot to a long plateau green among the dunes, and the 15th, a brutish par-3 where, depending on the wind, you will have to set the ball off over the out-of-bounds line and bring it back in on the wind. From there, it is a cracking finish, with the 17th, a penal par-4 where you'll do well to stay out of the bunkers, and the 18th, a fine hole, although it has lost some of its eccentricity since the home green was moved from hard by the club-house.

On a fine day there are few better places in Ireland to play golf than at Portmarnock. And with Portmarnock Links nearby, you don't need much more encouragement.

Secretary:	Mr J. Quigley	Tel: 01 846 2968
		Fax: 01 846 2601
Professional:	Mr J. Purcell	Tel: 01 846 2634

Playing: Midweek: round €165; day n/a. Weekend: round €190; day n/a.

Facilities: Bar: 10.30am–11pm. Food: Lunch and dinner from 11am–9pm. Bar snacks.

Comments: Brilliant course and an outstanding pro shop ... Classic links that does not suffer fools gladly ... Not a patch on County Down or Sligo ... Fair links unlike many of the heralded ones in Ireland ... Had the time of my life ... Who could criticise this outstanding piece of natural golfing terrain? ... Expected a lot but nothing prepared me for this ... Quite simply the best course in the British Isles.

Black Bush Golf Club   ★★

Thomastown, Dunshaughlin, County Meath
E-mail: golf@blackbush.iol.ie
Nearest main town: Dublin

Secretary:	Mr M. Connellan	Tel: 01 825 0021
		Fax: 01 825 0400
Professional:	Mr S. O'Grady	Tel: 01 825 0793
		Fax: 01 825 0400

Playing: Midweek: round €30; day n/a. Weekend: round €45; day n/a.

Facilities: Bar: 10.30am–11pm. Food: Lunch and dinner from 10am–9pm. Bar snacks.

Comments: A young club with great potential – very friendly ... Exciting 1st with drive over the lake ... Superb facilities ... Par-4s cater for average player ... Plenty of short par-4s.

Carlow Golf Club ★★★★

Deerpark, Carlow, County Carlow
Website: www.carlowgolfclub.com
E-mail: carlowgolfclub@eircom.net
Nearest main town: Carlow

Secretary:	Mr D. MacSweeney	Tel: 0503 31695
		Fax: 0503 40065
Professional:	Mr A. Gilbert	Tel: 0503 41745
		Fax: 0503 41745

Playing: Midweek: round €45; day n/a. Weekend: round €60; day n/a.

Facilities: Bar: 9.30am–11pm. Food: Breakfast, lunch and dinner from 9.30am–10pm. Bar snacks.

Comments: 16th and 17th are outstanding holes ... Always on my list to play ... Parkland with the best greens in Ireland ... Excellent value with panoramic view from the 8th tee ... All the challenges laid out fairly in front of you ... Well-thought-out layout with subtle protection to good scoring – liked it a lot ... Finishing hole is a par-5 falling all the way down to the clubhouse.

Castlewarden Golf & Country Club ★

Straffan, County Kildare
Website: www.castlewardengolfclub.com
Nearest main town: Dublin

Secretary:	Ms F. Kane	Tel: 01 458 9254
		Fax: 01 458 8972
Professional:	Mr G. Egan	Tel: 01 458 8219

Playing: Midweek: round €32 (Mon–Thurs before 1pm), €40 (after 2pm), €42 (Fri); day n/a. Weekend: round n/a; day n/a.

Facilities: Bar: 10.30am–11pm. Food: Lunch and dinner from 12pm–9pm.

Comments: Fairly new course with views of the Wicklow mountains
... Under ten years old with the best yet to come ... Nice
welcome at this attractive, basic course.

Charlesland Golf & Country Club   ★★★

Charlesland, Greystones, County Wicklow
Website: www.charlesland.com   E-mail: info@charlesland.com
Nearest main town: Dublin

Secretary:	Mr P. Bradshaw	Tel: 01 287 8200
		Fax: 01 287 8136
Professional:	Mr P. Duignan	Tel: 01 287 4350
		Fax: 01 287 4360

Playing: Midweek: round €45 (Mon–Thurs); day n/a. Weekend:
round €60 (Fri–Sun); day n/a.

Facilities: Bar: 10.30am–11pm. Food: Bar snacks.

Comments: Water hazards form course defence ... Not overly
impressed ... Setting can't be faulted ... Best views from
the 13th ... Located in the shadow of Sugarloaf
Mountain ... Club with friendly attitude.

Clontarf Golf Club   ★

Donnycarney House, Malahide Road, Dublin, County Dublin
Website: www.clontarfgolfclub.ie   E-mail: info.cgc@indigo.ie
Nearest main town: Dublin

Secretary:	Mr A. Cahill	Tel: 01 833 1892
		Fax: 01 833 1933
Professional:	Mr M. Callan	Tel: 01 833 1877
		Fax: 01 833 1933

Playing: Midweek: round €60; day n/a. Weekend: round €60;
day n/a.

Facilities: Bar: 10.30am–11pm. Food: Bar snacks.

Comments: Parkland course in Dublin suburbs ... Nearest course to
Dublin ... A little overused ... Clubhouse the star ...
12th played over a quarry ... Watch out for the trains
rattling by.

Courtown Golf Club ★★★

Kiltennel, Gorey, County Wexford
Website: www.courtowngolfclub.com   E-mail: courtown@iol.ie
Nearest main town: Gorey

Secretary: Mr D. Cleere   Tel: 055 25166
                                      Fax: 055 25553
Professional: Mr J. Coone   Tel: 055 25166

Playing: Midweek: round €38; day n/a. Weekend: round €43;
                  day n/a.

Facilities: Bar: 10.30am–11pm. Food: Lunch and dinner from
                  10am–9pm.

Comments: Friendly, quality golf ... Venue for learners ... Very few
                  doglegs ... Nice alternative to nearby 'super courses'
                  like the European ... Cheap and cheerful holiday golf
                  ... Needs toughening up ... Parkland course that
                  deserves praise.

Deer Park Golf Club ★★★

Deer Park Hotel, Howth Demesne, Howth, County Dublin
Nearest main town: Dublin

Secretary: Mr D. Daly   Tel: 01 832 3489
                                      Fax: 01 839 2405
Professional: None

Playing: Midweek: round €7.50–€8 (9 holes), €15.50–€16 (18
                  holes); day n/a. Weekend: round €11–€11.50 (9 holes),
                  €22.50–€23 (18 holes); day n/a.

Facilities: Bar: 10.30am–11pm. Food: Breakfast, lunch and
                  dinner from 7am–10pm. Bar snacks.

Comments: Huge golf complex with fine facilities ... Great value ...
                  A kind of hypermarket for all your golfing needs ...
                  Subtle course ... Very busy course – was it worth the
                  effort? ... Don't listen to the snobs, this is a great facility
                  for the high handicapper ... Boasts itself as Ireland's
                  largest golf complex ... Felt very welcome and enjoyed
                  every minute ... Nice views from fairways of so-so
                  course.

Delvin Castle Golf Club   ★

Clonyn, Delvin, County Westmeath
Nearest main town: Mullingar

Secretary: Mr P. Murphy   Tel: 044 64315
Professional: Mr D. Keenaghan

Playing: Midweek: round €26 (18 holes), €18 (9 holes); day n/a.
                    Weekend: round €30 (18 holes), €20 (9 holes); day n/a.

Facilities: Bar: 10.30am–11pm. Food: Bar snacks.

Comments: Basic course near Clonyn Castle ... Unmemorable ...
                    Suitable for beginners ... New facility for beginners but
                    not for those seeking new experiences ... New club that
                    tries hard.

Druid's Glen Golf Club

Newtownmountkennedy, Greystones, County Wicklow
Website: www.druidsglen.ie   E-mail: info@druidsglen.ie
Nearest main town: Newtownmountkennedy

Secretary: Mr D. Flinn   Tel: 01 287 3600
                                          Fax: 01 287 3699
Professional: Mr G. Henry

Playing: Midweek: round €150 (Druid's Glen), €110 (Druid's
                    Heath); day n/a. Weekend: round €150 (Druid's Glen),
                    €110 (Druid's Heath); day n/a.

Facilities: Bar: 11am–11pm. Food: Breakfast, lunch and dinner
                    from 9am–11pm. Bar snacks.

Comments: Complete luxury ... Like Mount Juliet for comfort, but
                    course not as good ... Condition out of this world ...
                    Too expensive and exclusive ... Doesn't feel like Irish golf
                    ... Who wants this when you can have some of the great
                    Dublin courses nearby ... Not much of a craic here ...
                    Generous fairways and greens – too easy ... Condition
                    first class ... Never seen fairways and greens so good ...
                    Watch out for Amen Corner.

Dundalk Golf Club   ★★★

Blackrock, Dundalk, County Louth
E-mail: dkgc@iol.ie
Nearest main town: Dundalk

Secretary: Mr T. Sloane   Tel: 042 932 1731
                                         Fax: 042 932 2022

Professional: Mr L. Walker

Playing: Midweek: round €55; day n/a. Weekend: round €55;
                   day n/a.

Facilities: Bar: 10.30am–11pm. Food: Lunch and dinner from
                   12pm–9pm. Bar snacks.

Comments: Not as good as nearby County Down but a cracker …
                   Mountains of Mourne form a marvellous canvas for
                   shots … Forget the bump-and-run of nearby County
                   Down, you need to hit them high here … Get to the turn
                   in good shape and you should score well … Nice
                   welcome … This and Greenore give excellent, good-
                   value golf.

Edmondstown Golf Club   ★

Rathfarnham, Dublin, County Dublin
Website: www.edmondstowngolfclub.ie
E-mail: info@edmondstowngolfclub.ie
Nearest main town: Dublin

Secretary: Mr S. Davies   Tel: 01 493 1082
                                         Fax: 01 493 3152
Professional: Mr A. Crofton   Tel: 01 494 1049

Playing: Midweek: round €55; day n/a. Weekend: round €65;
                   day n/a.

Facilities: Bar: 10.30am–11pm. Food: Lunch and dinner from
                   12pm–9pm. Bar snacks.

Comments: Nothing special about this parkland course …
                   Overpriced … Pleasant enough … Convenient if
                   you're staying in Dublin … Better courses to be found
                   nearby.

Glasson Golf & Country Club   ★★★★

Glasson, Athlone, County Westmeath
Website: www.glassongolf.ie   E-mail: glasgolf@iol.ie
Nearest main town: Athlone

Secretary: Mrs F. Reid   Tel: 090 648 5120
                                       Fax: 090 648 5444

Professional: None

Playing: Midweek: round €55 (Mon–Thurs); day n/a. Weekend:
                  round €60 (Fri & Sun), €70 (Sat); day n/a.

Facilities: Bar: 10.30am–11pm. Food: Breakfast, lunch and
                  dinner from 9am–9pm. Bar snacks.

Comments: Most enjoyable ... Remarkable location ... Great addi-
                  tion to Ireland's courses ... A little hilly but scenery takes
                  your mind off it ... Worth the drive ... Set in the heart of
                  Ireland, this is a picture ... Situated on a peninsula
                  bordering Lough Ree – magnificent ... What do you
                  expect from Christy O'Connor Jnr? ... The course on
                  everyone's lips ... Tee and green situated in a lake at the
                  15th.

Greenore Golf Club   ★★

Greenore, County Louth
Website: www.greenoregolf.com
E-mail: greenoregolfclub@eircom.net
Nearest main town: Dundalk

Secretary: Ms L. Clarke   Tel: 042 937 3212
                                        Fax: 042 938 3898

Professional: Mr R. Giles   Tel: 042 937 3212 (Ext 23)
                                        Fax: 042 938 3898

Playing: Midweek: round €32; day n/a. Weekend: round €45;
                  day n/a.

Facilities: Bar: 10.30am–11pm. Food: Lunch and dinner from
                  12pm–9pm. Bar snacks.

Comments: Part links, part woodland ... Variety in buckets – links,
                  woods, a railway line and blind greens ... A new chal-
                  lenge at every turn ... Had a ball ... Will go back as
                  soon as possible.

Headfort Golf Club   ★★★

Kells, County Meath
Nearest main town: Dublin

Secretary:	Mrs E. Carroll	Tel: 046 40146
		Fax: 046 49282
Professional:	Mr B. McGovern	Tel: 046 40639

Playing: Midweek: round €40 (Mon–Thurs, Old), €55 (New); day
n/a. Weekend: round €45 (Fri–Sun, Old), €60 (New);
day n/a.

Facilities: Bar: 10.30am–11pm. Food: Lunch and dinner from
10am–9pm. Bar snacks.

Comments: Beautiful parkland, hundreds of mature trees ... Value
... Excellent greens and fairways ... Excellent parkland
course ... Greens fast and fair ... Easy to get a game,
never overcrowded ... One of the top parkland courses
in Ireland.

The Heath (Portlaoise) Golf Club   ★

Portlaoise, County Laois
Nearest main town: Portlaoise

Secretary:	Mr D. O'Brien	Tel: 0502 62727
		Fax: 0502 46866
Professional:	Mr E. Doyle	Tel: 0502 46622

Playing: Midweek: round €18 (€13 with member); day n/a.
Weekend: round €34 (€23 with member); day n/a.

Facilities: Bar: 10.30am–11pm. Food: Lunch and dinner from
12pm–6pm.

Comments: Heather and gorse the main feature of this old course ...
Old course a little ragged around the edges ... Very
natural but very average.

Hermitage Golf Club   ★★★

Lucan, County Dublin
Nearest main town: Dublin

Secretary:	Mr P. Maguire	Tel: 01 626 8491
		Fax: 01 626 8491
Professional:	Mr S. Byrne	Tel: 01 626 8072

Playing:	Midweek: round €75; day n/a. Weekend: round €90; day n/a.
Facilities:	Bar: 10.30am–11pm. Food: Lunch and dinner from 12.30pm–9pm. Bar snacks.
Comments:	Nicely laid out, in good condition with good facilities ... Pretty inland course with unusual features ... Run-of-the-mill parkland track ... A few steep climbs ... Patience required with a few blind shots ... 10th a fine par-3 ... Seemingly simple course but danger lurks everywhere.

Hollywood Lakes Golf Club ★★

Ballyboughal, County Dublin
E-mail: austinbrogan@hotmail.com
Nearest main town: Dublin

Secretary:	Mr A. Brogan	Tel: 01 843 3406
		Fax: 01 843 3002
Professional:	None	
Playing:	Midweek: round €35 (Mon–Thurs), €40 (Fri); day n/a. Weekend: round €45; day n/a.	
Facilities:	Bar: 11am–11pm. Food: Lunch from 12pm–4pm. Dinner by arrangement.	
Comments:	Very long parkland course built to high specifications ... Modern course with water everywhere ... Fun course with water and 600-plus-yard par-5 ... Dreary new design ... Average condition for fairly new course ... Modern club with average facilities.	

The Island Golf Club ★★★★

Corballis, Donabate, County Dublin
Website: www.theislandgolfclub.com
E-mail: reservations@theislandgolfclub.com
Nearest main town: Dublin

Secretary:	Mr P. McDunphy	Tel: 01 843 6205
		Fax: 01 843 6860
Professional:	Mr K. Kelliher	Tel: 01 843 5002
		Fax: 01 843 6860

Playing: Midweek: round €110; day n/a. Weekend: round €110; day n/a.

Facilities: Bar: 10.30am–11pm. Food: Lunch and dinner from 10am–9pm.

Comments: Good all-round facilities with best holes the 5th, 6th, 10th and 15th ... True links ... Best course in Dublin but needs to be more welcoming ... 1st, 3rd and the 7th are the best holes on the front nine ... Surrounded on three sides by water ... Imposing sandhills in places.

The K Club (North)   ★★★★

Kildare Hotel & Country Club, Straffan, County Kildare
Website: www.kclub.ie
Nearest main town: Dublin

Secretary: Mr P. Crowe   Tel: 01 601 7300
                                        Fax: 01 601 7399
Professional: Mr J. McHenry   Tel: 01 601 7321

Playing: Midweek: round €185 (Apr & Oct), €265 (May–Sept); day n/a. Weekend: round €185 (Apr & Oct), €265 (May–Sept); day n/a.

Facilities: Bar: 10.30am–11pm. Food: Breakfast, lunch and dinner from 7am–10pm. Bar snacks.

Comments: Ideal Ryder Cup venue – superb ... Four hours of my life I'll never get back – dreadful ... I don't reckon Arnie would finish this long, punishing track ... Thinking man's course ... Superb ... Good if you are good, a nightmare if you are bad ... High-class professional approach here ... Fantastic condition ... No expense spared here.

Kilkea Castle Golf Club   ★

Kilkea, Castle Dermot, County Kildare
Website: www.kilkeacastlehotelgolf.com
E-mail: kilkeagolfclub@eircom.net
Nearest main town: Carlow

Secretary: Mrs A. Molloy   Tel: 059 914 5555
                   (Manager)   Fax: 059 914 5505
Professional: On request

Playing:	Midweek: round €40 (Mon–Thurs); day n/a. Weekend: round €45 (Fri–Sun); day n/a.
Facilities:	Bar: 10.30am–11pm. Food: Lunch from 12pm–2pm. Dinner from 6pm–9pm.
Comments:	12th-century castle dominates this magical parkland course ... Natural and in immaculate condition on visit ... Clubhouse a perfect 19th ... Course does not match the opulence of the surroundings ... Two man-made lakes and stream are primary defence of this layout.

Kilkenny Golf Club   ★★★

Glendine, Kilkenny, County Kilkenny
Nearest main town: Kilkenny

Secretary:	Mr S. O'Neill	Tel: 056 776 5400
		Fax: 056 772 3593
Professional:	Mr N. Leahy	Tel: 056 776 1730
Playing:	Midweek: round €35; day n/a. Weekend: round €40 (Sat only); day n/a.	
Facilities:	Bar: 10.30am–11pm. Food: Lunch and dinner from 10am–9pm.	
Comments:	Lovely mature parkland that is a tough test ... Tree-lined course, well established ... Pleasant day's golf on fairly easy track.	

Killeen Golf Club   ★★

Killeenbeg, Kill, County Kildare
Nearest main town: Sallins

Secretary:	Mr P. Carey	Tel: 045 866 003
		Fax: 045 875 881
Professional:	None	
Playing:	Midweek: round €35 (Mon–Thurs), €40 (Fri); day n/a. Weekend: round €50; day n/a.	
Facilities:	Bar: 10.30am–11pm. Food: Lunch and dinner from 10am–9pm. Bar snacks.	
Comments:	Tight driving course, a pleasure to walk and play ... Short course, fairly tight ... Some holes designed around lakes ... Little of interest at this parkland venue.	

Knockanally Golf Club   ★★

Donadea, North Kildare, County Kildare
Nearest main town: Dublin

Secretary:	Mr N. Lyons	Tel: 045 869 322
		Fax: 045 869 322
Professional:	Mr M. Darcy	

Playing: Midweek: round €30; day n/a. Weekend: round €45; day n/a.

Facilities: Bar: 10.30am–11pm. Food: Bar snacks. Dinner by arrangement.

Comments: One of the toughest opening holes in all of golf ... Clubhouse magnificent ... Undulating course that tails off after the opening hole ... Popular parkland course, can get busy.

Luttrellstown Castle Golf & Country Club   ★★★

Castleknock, Dublin 15, County Dublin
Website: www.luttrellstown.ie   E-mail: golf@luttrellstown.ie
Nearest main town: Dublin

Secretary:	None	Tel: 01 808 9988
		Fax: 01 808 9989
Professional:	Mr E. Doyle	Tel: 01 808 9988
		Fax: 01 808 9989

Playing: Midweek: round €85 (Sun–Thurs); day n/a. Weekend: round €95 (Fri & Sat); day n/a.

Facilities: Bar: 10.30am–11pm. Food: Lunch and dinner from 12pm–9pm. Bar snacks.

Comments: Excellent fairways and greens on a well-designed, tough-but-fair course ... Beautiful and challenging ... The day I win the Lotto is the day I join this great course ... Interesting, tough holes ... Excellent clubhouse and brilliant food ... Unknown designer means this course is underrated ... Lots of water fun, not so good for the traditionalist ... Loved it ... Always find time to play it ... One of the best newer courses in Ireland.

Malahide Golf Club   ★★

Beechwood, The Grange, Malahide, County Dublin
Website: www.malahidegolfclub.ie   E-mail: malgc@clubi.ie
Nearest main town: Dublin

Secretary:	Mr P. Smyth	Tel: 01 846 1611
		Fax: 01 846 1270
Professional:	Mr J. Murray	Tel: 01 846 0002

Playing: Midweek: round €50; day n/a. Weekend: round €85; day n/a.

Facilities: Bar: 10.30am–11pm. Food: Lunch and dinner from 11am–9pm. Bar snacks.

Comments: Very popular, friendly course ... Not a classic design but kept in excellent shape ... For all the challenge from the tee and fairway, the greens are generally flat ... Very fair to the once-in-a-while player ... Scoring usually good here ... Facilities excellent at this popular Dublin parkland course ... Clever use of water hazards.

Mount Temple Golf Club   ★★★

Mount Temple Village, Moate, County Westmeath
Website: www.mounttemplegolfclub.com   E-mail: mttemple@iol.ie
Nearest main town: Moate

Secretary:	Ms M. Allen	Tel: 090 648 1841
		Fax: 090 648 1957
Professional:	Mr D. Keenan	Tel: 090 648 1841
		Fax: 090 648 1957

Playing: Midweek: round €35; day n/a. Weekend: round €40; day n/a.

Facilities: Bar: 11am–11pm. Food: Bar snacks.

Comments: It's a beast but worth the pain ... Long and difficult course ... Extremely natural layout ... Undulating fairways and hard, unwatered greens make this a test of your imagination ... Shot-maker's course.

Mount Wolseley Golf Club   ★★

Tullow, County Carlow
Nearest main town: Tullow

Secretary: Mr S. McDonagh   Tel: 059 915 1674
Fax: 059 915 2123

Professional: Mr J. Bolger

Playing: Midweek: round €50; day n/a. Weekend: round €70 (Sat), €50 (Sun); day n/a.

Facilities: Bar: 11am–11pm. Food: Lunch and dinner from 11am–10pm. Bar snacks.

Comments: Very fun course ... Relatively new course in super condition ... A dream to play ... Can't wait to go back.

Mountrath Golf Club ★

Knockanina, Mountrath, County Laois
Nearest main town: Portlaoise

Secretary: Ms D. Kingsley   Tel: 0502 32558
Fax: 0502 32643

Professional: None

Playing: Midweek: round €20; day n/a. Weekend: round €20 (when available); day n/a.

Facilities: Bar: 10.30am–11pm. Food: Bar snacks.

Comments: Sheep the main hazard on this nine-hole course ... Fun course open to everyone ... A beginner's course.

Mullingar Golf Club

Belvedere, Mullingar, County Westmeath
Nearest main town: Mullingar

Secretary: Mrs A. Cully   Tel: 044 48366
Fax: 044 41499

Professional: Mr J. Burns   Tel: 044 40085

Playing: Midweek: round €32; day n/a. Weekend: round €40; day n/a.

Facilities: Bar: 10.30am–11pm. Food: Lunch and dinner from 12pm–9pm. Bar snacks.

Comments: Tactical short course ... Despite being less than 6000 yards, this course has stood the test of time ... Tight course ... Greens cleverly protected ... Bunkering protects this short course ... Will remember it for the par-3s ... Always a warm welcome.

Old Conna Golf Club ★

Ferndale Road, Bray, County Wicklow
Website: www.oldconna.com
Nearest main town: Dublin

Secretary:	Mr D. Diviney	Tel: 01 282 6055
		Fax: 01 282 5611
Professional:	Mr P. McDaid	Tel: 01 272 0022

Playing: Midweek: round €50; day n/a. Weekend: round €60; day n/a.

Facilities: Bar: 10.30am–11pm. Food: Lunch and dinner from 10am–9pm. Bar snacks.

Comments: New course near Dublin that has a bright future ... Time will tell whether this Hackett course will make it ... Three of the last four holes are 420-plus yards ... Overly long new course ... New players don't need to cover 6000-plus yards.

Portmarnock Hotel & Golf Links

Strand Road, Portmarnock, Dublin, County Dublin
Website: www.portmarnock.com   E-mail: golf@portmarnock.com
Nearest main town: Portmarnock

Secretary:	Mrs M. Cassidy	Tel: 01 846 1800
	(Golf Director)	Fax: 01 846 1077
Professional:	Mr D. Clarke	

Playing: Midweek: round €85 (resident), €120 (non-resident); day n/a. Weekend: round €85 (resident), €120 (non-resident); day n/a.

Facilities: Bar: 11am–11pm. Food: Breakfast, lunch and dinner from 9am–11pm. Bar snacks.

Comments: New links, a real credit to designers ... This course completely devoured me ... Slow start but gets better ... Better than the Old course ... Golf this good is rare ... So natural ... Have bored my friends rigid with tales of this one ... Condition exceptional for a links ... Very exposed ... In years to come will be one of the best in Ireland ... A fresh look at links golf.

Powerscourt Golf Club   ★★★

Enniskerry, County Wicklow
Website: www.powerscourt.ie   E-mail: golfclub@powerscourt.ie
Nearest main town: Bray

Secretary:	Mr B. Gibbons	Tel: 01 204 6033
		Fax: 01 276 1303
Professional:	Mr P. Thompson	Tel: 01 204 6033
		Fax: 01 276 1303

Playing: Midweek: round €110; day n/a. Weekend: round €110; day n/a.

Facilities: Bar: 9am–11pm. Food: Lunch and dinner from 12pm–9pm.

Comments: Wicklow mountains provide a stunning backdrop ... Dublin golfers are becoming very spoilt ... Par-5 17th of 698 yards not quite what I'm used to ... Inventive course but not much soul ... Felt very welcome ... Condition a tribute to the club.

Rathsallagh Golf & Country Club   ★★★★

Dunlavin, County Wicklow
Website: www.rathsallagh.com   E-mail: info@rathsallagh.com
Nearest main town: Naas

Secretary:	Mr J. O'Flynn	Tel: 045 403 316
		Fax: 045 403 295
Professional:	Mr B. McDaid	Tel: 045 403 316
		Fax: 045 403 295

Playing: Midweek: round €60 (Mon–Thurs); day n/a. Weekend: round €75 (Fri–Sun and bank holidays); day n/a.

Facilities: Bar: 10.30am–11pm. Food: Lunch and dinner from 12pm–9pm. Bar snacks.

Comments: Difficult, long course suitable for players of all abilities ... Beautiful setting and good value ... So much variety ... A bit of everything at this Peter McEvoy-designed course ... Watch out for the 6th ... Hard as nails ... Homely club ... Simple from the tee, but the trouble starts when you start firing at the flags.

Rosslare Golf Club   ★★★

Rosslare Strand, County Wexford
Website: www.rosslaregolf.com   E-mail: office@rosslaregolf.com
Nearest main town: Wexford

Secretary:	Mr J. Hanrick	Tel: 053 32203
		Fax: 053 32263
Professional:	Mr J. Young	Fax: 053 32263

Playing: Midweek: round n/a; day €35. Weekend: round n/a; day €50.

Facilities: Bar: 10.30am–11pm. Food: Lunch from 10am–9pm. Bar snacks.

Comments: Very pleasant links that lacks length ... Underrated due to its length ... Great welcome at this old-style links ... Very exposed – can spoil the fun ... Rough gets too high on occasions ... Charming little course – will be back.

Royal Dublin Golf Club   ★★★★

North Bull Island, Dollymount, Dublin, County Dublin
Website: www.theroyaldublingolfclub.com
Nearest main town: Dublin

Secretary:	Mr J. Lambe	Tel: 01 833 6346
		Fax: 01 833 6504
Professional:	Mr L. Owens	Tel: 01 833 6477

Playing: Midweek: round prices on application; day n/a. Weekend: round n/a; day n/a.

Facilities: Bar: 10.30am–11pm. Food: Breakfast, lunch and dinner from 7am–10pm. Bar snacks.

Comments: Welcoming atmosphere ... Superb links and great pro shop ... Past its best ... A stunning natural course with deep greenside bunkers ... Very busy with visitors from Dublin ... Hard-to-master course with blind drives.

Rush Golf Club   ★

Sandyhills, Rush, County Dublin
E-mail: info@rushgolfclub.com
Nearest main town: Dublin

| Secretary: | Ms N. Quirke | Tel: 01 843 8177 |
| Professional: | None | Fax: 01 843 8177 |

Playing: Midweek: round €32; day n/a. Weekend: round n/a; day n/a.

Facilities: Bar: 10.30am–11pm. Food: Bar snacks.

Comments: Nine-hole links with pot bunkers and undulating fairways ... Bunkers the main hazard at this neat little course ... Natural course in average condition ... Excellent fun and a bracing wind ... Good value for a unique golf experience.

St Helens Bay Golf Resort   ★★

Kilrane, Rosslare Harbour, County Wexford
Website: www.sthelensbay.com   E-mail: sthelens@iol.ie
Nearest main town: Wexford

Secretary:	Mr L. Byrne	Tel: 053 33234
		Fax: 053 33803
Professional:	Mr L. Bowler	Tel: 053 33234
		Fax: 053 33803

Playing: Midweek: round €27–38; day n/a. Weekend: round €34–45; day n/a.

Facilities: Bar: 10.30am–11pm. Food: Lunch and dinner from 12pm–9pm. Bar snacks.

Comments: Part links, part parkland ... Sleeping giant of a course ... Course suffers from identity crisis – is it parkland, is it links? ... Course finishes on right note with some cracking closing holes ... Simple course with potential ... Condition leaves a lot to be desired ... Ideal matchplay venue.

St Margarets Golf & Country Club   ★★★

St Margarets, Dublin, County Dublin
Nearest main town: Dublin

Secretary:	Mr T. Judge	Tel: 01 864 0400
	(Chief Exec)	Fax: 01 864 0289
Professional:	Mr D. Loys-Moroney	

Playing: Midweek: round €75 (Mon–Thurs); day n/a. Weekend: round €90 (Fri–Sun); day n/a.

Facilities: Bar: 10.30am–11pm. Food: Breakfast, lunch and dinner from 9am–9pm. Bar snacks.

Comments: Good championship course, but will be outstanding in ten years' time ... Best greens I have ever putted on ... Flat farmland transformed into a rolling, modern master-piece ... No bump-and-run here, high iron shots needed ... 8th and the 12th are excellent par-5s ... Fairly straightforward with shallow bunkers and easy-to-read greens ... Manufactured course, nothing you wouldn't find at the K Club ... Excellent facilities and course for the average player.

Tullamore Golf Club ★★★

Brookfield, Tullamore, County Offaly
Website: www.tullamoregolfclub.ie
E-mail: tullamoregolfclub@eircom.net
Nearest main town: Tullamore

Secretary: Ms J. Barber-Loughnane   Tel: 0506 21439
                                        Fax: 0506 41806

Professional: Mr D. McArdle   Tel: 0506 51757
                                        Fax: 0506 41806

Playing: Midweek: round €37; day n/a. Weekend: round €48; day n/a.

Facilities: Bar: 10.30am–11pm. Food: Lunch and dinner from 11am–9pm.

Comments: Pure golf and great 14th hole ... Generous course where good shots are always rewarded ... Nothing tricky about this warm, friendly club ... Best course for miles around.

Wicklow Golf Club ★★

Dunbur Road, Wicklow, County Wicklow
Nearest main town: Wicklow

Secretary: Mr J. Kelly   Tel: 0404 67379
Professional: Mr D. McLoughlin   Tel: 0404 66122

Playing: Midweek: round €40; day n/a. Weekend: round €40; day n/a.

Facilities: Bar: 10.30am–11pm. Food: Lunch and dinner from 10am–10pm. Bar snacks.

Comments: Beautiful scenery on a thinking man's course ... Views of Wicklow mountains best thing about this place ... Short nine-holer that offers little but views ... Wouldn't rush back ... There's better nine-holers elsewhere.

Woodbrook Golf Club   ★★★

Dublin Road, Bray, County Wicklow
Website: www.woodbrook.ie
Nearest main town: Dublin

Secretary: Mr J. Melody   Tel: 01 282 4799
                                        Fax: 01 282 1950
Professional: Mr W. Kinsella

Playing: Midweek: round €85; day n/a. Weekend: round €95 (members' guests only); day n/a.

Facilities: Bar: 10.30am–11pm. Food: Lunch and dinner from 11am–9pm. Bar snacks.

Comments: Club prides itself on condition of course ... Not a traditional links but a fun place to play ... 36 out, 36 home – nicely balanced course ... A facile links ideal for beginners ... Don't go out of your way.

Woodenbridge Golf Club   ★★★

Vale of Avoca, Arklow, County Wicklow
Website: www.woodenbridgegolfclub.com   E-mail: wgc@eircom.net
Nearest main town: Arklow

Secretary: Mr P. Smyth   Tel: 0402 35202
                                        Fax: 0402 35754
Professional: None

Playing: Midweek: round €51; day n/a. Weekend: round €63; day n/a.

Facilities: Bar: 11am–11pm. Food: Lunch from 11am–3pm. Dinner from 6pm–11pm. Bar snacks.

Comments: Can get very busy during the weekend ... Delightful course in the spring ... Pretty parkland which is very fair ... Setting and vegetation make this course ... Very popular ... Never have a bad round.

Ulster

Royal County Down Golf Club ★★★★★

Golf Links Road, Newcastle, County Down, BT33 0AN
Website: www.royalcountydown.org
E-mail: golf@royalcountydown.org
Nearest main town: Belfast

Along with Royal Dornoch in the nether reaches of Scotland, Royal County Down is arguably the finest links never to have held an Open Championship. Praise for this beautiful links, which is towered over by the spectacular range of the Mountains of Mourne, has come from far and wide.

Dai Rees felt it to be second only to Pine Valley as the toughest course in the world. Tom Watson, as qualified as anyone to comment on the merits of links courses having won the Open on five different ones, commented after his 1989 visit that the first eleven holes were 'the finest consecutive holes of links golf' he had ever played.

County Down's charm lies in the old-fashioned flavour of both the terrain and the layout. Some other courses are blessed with a similar mix of rugged dunes coloured by a blend of purple heather and yellow flowering gorse, but few combine them to such dramatic effect.

The fairways and greens are no less than you would expect from a championship seaside course, but the rough has a delightfully unkempt appearance which gives the feel of playing golf in the last century. Sea grasses grow from the lip of the bunkers in such thick tufts that it is better to land in the traps than to just clear them. The huge spines of dunes that bisect the course have resulted in the five blind tee shots, which are naturally a target of criticism in these days of laser-measured yardage charts.

But at County Down they add to the drama. Take the 486-yard 9th, where, following a blind tee shot, you walk to the top of the ridge to see the glory of one of golf's most photographed fairways unfold far below you, with the 2300-foot peak of Slieve Donard in the distance overseeing proceedings. The short par-4 16th, driveable with a big blow from a hilltop, has also come in for criticism, but perhaps the only thing out of place at County Down is the small lake in the middle of the 17th fairway, which seems unnecessarily contrived.

Secretary:	Mr J. Laidler	Tel: 028 4372 3314
		Fax: 028 4372 6281
Professional:	Mr K. Whitson	Tel: 028 4372 2419

Playing: Midweek: round £110 (am), £95 (pm); day n/a.
Weekend: round £125 (Sunday only); day n/a.

Facilities: Bar: 11am–11pm. Food: Lunch from 12pm–3pm. Bar snacks.

Comments: Weekend play only on Sunday from 1pm–2.30pm ... Best course in British Isles ... Deserving of its ultra-challenging reputation ... Inspiring setting ... The best first 11 holes on any course in the world, but a shame about the rest ... Stunning, breathtaking ... Hard to concentrate on your game in such surroundings ... Friendly, well-informed pro ... Best course I have ever played ... The course is a dream and the 9th hole is the pick of the bunch ... Maybe the best course in Ireland ... Not a bad hole here ... Breathtakingly beautiful, but don't take your eyes off the course ... Very narrow, very dangerous ... Too long, too hard, especially in the wind and rain – but I love it.

Royal Portrush Golf Club (Dunluce)   ★★★★★

Dunluce Road, Portrush, County Antrim, BT56 8JQ
Website: www.royalportrushgolfclub.com   E-mail: rpgc@dnet.co.uk
Nearest main town: Portrush

Few approaches to a golf course stir the passions more than the road to Royal Portrush. Shortly after passing the ruins of Dunluce Castle, you turn a corner and there, spread before you, is an expanse of crumpled links, rolling out towards the shimmering sea. In the distance are the brooding headlands of Inishowen and, on a clear day, you can see the Scottish landmarks of the Paps of Jura. It is a marvellously evocative setting.

Royal Portrush held the Open Championship in 1951 (the only course in Ireland to do so), but as the demands on space for hospitality grew, so its viability as a venue fell. It is certainly a course worthy of the event, and players walking off the 18th breathe a heavy sigh of satisfaction after what is an incredibly imaginative experience.

Essentially it is a driving course. The curves of the fairways and slopes of the terrain are intimidating from the tee and, although there are very few bunkers, the wind is a constant factor, and the rough is untamed and unruly, gobbling up any loose shot. The opening holes run fairly straight away from the clubhouse and it is not until the turn that the course starts to show its teeth. The holes swing back and forth, doglegging around dunes and greens backing onto the sea, most spectacularly at the 5th. What strikes you is that, although this is the most difficult part of the course, there are very few greenside bunkers, the small putting surfaces protected purely by small hummocks and hills.

The 14th, named 'Calamity Corner', is Portrush's most famous hole, a par-3 that is played to an elevated green located on a spine of rising land. All along the right is a hideous drop into a valley of bushes and scrub and, on the left, dangerous rough clinging to the banks.

Secretary: Miss W. Erskine   Tel: 028 7082 2311
                                      Fax: 028 7082 3139

Professional: Mr G. McNeill

Playing: Midweek: round £90.00; day n/a. Weekend: round £110.00; day n/a.

Facilities: Bar: 11am–11pm. Food: Lunch from 11am–3pm. Dinner by arrangement.

Comments: Magnificent links ... Great setting ... Grandiose ... Take the Open Championship there as soon as possible ... You need the heart of a lion for this one ... A must-play course with great views and wonderful company ... Must be played ... Gruelling ... Just magic ... An unbelievable experience for the overseas golfer.

Ardglass Golf Club   ★★★

Castle Place, Ardglass, County Down, BT30 7TP
Nearest main town: Downpatrick

Secretary: Miss D. Polly   Tel: 028 4484 1219
                                      Fax: 028 4484 1841

Professional: Mr P. Farrell   Tel: 028 4484 1022

Playing: Midweek: round £18.00; day £24.00. Weekend: round n/a; day n/a.

Facilities: Bar: 11am–11pm. Food: Lunch and dinner from 12pm–9pm, except Monday.

Comments: A jaw-dropping opening hole, delicious food, most notably the steaks! ... Beautiful track by the sea ... Many blind drives will send you potty ... An historic course ... First four holes perched on the cliffs ... Par-3 11th blows your socks off ... Very fair, the test of a great golf course.

Ballybofey & Stranorlar Golf Club   ★★★

The Glebe, Stranorlar, County Donegal
Nearest main town: Stranorlar

Secretary: Mr J. McCaughan   Tel: 074 943 1093
                                        Fax: 074 943 1058
Professional: None

Playing: Midweek: round n/a; day €20. Weekend: round n/a;
                    day €27.50.

Facilities: Bar: 11am–11pm. Food: Lunch and dinner from
                    12pm–9pm. Bar snacks.

Comments: A gentle, fun course … Intoxicating atmosphere in the
                    clubhouse … Impossible to leave bar until after midnight
                    … Warm welcome guaranteed … Parkland course more
                    renowned for its welcome than quality of golf … Good
                    course with views of the Donegal Hills.

Ballycastle Golf Club   ★★★

2 Cushendall Road, Ballycastle, County Antrim, BT64 6QP
Website: www.ballycastlegolfclub.com
E-mail: info@ballycastlegolfclub.com
Nearest main town: Portrush

Secretary: Mr B. Dillon   Tel: 028 2076 2536
                                          Fax: 028 2076 9909
Professional: Mr I. McLaughlin   Tel: 028 2076 2506
                                          Fax: 028 2076 9909

Playing: Midweek: round £20.00; day n/a. Weekend: round
                    £30.00; day n/a.

Facilities: Bar: 11am–11pm. Food: Lunch from 12pm–2pm.
                    Dinner by arrangement.

Comments: Three courses in one … Mixed parkland/links … Great
                    character … Parts played around ruins of 13th-century
                    friary … Thoughtful course of some standing.

Ballyliffin Golf Club (Glashedy) ★★★★

Ballyliffin, Clonmany, Inishowen, County Donegal
Website: www.ballyliffingolfclub.com
E-mail: info@ballyliffingolfclub.com
Nearest main town: Londonderry

Secretary:	Mr C. Doherty	Tel: 074 937 6119
		Fax: 074 937 6672
Professional:	Mr F. Howley	Tel: 074 937 8100
		Fax: 074 937 6672

Playing: Midweek: round €60; day n/a. Weekend: round €70; day n/a.

Facilities: Bar: 10.30am–11pm. Food: Lunch and dinner from 12pm–9pm.

Comments: Great value ... Don't go and play here and miss out on the Old course ... Lunar landscape with dunes like ocean liners ... Everything you need for a challenge – wind, doglegs, subtle greens, deep bunkers and tangly rough ... Better than the Old ... 12th, 13th and 14th just can't be bettered ... Magnificent new course, thank you Ruddy and Craddock ... Not as natural as the Old ... Could while away the rest of my life here ... Glashedy Rock reminiscent of Turnberry ... Fairly new course that feels 100 years old.

Ballyliffin Golf Club (Old) ★★★★

Ballyliffin, Clonmany, Inishowen, County Donegal
Website: www.ballyliffingolfclub.com
E-mail: info@ballyliffingolfclub.com
Nearest main town: Londonderry

Secretary:	Mr C. Doherty	Tel: 074 937 6119
		Fax: 074 937 6672
Professional:	Mr F. Howley	Tel: 074 937 8100
		Fax: 074 937 6672

Playing: Midweek: round €45; day n/a. Weekend: round €50; day n/a.

Facilities: Bar: 10.30am–11pm. Food: Lunch and dinner from 12pm–9pm.

Comments: Natural links course set in magnificent scenery ... Faldo calls it 'the most natural golf course ever' ... Watch out for 'The Tank' ... So beautiful ... Shorter than you would expect but so charming ... Never a flat lie on these fairways ... Stark beauty to this golfscape ... I do my best thinking out here ... Will never forget my time here ... Just so beautiful ... A haven of tranquillity from the modern world.

Balmoral Golf Club   ★★★

518 Lisburn Road, Belfast, BT9 6GX
Nearest main town: Belfast

Secretary: Mr R. McConkey   Tel: 028 9038 1514
                                        Fax: 028 9066 6759
Professional: Mr G. Bleakley   Tel: 028 9066 7747

Playing: Midweek: round £20.00; day n/a. Weekend: round £30.00; day n/a.

Facilities: Bar: 11am–11pm. Food: Breakfast, lunch and dinner from 9am–9pm. Bar snacks.

Comments: Good course near Belfast city centre ... Very beautiful ... Relaxed clubhouse ... Excellent greens on visit ... Impressive clubhouse ... Fairly short but with plenty of natural hazards ... Tree-lined course with some potential.

Bangor Golf Club   ★★★

Broadway, Bangor, County Down, BT20 4RH
Nearest main town: Bangor

Secretary: Mr D. Ryan   Tel: 028 9127 0922
                                        Fax: 028 9145 3394
Professional: Mr M. Bannon

Playing: Midweek: round £20.00; day £30.00. Weekend: round £25.00; day n/a.

Facilities: Bar: 11am–11pm. Food: Bar snacks. Dinner by arrangement.

Comments: Good course for the beginner and more experienced player ... Remote course but fun to play ... Numerous doglegs ... Another James Braid triumph ... Natural golf for the purist.

The Belvoir Park Golf Club   ★★★★

Church Road, Newtownbreda, Belfast, County Belfast, BT8 4AN
Nearest main town: Belfast

Secretary: Ms A. Vaughan   Tel: 028 9049 1693
                                           Fax: 028 9064 6113
Professional: Mr M. McGivern   Tel: 028 9064 6714

Playing: Midweek: round £33.00; day £33.00. Weekend: round
                    £38.00; day £38.00.

Facilities: Bar: 11am–11pm. Food: Lunch and dinner from
                    11am–9pm. Bar snacks.

Comments: Best inland course in Northern Ireland ... Lush fairways
                    on this rejuvenated course ... Hilly in places ... Highly
                    rated ... Close to Belfast but an apparent oasis of calm
                    ... Nice pro shop and accommodating to visitors.

Cairndhu Golf Club   ★★★

192 Coast Road, Larne, County Antrim, BT40 2QG
E-mail: cairndhu@globalgolf.com
Nearest main town: Larne

Secretary: Mr N. Moore   Tel: 028 2858 3324
                                           Fax: 028 2858 3324
Professional: Mr R. Walker   Tel: 028 2858 3417

Playing: Midweek: round £20.00; day n/a. Weekend: round
                    £25.00 (Sunday); day n/a.

Facilities: Bar: 11am–11pm. Food: Lunch and dinner from
                    11am–9pm. Bar snacks.

Comments: Don't be intimidated by the scenery ... Built on the side
                    of a hill ... Views to the Antrim Hills ... 3rd tee shot is
                    from way up high and has to carry 170 yards ... Small
                    greens make this so tough.

Castle Hume Golf Club   ★★

Belleek Road, Enniskillen, County Fermanagh, BT93 7ED
Website: www.castlehumegolf.com   E-mail: info@castlehumegolf.com
Nearest main town: Enniskillen

Secretary: Mrs W. Connor   Tel: 028 6632 7077
                    (Office Administrator) Fax: 028 6632 7076

Professional: Mr S. Donnelly   Tel: 028 6632 7077

Playing: Midweek: round £22/€32; day n/a. Weekend: round £28/€40; day n/a.

Facilities: Bar: 11am–11pm. Food: Breakfast, lunch and dinner from 9am–9pm. Bar snacks.

Comments: Fairly bland piece of land ... Average course for the area ... Good value ... Nice club course but not one for the visitor ... Rolling fairways, water hazards and clever bunkering make this a nice afternoon stroll.

Castlerock Golf Club   ★★★★

65 Circular Road, Castlerock, County Londonderry, BT51 4TJ
Website: www.castlerockgc.co.uk   E-mail: info@castlerockgc.co.uk
Nearest main town: Coleraine

Secretary: Mr M. Steen   Tel: 028 7084 8314
                                       Fax: 028 7084 9440
Professional: Mr I. Blair   Tel: 028 7084 9424
                                       Fax: 028 7084 9440

Playing: Midweek: round £35.00; day £50.00. Weekend: round £60.00; day n/a.

Facilities: Bar: 11am–11pm. Food: Breakfast, lunch and dinner from 9am–9pm. Bar snacks.

Comments: So hard, even for the members ... Good par-3s ... Pleasure to play ... Some unforgettable holes ... Does the wind ever blow gently? ... Friendly bunch of members ... White-knuckle stuff when the wind blows ... Great course and good welcome.

Clandeboye Golf Club (Ava)   ★★★

Tower Road, Conlig, Newtownards, County Down, BT23 7PN
Website: www.cgc-ni.com   E-mail: contact@cgc-ni.com
Nearest main town: Bangor

Secretary: Ms R. Eddis   Tel: 028 9127 1767
                                       Fax: 028 9147 3711
Professional: Mr P. Gregory   Tel: 028 9127 1750

Playing: Midweek: round £22.00; day n/a. Weekend: round £27.50; day n/a.

Facilities: Bar: 11am–11pm. Food: Breakfast, lunch and dinner from 9am–9pm. Bar snacks.

Comments: Short and good fun ... Par-5 second a beauty ... So much fun on this charming little course ... Views of Strangford Lough ... Keep your wits about you on this beguiling course.

Clandeboye Golf Club (Dufferin)   ★★★

Tower Road, Conlig, Newtownards, County Down, BT23 7PN
Website: www.cgc-ni.com   E-mail: contact@cgc-ni.com
Nearest main town: Bangor

Secretary: Ms R. Eddis   Tel: 028 9127 1767
                                  Fax: 028 9147 3711
Professional: Mr P. Gregory   Tel: 028 9127 1750

Playing: Midweek: round £27.50; day n/a. Weekend: round £33.00; day n/a.

Facilities: Bar: 11am–11pm. Food: Breakfast, lunch and dinner from 9am–9pm. Bar snacks.

Comments: Elevated greens, blind drives, streams, ditches – always something to watch out for ... Some long carries off the tee ... Woodland and heathland ... Drive on the 4th a terror ... High skill levels for this mature course.

County Cavan Golf Club   ★★

Arnmore House, Drumelis, Cavan, County Cavan
E-mail: info@cavangolf.ie
Nearest main town: Cavan

Secretary: Mr J. Fraher   Tel: 049 433 1541
                                  Fax: 049 433 1541
Professional: Mr C. Carroll

Playing: Midweek: round €25; day n/a. Weekend: round €30; day n/a.

Facilities: Bar: 10.30am–11pm. Food: Lunch and dinner from 10.30am–10pm. Bar snacks.

Comments: Parkland course ... Can get unplayable in winter ... Local knowledge helps ... Very cheap green fee ... Fair value for money for this unimaginative course.

Cruit Island Golf Club ★★

Kincasslagh, Dunglow, County Donegal
Nearest main town: Donegal

Secretary: Mr T. Gallagher   Tel: 074 954 3296
                                          Fax: 074 954 8028

Professional: None

Playing: Midweek: round €23; day n/a. Weekend: round €23;
                    day n/a.

Facilities: Bar: 11.30am–4pm. Food: Bar snacks.

Comments: Nine-hole course perched on the edge of the Atlantic
                    Ocean ... The 6th hole over the cove defies belief ...
                    With the Atlantic crashing against the rocks this is an
                    evocative experience ... Not in great condition but this
                    is golf back to its roots ... Don't let the fact it's half a
                    course put you off ... A blinder.

Donegal Golf Club ★★★★

Murvagh, Laghey, County Donegal
Website: www.donegalgolfclub.ie   E-mail: info@donegalgolfclub.ie
Nearest main town: Donegal

Secretary: Mr P. Nugent   Tel: 074 973 4054
                    (General Manager)   Fax: 074 973 4377
Professional: Mr L. Robinson   Tel: 074 973 4054
                                          Fax: 074 973 4377

Playing: Midweek: round €50 (Mon–Thurs); day n/a. Weekend:
                    round €65 (Fri–Sun); day n/a.

Facilities: Bar: 10.30am–11pm. Food: Lunch and dinner from
                    10am–9pm.

Comments: A sensational links ... Can't be bettered ... The match
                    of any of Ireland's links legends ... Opened in 1960 but
                    has an older feel to it ... A gruelling course ... Course
                    goes on and on ... Blue Stack Mountains dominate the
                    course ... 5th named the 'Valley of Tears' and rightly so
                    ... Staggering ... Long course putting great pressure on
                    the short game ... Longest course in Ireland ... Course
                    that fires the imagination ... Pray your driver is working
                    ... Drive badly and you're out with the washing ... A
                    Goliath of a course, felt like David ... Exciting ...
                    Exhilarating.

Dungannon Golf Club

34 Springfield Lane, Dungannon, County Tyrone, BT70 1QX
Website: www.dungannongolfclub.com
E-mail: dungannongolfclub@btopenworld.com
Nearest main town: Dungannon

Secretary: Ms B. McKenna   Tel: 028 8772 2098
                                   Fax: 028 8772 7338

Professional: Ms V. Teague

Playing: Midweek: round £20.00; day n/a. Weekend: round £25.00; day n/a.

Facilities: Bar: 11am–11pm. Food: Lunch and dinner from 12pm–7pm. Bar snacks.

Comments: Hilly in places but good way to work off hospitality ... Always enjoy society days here ... Established course with a nice feel ... Standard scratch is three under par ... A proper club with progressive attitude.

Dunmurry Golf Club

91 Dunmurry Lane, Dunmurry, BT17 9JS
Nearest main town: Belfast

Secretary: Mr I. McBride   Tel: 028 9061 0834
                                  Fax: 028 9060 2540

Professional: Mr J. Dolan   Tel: 028 9062 1314

Playing: Midweek: round £20.00; day n/a. Weekend: round £30.00; day n/a.

Facilities: Bar: 10.30am–11pm. Food: Lunch and dinner from 9am–9pm, except Mondays.

Comments: Nice club with a relaxed atmosphere ... Popular venue but course is suffering ... Opened in 1983 but has matured well ... Fair value at this open-to-all, friendly club.

Kilkeel Golf Club ★★

Mourne Park, Ballyardle, Kilkeel, County Down, BT34 4LB
E-mail: s.rooney@mail.com
Nearest main town: Kilkeel

Secretary:	Mr S. McBride	Tel: 028 4176 5095
		Fax: 028 4176 5579
Professional:	None	

Playing: Midweek: round n/a; day £20.00. Weekend: round n/a; day £25.00.

Facilities: Bar: 11am–11pm. Food: Lunch and dinner from 12pm–8pm. Bar snacks.

Comments: An excellent test on a scenic course ... Kept in reasonable condition ... Beautiful views in every direction ... Parkland course at the foot of the Mourne Mountains ... Quite an English feel to this parkland course ... Inland gem with great potential ... Mature woodland lends this course a regal air.

Kirkistown Castle Golf Club   ★★★

142 Main Road, Cloughey, Newtownards, County Down, BT22 1JA
Website: www.kcgc.org   E-mail: kirkistown@supanet.com
Nearest main town: Belfast

Secretary:	Ms R. Coulter	Tel: 028 4277 1233
		Fax: 028 4277 1699
Professional:	Mr J. Peden	Tel: 028 4277 1004

Playing: Midweek: round £20.75; day n/a. Weekend: round £27.75; day n/a.

Facilities: Bar: 11am–11pm. Food: Breakfast, lunch and dinner from 9am–9pm. Bar snacks.

Comments: A hidden gem that is worth taking the trouble to find ... Never gets wet underfoot ... Parkland/links with strategic bunkering ... Stunning location and excellent condition ... Drainage super ... Consistent, quality course.

The Knock Golf Club Ltd   ★★★

Summerfield, Dundonald, BT16 2QX
E-mail: knockgolfclub@btconnect.com
Nearest main town: Belfast

Secretary:	Mrs A. Armstrong	Tel: 028 9048 3251
		Fax: 028 9048 7277
Professional:	Mr G. Fairweather	Tel: 028 9048 3825
		Fax: 028 9048 7277

Playing: Midweek: round £25.00; day n/a. Weekend: round £40.00 (£30.00 after 2pm Sunday); day n/a.

Facilities: Bar: 11am–11pm. Food: Lunch and dinner from 11am–9pm. Bar snacks.

Comments: A tree-lined course that can get wet in winter ... Have a hearty breakfast before you go out ... Needs good drives ... Busy at weekends ... Most fairways tree-lined ... Watch your driving ... All the problems laid out clearly before you.

Letterkenny Golf Club ★

Barnhill, Letterkenny, County Donegal
Nearest main town: Letterkenny

Secretary: Mr I. Mackensie   Tel: 074 912 1150
Professional: None

Playing: Midweek: round €25; day n/a. Weekend: round €30; day n/a.

Facilities: Bar: 10.30am–11pm. Food: Bar snacks.

Comments: Lovely new clubhouse but course prone to damp ground ... Well presented and enjoyable ... Beautiful 11th hole ... Two halves to this course, the plateau holes get the nod ... Not much variety ... Not in the top rank for Donegal ... Did not do much for my game.

Lisburn Golf Club ★★

68 Eglantine Road, Lisburn, County Antrim, BT27 5RQ
E-mail: lisburngolfclub@aol.com
Nearest main town: Lisburn

Secretary: Mr G. McVeigh   Tel: 028 9267 7216
(Manager)   Fax: 028 9260 3608
Professional: Mr B. Campbell   Tel: 028 9267 7217

Playing: Midweek: round £25.00; day n/a. Weekend: round £30.00; day n/a.

Facilities: Bar: 11am–11pm. Food: Lunch and dinner from 11am–9pm. Bar snacks.

Comments: Well laid out with lots of bunkers ... Good pro shop ... Well maintained with picturesque holes ... Very tranquil ... Finishes with a wonderful par-3.

Lurgan Golf Club ★★

Demesne, Lurgan, County Armagh, BT67 9BN
Website: www.lurgangolfclub.com   E-mail: lurgan@btclick.com
Nearest main town: Lurgan

Secretary:	Mrs M. Sharpe	Tel: 028 3832 2087
		Fax: 028 3831 6166
Professional:	Mr D. Paul	Tel: 028 3832 1068

Playing: Midweek: round £15.00; day n/a. Weekend: round £20.00; day n/a.

Facilities: Bar: 11am–11pm. Food: Lunch and dinner by arrangement.

Comments: Internal out-of-bounds is annoying ... Set by Lurgan Lake ... Opportunity to open your shoulders on this flat expanse of a golf course ... Not high quality but cheap and cheerful.

Mahee Island Golf Club ★★

Comber, Newtownards, Belfast, County Down, BT23 6EP
Nearest main town: Belfast

Secretary:	Mr M. Marshall	Tel: 028 9754 1234
Professional:	Mr A. McCracken (Shop)	

Playing: Midweek: round £10.00; day n/a. Weekend: round £15.00; day n/a.

Facilities: Bar: 11am–11pm. Food: Lunch and dinner from 12pm–3pm. Bar snacks.

Comments: Top-of-the-drawer nine-hole course on island in Strangford Lough ... Idyllic location on an island ... Best-maintained nine-hole course in Ireland ... Bizarre but beautiful ... Predominantly in good condition ... One primarily for the enthusiast ... Poor off-course facilities.

Malone Golf Club

240 Upper Malone Road, Dunmurry, BT17 9LB
Website: www.malonegolfclub.co.uk
E-mail: manager@malonegolfclub.co.uk
Nearest main town: Belfast

Secretary:	Mr N. Agate	Tel: 028 9061 2758
		Fax: 028 9043 1394
Professional:	Mr M. McGee	Tel: 028 9061 4917
		Fax: 028 9043 1394

Playing: Midweek: round £40.00 (Main), £18 (Edenderry Nine); day n/a. Weekend: round £45.00 (Main), £20 (Edenderry Nine); day n/a.

Facilities: Bar: 11am–11pm. Food: Breakfast, lunch and dinner from 9am–9pm. Bar snacks.

Comments: One of the best parkland courses in the area ... In top condition, hardly a divot to be seen ... Rolling hills, water, sand – it has it all ... Magnificent clubhouse ... Very British course ... Opened in the 1960s and still in fine condition.

Massereene Golf Club ★★★

51 Lough Road, Antrim, County Antrim, BT41 4DQ
Website: www.massereenegolfclub1895.com
E-mail: massereenegc@utvinternet.com
Nearest main town: Antrim

Secretary:	Mr K. Stevens	Tel: 028 9442 8096
		Fax: 028 9448 7661
Professional:	Mr J. Smyth	Tel: 028 9442 8096
		Fax: 028 9448 7661

Playing: Midweek: round £20.00; day n/a. Weekend: round £25.00; day n/a.

Facilities: Bar: 11am–11pm. Food: Lunch from 11am–9pm.

Comments: A well-manicured, attractive course, very pleasing to the eye ... Very underrated but they like it that way ... Course has been fiddled with over the years ... Sporting and stylish ... Will make a point of returning to this parkland course.

Narin & Portnoo Golf Club

Narin, Portnoo, County Donegal
Nearest main town: Ardara

| Secretary: | Mr E. Bonner | Tel: 074 954 5407 |
| | | Fax: 074 944 5407 |

Professional: None

Playing: Midweek: round €30; day n/a. Weekend: round €35; day n/a.

Facilities: Bar: 10.30am–11pm. Food: Bar snacks.

Comments: Terrific potential – remove the cattle and caravans at the start and finish, upgrade the clubhouse, a few new tees and you would have a great course ... Windswept links ... Great hospitality and places to stay ... Starts poorly but gets better ... Popular course ... Respected venue almost deserted outside summer ... Short course protected by tight fairways ... Wonderful scenery.

North West Golf Club   ★

Lisfannon, Fahan, County Donegal
Nearest main town: Buncrana

Secretary: Mr D. Coyle   Tel: 074 936 1027
                                          Fax: 074 936 3284
Professional: Mr S. McBriarty   Tel: 074 936 1715

Playing: Midweek: round €25; day n/a. Weekend: round €30; day n/a.

Facilities: Bar: 10.30am–11pm. Food: Lunch and dinner from 12pm–9pm.

Comments: A second-string course in Donegal but has attractions in itself ... Flattish links near the Mouldy mountains ... Good atmosphere at this out-of-the-way club.

Nuremore Hotel & Golf Club   ★★

Carrickmacross, County Monaghan
Website: www.nuremore-hotel.ie   E-mail: nuremore@eircom.net
Nearest main town: Carrickmacross

Secretary: Mr A. Capaldi   Tel: 087 250 3771
Professional: Mr M. Cassidy   Tel: 042 966 4016
                                          Fax: 042 966 1853

Playing: Midweek: round €35; day n/a. Weekend: round €45; day n/a.

Facilities: Bar: 10.30am–11pm. Food: Breakfast, lunch and dinner from 9am–9pm. Bar snacks.

Comments: Scary tee shot on the 10th ... Hotel dominates this attractive parkland course ... Some short par-4s that make you think ... Picturesque drumlins and lakes ... Impressive finishing hole.

Portadown Golf Club ★

192 Gilford Road, Portadown, County Armagh, BT63 5LF
E-mail: portadowngc@btconnect.com
Nearest main town: Portadown

Secretary:	Mrs M. Holloway	Tel: 028 3835 5356
		Fax: 028 3839 1394
Professional:	Mr P. Stevenson	Tel: 028 3833 4655

Playing: Midweek: round £18.00; day n/a. Weekend: round £23.00; day n/a.

Facilities: Bar: 11am–11pm. Food: Lunch and dinner from 11am–9pm, except Mondays.

Comments: Flattish, fun course in parkland setting ... River Bann provides a nice natural framing for a few holes ... 9th over the river is impressive ... Variety of doglegs and straightaway holes.

Portsalon Golf Club

Portsalon, Fanad, County Donegal
E-mail: portsalongolfclub@eircom.net
Nearest main town: Letterkenny

Secretary:	Mr P. Doherty	Tel: 074 915 9459
		Fax: 074 915 9919
Professional:	None	

Playing: Midweek: round €35.00; day n/a. Weekend: round €40.00; day n/a.

Facilities: Bar: 10.30am–11pm. Food: Lunch and dinner from 12pm–9pm.

Comments: Try playing to your handicap here ... A course to play for the rest of your life ... Better than nearby Rosapenna ... Great names – the Ballymostocker Bay and Knockalla mountains ... Basic club ... Learn all about the unpredictability of links golf here ... In the summer the ball kicks everywhere ... Charming people ... Made welcome ... So unique ... Can't wait to return.

Portstewart Golf Club (Strand)   ★★★★

117 Strand Road, Portstewart, County Londonderry, BT55 7PG
Nearest main town: Portstewart

Secretary:	Mr M. Moss	Tel: 01265 833839
		Fax: 01265 834097
Professional:	Mr A. Hunter	Tel: 01265 832601

Playing: Midweek: round £50.00; day £65.00. Weekend: round £70.00; day n/a.

Facilities: Bar: 11am–11pm. Food: Breakfast, lunch and dinner from 9am–9pm. Bar snacks.

Comments: Exhilarating experience ... The pro seems to remember every visitor ... Beautiful nine holes out ... Staff and members top drawer ... Wonderful first nine holes designed by the club's members ... Very exciting to play ... First nine just a dream ... Very friendly pro and staff ... Cosy, friendly clubhouse ... Can I play this course every day for the rest of my life? ... Front nine simply golf heaven ... Could not believe the tee shot at the 2nd ... Redesigned in 1990 with seven new holes.

Radisson Roe Park Golf Club   ★★★

Limavaddy, County Londonderry, BT49 9LB
Nearest main town: Limavaddy

Secretary:	Mr D. Brockerton	Tel: 01504 722212
		Fax: 01504 722313
Professional:	Mr S. Duffy	

Playing: Midweek: round £20.00; day £20.00. Weekend: round £20.00; day £20.00.

Facilities: Bar: 11am–11pm. Food: Breakfast, lunch and dinner from 9am–9pm. Bar snacks.

Comments: Very testing parkland course with excellent facilities at good prices ... Interesting layout with pleasant club-house ... Lough Foyle and the Inishowen peninsula form the backdrop ... Beautifully sculpted course with US-style features.

Rosapenna Hotel Golf Club   ★★★★

Rosapenna, Downings, County Donegal
Website: www.rosapenna.ie   E-mail: rosapenna@eircom.net
Nearest main town: Londonderry

Secretary: Mr J. Sweeney   Tel: 074 915 5301
                                          Fax: 074 915 5128

Professional: None

Playing: Midweek: round €45 (Old Tom Morris), €60 (Sandy Hills
                    Links); day n/a. Weekend: round €50 (Old Tom Morris),
                    €60 (Sandy Hills Links); day n/a.

Facilities: Bar: 10.30am–11pm. Food: Breakfast, lunch and
                    dinner from 7am–10pm. Bar snacks.

Comments: A peaceful place to play with 18 holes of good standard
                    ... Laid out by Old Tom Morris ... This, Portsalon and
                    Ballyliffin should meet all your golfing needs in Donegal
                    ... Unknown links of substantial character ... Fairly
                    facile links without ruggedness of other Irish courses ...
                    A course to learn over time ... If you play here only on
                    holidays, you will never match your handicap ... Remote
                    links of tranquillity.

The Royal Belfast Golf Club   ★★

Station Road, Craigavad, Holywood, County Down, BT18 0BP
Website: www.royalbelfast.co.uk   E-mail: royalbelfastgc@btclick.com
Nearest main town: Belfast

Secretary: Mrs S. Morrison   Tel: 028 9042 8165
                                          Fax: 028 9042 1404
Professional: Mr C. Spence   Tel: 028 9042 8586
                                          Fax: 028 9042 1404

Playing: Midweek: round £45.00; day n/a. Weekend: round
                    £55.00; day n/a.

Facilities: Bar: 11am–11pm. Food: Lunch from 12pm–3pm.
                    Dinner by arrangement.

Comments: Very exclusive club ... If you can get on, fairly cheap for
                    an exclusive club ... Oldest established club in Ireland
                    ... Course condition always good ... Not as windy as
                    other links ... Protected by over 60 bunkers ... Simple
                    off the tee, problems start around the greens.

Royal Portrush Golf Club (Valley)   ★★★★

Dunluce Road, Portrush, County Antrim, BT56 8JQ
Nearest main town: Portrush

Secretary:	Miss W. Erskine	Tel: 028 7082 2311
		Fax: 028 7082 3139
Professional:	Mr G. McNeill	Tel: 028 7082 3335

Playing: Midweek: round £32.50; day n/a. Weekend: round £37.50; day n/a.

Facilities: Bar: 11am–11pm. Food: Lunch (included in round fee) from 11am–3pm. Dinner by arrangement.

Comments: A deserved respite after the Dunluce ... Bites hard when you least expect it ... Wee sister to the Dunluce but top of my list every time ... 'Feel' course ... Didn't even consider playing it after the Dunluce ... A bit 'after the Lord Mayor's show'.

Slieve Russell Golf Club   ★★★

Ballconnell, County Cavan
E-mail: slieve-golf-club@quinnhotels.com
Nearest main town: Cavan

Secretary:	Mr I. Hewson	Tel: 049 952 5091
	(Golf Director)	Fax: 049 952 6640
Professional:	Mr L. McCool	Tel: 049 952 6444
		Fax: 049 952 6640

Playing: Midweek: round €60 (Sun–Fri); day n/a. Weekend: round €75 (Sat); day n/a.

Facilities: Bar: 10.30am–11pm. Food: Lunch and dinner from 10.30am–9pm. Bar snacks.

Comments: Excellent new course ... Facilities and course first class ... Very linksy feel to this parkland beauty with huge contoured greens and deep greenside bunkers ... Exciting par-3s and birdieable par-5s ... Had a memorable weekend at the hotel and course – will return one day.

Warrenpoint Golf Club   ★★

Lower Dromore Road, Warrenpoint, County Down, BT34 3LN
Website: www.warrenpointgolf.com   E-mail: office@warrenpointgolf.com
Nearest main town: Newry

Secretary:	Mrs M. Trainor	Tel: 028 4175 3695
		Fax: 028 4175 2918
Professional:	Mr N. Shaw	Tel: 028 4175 2371
		Fax: 028 4175 2918

Playing: Midweek: round £22.00; day n/a. Weekend: round £28.00; day n/a.

Facilities: Bar: 11am–11pm. Food: Lunch and dinner from 12pm–9pm. Bar snacks.

Comments: Simply breathtaking scenery ... Very hilly parkland course ... Not very hard but you come here for the views not the golf ... If you're in the area you're probably coming to County Down, not here.

Connacht

County Sligo Golf Club ★★★★★

Rosses Point, County Sligo
Nearest main town: Sligo

The rich seams of golf that exist in south-west Ireland gradually disappear as you pass through Galway and up through County Roscommon. Eventually you reach the town of Sligo, from where it is a short drive to Rosses Point, a golf course that is undoubtedly the best in this part of the Republic. Dominated by the majestic mountain of Ben Bulben, from which the small villages, beaches and crofters' cottages take their character, Rosses Point is a treat to play.

It is a traditional links course, the standard perils of bunkers, heavy rough and wind dictating the course and pace of play. But its character is not built on that alone. The subtleties of the slightly undulating fairways and positions and angles of the green make it a real 'feel' course, harmonising your game with the rhythm of the land.

The poetry of William Butler Yeats used to speak fondly of this part of the world (he is buried in nearby Drumcliff), and visitors do fall under its charm, many leaving with the impression of Rosses Point as the finest links in Ireland. Certainly, it is incredibly fair, far removed from the traditional image of a links with its harsh bounces and cruel kicks.

One of the course's most memorable holes is the 5th, with its astonishing view of Ben Bulben. A par-5 named 'The Jump', you drive from an elevated tee to a fairway that hugs the cliff line, from where, if you're lucky, you could be faced with a long iron or, more realistically, a lay-up in front of the tiny green. The feeling of the hole shrinking, and getting more difficult as you walk each yard from the tee, is technically very strong. That could also be said of the 17th, a par-4 played down into a gully before climbing spectacularly to a hidden green protected on all sides. The incline and green all slope back towards you and one can imagine professional players spinning the ball back down the slope.

You may prefer the gung-ho thrillers of Waterville or Tralee with their enormous dunes, but you can't fail to be impressed with Rosses Point.

Secretary:	Mr J. Ironside (Manager)	Tel: 071 917 7134 Fax: 071 917 7460
Professional:	Mr L. Robinson	Tel: 071 917 7171
Playing:	Midweek: round €65 (Mon–Thurs); day n/a. Weekend: round €80 (Fri–Sun); day n/a.	

Facilities: Bar: 10.30am–11pm. Food: Lunch and dinner from 10am–9pm. Bar snacks.

Comments: Great stretch of golf in the middle of the round ... Ben Bulben lends this links a mystical feel ... So natural, so magical ... Played it every year on holiday for the last 20 years ... Good putting green and clubhouse ... Very natural, the wind is its defence ... Hilly and exhausting, where are the carts? ... Basic facilities ... Views of the Atlantic and the Bay of Drumcliff ... Exceptional.

Athlone Golf Club ★★★

Hodson Bay, Athlone, County Roscommon
Nearest main town: Athlone

Secretary: Mr L. Fagan   Tel: 090 649 2073
Fax: 090 649 4080

Professional: Mr M. Quinn

Playing: Midweek: round €30; day n/a. Weekend: round €35; day n/a.

Facilities: Bar: 10.30am–11pm. Food: Breakfast, lunch and dinner from 9am–9pm. Bar snacks.

Comments: Warmth and hospitality through and through ... Overlooking Lough Ree ... Fun course with short par-5s ... Straightforward course where you can feel good about your game ... Bunkers provide major headache.

Carne Golf Links ★★★★

Carne, Belmullet, County Mayo
Website: www.carnegolflinks.com   E-mail: carngolf@iol.ie
Nearest main town: Belmullet

Secretary: Mr J. O'Hara   Tel: 097 82292
Fax: 097 81477

Professional: None

Playing: Midweek: round n/a; day €50 Mar–Oct. Weekend: round n/a; day €50 Mar–Oct.

Facilities: Bar: 10.30am–11.30pm Mon–Fri; 10.30am–12.30am Sat/Sun. Food: Breakfast, lunch and dinner.

Comments: If you ever see bigger sand dunes than these I'd like to know about it ... An undiscovered gem, playing here is a total adventure ... I didn't expect to find much all the way out here, but I was so wrong. One of the great Irish links.

Connemara Golf Club   ★★★★

Ballyconneely, County Galway
Website: www.westcoastlinks.com   E-mail: links@iol.ie
Nearest main town: Clifden

Secretary: Mr R. Flaherty   Tel: 095 23502/23602
                                          Fax: 095 23662
Professional: Mr H. O'Neill   Tel: 095 23502
                                          Fax: 095 23662

Playing: Midweek: round €50; day n/a. Weekend: round €55; day n/a.

Facilities: Bar: 10.30am–11pm. Food: Lunch and dinner from 10am–9pm.

Comments: Great location and excellent food ... Course in need of more rough ... Spectacular setting and true Irish weather ... Very challenging ... Stunning setting ... Should be on every golfer's 'must-play' list ... Romantic course that gets going on the back nine ... Rough and fairway bunkers will catch you soon enough ... Disappointing front nine ... A course of two halves ... Would be the best in Ireland if you judged it on the back nine.

Enniscrone Golf Club   ★★★★

Enniscrone, County Sligo
Website: www.enniscronegolf.com
E-mail: enniscronegolf@eircom.net
Nearest main town: Enniscrone

Secretary: Mr M. Staunton   Tel: 096 36297
                   (Secretary/Manager)   Fax: 096 36657
Professional: Mr C. McGoldrick   Tel: 096 36666
                                          Fax: 096 36657

Playing: Midweek: round €50; day n/a. Weekend: round €63; day n/a.

Facilities: Bar: 10.30am–11pm. Food: Lunch and dinner from 10am–9pm. Bar snacks.

Comments: Beautiful location with great variety of holes ... A natural links, play it two or three times to know it ... A gem for very little money to play and eat ... Best holes are on the back nine among the dunes ... Contrasting nines, but both have their own appeal.

Galway Golf Club ★★★

Blackrock, Salthill, Galway, County Galway
Website: www.galwaygolf.com   E-mail: galwaygolf@eircom.net
Nearest main town: Galway

Secretary:	Mr P. Fahy	Tel: 091 522 033
		Fax: 091 529 783
Professional:	Mr D. Wallace	Tel: 091 523 038
		Fax: 091 529 783

Playing: Midweek: round €50; day n/a. Weekend: round €60; day n/a.

Facilities: Bar: 10.30am–11pm. Food: Lunch and dinner from 10am–9pm.

Comments: Views over Galway Bay ... Outdated course in need of spicing up ... Greens variable on visit ... Old course with an indefinable spirit and mystery ... Very tight and difficult ... Came away having ballooned over my handicap.

Galway Bay Golf & Country Club

Renville, Oranmore, County Galway
Website: www.gbaygolf.com   E-mail: gbay@iol.ie
Nearest main town: Galway

Secretary:	Ms A. Muleyan	Tel: 091 790 503
		Fax: 091 792 510
Professional:	Mr E. O'Connor	Tel: 091 790 503
		Fax: 091 792 510

Playing: Midweek: round €25 (Nov–Mar), €55 (Apr–Oct); day n/a. Weekend: round €35 (Nov–Mar), €70 (Apr–Oct); day n/a.

Facilities: Bar: 10.30am–11pm. Food: Breakfast, lunch and dinner from 7am–10pm. Bar snacks.

Comments: If there was no wind it would be a doddle ... Wind can get horrific ... Play this with a hangover and you'll soon blow the cobwebs away ... Exhilarating experience which I'll never forget ... Overlooking the Atlantic and Galway Bay ... Ordinary land turned into something special by Christy O'Connor Jnr.

Gort Golf Club   ★

Castlequater, Gort, County Galway
Nearest main town: Galway

Secretary: Mr S. Devlin   Tel: 091 632 244
Professional: None

Playing: Midweek: round €25; day n/a. Weekend: round €30; day n/a.

Facilities: Bar: 10.30am–11pm. Food: Bar snacks.

Comments: An old club built on a new site ... Excellent greens and tight fairways ... Opened fairly recently and excellent addition to region's quota of courses.

Loughrea Golf Club   ★

Graigue, Loughrea, County Galway
Nearest main town: Galway

Secretary: Mrs M. Hawkin   Tel: 091 841 049
Professional: None

Playing: Midweek: round €20; day n/a. Weekend: round €20; day n/a.

Facilities: Bar: 10.30am–11pm. Food: Breakfast, lunch and dinner from 9am–9pm. Bar snacks.

Comments: Very short and cheap course ... Great value for money ... Nothing special about the course ... Parkland course extended to 18 holes in early 1990s.

Strandhill Golf Club Ltd   ★

Strandhill, County Sligo
Website: www.strandhillgc.net   E-mail: strandhillgc@eircom.net
Nearest main town: Sligo

Secretary: Mr H. Gallagher   Tel: 071 916 8188
                  (Hon Sec)   Fax: 071 916 8811
Professional: Mr A. Gray   Tel: 071 916 8188
                                          Fax: 071 916 8811

Playing: Midweek: round €40; day n/a. Weekend: round €50;
                  day n/a.

Facilities: Bar: 10.30am–11pm. Food: Lunch and dinner from
                  12pm–9pm. Bar snacks.

Comments: Underrated, can be very tough with some unusual
                  par-3s ... Unknown links with views of mountains ...
                  Some memorable, friendly times here ... Too short to test
                  the advanced player.

Westport Golf Club   ★★★

Carrowholly, Westport, County Mayo
Website: www.golfwestport.com   E-mail: wpgolf@eircom.net
Nearest main town: Westport

Secretary: Mr P. Neill   Tel: 098 28262
                                          Fax: 098 27217
Professional: Mr A. Mealia   Tel: 098 28262
                                          Fax: 098 27217

Playing: Midweek: round €36–€40; day n/a. Weekend: round
                  €43–€50; day n/a.

Facilities: Bar: 10.30am–11pm. Food: Lunch and dinner from
                  10am–9pm. Bar snacks.

Comments: Excellent back nine ... Impressive locker room in
                  friendly, welcoming clubhouse ... Views make it ...
                  Don't give up, it gets better on the back nine ... Views of
                  Croagh Patrick ... Long, tough, scenic inland course ...
                  Course doesn't look great until the back nine ... 12th
                  and 15th just great golf holes.

Index of Courses